Condemned for a murder he had not committed, Henri Charrière (nicknamed Papillon) was sent to the penal colony of French Guiana. Forty-two days after his arrival he made his first break, travelling a thousand gruelling miles in an open boat. Recaptured, he suffered solitary confinement and was sent eventually to Devil's Island, a hell-hole of disease and brutality. No one had ever escaped from this notorious prison – no one until Papillon took to the shark-infested sea supported only by a makeshift coconut-sack raft. In thirteen years he made nine daring escapes, living through many fantastic adventures while on the run – including a sojourn with South American Indians whose women Papillon found welcomely free of European restraints . . .

Papillon is filled with tension, adventure and high excitement. It is also one of the most vivid stories of human endurance ever written.

Banco continues the adventures of Papillon in Venezuela, where he has finally won his freedom after thirteen years of escape and imprisonment. Despite his resolve to become an honest man, Papillon is soon involved in hair-raising exploits with goldminers, gamblers, bank-robbers and revolutionaries – robbing and being robbed, his lust for life as strong as ever.

Henri Charrière died in 1973 at the age of 66.

HENRI CHARRIÈRE

PAPILLON

BANCO

Translated from the French by
Patrick O'Brian

Grafton

HarperCollins*Publishers*
77-85 Fulham Palace Road
Hammersmith, London W6 8JB

www.harpercollins.co.uk

This omnibus edition published in 2004
by HarperCollins*Publishers*

Papillon
Copyright © Robert Laffont 1969

Banco
Copyright © Editions Robert Laffont 1972
This translation copyright © Hart-Davis, MacGibbon Ltd 1973

The author asserts the moral right
to be identified as the author of these works

ISBN 0 007 71209 X

Set in Postscript Linotype Times
by Rowland Phototypesetting Ltd
Bury St Edmunds, Suffolk

Printed and bound in Great Britain by
Mackays of Chatham plc, Chatham, Kent

PAPILLON

Contents

To the people of Venezuela, to the humble fishermen of the Gulf of Paria, to all those, intellectuals, soldiers and others who gave me my chance to make a new life.

To Rita, my wife, my best friend.

CARIBBEAN SEA

Güiria
Gulf of Paria
Port of Spain
TRINIDAD
San Fernando

Callao
El Dorado
Georgetown
Mackenzie
Paramaribo
Albina
St-Laurent
Maroni
ILES DU SALUT
Kourou
Cayenne

SURINAM

GUYANA

FRENCH GUIANA

—— 1933–1934
- - - 1941

All this last year France has been talking about Papillon, about the *phénomène Papillon*, which is not merely the selling of very large numbers of an unusually long book, but the discovery of a new world and the rediscovery of a kind of direct, intensely living narrative that has scarcely ever been seen since literature became self-conscious.

The new world in question is of course the underworld, seen from within and described with extraordinary natural talent by one who knows it through and through and who accepts its values, which include among others courage, loyalty and fortitude. But this is the real underworld, as different from the underworld of fiction as the act of love is different from adolescent imaginings, a world the French have scarcely seen except here and there in the works of Jean Genet and Albertine Sarrazin, or the English since Defoe; and its startling fierce uncompromising reality, savagely contemptuous of the Establishment, has shocked and distressed many a worthy bourgeois. Indeed, we have a minister's word for it (a minister, no less) that the present hopeless moral decline of France is due to the wearing of miniskirts and to the reading of *Papillon*.

Nevertheless all properly equipped young women are still wearing miniskirts, in spite of the cold, and even greater numbers of Frenchmen with properly equipped minds are still reading *Papillon*, in spite of the uncomfortable feelings it must arouse from time to time. And this is one of the most striking things about the *phénomène Papillon*: the book makes an immense appeal to the whole range of men of good will, from the Académie française to the cheerful young mason who is working on my house. The literary men are the most articulate in their praise, and I will quote from François Mauriac, the most literary and articulate of them all, for his praise sums up all the rest and expresses it better. This piece comes from his *Bloc-notes* in the *Figaro littéraire*.

I had heard that it was a piece of oral literature, but I do not agree at all: no, even on the literary plane I think it an extraordinary talented book. I have believed that there is no great success, no overwhelming success, that is undeserved.

It always has a deep underlying reason ... I think that *Papillon*'s immense success is in exact proportion to the book's worth and to what the author has lived through. But another man who had had the same life and had experienced the same adventures would have produced nothing from it at all. This is a literary prodigy. Merely having been a transported convict and having escaped does not mean a thing: you have to have talent to give this tale its ring of truth. It is utterly fascinating reading. This new colleague of ours is a master!

A thing that struck me very much in the book is that this man, sentenced for a killing that he did not commit ... takes a very sanguine view of mankind. At the beginning of his first escape he was taken in and given shelter on a lepers' island. The charity these most unfortunate, most forsaken of men showed to the convicts is truly wonderful. And it was the lepers who saw to it that they were saved. The same applies to the way they were welcomed in Trinidad and at Curaçao, not as criminals but as men who deserved admiration for having made that voyage aboard a nutshell. There is this human warmth all round them, and all through the book we never forget it. How different from those bitter, angry, disgusted books – Céline's, for example.

Man's highest virtues are to be found in what is called the gutter, the underworld; and what gangsters do is sometimes the same as what heroes do. I have already confessed that when I am very low in my mind I read detective stories. In these books, where everything is made up, the human aspect of the characters, the 'humanity', is appalling. But in Papillon's tale, which is true, we meet a humanity that we love in spite of its revolting side. This book is a good book, in the deep meaning of the word.

When one has read a little way into *Papillon* one soon comes to recognize the singular truthfulness of the writing, but at first some readers, particularly English readers, wonder whether such things can be; and so that no time, no pleasure, should be lost, a certain amount of authentication may be in place.

Henri Charrière was born in 1906, in the Ardèche, a somewhat remote district in the south of France where his father was the master of a village school. After doing his military service in the navy, Charrière went to Paris, where, having acquired the nickname of Papillon, he soon carved himself out a respected place in the underworld: he had an intuitive perception of its laws and standards, and he respected them scrupulously. Papillon was not a killer at that time, but he fell foul of the police and when he was taken up on the charge of murdering a ponce he was convicted. The perjury of a witness for the prosecution, the thick stupidity of the jury, the utter inhumanity of the prosecuting counsel, and the total injustice of the sentence maddened him, for like many of his friends he had a far more acute sense of justice than is usual in the bourgeois world. What is more, the sentence was appallingly severe – transportation to the penal settlements in French Guiana and imprisonment for life without a hope of remission: and all this at the age of twenty-five. He swore he would not serve it, and he did not serve it. This book is an account of his astonishing escapes from an organization that was nevertheless accustomed to holding on to thousands of very tough and determined men, and of the adventures that were the consequences of his escapes. But it is also a furious protest against a society that can use human beings so, that can reduce them to despair and that can for its own convenience shut them up in dim concrete cells with bars only at the top, there to live in total silence upon a starvation diet until they are tamed, driven mad or physically destroyed – killed. The horrible, absolutely convincing account of his years in solitary confinement is very deeply moving indeed.

After years on the run, years of being taken and then escaping again even though he was on the 'very dangerous' list, Papillon finally got away from Devil's Island itself, riding over many miles of sea to the mainland on a couple of sacks filled with coconuts. He managed to reach Venezuela, and eventually the Venezuelans gave him his chance, allowing him to become a Venezuelan citizen and to settle down to live in Caracas as quietly as his fantastic vitality would allow.

It was here that he chanced upon Albertine Sarrazin's wonderful *l'Astragale* in a French bookshop. He read it. The red band round the cover said *123rd thousand*, and Papillon said, 'It's pretty good: but if that chick, just going from hideout to hideout with that broken bone of hers, could sell 123,000 copies, why, with my thirty years of adventures, I'll sell three times as many.' He bought two schoolboys' exercise books with spiral bindings and in two days he filled them. He bought

13

eleven more, and in a couple of months they too were full.

It is perhaps this extraordinary flow that accounts for some of the unique living quality of the book. A professional writer who puts down between one and two thousand words a day is doing very well: Papillon must have written about five thousand a day, and the result is very like the flow of a practised raconteur – indeed the book has been called a masterpiece of oral literature, and although this is not Mauriac's view, with the utmost diffidence I (having lived with *Papillon* for months) venture to agree with it.

As luck would have it the manuscript was sent to Jean-Pierre Castelnau, the publisher who had discovered Albertine Sarrazin; and here I quote from his preface.

His manuscript reached me in September. Three weeks later Charrière was in Paris. Jean-Jacques Pauvert and I had launched Albertine: Charrière entrusted me with his book. . . .

I have left this book, poured red-hot from his glowing memory and typed by various enthusiastic but not always very French hands, virtually untouched. All I have done is to put some order into the punctuation, change a few almost incomprehensible Spanish turns of phrase, and straighten out certain muddles and inversions that arise from his daily use of three or four different languages in Caracas, all learnt by ear.

I can vouch for the basic authenticity of the book. Charrière came to Paris twice and we talked a great deal. Whole days: and some nights too. Clearly, in thirty years some details may have grown dim and memory may have altered others. They are not of any importance. As for the background, one has but to glance at Professor Devèze's *Cayenne* (*Collection Archives*, Julliard, 1965) to see that Charrière has by no means exaggerated either the way of life and morality of the penal settlement or its horror. Far from it.

As a matter of principle we have changed the names of all the convicts, warders and governors of the prison service, this book's intention being not to attack individuals but to describe given characters and a given community. We have done the same with the dates: some are exact, others merely give a general notion of the period. That is all that is required.

Perhaps I should add something about the translation of the book. To begin with it was one of the hardest I have ever undertaken, partly because Papillon could not get into his stride, and I had to stumble along with him, for I resent 'improvements' in translation – they do not seem to me right. (Once, in one of my own novels, an Italian translator improved a difficult poem right out of existence.) And then there was the problem of his slang: Papillon does not use very much – nothing to compare with Albertine Sarrazin or Céline, for example – and it offers no great difficulty from the point of view of comprehension; but what he does use is strongly alive, far more immediate and personal than the comparatively limited vocabulary of the English underworld. So I was obliged to draw upon the more copious and vivid American: but then Papillon's prison days were in the thirties and forties, so the slang had to belong to that period. Occasionally I have fallen into anachronism rather than sacrifice vividness, but on the whole I think the language, particularly the dialogue, is a reasonably faithful reflection of the original. Then again there was the question of obscenities. French of course makes a very free use of expressions such as *con* and *merde* whose literal equivalents are less often heard in English and therefore have a rather stronger effect; but on the other hand no one can be so simple as to suppose that thousands of ill-treated convicts herded together sound anything like a Sunday-school, so I have tried to steer between unnecessary grossness and inaccurate insipidity.

By the time I had settled these points Papillon had thoroughly hit his stride, and then I found that the best way of following his breakneck pace was to keep up with him. It is a pace that I am used to, for I have lived half my life among the most loquacious people in France, and although I could not translate quite as fast as Papillon wrote, I still finished the book in three months, treating it (to use Jean-Pierre Castelnau's words) as the flow of 'a sunlit, rather husky southern voice that you can listen to for hours on end'. And I may say that although in places it was tough going, all in all it was one of the most full and rewarding experiences in a literary life that has not been sparing in delights.

PATRICK O'BRIAN
Collioure, 1970

15

The Assizes

The blow was such a stunner that it was thirteen years before I could get back on to my feet again. It was not the usual kind of blow either, and they clubbed together to let me have it.

This was 26 October 1931. At eight in the morning they had taken me out of my cell in the Conciergerie – the cell I had been living in for the past year. I was well shaved and well dressed: I looked as smooth as they come in my made-to-measure suit and white shirt with a pale-blue bow-tie to add the finishing touch.

I was twenty-five and I looked twenty. The gendarmes were rather impressed by my posh clothes, and they treated me civilly. They even took off the handcuffs. There we were, all six of us, the five gendarmes and me, sitting on two benches in a bare room. A dreary sky outside. The door opposite us must lead into the assize-court, for this building, this Paris building, was the Palais de Justice of the Seine.

In a few moments I was to be indicted for wilful homicide. My counsel, Maître Raymond Hubert, came in to see me. 'There's no solid evidence against you: I fully expect us to be acquitted.' That 'us' made me smile. Anyone would have thought that Maître Hubert was going to appear in the dock too, and that if the verdict was guilty he too would have to serve time.

An usher opened the door and told us to come in. With four gendarmes round me and the sergeant to one side, I made my entrance through the wide-open double doors into an enormous court-room. They had done the whole place up in red, blood red, so as to hand me out this crushing blow – all red, the carpets, the curtains at the big windows and even the robes of the judges who were going to deal with me in two or three minutes' time.

'Gentlemen, the court!'

In single file six men appeared through a door on the right.

The president of the court and then five other lawyers with their official hats, their toques, on their heads. The presiding judge stopped at the seat in the middle and his colleagues arranged themselves to the right and the left. There was an impressive silence in the room, and everybody was standing up, including me. The court took its seat, and so did everybody else.

The president was a fat-faced man with pink cheeks and a cold eye; he looked straight at me without letting any sort of feeling show. His name was Bevin. When things were under way he ran the trial fairly and he made it clear to one and all that as a professional lawyer he was not sure that either the witnesses or the police were all that straight. No: he had no responsibility for the crusher: all he did was to pass it on to me.

The public prosecutor was a lawyer called Pradel, and all the barristers were frightened of him. He had the evil reputation of sending more victims to the guillotine and the convict prisons in France and overseas than any other man.

Pradel stood for the vindication of society. He was the official prosecutor and there was nothing human about him. He represented the Law, the scales of justice: he was the one who handled them, and he did everything he possibly could to make them come down on the right side for him. He lowered the lids over his vulturish eyes and stared at me piercingly from his full height. From the height of his rostrum in the first place, which made him tower over me, and then from his own natural height, an arrogant six feet. He did not take off his red robe, but he put his toque down in front of him, and he leaned on his two great ham-sized hands. There was a gold ring to show he was married, and a ring on his little finger made of a highly polished horseshoe nail.

He leant over a little so as to dominate me all the more, and he looked as though he were saying, 'If you think you can get away from me, young cock, you've got it wrong. My hands may not look like talons, but there are claws in my heart that are going to rip you to pieces. And the reason why all the barristers are afraid of me, the reason why the judges think the world of me as a dangerous prosecutor, is that I never let my prey escape. It's nothing to do with me whether you're guilty or innocent: all I'm here for is to make use of everything that can be said against you – your disreputable, shiftless life in Montmartre, the evidence the police have worked up and the statements of the police themselves. What I am to do is to take hold of all the disgusting filth piled up by the investigating magistrate and manage to make you look so revolting that the jury will see that you vanish from the community.' Either I was dreaming or I could hear him perfectly distinctly: this man-eater really shook me. 'Prisoner at the bar, just you keep quiet, and above all don't you attempt to defend yourself. I'll send you down the drain, all right. And I trust you've no faith in the jury? Don't you kid yourself. Those twelve men know nothing whatsoever about life. Look at them, lined up there opposite you. Twelve bastards brought up to Paris from some perishing village in the country: can you see them clearly? Small shopkeepers, pensioners, tradesmen. It's not worth describing them to you in detail. Surely you don't expect *them* to understand the life you lead in Montmartre or what it's like to be twenty-five? As far as they're concerned Pigalle and the Place Blanche are exactly the same as hell and all night-birds are the natural enemies of society. They are all unspeakably proud of being jurymen at the Seine Assizes. And what's more, I can tell you that they loathe their status – they loathe belonging to the pinched, dreary lower middle class. And now you make your appearance here, all young and handsome. Do you really suppose for a moment that I'm not going to make them see you as a night-prowling Montmartre Don Juan? That will put them dead against you right away. You're too well dressed: you ought to have come in something very modest indeed. That was a huge tactical error of yours. Can't you see how jealous of your suit they are? They all buy their clothes off the peg – they've never even dreamt of having a suit made to measure by a tailor.'

Ten o'clock, and we were all ready for the trial to start. Six official lawyers there in front of me, one of them a fierce, driving prosecutor who was going to use all his Machiavellian strength and all his intelligence to convince these twelve innocents that in the first place I was guilty and in the second that the only proper sentence was either penal servitude or the guillotine.

I was to be tried for the killing of a pimp, a police-informer belonging to the Montmartre underworld. There was no proof, but the cops (who get credit every time they find out who has committed a crime) were going to swear blind that I was guilty.

Seeing they had no proof, they said they had 'confidential' information that left the matter in no doubt. The strongest piece of the prosecution's evidence was a witness they had primed, a human gramophone-record manufactured at 36 quai des Orfèvres, their headquarters – a guy by the name of Polein. At one point, when I was saying over and over again that I did not know him, the president very fairly asked me, 'You say this witness is lying. Very well. But why should he want to lie?'

'Monsieur le Président, I've had sleepless nights ever since I was arrested, but not out of remorse for having killed Roland le Petit, because I never did it. It's because I keep trying to make out what kind of motive this witness can have for attacking me so ferociously and for bringing fresh evidence to support the charge every time it seems to weaken. I've come to the conclusion, Monsieur le Président, that the police picked him up in the act of committing some serious crime and that they made a bargain with him – we'll forget it, so long as you denounce Papillon.'

At the time I didn't think I was so close to the truth. A few years later this Polein, who had been held up at the assizes as an honest man with no criminal record, was arrested and found guilty of peddling cocaine.

Maître Hubert tried to defend me, but he was not up to the size of the prosecutor. Maître Bouffay, with his warm-hearted indignation, was the only one to make Pradel struggle for a while. But it didn't last, and the prosecutor's skill soon got him on top again. What's more, he flattered the jury, who swelled with pride at being treated as equals and as colleagues by this awe-inspiring character.

By eleven o'clock at night the game of chess was over. It was checkmate for my counsel. And I, an innocent man – I was found guilty.

In the person of Pradel, the public prosecutor, Society wiped out a young man of twenty-five for the term of his natural life. And none of your reductions, thank you very much! It was the president, Bevin, who handed me out this overflowing dish.

'Prisoner, stand up,' he said in a toneless voice.

I got to my feet. There was a complete silence in the court; people were holding their breath, and my heart beat a little faster. Some jurymen watched me; others hung their heads; they looked ashamed.

20

'Prisoner, since the jury has answered yes to all the questions except for that of premeditation, you are sentenced to undergo penal servitude for life. Have you anything to say?'

I did not flinch; I stood there naturally; all I did was to grip the bar of the dock a little harder. 'Yes, Monsieur le Président: what I have to say is that I am truly innocent and that I am the victim of a plot worked up by the police.' I heard a murmur from the place where there were some fashionably-dressed women, distinguished visitors, sitting behind the judges. Without raising my voice I said to them, 'Shut up, you rich women who come here for dirty thrills. The farce is over. A murder has been solved by your clever police and your system of justice – you've had what you came for.'

'Warders,' said the President, 'take the prisoner away.'

Before I vanished I heard a voice calling out, 'Don't you worry, sweetheart. I'll come out there and find you.' It was my brave, splendid Nénette giving full voice to her love. In the body of the court my friends of the underworld applauded. They knew perfectly well what to think about this killing, and this was their way of showing me that they were proud I had not given anything away or put the blame on anybody else.

Once we were back in the little room where we had been before the trial the gendarmes put the handcuffs on me, and one of them arranged a short chain, fixing my right wrist to his left. Not a word. I asked for a cigarette. The sergeant gave me one and lit it for me. Every time I took it out or put it back to my mouth the gendarme had to raise his arm or lower it to follow my movement.

I stood there until I had smoked about three-quarters of the cigarette. No one uttered a sound. I was the one who looked at the sergeant and said, 'Let's go.'

Down the stairs, surrounded by a dozen gendarmes, and I came to the inner yard of the law-courts. Our black maria was waiting for us there. It was not the sort with compartments: we sat on benches, about ten of us. The sergeant said, 'Conciergerie.'

When we reached this last of Marie-Antoinette's palaces, the gendarmes handed me over to the head warder, who signed a paper, their receipt. They went off without saying anything, but before they left the sergeant shook my two handcuffed hands. Surprise!

The head warder said to me, 'What did they give you?'

'Life.'

'It's not true?' He looked at the gendarmes and saw that it *was* true. This fifty-year-old warder had seen plenty and he knew all about my business: he had the decency to say this to me – 'The bastards! They must be out of their minds!'

Gently he took off my handcuffs, and he was good-hearted enough to take me to the padded cell himself, one of those kept specially for men condemned to death, for lunatics, very dangerous prisoners and those who have been given penal servitude.

'Keep your heart up, Papillon,' he said, closing the door on me. 'We'll send you some of your things and the food from your other cell. Cheer up!'

'Thanks, chief. My heart's all right, believe me; I hope their penal bleeding servitude will choke them.'

A few minutes later there was a scratching outside the door. 'What's up?' I said.

'Nothing,' said a voice. 'It's only me putting a card on the door.'

'Why? What's it say?'

'Penal servitude for life. To be watched closely.'

They're crazy, I thought: do they really suppose that this ton of bricks falling on my head is going to worry me to the point of committing suicide? I am brave and I always shall be brave. I'll fight everyone and everything. I'll start right away, tomorrow.

As I drank my coffee the next day I wondered whether I should appeal. What was the point? Should I have any better luck coming up before another court? And how much time would it waste? A year: maybe eighteen months. And all for what – getting twenty years instead of life?

As I had thoroughly made up my mind to escape, the number

of years did not count: I remembered what a sentenced prisoner had said to an assize judge. 'Monsieur, how many years does penal servitude for life last in France?'

I paced up and down my cell. I had sent one wire to comfort my wife and another to a sister who, alone against the world, had done her best to defend her brother. It was over: the curtain had fallen. My people must suffer more than me, and far away in the country my poor father would find it very hard to bear so heavy a cross.

Suddenly my breath stopped: *but I was innocent*! I was indeed; but for whom? Yes, who was I innocent for? I said to myself, above all don't you ever arse about telling people you're innocent: you'll only get laughed at. Getting life on account of a ponce and then saying it was somebody else that took him apart would be too bleeding comic. Just you keep your trap shut.

All the time I had been inside waiting for trial, both at the Santé and the Conciergerie, it had never occurred to me that I could possibly get a sentence like this, so I had never really thought about what 'going down the drain' might be like.

All right. The first thing to do was to get in touch with men who had already been sentenced, men who might later be companions in a break. I picked upon Dega, a guy from Marseilles. I'd certainly see him at the barber's. He went there every day to get a shave. I asked to go too. Sure enough, when I came in I found him standing there with his nose to the wall. I saw him just as he was making another man move round him so as to have longer to wait for his turn. I got in right next to him, shoving someone else aside. Quickly I whispered, 'You OK, Dega?'

'OK, Papi. I got fifteen years. What about you? They say you really copped it.'

'Yes: I got life.'

'You'll appeal?'

'No. The thing to do is to eat well and to keep fit. Keep your strength up. Dega: we'll certainly need good muscles. Are you loaded?'

'Yes. I've got ten bags* in pounds sterling. And you?'

'No.'

* 10,000 francs

'Here's a tip: get loaded quick. Your counsel was Hubert, wasn't he? He's a square and he'd never bring you in your charger. Send your wife with it, well filled, to Dante's. Tell her to give it to Dominique le Riche and I guarantee it'll reach you.'

'Ssh. The screw's watching us.'

'So we're having a break for gossip, are we?' asked the screw.

'Oh, nothing serious,' said Dega. 'He's telling me he's sick.'

'What's the matter with him? Assizes colic?' And the fat-arsed screw choked with laughter.

That was life all right. I was on the way down the drain already. A place where you howl with laughter, making cracks about a boy of twenty-five who has been sentenced for the whole of the rest of his life.

I got the charger. It was a beautifully polished aluminium tube that unscrewed exactly in the middle. It had a male half and a female half. There was 5,600 francs in new notes inside. When it was passed to me I kissed it: yes, I kissed this three-and-a-half-inch thumb-thick tube before shoving it into my anus. I drew a deep breath so that it should get right up to my colon. It was my safe-deposit. They could strip me, make me open my legs, make me cough and bend double, but they could never find out whether I had anything. It went up very high into my big intestine. It was part of me. This was life and freedom that I was carrying inside me – the path to revenge. For I was thoroughly determined to have my revenge. Indeed, revenge was all I thought of.

It was dark outside. I was alone in the cell. A strong ceiling light let the screw see me through the little hole in the door. It dazzled me, this light. I laid my folded handkerchief over my eyes, for it really hurt. I was lying on a mattress on an iron bed – no pillow – and all the details of that horrible trial passed through my mind.

Now at this point perhaps I have to be a little tedious, but in order to make the rest of this long tale understandable and in order to thoroughly explain what kept me going in my struggle I must tell everything that came into my mind at that point, everything I really saw with my mind's eye during those first days when I was a man who had been buried alive.

How was I going to set about things once I had escaped?

Because now that I possessed my charger I hadn't a second's doubt that I was going to escape. In the first place I should get back to Paris as fast as possible. The first one to kill would be Polein, the false witness. Then the two cops in charge of the case. But just two cops was not enough: I ought to kill the lot. All the cops. Or at least as many as possible. Ah, I had the right idea. Once out, I would get back to Paris, I'd stuff a trunk with explosive. As much as it would hold. Ten, twenty, maybe forty pounds: I wasn't sure quite how much. And I began working out what it would take to kill a great many people.

Dynamite? No, cheddite was better. And why not nitroglyc-erine? Right, I'd get advice from the people inside who knew more about it than me. But the cops could really rely upon me to provide what was coming to them, and no short measure, either.

I still had my eyes closed, with the handkerchief keeping them tight shut. Very clearly I could see the trunk, apparently innocent but really crammed with explosives, and the exactly set alarm-clock that would fire the detonator. Take care: it had to go off at ten in the morning in the assembly room of the Police Judiciaire* on the first floor of 36, quai des Orfèvres. At that moment there would be at least a hundred and fifty cops gathered to hear the report and to get their orders. How many steps to go up? I mustn't get it wrong.

I should have to work out the exact time it would take for the trunk to get up from the street to the place where it was to explode – work it out to the second. And who was going to carry it? OK: I'd get it in by bluff. I'd take a cab to the door of the Police Judiciaire and in a commanding voice I'd say to the two slops on guard, 'Take this trunk up to the assembly room for me: I'll follow. Tell Commissaire Dupont that it's from Inspecteur chef Dubois, and that I'll be there right away.'

But would they obey? What if I chanced upon the only two intelligent types among all those idiots? In that case it was no go. I'd have to find something else. Again and again I racked my brains. Deep inside I had no doubt that I should succeed in finding some hundred per cent certain way of doing it.

I got up for a drink of water. All that thinking had given

* The branch of the police particularly concerned with crime.

me a headache. I lay down again without the cloth over my eyes: slowly the minutes dropped by. That light, dear God above, that light! I wetted the handkerchief and put it on again. The cold water felt good, and being heavier now the handkerchief fitted better over my eyelids. I would always do it that way from now on.

Those long hours during which I worked out my future revenge were so vivid that I could see myself carrying it out exactly as though the thing was actually being done. All through those nights and even during part of every day, there I was, moving about Paris, as though my escape was something that had already happened. I was dead certain that I should escape and that I should get back to Paris. And of course the first thing to do was to square the account with Polein: and after him, the cops. And what about the members of the jury? Were those bastards to go on living in peace? The poor silly bastards must have gone home very pleased with themselves for having carried out their duty with a capital D. Stuffed with their own importance, they would lord it over their neighbours and their drabble-tailed wives, who would have kept supper back for them.

OK. What was I to do about the jurymen? Nothing. They were poor dreary half-wits. They were in no way fitted to be judges. If one of them was a retired gendarme or a customs-man, he would react like a gendarme or a customs-man. And if he was a milkman, then he'd act like any other dim-wit pedlar. They had gone right along with the public prosecutor and he had had no sort of difficulty in bowling them over. They weren't really answerable. So that was settled: I'd do them no harm whatsoever.

As I write these thoughts that came to me so vividly all those years ago and that now come crowding back with such terrible clarity, I remember how intensely total silence and complete solitariness can stimulate an imaginary life, when it is inflicted upon a young man shut up in a cell – how it can stimulate the imagination before the whole thing turns to madness. So intense and vivid a life that a man literally divides himself into two people. He takes wing and he quite genuinely wanders wherever he feels inclined to go. His home, his father, mother, family, his childhood – all the various stages of his life. And then even more, there are all those castles in Spain that appear in his fertile mind with such an unbelievable vividness that he really comes to believe that he is living through everything that he dreams.

Thirty-six years have passed, and yet recording everything that came into my head at that moment of my life does not need the slightest effort.

No: I should do the members of the jury no harm: my pen races along. But what about the prosecuting counsel? I must not miss him, not at any cost. In any case, I had a ready-made recipe for him, straight out of Alexandre Dumas. Just like in *The Count of Monte Cristo*, and the guy they shoved into the cellar and let die of hunger.

As for that lawyer, yes, he was answerable all right. That red-robed vulture – there was everything in favour of putting him to death in the most hideous manner possible. Yes, that was what I should do: after Polein and the cops, I should devote my whole time to dealing with this creep. I'd rent a villa. It'd have to have a really deep cellar with thick walls and a very solid door. If the door wasn't thick enough I should sound-proof it myself with a mattress and tow. Once I had the villa I'd work out his movements and then kidnap him. The rings would be all ready in the wall, so I'd chain him up straight away. And then which of us was going to have fun?

I had him directly opposite me: under my closed eyelids I could see him with extraordinary exactness. Yes, I looked at him just as he had looked at me in court. The scene was so clear and distinct that I could feel the warmth of his breath on my face; for I was very close, face to face, almost touching him. His hawk's eyes were dazzled and terrified by the beam of a very powerful headlight I had focused on him. Great drops of sweat ran down his red, swollen face. I could hear my questions and I listened to his replies. I experienced that moment very vividly.

'Do you recognize me, you sod? I'm Papillon. Papillon, the guy you so cheerfully sent down the line for life. You sweated over your books for years and years so as to be a highly educated man; you spent your nights doing Roman law and all that jazz; you learnt Latin and Greek and you sacrificed your youth so as to become a great speaker. Do you think it was worth it? Where did it get you, you silly bastard? What did it help you do? To work out new, decent laws for the community? To persuade the people that peace is the finest thing on earth? To preach the philosophy of some terrific religion? Or even to use your influence, your superior college education, to persuade others to be better people or at least stop being wicked? Tell me, have you used your knowledge to pull men out of the water or to drown them? You've never helped a soul: you've only had one single motive – ambition! Up, up. Up the steps of your lousy career. The penal settlements' best provider, the unlimited supplier of the executioner and the guillotine – that's your glory. If Deibler* had any sense of gratitude he'd send you a case of the best champagne every New Year. Isn't it thanks to you, you bleeding son of a bitch, that he's been able to lop off five or six more heads in the past twelve months? Anyhow, now I'm the one that's got you, chained good and hard to this wall. I can just see the way you grinned, yes, I can see your triumphant look when they read out my sentence after your speech for the prosecution. It seems only yesterday, and yet it was years ago. How many? Ten years? Twenty?'

But what was happening to me? Why ten years? Why twenty? Get a hold of yourself, Papillon; you're young, you're strong, and you've got five thousand six hundred francs in your gut. Two years, yes. I'd do two years out of my life sentence, and no more: I swore that to myself.

Snap out of it, Papillon, you're going crazy. The silence and this cell are driving you out of your mind. I've got no cigarettes. Finished the last yesterday. I'll start walking. After all, I don't have to have my eyes closed or my handkerchief over them to see what goes on. That's it; I'm on my feet. The cell's four yards long from the door to the wall – this is to say five short paces. I began walking, my hands behind my back. And I went on again, 'All right. As I was saying, I can see your triumphant look quite distinctly. Well, I'm going to change it for you: into something quite different. In one way it's easier for you than it was for me. I couldn't shout out, but you can. Shout just as much as you like; shout as loud as you like. What am I going to do to you? Dumas' recipe? Let you die of hunger, you sod? No: that's not enough. To start with I'll just put out your eyes. Eh? You still look triumphant, do you? You think that if I put your eyes out at least you'll have the advantage of not seeing me any longer, and that I'll be

* The executioner in 1932.

28

deprived of the pleasure of seeing the terror in them. Yes, you're right: I mustn't put them out. At least not right away. That'll be for later. I'll cut your tongue out, though, that terrible cutting tongue of yours, sharp as a knife; no, sharper – as sharp as a razor. The tongue that you prostituted to your splendid career. The same tongue that says pretty things to your wife, your kids and your girl-friend. Girl-friend? Boy-friend, more likely. Much more likely. You couldn't be anything but a passive, flabby pouffe. That's right: I must begin by doing away with your tongue, because next to your brain that's what does the damage. You see it very well, you know: so well you could persuade the jury to answer yes to the questions put to them. So well that you could make the cops look like they were straight and devoted to their duty: so well that that witness's cock and balls seemed to hold water. So well that those twelve bastards thought I was the most dangerous man in Paris. If you hadn't possessed this false, skilful, persuasive tongue, so practised at distorting people and facts and things, I should still be sitting there on the terrace of the Grand Café in the Place Blanche, and I'd never have had to stir. So we're all agreed, then, that I'm going to rip this tongue of yours right out. But what'll I do it with?'

I paced on and on and on. My head was spinning, but there I was, still face to face with him, when suddenly the electricity went out and a very faint ray of daylight made its way into the cell through the boarded window.

What? Morning already? Had I spent the whole night with my revenge? What splendid hours they had been! How that long, long night had flown by!

Sitting on my bed, I listened. Nothing. The most total silence. Now and then a little click at my door. It was the warder, wearing slippers so as to make no sound, opening the little metal flap and putting his eye to the peep-hole that let him see me without my being able to see him.

The machinery that the Republic of France had thought up was now entering its second phase. It was working splendidly: in its first run it had wiped out a man that might be a nuisance to it. But that was not enough. The man was not to die too quickly: he mustn't manage to get out of it by way of suicide. He was wanted. Where would the prison service be if there weren't any prisoners? In the shit. So he was to be watched. He had to go off alive to the penal settlements, where he would provide a living for still more state employees. I heard the click again, and it made me smile.

Don't you worry, you sod: I shan't escape. At least not the way you're afraid of – not by suicide. There's only one thing I want, and that's to keep alive and as fit as possible and to leave as soon as I can for that French Guiana where you're sending me, bloody fools that you are: thank God.

This old warder with his perpetual clicking was a fairy godmother in comparison with the screws over there: they were no choir-boys, not by any means. I'd always known that; for when Napoleon set up the penal settlements and they said to him. 'Who are you going to have to look after these hard cases?' he answered, 'Harder cases still.' Afterwards I found that the inventor of the penal settlements had not lied.

Clang clang: an eight-inch-square hole opened in the middle of my door. They passed me in coffee and a pound and a half of bread. Now I was sentenced I was no longer allowed to have things sent in from the restaurant, but if I could pay I could still buy cigarettes and a certain amount of food from the little canteen. That would last a few days more, then after that nothing. The Conciergerie was the stage just before penal internment. I smoked a Lucky Strike, enjoying it enormously: six francs sixty a packet they cost. I bought two. I was spending my official prison money because soon they would be confiscating it for the costs of the trial.

Dega sent a little note in my bread to tell me to go to the de-lousing centre. 'There are three lice in the matchbox.' I took out the matches and I found his fine healthy cooties. I knew what it meant. I showed them to the warder so that the next day he should send me and all my things, including the mattress, to a steam-room where all the parasites would be killed – except us, of course. And there the next day I met Dega. No warder in the steam-room. We were alone.

'You're a good guy, Dega. Thanks to you I've got my charger.'

'It doesn't bother you?'

'No.'

'Every time you go to the latrine, wash it well before you put it back.'

'Yes. I think it's completely water-tight. The folded notes are perfect, though I've had it in this last week.'

'That means it's all right, then.'

30

'What do you think you'll do, Dega?'

'I'm going to pretend to be mad. I don't want to go to Guiana. I'll do maybe eight or ten years here in France. I've got contacts and I can get five years remission at least.'

'How old are you?'

'Forty-two.'

'Then you're out of your mind! If you do ten out of your fifteen you'll come out an old man. Are you scared of penal?'

'Yes. I'm not ashamed of saying it to you, Papillon, but I'm scared. It's terrible in Guiana. Eighty per cent mortality every year. One convoy takes the place of the last, and each convoy has between eighteen hundred and two thousand men. If you don't get leprosy you get yellow fever or one of those kinds of dysentery there's no recovering from, or else consumption or malaria. And if you escape all that then it's very likely you'll get murdered for your charger, or else you'll die trying to make a break. Believe me, Papillon, I'm not trying to discourage you; but I've known a good many lags who've come back to France after doing short stretches – five to seven years – and I know what I'm talking about. They are absolute complete bleeding wrecks. They spend nine months of the year in hospital; and they say that making a break is nothing like what people think – not a piece of cake at all.'

'I believe you, Dega. But I believe in myself, too. I won't waste much time there. That's something you can be sure of. I'm a sailor and I understand the sea, and you can trust me when I say I shall make a break very soon. And what about you? Can you really see yourself doing ten years hard? Even if they do give you five off, which is not at all sure, do you really think you could do it without being driven crazy by the solitary? Take me now, all alone in that cell with no books, no going out, no being able to talk to anyone twenty-four hours every god-damned day – it's not sixty minutes you have to count in each hour but six hundred: and even then you're far short of the truth.'

'Maybe. But you're young and I'm forty-two.'

'Listen, Dega, tell me straight: what is it you're scared of most? The other lags, isn't it?'

'To tell you straight, Papi, yes it is. Everyone knows I'm a millionaire, and there's no distance between that and cutting my throat because they think I'm carrying fifty or a hundred thousand on me.'

'Listen, do you want us to make a pact? You promise me not to go crazy and I'll promise to keep right next to you all the time. Each can support the other. I'm strong and I move quick: I learnt how to fight when I was a kid and I'm terrific with a knife. So as far as the other lags are concerned you can rest easy: we'll be respected, and more than that we'll be feared. As for the break, we don't need anyone else. You've got cash, I've got cash: I know how to use a compass and I can sail a boat. What more do you want?'

He looked at me hard, right in the eye ... We embraced one another. The pact was signed.

A few moments later the door opened. He went off with his pack in one direction and I in the other. We were not very far apart and we saw one another from time to time at the barber's or the doctor's or in chapel on Sundays.

Dega had been sent down for the business of the phony National Defence bonds. A bright forger had produced them in a very unusual way: he bleached the five hundred franc bonds and overprinted them with the ten thousand franc text, absolutely perfectly. As the paper was the same, banks and businessmen accepted them just like that. It had been going on for years and the government's financial section was all at sea until the day they picked up a character named Brioulet – caught him red-handed.

Louis Dega was sitting there calmly, keeping an eye on his bar in Marseilles, where the pick of the southern underworld came every night and where the really hard guys from all over the world met one another – an international rendezvous. That was 1929 and he was a millionaire. Then one night a young, pretty, well-dressed woman turned up. She asked for Monsieur Louis Dega.

'That's me, Madame. What can I do for you? Come into the next room.'

'Look, I'm Brioulet's wife. He's in Paris in prison for passing forged bonds. I saw him in the visiting-room at the Santé: he gave me the address of this bar and told me to come and ask you for twenty thousand francs to pay the lawyer.'

It was at this point, faced with the danger of a woman who knew his part in the business, that Dega, one of the most esteemed crooks in France, made the one remark he never should have made. 'Listen, Madame, I don't know your husband from Adam, and if you need money, go on the streets.

You're young and pretty and you'll make more than you need.' Furious, the poor woman ran out in tears. She told her husband. Brioulet was mad and the next day he told the investigating magistrate everything he knew, directly accusing Dega of being the man who produced the forged bonds. A team of the most intelligent detectives in the country got on to Dega's trail. One month later Dega, the forger, the engraver and eleven accomplices were all arrested at the same moment in different places and put behind bars. They came up at the Seine Assizes and the trial lasted fourteen days. Each prisoner was defended by a famous lawyer. Brioulet would never take back a single word. And the result was that for a piddling twenty thousand francs and a damn-fool crack the biggest crook in France got fifteen years hard labour. There he was, ten years older than his age, and completely ruined. And this was the man I had just signed a treaty with – a life and death pact.

Maître Raymond Hubert came to see me. He wasn't very pleased with himself. I never uttered a word of blame.

One, two, three, four, five, about turn . . . One, two, three, four, five, about turn. It was a good many hours now that I had been walking up and down between the door and the window of my cell. I smoked: I felt I was well in control, steady-handed and able to cope with anything at all. I promised myself not to think about revenge for the time being. Let's leave the prosecuting counsel just there where I left him, chained to the rings in the wall, opposite me, without yet making up my mind exactly how I'd do him in.

Suddenly a shriek, a desperate, high-pitched, hideously dying shriek made its way through the door of my cell. What was it? It was like the sound of a man under torture. But this was not the Police Judiciaire. No way of telling what was going on. They turned me right up, those shrieks in the night. And what strength they must have had, to pierce through that padded door. Maybe it was a lunatic. It's so easy to go mad in these cells where nothing ever gets through to you. I talked aloud there all by myself: I said to myself what the hell's it got to do with you? Keep your mind on yourself, nothing but yourself and your new side-kick Dega. I bent down, straightened up and hit myself hard on the chest. It really hurt: so everything was all right – the muscles of my arms were working perfectly. And what about your legs, man? You can congratulate them, because you've been walking more than sixteen hours now and you're not even beginning to feel tired.

The Chinese discovered the drop of water that falls on your head. The French discovered silence. They do away with everything that might occupy your mind. No books, no paper, no pencil: the heavily-barred window entirely boarded up: only a very little light filtering through a few small holes.

That piercing shriek had really shaken me, and I went up and down like an animal in a cage, I had the dreadful feeling that I had been left there, abandoned by everybody, and that I was literally buried alive. I was alone, absolutely alone: the only thing that could ever get through to me was a shriek.

The door opened. An old priest appeared. Suddenly you're not alone: there's a priest there, standing in front of you.

'Good evening, my son. Forgive me for not having come before, but I was on holiday. How are you?' And the good old curé walked calmly into the cell and sat right down on my pad. 'Where do you come from?'

'The Ardèche.'

'And your people?'

'Mum died when I was eleven. Dad was very good to me.'

'What did he do?'

'School-teacher.'

'Is he alive?'

'Yes.'

'Why do you speak of him in the past if he is still alive?'

'Because although *he's* alive all right, I'm dead.'

'Oh, don't say that! What did you do?'

In a flash I thought how square it would sound to say I was innocent: I replied, 'The police say I killed a man; and if they say it, it must be true.'

'Was it a tradesman?'

'No. A ponce.'

'And they've sentenced you to hard labour for life for something that happened in the underworld? I don't understand. Was it murder?'

'No. Manslaughter.'

'My poor boy, it's unbelievable. What can I do for you? Would you like to pray with me?'

'I never had any religious instruction. I don't know how to pray.'

'That doesn't matter, my son: I'll pray for you. God loves

all His children, whether they are christened or not. Repeat each word as I say it, won't you?' His eyes were so gentle, and such kindness beamed from his round face that I was ashamed to refuse; and as he had gone down on his knees I did the same. 'Our Father which art in heaven . . .' Tears came into my eyes: the dear priest saw them and with his plump finger he gathered a big drop as it ran down my cheek. He put it to his mouth and drank it. 'My son,' he said, 'these tears are the greatest reward God could ever have sent me today, and it comes to me through you. Thank you.' And as he got up he kissed me on the forehead.

We sat there, side by side on the bed again. 'How long is it since you wept?'

'Fourteen years.'

'Why fourteen years ago?'

'It was the day Mum died.'

He took my hand in his and said, 'Forgive those who have made you suffer so.'

I snatched it away and sprang into the middle of my cell – an instinctive reaction. 'Not on your life! I'll never forgive them. And I'll tell you something, Father. There's not a day, not a night, not an hour or minute when I'm not busy working out how I'll kill the guys that sent me here – how, when and what with.'

'You say that, my son, and you believe it. You're young, very young. As you grow older you'll give up the thought of punishment and revenge.' Thirty-four years have passed now, and I am of his opinion. 'What can I do for you?' asked the priest again.

'A crime, Father.'

'What crime?'

'Going to cell 37 and telling Dega to get his lawyer to ask for him to be sent to the central prison at Caen – tell him I've done the same today. We have to get out of the Conciergerie quick and leave for one of the centrals where they make up the Guiana convoys. Because if you miss the first boat you have to wait another two years in solitary before there's another. And when you've seen him, Father, will you come back here?'

'What reason could I give?'

'You could say that you forgot your breviary. I'll be waiting for the answer.'

'And why are you in such a hurry to go off to such a hideous place as the penal settlement?'

I looked at him hard, this great-hearted salesman of the good word, and I was certain he would not betray me. 'So as to escape all the sooner, Father.'

'God will help you, my boy, I am sure of it; and I feel that you will remake your life. I can see in your eyes that you are a decent fellow and that your heart is in the right place. I'll go to cell 37 for you. You can expect an answer.'

He was back very soon. Dega agreed. The curé left me his breviary until the next day.

What a ray of sunlight that was! Thanks to that dear good man my cell was filled with it – all lit up. If God exists why does He allow such different sorts of human being on earth? Creatures like the prosecuting counsel, the police, Polein – and then this chaplain, the chaplain of the Conciergerie?

That truly good man's visit set me up, healed me: and it was useful, too. Our requests went through quickly and a week later there we were, seven of us lined up in the corridor of the Conciergerie at four in the morning. All the screws were there too, a full parade.

'Strip!' Everybody slowly took off his clothes. It was cold and I had goose-pimples.

'Leave your things in front of you. About turn. One pace backwards.' And there in front of each of us was a heap of clothes.

'Dress yourselves.' The good linen shirt I had been wearing a few moments earlier was replaced by a rough undyed canvas job and my lovely suit by a coarse jacket and trousers. No more shoes: instead of them I put my feet into a pair of wooden sabots. Up until then I'd looked like any other ordinary type. I glanced at the other six – Jesus, what a shock! No individuality left at all: they had turned us into convicts in two minutes.

'By the right, dress. Forward march!' With a escort of twenty warders we reached the courtyard and there, one after another, each man was shoved into a narrow cupboard in the cellular van. All aboard for Beaulieu – Beaulieu being the name of the prison at Caen,

The moment we got there we were taken into the governor's office. He was sitting in pomp behind an Empire desk on a dais some three feet high.

'Shun! The governor is going to speak to you.'

'Prisoners, you are here in transit until you can be sent off to the penal settlement. This is not an ordinary prison. Compulsory silence all the time: no visits: no letters from anyone. You obey or you are broken. There are two doors you can go out by. One leads to the penal settlement, if you behave well. The other to the graveyard. And just let me tell you about bad behaviour: the slightest error will get you sixty days in the punishment-cell on bread and water. No one has yet survived two consecutive sentences to the black-hole. You get my meaning?' He turned to Pierrot le Fou, who had been extradited from Spain. 'What was your calling in civil life?'

'Bullfighter, Monsieur le Directeur.'

The reply infuriated the governor and he bawled out 'Take him away! Double-quick time!' Before you could blink, the bullfighter had been knocked down, clubbed by four or five screws and hurried away from us. He could be heard shouting 'You bastards – five against one. With clubs too, you cowardly shits!' Then an *ah* like an animal given its death-wound: and nothing more. Only the sound of something being dragged along the concrete floor.

If we did not get the governor's meaning after that performance we should never get it at all. Dega was next to me. He moved one finger, just one, and touched my trousers. I understood his signal: 'Look out for yourself if you want to reach Guiana alive.' Ten minutes later each one of us was in a cell in the punishment block – each one of us except for Pierrot le Fou, who had been taken down below ground-level to a vile black-hole.

As luck would have it Dega was in the next cell to mine. Before this we had been shown to a kind of red-headed, one-eyed ogre, well over six feet tall, with a brand-new bull's pizzle in his right hand. This was the provost, a prisoner who acted as torturer under the orders of the screws. He was the terror of the convicts. With him at hand the warders could beat and flog the prisoners not only without tiring themselves out but also without getting blamed by the authorities in case anyone died of it.

Later, when I was doing a short spell in the hospital, I learnt the story of this human brute. The governor really ought to have been congratulated on choosing his executioner so well. This guy was a quarryman by trade. He lived in a little town up in Flanders, and one day he made up his mind to do away with himself and to kill his wife at the same time. He used a fair-sized stick of dynamite for the job. He lay down next to his wife, who was in their bedroom on the second floor of a six-storey building. She was asleep. He lit a cigarette and used it to light the fuse, holding the stick in his left hand between his own head and his wife's. God-almighty bang. Result: wife had to be scooped up with a spoon – she was literally mince-meat. Part of the house collapsed, killing three children and a seventy-year-old woman. And everybody else in it more or less dangerously hurt. As for this Tribouillard, the guy in question, he lost some of his left hand (only his little finger and half his thumb remaining) and his left eye and ear. His head was bashed badly enough to need trepanning. After his conviction they made him provost in the punishment block of the central prison. This half-maniac had complete power over the wretched prisoners who landed up there.

One, two, three, four, five, about turn . . . one, two, three, four, five, about turn . . . the unending to-and-fro between the door of the cell and the wall had begun.

You were not allowed to lie down during the daytime. At five in the morning everyone was woken by a piercing blast on a whistle. You had to get up, make your bed, wash, and then either walk about or sit on a stool clamped to the wall. You were not allowed to lie down all day long. And to put the last touch to the penal system the bed was made to fold up against the wall and hook there. That way the prisoner was unable to stretch himself out and he could be watched all the easier.

One, two, three, four, five . . . fourteen hours of pacing. To get into the way of this unceasing, mechanical rhythm you have to learn to keep your head down, your hands behind your back, and to walk neither too fast nor too slow, paces all the same length, turning automatically at each end of the cell, left foot one end, right the other.

One, two, three, four, five . . . The cells were better lit than at the Conciergerie and noises from outside could be heard – some noises from the punishment block and some that reached us from the countryside. At night you could make out the whistling or the singing as the farm-workers went home, happy after their cider.

I had my Christmas present. There was a crack in the plants blocking the window and through it I saw the snowy fields and a few tall black trees with the full moon lighting them up. Anyone would have said it was one of those cards you send at Christmas. The trees had been shaken by the wind and they had got rid of their covering of snow, so you could distinguish them quite clearly. They stood out as great dark patches against all the rest.

It was Christmas for everybody: it was even Christmas in one part of the prison. The authorities had made an effort for the convicts in transit – we were allowed to buy two bars of chocolate. I really mean two bars and not two slabs. My 1931 Christmas dinner consisted of these two bits of Aiguebelle chocolate.

One, two, three, four, five . . . The Law's repression had turned me into a pendulum: my whole world was this going to and fro in a cell. It had been scientifically worked out. Nothing, absolutely nothing, was allowed to remain in the cell. Above all the prisoner must never be allowed to turn his mind to other things. If I were caught looking through that crack in the window planks I should be severely punished. And after all, weren't they right, since as far as they were concerned I was merely a living corpse? What right had I to delight in the landscape?

There was a butterfly, a pale blue butterfly with a little black stripe, flying close to the window, and a bee humming not far from the butterfly. What on earth were they looking for in this place? They seemed to have gone out of their wits at the sight of the winter sun: unless maybe they were cold and wanted to get into the prison. A butterfly in winter is something that has come to life again. How come it wasn't dead? And how come that bee had left its hive? What a nerve – if only they had known it – to come here! Fortunately the provost had no wings, or they wouldn't be alive for long.

This Tribouillard was a bleeding sadist and I had a strong feeling there would be trouble with him. I wasn't wrong either, more's the pity. The day after those lovely insects came to see me I reported sick. I couldn't bear it any more – the loneliness was smothering me and I had to see a face and hear a voice, even an unpleasant one. For it would still be a voice; and something I just had to hear.

Stark naked in the icy corridor I stood there facing the wall, my nose three inches from it: I was the last but one in a line of eight, and I was waiting my turn to go in front of the doctor. I had wanted to see people: and I succeeded all right! The provost caught us just as I was whispering a few words to Julot, the one they called the hammer-man. The red-headed maniac's reaction was appalling. He half knocked me out with a punch on the back of my head, and as I'd not seen the blow coming my nose went smash against the wall. The blood spurted out, and as I got up – for I had fallen – I shook myself, trying to grasp what had happened. I made a faint movement of protest. That was the very thing the huge brute had been waiting for and with a kick in the belly he flattened me again and started flogging me with his bull's pizzle. Julot couldn't bear this. He jumped on him and a frightful dog-fight began: as Julot was getting the worst of it the warders stood calmly looking on. I got up. No one took any notice of me. I glanced round to see whether I could see anything to use as a weapon. Suddenly I saw the doctor leaning over his armchair in his surgery, trying to make out what was going on in the corridor: and at the same moment I caught sight of a saucepan-lid rising under the push of the steam. The big enamel saucepan was sitting on a stove that warmed the doctor's room. The steam was meant to purify the air, no doubt.

Then, moving very fast, I caught the pot by the handles – it burnt but I didn't drop it – and in one swing I flung all the boiling water into the provost's face. He was so busy with Julot he never saw me coming. The big bastard uttered a hideous, tearing shriek. He had really copped it. There he was writhing on the ground, trying to tear off his three woollen vests, one after the other. When at last he got to the third his skin came off with it. It was a narrow-necked vest and as he ripped it off the skin of his chest, part of the skin of his neck and all on his cheek came too, sticking to the wool. His one eye had been scalded as well, and he was blind. At last he got up, hideous, oozing with blood, flayed; and Julot took advantage of it to give him a terrible kick right in the balls. The huge brute went down, vomiting and frothing at the mouth. He was finished. As for us, we lost nothing by waiting for what was coming to us. The two warders who had been watching this performance hadn't the guts to tackle us. They sounded the alarm for reinforcements. They came in from all sides and the truncheon-blows rained down on us thick as hail. I had the luck to be knocked out very early, which prevented me from feeling much.

I woke up two storeys lower down, stark naked, in a flooded black-hole. Slowly I came to. I ran my hand all over my aching body. There were at least fourteen or fifteen lumps on my head. What was the time? I couldn't tell. Down here there was neither night nor day: no light of any kind. I heard a knocking on the wall, a knocking that came from a great way off.

Thump, thump, thump, thump, thump. This knocking was how we communicated with each other. I had to knock twice if I wanted to answer. Knock: but what with? In the darkness I couldn't make out anything I could use. Fists were no good – their blows were not sharp or distinct enough. I moved over to where I imagined the door was, for it was a little less dark over there. I came up hard against bars I had not seen. Reaching out in the darkness I came to understand that the cell was closed by a door about a yard from me, and that these bars I was touching prevented me from getting to it. This way, when anyone wants to go into a dangerous prisoner's cell he is in no danger of being touched, because the prisoner is in a cage. You can talk to him, soak him, throw his food in and insult him without the least risk. But there's this advantage – he can't be hit without danger, because in order to hit him you have to open the bars.

From time to time the knocking was repeated. Who could it be that was calling me? The guy deserved to be answered, because he was running a diabolical risk if he was caught. As I moved about I very nearly came down on my face. I had trodden on something hard and round. I felt for it: a wooden spoon. I grabbed it and got ready to answer. I waited there, with my ear hard up against the wall. Thump, thump, thump, thump, pause: thump, thump. Thump-thump, I replied. These two knocks meant to the man the other end, Go ahead, I'm taking the call. The knocking began again: thump, thump, thump . . . The alphabet ran by quickly – a b c d e f g h i j k l m n o p: stop. He was stopping at the letter p. I struck one hard blow. Thump. So he knew I had got the letter. Then came an a, a p, an i, and so on. He was saying, 'Papi, you OK? You got it bad. I have a broken arm.' It was Julot.

We talked to one another in this way for more than two hours without worrying about being caught. We were absolutely delighted, exchanging our messages. I told him I had nothing broken, that my head was covered with lumps, but that I was not wounded anywhere.

He had seen me going down, dragged by one foot, and he told me that at each stair my head had banged on the step before. He had never lost consciousness. He thought that Tribouillard had been very seriously scalded and that with the help of the wool the burns had gone deep – he was not going to get over it in a hurry.

Three very fast, repeated knocks told me there was something up. I stopped. And indeed a few moments later the door opened. There was a shout, 'Get to the back, you sod! Get to the back of your cell and stand to attention.' It was the new provost speaking. 'Batton's my name, my real name. I've got the name of the job, you see.' He lit up the black-hole and my naked body with a big ship's lantern. 'Here's something to put on. Don't you stir from back there. Here's some bread and water.* Don't stuff it all down at one go: you won't get anything more for another twenty-four hours.'

He shouted at me like a brute and then he raised the lantern to his face. I saw he was smiling, but not wickedly. He laid a finger on his lips and pointed at the things he had left. There must have been a warder in the passage, but he wanted to make me understand he was not an enemy.

True enough, inside the hunk of bread I found a big piece of boiled meat and in the pocket of the trousers – Christ, what wealth! – a packet of cigarettes and a dry lighter – a tinder lighter with a bit of tinderwick in it. Presents like this were worth millions here. Two shirts instead of one, and woollen drawers that came down to my ankles. I'll never forget him, that Batton. He was rewarding me for having wiped out Tribouillard. Before the dust-up he had only been assistant-provost. Now, thanks to me, he had risen to be the great man himself. In a word, he owed his promotion to me and he was showing his gratitude. And because we were safe with Batton, Julot

* 1 lb. of bread and one-and-three-quarter pints of water.

42

and I sent one another telegrams all day long. I learnt from him that our departure for the penal settlement was no great way off – three or four months.

Two days later we were brought out of the punishment cells and taken up to the governor's office, two warders to each of us. There were three men sitting there opposite the door, behind a table. It was a kind of court. The governor acted as president, and the deputy-governor and chief warders as assessors.

'Ah-ha, my young friends, so here you are! What have you got to say?'

Julot was very white and his eyes were swollen: he certainly had a temperature. His arm had been broken three days ago, and he must have been in shocking pain. Quietly he said, 'My arm's broken.'

'You asked for it. That'll teach you to fly at people. You'll see the doctor when he comes. I hope it will be within a week. The waiting will be good for you, because the pain will perhaps be a lesson. But you don't think I'm going to send for a doctor especially for a fellow like you? You can just wait until the prison doctor has time to come, and he will look after you. But nevertheless I sentence you both to the black-hole until further orders.'

Julot looked full at me, right in the eye. He seemed to be saying, 'This well-dressed gent disposes of other people's lives very easily.'

I turned towards the governor again and looked at him. He thought I meant to speak. He said, 'And what about you? The sentence doesn't seem to be to your liking? Have you anything to say against it?'

I said, 'Absolutely nothing, Monsieur le Directeur. The only thing I feel is an urge to spit in your eye; but I don't like to do so, in case it should dirty my spit.'

He was taken aback, he reddened and for a moment he couldn't grasp what I'd said. But the chief warder grasped it all right. He roared at the screws, 'Take him out and look after him properly. I want to see him here again in an hour's time, begging pardon on his hands and knees. We'll tame him! I'll make him polish my boots with his tongue, soles and all. Don't be lenient with him – he's all yours.'

Two warders twisted my right arm, two others my left. I was flat on my face with my hands right up against my shoulder-blades. They put on handcuffs with a thumb-piece, fixing my left forefinger to the thumb of my right hand, and the top warder picked me up by the hair like an animal.

There's no point telling you what they did to me. I'll just say I had the handcuffs on behind my back for eleven days. I owed my life to Batton. Every day he tossed the regulation hunk of bread into my cell, but since I couldn't use my hands it was impossible to eat it. Even when I had it wedged up against the bars I couldn't manage to bite into the lump. But Batton also tossed in bits the size of a mouthful, and he tossed in enough to keep me alive. I heaped them up with my foot and flat on my belly I ate them like a dog. I chewed each bit very thoroughly, so as not to lose anything at all.

When they took the handcuffs off me on the twelfth day the steel had eaten in, and in some places the metal was covered with bruised flesh. The head warder got scared, particularly as I fainted away with the pain. After they had brought me round they took me to the hospital, where they cleaned me up with hydrogen peroxide. The attendant insisted on my being given an anti-tetanus shot. My arms had stiffened and could not go back to their natural position. It took more than half an hour of rubbing them with camphorated oil before I could bring them down to my sides.

I went back to the black-hole, and the chief warder, seeing the eleven hunks of bread, said, 'You can have a proper banquet now! But it's funny – you haven't got all that thin after eleven days of starving.'

'I drank plenty of water, chief.'

'Ah, so that's it. I get you. Well, now eat plenty to get your strength back.' And he went away.

The poor bloody half-wit! He said that because he was sure I hadn't eaten anything for eleven days and because if I stuffed myself all at once I should die of it. Not bleeding likely. Towards nightfall Batton sent me in some tobacco and ciga-rette-paper. I smoked and smoked, breathing out into the cen-tral-heating pipe – it never worked, of course, but at least it served that purpose.

Later I called up Julot. He too thought I had eaten nothing for eleven days and he advised me to go easy. I did not like to let him know the truth, because I was afraid of some bastard picking up the message. His arm was in plaster; he was in good form; he congratulated me on holding out. According to him the convoy was close at hand. The medical orderly had told him the shots the convicts were to be given before they left had already arrived. They usually came a month before the convoy left. Julot wasn't very cautious, for he also asked me whether I had managed to keep my charger.

Yes, I had kept it all right, but I can't describe what I had had to do not to lose it. There were some cruel wounds in my anus.

Three weeks later they took us out of the punishment cells. What was up? They gave us a marvellous shower with soap and hot water. I felt myself coming to life again. Julot was laughing like a child and Pierrot le Fou beamed all over himself with happiness.

Since we had come straight out of the black-hole we knew nothing about what was happening. The barber wouldn't answer when I whispered, 'What's up?' A wicked-looking character I didn't know said, 'I think we're amnestied from the punishment cells. Maybe they're scared of an inspector who's coming by. The great thing is they have to show us alive.' Each of us was taken to an ordinary cell. At noon, as I ate my first bowl of hot soup for forty-three days, I found a bit of wood. On it I read 'Leave in a week's time. Shots tomorrow.'

Who had sent it? I never knew. It must have been some convict who was decent enough to give us warning. He knew that if one of us knew it we all should. It was just chance that the message came to me. I called Julot right away and told him. 'Pass it on,' I said.

I heard telephoning all night long. As for me, once I'd sent it out I stopped. I was too comfortable in my bed. I didn't want any sort of trouble. And the prospect of going back to the black-hole didn't attract me at all. Today less than any other time.

Saint-Martin-de-Ré

That evening Batton sent me in three cigarettes and a piece of paper that read, 'Papillon, I know you'll remember me kindly when you go. I'm provost, but I try to hurt the prisoners as little as possible. I took the job because I've got nine children and I can't wait for a pardon. I'm going to try to earn it without doing too much harm. Good-bye. Good luck. The convoy is for the day after tomorrow.'

And in fact the next day they assembled us in the corridor of the punishment-block in groups of thirty. Medical orderlies from Caen gave us shots against tropical diseases. Three shots for each man, and three and a half pints of milk. Dega was close to me: he looked thoughtful. We no longer paid any attention to the rules of silence for we knew they couldn't put us in the punishment cell just after having our injections. We gossiped in an undertone right there in front of the screws, who dared not say anything because of the orderlies from the town.

Dega said to me, 'Are they going to have enough cellular vans to take us all in one go?'

'I don't think so.'

'It's a good way off, Saint-Martin-de-Ré, and if they take sixty a day, it'll last ten days, because we're close on six hundred here alone.'

'The great thing is to have the injections. That means you're on the list and soon you'll be in Guiana. Keep your chin up, Dega: the next stage is beginning now. Count on me, just as I count on you.'

He looked at me, his eyes shining with pleasure; he put his hand on my arm and once again he said, 'Life or death, Papi.'

There was nothing really much to say about the convoy, except that each man very nearly stifled in his little cupboard in the cellular van. The warders wouldn't let us have any air, not even by letting the doors stand just ajar. When we reached

La Rochelle two of the people in our van were found dead, asphyxiated.

There were people standing around on the quay – for Saint-Martin-de-Ré is an island and we had to take a boat to cross – and they saw those two poor unfortunate bastards being found. Not that they showed feelings of any sort for us, I may add. And since the gendarmes had to hand us over at the citadel, living or dead, they loaded the corpses on to the boat along with the rest of us.

It was not a long crossing, but it gave us a real breath of sea-air. I said to Dega, 'It smells of a break.' He smiled. And Julot, next to us, said, 'Yes. It smells of a break. I'm on my way back to the place I escaped from five years ago. Like a silly bastard I let myself be picked up just as I was on the point of carving up the fence who'd done the Judas on me at the time of my little trouble ten years ago. Let's try and stay together, because at Saint-Martin they put you ten to a cell in any old order, just as you come to hand.'

He'd got that one wrong, brother Julot. When we got there he and two others were called out and set apart from the rest. They were three men who had got away from the penal settlement: they had been retaken in France and now they were going back for the second time.

Grouped ten by ten in our cells, we began a life of waiting. We were allowed to talk and smoke, and we were very well fed. The only danger during this period was for your charger. You could never tell why, but suddenly you would be called up, stripped and very carefully searched. The whole of your body first, even the soles of your feet, and then all your clothes. 'Get dressed again!' And back you went to where you came from.

Cells: dining-hall: the courtyard where we spent hours and hours marching in single file. 'Left, right! Left, right! Left, right!' We marched in groups of five hundred convicts. A long, long crocodile; wooden shoes going clack-clack. Compulsory total silence. Then, 'Fall out!' Everyone would sit down on the ground, forming groups according to class or status. First came the men of the genuine underworld: with them it scarcely mattered where you came from, and there were Corsicans, men from Marseilles, Toulouse, Brittany, Paris and so on. There was even one from the Ardèche, and that was me. I must say this for the Ardèche – there were only two

Ardéchois in the whole convoy of one thousand nine hundred men, a gamekeeper who had killed his wife, and me. Which proves that the Ardéchois are good guys. The other groups came together more or less anyhow, because more flats than sharps go to the penal settlements, more squares than wide boys. These days of waiting were called observation days. And it was true enough they observed us from every possible angle.

One afternoon I was sitting in the sun when a man came up to me. A little man, spectacled, thin. I tried to place him, but with our clothing all being the same it was very difficult.

'You're the one they call Papillon?' He had a very strong Corsican accent.

'That's right. What do you want with me?'

'Come to the latrine,' he said. And he went off.

'That guy,' said Dega, 'he's some square from Corsica. A mountain bandit, for sure. What can he possibly want with you?'

'I'm going to find out.'

I went towards the latrines in the middle of the courtyard and when I got there I pretended to piss. The man stood next to me, in the same attitude. Without looking round he said, 'I'm Pascal Matra's brother-in-law. In the visiting-room he told me to come to you if I needed help – to come in his name.'

'Yes: Pascal's a friend of mine. What do you want?'

'I can't keep my charger in any more. I've got dysentery. I don't know who to trust and I'm afraid it'll be stolen or the screws will find it. Please, Papillon, please carry it for me a few days.' And he showed me a charger much bigger than mine. I was afraid he was setting a trap – asking me to find out whether I was carrying one myself. If I said I was not sure I could hold two, he'd know. Without any expression I said, 'How much has it got in it?'

'Twenty-five thousand francs.'

Without another word I took the charger – it was very clean, too – and there in front of him I shoved it up, wondering whether a man could hold two. I had no idea. I stood up, buttoned my trousers . . . it was all right. It did not worry me.

'My name's Ignace Galgani,' he said, before going. 'Thanks, Papillon.'

I went back to Dega and privately I told him about what had happened.

'It's not too heavy?'

'No.'

'Let's forget it then.'

We tried to get in touch with men who were being sent back after having made a break: Julot or Guittou, if possible. We were eager for information – what it was like over there, how you were treated, how you ought to set about things so as to be left paired with a friend, and so on. As luck would have it we chanced upon a very odd guy, a case entirely on his own. He was a Corsican who had been born in the penal settlement. His father had been a warder there, living with his mother on the Isles du Salut. He had been born on the Ile Royale, one of the three – the others are Saint-Joseph and Devil's Island. And (irony of fate!) he was on his way back, not as a warder's son but as a convict.

He had copped twelve years for housebreaking. Nineteen: frank expression and open face. Both Dega and I saw at once that he had been sold down the river. He only had a vague notion of the underworld; but he would be useful to us because he could let us know about what was in store. He told us all about life on the islands, where he had lived for fourteen years. For example, he told us that his nurse on the islands had been a convict, a famous tough guy who had been sent down after a knife-fight in Montmartre, a duel for the love of the beautiful Casque d'Or. He gave us some very valuable advice – you had to make your break on the mainland, because on the islands it was no go at all: then again you mustn't be listed dangerous, because with that against your name you would scarcely step ashore at Saint-Laurent-du-Maroni before they shut you right away – interned you for a certain number of years or for life, according to how bad your label was. Generally speaking, less than five per cent of the convicts were interned on the islands. The others stayed on the mainland. The islands were healthy, but (as Dega had already told me) the mainland was a right mess that gradually ate the heart out of you with all sorts of diseases, death in various shapes, murder, etc.

Dega and I hoped not to be interned on the islands. But there was a hell of a feeling there in my throat – what if I had been labelled dangerous? What with my lifer, the business with Tribouillard and that other one with the governor, I'd be lucky to get away with it.

One day a rumour ran through the prison – don't go to the

sick-bay whatever happens, because everybody who is too weak or too ill to stand the voyage is poisoned. It was certainly all balls. And indeed a Parisian, Francis la Passe, told us there was nothing in it. There had been a type who died of poison there, but Francis' own brother, who worked in the sick-bay, explained just what had happened.

The guy had killed himself. He was one of the top safebreaking specialists, and it seems that during the war he had burgled the German embassy in Geneva or Lausanne for the French Intelligence. He had taken some very important papers and had given them to the French agents. The police had brought him out of prison, where he was doing five years, specially for this job. And ever since 1920 he had lived quietly, just operating once or twice a year. Every time he was picked up he brought out his little piece of blackmail and the Intelligence people hurriedly stepped in. But this time it hadn't worked. He'd got twenty years and he was to go off with us. So as to miss the boat he had pretended to be sick and had gone into hospital. According to Francis la Passe's brother a tablet of cyanide had put paid to his capers. Safe deposits and the Intelligence Service could sleep in peace.

The courtyard was full of stories, some true, some false. We listened to them in either case – it passed the time.

Whenever I went to the latrines, either in the courtyard or in the cell, Dega had to go with me, on account of the chargers. He stood in front of me while I was at it and shielded me from over-inquisitive eyes. A charger is a bleeding nuisance at any time, but I had two of the things still, for Galgani was getting sicker and sicker. And there was a mystery about the whole affair: the charger I shoved up last always came out last, and the first always first. I've no idea how they turned about in my guts, but that's how it was.

At the barber's yesterday someone had a go at murdering Clousiot while he was being shaved. Two knife-stabs right next to his heart. By some miracle he didn't die. I heard about the whole thing from a friend of his. It was an odd story and I'll tell it one day. The attack was by way of settling accounts. The man who nearly got him died six years after this at Cayenne, having eaten bichromate of potassium in his lentils. He died in frightful agony. The attendant who helped the doctor at the post-mortem brought us five inches of gut. It had seventeen holes in it. Two months later this man's murderer was

50

found strangled in his hospital bed. We never knew who by.

It was twelve days now that we had been at Saint-Martin-de-Ré. The fortress was crammed to overflowing. Sentries patrolled on the ramparts night and day.

A fight broke out between two brothers, in the showers. They fought like wild-cats and one of them was put into our cell. André Baillard was his name. He couldn't be punished, he told me, because it was the authorities' fault: the screws had been ordered not to let the brothers meet on any account whatsoever. When you knew their story, you could see why.

André had murdered an old woman with some money, and his brother Emile hid the proceeds. Emile was shopped for theft and got three years. One day, when he was in the punishment cell with some other men, he let the whole thing out: he was mad with his brother for not sending him in money for cigarettes and he told them everything – he'd get André, he said; and he explained how it was André who had done the old woman in and how it was he, Emile, who had hidden the money. What's more, he said, when he got out he wouldn't give André a sou. A prisoner hurried off to tell the governor what he had heard. Things moved fast. André was arrested and the two brothers were sentenced to death. In death alley at the Santé their condemned cells were next door to one another. Each put in for a reprieve. Emile's was granted the forty-third day, but André's was turned down. Yet out of consideration for André's feelings Emile was kept in the condemned cell and the two brothers did their daily exercise together, the one behind the other, with chains on their legs.

On the forty-sixth day at half-past four in the morning André's door opened. They were all there, the governor, the registrar and the prosecuting counsel who had asked for his head. This was the execution. But just as the governor stepped forward to speak André's lawyer appeared, running, followed by someone else who handed the prosecutor a paper. Everyone went back into the corridor. André's throat was so tight and stiff he couldn't swallow his spit. This wasn't possible – executions were never interrupted once they had begun. And yet this one was. Not until the next day, after hours of dreadful doubt, did he hear from his lawyer that just before his execution President Doumer had been murdered by Gorguloff. But Doumer hadn't died right away. The lawyer had stood there all night outside the hospital, having told the Minister of Justice that if the President died before the time of the execution (between half-past four and five in the morning) he would call for a postponement on the grounds that there was no head of state. Doumer died at two minutes past four. Just time to warn the ministry, jump into a cab, followed by the man with the order for putting it off; but he got there three minutes too late to stop them opening André's door. The two brothers' sentences were commuted to transportation and hard labour for life: for on the day of the new president's election the lawyer went to Versailles, and as soon as Albert Lebrun was chosen, the lawyer handed him the petition for a reprieve. No president ever refuses the first reprieve he is asked for. 'Lebrun signed,' said André, 'and here I am, mate, alive and well, on my way to Guiana.' I looked at this character who had escaped the guillotine and I said to myself that in spite of all I had gone through it was nothing to what he must have suffered.

Yet I never made friends with him. The idea of his killing a poor old woman to rob her made me feel sick. This André was always a very lucky man. He murdered his brother on the Ile Saint-Joseph some time later. Several convicts saw him. Emile was fishing, standing there on a rock and thinking about nothing but his rod. The noise of the heavy waves drowned every other sound. André crept up on his brother from behind with a thick ten-foot bamboo in his hand and shoved him off his balance with a single push. The place was stiff with sharks and precious soon Emile had become their lunch. He wasn't there at the evening roll-call and he was put down as having disappeared during an attempt to escape. No one talked about him any more. Only four or five convicts gathering coconuts high up on the island had seen what happened. Everyone knew, of course, except for the screws. André Baillard never heard another word about it.

He was let out of internment for 'good conduct' and he had a privileged status at Saint-Laurent-du-Maroni. They gave him a little cell to himself. He had a disagreement with another convict and one day he treacherously asked him into this cell: there he killed him with a stab right to the heart. They wore his plea of self-defence and he was acquitted. Then, when the penal settlement was abolished, he was pardoned, still on account of his 'good conduct'.

Saint-Martin-de-Ré was stuffed with prisoners. Two quite different sorts: eight hundred or a thousand real convicts and nine relégués – men in preventive detention. To be a convict you have to have done something serious or at least to have been accused of an important crime. The mildest sentence is seven years hard labour and then it goes up by stages to life, or perpetuity, as they say. A commuted death-sentence automatically means perpetuity. Preventive detention, or relegation, that's something quite different. If he's sentenced from three to seven times, a man can be relegated. It's true they're all incorrigible thieves and you can see that society has to protect itself. But still it's shameful that a civilized nation should have this extra sentence of preventive detention. They are small-time thieves – clumsy operators, since they are shopped so often – who get relegation (and in my time that meant the same as life) and who have never stolen as much as ten thousand francs in their whole career as thieves. That's the greatest bit of meaningless balls French civilization has to offer. A nation has no right to revenge itself nor to wipe out the people who hinder the workings of society. They are people who ought to be treated rather than be punished in such an inhuman way.

Now we had been seventeen days at Saint-Martin-de-Ré. We knew the name of the ship that was to carry us to the settlement: she was the *Martinière*. She was going to take one thousand eight hundred and seventy prisoners aboard. That morning eight or nine hundred convicts were assembled in the inner court of the fortress. We had been standing there for about an hour, lined up in ranks of ten, filling the square. A gate opened and in came men who were not dressed like the warders we were used to. They wore good, military kind of clothes: sky-blue. It wasn't the same as a gendarme and it wasn't the same as a soldier. They each had a broad belt with a holster; the revolver grip showed. There were about eighty of them. Some had stripes. They were all sunburnt and they were of any age between thirty-five and fifty. The old ones looked pleasanter than the young, who threw a chest and looked important – gave themselves airs. Along with these men's officers there came the governor of Saint-Martin-de-Ré, a gendarmerie colonel, three or four quacks in overseas army uniform and two priests in white cassocks. The gendarmerie colonel picked up a speaking-trumpet and put it to his mouth. We expected *shun*! but nothing of the kind. He said, 'Listen carefully, all of you. From this moment on you are taken over by the authorities of the Ministry of Justice, representing the penitentiary administration of French Guiana, whose administrative centre is the town of Cayenne. Major Barrot, I hereby hand over to you the eight hundred and sixteen convicts now present, and this is the list of their names. Be so good as to check that they are all here.'

The roll-call began straight away. 'So-and-so, present. So-and-so . . .' etc. It lasted two hours and everything was correct. Then we watched the two authorities exchanging signatures on a little table brought for the purpose.

Major Barrot had as many stripes as the colonel, but they were gold and not the gendarmerie's silver: he took his turn at the megaphone.

'Transportees, from now on that is the name you'll always be called by – transportee so-and-so or transportee such-and-such a number – the number that will be allotted to you. From now on you are under the special penal settlement laws and regulations: you come under its own particular tribunals which will take the necessary decision with regard to you as the case arises. For crimes committed in the penal settlement these courts can condemn you to anything from imprisonment to death. These disciplinary sentences, such as prison or solitary confinement, are of course served in different establishments that belong to the administration. The officers you see opposite you are called supervisors. When you speak to them you will say "Monsieur le surveillant". After you have eaten you will be given a kitbag containing the settlement uniform. Everything has been provided for and you will not need anything but what is in the bag. Tomorrow you will go aboard the *Martinière*. We shall travel together. Don't lose heart at leaving this country: you will be better off in the settlement than in solitary confinement in France. You can talk, amuse yourselves, sing and smoke; and you needn't be afraid of being treated roughly so long as you behave yourselves. I ask you to leave the settling of your private disagreements until we reach Guiana. During the voyage discipline has to be very strict, as I hope you will understand. If there are any men among you who don't feel up to making the voyage, they may report to the infirmary, where they will be examined by the medical officers who are accompanying the convoy. I wish you all a pleasant trip.' The ceremony was over.

'Well, Dega, what do you think about it?'

'Papillon, old cock, I see I was right when I told you that the other convicts were the worst danger we'd have to cope with. That piece of his about "leave the settling of your private disagreements until we reach Guiana" meant plenty. Christ, what killings and murdering must go on there!'

'Never worry about that: just rely on me.'

I found Francis la Passe and said, 'Is your brother still a medical attendant?'

'Yes. He's not a real convict, only a bleeding relégué.'

'Get into touch with him as quick as possible: ask him to give you a scalpel. If he wants money for it, tell me how much. I'll pay.'

Two hours later I had a very strong steel-handled scalpel. Its only fault was that it was rather big; but it was a formidable weapon.

I went and sat very near the latrines in the middle of the courtyard and I sent for Galgani to give him back his charger; but it was going to be very hard to find him in that milling crowd – a huge yard crammed with eight hundred men. We had never caught sight of Julot, Guittou or Suzini since we got there.

The advantage of communal life is that you belong to a new society, if this could be called a society – you live in it, talk in it, become part of it. There are so many things to say, to hear and to do that you no longer have any time to think. And it seemed to me, as I saw how the past faded away, growing less important in comparison with everyday life, it seemed to me that once you got to the penal settlement you must almost forget what you have been, how or why you had landed up there, and concentrate upon one thing alone – escape. I was wrong, because the most important and most engrossing thing is above all to keep yourself alive.

Where were the cops, the members of the jury, the assizes, the judges, my wife, my father, my friends? They were there all right, thoroughly alive, each one in his place in my heart; but what with the intense excitement of leaving, of this great leap into the unknown, these new friendships and new aspects of life, they seemed to have less importance than before. But that was only a mere impression. When I wanted, and whenever my mind chose to open each one's file, they were all instantly alive once more.

Now here was Galgani, being led towards me, for even with

his thick pebble-lenses he could scarcely see. He looked better. He came up to me and shook my hand without a word.

I said, 'I want to give you back your charger. Now you're well you can carry it yourself. It's too much responsibility for me during the voyage; and then who knows whether we'll be in touch at the settlement, or whether we'll even see one another? So it's better you should have it back.' Galgani looked at me unhappily. 'Come on,' I said. 'Come into the latrine and I'll give it back to you.'

'No, I don't want it. You keep it – I give it to you. It's yours.'

'Why do you say that?'

'I don't want to get myself murdered for my charger. I'd rather live without money than have my throat slit for it. I give it to you, for after all there's no reason why you should risk your life, looking after my lolly for me. If you run the risk it might as well be for your own sake.'

'You're scared, Galgani. Have you been threatened already? Does anyone suspect you're loaded?'

'Yes: there are three Arabs who follow me all the time. That's why I've never come to see you, so they won't suspect we're in touch. Every time I go to the latrine, day or night, one of these three comes and puts himself next to me. Without making it obvious I've shown them absolutely plain that I'm *not* loaded, but in spite of all I can do they never let up. They think someone else has my charger; they don't know who; and they keep behind me to see when I'll get it back again.'

I looked hard at Galgani and I saw he was terror-stricken, really persecuted. I said, 'What part of the courtyard do they keep to?'

He said, 'Over towards the kitchen and the laundry.'

'Right, you stay here. I'll be back. But no, now I come to think of it, you come with me.' With Galgani at my side I went over towards the Arabs. I'd taken the scalpel out of my cap and I had the blade up my right sleeve, with the handle in my palm. When we had crossed the court, sure enough I saw them. Four of them. Three Arabs and a Corsican, a character by the name of Girando. I grasped the situation right away. It was the Corsican who had been cold-shouldered by the real hard men and who had put the Arabs up to this job. He must have known that Galgani was Pascal Matra's brother-in-law and that it wasn't possible for him *not* to have a charger.

'Hi, Mokrane. OK?'

'OK, Papillon. You OK too?'

'Hell, no. Far from it. I've come to see you guys to tell you Galgani is my friend. If anything happens to him, it's you who cop it first, Girando. And then the rest of you. And you can take that just how you like.'

Mokrane stood up. He was as tall as me – about five foot eight – and as broad-shouldered. The words had needled him and he was on the point of moving in to start things when I flashed the scalpel and with it right there shining-new in my hand I said, 'If you stir I'll kill you like a dog.'

He was knocked sideways by seeing me armed in a place where everybody was searched all the time, and he was shaken by my attitude and the length of the blade. He said, 'I got up to talk, not to fight.'

I knew it was not true, but it was to my advantage to save his face in front of his friends. I left the door open for him wide and handsome. 'OK, since you just got up to talk . . .'

'I didn't know Galgani was your friend. I thought he was a square. And you know very well, Papillon, that when you're skint you have to find cash somewhere to make a break.'

'Fair enough. You certainly have the right to struggle for your life, Mokrane, like anyone else. Only keep away from Galgani, see? You've got to look somewhere else.'

He held out his hand: I shook it hard. Jesus, I was well out of that one; for looking at it rightly, if I had killed that guy, I should never have left the next day. A little later I realized I had made a bleeding error. Galgani and I walked away. I said, 'Don't tell anyone about this caper. I don't want to have old Dega bawling me out.'

I tried to persuade Galgani to take the charger. He said, 'Tomorrow, before we leave.' The next day he lay so low that I set out for penal with two chargers aboard.

That night not one of us – and we were about eleven in the cell – not one of us said a word. For we all had more or less the same thought in our minds – this was the last day we should pass on French soil. Each of us was more or less filled with homesickness at the idea of leaving France for ever, with an unknown land and an unknown way of life at the end of our journey.

Dega did not speak. He sat next to me close to the barred door on to the corridor, where the air was a little fresher. I felt completely at sea. The information we had about what was coming was so contradictory that I did not know whether to be pleased or wretched or downright hopeless.

The other men in the cell were all genuine underworld characters. The only one who did not belong was the little Corsican who had been born in the settlement. All these men were in a grey, floating state of mind. The seriousness of the moment and its importance had made them almost entirely dumb. The cigarette-smoke wafted out of the cell into the corridor like a cloud, and if you didn't want your eyes to sting you had to sit lower than the heavy fog-blanket. No one slept except for André Baillard; it was natural enough for him, since his life had already been lost, as it were. As far as he was concerned everything else could only be unlooked-for heaven.

My life passed before my eyes like a film – childhood in a family filled with love, affectionate discipline, decent ways and good-heartedness; the wild flowers, the murmur of streams, the taste of the walnuts, peaches and plums that our garden gave us in such quantities; the smell of the mimosa that flowered every spring in front of our door; the outside of our house, and the inside with my family there – all this ran by before my eyes. It was a talking picture, one in which I heard the voice of my mother (she had loved me so), and then my father's – always affectionate and kind – and the barking of Clara, his gun-dog, calling me into the garden to play. The boys and girls of my childhood, the ones I had played with during the happiest days of my life. All this – this film I was watching without ever having meant to see it, this magic lantern that my subconscious had lit against my will – all this filled the night of waiting before the leap into the great unknown with sweet, gentle memories and emotions.

Now was the time to get things clear in my mind. Let's see: I was twenty-six and very fit; I had five thousand six hundred francs belonging to me in my gut and twenty-five thousand belonging to Galgani. Dega, there beside me, had ten thousand. It seemed to me I could count on forty thousand francs, for if Galgani couldn't look after his dough here he'd be even less capable of doing so aboard the ship or in Guiana. What's more, he knew it: and that's why he never came to ask for his charger. So I could count on that money – taking Galgani with me, of course. He'd have to profit by it – it was his cash, not mine. I'd use it for his good; but I should gain by it too. Forty thousand francs was a lot of money, so I should find it easy to buy helpers – convicts serving their time, men who had been let out, warders.

The conclusion was positive. As soon as I got there I must escape together with Dega and Galgani, and that was the only thing I was to concentrate upon at this point. I touched the scalpel, and the feel of the cold steel handle pleased me. It gave me confidence, having such a formidable weapon as that upon me. I had already proved how useful it could be in that business with the Arabs.

About three o'clock in the morning the men for solitary piled up eleven kitbags in front of the bars of the cell: they were all crammed full and each had a big label on it. I could read one that hung in through the bars. C –, Pierre, thirty years old, five foot eight and a half, waist size forty-two, shoes eight and a half, number x. This Pierre C – was Pierrot le Fou, a guy from Bordeaux who had got twenty years hard in Paris for homicide.

He was a good type, a decent, straightforward member of the underworld, and I knew him well. The label showed me how precise and well-organized the authorities in charge of the penal settlement were. It was better than the army, where they make you try your things on by guesswork. Here everything was written down and so each man would get things his own size. I could see from a bit of canvas at the top of the bag that the uniform was white with vertical red stripes. Dressed like that, you could scarcely pass unnoticed.

I tried to force my mind to make pictures of the assizes, the jurymen, the prosecuting counsel, etc. It flatly refused to obey me, and I could only get it to produce ordinary images. It came to me that if you want to live through anything imaginary as vividly as I did at the Conciergerie or at Beaulieu you have to be alone, utterly alone. It was a relief to understand this, and I saw that the communal life that was coming would bring other needs with it, other reactions and other plans.

Pierrot le Fou came up to the bars and said, 'OK, Papi?'

'What about you?'

'Well, as far as I'm concerned, I'd always dreamed of going to America; but I was a gambler, so I could never save enough for the trip. The cops had the idea of making me a present of it. You can't deny it was kind of them, Papillon.' He was speaking naturally. There was no bragging about what he said. You could feel that right down he was sure of himself. 'The cops' free trip to America has something to be said for it, you know. I'd much rather go to Guiana than sweat out fifteen years of solitary in France.'

'As I see it going crazy in a cell or just falling apart in some solitary confinement hole in France is even worse than dying of leprosy or yellow fever.'

'That's how I see it too,' he said.

'Look, Pierrot, this label is yours.'

He bent down, looking very close to read it, and slowly he made out the words. 'I can't wait to put these clothes on. I've a mind to open the bag – no one will say anything. After all, they're meant for me.'

'You leave it alone and wait till they tell you. This isn't the time to ask for trouble, Pierre. I need some peace and quiet.' He grasped what I meant and moved away from the bars.

Louis Dega looked at me and said, 'This is our last night, boy. Tomorrow they're taking us far away from our beautiful country.'

'Our beautiful country hasn't got such a very beautiful system of justice, Dega. Maybe we'll come to know countries that aren't so beautiful but that have a slightly more human way of treating people who have slipped up.' I didn't think I was so near the truth: the future was to show me that I was dead right. Total silence fell again.

Leaving for Guiana

Six o'clock, and everything was in motion. Convicts came round with coffee and then four warders appeared. Today they were in white; they still carried their revolvers. Spotless white tunics and buttons that shone like gold. One had three gold chevrons on his left sleeve: nothing on his shoulders.

'Transportees, come out into the corridor in twos. Each man will find the bag with his name on the label. Take the bag and move back against the wall, facing the corridor with your bag in front of you.'

It took twenty minutes before we were all lined up with our kitbags at our feet.

'Strip: roll up your things, put them into the jacket, bundle it all up and tie the sleeves . . . right. You over there, pick up the rolls and put them into the cell. Now dress. Put on vest, drawers, striped drill trousers, drill jacket, shoes and socks . . . You're all dressed?'

'Yes, Monsieur le surveillant.'

'Right. Keep the woollen jersey out of the bag in case it rains or turns cold. Bags on your left shoulder. In double file, follow me.'

With the sergeant in front, two warders at the sides and the fourth behind, our little column moved out to the courtyard. In under two hours eight hundred and ten convicts were lined up there. Forty men were called out, including Dega and me and the three who were being sent back after their escape – Julot, Galgani and Santini. These forty men were lined up in rows of ten. Each rank of the column that was taking shape had a warder beside it. No chains, no handcuffs. Three yards in front of us, walking backwards, ten gendarmes. They faced us, rifle in hand, and they marched like that all the way, each steered by another gendarme holding his shoulder-belt.

The great gate of the citadel opened, and slowly the column began to move. As the line emerged from the fortress so more gendarmes, carrying rifles or light machine-guns, joined the convoy, staying a couple of yards from it and keeping pace. Other gendarmes held back a huge crowd that had come to watch us leaving for the penal settlements. Half way to the quay I heard a quiet whistle from the windows of a house. I looked up and saw Nénette, my wife, and my friend Antoine D – at one window; Paula, Dega's wife, and his friend Antoine Giletti were at the other. Dega saw them too, and we marched with our eyes fixed on those windows as long as we could see them. That was the last time I ever set eyes on my wife: or my friend Antoine, who died much later in an air-raid on Marseilles. No one spoke. There was a total silence. No prisoner, no warder, no gendarme, no person in the crowd disturbed that truly heart-rending moment when everyone knew

61

that one thousand eight hundred men were about to vanish from ordinary life for ever.

We went aboard. The forty in front – that is to say us – were sent to the bottom of the hold, into a cage with thick bars. There was a marker on it. I read 'Hall no. 1. 40 men top special category. Strict, continual surveillance.' Each man was given a rolled-up hammock. There were quantities of rings to hang them by. Someone seized me in his arms: it was Julot. He knew all about this, because he had already made the voyage ten years before. He knew how to cope. He said, 'This way, quick. Hang your bag where you're going to hang your hammock. This place is near two closed port-holes, but they'll be opened when we're at sea, and we'll be able to breathe better here than anywhere else in the cage.'

I introduced Dega. We were talking when a man came our way. Julot put out his arm and blocked the path. He said, 'Never come over this side if you want to reach penal alive. Get it?' 'Yes,' said the other man. 'You know why?' 'Yes.' 'Then bugger off.' The guy went. Dega was delighted with this show of strength and he didn't hide it. 'With you two, I'll be able to sleep easy.' Julot said, 'With us, you're safer here than in any villa on the coast that has a single window open.'

The voyage lasted eighteen days. Only one piece of excitement. Everyone was woken by an enormous shriek in the night. A character was found dead with a long knife deep between his shoulders. The knife had been driven from below upwards and it had passed through the hammock before reaching him. A really dangerous weapon, a good eight inches long in the blade. Immediately twenty-five or thirty warders turned their revolvers or rifles on us, shouting, 'Everyone strip. Double quick time!'

Everyone stripped. I saw there was going to be a search and I put my bare right foot over the scalpel, taking my weight on the left, because the blade was cutting into me. Nevertheless my foot covered the scalpel. Four warders came inside the cage and began rummaging through the shoes and clothes. Before they came in they left their weapons outside and the door was closed on them, but those who were the other side of the bars kept watch on us, keeping us covered. 'The first man to stir is a goner,' said a head screw's voice. During the search they found three knives, two long roofing-nails, sharpened, a corkscrew, and a gold charger. Six men were brought out on to the deck, still naked. Major Barrot, the officer in command of the convoy, appeared together with two colonial army doctors and the captain of the ship. When the screws left our cage everyone dressed again, without waiting for the order. I picked up my scalpel.

The warders moved back to the far end of the deck. In the middle there was Barrot, just by the companion-way, with the other officers. The six naked men were lined up opposite them, standing to attention.

'This is his,' said the screw who had conducted the search, picking up a knife and pointing to its owner.

'Fair enough. It's mine.'

'Right,' said Barrot. 'He'll make the rest of the voyage in a cell over the engines.'

Each man was pointed out as responsible either for the nails, or the corkscrew or the knives, and each acknowledged that the weapon that had been found belonged to him. Each one, still naked, went up the ladder, accompanied by two screws. Lying there on the floor there was still one knife and the gold charger: and only one man for both of them. He was young – twenty-three or twenty-five – well-built, at least five foot ten, athletic, blue eyes.

'This is yours, isn't it?' said the screw, holding out the gold charger.

'Yes, it's mine.'

'What's in it?' asked Major Barrot, taking it.

'Three hundred pounds sterling, two hundred dollars and two five-carat diamonds.'

'Right. We'll have a look.' He opened it. The major was surrounded by other people and we couldn't see a thing. But we heard him say, 'Just so. What's your name?'

'Salvidia Romeo.'

'You're Italian?'

'Yes, sir.'

'You'll not be punished for the charger: but you will be for the knife.'

'Excuse me, but the knife isn't mine.'

'Don't talk balls,' said the screw, 'I found it in your shoe.'

'I say again the knife isn't mine.'

'So I'm lying, am I?'

'No, you're just mistaken.'

'Whose is the knife, then?' asked Major Barrot. 'If it's not yours, it must be somebody's.'

'It's not mine, that's all.'

'If you don't want to be put in the punishment cell – and you'll fry there, because it's over the boiler – just tell me whose the knife is.'

'I don't know.'

'Are you trying to make a fool of me? A knife's found in your shoe and you don't know whose it is? Do you think I'm a fool? Either it's yours or you know whose it is. Speak up.'

'It's not mine and it's not for me to say whose it is. I'm not an informer. You don't by any chance think I look like a bleeding prison officer, do you?'

'Warder, put on the handcuffs. This kind of undisciplined conduct costs a packet, my friend.'

The two commanding officers, the captain of the ship and the head of the convoy, talked privately. The captain gave an order to a quartermaster, who went up on deck. A few moments later a Breton sailor appeared, a giant of a man, with a wooden bucket of sea water and a rope as thick as your wrist. The convict was tied to the bottom step of the ladder, on his knees. The sailor wetted the rope in the bucket and then deliberately, with all his strength, he set about flogging the poor devil's back and buttocks. Not a sound came from the convict: blood flowed from his buttocks and his sides. A shout from our cage broke the graveyard silence. 'You bloody sods!'

That was all that was needed to start everybody roaring. 'Murderers! Swine! Bastards!' The more they threatened to fire if we did not shut up the more we bellowed until suddenly the captain shouted, 'Turn on the steam!'

Sailors turned various wheels and jets of steam shot out at us with such force that in a split second everyone was flat on his belly. The jets came at chest-height. We were all struck with panic. The men who had been scalded dared not cry out. The whole thing lasted under a minute, but it terrified every man there.

'I hope you obstinate brutes have grasped what I mean. The slightest trouble, and I turn on the steam. You get me? Stand up!'

Only three men had been seriously scalded. They were taken to the sick-bay. The man who had been flogged was put back with us. Six years later he died while making a break with me.

During those eighteen days of the voyage we had plenty of time to try to learn about what was coming or to get at least some notion of the penal settlement. Yet when we got this nothing turned out quite as we had expected, although Julot had done his very best to pass on his knowledge.

We did know that Saint-Laurent-du-Maroni was a village seventy-five miles from the sea on a river called the Maroni. Julot told us about it. 'That's the village that has the prison, the one that's the centre of the penal settlement. That's where they sort you out according to your category. The preventive detentions go straight to a prison called Saint-Jean, about ninety miles away. The right convicts are separated into three groups. First the ones labelled *very dangerous*: as soon as they arrive they're called out and shoved into cells in the punishment-block until they can be transferred to the Iles du Salut. There they are interned either for a given number of years or for life. These islands are three hundred miles and more from Saint-Laurent and sixty from Cayenne. There are three of them. Royale, the biggest; Saint-Joseph, which has the settlement's solitary-confinement prison; and Devil's Island, the smallest of them all. Apart from a very few exceptions, convicts don't go to Devil's Island. The people there are politicals. Then comes *dangerous, second category*: they stay at the Saint-Laurent camp, and they're put to gardening and working on the land. Whenever there's a need for men they're sent to the very tough camps – Camp Forestier, Charvin, Cascade, Crique Rouge and Kilomètre 42, the one they call the death camp. Then there's the ordinary category: they're given jobs in the offices and kitchens, or put to cleaning in the village and the camp, or they're sent to the different workshops – carpentry, painting, blacksmith's shop, electricity, mattress-making, tailor's shop, laundry and so on. So zero hour is the moment you get there. If you're called out and taken to a cell, that means you're going to be interned on the islands, so good-bye to any hope of escape. There's only one chance, and that's to mutilate yourself quick – open your knee or your belly so as to get into the hospital and escape from there. At all costs you have to avoid going to the islands. There's one other hope: if the ship that's to take the internees to the islands isn't ready you can bring out your money and offer it to the medical orderly. He'll give you a shot of turpentine in a joint or draw a urine-soaked hair through a cut so that it'll go bad. Or he'll give you sulphur to inhale and then tell the doctor you've got a temperature of 102. During those few days of waiting you have to get into hospital, no matter what it costs.

'If you're not called out but left with the others in the huts at the camp, then you have time to get working. If this happens, you mustn't look for a job inside the camp. What you want to do is to pay the clerk to be given a scavenger's or a sweeper's job in the village, or else to get taken on at an outside firm's sawmills. Going out of the prison to work and coming back into the camp every night gives you time to get in touch with the time-expired convicts who live in the village or with the Chinese, so that they can get your break ready for you. Avoid the camps outside the village. Everybody dies quickly in them – there are some where no one has been able to stand it for three months. Out there in the deep bush, men are forced to cut a cubic yard of wood every day.'

Throughout the voyage Julot had gone over and over all this valuable information. For his part, he was quite ready. He knew that he was going straight to the punishment cell, because he was an escaped man who had been retaken. So he had a very small blade, not much more than a penknife, in his charger. When we got there he was going to take it out and rip his knee open. As we came down the gangway he was going to fall, right there in front of everyone. He thought he'd be taken straight from the quay to the hospital. And that indeed was exactly what happened.

Saint-Laurent-Du-Maroni

The warders had gone off in relays to change. Each in turn came back dressed in white with a sun-helmet instead of a képi. Julot said. 'We're almost there.' It was appallingly hot, for they had shut the port-holes. Through the glass you could see the bush. So we were in the Maroni. The water was muddy. Untouched virgin forest, green and impressive. Disturbed by the ship's siren, birds rose and flew across the sky. We went very slowly, and that allowed us to pay close attention to the thick, dark-green, overflowing vegetation. We saw the first wooden houses, with their corrugated iron roofs. Black men and women stood at their doors, watching the ship go by. They were quite used to seeing it unload its human cargo, and so they never even bothered to wave as it passed. Three blasts on the siren and the churning of the propeller told us that we were there, and then the engines stopped entirely. Not a sound: you could have heard the buzzing of a fly.

Nobody spoke. Julot had his knife open and he was cutting his trousers at the knee, making the edges of the slash look like a tear. It was only on deck that he was going to cut his knee, so as not to leave a trail of blood. The warders opened the door of the cage and lined us up in threes. We were in the fourth rank, with Julot between Dega and me. Up on deck. It was two o'clock in the afternoon and suddenly the blazing sun hit my cropped head and my eyes. We were formed up on the deck and then we moved towards the gangway. When the column hesitated for a moment, just as the first man stepped on to the gangway. I held Julot's kitbag in place on his shoulder while he used both hands to stretch the skin of his knee, drive the knife in and slash through three or four inches of flesh in one sweep. He passed me the knife and held the kitbag himself. The moment we set foot on the gangway he fell and rolled right down to the bottom. They picked him up, and finding that he was hurt they called the stretcher-bearers. Everything ran just as he had worked it out, and he disappeared, carried by two men on a stretcher.

A motley crowd watched us with some curiosity. Negroes, half-castes, Indians, Chinese and wrecks of white men (they were certainly freed convicts) stared at each one of us as he set foot on land and lined up behind the others. On the other side there were warders, well-dressed civilians, women in summer dresses and children, all with sun-helmets on. They too watched the new arrivals. When there were two hundred of us ashore, the column moved off. We marched for some ten minutes and came to a very high gate made of massive beams, with the words *Penitentiary of Saint-Laurent-du-Maroni. Capacity, 3,000 men.* The gate opened and we went in by

ranks of ten. 'Left, right. Left, right. Left, right!' A good many
convicts watched us come in. They had climbed up on the
windows or on big stones to see us better.

When we reached the middle of the court a voice shouted,
'Halt. Put your bags down in front of you. You there, hand
out the hats.' They gave us each a straw hat, and we needed
it – two or three men had already dropped from sunstroke.
Dega and I exchanged a glance, for a screw with stripes had
a list in his hand. We thought of what Julot had told us. Guittou
was called. 'Here!' he said. Two warders took him away.
Suzuni, the same: Girasol likewise.

'Jules Pignard!'

'Jules Pignard (that was our Julot) has been hurt. He's gone
to hospital.'

'Right.' Those were the internees for the islands. Then the
warder went on, 'Listen carefully. Each man whose name I
call is to step from the ranks with his kitbag on his shoulder
and go and line up in front of that yellow hut, number one.'

The roll-call went on, with So-and-so – Present, etc., and
Dega, Carrier and I ended up with the others, in line over
against the hut. They opened the door and we went into a
rectangular hall some twenty yards long. Down the middle ran
a passage about two yards wide with an iron bar on either
side, the whole length of the room. Canvas hammocks were
slung between the bar and the wall, and each held a blanket.
Every man chose his own place. Dega, Pierrot le Fou, Santori,
Grandet and I moved in all next to one another, and little
groups began to take shape at once. I went down to the far
end of the room: showers on the right, latrines on the left: no
running water.

The men who had left the ship after us began to arrive, and
we watched them, clinging to the bars over the windows. Louis
Dega, Pierrot le Fou and I were delighted – since we were in
an ordinary barrack-room it meant we weren't going to be
interned. Otherwise we'd already have been put into a cell, as
Julot had explained. Everybody was very pleased until about
five o'clock, when it was all over; but then Grandet said, 'It's
funny, but they haven't called out a single man for internment
in this whole convoy. Odd. Still, so much the better, as far as
I'm concerned.' Grandet was the man who stole the safe from
one of the central prisons, a job that had made the whole
country laugh.

In the tropics day and night come without any sort of twilight. You go straight from the one to the other, and at the same time all through the year. Suddenly, at half-past six, it's night. And at half-past six two old convicts brought two oil lamps that they hung on a hook in the ceiling and that gave a very little light. Three-quarters of the room was perfectly dark. By nine o'clock everybody was asleep, for now that the excitement of our arrival was over, we were quite overcome by the heat. Not a breath of air, and everyone was stripped to his drawers. My hammock was between Dega and Pierrot le Fou: we whispered a while and then went back to sleep.

It was still dark the next morning when the bugle blew. Everyone got up, washed and dressed. They gave us coffee and a hunk of bread. There was a plank fixed to the wall for your bread, mug and other belongings. At nine o'clock two warders came in, together with a young convict dressed in white without stripes. The two screws were Corsicans, and they talked Corsican to the convicts from their country. Meanwhile the medical orderly walked about the room. When he reached me he said, 'How goes it, Papi? Don't you recognize me?'

'No.'

'I'm Sierra l'Algérois: I knew you in Paris, at Dante's.'

'Oh, yes, I recognize you now. But you were sent down in '29. It's '33 now: how come you're still here?'

'Yes. There's no getting out of here in a hurry. You report sick, will you? Who's this guy?'

'He's Dega, a friend of mine.'

'I'll put you down for the doctor too, Dega. Papi, you've got dysentery. And you, dad, you've got fits of asthma. I'll see you at the medical at eleven o'clock. There's something I've got to tell you.' He went on his way, calling out 'Who's sick there?', going over to those who held up their hands, and writing down their names. When he came back he had a warder with him, an elderly sunburnt man. 'Papillon, let me introduce my boss, Medical-Warder Bartiloni. Monsieur Bartiloni, these two are the friends I told you about.'

'OK, Sierra, we'll see to that at the medical: rely on me.'

At eleven they came for us. There were nine men going sick. We walked through the camp among the hutments. When we reached a newer building than the rest, the only one painted white with a red cross on it, we went in and found a waiting-room with about sixty men in it. Two warders in each corner. Sierra appeared, in spotless medical overalls. He said, 'You, you and you: go in.' We went into a room that was obviously the doctor's. He talked to the three older men in Spanish. There was one Spaniard there I recognized straight away: he was Fernandez, the one who killed the three Argentines at the Café de Madrid in Paris. After they had exchanged a few words Sierra showed him to a little room communicating with the main hall and then came back to us. 'Papi, let me embrace you. I'm delighted to be able to do you and your friend a very good turn. You're both of you down for internment ... No, let me finish. You're down for life, Papillon; and Dega, you're down for five years. You got any cash?'

'Yes.'

'Then give five hundred francs apiece and tomorrow morning you'll be sent to hospital. You for dysentery. And you, Dega, you must bang on the door during the night – or better still, let someone call the screw and ask for the orderly, because Dega's asthma's killing him. I'll look after the rest of it. There's just one thing I ask of you, Papillon, and that is to give me fair warning if you clear out: I'll be there when you say. They'll be able to keep you in the hospital for a month, at a hundred francs a week each. You must move fast.'

Fernandez came out of the little room and in front of us he handed Sierra five hundred francs. Then I went in, and when I came out I gave him not a thousand but fifteen hundred francs. He refused the five hundred. I did not like to press him. He said, 'This dough you're giving me's for the screw. I don't want anything for myself. We're friends, aren't we?'

The next day Dega, Fernandez and I were in an enormous cell in the hospital. Dega was hurried in during the middle of the night. The attendant in charge of the ward was a man of thirty-five called Chatal. He knew all about us three from Sierra. When the doctor came round he was to show a motion that would make me look like I was falling apart with amoebas. Ten minutes before the inspection he was to burn a little sulphur for Dega and make him breathe the gas with a towel over his head. Fernandez had an enormously swollen face: he had pierced the skin inside his cheek and had blown as hard as he could for an hour. He had done it so conscientiously that the swelling closed one eye. The cell was on the first floor and there were about seventy patients in it, many of them dysentery cases. I asked Chatal where Julot was. He said, 'In the building just over the way. You want me to tell him something?'

'Yes. Tell him Papillon and Dega are here; ask him to show himself at the window.'

The attendant could come and go as he liked. All he had to do was to knock at the ward door and an Arab would open it. The Arab was a turnkey, a convict acting as an auxiliary to the warders. There were chairs on the right and the left of the door, and three warders sat there, rifles on their knees. The bars over the windows were lengths of railway line: I wondered how one could ever get through them. I sat there at the window.

Between our building and Julot's there was a garden full of pretty flowers. Julot appeared at a window: he had a slate in his hand, and he had chalked BRAVO on it. An hour later the attendant brought me a letter from him. It said, 'I'm trying to get into your ward. If I fail, try to get into mine. The reason is you've got enemies in your ward. So it seems you're interned? Keep your heart up: we'll do them in the eye yet.'

Julot and I were very close to one another because of that business at Beaulieu, where we had suffered together. Julot specialized in the use of a wooden mallet, and that was why they called him the hammer-man. He would drive up to a jeweller's shop in the middle of the day, when all the finest jewels were on show in their cases. Someone else would be at the wheel, and they'd pull up with the engine running. Julot hopped out with his mallet, smashed the window with one blow, grabbed as many jewel-cases as he could hold and darted back into the car, which shot away with a scream of tyres. He brought it off in Lyons, Angers, Tours and Le Havre, and then he had a go at a big Paris shop, at three in the afternoon, getting away with jewels to the value of close on a million. He never told me how or why he was identified. He was sentenced to twenty years and he escaped at the end of four. And as he told us, it was in coming back to Paris that he was arrested: he was looking for his fence, so as to kill him, for the fence had never given Julot's sister the large sum he owed him. The fence saw him prowling in the street where he lived and tipped off the police. Julot was picked up and he went back to Guiana with us.

It was a week now that we had been in hospital. Yesterday I gave Chatal two hundred francs: that was the weekly price

71

for keeping both of us. By way of making ourselves popular we gave tobacco to the people who had nothing to smoke. A sixty-year-old tough guy from Marseilles, one Carora, had made friends with Dega. He was his adviser. Many times a day he told him that if he had plenty of money and it was known in the village (the French papers gave the news about all the important cases), then it was much better for him not to escape, because the freed convicts would kill him for his charger. Old Dega told me about his conversations with old Carora. It was in vain that I said the antique was certainly no sort of use, since he had stayed here for twenty years: he paid no attention. The old man's tales made a great impression on Dega, and although I kept his courage up as well as I could it was heavy going.

· I sent a note to Sierra asking him to let me see Galgani. It didn't take long. Galgani was in hospital the next day, but in an unbarred ward. How was I to set about giving him back his charger? I told Chatal it was absolutely necessary for me to talk to Galgani: I let him imagine we were preparing a break. He told me he could bring him at five to twelve on the nose. Just as the guard was being changed he would bring him up on to the verandah to talk to me through the window; and he'd do it for nothing. Galgani was brought to me at the window at noon: straight away I put his charger into his hands. He stood there before me and wept. Two days later I had a magazine from him with five thousand-franc notes in it and the single word, *Thanks*.

Chatal passed me the magazine; and he had seen the money. He did not mention it, but I wanted to give him some: he would not take it. I said, 'We want to get out. Would you like to come with us?'

'No, Papillon, I'm fixed elsewhere. I don't want to try to escape for five months, when my mate will be free. The break will be better prepared that way, and it'll be more certain. Being down for internment, I know you're in a hurry: but getting out of here, with all these bars, is going to be very difficult. Don't count on me to help you – I don't want to risk my job. Here I can wait in peace until my friend comes out.'

'OK, Chatal. It's better to speak straight. I won't ever talk to you about this again.'

'But still,' he said, 'I'll carry notes for you and deliver messages.'

'Thanks, Chatal.'

That night we heard bursts of machine-gun fire. Next day we heard it was the hammer-man who had got away. God be with him: he was a good friend. He must have seen a chance and made the most of it. So much the better for him.

Fifteen years later, in 1948, I was in Haïti, and there, together with a Venezuelan millionaire, I was working out a deal with the chief of the casino for a contract to run the gambling in those parts. One night I came out of a club where we had been drinking champagne, and one of the girls who was with us – coal-black, but as well brought up as the daughter of a good French provincial family – said to me, 'My grandmother's a voodoo priestess, and she lives with an old Frenchman. He escaped from Cayenne. He's been with us now for fifteen years, and he's almost always drunk, Jules Marteau is his name.'

I sobered up instantly. 'Chick, you take me to your grandma's right away.'

She spoke to the cab-driver in Haïtian patois and he drove off at full speed. We passed a night-bar, still open and all lit up. 'Stop.' I went in, bought a bottle of Pernod, two of champagne and two of local rum. 'Let's go.' We reached a pretty little red tiled white house on the beach. The sea almost lapped its steps. The girl knocked and knocked, and first there came out a big black woman with completely white hair. She was wearing a wrapper that came down to her ankles. The two women spoke in patois and then she said, 'Come in, Monsieur: the house is all yours.' An acetylene lamp lit up a very clean room, filled with birds and fishes. 'Would you like to see Julot? He's just coming. Jules! Jules! Here's someone who wants to see you.'

An old man appeared, barefoot and wearing striped blue pyjamas that reminded me of our prison uniform. 'Why, Snowball, who can be coming to see me at this time of night? Papillon! No! It can't be true!' He clasped me in his arms. He said, 'Bring the lamp closer, Snowball, so that I can see my old friend's face. It's you all right, mate! It's certainly you! Welcome, welcome, welcome! This kip, what little dough I've got, and my old woman's grand-daughter – they're all yours. You only have to say the word.'

We drank the Pernod, the champagne and the rum; and from time to time Julot sang. 'So we did them in the eye after all, didn't we, Papi? There's nothing like bashing around. Take me, I came through Colombia, Panama, Costa Rica and Jamaica; and then, about fifteen years ago now, I reached here; and I'm happy with Snowball – she's the best woman a man could ask for. When are you leaving? Are you here for long?'

'No. A week.'

'What did you come for?'

'To take over the casino, with a contract between us and the president himself.'

'Brother, I'd love you to spend the rest of your life here with me in this bleeding wilderness; but if it's the president you're in touch with, don't you fix any sort of deal at all. He'll have you killed the minute he sees your joint is making a go of it.'

'Thanks for the advice.'

'Hey there, Snowball! Get ready for your not-for-tourists voodoo dance. The one and only genuine article for my friend.' Another time I'll tell you about this terrific not-for-tourists voodoo dance.

So Julot escaped, and here were we, Dega, Fernandez and me, still hanging about. Now and then, without seeming to, I looked at the bars over the windows. They were lengths of genuine railway line and there was nothing to be done about them. The only possibility was the door. It was guarded night and day by three armed warders. Since Julot's escape the watch had been much sharper. The patrols came round at shorter intervals and the doctor was not so friendly. Chatal only came into the ward twice a day, to give the injections and to take the temperatures. A second week went by and once more I paid two hundred francs. Dega talked about everything except escape. Yesterday he saw my scalpel and he said, 'You've still got that? What for?'

Angrily I replied, 'To look after myself, and you too if necessary.'

Fernandez was not a Spaniard: he was an Argentine. He was a fine sort of a man, a genuine high-flier; but old Carora's crap had left its mark on him too. One day I heard him say to Dega. 'It seems the islands are very healthy, not like here: and it's not hot over there. You can catch dysentery in this ward just going to the lavatory, because you may pick up germs.' In this ward of seventy men, one or two died of dysentery every day. It was an odd thing, but they all died at low tide in the afternoon or the evening. No sick man ever died in the morning. Why? One of nature's mysteries.

Tonight I had an argument with Dega. I told him that sometimes the Arab turnkey was stupid enough to come in at night and pull the sheet off the faces of the very sick men who had covered themselves up. We could knock him out and put on his clothes (we wore shirt and sandals – that was all). Once dressed I'd go out, suddenly snatch a rifle from one of the screws, cover them, make them go into a cell and close the door. Then we'd jump the hospital wall on the Maroni side, drop into the water and let ourselves go with the current. After that we'd make up our minds what to do next. Since we had money, we could buy a boat and provisions to get away by sea. Both of them turned my plan down flat, and they even criticized it. I felt they'd quite lost their guts: I was bitterly disappointed: and the days dropped by.

Now it was three weeks all but two days we had been here. There were ten left to try making a dash for it, or fifteen at the most. Today, 21 November 1933, a day not to be forgotten, Joanes Clousiot came into the ward – the man they had tried to murder at Saint-Martin, in the barber's. His eyes were closed and almost sightless: they were full of pus. As soon as Chatal had gone I went over to him. Quickly he told me that the other men for internment had gone off to the islands more than a fortnight ago, but he had been overlooked. Three days back a clerk had given him the word. He had put a castor-oil seed in each eye, and all this pus had got him into hospital. He was dead keen to escape. He told me he was ready for anything, even killing if need be: he would get out, come what may. He had three thousand francs. When his eyes were washed with warm water he could see properly right away. I told him my plan for a break: he liked it, but he said that to catch the warders by surprise two of us would have to go out, or if possible three. We could undo the legs of the beds, and with an iron bed-leg apiece, we could knock them cold. According to him they wouldn't believe you would fire even if you had a gun in your hands, and they might call the other screws on guard in the building Julot escaped from, not twenty yards away.

Escape from the Hospital

That evening I put it to Dega straight, and then to Fernandez. Dega told me he did not believe in the plan and that he was thinking of paying a large sum of money, if necessary, to have his internment label changed. He asked me to write to Sierra, telling him this had been suggested, and asking whether it was on the cards. Chatal carried the note that same day, and brought back the answer. 'Don't pay anyone anything for having your internment changed. It's decided in France, and no one, even the governor, can touch it. If things are hopeless in the hospital, you can try to get out the day after the *Mana*, the boat for the islands, has left.'

We should stay a week in the cellular block before going across to the islands where it might be easier to escape than from the hospital ward we had landed up in. In the same note Sierra told me that if I liked he'd send a freed convict to talk about getting me a boat ready behind the hospital. He was a character from Toulon called Jesus: the one who prepared Dr. Bougrat's escape two years before. To see him I should have to go and be X-rayed in the special wing. It was inside the hospital walls, but the freed men could get in on a forged pass for an X-ray examination. He told me to take out my charger before I was looked at, or the doctor might look lower than my lungs and catch sight of it. I wrote to Sierra telling him to get Jesus to the X-ray and to fix things with Chatal so that I should be sent too. That very evening Sierra let me know that it was for nine o'clock the day after next.

The next day Dega asked permission to leave hospital, and so did Fernandez. The *Mana* had left that morning. They hoped to escape from the cells in the camp: I wished them good luck, but as for me I did not change my plan.

I saw Jesus. He was an old time-expired convict, as dry as a smoked haddock, and his sunburnt face was scarred with two hideous wounds. One of his eyes wept all the time when he looked at you. A wrong 'un's face: a wrong 'un's eye. I didn't have much confidence in him and as things turned out I was dead right. We talked fast. 'I can get a boat ready for you: it'll hold four – five at the outside. A barrel of water, victuals, coffee, tobacco; three paddles, empty flour sacks and a needle and thread for you to make the mainsail and jib yourself; a compass, an axe, a knife, five bottles of tafia [the local rum]. Two thousand five hundred francs the lot. It's the dark of the moon in three days. If it's a deal, in four days time I'll be there in the boat on the river every night for a week from eleven till three in the morning. After the first quarter I shan't wait any longer. The boat will be exactly opposite the lower corner of the hospital wall. Guide yourself by the wall, because until you're right on top of the boat you won't be able to see it, not even at two yards.' I didn't trust him, but even so I said yes.

'And the cash?' said Jesus.

'I'll send it you by Sierra.' We parted without shaking hands. Not so hot.

At three o'clock Chatal went off to the camp, taking the money to Sierra: two thousand five hundred francs. I thought: 'I can afford this bet thanks to Galgani; but it's an outside chance, all right. I hope to God he doesn't drink the whole bleeding lot in tafia.'

Clousiot was overjoyed: he was full of confidence in himself, in me and in the plan. There was only one thing that worried him: although the Arab turnkey did come very often it was not every night that he came into the ward itself; and when he did it was rare that he came in very late. Another question: who could we have as a third? There was a Corsican belonging to the Nice underworld, a man called Biaggi. He had been in penal since 1929 and he was in this high-security ward because he had recently killed a guy – he was being held while that charge was investigated. Clousiot and I wondered whether we ought to put it up to him, and if so, when. While we were talking about this in an undertone an eighteen-year-old fairy came towards us, as pretty as a girl. Maturette was his name, and he had been condemned to death but reprieved because of his youth – seventeen when he murdered this taxi-driver. There were these two kids of sixteen and seventeen in the dock at the assizes, and instead of the one laying the blame on the other, each claimed that he had killed the man. But the taxi-driver had only one bullet in him. The kids' attitude at the time of the trial had won them the convicts' esteem.

Very much the young lady, Maturette came up to us and speaking in a girlish voice he asked us for a light. We gave him one; and more than that, I made him a present of four cigarettes and a box of matches. He thanked me with a languishing, come-on smile and we let him go. All at once Clousiot said, 'Papi, we're saved. The Arab's going to come in as often as we like and when we like. It's in the bag.'

'How come?'

'It's simple. We'll tell this little Maturette to make the Arab fall for him. Arabs love boys – everyone knows that. Once that's done, there's no great difficulty in getting him to come by night to have a swig at the boy. All the kid has to do is to go coy and say he's afraid of being seen, for the Arab to come just when it suits us.'

'Leave it to me.'

I went over to Maturette, who welcomed me with a winning smile. He thought he had aroused me with his first simper. Straight away I said, 'You've got it wrong. Go to the lavatory.' He went, and when we were there I said, 'If you repeat a word of what I'm going to say. I'll kill you. Listen: will you do so-and-so and so-and-so and so-and-so for money? How much? As a paid job for us, or do you want to go with us?'

'I'd like to go with you. OK?' Done. We shook hands.

He went to bed, and after a few words with Clousiot I went too. At eight o'clock that evening Maturette went and sat at the window. He didn't have to call the Arab: he came all by himself, and they fell into a murmured conversation. At ten Maturette went to bed. We had been lying down, one eye open, since nine. The Arab came in, went his rounds and found a dead man. He knocked on the door and a little while later two stretcher-bearers came and took the corpse away. This dead man was going to be useful to us, because he would make the Arab's inspections at any time of the night seem quite reasonable. The next day, advised by us, Maturette fixed to see the Arab at eleven. When the time came round the turnkey appeared, passed in front of the kid's bed, pulled his foot to wake him up, and went off towards the lavatory. Maturette followed him. A quarter of an hour later the turnkey came out, went straight to the door and out through it. Just after that Maturette returned to his bed without speaking to us. To cut it short, the next day was the same, only at midnight. Everything was set up: the Arab would come exactly when the kid said.

On 27 November 1933 there were two bed-legs ready to be removed and used as clubs, and at four o'clock in the afternoon. I was waiting for a note from Sierra. Chatal, the attendant, appeared: he had nothing in writing: he just said to me, 'François Sierra told me to say Jesus is waiting for you at the place you know. Good luck.'

At eight that night Maturette said to the Arab, 'Come after midnight, because that way we can stay longer together.'

The Arab said he'd come after midnight. Dead on midnight we were ready. The Arab came in at about a quarter past twelve; he went straight to Maturette's bed, tweaked his foot and went on to the lavatory. Maturette went in after him. I wrenched the leg off my bed: it made a little noise as it lurched over. No sound from Clousiot's. I was to stand behind the lavatory door and Clousiot was to walk towards it to attract the Arab's attention. There was a twenty-minutes' wait and then everything moved very fast. The Arab came out of the lavatory and, surprised at seeing Clousiot, said, 'What are you doing here in the middle of the ward at this time of night? Get back to bed.'

At that moment I hit him on the back of the neck and he dropped without a sound. Quickly I put on his clothes and shoes: we dragged him under a bed, and before shoving him completely out of sight I gave him another crack on the nape. That put paid to him.

Not a single one of the eighty men in the ward had stirred. I went quickly towards the door, followed by Clousiot and Maturette, both of them in their shirts. I knocked. The warder opened. I brought my iron down on his head. The other, opposite him, dropped his rifle: he'd certainly been asleep. Before he could move I knocked him out. My two never uttered: Clousiot's went 'Ah!' before he dropped. My two stayed there in their chairs, stunned. The third was stretched out on the floor. We held our breath. It seemed to us that everybody must have heard that 'Ah!' It had indeed been pretty loud; and yet nobody moved.

We didn't heave them into the ward: we went straight off with the three rifles. Clousiot first, then the kid, then me: down the stairs, half-lit by a lantern. Clousiot had dropped his iron;

I still had mine in my left hand, and in my right the rifle. At the bottom of the stairs, nothing. Ink-black night all round us. We had to look hard to make out the wall over on the river side. We hurried towards it. Once we were there, I bent down. Clousiot climbed up, straddled the top, hauled Maturette up and then me. We let ourselves drop into the darkness on the far side. Clousiot fell badly into a hole, twisting his foot. Maturette and I landed properly. We two got up: we had left the rifles before we went over. Clousiot tried to get to his feet but couldn't: he said his leg was broken. I left Maturette with Clousiot and ran towards the corner of the wall, feeling it all the way with my hand. It was so dark that when I got to the end of the wall I didn't know it, and with my hand reaching out into emptiness I fell flat on my face. Over on the river side I heard a voice saying, 'Is that you?'

'Yes. That Jesus?'

'Yes.' He flicked a match for half a second. I fixed his position, plunged in and swam to him. There were two of them in the boat.

'You in first. Which are you?'

'Papillon.'

'Good.'

'Jesus, we must pull upstream. My friend's broken his leg jumping off the wall.'

'Take this paddle, then, and shove.'

The three paddles dug into the water and the light boat shot across the hundred yards between us and the place where I supposed the others were – you could see nothing. I called, 'Clousiot!'

'For Christ's sake shut up! Fatgut, flick your lighter.' Sparks flashed: they saw it. Clousiot whistled between his teeth the way they do in Lyons; it's a whistle that makes no noise at all but that you hear very clearly. You'd say it was a snake hissing. He kept up this whistling all the time, and it led us to him. Fatgut got out, took Clousiot in his arms and put him into the boat. Then Maturette got in and then Fatgut. There were five of us and the water came to within two inches of the gunwale.

'Don't anyone move without saying,' said Jesus. 'Papillon, stop paddling. Put the paddle across your knees. Fatgut, shove!' And quickly, helped by the current, the boat plunged into the night.

80

Half a mile lower down, when we passed the prison, ill-lit by the current from a third-rate dynamo, we were in the middle of the river and the tide was tearing us along at an unbelievable rate. Fatgut had stopped paddling. Only Jesus had his out, with its handle tight against his thigh, just to keep the boat steady. He was not rowing at all, only steering.

Jesus said, 'Now we can talk and have a smoke. I think we've brought it off. Are you certain you didn't kill anyone?'

'I don't think so.'

'Christ, Jesus, you've double-crossed me!' said Fatgut. 'You told me it was a harmless little break and no fuss, and now it turns out to be an internees' break, from what I can gather.'

'Yes, they're internees. I didn't feel like telling you, Fatgut, or you wouldn't have helped me: and I needed someone. But why should you worry? If we're shopped I'll take it all on myself.'

'That's the right way of looking at it, Jesus. I don't want to risk my head for the hundred francs you've paid me; nor a lifer if there's anyone wounded.'

I said, 'Fatgut, I'll give you a present of a thousand francs between you.'

'OK, then, brother. That sounds like a square deal to me. Thanks, because we starve to death there in the village. It's worse being outside than in. If you're in, at least you can fill your belly every day; and they find you in clothes.'

'It doesn't hurt you too much, mate?' said Jesus to Clousiot.

'It's all right,' said Clousiot. 'But what are we going to do, Papillon, with my leg broken?'

'We'll see. Where we going, Jesus?'

'I'm going to hide you in a creek twenty miles from the mouth of the river. There you can lie up for a week and let the worst of the warders' and trackers' hunt blow over. You must give them the idea you went right down the Maroni and out to sea this very night. The trackers go in boats with no motor, and they're the most dangerous. If they're on the watch, it can be fatal to you to talk or cough or have a fire. As for the screws, they're in motor-boats that are too big to go up the creeks – they'd run aground.'

The darkness was lessening. For a long time we searched for a landmark known only to Jesus, and it was almost four o'clock before we found it: then we literally went right into the bush. The boat flattened the small undergrowth, which straightened up again behind us, making a very thick protective curtain. You had to be a wizard to know whether there was enough water to float a boat. We went in, pushing aside the branches that barred our passage and thrusting into the bush for more than an hour. All at once we were there, in a kind of canal, and we stopped. There was clean grass on the bank; and now, at six o'clock, the light did not penetrate the leaves of the huge trees. Beneath this impressive roof there were the sounds of hundreds of creatures quite unknown to us. Jesus said, 'Here is where you have to wait for a week. I'll come on the seventh day and bring you food.' From under the thick vegetation he pulled a very small canoe, about six feet long. Two paddles in it. This was the craft he was going back to Saint-Laurent in, on the flood-tide.

Now we took care of Clousiot, who was lying there on the bank. He was still in his shirt, so his legs were bare. We trimmed dry branches with the axe, making splints of them. Fatgut heaved on his foot; Clousiot sweated hard and then at a given moment he cried, 'Stop! It hurts less in this position, so the bone must be in its right place.' We put on the splints and tied them with new hemp cord from the boat. His pain was eased. Jesus had bought four pairs of trousers, four shirts and four relégués' woollen lumber-jackets. Maturette and Clousiot put them on: I stayed in the Arab's clothes. We had a tot of rum. This was the second bottle since we left – it warmed us, which was a good thing. The mosquitoes did not give us a moment's peace: we had to sacrifice a packet of tobacco. We put it to soak in a calabash and smeared the nicotine-juice over our faces, hands and feet. The woollen jackets were splendid; they kept us warm in spite of this penetrating damp.

Fatgut said, 'We're off. What about this thousand francs you promised?' I went behind a bush and came back with a brand-new thousand note.

'Be seeing you. Don't stir from here for eight days,' said Jesus. 'We'll come on the seventh. The eighth you can get out to sea. Meanwhile make the mainsail and jib; put the boat to rights, everything in its place. Fix the pintle – the rudder's not shipped. If we don't come within ten days, it means we've been arrested in the village. As there was an attack on a warder, which adds some spice to the break, there will surely be the most God-almighty bleeding rampage about it all.'

Clousiot had told us he didn't leave the rifle at the bottom of the wall. He had flung it over, and the water was so close (which he hadn't known) that it must certainly have gone into the river. Jesus said that was fine, because if it was not found the trackers were going to think we were armed. And since they were the really dangerous ones, we should therefore have nothing to be afraid of. Because they only had a revolver and a jungle-knife and if they thought we had rifles, they would never risk it.

Good-bye. Good-bye. If we were found and we had to leave the boat, we should go up the little stream as far as the dry bush and then steer by compass, always keeping north. In two or three days' march we were likely to come across the death-camp called Charvin. There we should have to pay someone to tell Jesus we were in such and such a place. The two old lags pushed off. A few moments later their canoe had vanished: we neither heard nor saw anything more at all.

Daylight comes into the bush in a very special way. You would think you were in an arcade whose top caught the sun and never let a single ray make its way down to the bottom. It began to grow hot. And now here we were, Maturette, Clousiot and me, quite alone. Our first reaction was to laugh – the whole thing had run on oiled wheels. The only hitch was Clousiot's broken leg, though he said himself that now it was held between flat pieces of wood, it was all right. We could brew the coffee straight away. This we did very quickly, making a fire and drinking a great mug of black coffee apiece, sweetened with brown sugar. It was marvellous. We had used ourselves up so much since the evening before that we hadn't the energy to look at the things or to inspect the boat. We'd see to all that later. We were free, free, free. Exactly thirty-seven days had passed since I reached Guiana. If we brought this break off, my lifer wouldn't have been a very long one. I said aloud, 'Monsieur le Président, how many years does penal servitude for life last in France?' and I burst out laughing. So did Maturette – he had a lifer too. Clousiot said, 'don't crow too soon. Colombia's a long way off, and this hollowed-out tree-trunk doesn't seem to me much of a thing to go to sea in.'

I did not reply, because to tell the truth until the last moment I had thought it was just the canoe meant to take us to the real boat, the boat for the sea voyage. When I found I was wrong, I did not like to say anything, so as not to discourage my friends in the first place, and in the second not to give Jesus the idea that I didn't know what kind of boats were usually used for a break – he seemed to think it perfectly natural.

We spent the first day talking and getting to know a little about the bush – it was completely strange to us. Monkeys and squirrels of some kind flung themselves about overhead in the most astonishing way. A herd of peccaries came down to drink: they are a kind of small wild pig. There were at least two thousand of them. They plunged into the creek and swam about, tearing off the hanging roots. An alligator emerged from God knows where and caught one pig by the foot: it started to shriek and squeal like a steam-engine, and all the others rushed at the alligator, clambering on to it and trying to bite the corners of its enormous mouth. At every blow of the alligator's tail a pig flew into the air, one to the left, the next to the right. One pig was stunned and it floated there, belly up. Instantly its companions ate it. The creek was red with blood. This scene lasted twenty minutes and then the alligator escaped into the water. We never saw it again.

We slept well, and in the morning we made our coffee. I took off my jacket so as to wash with a big bar of common soap we found in the boat. Using my scalpel, Maturette shaved me, more or less, and then he shaved Clousiot. He himself had no beard. When I picked up my jacket to put it on again, a huge, hairy, blackish-purple spider fell out. Its hairs were very long and each ended in a little shining ball. The monstrous thing must have weighed at least a pound: I squashed it, feeling disgusted. We took everything out of the boat, including the little water-barrel. The water was violet, and it seemed to me Jesus had put in too much permanganate to make it keep. There were well-corked bottles with matches and strikers. The compass was only a schoolboy's job – it just gave north, south, east and west: no graduations. The mast was no more than eight feet long, so we sewed the flour-sacks into a lug-sail with a border of rope to strengthen it. And I made a little triangular jib to help make the boat lie close.

When we stepped the mast I found the boat's bottom was not sound: the slot for the mast was eaten away and badly worn. When I put in the spikes for the hinges that were to hold the rudder, they went in as if the hull were butter. The boat was rotten. That sod Jesus was sending us to our death. Very unwittingly I explained all this to the others: I had no right to hide it from them. What were we going to do about it? Make Jesus find us a sounder boat when he came, that's what. We'd take his weapons from him, and carrying a knife and the axe I'd go to the village with him and look for another boat. It was a great risk to take; but not so great as putting to sea in a coffin. The stores were all right: there was a wicker-covered bottle of oil and some tins full of manioc flour. We could go a long way on that.

That morning we saw a wonderfully strange sight: a troop of grey-faced monkeys had a battle with monkeys whose faces were black and woolly. During the struggle Maturette came in for a piece of wood on the head that gave him a lump the size of a walnut.

Now we had been there five days and four nights. Last night rain fell in torrents. We sheltered ourselves under wild banana leaves. Their shiny sides poured with water, but we were not wetted at all, only our feet. This morning, as we drank our coffee, I thought about Jesus's wickedness. Taking advantage of our lack of experience to palm off this rotting boat on us! Just to save five hundred or a thousand francs he was sending three men to certain death. I wondered whether I shouldn't kill him once I had forced him to get us another boat.

Suddenly we were startled by a noise like jays, a shrieking so harsh and unpleasant that I told Maturette to take the jungle-knife and go and see what was up. Five minutes later he came back, beckoning. I followed him and we reached a spot about a hundred and fifty yards from the boat: hanging there I saw a great pheasant or wild-fowl, twice the size of a cock. It was caught in a noose and it was hanging by its foot from a branch. With one blow of the jungle-knife I took off its head, to stop its ghastly shrieks. I felt its weight: it must have been at least ten pounds. It had spurs like a cock. We decided to eat it, but while we were thinking it over, it occurred to us that somebody must have set that snare and that there might be others. We went to have a look. When we were back there we found something very odd — a positive fence or wall about a foot high, made of woven leaves and creepers, some ten yards from the creek. This barrier ran parallel with the water. Every now and then there was a gap, and in this gap, hidden by twigs, the end of a noose of brass wire fixed to a bent-over whippy branch. I saw at once that the creature must come up against this hedge and then go along it, trying to get past. On finding the gap, it would pass through, but its feet would catch in the wire and spring the branch. Then there it would be, hanging in the air until the owner of the snares came to take it.

This discovery worried us badly. The hedge seemed to be well kept, so it wasn't old: and we were in danger of being found. We mustn't light a fire in the daytime: but at night the hunter wouldn't come. We decided to take it in turns to keep watch in the direction of the traps. We hid the boat under branches and all the stores in the bush.

The next day at ten o'clock I was on guard. For supper we had eaten that pheasant or cock or whatever it was. The soup had done us an enormous amount of good, and although the meat was only boiled it was still delicious. We had each eaten two bowls full. So I was on guard: but I was so taken up with the goings-on of the huge black manioc ants, each carrying a piece of leaf to the enormous ant-hill, that I forgot to keep watch. These ants were close on an inch long and they stood high on their legs. Each one was carrying this enormous piece of leaf. I followed them to the plant they were stripping and I discovered the whole thing was thoroughly organized. First there were the cutters, who did nothing but get the pieces ready: they were working away on a gigantic leaf something like the ones on a banana palm, very skilfully and very quickly cutting off pieces all the same size, which they dropped to the ground. Down below there were ants of the same sort but slightly different. These ones had a grey stripe on the side of their jaws: and they stood in a half circle, supervising the carriers. The carriers came filing in from the right and they went off towards the left in the direction of the ant-hill. They snatched up their loads before getting into line, but sometimes, what with their hurry in trying to load and to get into position, there was a jam. Then the police-ants would step in and shove the workers into their proper places. I couldn't understand the crime one worker had committed, but she was brought out of the ranks and one police-ant bit off her head while another divided her body in two in the middle. The police-ants stopped two workers; they put down their loads, scratched a hole, buried the three parts of the ant – head, chest, bottom piece – and covered them over with earth.

I was so taken up with watching these creatures and following the soldiers to see whether their policing went as far as the entrance to the ant-hill, that I was taken utterly by surprise when a voice said, 'Don't move or you're a dead man. Turn round.'

It was a man bare from the waist up, wearing khaki shorts and long red leather boots. He had a double-barrelled gun in his hands. Medium-sized and thickset: sunburnt. He was bald and his eyes and nose were covered with a bright blue tattooed mask. And in the middle of his forehead there was a tattooed black-beetle.

'You armed?'

'No.'

'Alone?'

'No.'

'How many of you are there?'

'Three.'

'Take me to your friends.'

'I wouldn't like to do that: one has a rifle, and I wouldn't like to get you killed before I know what you mean to do.'

'Ah? Don't you move an inch, then; and just you talk quiet. You're the three guys that escaped from the hospital?'

'Yes.'

'Which is Papillon?'

'That's me.'

'Well then, I can tell you you've stirred things up good and proper in the village, with your escape! Half the time-expired men are under arrest at the gendarmerie.' He came towards me, and lowering his gun he stretched out his hand. 'I'm the Masked Breton,' he said. 'You've heard of me?'

'No, but I can see you're not a tracker.'

'You're right there. I set traps round about here to catch hoccos. A jaguar must have eaten one for me, unless it was you guys.'

'It was us.'

'You want some coffee?' He had a thermos in a knapsack: he gave me a little and drank some himself. I said, 'Come and see my friends.' He came and sat down with us. He was amused at my having pulled the rifle trick with him. He said, 'I fell for it, particularly as everyone knows you left carrying a gun, and there's no tracker who'll go after you.'

He told us he had been in Guiana twenty years and that he'd been free these last five. He was forty-five. Because of the silly caper of having had that mask tattooed on his face, life in France didn't mean anything to him. He worshipped the bush and lived off it entirely – snakes' and jaguars' skins, butterfly collections, and above all catching live hoccos, the bird we'd eaten. He could sell them for two hundred or two hundred and fifty francs. I suggested paying for it, but he refused indignantly. This is what he told us: 'The bird is a sort of wild bush cock. Of course, it's never so much as seen an ordinary hen or a cock or a human being. Well, I catch one, I take it to the village and I sell it to someone who has a hen-run – they're always in demand. Right. You don't have to clip his wings, you don't have to do anything at all: at nightfall you put him into the henhouse and when you open the door in the morning there he is, standing by, looking like he was counting the cocks and hens as they come out. He comes out after them, and although he eats alongside of them, all the time he's watching – he looks up, he looks sideways and he looks into the bushes all round. There's no watchdog to touch him. In the evening he stands there at the door and although no one can tell how, he knows if there's a hen or two missing, and he goes and finds them. And whether it's a cock or whether it's a hen, he drives them in, pecking them like mad to teach them to keep an eye on the clock. He kills rats, snakes, shrews, spiders and centipedes; and a bird of prey has hardly appeared in the sky before he sends everyone off to hide in the grass while he stands there defying it. He never quits the hen-run for a moment.' And this was the wonderful bird we had eaten like any common barnyard cock.

The Masked Breton told us that Jesus, Fatgut and some thirty other freed men were in prison in the Saint-Laurent gendarmerie, being investigated to see whether any of them could be recognized as having been seen prowling about the building we escaped from. The Arab was in the black-hole of the gendarmerie. He was in solitary, accused of having helped us. The two blows that knocked him out had left no mark, whereas each of the screws had a little lump on the head. 'For my part, I wasn't interfered with at all, because everybody

knows I never have anything to do with preparing a break.'
He told us Jesus was a sod. When I spoke to him about the
boat he asked to see it. He'd scarcely caught sight of it before
he cried, 'But the bastard was sending you to your death! This
canoe could never live for an hour in the sea. The first wave
of any size, and it'd split in two as it came down. Don't go
off in that thing – it'd be suicide.'

'What can we do, then?'

'Got any money?'

'Yes.'

'Then I'll tell you what to do: and what's more, I'll help
you. You deserve it. You mustn't go anywhere near the village
– not at any price. To get hold of a decent boat you have to
go to Pigeon Island. There are about two hundred lepers there.
There's no warder, and no healthy man ever goes, not even
the doctor. At eight o'clock every day a boat takes food for
twenty-four hours: uncooked food. A hospital orderly hands
over a case of medicine to the two attendants, lepers themselves, who look after the patients. No one sets foot on the
island, whether he's warder, tracker or priest. The lepers live
in little straw huts they make themselves. They have a central
building where they meet. They raise hens and ducks, and that
helps them out with their rations. Officially they aren't allowed
to sell anything off the island, so they have an illicit trade
with Saint-Laurent, Saint-Jean and the Chinese of Albina in
Dutch Guiana. They're all dangerous murderers. They don't
often kill one another but they do a fair amount of villainy
when they get out of the island on the quiet – they go back
and hide there when it's over. They have some boats stolen
from the nearby village for these excursions. Possessing a boat
is the worst crime they can commit. The warders fire on any
canoe that comes or goes from Pigeon Island. So the lepers
sink their boats, filling them with stones: when they need one
they dive down, take out the stones, and the boat comes up.
There are all kinds on the island, every colour and nation and
from every part of France. What it comes to is this – your
canoe is only any use to you on the Maroni, and without much
in it, at that. To get out to sea, you've got to find another boat,
and the best place for that is Pigeon Island.'

'How are we to set about it?'

'This is how. I'll come with you up the river until we're in
sight of the island. You wouldn't find it, or at any rate you

might go wrong. It's about a hundred miles from the mouth, so you have to go upstream again. It's about thirty miles from Saint-Laurent. I'll guide you in as close as I can and then I'll get into my canoe – we'll tow it behind. Then, once on the island, it's all up to you.'

'Why won't you come on to the island with us?'

'Ma Doué,' said the Breton, 'I just set foot on the landing stage one day, the jetty where the official boats come in. Just once. It was in full daylight, but even so, what I saw was quite enough for me. No, Papi: I'll never set foot on that island again in my life. Anyhow, I'd never be able to hide my disgust at being near them, talking to them, dealing with them. I'd do more harm than good.'

'When do we go?'

'At nightfall.'

'What's the time now, Breton?'

'Three o'clock.'

'OK. I'll get a little sleep.'

'No. You've got to load everything properly aboard your canoe.'

'Nothing of the sort. I'll go with the empty canoe and then come back for Clousiot. He can stay here with the things.'

'Impossible. You'd never be able to find the place again, even in the middle of the day. And you must never, never be on the river in daylight. The search for you isn't over, so don't think that. The river is still very dangerous.'

Evening came. He brought his canoe and we tied it behind ours. Clousiot lay next to the Breton, who took the steering paddle, and then came Maturette, and then me in front. We made our slow way out of the creek and when we came into the river, night was just about to come down. Over towards the sea a huge brownish-red sun lit up the horizon. The countless fireworks of an enormous display fought to be the most brilliant, redder than the red, yellower than the yellow, more fantastically striped where the colours were mixed. Ten miles away, we could distinctly make out the estuary of the splendid river as it ran gleaming pink and silver into the sea.

The Breton said, 'It's the last of the ebb. In an hour we should feel the flood-tide: we'll make use of it to run up the Maroni: the current will take us up without any effort, and we'll reach the island pretty soon.' The darkness came down in a single sweep.

'Give way,' said the Breton. 'Paddle hard and get into the middle of the stream. Don't smoke.' The paddles dug into the water and we moved quite fast across the current. Shoo, shoo, shoo. The Breton and I kept stroke beautifully; Maturette did his best. The nearer we got to the middle of the river the more we felt the thrust of the tide. We slid on rapidly, and every half hour we felt the difference. The tide grew in strength, pushing us faster and faster. Six hours later we were very close to the island and heading straight for it – a great patch of darkness almost in the middle of the river, slightly to the right. 'That's it,' said the Breton in a low voice. The night was not very dark, but it would have been almost impossible to see us from any distance because of the mist over the face of the water. We came closer. When the outline of the rocks was clearer, the Breton got into his canoe and cast off quickly, just murmuring, 'Good luck, you guys.'

'Thanks.'

'Think nothing of it.'

As the boat no longer had the Breton steering it, we went straight for the island, drifting sideways. I tried to straighten out, turning it right round, but I made a mess of it and the current thrust us deep into the vegetation overhanging the water. We came in with such force, in spite of my braking with my paddle, that if we had hit a rock instead of leaves and branches the canoe would have been smashed and everything lost – stores, food, the lot. Maturette jumped into the water and heaved; we slid under a huge clump of bushes. He pulled and pulled and we tied the boat to a branch. We had a shot of rum and then I climbed the bank alone, leaving my two friends in the boat.

I went along with the compass in my hand, breaking several branches as I went, tying on scraps of flour-sack that I had put aside before we left. I saw a lighter patch in the darkness and then all at once I made out three huts and heard the sound of voices. I went forward, and as I had no idea how to make myself known, I decided to let them find me. I lit a cigarette. The moment the match sparked a little dog rushed out, barking and jumping up to bite my legs. 'Christ, I hope it's not a leper,' I thought. 'Don't be a fool: dogs don't get leprosy.'

'Who's there? Who is it? Marcel, is that you?'

'It's a guy on the run.'

'What are you doing here? Trying to knock something off? Do you think we've got anything to spare?'

'No. I want help.'

'For free or for cash?'

'You shut your bloody trap, La Chouette.' Four shadows came out of the hut. 'Come forward slowly, brother. I'll bet any money you're the character with the rifle. If you've got it with you, put it down: there's nothing to be afraid of here.'

'Yes, that's me. But the rifle's not here.' I walked forward; I was close to them; it was dark and I could not make out their faces. Like a fool I held out my hand: nobody took it. Too late I grasped that this was the wrong move here – they didn't want to infect me.

'Let's go into the hut,' said La Chouette. It was lit by an oil lamp standing on the table. 'Sit down.'

I took a straw chair without a back. La Chouette lit three other lamps and set one on the table just in front of me. The wick gave off a sickening reek – the smell of coconut-oil. I sat there: the five others stood. I couldn't make out their faces. Mine was lit up by the lamp, which was what they had wanted. The voice that had told La Chouette to shut up said, 'L'Anguille, go to the house and ask if they want us to take him there. Come back with the answer quick, particularly if Toussaint says yes. We can't give you anything to drink here, mate, unless you'd like a raw egg.' He pushed a plaited basket full of eggs towards me.

'No, thanks.'

Very close to me on my right one of them sat down and it was then that I saw my first leper's face. It was horrible and I made an effort not to turn away or show what I felt. His nose, flesh and bone, was entirely eaten away: a hole right in the middle of his face. I mean *a* hole, not two. Just one hole, as big as a two-franc piece. On the right-hand side his lower lip was eaten away, and three very long yellow teeth showed in the shrunken gum: you could see them go into the naked bone of the upper jaw. Only one ear. He put his bandaged hand on the table. It was his right hand. In the two fingers that he still had on the other he held a long, fat cigar: he must certainly have rolled it himself from a half-cured leaf, for it was greenish. He had an eyelid only on his left eye: the right had none, and a deep wound ran upwards from the eye into his thick grey hair. In a hoarse voice he said, 'We'll help you, mate: you mustn't stay in Guiana long enough to get the way I am. I don't want that.'

'Thanks.'

'They call me Jean sans Peur: I'm from Paris. I was better looking, healthier and stronger than you when I reached the settlement. Ten years, and now look at me.'

'Don't they give you any treatment?'

'Yes, they do. I've been better since I started chaulmoogra oil injections. Look.' He turned his head and showed me the left side. 'It's drying up here.'

I had an overwhelming feeling of pity and to show my friendliness I put my hand up towards his left cheek. He started back and said, 'Thanks for meaning to touch me. But don't ever touch a sick man, and don't eat or drink out of his bowl.' This was still the only leper's face I had seen – the only one who had the courage to bear my looking at him.

'Where's this character you're talking about?' The shadow of a man only just bigger than a dwarf appeared in the doorway. 'Toussaint and the others want to see him. Bring him over.'

Jean sans Peur stood up and said, 'Follow me.' We all went out into the darkness, four or five in front, me next to Jean sans Peur, the rest behind. In three minutes we reached a broad open place, a sort of square, which was lit by a scrap of moon. This was the flat topmost point of the island. A house in the middle. Light coming out of two windows. About twenty men waiting for us in front of the door: we went towards them. As we reached the door they stood aside to let us go through. It was a room some thirty feet long and twelve wide with a log fire burning in a kind of fireplace made of four huge stones all the same height. The place was lit by two big hurricane lamps. An ageless man with a white face sat there on a stool. Five or six others on a bench behind him. He had black eyes and he said to me. 'I'm Toussaint the Corsican: and you must be Papillon.'

'Yes.'

'News travels fast in the settlement; as fast as you move yourself. Where have you put the rifle?'

'We tossed it into the river.'

'Where?'

'Opposite the hospital wall, just where we jumped.'

'So it could be got at?'

'I think so; the water's not deep there.'

'How do you know?'

'We had to get in to carry my wounded friend into the boat.'

'What's wrong with him?'

'A broken leg.'

'What have you done about it?'

'I've split branches down the middle and put a kind of cage round his leg.'

'Does it hurt?'

'Yes.'

'Where is he?'

'In the canoe.'

'You said you'd come for help. What sort of help?'

'A boat.'

'You want us to let you have a boat?'

'Yes. I've got money to pay for it.'

'OK. I'll sell you mine. It's a splendid boat, quite new – I stole it only last week in Albina. Boat? It's not a boat: it's a liner. There's only one thing it lacks, and that's a keel. It hasn't got one: but we'll put one on for you in a couple of hours. There's everything there – a rudder and its tiller, a thirteen-foot iron-wood mast and a brand-new canvas sail. What'll you give me?'

'You name a price. I don't know the value of things here.'

'Three thousand francs, if you can pay it: if not, go and fetch the rifle tomorrow night and we'll do a swap.'

'No. I'd rather pay.'

'OK, it's a deal. La Puce, let's have some coffee.'

La Puce, the near-dwarf, who had come for me, went to a plank fixed to the wall over the fire, took down a mess-tin shining with cleanliness and newness, poured coffee into it from a bottle and set it on the fire. After a while he took it off, poured coffee into various mugs standing by the stones for Toussaint to pass to the men behind him, and gave me the mess-tin, saying 'Don't be afraid of drinking. This one's for visitors only. No sick man ever uses it.'

I took the bowl, drank, and then rested it on my knee. As I did so I noticed a finger sticking to its side. I was beginning to grasp the situation when La Puce said, 'Hell, I've lost another finger. Where the devil can it have got to?'

'Here it is,' I said, showing him the tin. He picked off the finger, threw it in the fire and gave me back the bowl.

'It's all right to drink,' he said, 'because I've only got dry leprosy. I come to pieces spare part by spare part, but I don't rot – I'm not catching.'

I smelt burning meat. I thought, 'That must be the finger.'

Toussaint said, 'You'll have to spend the whole day here until the evening ebb. You must go and tell your friends. Carry the one with the broken leg up to a hut, empty the canoe and sink it. There's no one here can give you a hand – you know why, of course.'

I hurried back to the others. We lifted Clousiot out and then carried him to a hut. An hour later everything was out of the canoe and carefully arranged on the ground. La Puce asked for the canoe and a paddle as a present. I gave it to him and he went off to sink it in a place he knew. The night passed quickly. We were all three of us in the hut, lying on new blankets sent by Toussaint. They reached us still wrapped in their strong backing paper. Stretched out there at my ease. I told Clousiot and Maturette the details of what had happened since I went ashore and about the deal I had made with Toussaint. Then, without thinking, Clousiot said a stupid thing. 'So the break's costing six thousand five hundred. I'll give you half, Papillon – I mean the three thousand francs that I have.'

'We don't want to muck about with accounts like a bunch of bank-clerks. So long as I've got the cash, I pay. After that – well, we'll see.'

None of the lepers came into the hut. Day broke, and Toussaint appeared. 'Good morning. You can go out without worrying. No one can come on you unexpectedly here. Up a coconut-palm on the top of the island there's a guy watching to see if there are any screws' boats on the river. There's none in sight. So long as that bit of white cloth is up there, it means no boats. If he sees anything he'll come down and say. You can pick papayas yourselves and eat them, if you like.'

I said, 'Toussaint, what about the keel?'

'We'll make it out of a plank from the infirmary door. That's heavy snake-wood. Two planks will do the job. We took advantage of the night to haul the boat up to the top. Come and have a look.' We went. It was a splendid sixteen-foot boat, quite new, with two thwarts – one had a hole for the mast. It was so heavy that Maturette and I had a job turning it over. The sail and rigging were brand-new. There were rings in the sides to lash things to, such as the water-barrel. We set to work. By noon a keel, deepening as it ran aft, was firmly fixed with long screws and the four spikes I had with me.

Standing there in a ring, the lepers silently watched us work. Toussaint told us how to set about it and we followed his instructions. Toussaint's face looked natural enough – no bad places on it. But when he spoke you noticed that only one half of his face moved, the left half. He told me that; and he also told me he had dry leprosy. His chest and his right arm were paralysed too, and he was expecting his right leg to go presently. His right eye was as set as one made of glass: it could see, but not move. I won't give any of the lepers' names. Maybe those who knew or loved them were never told the hideous way they rotted alive.

As I worked I talked to Toussaint. No one else said a word. Except once, when I was just going to pick up some hinges they had wrenched off a piece of furniture in the infirmary to strengthen the hold of the keel: one said, 'Don't take them yet. Leave them there. I cut myself getting one off, and although I wiped it there's still a little blood.' Another leper poured rum over the hinge and lit it twice. 'Now you can use it,' he said.

During our work Toussaint said to one of the lepers, 'You've escaped a good many times; tell Papillon just what he ought to do, since none of these three has ever made a break.'

Straight away the leper began, 'The ebb will start very early this afternoon. The tide'll change at three. By nightfall, about six o'clock, you'll have a very strong run that'll take you to about sixty miles from the mouth of the river in less than three hours. When you have to pull in, it'll be about nine. You must tie up good and solid to a tree in the bush during the six hours of flood: that brings you to three in the morning. Don't set off then, though, because the ebb doesn't run fast enough. Get out into the middle at say half past four. You'll have an hour and a half to cover the thirty odd miles before sunrise. Everything depends on that hour and a half. At six o'clock, when the sun comes up, you have to be out at sea. Even if the screws do see you, they can't follow, because they'd reach the bar at the mouth of the river just as the flood begins. They can't get over it, and you'll already be across. You've got to have that lead of half a mile when they see you – it's life or death. There's only one sail here. What did you have on the canoe?'

'Mainsail and jib.'

'This is a heavy boat: it'll stand two jibs – a staysail and an outer jib to keep her bows well up. Go out of the river with everything set. There are always heavy seas at the mouth there, and you want to take them head on. Make your friends lie down in the bottom to keep her steady and get a good grip on the tiller. Don't tie the sheet to your leg, but pass it through that fairlead and hold it with a turn round your wrist. If you see that the wind and a heavy sea are going to lay you right over, let everything go and you'll straighten up right away. If that happens, don't you stop, but let the mainsail spill the wind and carry right on with the jib and staysail full. When you're out in the blue water you'll have time enough to put it all to rights – not before that. Do you know your course?'

'No. All I know is that Venezuela and Colombia lie north-west.'

'That's right; but take care not to be forced back on shore. Dutch Guiana, on the other side of the river, hands escaped men back, and so does British Guiana. Trinidad doesn't, but they make you leave in a fortnight. Venezuela returns you, after you've worked on the roads for a year or two.'

I listened as hard as I could. He told me he went off from time to time, but since he was a leper everybody sent him away at once. He admitted he had never been farther than Georgetown, in British Guiana. His leprosy could only be seen on his feet, which had lost all their toes. He was barefoot. Toussaint told me to repeat all the advice I had been given, and I did so without making a mistake. At this point Jean sans Peur said, 'How long ought he to sail out to sea?'

I answered first, 'I'll steer north-north-east for three days. Reckoning the leeway that'll make dead north. Then the fourth day I'll head north-west, which will come to true west.'

'That's right,' said the leper. 'Last time I only stood out two days, so I ended up in British Guiana. With three days standing on, you'll go north past Trinidad or Barbados, and then you go right by Venezuela without noticing it and land up in Curaçao or Colombia.'

Jean sans Peur said, 'Toussaint, what did you sell your boat for?'

'Three thousand,' said Toussaint. 'Was that dear?'

'No, that wasn't why I asked. Just to know, that's all. Can you pay, Papillon?'

'Yes.'

'Will you have any money left?'

'No. That's all we've got – exactly the three thousand my friend Clousiot has on him.'

'Toussaint,' said Jean sans Peur, 'I'll let you have my revolver. I'd like to help these guys. What'll you give me for it?'

'A thousand francs,' said Toussaint. 'I'd like to help them too.'

'Thanks for everything,' said Maturette, looking at Jean sans Peur.

'Thanks,' said Clousiot.

Now I was ashamed of having lied and I said, 'No. I can't take it. There's no reason why you should give us anything.'

He looked at me and said, 'Yes, there is a reason all right. Three thousand francs is a lot of money; but even so, Toussaint's dropping two thousand at least on the deal, because it's a hell of a good boat he's letting you have. There's no reason why I shouldn't do something for you too.'

And then something very moving happened. La Chouette put a hat on the ground and the lepers began throwing notes or coins into it. Lepers appeared from everywhere, and every one of them put something in. I was overcome with shame. Yet it just wasn't possible to say I still had money left. Christ, what was I to do? Here was this great-hearted conduct and I was behaving like a shit. I said, 'Please, please don't sacrifice all this.' A coal-black Negro, terribly mutilated – two stumps for hands, no fingers at all – said, 'We don't use the money for living. Don't be ashamed to take it. We only use it for gambling or for stuffing the leper-women who come over from Albina now and then.' What he said was a relief to me and it stopped me confessing I still had some money.

The lepers had boiled two hundred eggs. They brought them in a wooden box with a red cross on it. It was the box they had had that morning with the day's medicines. They also brought two live turtles weighing at least half a hundredweight each, carefully laid on their backs, tobacco in leaves and two bottles full of matches and strikers; a sack of at least a hundredweight of rice, two bags of charcoal; the Primus from the infirmary and a wicker bottle of paraffin. The whole community, all these terribly unfortunate men, felt for us; they all wanted to help us succeed. Anyone would have said this was their escape rather than ours. We hauled the boat down near to the place where we had landed. They counted the money in the hat: eight hundred and ten francs. I only had to give Toussaint one thousand two hundred. Clousiot passed me his charger. I opened it there in front of everybody. It held a thousand-franc note and four five hundreds. I gave Toussaint one thousand five hundred. He gave me three hundred change and then he said, 'Here. Take the revolver – it's a present. You're staking everything you've got, and it mustn't go wrong at the last moment just for want of a weapon. I hope you won't have to use it.'

I didn't know how to say thank you, to Toussaint first and then to all the others. The medical orderly had put up a little tin with cotton-wool, alcohol, aspirin, bandages, iodine, a pair of scissors and some sticking-plaster. Another leper brought two slim, well-planed pieces of wood and two strips of antiseptic binding still in its packet, perfectly new. They were a present so that I could change Clousiot's splints.

About five it began to rain. Jean sans Peur said, 'You're lucky. There's no danger of your being seen, so you can get off right away and gain at least half an hour. That way you'll be nearer the mouth when you start again at half-past four in the morning.'

'How shall I know the time?' I asked him.

'The tide'll tell you, coming in or out.'

We launched the boat. It was not like the canoe at all. Even with us and all our things aboard, the gunwale was a good eighteen inches from the water. The mast, wrapped in the sail, lay flat fore and aft, because we were not to put it up until we were about to run out of the river. We shipped the rudder, with its safety-bar and tiller, and put a pad of creepers for me to sit on. We made a comfortable place in the bottom of the boat with the blankets for Clousiot, who had not wanted to have his bandages changed. He lay at my feet, between me and the water-barrel. Maturette was in the bottom too, but up forward. Straight away I had a feeling of safety and solidity that I had never had in the canoe.

It was still raining. I was to go down the middle of the river, but rather to the left, over on the Dutch side. Jean sans Peur said, 'Good-bye. Push off quick.'

'Good luck,' said Toussaint, and he gave the boat a great shove with his foot.

'Thanks, Toussaint. Thanks, Jean. Thanks, everybody,

thanks a thousand times over!' And we vanished at great speed, swept along by the ebb-tide that had begun quite two and a half hours ago and that was now running at an unbelievable pace.

It rained steadily: we couldn't see ten yards in front of us. There were two little islands lower down, so Maturette leant out over the bows, staring ahead so we shouldn't run on their rocks. Night fell. For a moment we were half caught in the branches of a big tree that was going down the river with us, but fortunately not quite so fast. We quickly got free and carried on at something like twenty miles an hour. We smoked: we drank rum. The lepers had given us half a dozen of those straw-covered Chianti bottles, but filled with tafia. It was odd, but not one of us mentioned the hideous mutilations we had seen among the lepers. The only thing we talked about was their kindness, their generosity, their straightness and our good luck in having met the Masked Breton, who took us to Pigeon Island. It rained harder and harder and I was wet through: but those woollen jackets were such good quality they kept you warm even when they were soaked. We were not cold. The only thing was my hand on the tiller – the rain made it go stiff.

'We're running at more than twenty-five miles an hour now,' said Maturette, 'How long do you think we've been gone for?'

'I'll tell you,' said Clousiot. 'Just a moment. Three and a quarter hours.'

'Are you crazy, man? How can you possibly tell?'

'I've been counting ever since we left and at each three hundred seconds I've torn off a piece of cardboard. There're thirty-nine bits now. At five minutes a go, that makes three hours and a quarter. Unless I've got it wrong, in fifteen or twenty minutes we shan't be running down any more, but going back to where we came from.'

I thrust the tiller over to my right to slant across the stream and get into the bank on the Dutch side. Before we reached the shore the current had stopped. We were no longer going down; and we weren't going up, either. It was still raining. We no longer smoked; we no longer talked – we whispered. 'Take the paddle and shove.' I paddled too, holding the tiller wedged under my right leg. Gently we came up against the bush: we seized branches and pulled, sheltering beneath them. We were in the darkness of the vegetation. The river was grey, quite covered with thick mist. If we had not been able to rely upon the ebb and flow of the tides, it would have been impossible to tell where the sea lay and where the landward river.

Right Out and Away

The flood-tide would last six hours. Then there was the hour and a half to wait for the ebb. I should be able to sleep for seven hours, although I was very much on edge. I had to get some sleep, because once out at sea, when should I be able to lie down? I stretched out between the barrel and the mast; Maturette laid a blanket over the thwart and the barrel by way of a cover, and there in the shelter I slept and slept. Dreams, rain, cramped position – nothing disturbed that deep, heavy sleep.

I slept and slept until Maturette woke me. 'Papi, we think it's time, or just about. The ebb has been running a good while.'

The boat had turned towards the sea and under my fingers the current raced by. It was no longer raining, and by the light of a quarter moon we could distinctly see the river a hundred yards in front of us, carrying trees, vegetation and dark shapes upon its surface. I tried to distinguish the exact place where the sea and river met. Where we were lying there was no wind. Was there any out in the middle? Was it strong? We pushed out from under the bush, the boat still hitched to a big root. Looking at the sky I could just make out the coast, where the river ended and the sea began. We had run much farther down than we had thought, and it seemed to me that we were under six miles from the mouth. We had a stiff tot of rum. Should we step the mast now? Yes, said the others. It was up, very strongly held in its heel and the hole in the thwart. I hoisted the sail without unfurling it, keeping it tight to the mast. Maturette was ready to haul up the staysail and jib when I said. All that was needed to fill the sail was to cast loose the line holding it close to the mast, and I'd be able to do that from where I sat. Maturette had one paddle in the bows and I had another in the stern: we should have to shove out very strong and fast, for the current was pressing us tight against the bank.

'Everybody ready. Shove away. In the name of God.'

'In the name of God,' repeated Clousiot.

'Into Thy hands I entrust myself,' said Maturette.

And we shoved. Both together we shoved on the water with our blades – I thrust deep and I pulled hard: so did Maturette. We got under way as easy as kiss my hand. We weren't a stone's throw from the bank before the tide had swept us down a good hundred yards. Suddenly there was the breeze, pushing us out towards the middle.

'Hoist the staysail and jib – make all fast.' They filled: the boat reared-like a horse and shot away. It must have been later than the time we'd planned, because all of a sudden the river was as light as though the sun was up. About a mile away on our right we could see the French bank clearly, and perhaps half a mile on the left, the Dutch. Right ahead, and perfectly distinct the white crests of the breaking ocean waves.

'Christ, we got the time wrong,' said Clousiot. 'Do you think we'll have long enough to get out?'

'I don't know.'

'Look how high the waves are, and how they break so white! Can the flood have started?'

'Impossible. I can see things going down.'

Maturette said, 'We shan't be able to get out. We shan't be there in time.'

'You shut your bloody mouth and sit there by the jib and staysail sheets. You shut up too, Clousiot.'

Bang. Bang. Rifles, shooting at us. I distinctly spotted the second. It was not screws firing at all: the shots were coming from Dutch Guiana. I hoisted the mainsail and it filled with such strength that the sheet tearing at my wrist nearly had me in the water. The boat lay over at more than forty-five degrees. I bore away as fast as I could – it wasn't hard, for there was wind and to spare. Bang, bang, bang, and then no more. We had run farther towards the French side than the Dutch, and that was certainly why the firing stopped.

We tore along at a blinding speed, with a wind fit to carry

everything away. We were going so fast that we shot across the middle of the estuary, and I could see that in a few minutes' time we should be right up against the French bank. I could see men running towards the shore. Gently, as gently as possible, I came about, heaving on the sheet with all my strength. We came up into the wind: the jib went over all by itself and so did the staysail. The boat turned, turned, I let go the sheet and we ran out of the river straight before the wind. Christ, we'd done it! It was over! Ten minutes later a sea-wave tried to stop us; we rode over it smooth and easy, and the shwit shwit that the boat had made in the river changed to thumpo-thumpo-thump. The waves were high, but we went over them as easy as a kid playing leap-frog. Thump-o-thump, the boat went up and down the slopes without a shake or a tremble, only that thud of her hull striking the water as it came down.

'Hurray, hurray! We're out!' roared Clousiot with the full strength of his lungs.

And to light up our victory over the elements the Lord sent us an astonishing sunrise. The waves came in a steady rhythm. Their height grew less the farther we went from the shore. The water was filthy – full of mud. Over towards the north it looked black; but later on it was blue. I had no need to look at my compass: with the sun there on my right shoulder I steered straight ahead going large but with the boat lying over less, for I had slackened off the sheet until the sail was just drawing pleasantly. The great adventure had begun.

Clousiot heaved himself up. He wanted to get his head and shoulders out to see properly. Maturette came and gave him a hand, sitting him up there opposite me with his back against the barrel: he rolled me a cigarette, lit it and passed it. We all three of us smoked.

'Give me the tafia,' said Clousiot. 'This crossing of the bar calls for a drink.' Maturette poured an elegant tot into three tin mugs; we clinked and drank to one another. Maturette was sitting next to me on my left: we all looked at one another. Their faces were shining with happiness, and mine must have been the same. Then Clousiot said to me, 'Captain, sir, where are you heading for, if you please?'

'Colombia, if God permits.'

'God will permit all right, Christ above!' said Clousiot.

The sun rose fast and we dried out with no difficulty at all. I turned the hospital shirt into a kind of Arab burnous. Wetted, it kept my head cool and prevented sunstroke. The sea was an opal blue; the ten-foot waves were very wide apart, and that made sailing comfortable. The breeze was still strong and we moved fast away from the shore; from time to time I looked back and saw it fading on the horizon. The farther we ran from that vast green mass, the more we could make out the lie of the land. I was gazing back when a vague uneasiness called me to order and reminded me of my responsibility for my companions' lives and my own.

'I'll cook some rice,' said Maturette.

'I'll hold the stove and you hold the pot,' said Clousiot.

The bottle of paraffin was made fast right up forward where no one was allowed to smoke. The fried rice smelt good. We ate it hot, with two tins of sardines stirred into it. On top of that we had a good cup of coffee. 'Some rum?' I refused: it was too hot. Besides, I was no drinker. Clousiot rolled me cigarette after cigarette and lit them for me. The first meal aboard had gone off well. Judging from the sun, we thought it was ten o'clock in the morning. We had had only five hours of running out to sea and yet you could already feel that the water beneath us was very deep. The waves were not so high now, and as we ran across them the boat no longer thumped. The weather was quite splendid. I realized that during daylight I should not have to be looking at the compass all the time. Now and then I fixed the sun in relation to the needle and I steered by that – it was very simple. The glare tired my eyes and I was sorry I had not thought to get myself a pair of dark glasses.

Out of the blue Clousiot said, 'What luck I had, finding you in hospital!'

'It was just as lucky for me – you're not the only one.' I thought of Dega and Fernandez . . . if they'd said yes, they would have been here with us.

'That's not so certain,' said Clousiot. 'But it might have been tricky for you to get the Arab into the ward just at the right moment.'

'Yes, Maturette has been a great help to us. I'm very glad we brought him, he's as reliable as they come, brave and clever.'

'Thanks,' said Maturette. 'And thank you both for believing in me, although I'm so young and although I'm you know what. I'll do my best not to let you down.'

Then after a while I said, 'François Sierra too, the guy I'd so much wanted to have with us; and Galgani . . .'

'As things turned out, Papillon, it just wasn't on. If Jesus had been a decent type and if he had given us a decent boat, we could have lain up and waited for them — we could have waited for Jesus to get them out and bring them. Anyhow, they know you, and they know that if you didn't send for them, it was on account of it just wasn't possible.'

'By the way, Maturette, how come you were in the high-security ward?'

'I never knew I was to be interned. I reported sick because I had a sore throat and because I wanted the walk, and when the doctor saw me he said, "I see from your card that you're for internment on the islands, Why?" "I don't know anything about it, Doctor. What's internment mean?" "All right. Never mind. Hospital for you." And there I was: that's all there was to it.'

'He meant to do you a good turn,' said Clousiot.

'What on earth did the quack want, sending me to hospital? Now he must be saying "My angel-faced boy wasn't such a wet after all, seeing he's got out — he's on the run".'

We talked and laughed. I said, 'Who knows but we may come across Julot, the hammer-man. He'll be far off by now, unless he's still lying up in the bush.' Clousiot said, 'When I left I put a note under my pillow saying, "Gone without leaving an address".' That made us roar with laughter.

Five days we sailed on with nothing happening. The east-west passage of the sun acted as my compass by day: by night I used the compass itself. On the morning of the sixth day we were greeted by a brilliant sun; the sea had suddenly calmed, and flying-fishes went by not far away. I was destroyed with fatigue. During the night Maturette had kept wiping my face with a wet cloth to keep me from sleeping; but even so I went off, and Clousiot had had to burn me with his cigarette. Now it was dead calm, so I decided to get some sleep. We lowered the mainsail and the jib, keeping just the staysail, and I slept like a log in the bottom of the boat, the sail spread to keep me from the sun.

I woke up with Maturette shaking me. He said, 'It's noon or one o'clock, but I'm waking you because the wind is getting stronger and on the horizon where it's coming from, every-thing's black.' I got up and went to my post. The one sail we had set was carrying us over the unruffled sea. In the east, behind me, all was black, and the breeze was strengthening steadily. The staysail and the jib were enough to make the boat run very fast. I furled the mainsail against the mast, carefully, and made all tight. 'Look out for yourselves, because what's coming is a storm.'

Heavy drops began to fall on us. The darkness came rushing forwards at an astonishing speed, and in a quarter of an hour it had spread from the horizon almost as far as us. Now here it came: an incredibly strong wind drove straight at us. As if by magic the sea got up faster, waves with foaming white tops: the sun was wiped right out, rain poured down in torrents, we could see nothing, and as the seas hit the boat so they sent packets of water stinging into my face. It was a storm all right, my first storm, with all the terrific splendour of nature unrestrained – thunder, lightning, rain, waves, the howling of the wind over and all around us.

The boat was carried along like a straw; she climbed unbelievable heights and ran down into hollows so deep you felt she could never rise up again. Yet in spite of these astonishing depths she did climb up the side of the next wave, go over the crest, and so begin once more – right up and down again and again. I held the tiller with both hands; and once, when I saw an even bigger wave coming I thought I should steer a little against it. No doubt I moved too fast, because just as we cut it, I shipped a great deal of water. The whole boat was aswim. There must have been about three foot of water aboard. Without meaning to I wrenched the boat strongly across the next wave – a very dangerous thing to do – and she leant over so much, almost to the point of turning turtle, that she flung out most of the water we had shipped.

'Bravo!' cried Clousiot. 'You're a real expert, Papillon! You emptied her straight away.'

I said, 'You see now how it's done, don't you?'

If only he'd known that my lack of experience had very nearly turned us upside down, right out in the open sea! I decided not to struggle against the thrust of the waves any more, not to worry about what course to steer, but just to keep the boat as steady as possible. I took the waves three-quarters on; I let the boat run down and rise just as the sea would have it. Very soon I realized that this was an important discovery and that I'd done away with ninety per cent of the danger.

The rain stopped: the wind was still blowing furiously, but now I could see clearly in front and behind. Behind, the sky was clear; in front it was black. We were in the middle of the two.

By about five it was all over. The sun was shining on us again, the breeze was its usual self, the sea had gone down: I hoisted the mainsail and we set off once more, pleased with ourselves. We baled the boat with the saucepans and we brought out the blankets to dry them by hanging them to the mast. Rice, flour, oil and double-strength coffee: a comforting shot of rum. The sun was about to set, lighting up the blue sea and making an unforgettable picture – reddish-brown sky, great yellow rays leaping up from the half-sunk orb and lighting the sky, and the few white clouds, and the sea itself. As the waves rose they were blue at the bottom, then green; and their crests were red, pink or yellow, according to the colour of the rays that hit them.

I was filled with a wonderfully gentle peace; and together with the peace a feeling that I could rely upon myself. I had stuck it out pretty well; this short storm had been very valuable to me. All by myself I had learnt how to handle the boat in such circumstances. I'd look forward to the night with a completely easy mind.

'So you saw how to empty a boat, Clousiot, did you? You saw how it was done?'

'Listen, brother, if you hadn't brought it off, and if another wave had caught us sideways, we'd have sunk. You're all right.'

'You learnt all that in the navy?' said Maturette.

'Yes. There's something to be said for a naval training, after all.'

We must have made a great deal of leeway. Who could tell how far we had drifted during those four hours, with a wind and waves like that? I'd steer north-west to make it up: that's what I'd do. The sun vanished into the sea, sending up the last flashes of its firework display – violet this time – and then at once it was night.

For six more days we sailed on with nothing to worry us except for a few squalls and showers – none ever lasted more than three hours and none were anything like that first everlasting storm.

Ten o'clock in the morning and not a breath of wind: a dead

calm. I slept for nearly four hours. When I woke my lips were on fire. They had no skin left; nor had my nose either; and my right hand was quite raw. Maturette was the same; so was Clousiot. Twice a day we rubbed our faces and hands with oil, but that was not enough – the tropical sun soon dried it.

By the sun it must have been two o'clock in the afternoon. I ate, and then, seeing it was dead calm, we rigged the sail as an awning. Fish came round the boat where Maturette had done the washing-up. I took the jungle-knife and told Maturette to throw in some rice – anyhow it had begun to ferment since the water had got at it. The fish all gathered where the rice struck the water, all on the surface; and as one of them had his head almost out of the water I hit at him very hard. The next moment there he was, belly up. He weighed twenty pounds: we gutted him and cooked him in salt water. We ate him that evening with manioc flour.

Now it was eleven days since we had set out to sea. In all that time we had only seen one ship, very far away on the horizon. I began to wonder where the hell we were. Far out, that was for sure; but how did we lie in relation to Trinidad or any of the other English islands? Speak of the devil . . . and indeed there, right ahead, we saw a dark speck that gradually grew larger and larger. Would it be a ship or a deep-sea fishing boat? We'd got it all wrong: it was not coming towards us. It was a ship: we could see it clearly now, but going across. It was coming nearer, true enough, but its slanting course was not going to bring us together. There was no wind, so our sails drooped miserably: the ship would surely not have seen us. Suddenly there was the bowl of a siren and then three short blasts. The ship changed course and stood straight for our boat.

'I hope she doesn't come too close,' said Clousiot.

'There's no danger: it's as calm as a millpond.'

She was a tanker. The nearer she came, the more clearly we could make out the people on deck. They must have been wondering what this nutshell of a boat was doing there, right out at sea. Slowly she approached, and now we could see the officers and the men of the crew. And the cook. Then women in striped dresses appeared on deck, and men in coloured shirts. We took it these were passengers. Passengers on a tanker – that struck me as odd. Slowly the ship came close and the captain hailed us in English, 'Where do you come from?'

'French Guiana.'

'Do you speak French?' asked a woman.

'Oui, Madame.'

'What are you doing so far out at sea?'

'We go where God's wind blows us.'

The lady spoke to the captain and then said, 'The captain says to come aboard. He'll haul your little boat on deck.'

'Tell him we say thank you very much but we're quite happy in our boat.'

'Why don't you want help?'

'Because we are on the run and we aren't going in your direction.'

'Where are you going?'

'Martinique or even farther. Where are we?'

'Far out in the ocean.'

'What's the course for the West Indies?'

'Can you read an English chart?'

'Yes.'

A moment later they lowered us an English chart, some packets of cigarettes, a roast leg of mutton and some bread. 'Look at the chart.'

I looked and then I said, 'I must steer west by south to hit the British West Indies, is that right?'

'Yes.'

'About how many miles?'

'You'll be there in two days,' said the captain.

'Good-bye! Thank you all very much.'

'The captain congratulates you on your fine seamanship.'

'Thank you. Good-bye!'

The tanker moved gently off, almost touching us; I drew away to avoid the churning of the propellers and just at that moment a sailor tossed me a uniform cap. It dropped right in the middle of the boat; it had a gold band and an anchor, and it was with this cap on my head that we reached Trinidad two days later, with no further difficulty.

Long before we saw it, the birds had told us land was near. It was half-past seven in the morning when they began to circle round us. 'We're getting there, man! We're getting there! The first part of the break, the hardest part – we've brought it off. Freedom, freedom, freedom for ever!' Joy made us shout like schoolboys. Our faces were plastered with the coconut-butter that the tanker had given us for our sunburn. At about nine o'clock we saw the land. A breeze carried us in quite fast over a gentle sea. It was not until four in the afternoon that we could make out the details of a long island, fringed with little clumps of white houses and topped with great numbers of coconut-palms. So far we could not tell whether it was really an island or a peninsula, nor whether these houses were lived in. We had to wait another hour and more before we could distinguish people running towards the beach where we were going to land. In under twenty minutes a highly-coloured crowd had gathered. The entire little village had come out on to the shore to welcome us. Later we learnt that it was called San Fernando.

Three hundred yards from the beach I dropped the anchor: it bit at once. I did so partly to see how the people would take it and partly so as not to damage my boat when it grounded, supposing the bottom was coral. We furled the sails and waited. A little boat came towards us. Two blacks paddling and one white man with a sun-helmet on.

'Welcome to Trinidad,' said the white man in perfect French. The black men laughed, showing all their teeth.

'Thank you for your kind words, Monsieur. Is the bottom coral or sand?'

'It's sand. You can run in without any danger.'

We hauled up the anchor, and the waves gently pushed us in towards the beach. We had scarcely touched before ten men waded in and with a single heave they ran the boat up out of the water. They gazed at us and stroked us, and Negro or Indian coolie women beckoned to invite us in. The white man who spoke French explained that they all wanted us to stay with them. Maturette caught up a handful of sand and kissed it. Great enthusiasm. I had told the white man about Clousiot's condition and he had him carried to his house, which was very close to the beach. He told us we could leave all our belongings in the boat until tomorrow – no one would touch anything. They all called out, 'Good captain, long ride in little boat.'

Night fell, and when I had asked them to heave the boat a little higher up I tied it to a much bigger one lying on the beach; then I followed the Englishman and Maturette came after me. There I saw Clousiot looking very pleased with himself in an armchair, with a lady and a girl beside him and his wounded leg stretched out on a chair.

'My wife and my daughter,' said the gentleman. 'I have a son at the university in England.'

'You are very welcome in this house,' said the lady in French.

'Sit down, gentlemen,' said the girl, placing us two wicker armchairs.

'Thank you, ladies, but please don't put yourselves out for us.'

'Why? We know where you come from, so be easy; and I say again, you are very welcome in this house.'

The Englishman was a barrister. Mr. Bowen was his name, and he had his office in Port of Spain, the capital, twenty-five miles away. They brought us tea with milk, toast, butter and jam. This was our first evening as free men, and I shall never forget it. Not a word about the past, no untimely questions: only how many days had we been at sea and what kind of voyage we had had. Whether Clousiot was in much pain and whether we should like them to tell the police tomorrow or wait for another day: whether we had any living relations, such as wives or children. If we should like to write to them, they would post the letters. What can I say? It was a wonderful welcome, both from the people on the shore and from this family with their extraordinary kindness to three men on the run.

Mr. Bowen telephoned a doctor, who told him to bring the wounded man in to his nursing-home tomorrow afternoon so that he could X-ray him and see what needed doing. Mr. Bowen also telephoned the head of the Salvation Army in Port of Spain. He said this man would have a room ready for us in the Salvation Army hostel and that we could go whenever we liked; he said we should keep our boat if it was any good, because we'd need it for leaving again. He asked if we were convicts or relégués and we told him convicts. He seemed pleased we were convicts.

'Would you like to have a bath and a shave?' asked the girl. 'Don't feel awkward, whatever you do – it doesn't worry us in the least. You'll find some things in the bathroom that I hope will fit you.'

I went into the bathroom, had a bath, shaved and came out again with my hair combed, wearing grey trousers, a white shirt, tennis shoes and white socks.

An Indian knocked on the door: he was carrying a parcel which he gave to Maturette, telling him the doctor had noticed that as I was roughly the same size as the lawyer I wouldn't need anything; but little Maturette wouldn't find anything to fit, because there was no one as small as him in Mr. Bowen's house. He bowed in the Moslem way and went out. What is there I can say about such kindness? There is no describing the feelings in my heart. Clousiot went to bed first, then the five of us talked about a great number of things. What interested those charming women most was how we thought of remaking a life for ourselves. Not a word about the past: only the present and the future. Mr. Bowen said how sorry he was Trinidad wouldn't permit escaped men to settle on the island. He'd often tried to get permission for various people to stay, he told us, but it had never been allowed.

The girl spoke very good French, like her father, with no accent or faulty pronunciation. She had fair hair and she was covered with freckles; she was between seventeen and twenty – I did not like to ask her age. She said, 'You're very young and your life is ahead of you: I don't know what you were sentenced for and I don't want to know, but the fact of having taken to sea in such a small boat for this long, dangerous voyage proves that you're willing to pay absolutely anything for your freedom; and that is something I admire very much.'

We slept until eight the next morning. When we got up we found the table laid. The two ladies calmly told us that Mr. Bowen had left for Port of Spain and would only be back that afternoon, bringing the information he needed to see what could be done for us.

By leaving his house to three escaped convicts like this he gave us a lesson that couldn't have been bettered: it was as though he were saying, 'You are normal decent human beings; you can see for yourselves how much I trust you, since I am

leaving you alone in my house with my wife and daughter.'
We were very deeply moved by this silent way of saying,
'Now that I've talked to you, I see that you are perfectly
trustworthy – so much so that I leave you here in my home
like old friends, not supposing for a moment that you could
possibly do or say anything wrong.'

Reader – supposing this book has readers some day – I am
not clever and I don't possess the vivid style, the living power,
that is needed to describe this immense feeling of self-respect
– no, of rehabilitation, or even of a new life. This figurative
baptism, this bath of cleanliness, this raising of me above the
filth I had sunk in, this way of bringing me overnight face to
face with true responsibility, quite simply changed my whole
being. I had been a convict, a man who could hear his chains
even when he was free and who always felt that someone
was watching over him; I had been all the things I had seen,
experienced, undergone, suffered; all the things that had urged
me to become a marked, evil man, dangerous at all times,
superficially docile yet terribly dangerous when he broke out:
but all this had vanished – disappeared as though by magic.
Thank you, Mr. Bowen, barrister in His Majesty's courts of
law, thank you for having made another man of me in so short
a time!

The very fair-haired girl with eyes as blue as the sea around
us was sitting with me under the coconut-palms in her father's
garden. Red, yellow and mauve bougainvillaeas were all in
flower, and they gave the garden the touch of poetry that the
moment called for. 'Monsieur Henri, [she called me Monsieur!
How many years had it been since anyone called me Monsieur?] as Papa told you yesterday, the British authorities are so
unfair, so devoid of understanding, that unfortunately you can't
stay here. They only give you a fortnight to rest and then you
must go off to sea again. I went to have a look at your boat
early this morning: it looks very small and frail for such a
long voyage as you have to make. Let's hope you reach a more
hospitable, understanding country than ours. All the English
islands do the same in these cases. If you have a horrid time
in the voyage ahead of you, I do ask you not to hold it against
the people who live in these islands. They are not responsible
for this way of looking at things: these are orders that come
from England, from people who don't know you. Papa's
address is 101 Queen Street, Port of Spain, Trinidad. If it's

God's will that you can do so. I beg you to send us just a line to tell us what happens to you.'

I was so moved I didn't know what to say. Mrs. Bowen came towards us. She was a very beautiful woman of about forty with chestnut hair and green eyes. She was wearing a very simple white dress with a white belt, and a pair of light-green sandals. 'Monsieur, my husband won't be home till five. He's getting them to allow you to go to Port of Spain in his car without a police escort. He also wants to prevent your having to spend the first night in the Port of Spain police-station. Your wounded friend will go straight to a nursing-home belonging to a friend of ours, a doctor; and you two will go to the Salvation Army hostel.'

Maturette joined us in the garden: he'd been to see the boat, and he told us it was surrounded by an interested crowd. Nothing had been touched. The people looking at it had found a bullet lodged under the rudder: someone had asked whether he might pull it out as a souvenir. Maturette had replied, 'Captain, captain,' and the Indian had understood that the captain had to be asked. Maturette said, 'Why don't we let the turtles go?'

'Have you got some turtles?' cried the girl. 'Let's go and see them.'

We went down to the boat. On the way a charming little Hindu girl took my hand without the least shyness. All these different-coloured people called out 'Good afternoon.' I took the turtles out. 'What shall we do? Put them back into the sea? Or would you like them for your garden?'

'The pool at the bottom is sea-water. We'll put them there, and then I'll have something to remember you by.'

'Fine.' I gave the onlookers everything in the boat except for the compass, the tobacco, the water-cask, the knife, the machete, the axe, the blankets and the revolver, which I hid under the blankets – no one had seen it.

At five o'clock Mr. Bowen appeared. 'Gentlemen, everything is in order. I'll drive you to the capital myself. First we'll drop the wounded man in at the nursing-home and then we'll go to the hostel.' We packed Clousiot into the back seat of the car: I was saying thank you to the girl when her mother came out bringing a suitcase and said to us, 'Please take these few things of my husband's – we give them to you with all our heart.' What could we say in the face of such very great

114

kindness? 'Thank you, thank you again and again and again.'
We drove off in the car. At a quarter to six we reached the
nursing-home – Saint George's nursing-home. Nurses carried
Clousiot's stretcher to a ward with a Hindu in it, sitting up in
his bed. The doctor came, and shook Bowen's hand: he spoke
no French but through Mr. Bowen he told us that Clousiot
would be well looked after and that we could come and see
him as often as we liked. We went through the town in Mr.
Bowen's car.

It astonished us, with all its lights and cars and bicycles.
White men, black men, yellow men, Indians and coolies all
mingled there, walking along the pavements of Port of Spain,
a town of wooden houses. We reached the Salvation Army, a
building whose ground floor alone was made of stone – the
rest of wood. It was well placed in a brightly-lit square whose
name I managed to read – Fish Market. We were welcomed
by the captain of the Salvation Army together with all his
staff, both men and women. He spoke a little French and all
the others said things to us in English, which we did not
understand; but their faces were so cheerful and their eyes so
welcoming that we were sure the words were kind.

We were taken to a room on the second floor with three
beds in it – the third being laid on for Clousiot. There was a
bathroom just at hand, with towels and soap for us. When he
had shown us our room, the captain said, 'If you would like
to eat, we all have supper together at seven o'clock, that is to
say in half an hour's time.'

'No. We're not hungry.'

'If you'd like to walk about the town, here are two West
Indies dollars to have some tea or coffee, or an ice. Take great
care not to get lost. When you want to come back just ask
your way by saying "Salvation Army, please".'

Ten minutes later we were in the street. We walked along
the pavements; we pushed our way among other people;
nobody looked at us or paid any attention to us: we breathed
deeply, appreciating these first steps, free in a town, to the
full. This continual trust in us, letting us go free in a fair-sized
city, warmed our hearts: it not only gave us self-confidence
but made us aware that we must wholly deserve this trust.
Maturette and I walked slowly along in the midst of the throng.
We needed to be among people, to be jostled, to sink into the
crowd and form part of it. We went into a bar and asked for

two beers. It seems nothing much just to say 'Two beers, please.' It's so natural, after all. Yet still to us it seemed absolutely extraordinary when the Indian girl with the gold shell in her nose served us and then said, 'Half a dollar, sir.' Her pearly smile, her big dark violet eyes a little turned up at the corners, her shoulder-long black hair, her low-cut dress that showed the beginning of her breasts and let one guess the rest was splendid – all these things that were so trifling and natural for everybody else seemed to us to belong to some unheard-of fairyland. Hold it, Papi: this can't be true. It can't be true that you are turning from a convict with a life sentence, a living corpse, into a free man so quickly!

It was Maturette who paid: he had only half a dollar left. The beer was beautifully cool and he said, 'What about another?' It seemed to me that this second round was something we shouldn't do. 'Hell,' I said, 'it's not an hour since you've been really free and you're already thinking of getting drunk?'

'Easy, easy now, Papi! Having two beers and getting drunk, those are two very different things.'

'Maybe so. But it seems to me that rightly speaking, we shouldn't fling ourselves on the first pleasures that come to hand. I think we ought to just taste them little by little and not stuff ourselves like hogs. Anyhow, to begin with this money's not ours.'

'Fair enough: you're right. We must learn how to be free in slow stages – that's more our mark.'

We went out and walked down Watters Street, the main avenue that runs clean through the town; and we were so wonderstruck by the trams going by, the donkeys with their little carts, the cars, the lurid cinema and dance-hall advertisements, the eyes of the young black or Indian girls, who looked smilingly at us, that we went all the way to the harbour without noticing it. There in front of us were ships all lit up – tourist ships with bewitching names, Panama, Los Angeles, Boston, Quebec; cargo-ships from Hamburg, Amsterdam and London. And side by side all along the quay there were bars, pubs and restaurants, all crammed with men and women jammed together, drinking, singing, bawling one another out. Suddenly I felt an irresistible urge to mingle with this crowd – common maybe, but so full of life. On the terrace of one bar there were oysters, sea-eggs, shrimps, solens and mussels arranged on ice, a whole display of sea-food to excite the appetite of the passer-by. There were tables with red-and-white checked cloths to invite us to sit down – most of them were occupied. And there were coffee-coloured girls with delicate profiles, mulattoes without a single negroid feature, tight in their many-coloured, low-cut blouses, to make you feel even more eager to make the most of what was going.

I went up to one of them and said, 'French money good?' showing her a thousand-franc note. 'Yes, I change for you.' 'OK.' She took the note and vanished into a room crammed with people. She came back. 'Come here.' And she led me to the cash desk, where there was a Chinese sitting.

'You French?'

'Yes.'

'Change thousand francs?'

'Yes.'

'All West Indies dollars?'

'Yes.'

'Passport?'

'Got none.'

'Sailor's card?'

'Got none.'

'Immigration papers?'

'Got none.'

'Fine.' He said something to the girl: she looked over the room, went up to a nautical character with a cap like mine – gold band and anchor – and brought him to the cash desk. The Chinese said, 'Your identity card?'

'Here.'

And calmly the Chinese wrote out an exchange-form for a thousand francs in the stranger's name and made him sign it; then the girl took him by the arm and led him away. He certainly never knew what had happened. I got two hundred and fifty West Indies dollars, fifty of them in one and two-dollar notes. I gave the girl one dollar; we went outside, and sitting there at a table we treated ourselves to an orgy of sea-food, washed down with a delightful dry white wine.

Trinidad

I can still see our first night of freedom in that English town as clearly as though it was yesterday. We went everywhere, drunk with the light and the warmth in our hearts, and we plunged deep into the very being of the jolly, laughing crowd, overflowing with happiness. A bar, full of sailors and the tropical girls who were waiting there to pluck them. But there was nothing squalid about these girls; they were nothing like the women of the gutters of Paris, Le Havre or Marseilles. It was something else again – quite different. Instead of those overmade-up, vice-marked faces with their avid, cunning eyes, these were girls of every colour from Chinese yellow to African black, from light chocolate with smooth hair to the Hindu or Javanese whose parents had come together in the cocoa or sugar plantations, and so on to the Chinese-Indian girl with the gold shell in her nose and to the Llapane with her Roman profile and her copper-coloured face lit by two huge shining black eyes with long lashes, pushing out her half-covered bosom as though to say, 'Look how perfect they are, my breasts.' Each girl had different coloured flowers in her hair, and they were all of them the outward show of love; they made you long for women, without anything dirty or commercial about it. You didn't feel they were doing a job – they were really having fun and you felt that money was not the main thing in their lives.

Like a couple of moths drawn by the light, Maturette and I went blundering along from bar to bar. It was as we were coming out into a little brightly-lit square that I noticed the time on a church clock. Two. It was two o'clock in the morning! Quick, quick, we must hurry back. We had been behaving badly. The Salvation Army captain would have a pretty low opinion of us. We must get back at once. I hailed a taxi, which took us there. Two dollars. I paid and we walked into the hostel, very much ashamed of ourselves. A really young blonde

118

woman-soldier of the Salvation Army, twenty-five or thirty years old, welcomed us pleasantly in the hall. She seemed neither astonished nor vexed at our coming home so late. After a few words in English – we felt they were good-natured and kind – she gave us the key of our room and said good night. We went to bed. In the suitcase I found a pair of pyjamas. As we were putting out the light, Maturette said, 'Still, I think we might say thank you to God for having given us so much so quickly. What do you think, Papi?'

'You thank Him for me – he's a great guy, your God. And you're dead right. He's been really generous with us. Good night.' And I turned the light out.

This rising from the dead, this breaking out from the grave-yard in which I had been buried, these emotions all crowding one upon another, this night of bathing in humanity, reintegrat-ing myself with life and mankind – all these things had been so exciting that I could not get off to sleep. I closed my eyes, and in a kind of kaleidoscope all sorts of pictures, things and feelings appeared, but in no order at all; they were sharp and clear, but they came without any regard for time – the assizes, the Conciergerie, then the lepers, then Saint-Martin-de-Ré, Tribouillard, Jesus, the storm . . . It was as though everything I had lived through for the past year was trying to appear at the same moment before the eye of memory in a wild, nightmarish dance. I tried to brush these pictures aside, but it was no good. And the strangest part of it was that they were all mixed up with the noise of the pigs, the shrieks of the hocco, the howling of the wind and the crash of waves, the whole wrapped in the sound of the one-stringed fiddles the Indians had been playing just a little while ago in the various bars we had visited.

Finally, at dawn, I dropped off. Towards ten o'clock there was a knock on the door. Mr. Bowen came in, smiling. 'Good morning, friends. Still in bed? You must have come home late. Did you have a good time?'

'Good morning. Yes, we came in late. We're sorry.'

'Come, come: not at all. It's natural enough, after all you've been through. You certainly had to make the most of your first night as free men. I've come so as to go to the police-station with you. You have to appear before them to make an official declaration of having entered the country illegally. When that formality's over we'll go and see your friend. They

X-rayed him very early this morning. They will know the results later on.'

We washed quickly and went down to the room below, where Bowen was waiting for us with the captain.

'Good morning, my friends,' said the captain in bad French. 'Good morning, everybody.'

A woman officer of the Salvation Army said, 'Did you like Port of Spain?'

'Oh yes, Madame! It was quite a treat for us.'

After a quick cup of coffee we went to the police-station. We walked – it was only about two hundred yards. All the policemen greeted us; they looked at us without any particular curiosity. Having passed two ebony sentries in khaki uniform we went into an impressive, sparsely-furnished office. An officer of about fifty stood up: he wore shorts, a khaki shirt and tie, and he was covered with badges and medals. Speaking French he said, 'Good morning. Sit down. I should like to talk to you for a while before officially taking your statement. How old are you?'

'Twenty-six and nineteen.'

'What were you sentenced for?'

'Manslaughter.'

'What was your sentence?'

'Transportation and hard labour for life.'

'Then it was for murder, not manslaughter?'

'No, Monsieur, in my case it was manslaughter.'

'It was murder in mine,' said Maturette. 'I was seventeen.'

'At seventeen you know what you're doing,' said the officer. 'In England, if it had been proved, you would have been hanged. Right. The British authorities are not here to judge the French penal system. But there's one thing we don't agree with, and that's the sending of criminals to French Guiana. We know it's an inhuman punishment and one quite unworthy of a civilized nation like France. But unfortunately you can't stay in Trinidad, nor on any other British island. It's impossible. So I ask you to play it straight and not try to find any excuse – sickness or anything like that – to delay your departure. You may stay here quite freely in Port of Spain for from fifteen to eighteen days. It seems that your boat is a good one. I'll have it brought round to the harbour for you. If there are any repairs needed the Royal Navy shipwrights will carry them out for you. On leaving you will be given the necessary stores,

120

a good compass and a chart. I hope the South American countries will take you in. Don't go to Venezuela, because there you'll be arrested and forced to work on the roads until finally they hand you back to the French authorities. Now a man is not necessarily lost for ever because he has gone very badly wrong on one occasion. You are young and healthy and you look decent fellows, so I hope that after what you've been through you will not let yourselves be defeated for good. The fact of your having come as far as here is proof enough that that's not the case. I'm glad to be one of the factors that will help you to become sound, responsible men. Good luck. If you have any difficulties, call this number. We'll answer in French.' He rang a bell and a civilian came for us. Our statement was taken in a large room where several policemen and civilians were working at their typewriters.

'Why did you come to Trinidad?'

'To recover our strength.'

'Where did you come from?'

'French Guiana.'

'In your escape, did you commit any crime? Did you kill anyone or cause grievous bodily harm?'

'We didn't hurt anyone seriously.'

'How do you know?'

'We were told before we left.'

'Your age, legal position with regard to France . . .' And so on. 'Gentlemen, you have fifteen to eighteen days in which to rest here. During that time you are entirely free to do what you like. If you change your hotel, let us know. I am Sergeant Willy. There are two telephone numbers on my card: this one is the official police number and the other my home. If anything happens and you want my help, call me at once. We know our trust in you is well placed. I'm sure you will behave well.'

A few moments later Mr. Bowen took us to the nursing-home. Clousiot was very glad to see us. We told him nothing about our night on the town. We only said they had left us free to go wherever we liked. He was so astonished that he said, 'Without even an escort?'

'Yes, without even an escort.'

'Well, they must be a quaint lot, these rosbifs.'

Bowen had gone to see the doctor and now he came back with him. He said to Clousiot, 'Who reduced the fracture for you, before splinting your leg?'

'Me and another guy who's not here.'

'You did it so well there's no need to break the leg again. The broken fibula was put back very neatly. We'll just plaster it and give you an iron so that you can walk a little. Would you rather stay here or go with your friends?'

'Go with them.'

'Well, tomorrow you'll be able to join them.'

We poured out our thanks. Mr. Bowen and the doctor left and we spent the rest of the morning and part of the afternoon with our friend. The next day we were delighted to find ourselves all together once more, the three of us in our hostel bedroom, with the window wide open and the fans going full blast to cool the air. We congratulated one another upon how fit we looked, and we said what fine fellows we were in our new clothes. When I saw the talk was going back over the past I said, 'Now let's forget the past as soon as possible and concentrate on the present and the future. Where shall we go? Colombia? Panama? Costa Rica? We ought to ask Bowen about the countries where we're likely to be admitted.'

I called Bowen at his chambers: he wasn't there. I called his house at San Fernando, and it was his daughter who answered. After some pleasant words she said, 'Monsieur Henri, in the Fish Market near the hostel there are buses for San Fernando. Why don't you come and spend the afternoon with us? Do come: I'll be expecting you.' And there we were, all three of us on the way to San Fernando. Clousiot was particularly splendid in his snuff-coloured semi-military uniform.

We were all three deeply moved by this return to the house that had taken us in with such kindness. It seemed as though the ladies understood our emotion, for both speaking together they said, 'So here you are, home again! Sit yourselves down comfortably.' And now, instead of saying Monsieur each time they spoke to us, they called us by our Christian names – 'Henri, please may I have the sugar? André [Maturette's name was André], a little more pudding?'

Mrs. Bowen and Miss Bowen, I hope that God has rewarded you for all the great kindness you showed us, and that your noble hearts – hearts that gave us so much joy – have never known anything but perfect happiness all your lives.

With a map spread out on the table, we asked their advice. The distances were very great: seven hundred and fifty miles to reach Santa Marta, the nearest Colombian port, thirteen hundred miles to Panama; one thousand four hundred and fifty to Costa Rica. Mr. Bowen came home. 'I've telephoned all the consulates, and I've one piece of good news – you can stay a few days at Curaçao to rest. Colombia has no set rules about escaped prisoners. As far as the consul knows no one has ever reached Colombia by sea. Nor Panama nor anywhere else, either.'

'I know a safe place for you,' said Margaret, Mr. Bowen's daughter. 'But it's a great way off – one thousand eight hundred miles at least.'

'Where's that?' asked her father.

'British Honduras. The governor is my godfather.'

I looked at my friends and said, 'All aboard for British Honduras.' It was a British possession with the Republic of Honduras on the south and Mexico on the north. Helped by Margaret and her mother we spent the afternoon working out the course. First leg, Trinidad to Curaçao, six hundred and twenty-five miles: second leg, Curaçao to some island or other on our route: third leg, British Honduras.

As you can never tell what will happen at sea, we decided that in addition to the stores the police would give us, we should have a special case of tinned tings to fall back on – meat, vegetables, jam, fish, etc. Margaret told us that the Salvatori Supermarket would be delighted to make us a present of them. 'And if they won't,' she said simply, 'Mama and I will buy them for you.'

'No, Mademoiselle.'

'Hush, Henri.'

'No, it's really not possible, because we have money and it wouldn't be right to profit by your kindness when we can perfectly well buy these stores ourselves.'

The boat was at Port of Spain, afloat in a Royal Navy dock. We left our friends, promising to see one another again before we finally sailed away. Every evening we went out punctually at eleven o'clock. Clousiot sat on a bench in the liveliest square and Maturette and I took it in turns to stay with him while the other wandered about the town. We had been here now for ten days. Thanks to the iron set in his plaster, Clousiot could walk without too much difficulty. We had learnt to get to the harbour by taking a tram. We often went in the afternoons and always at night. We were known and adopted in some of the bars down there. The police on guard saluted us and everybody knew who we were and where we came from, though there was never the slightest allusion to anything whatsoever. But we noticed that in the bars where we were known they charged us less for what we ate or drank than the sailors. It was the same with the tarts. Generally speaking, whenever they sat down at a table with sailors or officers or tourists they drank non-stop and always tried to make them spend as much as possible. In the bars where there was dancing, they would never dance with anyone unless he stood them a good many drinks first. But they all behaved quite differently with us. They would stay with us for quite a time and we had to press them before they'd drink anything at all: and then it wasn't their notorious tiny glass, but a beer or a genuine whiskey and soda. All this pleased us very much, because it was an indirect way of saying that they knew how we were fixed and that they were on our side.

The boat had been repainted and the gunwale raised six inches. The keel had been strengthened. None of her ribs had suffered, and the boat was quite sound. The mast had been replaced by a longer but lighter spar, and the flour-sack jib and staysail by good ochre-coloured canvas. At the naval basin a captain gave me a fully-graduated compass and showed me how I could find roughly where I was by using the chart. Our course for Curaçao was marked out – west by north.

The captain introduced me to a naval officer in command of the training-ship *Tarpon*, and he asked me if I would be so good as to go to sea at about eight the next morning and run a little way out of the harbour. I did not understand why, but I promised to do so. I was at the basin next day at the appointed time, with Maturette. A sailor came aboard with us and I sailed out of the harbour with a fair wind. Two hours later, as we were tacking in and out of the port, a man-of-war came towards us. The officers and crew, all in white, were lined up on the deck. They went by close to us and shouted 'Hurrah!' They turned about and dipped their ensign twice. It was an official salute whose meaning I didn't grasp. We went back to the naval basin, where the man-of-war was already tied up at the landing-stage. As for us, we moored alongside the quay. The sailor made signs to us to follow him; we went aboard and the captain of the ship welcomed us at the top of the gangway. The bosun's pipe saluted our coming aboard, and when we had been introduced to the officers they led us past the cadets and petty-officers lined up and standing to attention. The captain said a few words to them in English and then they fell out. A young officer explained that the captain had just told the cadets we deserved a sailor's respect for having made such a long voyage in that little boat; he also told them we were about to make an even longer and more dangerous trip. We thanked the officer for the honour we had been paid. He made us a present of three oilskins – they were very useful to us afterwards. They were black, and they fastened with a long zip: they had hoods.

Two days before we left, Mr. Bowen came to see us with a message from the police superintendent asking us to take three relégués with us – they had been picked up a week before. These relégués had been landed on the island and according to them their companions had gone on to Venezuela. I didn't much care for the idea, but we had been treated too handsomely to be able to refuse to take the three men aboard. I asked to see them before giving my answer. A police-car came to fetch me. I went to see the superintendent, the high-ranking officer who had questioned us when we first came. Sergeant Willy acted as interpreter.

'How are you?'

'Very well, thanks. We should like you to do us a favour.'

'With pleasure, if it's possible.'

'There are three French relégués in our prison. They were on the island illegally for some weeks and they claim that their friends marooned them here and then sailed away. We believe it's a trick to get us to provide them with another boat. We have to get them off the island: it would be a pity if I were forced to hand them over to the purser of the first French ship that goes by.'

'Well, sir, I'll do the very best I possibly can; but I'd like to talk to them first. It's a risky thing to take three unknown men aboard, as you will certainly understand.'

'I understand. Willy, give orders to have the three Frenchmen brought out into the courtyard.'

I wanted to see them alone and I asked the sergeant to leave us to ourselves. 'You're relégués?'

'No. We're convicts.'

'What did you say you were relégués for, then?'

'We thought they'd rather have a man who'd done small crimes rather than big ones. We got it wrong: we see that now. And what about you? What are you?'

'Convict.'

'Don't know you.'

'I came on the last convoy. When did you?'

'The 1929 shipment.'

'Me on the '27,' said the third man.

'Listen: the superintendent sent for me to ask me to take you aboard – there are three of us already. He said that if I won't and that as there's not one of you who knows how to handle a boat, he'll be forced to put you aboard the first French ship that goes by. What have you got to say about it?'

'For reasons of our own we don't want to take to the sea again. We could pretend to leave with you and then you could drop us at the end of the island and carry on with your own break.'

'I can't do that.'

'Why not?'

'Because they've been good to us here and I'm not going to pay them back with a kick in the teeth.'

'Listen, brother, it seems to me you ought to put a convict before a rosbif.'

'Why?'

'Because you're a convict yourself.'

'Yes. But there are so many different kinds of convict that maybe there's more difference between you and me than there is between me and the rosbifs. It all depends on where you sit.'

'So you're going to let us be handed over to the French authorities?'

'No. But I'm not going to put you ashore before Curaçao, either.'

'I don't think I've the heart to begin all over again,' said one of them.

'Listen, have a look at the boat first. Perhaps the one you came in was no good.'

'Right. Let's have a go,' said the two others.

'OK. I'll ask the superintendent to let you come and have a look at the boat.'

Together with Sergeant Willy we all went down to the harbour. The three guys seemed more confident once they had seen the boat.

Two days later we and the three strangers left Trinidad. I can't tell how they knew about it, but a dozen girls from the bars came down to see us go, as well as the Bowens and the Salvation Army captain. When one of the girls kissed me, Margaret laughed, and said, 'Why, Henri, engaged so soon? You *are* a quick worker.'

'Au revoir, everybody! No: good-bye! But just let me say what a great place you have in our hearts – nothing'll ever change that.'

And at four in the afternoon we set out, towed by a tug. We were soon out of harbour, but we did not leave without wiping away a tear and gazing until the last moment at the people who had come to say good-bye and who were waving their white handkerchiefs. The moment the tug cast us off we set all our sails and headed into the first of the countless waves that we were to cross before we reached the end of our voyage.

There were two knives aboard: I wore one and Maturette the other. The axe was next to Clousiot, and so was the jungle-knife. We were certain that none of the others had any weapon. We arranged it so that only one of us should ever be asleep during the passage. Towards sunset the training-ship came and sailed along with us for half an hour. Then she dipped her ensign and parted company.

'What's your name?'

'Leblond.'

'Which convoy?'

'27.'

'What sentence?'

'Twenty years.'

'What about you?'

'Kargueret, 1929 convoy: fifteen years. I'm a Breton.'

'You're a Breton and you can't sail a boat?'

'That's right.'

The third said, 'My name's Dufils and I come from Angers. I got life for a silly crack I made in court: otherwise it'd have been ten years at the outside. 1929 convoy.'

'What was the crack?'

'Well, I'd killed my wife with a flat-iron, you see. During the trial a juryman asked me why the flat-iron. I don't know what possessed me but I told him I'd used a flat-iron on account of she needed smoothing out. According to my lawyer it was that bloody-fool remark that made them give me such a dose.'

'Where did you all make your break from?'

'A logging camp they call Cascade, fifty miles from Saint-Laurent. It wasn't hard to get out – they give you a lot of freedom there. We just walked off, the five of us – nothing simpler.'

'How come, five? Where are the other two?'

An awkward silence. Clousiot said, 'Man, there are only straight guys here, and since we're together we've got to know. Tell.'

'I'll tell you, then,' said the Breton. 'We were five when we left, all right: but the two missing guys who aren't here now were from Cannes and they'd told us they were fishermen back at home. They paid nothing for the break because they said their work in the boat would be worth more than any money. Well, on the way we saw that neither the one nor the other knew the first thing about the sea. We were on the edge of drowning twenty times. We went creeping along the shore – first the coast of Dutch Guiana, then British Guiana, and then finally Trinidad. Between Georgetown and Trinidad I killed the one who said he would act as leader of the break. The guy had it coming to him, because to get off not paying he had lied to everyone about what a seaman he was. The other thought he was going to be killed too and he threw himself into the sea during a squall, letting go the tiller. We managed as best we could. We let the boat fill with water a good many times and in the end we smashed against a rock – it was a miracle we got out alive. I give you my word of honour everything I've said is the exact truth.'

'It's true,' said the two others. 'That's just how it happened, and we all three of us agreed about killing the guy. What do you say about it, Papillon?'

'I'm in no position to judge.'

'But what would you have done in our place?' insisted the Breton.

'I'd have to think it over. You want to live through things like that to know what's right and what's not: otherwise you just can't tell where the truth lies.'

Clousiot said, 'I'd have killed him, all right. That lie might have caused the death of everyone aboard.'

'OK. Let's scrub it. But I've got a hunch you were scared through and through. You're still scared, and you're only at sea because there's no choice. Is that right?'

'Bleeding right,' they answered all together.

'Well then, there's not got to be any panic here, whatever happens. Whatever happens nobody's got to show he's afraid. If anyone's scared, just let him keep his trap shut. This is a good boat: it's proved that. We're heavier laden than we were, but then she's been raised six inches all round. That more than compensates.'

We smoked; we drank coffee. We had had a good meal before leaving and we decided not to have another before next morning.

This was 9 December 1933, forty-two days since the break had started in the high security ward of the hospital at Saint-Laurent. It was Clousiot, the company's accountant, who told us that. I had three very valuable things that we lacked when we set out – a waterproof steel watch bought in Trinidad, a real good compass in gimbals, and a pair of celluloid sunglasses. Clousiot and Maturette each had a cap.

Three days passed with nothing much happening, apart from our twice meeting with schools of dolphins. They made our blood run cold, because one band of eight started playing with the boat. First they'd run under it longways and come up just in front – sometimes one of them would touch us. But what really made us quake was the next caper. Three dolphins in a triangle, one in front and then two abreast, would race straight for our bows, tearing through the water. When they were within a hair's breadth of us they would dive and then come up on the right and the left of the boat. Although we had a good breeze and we were running right before it they went still faster than we did. The game lasted for hours: it was ghastly. The slightest mistake on their part and they would have tipped us over. The three newcomers said nothing, but you should have seen their miserable faces!

In the middle of the night of the fourth day a perfectly horrible storm broke out. It really was something quite terrifying. The worst part of it was that the waves didn't follow one another in the same direction. As often as not they collided and broke against one another. Some were long and deep, others choppy – there was no understanding it. Nobody uttered a word except for Clousiot; from time to time he called out, 'Go it, mate! You'll do this one, just like the rest.' Or 'Keep an eye out for the one behind!'

A very curious thing was that sometimes they would come three-quarters on, roaring and capped with foam. Fine: I'd have plenty of time to judge their speed and work out the right angle to take them. Then suddenly, unreasonably, there'd be one roaring right up over the boat's stern, immediately behind. Many a time they broke over my shoulders and then of course a good deal came into the boat. The five men baled non-stop with tins and saucepans. Still, I never filled her more than a quarter full and so we were never in danger of sinking. This party lasted a good half of the night, close on seven hours. Because of the rain we never saw the sun at all until eight.

We were all of us, including me, heartily glad to see this sun shining away with all its might after the storm. Before anything else, coffee. Scalding hot coffee with Nestlé's milk and ship's biscuits: they were as hard as iron, but once they were drunked in coffee they were wonderful. The night's struggle against the storm had worn me right out, and although there was still a strong wind and a heavy, uneven sea, I asked Maturette to take over for a while. I just had to sleep. I hadn't been lying down ten minutes before Maturette took a wave the wrong way and the boat was three quarters swamped. Every thing was afloat – tins, stove, blankets, the lot. I reached the tiller with the water up to my waist and I just had time to avoid a breaking wave coming right down upon us. With a heave of the tiller I put us stern-on: the sea did not come in but thrust us forward for a good ten yards.

Everyone baled. With the big saucepan Maturette flung out three gallons at a time. No one bothered about saving anything at all – there was only one idea and that was to empty the boat of all this water that was making her so heavy that she could not struggle against the sea. I must admit the three newcomers behaved well; and when the Breton's tin was swept away, alone he took the quick decision to ease the boat by letting go the water-cask, which he heaved overboard. Two hours later everything was dry, but we had lost our blankets, primus, charcoal stove and charcoal, the wicker bottle of paraffin and the water-cask, the last on purpose.

At midday I went to put on another pair of trousers, and it was then that I noticed that my little suitcase had gone overboard too, together with two of the three oilskins. Right at the bottom of the boat we found two bottles of rum. All the tobacco was either gone or soaked: the leaves and their water-tight tin had disappeared. I said, 'Brothers, let's have a good solid tot of rum to begin with, and then open the reserves and see what we can reckon on. Here's fruit juice: good. We'll ration ourselves for what we can drink. Here are some tins of biscuits: let's empty one and make a stove of it. We'll stow the other tins in the bottom of the boat and make a fire with the wood of the box. A little while ago we were all pretty scared, but the danger's over now: we've just got to get over it and not let the others down. From this moment on, no one must say "I'm thirsty", no one must say "I'm hungry"; and no one must say "I feel like a smoke". OK?'

'OK, Papi.'

Everyone behaved well and providentially the wind dropped so that we could make a soup with bully-beef for a basis. A mess tin full of this with ship's biscuits soaked in it gave us a comfortable lining, quite enough until tomorrow. We brewed a very little green tea for each man. And in an unbroken box we found a carton of cigarettes: they were little packets of eight, and there were twenty-four of them. The other five decided that I alone should smoke, to help me keep awake; and so there should be no ill-feeling, Clousiot refused to light them for me, but he did pass me the match. What with this good understanding aboard, nothing unpleasant happened at any time.

Now it was six days since we had sailed, and I had not yet been able to sleep. But this afternoon I did sleep, the sea being as smooth as glass: I slept, flat out, for nearly five hours. It was ten in the evening when I woke. A flat calm still. They had had a meal without me and I found a very well cooked kind of polenta made of maize flour – tinned, of course – and I ate it with a few smoked sausages. It was delicious. The tea was almost cold, but that didn't matter in the least. I smoked, waiting for the wind to make up its mind to blow.

The night was wonderfully starlit. The pole star shone with all its full brilliance and only the Southern Cross outdid it in splendour. The Great and the Little Bear were particularly clear. Not a cloud, and already the full moon was well up in the starry sky. The Breton was shivering. He had lost his jacket and he was down to his shirt. I lent him the oilskin.

We began the seventh day. 'Mates, we can't be very far from Curaçao. I have a hunch I made a little too much northing, so now I'll steer due west, because we mustn't miss the Dutch West Indies. That would be serious, now we've no fresh water left and all the food's gone except for the reserve.'

'We leave it to you, Papillon,' said the Breton.

'Yes, we leave it to you,' said all the others together. 'You do what you think right.'

'Thanks.'

It seemed to me that what I had said was best. All night long the wind had failed us and it was only about four in the morning that a breeze set us moving again. This breeze strengthened during the forenoon, and for thirty-six hours it blew strong enough to carry us along at a fair rate, but the waves were so gentle we never thumped at all.

Curaçao

Gulls. First their cries, because it was still dark, and then the birds themselves, wheeling above the boat. One settled on the mast, lifted off, then settled again. All this flying around lasted three hours and more until the dawn came up, with a brilliant sun. Nothing on the horizon showed any hint of land. Where the hell did all these gulls and sea-birds come from? Our eyes searched throughout the day, and searched in vain. Not the least sign of land anywhere near. The full moon rose just as the sun was setting; and this tropical moon was so strong that its glare hurt my eyes. I no longer had my dark glasses – they had gone with that diabolical old wave, as well as all our caps. At about eight o'clock, very far away in this lunar daylight, we saw a dark line on the horizon.

'That's land all right,' said I, the first of us all to say it.

'Yes, so it is.'

In short, everybody agreed that they could see a dark line that must be land of some sort. All through the rest of the night I kept my bows pointed towards this shadow, which grew clearer and clearer. We were getting there. No clouds, a strong wind and tall but regular waves, and we were running in as fast as we could go. The dark mass did not rise high over the water, and there was no way of telling whether the coast was cliffs, rocks or beach. The moon was setting on the far side of the land, and it cast a shadow that prevented me from seeing anything except a line of lights at sea-level, continuous at first and then broken. I came closer and closer, and then, about half a mile from the shore, I dropped anchor. The wind was strong, the boat swung round and faced the waves, which it took head-on every time. It tossed us around a great deal and indeed it was very uncomfortable. The sails were lowered and furled, of course. We might have waited until daylight in this unpleasant but safe position, but unhappily the anchor suddenly lost its hold. To steer a boat, it has to be moving: otherwise the rudder has no bite. We hoisted the jib and stay-sail, but then a strange thing happened – the anchor would not get a grip again. The others hauled the rope aboard: it came in without any anchor. We had lost it. In spite of everything I could do the waves kept heaving us in towards the rocks of this land in such a dangerous way that I decided to hoist the mainsail and run in on purpose – run in fast. This I carried out so successfully that there we were, wedged between two rocks, with the boat absolutely shattered. No one bawled out in panic, but when the next wave came rolling in we all plunged into it and ended up on shore, battered, tumbled, soaked, but alive. Only Clousiot, with his plastered leg, had a worse time than the rest of us. His arm, face and hands were badly scraped. We others had a few bangs on the knees, hands and ankles. My ear had come up against a rock a little too hard, and it was dripping with blood.

Still, there we were, alive on dry land, out of the reach of the waves. When day broke we picked up the oilskin and I turned the boat over – it was beginning to go to pieces. I managed to wrench the compass from its place in the stern-sheets. There was no one where we had been cast up, nor anywhere around. We looked at the line of lights, and later we learned that they were there to warn fishermen that the place was dangerous. We walked away, going inland; and we saw nothing, only cactuses, huge cactuses, and donkeys. We reached a well, tired out, for we had had to carry Clousiot, taking turns with two of us making a kind of chair with joined hands. Round the well there were the dried carcasses of goats and asses. The well was empty, and the windmill that had once worked it was now turning idly, bringing nothing up. Not a soul; only these goats and donkeys.

We went on to a little house whose open doors invited us to walk in. We called out 'Haloo! Haloo!' Nobody. On the chimney-piece a canvas bag with its neck tied by a string; I took it and opened it. As I opened it the string broke – it was full of florins, the Dutch currency. So we were on Dutch territory: Bonaire, Curaçao or Aruba. We put the bag back without touching anything; we found water and each drank in turn out of a ladle. No one in the house, no one anywhere near. We left, and we were going along very slowly, because of Clousiot, when an old Ford blocked our path.

'Are you Frenchmen?'

'Yes, Monsieur.'

'Get into the car, will you?' Three got in behind and we settled Clousiot on their knees; I sat next to the driver and Maturette next to me.

'You've been wrecked?'

'Yes.'

'Anyone drowned?'

'No.'

'Where do you come from?'

'Trinidad.'

'And before that?'

'French Guiana.'

'Convicts or relégués?'

'Convicts.'

'I'm Dr. Naal, the owner of this property; it's a peninsula running out from Curaçao. They call it Ass's Island. Goats and asses live here, feeding on the cactuses, in spite of the long thorns. The common nickname for those thorns is the young ladies of Curaçao.'

I said, 'That's not very flattering for the real young ladies of Curaçao.' The big, heavy man laughed noisily. With an asthmatic gasp the worn-out Ford stopped of its own accord. I pointed to a herd of asses and said, 'If the car can't manage it any more, we can easily have ourselves pulled.'

'I've got a sort of harness in the boot, but the great difficulty is to catch a couple and then put the harness on.' The fat fellow opened the bonnet and found that a particularly heavy lurch had disconnected a plug. Before getting in he gazed all round, looking uneasy. We set off again, and having bumped along rough tracks we came to a white barrier across the road. Here there was a little white cottage. He spoke in Dutch to a very light-coloured, neatly-dressed Negro who kept saying, 'Ya, master; ya, master.' Then he said, 'I've given this man orders to stay with you until I come back and give you something to drink if you're thirsty. Will you get out?' We got out and sat on the grass in the shade. The aged Ford went gasping away. It had scarcely gone fifty yards before the black, speaking papiamento – a Dutch West Indies patois made up of English, Dutch, French and Spanish words – told us that his boss, Dr. Naal, had gone to fetch the police, because he was very frightened of us: he had told him to look out for himself, we being escaped thieves. And the poor devil of a mulatto couldn't do enough to try to please us. He made us some coffee: it was very weak, but in that heat it did us good. We waited for more than an hour and then there appeared a big van after the nature of a black maria with six policemen dressed in the German style, and an open car with a uniformed chauffeur and three gentlemen behind, one of them being Dr. Naal.

They got out, and the smallest, who looked like a new-shaven priest, said to us, 'I am the superintendent in charge of security for the island of Curaçao. My position obliges me to place you under arrest. Have you committed any crimes since your arrival upon the island and if so what? And which of you?'

'Monsieur, we are escaped prisoners. We have come from Trinidad, and only a few hours ago we wrecked our boat on your rocks. I am the leader of this little band and I can assure you not one of us has committed the slightest crime.'

The superintendent turned towards Dr. Naal and spoke to him in Dutch. They were both talking when a fellow hurried up on a bicycle. He talked loud and fast, as much to Dr. Naal as to the policeman.

'Monsieur Naal,' I said, 'why did you tell this man we were thieves?'

'Because before I met you this fellow told me he watched you from behind a cactus and he had seen you go into his

135

house and then come out of it again. He's an employee of mine – he looks after some of my asses.'

'And just because we went into the house does that mean we're thieves? What you say doesn't make sense, Monsieur: all we did was to take some water – you don't call that theft, do you?'

'And what about the bag of florins?'

'Yes, I did open that bag; and in fact I broke the string as I did so. But I most certainly didn't do anything but look to see what kind of money it had in it, and so to find out what country we had reached. I scrupulously put the money and the bag back where they were, on the chimney-piece.'

The policeman looked me right in the eye, and then turning he spoke to the character on the bicycle very severely. Dr. Naal made as though to speak. Harshly, in the German style, the superintendent cut him short. Then he made the newcomer get into the open car next to the chauffeur, got in himself with two policemen and drove off. Naal and the other man who had come with him walked into the house with us.

'I must explain,' he said. 'That man had told me the bag had vanished. Before having you searched, the superintendent questioned him, because he thought he was lying. If you're innocent, I'm very sorry about the whole thing; but it wasn't my fault.'

Less than a quarter of an hour later the car came back and the superintendent said to me, 'You told the truth: that man was a disgusting liar. He will be punished for having tried to damage you like this.' Meanwhile the fellow was being loaded aboard the black maria: the five others got in too and I was about to follow when the superintendent held me back and said, 'Get into my car next to the driver.' We set out ahead of the van and very quickly we lost sight of it. We took proper macadamed roads and then came to the town with its Dutch-looking houses. Everything was very clean, and most of the people were on bicycles – there were hundreds of them coming and going in every direction. We reached the police-station. We went through a big office with a good many policemen in it, all dressed in white and each at his own desk, and we came to an inner room. It had air-conditioning, and it was cool. A big fat fair-haired man of about forty was sitting there in an armchair. He got up and spoke in Dutch. When their first remarks were over the superintendent, speaking

French, said, 'This is the chief of police of Curaçao. Chief, this Frenchman is the leader of the band of six we've just picked up.'

'Very good, Superintendent. As shipwrecked men, you are welcome to Curaçao. What's your name?'

'Henri.'

'Well, Henri, you have had a very unpleasant time with this business of the bag of money, but from your point of view it's all for the best, because it certainly proves you are an honest man. I'll give you a sunny room with a bunk in it so you can get some rest. Your case will be put before the governor and he will take appropriate measures. The superintendent and I will speak in your favour.' He shook hands and we left. In the courtyard Dr. Naal apologized and promised to use his influence on our behalf. Two hours later we were all shut up in a very large kind of ward with a dozen beds in it and a long table and benches down the middle. Through the open window we asked a policeman to buy us tobacco, cigarette-paper and matches, with Trinidad dollars. He did not take the money and we didn't understand his reply.

'That coal-black character seems too devoted to his duty by half,' said Clousiot. 'We still haven't got that tobacco.'

I was just about to knock on the door when it opened. A little man looking something like a coolie and wearing prison uniform with a number on the chest so that there should be no mistake, said, 'Money, cigarettes.' 'No. Tobacco, matches and paper.' A few minutes later he came back with all these things and with a big steaming pot – chocolate or cocoa. He brought bowls too, and we each of us drank one full.

I was sent for in the afternoon, and I went to the chief of police's office again. 'The governor has given me orders to let you walk about in the prison courtyard. Tell your companions not to try to escape, for that would lead to very serious consequences for all of you. Since you are the leader, you may go into the town for two hours every morning, from ten until twelve, and then in the afternoon from three until five. Have you any money?'

'Yes. English and French.'

'A plain-clothes policeman will go with you wherever you choose during your outings.'

'What are they going to do to us?'

'I think we'll try to get you aboard tankers one by one –

tankers of different nationalities. Curaçao has one of the biggest oil refineries in the world: it treats oil from Venezuela, and so there are twenty or twenty-five tankers from all countries coming and going every day. That would be the ideal solution for you, because then you would reach the other countries without any sort of difficulty.'

'What countries, for example? Panama, Costa Rica, Guatemala, Nicaragua, Mexico, Canada, Cuba, the United States or the countries which have English laws?'

'Impossible. Europe's just as impossible too. Don't you worry: just you rely on us and let us do our best to help you make a new start in life.'

'Thank you, Chief.'

I repeated all this very exactly to my companions. Clousiot, the sharpest crook of us all, said, 'What do you think of it, Papillon?'

'I don't know yet. I'm afraid it may be a piece of soap so we'll keep quiet and not escape.'

'I'm afraid you may be right,' he said.

The Breton believed in this wonderful scheme. The flat-iron guy was delighted: he said, 'No more boats, no more adventures, and that's for sure. We each of us land up in some country or other aboard a big tanker and then we fade right away.' Leblond was of the same opinion.

'What about you, Maturette?'

And this kid of nineteen, this little wet-leg who had accidentally been turned into a convict, this boy with features finer than a girl, raised his gentle voice and said, 'And do you people really think these square-headed cops are going to produce bent papers for each one of us? Or even actually forge them? I don't. At the most they might close their eyes if we went off one by one, and illegally got aboard a tanker on its way out: but nothing more. And even then they'd only do so to get rid of us without a headache. That's what I think. I don't believe a word of it.'

I went out very little: just now and then in the mornings, to buy things. We had been here a week now, and nothing had happened. We were beginning to feel anxious. One evening we saw three priests accompanied by policemen going round the cells and wards. They stopped for a long while in the cell nearest to us, where a Negro accused of rape was shut up. We thought they might come to see us, so we went back into the ward and sat there, each on his bed. And indeed all three of them did come in, together with Dr. Naal, the chief of police and someone in a white uniform I took to be a naval officer.

'Monseigneur, here are the Frenchmen,' said the chief of police in French. 'Their behaviour has been excellent.'

'I congratulate you, my sons. Let us sit down on the benches round this table; we shall be able to talk better like that.' Everyone sat down, including the people who were with the bishop. They brought a stool that stood by the door in the courtyard and put it at the head of the table. That way the bishop could see everybody. 'Nearly all Frenchmen are Catholics: is there any one among you who is not?' Nobody put up his hand. It seemed to me that I too ought to look upon myself as a Catholic. 'My friends, I descend from a French family. My name is Irénée de Bruyne. My people were Huguenots, Protestants who fled to Holland at the time Catherine de Medicis was hunting them down. So I am a Frenchman by blood. I am the bishop of Curaçao, a town where there are more Protestants than Catholics, but where the Catholics are very zealous and attentive to their duties. What is your position?'

'We are waiting to be put aboard tankers, one by one.'

'How many of you have left in this way?'

'None, so far.'

'Hmmm. What have you to say to that, Chief? Be so kind as to answer in French – you speak it so well.'

'Monseigneur, the governor really did have the idea of helping these men in this way, but in all frankness I must tell you that so far not a single captain has agreed to take one, principally because they have no passports.'

'That's where we must start, then. Couldn't the governor give each one a special passport for the occasion?'

'I don't know. He's never talked to me about that.'

'The day after tomorrow I shall say a mass for you. Would you like to come to confession tomorrow afternoon? I'll confess you myself – I'll do all I can for you so that the good Lord will forgive your sins. Is it possible for you to have these men sent to the cathedral at three o'clock?'

'Yes.'

'I should like them to come in a taxi or a private car.'

'I'll bring them myself, Monseigneur,' said Dr. Naal.

'Thank you. My sons, I promise you nothing. Just one perfectly true word – from now on I shall try to be as useful to you as I possibly can.'

When we saw Naal kiss his ring and then the Breton do the same we all touched it with our lips and went with him as far as his car, which was parked in the courtyard.

The next day everybody went to the bishop for confession. I was the last.

'Come, my son, let us begin with the gravest sin.'

'Father, to begin with I'm not baptized; but a priest in the prison in France told me that whether you were baptized or not, everyone was God's child.'

'He was right. Very well. Let us leave the confessional and you can tell me all about it.'

I told him the story of my life in detail. At great length, patiently and very attentively this prince of the Church listened to me without interrupting. He took my hands in his and often he looked me full in the faces and then sometimes, when I came to passages that were hard to bring out, he lowered his eyes to help me in my confession. This sixty-year-old priest's eyes and face were so pure that there was an almost child-like reflection in them. The transparent cleanliness of his soul (full of boundless kindness, I was sure) shone in all his features; and the gaze of his pale grey eyes entered into me, as soothing as balm to a wound. Gently, very gently, and still holding my hands in his, he spoke to me in so quiet a voice that it was almost a whisper. 'God sometimes requires His children to bear with human wickedness, so that the one He has chosen as a victim may emerge stronger and nobler than before. Reflect, my son: if you had not been forced to undergo this calvary you would never have been able to raise yourself to such heights or to bring yourself so close to divine truth. I will go even farther. The people, the system, the workings of this horrible machine that has ground you down, and the fundamentally evil beings who in their different ways have tormented and harmed you, have in fact done you the greatest service they possibly could. They have brought a new person into being inside you, better than the first; and it is to them that you owe it that now you possess a sense of honour, kindness and charity, as well as the will-power needed to conquer all these difficulties and to become a finer man. In a person like you these notions of revenge cannot prosper; nor can the idea of punishing each one according to the harm he

140

has done you. You must be a saver of men. You must not live to hurt others, even though you may think it justified. God has been open-handed towards you; He has said to you "Help yourself, and I will help you". He has helped you in everything, and He has even allowed you to save others and to bring them to freedom. Above all, do not suppose that the sins you have committed are so very grave. There are plenty of highly-placed people who are guilty of much more serious misconduct than yours. Yet the punishment inflicted by human justice has not given them the opportunity of rising above themselves as you have done.'

'Thank you, Father. You have done me an enormous amount of good: it will last me all my life. I shall never forget it.' And I kissed his hands.

'You must set off again, my son, and come face to face with other perils. I should like to christen you before you go. What do you say?'

'Father, leave me like this for a moment. My father brought me up without any religion. He has a heart of gold. When Maman died he somehow managed to take her place, with all the things a mother would say or do, and all a mother's affection. It seems to me that if I let myself be christened, I should somehow be betraying him. Just let me be completely free for a while, with a proper set of papers and an ordinary way of earning my living, so that when I write to him I can ask whether I can leave his philosophy – whether I can be christened without grieving him.'

'I understand, my son, and I am sure God is with you. I give you my blessing and I beg that God will protect you.'

'There,' said Dr. Naal, 'you see how Monseigneur Irénée de Bruyne's sermon shows you the whole man himself?'

'Certainly I do. Tell me, what are you thinking of doing now?'

'I am going to ask the governor to give orders for me to have the preference in the next sale of confiscated smuggling boats. You will come with me to tell me your opinion and pick the one you think most suitable. For the rest, stores and clothes, it will be easy.'

From the day of the bishop's sermon we had a constant flow of visitors, particularly at about six in the evening. They were people who wanted to know us. They sat on the benches by the table and each brought something that he would put down on a bed and leave without saying anything about it. About two in the afternoon the Little Sisters of the Poor would appear, accompanied by their Superior; they spoke French very well. Their basket was always full of good things they had cooked themselves. The Mother Superior was very young – less than forty. You could not see her hair, because it was hidden under her white coif, but her eyes were blue and her eyebrows fair. She belonged to a great family in Holland (Dr. Naal told us) and she had written home to see whether something could be done for us instead of our being sent off to sea again. We spent some pleasant hours together and she would ask me to tell the story of our escape. Sometimes she would ask me to tell the nuns who came with her and who spoke French. And if I forgot a detail or skipped it she would gently call me to order. 'Henri, not so fast. You have skipped the story of the hocco . . . Why are you forgetting the ants today? They are very important, since it was because of the ants that the Masked Breton came upon you by surprise.' I tell all this, because those were such gentle, kindly moments and so wholly unlike everything we had lived through that our horrible rotting former life seemed to be lit up by a heavenly light and to become unreal.

I saw the boat, a splendid twenty-five-foot craft with a deep keel, a very long mast and a huge spread of sail. It was perfectly designed for smuggling. It was fully equipped, but there were wax customs seals all over it. At the auction someone began the bidding at six thousand florins, or round about a thousand dollars. To cut the story short, after a few whispered words between this man and Dr. Naal they let us have it for six thousand and one florins.

In five days we were ready. Newly painted and crammed with stores all carefully stowed below, this half-decked boat was a kingly gift. A suitcase for each man, six suitcases filled with new clothes, shoes and everything necessary, were lined up in a waterproof tarpaulin and then stowed on the deck.

We left at dawn. The doctor and the nuns came to say goodbye. We slipped our moorings easily; the wind took us right away and we sailed out of the harbour. A brilliant sun came up and we had an untroubled day before us. In no time I found that the boat had too much in the way of sail and not enough ballast. I made up my mind to be very cautious. We raced along: from the point of view of speed this boat was a thoroughbred but she was both touchy and nervous. I steered due west.

It had been decided that we should land our three passengers from Trinidad illegally on the coast of Colombia. They wouldn't have anything whatever to do with a long voyage; they said they trusted in me all right, but not in the weather. And in fact the forecasts in the papers we had read in prison spoke of storms and even hurricanes. I acknowledged they were within their rights and it was agreed we should land them on a barren, uninhabited peninsula called Goajira. As for us, we should set off again for British Honduras.

The weather was magnificent, and the starlit night with a brilliant half moon made our scheme for landing them all the easier. We ran straight for the Colombian coast: I dropped anchor and foot by foot we sounded to see when they could go ashore. Unhappily the water was very deep and we had to go dangerously close to the rocky coast before we had less than five feet. We shook hands: each of them got out, stood there in the sea with his suitcase on his head, and waded to the land. We watched them closely and rather sadly. They were companions who had faced up to things well; they had never let us down at any time. It was a pity they were leaving the boat. While they were making their way ashore the wind dropped entirely. Hell! What if we were seen from the village shown on the map – the village called Rio Hacha? That was the nearest port with police in it. Let's hope not. I had the feeling we were much nearer than we had meant to be, because of that lighthouse on the headland we had just passed.

Wait, wait . . . The three men had disappeared, having waved good-bye with a white handkerchief. A breeze, for God's sake! A breeze to carry us away from this Colombian coast: for as far as we were concerned the country was one big question mark. No one knew whether they handed escaped prisoners back or not. All three of us would rather have the certainty of British Honduras than this unknown Colombia. It was not until three in the afternoon that there was a wind and we were able to get under way. I set everything, and with perhaps too much aboard we sailed along for a couple of hours: then a launch filled with men appeared, steering straight for us and firing shots in the air to make us stop. I ran on without obeying, trying to get out to sea, out of territorial waters. Impossible. The powerful launch caught up with us in less than an hour and a half's chase, and with ten rifles pointing at us we were forced to surrender.

The soldiers or maybe policemen who had arrested us all had much the same look: they all wore dirty trousers that had once been white and ragged singlets that had never been washed at any time, and they were all of them, except for the 'captain', barefoot – he was better dressed and cleaner. But although they were badly dressed they were very well armed: a full cartridge-belt round their waists, well-kept rifles and a long sheathed dagger into the bargain, the hilt just at hand. The one they called captain looked like a half-caste and a murderer. He had a heavy revolver, and he too wore it with a well-filled bandolier. As they only spoke Spanish we could not make out their meaning, but neither their looks nor their motions nor their tone of voice were friendly: far from it.

We walked from the harbour to the prison, going through the village, which was indeed Rio Hacha, escorted by six toughs with three more a couple of paces behind, their guns trained on us. It was not the most friendly of welcomes.

We reached the courtyard of a prison with a little wall round it. There were about twenty dirty, bearded prisoners sitting about or standing, and they looked at us with hostile eyes. 'Vamos, vamos.' We understood the soldiers to mean. 'Come on, come on,' which was hard for us, because although Clousiot was a good deal better he still had to walk on the iron in his plastered leg and he could not go fast. The 'captain' had stayed behind and now he caught us up with the compass and the oilskin under his arm. He was eating our biscuits and chocolate and we instantly grasped that we were going to be stripped bare. And we weren't mistaken, either. They shut us up in a filthy room with heavy bars over the window. There were some planks on the ground with a kind of wooden pillow beside them; those were the beds. A prisoner came to the window after the police had left and called to us, 'Frenchmen, Frenchmen!'

'What do you want?'

'Frenchmen, no good, no good.'

'Who do you mean, no good?'

'Police.'

'Police?'

'Yes, police are no good.'

And he disappeared. Night fell; the room was lit by a bulb that must have been of a very low voltage, for it gave hardly any light. Mosquitoes buzzed round our ears and got into our noses.

'Well, a fine mess we're in! It's going to cost us a packet, having landed those guys.'

'That's how it is: we couldn't tell. The real thing was there was no wind.'

'You went in too close,' said Clousiot.

'Just you shut your trap, will you? This is no time for blame: this is when we've got to back one another up. We've got to hold together now more than ever.'

'Sorry: you're right, Papi. It was nobody's fault.'

Oh, it would be too unfair if the break were to come to an end here, so wretchedly, after we'd had such a struggle. They had not searched us. I had my charger in my pocket and I hurriedly stuffed it up. So did Clousiot. We had been wise not to throw them away. In any case they were watertight wallets, easy to carry, and they took up very little room. According to my watch it was eight in the evening. They brought us some dark brown sugar, a lump the size of your fist for each man, and three what you might call gobs of boiled and salted rice. 'Buenas noches.' 'That must mean good night,' said Maturette.

At seven the next day they gave us very good coffee in wooden bowls out there in the courtyard. At about eight the captain came by. I asked him for permission to go to the boat to fetch our things. He either didn't understand or he pretended not to. The more I saw him the more he seemed to me to have a murdering kind of a face. On the left-hand side of his belt he had a little bottle in a leather case: he took it out, uncorked it, drank a mouthful, spat and offered it to me. This was the first friendly gesture we had seen, so I took it and drank.

Fortunately I had only poured a very little into my mouth – it was liquid fire and it tasted like methylated spirits. Quickly I swallowed and began to cough, which made this half-black half-Indian laugh very cheerfully.

At ten o'clock several civilians appeared, dressed in white and wearing ties. There were six or seven of them, and they went into a building that seemed to be the prison's administrative centre. We were sent for. They were all sitting there in a semicircle in a room dominated by the picture of a very much decorated white officer – President Alfonso Lopez of Colombia. One of these gentlemen made Clousiot sit down, speaking to him in French; the rest of us remained standing. A thin, hook-nosed party in the middle who wore half-glasses began questioning me. The interpreter interpreted none of it but said to me, 'The man who has just spoken and who is going to interrogate you is the magistrate of the town of Rio Hacha; the others are prominent citizens, friends of his. I'm a Haïtian, and I look after the electricity in these parts: I act as interpreter. I believe some of the people here understand a little French, though they don't say so. Maybe even the magistrate.'

This preamble made the magistrate impatient, and he broke in with his interrogation in Spanish. The Haïtian translated the questions and answers as they came.

'Are you French?'

'Yes.'

'Where do you come from?'

'Curaçao.'

'And before that?'

'Trinidad.'

'And before that?'

'Martinique.'

'You're lying. More than a week ago our consul in Curaçao was warned that the coast should be watched because six men who had escaped from the French penal settlement were going to try to land in our country.'

'All right. We did escape from the penal settlement.'

'You're a Cayenero, then?'

'Yes.'

'If so noble a country as France sent you so far and punished you so severely, it must be because you are very dangerous malefactors.'

'Maybe.'

146

'Theft or murder?'

'Manslaughter.'

'Killing – it's all one. So you are matadors, then? Where are the other three?'

'They stayed in Curaçao.'

'You're lying again. You landed them thirty-five miles from here in a region called Castillette. Fortunately they have been arrested and they'll be here in a few hours. Did you steal the boat?'

'No. The Bishop of Curaçao gave it us as a present.'

'All right. You'll stay in prison here until the governor has made up his mind what is to be done with you. For the crime of landing three of your accomplices on Colombian territory and then trying to put out to sea again, I sentence you, the captain of the vessel, to three months imprisonment, and the other two to one month. You had better behave, if you don't want the police to inflict corporal punishment – they are very severe men. Have you anything to say?'

'No. I should just like to collect my belongings and the stores aboard the boat.'

'That's all confiscated by the customs, except for one pair of trousers, one shirt, one jacket and a pair of shoes for each man. All the rest is confiscated, so don't make a fuss. There's nothing to be said – it's the law.'

Everyone went out into the courtyard. The wretched local prisoners clustered round the magistrate, clamouring 'Doctor, Doctor!' He pushed right through them, swollen with his own importance, neither replying nor stopping. They walked out of the prison and disappeared.

At one o'clock our three friends arrived in a lorry, with seven or eight armed men. They got out, carrying their suitcases and looking thoroughly downcast. We went back indoors with them.

'What a bloody awful mistake we made – and made you make,' said the Breton. 'There's nothing to be said for us, Papillon. If you want to kill me, go right ahead: I shan't raise a finger. We aren't men: we're a set of pouffes. We did it because we were afraid of the sea. Well, after the glimpse I've had of Colombia and the Colombians, the perils of the sea are a fun-fair compared with the perils of being in the hands of these buggers. Was it because there was no wind they copped you?'

'That's right, Breton. There's no call for me to kill anyone: we all got it wrong. All I had to do was to refuse to land you and nothing would have happened.'

'You're too good, Papi.'

'No. I'm fair, that's all.' I told them about the interrogation. 'So in the end maybe the governor will let us go.'

'Bloody likely. Still, let's hope, since hope is what keeps you going, as the guy said in the story.'

As I saw it the authorities of this half-civilized hole could not decide upon our case. It was only much higher up that it would be laid down whether we could stay in Colombia, or whether we were to be handed back to France, or whether we should be put back in our boat to go farther off. It would be hellish unjust if these people were to take the worst decision, for after all we had done them no harm and we hadn't committed the slightest crime in their country.

We had been here a week now. No change of any kind apart from some talk of sending us under strong guard to a larger town called Santa Marta, a hundred and twenty-five miles away. These savage, piratical-looking police had not changed their attitude towards us. Yesterday I was on the very edge of being shot by one, just for having snatched my soap back from him in the wash-house. We were still in this room stiff with mosquitoes, but fortunately it was rather cleaner than the way we found it, thanks to Maturette and the Breton scrubbing it out every day. I began to despair, to lose confidence. These Colombians, this mixed race of Indians and Negroes, and Indians and the Spaniards who were once masters here, made me feel like giving up. A Colombian prisoner lent me an old Santa Marta paper. On the front page there were photos of us six and the police-captain underneath, wearing his huge felt hat and with a cigar in his mouth. And there was a picture of nine or ten police all armed with their rifles too. I gathered that the whole thing had been jazzed up and their part in it made much more dramatic. Anyone would have thought the whole of Colombia had been preserved from some terrible danger by our arrest. And yet the picture of the villains was pleasanter to look at than the one of the police. The villains really looked quite like decent people, whereas the police – oh, pardon me! You had only to look at the captain and your mind was made up. What were we to do? I began to learn a few words of Spanish. Escape, *fugarse*; prisoner, *preso*; kill, *matar*; chain, *cadena*; handcuffs, *esposas*; man, *hombre*; woman, *mujer*.

The Break from Rio Hacha

I made friends with a guy in the courtyard who wore handcuffs all the time. We smoked the same cigar; it was long, thin and terribly strong, but at least it was a smoke. I gathered he was a smuggler working between Venezuela and the island of Aruba. He was accused of having killed some coastguards and he was awaiting his trial. Some days he was wonderfully calm and then on others he would be all on edge and nervous. Finally I noticed that the calm days were when he chewed some leaves he was brought. One day he gave me half of one of these leaves and straight away I understood what it was all about. My tongue, palate and lips lost all feeling. These were the leaves of the coca plant. He was a man of thirty-five; his arms were hairy and his chest was covered with a mat of very black curly fur; he must have been most uncommonly strong. There was such a layer of thick horny skin on the soles of his bare feet that I often saw him pull out bits of glass or a nail which had gone right in without reaching the flesh.

'Fuga, you and me,' I said to the smuggler one afternoon. Once when the Haitian had come to see me I had asked him for a French-Spanish dictionary. The smuggler got my meaning and with a gesture he showed me he'd certainly like to escape, but what about the handcuffs? They were American handcuffs with a ratchet. They had a slot for the key, and the key must certainly be of the flat sort. With a piece of wire, flattened at the end, the Breton made me a hook. After several tries I could open my new friend's handcuffs whenever I wanted. He spent the night by himself in a *calabozo* (cell) whose bars were fairly thick. In ours they were thin, and they could be bent for

149

sure. So there would be only one bar to saw through – one of those in Antonio's cell (the Colombian was called Antonio). 'How can we get a *socette* (saw)?' '*Plata* (money).' '*Cuanto* (how much)?' 'A hundred pesos.' 'Dollars?' 'Ten.' To cut it short, he got two hacksaw blades with the ten dollars I gave him. Drawing on the ground in the yard I showed him how he was to mix the metal sawdust with the cooked rice they gave us and carefully cover up the slit every time he had sawed any depth. At the last moment, just before we all went in for the night, I used to open one of his handcuffs. In case they were checked, all he had to do was to push on it for it to shut automatically. He took three nights to saw through the bar. He told me he could finish the cut in under a minute and that he was sure he could bend it over with his hands. He was to come and fetch me.

It often rained, and he said that the '*primera noche de lluvia* (the first rainy night)' he would come. That very night it started pouring down. My friends knew what I was up to: not one of them wanted to accompany me, because they thought the region I meant to go to was too far. I wanted to reach the tip of the Colombian peninsula on the Venezualan frontier. Our map showed this part under the name of Goajira, and said it was disputed territory, neither Colombian nor Venezuelan. The Colombian said that '*eso es la tierra de los Indios* (this was Indian country)' and that there were no police in those parts, neither Colombian nor Venezuelan. Just a few smugglers passed through. It was dangerous, because the Goajira Indians would not allow a civilized man into their country. The farther inland, the more dangerous they were. There were fishing Indians on the coast, and these ones traded with the village of Castillette and a hamlet called La Vela through some rather more civilized Indians. Antonio himself didn't want to go there. Either he or his friends had killed some Indians during a battle that was fought when a boat filled with contraband took refuge on their coast by force one day. But Antonio undertook to lead me very near to Goajira, and after that I was to go on alone. I don't have to tell you how tedious it was, working all this out, because he used words that weren't in the dictionary.

So that night it was pouring with rain. There I was, standing near the window. Long before this a plank had been wrenched free from the bed-platform: we were going to use it as a lever to force the bars apart. We had made a trial two nights before, and we had seen they gave easily.

'*Listo* (ready).' Antonio's face appeared, stuck between the bars. Helped by Maturette and the Breton, I not only wrenched the bar aside with a single heave, but even unseated its bottom end. They shoved me up, and before I vanished they slapped my buttocks hard. This was my friends' good-bye. We were in the yard. The torrential rain made a hellish din as it thundered down on the corrugated iron roofs. Antonio took me by the hand and led me to the wall. Getting over it was child's play – it was only six feet high. Nevertheless I cut my hand on one of the bits of glass on top: it was nothing – let's go. Antonio, that phenomenon, could somehow guide himself through the downpour that prevented us from seeing anything ten feet away. He made the most of it and went right through the village itself; then we took a road between the bush and the coast. Very late that night we saw a light. We had to make a long detour through the bush before coming back to the road – fortunately it was not very thick. We walked on through the rain until daybreak. When we set out he had given me a coca-leaf and I chewed on it just as I had seen him do in prison. I was not at all tired when daylight came. Was it the leaf? It certainly was. We went on walking in spite of the light. From time to time he lay down and set his ear to the streaming ground. And then we'd go on again.

He had an odd way of getting along. It was neither running nor walking, but in a series of little jumps one after another, all the same length, with his arms out as though he was rowing through the air. He must have heard something, because he pulled me into the bush. It was still raining. And true enough, before our eyes there appeared a roller pulled by a tractor, to flatten the earth on the road, no doubt.

Half past ten in the morning. The rain had stopped and the sun had come out. We went into the bush after having walked nearly a mile on the grass and not on the road. We lay there under a very thick tuft, surrounded by dense, thorny vegetation: it seemed to me we had nothing to fear, and yet Antonio wouldn't let me smoke or even talk in a whisper. As Antonio swallowed the juice of his leaves all the time, I did the same, only rather less. He had a bag with more than twenty in it, and he showed it to me. His splendid teeth shone in the shadow as he laughed. There were mosquitoes everywhere, so he

151

chewed a cigar and with spit full of nicotine we daubed our faces and hands. After that they left us in peace. Seven in the evening. Night had fallen but there was too much moon lighting the road. He pointed to nine o'clock on my watch and said 'lluvia' (rain).' I grasped that at nine o'clock it was going to rain. And in fact at nine o'clock it did rain and we set off again. So as not to keep him back I learnt the knack of skipping along and rowing with my arms. It was not difficult, and without actually running I still got along faster than a quick walk. During the night we had to go into the bush three times to let a car, a lorry and a little cart pulled by two asses go by. Thanks to the coca-leaves I did not feel at all tired when day broke. The rain stopped at eight o'clock and then we did the same thing all over again – about a mile on the grass and then into the bush to hide. The awkward thing about these leaves was that they prevented you from sleeping. We had not had a wink since the beginning of the break. Antonio's pupils were so dilated that there was no iris left. No doubt mine were the same.

Nine in the evening. It was raining. Anyone would have said the rain waited for this time of night to start. Later on I learnt that in the tropics, when it starts raining at such and such a time, it'll go on doing so until the change of the moon – it'll start at that time and stop at just the same time too. When we began walking that night we heard voices and we saw lights. 'Castillette,' said Antonio. Without any hesitation this phenomenon took me by the hand; we went back into the bush, and after more than two hours of hard going we hit the road once more. We marched, or rather bounded along all the rest of that night and a good deal of the next morning. The sun dried our clothes on us. It was three days now that we had been soaked, and three days since we had eaten anything apart from a lump of brown sugar the first day. Antonio seemed almost certain we shouldn't meet with any evilly-disposed people now. He went along quite carefree, and it was hours since he had put his ear to the ground. Here the road ran along by the shore. Antonio cut himself a branch; we left the road and walked along the wet sand. Antonio stopped to look closely at a broad flattened track on the beach; it was about two feet wide and it ran up out of the sea to the dry sand. We followed it and reached a place where the track spread out into a circle. Antonio thrust his stick in. When he pulled it out there was something yellow sticking to it, like the yolk of an egg. I helped him make a hole, digging the sand away with our hands, and there indeed were eggs, three or four hundred – I can't tell how many. They were turtle eggs. They had no shells, only a skin. Antonio took off his shirt and we filled it full, maybe a hundred of them. We left the beach and crossed the road to hide in the bush. When we were quite hidden we began eating – the yolks only, as Antonio showed me. He ripped the skin with his wolfish teeth, let the white run out and then swallowed the yolk: one for him, one for me. He opened a great many, always one for him and one for me. When we had eaten to the point of bursting we both lay down, rolling up our jackets for pillows. Antonio said, '*Mañana tu sigues solo dos dias más. De mañana en adelante no hay policias* (Tomorrow you go on by yourself for two more days. From tomorrow on there will be no more police).'

At ten that evening, the last frontier post. We recognized it by the barking of the dogs and by a little house stuffed with lights. Antonio avoided it all with wonderful skill. Then we went on all night without taking any precautions whatsoever. It was not a wide road; indeed it was not much more than a track; but you felt it was quite well used, because there was absolutely no grass growing on it. This path was about two feet across, and it ran along the edge of the bush, some six feet above the shore; and here and there you could see the marks of horses' or asses' hoofs. Antonio sat down on a broad root and motioned to me to sit down too. The sun was beating down good and hard. According to my watch it was eleven o'clock, but by the sun it must have been noon – a twig pushed into the ground made no shadow at all. So noon it was, and I altered my watch accordingly. Antonio emptied his bag of coca-leaves. There were seven of them. He gave me four and kept three. I went a little way into the bush and came back with a hundred and fifty Trinidad dollars and sixty florins and held them out to him. He stared at me with great astonishment and touched the notes: he couldn't understand how they could look so new or how they had never got wet, since he had never seen me drying them. He thanked me, holding all the notes in his hand: he thought for a long while and then took six five-florin notes – that is thirty florins altogether – and gave me back the rest. I pressed him, but he would not accept any more. At this point something changed in his mind. It had been decided that we were going to part here, but now he looked as though he was going to stay with me for another day. I understood him to say that after that he would turn back. Right. When we had swallowed a few more egg-yolks and lit a cigar – it took more than half an hour of beating two stones together to kindle a little dry moss – we set off once more.

We had been going three hours when we reached a long straight piece of path, and there, coming directly towards us, was a man on a horse. He was wearing a huge straw hat and long boots, no trousers, but a kind of leather slip, a green shirt and a faded jacket, a more or less military jacket; and that was green too. For weapons he had a very fine rifle and an enormous revolver in his belt.

'*Carambal Antonio, hijo mio* (my son)!' Antonio had recognized the horseman from a great way off; he hadn't said anything to me, but it was perfectly obvious. The big copper-coloured guy – he was at least forty – got down from his horse and they thumped one another's shoulders. Later I often came across this way of embracing.

'Who's this?'

'*Compattero de fuga* (fellow-escaper). A Frenchman.'

'Where are you going?'

'As near as possible to the fishing Indians. He wants to go through the Indian country so as to get into Venezuela. There he means to find some way of going back to Curaçao or Aruba.'

'Goajira Indian bad,' said the man. 'You are not armed. *Toma* (take this).' He gave me a dagger with a polished horn handle and its leather sheath. We sat down at the edge of the path. I took off my shoes: my feet were all bloody. Antonio and the horseman spoke fast; it was clear they didn't like my idea of going through Goajira. Antonio made a sign that I was to get on to the horse: with my shoes hung over my shoulder my feet could stay bare and my wounds would dry. He conveyed all this to me by gestures. The horseman mounted. Antonio shook my hand, and before I had grasped what was happening there I was astride the horse, galloping off behind Antonio's friend. We galloped all that day and all that night. From time to time we stopped and he would pass me a bottle of anis: each time I drank a little. At daybreak he reined in. The sun rose: he gave me a piece of cheese as hard as a stone and two biscuits, six leaves of coca and (as a present) a special waterproof bag to carry them in, hung from one's belt. He clasped me in his arms, thumping my shoulders as I had seen him do with Antonio, got on to his horse again and galloped off at full speed.

The Indians

I walked until one in the afternoon. There was no more bush, not so much as a single tree on the horizon. The brilliant sea glittered under a blazing sun. I walked barefoot with my shoes still slung over my left shoulder. Just when I had made up my mind to lie down it seemed to me that I could make out five or six trees or perhaps rocks, lying well back from the shore. I tried to judge the distance: six miles, maybe. I picked out a large half-leaf, and chewing it I set off again, going quite fast. An hour later I could see what these things were for sure – huts with roofs thatched either with straw or light-brown leaves. Smoke was coming out of one of them. Then I saw people. They had seen me. One group was waving and calling out in the direction of the sea: I could hear and see them plainly. And now I saw four boats coming in fast and about ten men getting out of them. Everybody was gathered in front of the huts, looking towards me. I could clearly see that the men and women were naked, wearing only something that hung down to hide their private parts. I walked slowly towards them. There were three men leaning on their bows, and they had arrows in their hands. Not a movement, either of friendship or of enmity. A barking dog came rushing furiously out at me. It bit me low down on the calf, carrying away a piece of my trousers. As it was coming in to attack me again it was hit behind by a little arrow that came from I couldn't tell where (later I learnt it was a blow-pipe); it fled howling and seemed to go into one of the houses. I came nearer, limping, for it had bitten me badly. Now I was no more than ten yards from

155

the group. Not one of them had stirred or spoken: the children stood behind their mothers. They had splendid muscular naked bodies, the colour of copper. The women had high, firm, jutting-out breasts with huge tips. Only one had a heavy, sagging bosom.

The attitude of one of the men was so noble, his features were so clear-cut and he was so obviously of a superior kind that I went straight towards him. He had neither bow nor arrows. He was the same height as me; his hair was carefully cut with a heavy fringe at the level of his eyebrows. His hair hid his ears, for at the back it came down as far as their lobes; it was as black as jet, almost purple. Iron-grey eyes. No hair on his chest nor on his arms nor on his legs. Strong, muscular thighs and well-turned, delicate, copper-coloured legs. His feet were bare. Three yards from him, I stopped. He took two paces forward and looked me full in the face. The inspection lasted two minutes. Not the least movement on his visage – it was like a copper statue with almond eyes. Then he smiled and touched me on the shoulder. And now everybody came and touched me, and a young Indian woman took me by the hand and led me into the shade of one of the huts. There she pushed up the leg of my trousers. Everyone sat down in a circle round us. A man held me out a lit cigar; I took it and began to smoke. My way of smoking made them all burst out laughing; for with them both men and women smoke with the lit end inside their mouths. The wound was no longer bleeding, but a piece about half the size of a five-franc piece had been taken out. The young woman plucked out the hairs, and when everything was quite bare she washed the place with sea water that a little Indian girl had gone to fetch. At the same time she squeezed to make it bleed. She was not satisfied with the result, so she took a piece of sharpened iron and scraped each hole, widening it. I did my best not to flinch, because everybody was watching. Another Indian girl wanted to help, but mine thrust her back violently. Everyone laughed at this, and I grasped that she had meant to show the other one that I was her exclusive property: that was why everyone was so amused. Then she cut off the legs of my trousers well above the knee. Someone brought her seaweed: she prepared it on a stone, put it on to the wound and bound it there with strips torn from my trousers. She was pleased with her work, and she motioned me to get up.

I rose, taking off my jacket. As I did so, she saw the butterfly tattooed low on my back – it showed in the opening of my shirt. She looked closely, and then finding other tattooes she took my shirt off herself to see them better. All of them, men and women too, were deeply interested in the designs on my chest: on the right, a soldier of a punishment-battalion; on the left, a woman's face; on my stomach, a tiger's head; on my backbone, a big crucified sailor; and right across the lower part of my back, a tiger-hunt with hunters, palm-trees, elephants and tigers. When they saw these tattooes the men pushed the women aside, and carefully, slowly, they touched and inspected each design. When the chief had spoken, all the others gave their opinion. From that moment on the men adopted me for good. The women had done so from the moment the chief smiled and touched my shoulder.

We went into the biggest of the huts, and at the sight of it I was completely taken aback. The hut was made of brick-red beaten earth. It had eight doors: it was round, and in an inner corner brilliantly striped pure wool hammocks were hanging from the beams. In the middle there was a round, flat, brown, polished stone, and round it, other flat stones for sitting on. Against the wall, several double-barrelled guns, a military sword, and bows of every size hanging all over the place. I also noticed a turtle-shell so huge that a man could lie down in it; and a very well-built dry-stone chimney – no mortar at all. A table with half a calabash standing on it, and in the calabash two or three handfuls of pearls. They gave me a drink in a wooden bowl – it was fermented fruit-juice, bitter-sweet and very good. Then, on a banana leaf, they brought me a big fish; it must have weighed at least five pounds, and it had been cooked on the embers. I was invited to eat, and I ate slowly. When I had finished the delicious fish the young woman took me and led me to the beach, where I washed my hands and rinsed my mouth with sea-water. Then we went back again. We sat in a circle, the young woman next to me with her hand on my thigh, and with gestures and words we tried to exchange a certain amount of information about ourselves.

All at once the chief got up, went to the back of the hut, returned with a piece of white stone and drew on the table. First the naked Indians and their village, and then the sea. On the right of the Indian village, houses with windows and men and women wearing clothes. The men had either a rifle or a stick in their hands. On the left, another village, and ugly-looking brutes with rifles and hats: women in dresses. When I had carefully looked at the drawings he noticed he had forgotten something and he drew a road leading to the other village on the left. To show me how they lay with regard to his own village, he drew a sun on the Venezuelan side, on the right, a round circle with rays coming out of it all over; and on the side of the Colombian village another sun with a wavy line cutting it at the horizon. There was no mistaking him – on one side the sun was rising and on the other it was setting. The young chief gazed proudly at his work, and everybody looked at it in turn. When he saw that I had thoroughly understood what he meant, he took the chalk and drew criss-cross lines all over the two villages: only his own remained untouched. I understood that he meant to convey that people of the other villages were wicked, that he wanted to have nothing to do with them, and that only his village was good. As if he had to tell *me* that!

He wiped the table with a wet rag. When it was dry he put the piece of chalk into my hand, and now it was up to me to tell my story in pictures. It was harder than his. I drew a man with his hands tied and two armed men looking at him; then the same man running and the two others chasing him and aiming with their guns. I drew the same scene three times, but each time I was a little farther away from the men after me; and in the last drawing the police had stopped and I was still running in the direction of their village, which I drew with the Indians and the dog, and in front of them all the chief holding out his arms towards me.

My drawing can't have been so bad, because after a good deal of talking among the men the chief held out his arms like in the drawing. They had got my meaning.

That same night the Indian girl took me to her hut, where six women and four men were living. She slung a splendid striped woollen hammock, so broad that two could easily lie in it sideways. I got into it, but long-ways; and seeing that she got into another crossways. I did the same and she came and lay down next to me. She felt my body, ears, eyes and mouth with her long, thin but very rough-skinned fingers, all scarred – delicate, but wrinkled. They were the cuts from the coral when she dived for pearl-oysters. When in my turn I stroked her face she took my hand, and she was amazed to find it smooth and unhorny. After this hour in the hammock we got up and went back to the chief's great hut. They gave me the guns to look at – twelve and sixteen bores from Saint-Etienne. They had six boxes of cartridges.

The Indian girl was medium-sized and she had the same grey eyes as the chief; she had a very clean-cut profile and her plaited hair, parted in the middle, came down to her hips. She had beautifully-formed breasts, high and pear-shaped. Their tips were darker than her copper skin, and very long. By way of kissing, she nibbled: she didn't know how to kiss. I very soon taught her how it was done in the civilized world. When we walked, she would not go at my side: there was nothing to be done about it – she insisted on walking behind. One of the huts had nobody in it, and it was in poor repair. With the other women to help her, she fixed the coconut-leaf roof and patched the walls with dollops of very sticky red earth. The men had all kinds of edged tools and weapons – knives, daggers, machetes, axes, hoes and an iron-pronged fork. They had copper and aluminium saucepans, watering-cans, iron pots, a grindstone, an oven, and metal and wooden barrels. Extraordinarily big hammocks made of pure wool and decorated with plaited fringes and with very strongly coloured patterns – blood-red, Prussian blue, shining black and canary-yellow. Presently the house was finished and she began bringing in the things the other Indians gave her, such as an iron tripod to go over the fire, a hammock big enough for four grown-ups lying sideways, glasses, tin pots, saucepans and even an ass's harness.

We had been caressing one another for the fortnight I had been there, but she savagely refused to go all the way. I couldn't understand, for it was she who excited me and then just when everything was set up she wouldn't. She never put on a stitch of clothing apart from her loincloth, which had a very thin string round her slender waist, leaving her bottom quite bare. We set up house in the hut without the least cere-mony: it had three doors, the main one in the middle of the round and the other two opposite one another. In the circle of the round house, these doors formed an isosceles triangle. Each had its own function: I was always supposed to come in and go out of the northern one. And she was always supposed to go out and come in by the southern one. I was not to go in or out of hers, and she was not to use mine. Friends came in or went out by the main door, and neither she nor I could come in by it unless we had visitors with us.

It was only when we had settled in the house that she gave herself to me. I don't want to go into the details, but by instinct she made fiery and wonderfully skilful love, winding round me like a tropical creeper. When we were by ourselves, absolutely alone, I combed and plaited her hair. She was very happy when I did this; her face showed the most wonderful delight and yet at the same time fear in case anyone should see us. For I gathered that a man was not supposed to comb his woman's hair, nor smooth her hands with a stone like pumice, nor kiss her on the mouth or breasts in a certain way.

So there we were, Lali and me (Lali was her name), settled in this house. One thing surprised me very much, and that was that she never used iron or aluminium saucepans or frying-pans nor ever drank out of a glass; she did everything in the earthenware pots they made themselves. The watering-can was used for washing with, under the rose. The ocean was our lavatory.

I was there when the oysters were opened to be searched for pearls. The oldest of the women did this job. Every girl who went pearl-diving had her own bag. The pearls they found were divided like this – one share for the chief as the representative of the tribe; one for the fisherman; half a share for the oyster-opener; and a share and a half for the diving-girl. If she lived with her family, she gave her pearls to her uncle, her father's brother. I never understood why it was that it was also the uncle who first came into the house of a couple about to be married, took the girl's arm and put it round the man's waist and then the man's right arm, wrapping it round the girl's waist so that the forefinger went into her navel. Then, once that was done, he would go away.

So I was there when the oysters were opened; but I didn't go out fishing, because I had not been directly asked to get into a boat. They fished quite far from the shore, perhaps five hundred yards out. Some days Lali would come back with her ribs and thighs all scratched from the coral. The wounds bled sometimes, and then she would crush seaweed and rub it on the places. I never did anything unless they made signs, inviting me. I never went into the chief's house unless he or someone else led me in by the hand. Lali suspected that three

160

Indians girls of her own age came and lay in the grass as near as possible to our door to try and see or hear what we did when we were alone.

Yesterday I saw the Indian who travelled between our village and the nearest Colombian settlement, about a mile from the frontier post. This village was called La Vela. The Indian had two donkeys and he carried a Winchester repeater; he never put on a stitch, apart from the loin-cloth everybody wore. He did not speak a word of Spanish: so how did he carry out his trade, then? With the help of the dictionary I wrote on a piece of paper *agujas* (needles), red and blue Indian ink, and sewing cotton, because the chief often asked me to tattoo him. This travelling Indian was small and wizened. He had a terrible wound on the upper part of his body that started at his lower ribs, went clean across and ended up on his right shoulder. In healing the wound had made a rolled scar as thick as your finger. The pearls were put into a cigar-box. The box was divided into compartments and the pearls went into them according to size. When the Indian left, the chief gave me permission to go a little way with him. So as to make me come back, in his simple-minded fashion he lent me a double-barrelled gun and six cartridges. That way he was sure I'd be forced to return, because he was quite certain I'd never carry off anything that didn't belong to me. As the asses were not loaded the Indian got on to one and I got on to the other. All day we travelled along the same path I had taken to come; but at about a mile or two from the frontier post the Indian turned his back to the sea and plunged inland.

Towards five o'clock we reached the edge of a stream where there stood five Indian houses. They all came out to look at me. The Indian talked and talked and talked until at last there appeared a character who had everything of an Indian – eyes, hair, features – except the colour. He was dead white, and he had the red eyes of an albino. He wore khaki trousers. And at this point I grasped that the Indian from my village never went farther than this place. The white Indian said to me, '*Buenos dias* (good day). *Tu eres el matador que se fugó con Antonio?* (are you the killer who escaped with Antonio?) *Antonio es compadre mio de sangre* (Antonio is my blood-brother).' To be blood-brothers two men tie their arms together, the one to the other, and then each runs his knife over the other's arm cutting into it. Then each smears the other's arm with his own blood, and each licks the other's blood-stained hand. '*Que quieres* (What do you want)?'

'*Agujas, tinta china roja y azul* (Needles, and red and blue Indian ink). *Nada más* (Nothing else).'

'*Tu lo tendrás de aquí a un cuarto de luna* (You'll have them at the next quarter of the moon from now).'

He spoke Spanish better than I did and I had the impression he would know how to enter into contact with civilized men and organize barter, at the same time taking the greatest care of his own people's interests. Just as we were going he gave me a necklace made of very white Colombian silver coins: he said it was for Lali.

'*Vuelva a verme* (Come back and see me),' said the white Indian. To make sure I should return he gave me a bow.

I set off for the village again, but by myself; and I had not covered half the distance before I saw Lali, together with a young sister of hers – twelve or perhaps thirteen. Lali was certainly between sixteen and eighteen. She rushed at me furiously and scratched me, only getting at my chest, however, for I hid my face; and then she gave me a savage bite on the neck. Even using all my strength I found it hard to keep her off. Suddenly she calmed down. I put the younger girl on the donkey and I walked behind, my arm round Lali. Slowly we went back to the village. On the way I killed an owl. I fired without knowing what it was, just seeing these eyes glowing in the darkness. Lali insisted on taking it back, and she hung it on the ass's saddle. We got home at dawn. I was so tired I just had to wash. Lali washed me, and then, there in front of me, took off her sister's loin-cloth and set about washing her too. When she had finished she washed herself.

When they both came in again I was sitting there, waiting for the water to boil: I had put it on to have a hot lemon and sugar drink. And now there happened something that I never understood until long after. Lali pushed her sister between my legs and put my arm round her waist: I noticed that the sister had no loin-cloth on and that she was wearing the necklace I had given Lali. I didn't know how to get out of this delicate position, but I gently pulled the girl from between my legs, picked her up and put her to lie in the hammock. I took the necklace off her and passed it over Lali's head. Lali lay down next to her sister and me next to Lali. Long after I learnt that Lali had thought I had been finding out how to get away because maybe I wasn't happy with her; and she had thought that perhaps her sister would be able to keep me there. When I woke up there were Lali's hands over my eyes. The little sister wasn't there any more: it was very late – eleven in the morning. Lali gazed lovingly at me with her big grey eyes and gently nibbled the corner of my mouth. She was happy to make me understand that she knew I loved her and that I was not going to leave just because she couldn't hold me.

The Indian who usually paddled Lali's canoe was sitting there in front of the house. I saw that he was waiting for her. He smiled at me and closed his eyes in very well-acted pantomime – his way of telling me he knew Lali was asleep. I sat down next to him; he said a good many things I couldn't understand. He was a young man, athletic and wonderfully muscular. He gazed at my tattooes for a long while, examining them, and then by signs he showed he'd like me to tattoo him. I nodded to say yes, but it seemed to me he thought I didn't know how. Lali appeared. She had covered herself all over with oil. She knew I didn't care for it, but she made me understand that in this cloudy weather the water would be very cold. Her mimicry, half laughing and half serious, was so pretty that I made her go through it several times, pretending not to be able to follow. When I made a sign that she was to begin again she put on a face that said as clearly as could be, 'Are you stupid, or is it that I'm *torpe* (dull) at explaining why I put on this oil?'

The chief went by with two Indian women. They were carrying a huge green lizard weighing at least ten or twelve pounds and he had his bow and arrows. He had just killed the lizard, and he invited me to come and eat it with him later. Lali spoke to him; he touched my shoulder, pointing to the sea. I gathered that I could go with Lali if I wanted to. We went off all three of us, Lali, her usual fishing companion and me. It was a very light little boat made of balsa wood, and it was easy to launch. They waded down carrying it on their shoulders and then plunged in. Getting it out to sea was an odd business: the man got in first, in the stern, holding a huge paddle. Lali, with the water up to her bosom, held the canoe steady and prevented it from being pushed back on shore; I got in and sat in the middle; and then in one movement there was Lali aboard and at the same instant the Indian dug in his paddle and sent us out. The rollers were higher and higher the

163

farther we went from the shore. Five or six hundred yards out we found a kind of channel where two other boats were already fishing. Lali had tied her plaits close to her head with five red leather thongs, three across and two lengthways; the thongs themselves went round her neck. Carrying a stout knife in her hand, she went down the anchor, a thick iron bar weighing about thirty pounds that the man had lowered to the bottom. The boat stayed there at anchor, but it was never still, for it rose and fell with every roller.

For three hours and more Lali went up and down between the canoe and the bottom of the sea. The bottom could not be seen, but judging from the time she took, it must have been fifty and sixty feet down. Every time she brought oysters up in the sack the man emptied them into the canoe. During these three hours Lali never once got into the canoe. To rest, she clung to the side for five or ten minutes. We changed places twice without her getting in. In the second place the sack came up with more and bigger oysters. We turned back for the shore. Lali had got into the boat and the rollers soon ran us back to the beach. The old Indian woman was waiting there. Lali and I let her and the man carry the oysters up to the dry sand. When they were all ashore, Lali stopped the old woman from opening them: it was Lali herself who began. She quickly opened about thirty with the point of her knife before she found a pearl. I swallowed at least two dozen – that goes without saying: the water must have been cold down there, because their flesh was chilled. Gently she brought out a pearl, the size of one's little finger nail. It was a pearl nearer the larger than the medium size. How it gleamed! Nature had given it a wonderful variety of changing colours, none of them too pronounced. Lali took the pearl in her fingers, put it into her mouth, kept it there for a moment, and then, bringing it out, she put it into mine. With a mimic chewing she showed that she wanted me to crush it with my teeth and swallow it. At my first refusal she begged so prettily that I did what she wanted: I crushed the pearl between my teeth and I swallowed the fragments. She opened four or five oysters and gave them me to swallow, meaning the whole of the pearl to go down inside me. She pushed me back on the sand, and like a little girl she opened my mouth and looked to see whether there were any crumbs still there between my teeth. We walked off, leaving the two others to get on with the work.

I had been here a month now. I couldn't get that wrong, because I noted the day and the date on a piece of paper every morning. I had had the needles for some time, as well as red, blue and violet Indian ink. In the chief's hut I found three Solingen razors. They were never used for shaving, since the Indians had no beard. One came in useful for the even trimming of their hair. I tattooed Zato, the chief, on the arm. I did him an Indian with different-coloured feathers in his hair. He was delighted, and he made me understand that I was not to tattoo anyone else until I had done him a big picture on the chest. He wanted the same tiger's head that I had, with long teeth. I laughed: I wasn't good enough at drawing to do such fine work. Lali took all the hair off my whole body. She could scarcely see a hair before she would pluck it out and rub me with seaweed, crushed and mixed with ash. It seemed to me the hairs did not grow so strongly after this.

This Indian tribe was called Goajira. They lived on the coast and on the inland plain as far as the beginning of the mountains. In the mountains there were other tribes called Motilones. Years afterwards, I came into contact with them. As I said, the Goajiras were in indirect touch with civilization through their barter. The ones on the coast gave the white Indian their pearls and also turtles. The turtles were supplied alive, and sometimes they reached a weight of three hundred and fifty pounds. They never came up to the weight and size of the Orinoco or Maroni turtles, which reached nearly nine hundred pounds and whose shell could be as much as six feet long and more than three across. Once they are turned on their backs, these turtles cannot get up again. I've seen them carried off still alive after having lain there on their backs for three weeks without eating or drinking. As for the big green lizards, they are very good to eat. Their white, tender flesh is delicious; and their eggs, cooked by the sun in the sand, are very good too. Only their appearance puts you off a little.

Every time Lali went fishing she brought back her share of the pearls and gave them to me. I put them into a wooden bowl without sorting them – big, medium and small all mixed. The only ones I set aside, putting them in an empty matchbox, were two pink pearls, three black, and seven of a wonderfully beautiful metallic grey. I also had a big irregular bean-shaped pearl, the size of one of our white or red haricots at home. This baroque pearl had three colours one on top of the other, and according to the weather one would show more than the others – the black layer, the gunmetal or the silvery layer with its pinkish sheen. Thanks to these pearls and a few turtles, the tribe lacked for nothing. But they possessed some objects that were no use to them, while others they might have found valuable were not there. For example, there wasn't a single mirror in the whole tribe. I had to find a square of nickel-plated metal, about eighteen inches across that no doubt came from a wreck, before I could shave or see myself.

My policy towards my friends was simple: I did nothing that could lessen the chief's authority or wisdom, still less that of a very old Indian who lived by himself two miles away inland, together with various snakes, two goats and a dozen sheep. He was the medicine-man for certain Goajira villages. This behaviour of mine meant that no one felt jealous of me or wished me away. By the end of two months I was completely adopted by one and all. The medicine-man also had a score of hens. Seeing that in the two hamlets I knew there were no goats nor hens nor sheep, it occurred to me that owning domestic animals must be a medicine-man's privilege. Every morning, each taking her turn, an Indian woman would set off with a plaited basket on her head to carry him freshly-caught fish and seafood. They also took him maize cakes made that morning and roasted on stones in the fire. Sometimes, but not always, she would come back with eggs or sour milk. When the medicine-man wanted me to go and see him he sent three eggs for me personally and a highly-polished wooden knife. Lali went half of the way with me and then waited in the shade of a huge cactus. The first time she put the wooden knife in my hand and showed me I was to go in the direction she pointed out.

The old Indian lived in disgusting filth in a tent made of stretched cow-hides, the hairy side in. There were three stones in the middle with a fire that you felt must always be alight. He didn't sleep in a hammock but on a kind of bed made of branches, standing more than three feet high. It was quite a large tent – it must have covered twenty square yards. It had no walls, apart from a few branches on the windy side. I saw two snakes, the one ten feet long and as thick as your arm, and the other about three feet with a yellow V on its head; and I said to myself, 'Think of what those snakes must put away in eggs and chickens!' I could not understand how goats, hens, sheep and even the ass could all shelter in this one tent. The old Indian examined me from all sides. He made me take off the trousers Lali had turned into shorts, and when I was mother-naked he made me sit down on a stone near the fire. He put green leaves on to it; they made a great deal of smoke and they smelt of mint. The smoke all round nearly smothered me, but I scarcely coughed at all and for close on ten minutes I sat it out, waiting for it to finish. Then he burnt my trousers and gave me two Indian loin-cloths, one made of sheepskin and the other of snakeskin, as supple as a glove. He put a bracelet of goat, sheep and snakeskin strips round my arm. It was four or five inches broad and it was held by a snakeskin thong that could be tightened or loosened.

The medicine-man had an ulcer on his left ankle the size of a two-franc piece, covered with flies. From time to time he whisked at them, and when they bothered him too much he dusted the place with ash. When the medicine-man had finished my adoption I was about to go, but first he gave me a smaller wooden knife than the one he had sent me when he wanted to see me. Later Lali told me that if I wanted to see him, I was to send him the little knife; and if he agreed to let me come, he would send me the big one. I took leave of the very old Indian, noticing the wonderful wrinkles on his thin face and his neck. He only had five teeth left, three below and two above, in front. His eyes were almond-shaped like all Indians, and their lids were so thick that when he shut them it made two round balls. No eyebrows or lashes; but straight, perfectly black hair hanging down to his shoulders and neatly cut at the ends. Like all other Indians, he had a fringe coming down to his eyebrows.

I went away, feeling awkward with my buttocks bare. I felt peculiar all over. Still, this was all part of the break! The Indians were not to be taken lightly and it was well worth a little embarrassment to be free. Lali saw my loin-cloth and laughed heartily, showing all her teeth, as beautiful as the pearls she fished up from the bottom of the sea. She inspected the bracelet and the other loin-cloth, the snakeskin one. To see if I'd been through the smoke she smelt me. I may say the Indians have a very strong sense of smell.

I was growing used to this sort of life and I realized that I must not go on too long, or perhaps, I might never want to leave. Lali kept watch on me all the time: she would have liked to see me enter more thoroughly into the life of the tribe. For example, she had seen me go out to catch fish, and she knew I could paddle well and handle the little light canoe with great skill; so it was no time before she wanted me to be the one who managed the canoe for the pearl fishing. But the idea didn't suit me at all. Lali was the best diving-girl in the whole village. It was always her boat that brought back the best and biggest oysters – that is to say, those that had been found in the deepest water. I also knew that the young Indian who paddled her canoe was the chief's brother. If I were to go with Lali, it would be against his interests; so that was something I shouldn't do. When Lali saw I was pensive she went off to fetch her sister again. She came running, quite delighted, and used my door to come in by. This must have had an important meaning. That is to say, they both appeared together in front of the main door, the one facing the sea, and there they separated, Lali going round to her door and Zoraïma, the little one, to mine. Zoraïma's breasts were hardly the size of tangerines and her hair was quite short. It was cut square at chin level, and her fringe came down lower than her brows – almost to her eyes. Every time her sister brought her like this, they both bathed and when they came in they took off their loin-cloths and hung them up on the hammock. The younger one always went off very sad because I wouldn't have her. One day, when we were all three lying there, with Lali in the middle, she got up and then got in again leaving me pressed tight against Zoraïma's naked body.

Lali's fishing companion hurt his knee – a very deep, wide gash. He was carried to the medicine-man and came back with a white clay plaster over it. So that morning I went fishing with Lali. We launched the canoe just as usual, and everything went very well. I took her out rather farther than she generally went. Lali was perfectly delighted at having me in the canoe with her. Before diving she rubbed herself all over with oil. I reflected that down there – and the bottom was black as far as I could see – it must be very cold. Three sharks' fins passed quite close to us and I pointed them out; she didn't think they mattered in the least. It was ten o'clock in the morning, and the sun was shining. With her bag rolled round her left arm and her sheathed knife tight in her belt, she dived; and she did so without pushing the boat with her feet as an ordinary person would have done. She vanished downwards, towards the dark bottom, with extraordinary speed. Her first dive must have been just to explore, because there were few oysters in the sack when she came up. An idea occurred to me. There was a bundle of leather thongs aboard: I put a hitch round the sack, handed it back to Lali and paid out the thongs as she went down, taking the line with her. She must have understood the operation, because after a longish pause she came up again without the sack. She hung there to rest after this long dive and she made a sign that I was to pull it up. I heaved steadily, but at one point it caught, having fouled the coral. She dived and disentangled it: it came up half full and I emptied it into the canoe. In the course of that morning in eight fifty-foot dives we almost filled the canoe. When she got in again the gunwale was only two inches above the surface. We were so full of oysters that hauling up the anchor put us in danger of sinking. So I untied the anchor-rope and made it fast to the paddle, which would float there until we went back for it. We landed without any trouble.

The old woman was waiting for us and Lali's Indian was sitting there on the dry sand just where they always opened the oysters they had fished up. To begin with he was pleased we had brought in so many. Lali seemed to be explaining how I had tied the sack to the line, which made it easier for her to come up and also allowed her to put more oysters in. He looked carefully at my double hitch for holding the sack, and at the first try he tied it again perfectly. Then he looked at me, very proud of himself.

When the old woman opened the oysters, she found thirteen pearls. Usually Lali never stayed for this part of the job but waited for her share to be brought to her at home; but today she stayed until the last one was finished. I ate at least three dozen, and Lali ate five or six. The old woman divided out the shares. The pearls were all more or less the same size, about as big as a good pea. She put three aside for the chief, then three for me, two for her, and five for Lali. Lali took the three and gave them to me. I took them and handed them to the wounded Indian. He didn't want to take them, but I opened his hand and closed it over the pearls. Then he accepted them. His wife and daughter had been silently watching from a distance; at this they burst out laughing and came to join us. I helped carry the Indian to his hut.

This scene was repeated for close on a fortnight. Every time,

I handed over the pearls to the fisherman. Yesterday I kept one for myself, one out of the six that came to my share. When we got home I made Lali eat it. She was wild with delight and she sang all that afternoon. From time to time I went to see the white Indian. He told me to call him Zorrillo, which means little fox in Spanish. He told me the chief had asked him to ask me why I didn't tattoo the tiger's head for him, and I explained it was because I couldn't draw well enough. With the help of the dictionary I asked him to bring me a mirror with a surface as big as my chest, some transparent paper, a fine brush and a bottle of ink, and some carbon paper. Or if he couldn't get carbon paper, then a thick, very soft pencil. I also told him to bring me clothes of my size and to leave them at his place, together with three khaki shirts. I learnt that the police had questioned him about Antonio and me. He'd told them that I had crossed the mountains into Venezuela and that Antonio had died of a snake bite. Zorrillo also knew that the Frenchmen were in prison at Santa Marta.

In Zorrillo's house there was just the same mixture of things as I had seen in the chief's hut – a whole pile of earthenware pots decorated with the patterns the Indians loved, very artistic pots, both in their shapes and in their patterns and colours; splendid pure wool hammocks, some quite white and others coloured and fringed; the tanned skins of snakes, lizards and huge bull-frogs; baskets, some woven of white creepers and others of coloured. He told me that all these things were made by Indians of the same race as my tribe, but living in the forest, far inland, twenty-five days' march into the bush from here. That was where the coca-leaves that he gave me came from. He gave me more than twenty: whenever I felt low I was to chew one. When I left Zorrillo I asked him to get me all the things I had written down, and if he could some papers and magazines in Spanish, for with my dictionary I had learnt a lot in these two months. He had no news of Antonio: he only knew there had been another clash between coastguards and smugglers. Five coastguards and one smuggler had been killed and the boat had not been taken. I had never seen a drop of alcohol in the village, apart from that fermented fruit-juice stuff. Noticing a bottle of anis I asked him to give it to me. He wouldn't. If I liked I could drink it there, but not take it away. He was a wise man, that albino.

I left Zorrillo and went off on an ass he'd lent me – it would go home of its own accord the next day. The only things I took with me were a big bag of different-coloured sweets, each wrapped in thin paper, and sixty packets of cigarettes. Lali was waiting for me about two miles from the village, with her sister; she made no scene of any kind and consented to walk beside me, arm in arm. Now and then she stopped and kissed me on the lips in the civilized way. When we got there I went to see the chief and gave him the sweets and the cigarettes. We sat in front of the door, facing the sea. We drank the fermented stuff, cool out of its earthenware jars. Lali sat on my right with her arms round my thigh, and her sister in the same position on my left. They sucked away at the sweets. The bag was open there in front of us, and the women and children quietly helped themselves. The chief pushed Zoraïma's head towards mine and made me understand that she wanted to be my woman like Lali. Lali held her breasts in her hands and then pointed to Zoraïma's little bosom to show that that was the reason I didn't want her. I shrugged and everybody laughed. I could see Zoraïma was very miserable. I smoked a few cigarettes: the Indians tried them but soon threw them away and returned to their cigars, the lighted end inside their mouths. When I had said good-bye to everyone I went, taking Lali by the arm. But she would walk behind me and Zoraïma followed. We cooked some large fish over the embers – that was always a treat. And I buried a five-pound crayfish in the hot ashes; it was a delight to eat its tender flesh.

I received the mirror, the tracing paper and the carbon, a tube of glue that I hadn't asked for but that might come in handy, several medium-hard pencils, the pot of ink and the brush. I hung the mirror so that it was chest-height when I was sitting down. The tiger's head showed in it, life-size with all its details. Inquisitive and interested, Lali and Zoraïma watched me. I followed the outlines with the brush, but as the ink ran I turned to the glue and mixed them together. From then on everything went well. In three sittings of an hour apiece I managed to fix an exact copy of the tiger's head on the looking-glass.

Lali went to fetch the chief: Zoraïma took my hands and put them on her breasts. She looked so unhappy and longing and her eyes were so full of love and desire that hardly knowing what I was at I had her, there on the ground, in the middle of

171

the hut. She groaned a little but her body, all taut with pleasure, clasped me tight and would not let me go. Gently I disentangled myself and went to bathe in the sea, for I was all covered with earth: she came after me and we bathed together. I washed her back and she washed my legs and arms, and then we returned to the house together. Lali was sitting just where we had lain and when we came in she understood what had happened. She got up, put her arms round my neck and kissed me lovingly, and then she took her sister by the arm and made her go out by my door. Lali turned round and went out by hers. I heard knocking outside and when I went out I found Lali, Zoraïma and two other women trying to make a hole in the wall with an iron bar. I gathered that they were going to make a fourth door. So that it should not crack except where they wanted it too, they were wetting it with the watering-can. Presently the door was made. Zoraïma pushed the rubble out: from now on she alone would come and go by this opening – never again would she use mine.

The chief came with three other Indians and his brother, whose leg was almost healed. He looked at the drawing on the mirror and he looked at his own reflection. He was astonished at seeing the tiger so well drawn and at the sight of his own face. He did not understand what I meant to do. When everything was dry, I put the glass on the table with tracing-paper over it and I began copying. This was very easy and it went fast – the pencil ran accurately along all the lines. Before the interested gaze of all present. I produced a drawing as perfect as the original in under half an hour. One after the other they all took the sheet and inspected it, comparing the tiger on my chest with the one on the paper. I made Lali lie on the table, wetted her just a little with a damp cloth, put a piece of carbon-paper on her belly and then the sheet I had just drawn on over it. I drew a few strokes, and when they saw a small part of the drawing reproduced on Lali's skin they were all utterly amazed. It was only then that the chief grasped that it was for him I was taking all this trouble.

Human beings who do not have the hypocrisy of a civilized upbringing react naturally, as soon as they understand what is going on. It's in the living present that they're pleased or angry, happy or sad, concerned or indifferent. There is a striking superiority about pure-blooded Indians like these Goajiras. They outdo us in everything; if once they have adopted someone, everything they posses is his; and if he does the least thing for them, their very quick feelings are extraordinarily moved. I decided to trace the main outlines with a razor so that from the first sitting the chief features should be there, fixed for good in tattoo. I'd go over it all again afterwards, with three needles fixed in a little stick. The next day I began my work.

Zato lay on the table. When I had traced the drawing on a stronger piece of white paper I transferred it to his skin, which I had already prepared with a white clay wash that had been allowed to harden. It all came out quite perfect, and I let it dry thoroughly. The chief lay there stretched stiffly on the table, neither wincing nor even moving his head, so afraid was he of spoiling the picture, which I showed him in the mirror. I began on the lines with the razor. There was very little blood and each time a little showed I wiped it away at once. When I had gone over the whole thing very thoroughly, so that the drawing was replaced by thin red lines, I daubed his entire chest with blue ink. The blood prevented the ink taking only in the places where I had gone a little too deep, but almost all the picture stood out wonderfully. A week later Zato had his open-mouthed tiger's head with its pink tongue, white teeth and black eyes, nose and whiskers. I was pleased with my work: it was better than my own tattoo and its colours were livelier. When the scabs came off I went over some places again with the needles. Zato was so pleased he asked Zorrillo to get six more looking-glasses, one for each hut and two for his.

Days, weeks and months went by. We were in April, and now I had been here four months. My health was splendid. I was strong, and now that I was used to going barefoot I could go great distances without getting tired, hunting the big green lizards. I forgot to say that after my first visit to the medicine-man I asked Zorrillo to bring me iodine, peroxide, cotton-wool, bandages, quinine tablets and Stovarsol. I had once seen a convict in hospital with an ulcer as big as the medicine-man's. Chatal, the orderly, crushed a tablet of Stovarsol and put it on it. I sent the medicine-man the little wooden knife and he answered by sending me his. It was hard work to persuade him to be treated, and it took a long time. But after a few goes the ulcer was smaller by half: then he continued the treatment on his own, and one fine day he sent me the big knife so I should come and see that it was completely healed. Nobody ever knew that it was me who had cured him.

My wives never left me. When Lali was fishing, Zoraïma was with me. If Zoraïma went off to sea, Lali stayed to keep me company.

Zato had a son. His wife went down to the beach when her pains began: she chose a big rock that sheltered her from all eyes and another of Zato's wives took her a large basket with maize-cakes, fresh water and papelon, which is unrefined brown sugar, in five-pound loaves. She must have had the child about four in the afternoon, for at sunset there she was calling out as she came towards the village, holding the baby high in the air. Before she reached him, Zato knew it was a boy. It seemed to me they said that if it had been a girl she wouldn't have raised it in the air and called out happily, but would have come quietly, just holding the baby in her arms. Lali explained it all in pantomime. Zato's wife came forward, then having held up her child she stopped. Zato held out his arms, shouting, but he did not move. Then she got up, came forward another few yards, held up the child, called out, and stopped again. Once again Zato shouted and held out his arms. This happened five or six times during the last thirty or forty yards. Still Zato never stirred from the doorway of his hut. He stood in front of the main door, with everybody to his right and left. The mother stopped no more than five or six paces off: she lifted her baby high and cried out. Now Zato stepped forward, took the child under the arms and raised it high in his turn: he shouted three times, and three times he lifted it up. Then he set the child on his right arm, laid it across his chest and put its head under his armpit, hiding it with his left arm. He walked into his hut by the main door, never turning round. Everybody followed him, the mother coming last. We drank everything there was in the way of fermented juice.

All that week they sprinkled the ground in front of Zato's hut, and the men and women pounded the earth by stamping it. In this way they formed a very large circle of thoroughly tamped red clay. The next day they put up a great tent made of bullocks' hides and I guessed there was going to be a feast. Under the shelter they arranged at least twenty huge jars full of their favourite drink. Stones were set out, and all round them piles of wood, both green and dry, that mounted every day. A good deal of this wood had been cast up long ago by the sea; it was dry, white and polished. There were some very big trunks that had been rolled up far from the waves God knows how long ago. Upon these stones they set up two forked pieces of wood both the same height: these were the holders for an enormous spit. Four turned-over turtles; more than thirty live lizards, each as huge as the last and all with their feet and claws tied so they could not get away; two sheep: all this meat was there waiting to be knocked on the head and eaten. And at least two thousand turtle eggs.

One morning about fifteen horsemen arrived; they were all Indians wearing necklaces, very wide straw hats, loin-cloths and sleeveless sheepskin jackets with the wool turned in; their feet, legs and buttocks were naked. They all carried huge daggers in their belts, and two of them had double-barrelled guns. Their chief had a repeating rifle, a splendid jacket with black leather sleeves and a full cartridge-belt. The horses were beautiful: small, but very muscular, and all dapple grey. They carried bundles of hay on their cruppers. They announced their coming from a great way off by firing their guns, but as they came on at a full gallop they were with us very soon. The chief was wonderfully like a somewhat older version of Zato and his brother. He dismounted from his splendid horse and came towards Zato: each touched the other's shoulder. He went into the house alone and came out again holding the baby and followed by Zato. He held it out towards everybody and then he made the same motion as Zato: when he had held it out to the east, where the sun rose, he hid it under his left arm and went back into the house. Then all the other horsemen dismounted; they hobbled their horses a little way off and hung the bundle of hay from their necks. At about noon the Indian women arrived, in a huge waggon pulled by four horses. The driver was Zorrillo. In the waggon there were at least twenty young Indian girls, and seven or eight children, all of them little boys.

Before Zorrillo arrived I had been introduced to all the horsemen, starting with the chief. Zato pointed out that the little toe of his left foot was bent over the one next to it: his brother had the same thing, and so did the chief who had just come. After that he showed me that each of them had the same black mark, like a mole, under his arm. I gathered that the newcomer was his brother. Everyone greatly admired Zato's tattooing, particularly the tiger's head. All the Indian women who had just come had different-coloured patterns on their faces and bodies. Lali put coral necklaces round the necks of some of these girls, and strings of shells round others. I noticed one lovely Indian girl; she was taller than the rest, who were rather on the short side. She had the profile of an Italian – you would have said a cameo. Her hair was blue-black; her enormous eyes were a perfect jade-green and they had very long lashes and beautifully curved brows. She wore her hair in the Indian style – fringe, parting in the middle, and hair falling each side of her face and covering her ears. It was cut short a handsbreadth from the middle of her neck. Her very firm breasts started close together and spread most beautifully.

Lali introduced me and carried her off to our house with Zoraïma and another young girl who was carrying little pots and a kind of brush. For indeed the visiting Indian girls meant to paint those belonging to our village. I was there while the very pretty girl carried out a masterpiece on Lali and Zoraïma. Their brushes were made of a twig with a little piece of wool at its tip. She dipped it into various colours to make her pictures. Then I took up my brush, and starting at Lali's navel I drew a plant whose two branches went to the beginning of her breasts, and then I painted pink petals and put yellow on her nipples. It looked like a half-open flower with its pistil. The three others wanted me to do the same for them. I thought I had better ask Zorrillo. He came and told me I could paint them however I liked so long as they were willing. What did I leave undone! For more than two hours I painted all the visiting girls' bosoms and all the others' too. Zoraïma insisted upon having exactly the same picture as Lali. Meanwhile the men had been roasting the sheep on the spit, while two turtles, cut up, were cooking on the embers. The meat was a fine red – you might have taken it for beef.

I sat under the awning next to Zato and his father. The men ate on one side, and the women, apart from those who served us, on the other. Very late that night the feast ended with a sort of dance. For the dancing an Indian played a wooden flute that yielded a sharp, monotonous sound, and beat on two sheepskin drums. Many of the men and women were drunk, but nothing at all unpleasant happened. The medicine-man had come on his ass. Everyone looked at the pink scar where the ulcer had been – an ulcer known to one and all so they were astonished to see it healed. Zorrillo and I were the only ones to know what had really happened. Zorrillo told me the chief of the visiting tribe was Zato's father and that his name was Justo, which means Just. He was the one who judged the disputes that arose between the people of his own tribe and the other tribes of the Goajira nation. He also told me that when there were difficulties with the Iapus, another Indian nation, they all met to discuss whether they should have a war or whether they should settle things in a friendly way. If an Indian was killed by the member of another tribe and they wanted to avoid war, it would be agreed that the killer should pay for the death of the man of the other tribe. Sometimes it would go as high as two hundred head of cattle, for in the mountains and the foothills all the tribes had a great many cows and steers. Unfortunately they never vaccinated against foot-and-mouth disease and the outbreaks killed great numbers. From one point of view, said Zorrillo, it was a good thing, because if it weren't for these diseases there would be too many of them. The cattle would not officially be sold in Colombia or in Venezuela; they must always stay in the Indian territory in case they should bring foot-and-mouth into the two countries. But, said Zorrillo, there was a great deal of smuggling of cattle across the mountains.

Justo, the visiting chief, told me through Zorrillo to come and see him in his village, where there were more than a hundred huts, it seemed. He told me to come with Lali and Zoraïma and he would give me a house for us, and to bring nothing, because he would provide all we could need. He said I should just bring my tattooing things to do a tiger's head on him too. He took off his black leather wrist-band and gave it to me. According to Zorrillo this meant a great deal: it was the same as saying he was my friend and that he would have no strength to refuse anything I asked. He asked me if I should like a horse; I said yes, but I couldn't have one here because there was almost no grass. He said Lali and Zoraïma could go and fetch some whenever it was necessary, half a day's ride off. He said just where and explained that the grass in that place was long and good. I accepted the horse and he said he would send it presently.

I took advantage of Zorrillo's long visit to tell him I relied upon him and that I hoped he would not betray my idea of going off to Venezuela or Colombia. He told me of the dangers of the twenty miles on either side of the frontiers. According to what the smuggler said, the Venezuelan side was more dangerous than the Colombian. What's more, he could go with me almost as far as Santa Marta on the Colombian side; he added that I had already travelled over that road and that in his opinion Colombia was the right choice. He agreed I ought to buy another dictionary, or rather books for learning Spanish with everyday phrases in them. As he saw it, it would be a very good thing if I learnt to stammer a great deal: people would get irritated listening to it and they'd finish my sentences themselves, without paying much attention to the accent or pronunciation. We decided on that: he would bring me the books and the most accurate map he could get, and he also undertook to sell my pearls for Colombian money when the time came. Zorrillo told me that the Indians, from the chief downwards, would be for me in my decision to go, since that was what I wanted; they would be sorry about it, but they would understand it was natural for me to want to go back to my own people. The difficulty would be Zoraïma and even more Lali. Both one and the other, but above all Lali, was perfectly capable of shooting me. And then again I learnt something I hadn't known, still from Zorrillo – Zoraïma was pregnant. I hadn't noticed a thing: so I was amazed.

The feast was over, everybody had gone home, the hide tent was taken down and everything returned to what it had been, at least on the surface. My horse came, a splendid dapple-grey with a tail that almost touched the ground and a wonderful silvery-grey mane. Lali and Zoraïma were not at all pleased, and the medicine-man sent for me to tell me they had asked him whether they could, without danger, give the horse ground glass so it should die. He had told them not to do that because I was protected by some Indian saint or other and therefore the glass would go back to their own bellies. He said he thought there was no danger any more, but he wasn't dead certain. I was to take care. And what about me? No, he said. If they saw me making serious preparations for going, then all they were likely to do was to shoot me, particularly Lali. Could I try to persuade them to let me go, saying I should come back? No, no, not at all: I must never show I wanted to be off.

It was possible for the medicine-man to tell me all this because he had made Zorrillo come the same day, and he acted as interpreter. Zorrillo was of the opinion that things were too serious not to take all possible precautions. I went home. Zorrillo had both come to the medicine-man's place and left by a completely different road from mine. No one in the village knew that the medicine-man had sent for me at the same time as Zorrillo.

Six months had passed now, and I was impatient to get away. One day I came back and found Lali and Zoraïma studying the map. They were trying to make out what the shapes meant. What worried them most was the rose with its arrows showing the four cardinal points. They were uneasy; they guessed that this paper had something very important to do with our lives.

Zoraïma really began to look pregnant. Lali was rather jealous and she obliged me to make love at any hour of the day or night and in any convenient place. Zoraïma also wanted to be made love to, but fortunately only at night. I went to visit Justo, Zato's father; and Lali and Zoraïma went with me. Luckily I had kept my drawing, and I used it to trace the tiger's head on his chest. In six days it was done, for the first scabs had come off very quickly, thanks to his washing with water in which he had put a little piece of quicklime. Justo was so pleased that he gazed at himself in the mirror several times a day. Zorrillo came while I was staying there. Having asked my permission he spoke to Justo about my plan, because I wanted my horse to be changed. The dapple-grey Goajira horses did not exist in Colombia, but Justo had three reddish-brown ones, and they were Colombian. The moment Justo knew my scheme he sent for these horses. I chose the one that seemed to me the quietest; and he had a saddle, stirrups and an iron bit put on it; for theirs have no saddle and the bit is made of bone. Having set me up in the Colombian fashion, Justo put the brown leather reins into my hand, and there in front of me he counted out thirty-nine hundred-peso gold pieces. He gave them to Zorrillo; who was to keep them and hand them to me the day I left. He wanted to give me his repeating rifle, but I refused; and in any case Zorrillo said I couldn't go into Colombia armed. So then Justo gave me two arrows as long as your finger, wrapped in wool and kept in a little leather case. Zorrillo told me they were poisoned arrows, tipped with a very strong and extremely rare venom.

Zorrillo had never either seen or possessed poisoned arrows. He was to keep them too until I set off. I didn't know what to do to show how grateful I felt for Justo's splendid generosity.

Through Zorrillo he told me he knew a little about my life and that the part he didn't know must be very rich, because I was a complete man. He said this was the first time in his life he had ever known a white man: he had always considered them as enemies before, but now he was going to like them and try to find another like me. 'Think awhile,' he said, 'before going off into a land where you have many enemies; for here, in this land where we are, you have nothing but friends.'

He told me that Zato and he would watch over Lali and Zoraïma; and if he was a boy, of course Zoraïma's child would always have an honourable place in the tribe. 'I don't want to see you go. Stay, and I'll give you that beautiful girl you saw at the feast. She's a virgin, and she likes you. You could stay here with me. You'll have a big hut and as many cows and bullocks as you want.'

I left this open-handed, splendid man and went back to my village. Lali never said a word the whole journey. She was up behind me on the brown horse. The saddle must have been hurting her thighs, but she never once mentioned it. Zoraïma was behind another Indian on horseback. Zorrillo had gone off to his village by another road. It was rather cold during the night. I handed Lali a sheepskin jacket Justo had given me. She let me put it on her without saying a word or showing any emotion. Not a single movement. She let the jacket be put on her, that's all. Although the horse trotted rather hard at times, she never held me round the middle to stay on. When we reached the village and I went off to greet Zato, she took the horse and hitched it to the wall of the house with a pile of grass in front of it, without taking off its saddle and bridle. I spent a good hour with Zato and then went home.

When they are sad, Indian men and even more Indian women have impassive faces – not a muscle stirs; their eyes may be overwhelmed with sadness, but they never weep. They may groan, but they never weep. As I turned over I hurt Zoraïma's belly, and the pain made her cry out. So I got up in case it should happen again and went and lay in another hammock. It was a very low-slung hammock, and as I was lying there I felt someone touch it. I pretended to be asleep, Lali was sitting motionless on a stump of wood looking at me. A moment later I knew that Zoraïma was there: she had a way of rubbing orange-flowers on her skin by way of scent. She got them in little bags, trading with an Indian woman who came to the village now and then. When I woke up they were still there, immobile. The sun was up, and it was almost eight o'clock. I led them down to the beach and I lay there on the dry sand. Lali sat down and so did Zoraïma. I stroked Zoraïma's breasts and belly: she remained quite unmoved. I lay Lali down and kissed her: she closed her mouth. The fisherman came to wait for Lali. At the first sight of her face he understood what was going on and went away. I was really grieved, and the only thing I could think of doing was to stroke and kiss them to show I loved them. Not a single word did they utter. I was deeply upset at the sight of so much pain caused by the mere idea of what their life would be when I was gone. Lali tried to force herself to make love, giving herself to me with a kind of mad despair. What was her motive? There could only be one – to get herself with child by me.

This morning for the first time I saw her jealous of Zoraïma. We were lying in a sheltered hollow in the fine sand on the beach, and I was stroking Zoraïma's bosom and belly while she was nibbling the lobes of my ear when Lali appeared, took her sister by the arm, ran her hand over her rounded belly and then over her own, flat and smooth. Zoraïma got up and, as though she were saying. 'Yes, you're right', she let Lali have her place at my side.

The women gave me my food every day, but they ate nothing themselves. It was three days now since they had eaten anything at all. I took the horse and I very nearly committed a serious error, the first in more than five months – I went to see the medicine-man without asking permission. On the way I realized what I was doing, and instead of going to his tent I rode to and fro two hundred yards from it. He saw me and beckoned to me. As well as I could I made him understand that Lali and Zoraïma were no longer eating anything. He gave me a kind of nut that I was to put in the drinking-water at home. I went back and put the nut in the big jar. They drank several times, but even so they did not start eating. Lali no longer went fishing. Today, after four days of complete fasting, she did something very rash: she went nearly two hundred yards from the shore – swimming, not in a canoe – and came back with thirty oysters for me to eat. Their dumb misery upset me so much I could scarcely eat anything either. It had been going on for six days now. Lali was in bed feverish. In six days she had sucked a few lemons, nothing else. Zoraïma ate once a day, at noon. I no longer knew what to do. I sat there next to Lali. She was lying on the ground on a hammock that I had folded to make a sort of mattress for her: she stared steadily at the ceiling of the hut and never moved. I looked at her; I looked at Zoraïma with her peaked belly; and I don't know why, but I began to weep. For myself maybe? Maybe for them? God knows. I wept, and the heavy tears rolled down my cheeks. Zoraïma saw them and began to moan; at this Lali turned her head and saw me crying. With one spring she got up and sat between my legs, groaning gently. She kissed me and stroked me. Zoraïma put an arm round my shoulders and Lali began talking – talking on and on and moaning at the same time – and Zoraïma answered her. She seemed to be blaming Lali. Lali took a piece of sugar the size of a fist, showed me she was melting it in water, and I drank it off in two gulps. Then she went out with Zoraïma. I heard them pulling out the horse and when I came outside I found it ready saddled and bitted, with the reins round the pommel of the saddle. I took the sheepskin jacket for Zoraïma and Lali put a folded hammock for her to sit on in front. Zoraïma mounted first, almost on the horse's neck, then me in the middle and Lali behind. I was so upset I set off without saying anything to anyone or telling the chief.

I had supposed we were going to see the medicine-man and I set off in that direction; but no, Lali pulled the reins and said 'Zorrillo'. It was Zorrillo we were going to see. As we went, she held me tight by the belt and often she kissed the back of my neck. I had the reins in my left hand, and with my right I stroked Zoraïma. We reached Zorrillo's village just as he was coming back from Colombia with three asses and a horse, all very heavily laden. We went into the house. Lali spoke first, then Zoraïma.

And this is what Zorrillo told me: until the moment I wept, Lali had thought I was a white man who considered her as of no importance whatsoever. Lali knew very well I was going to go; but I was as false as a serpent because never had I told her or tried to make her understand. She said she was very, very deeply disappointed, because she had imagined an Indian girl like her could make a man happy – and a contented man did not go away. She thought there was no point in her going on living after such a disaster. Zoraïma said the same thing, and as well as all that she had been afraid her son would turn

182

out like his father – a false man with no word that could be relied upon, one who asked his wives, who would give their lives for him, things so hard they could not possibly understand him. Why was I running away from her as though she were the dog that had bitten me the day I arrived?

I answered, 'Lali, what would you do if your father was ill?'

'I'd walk over thorns to go and look after him.'

'What would you do, once you could stand up for yourself, to someone who had hunted you like an animal, trying to kill you?'

'I'd look for my enemy everywhere, so as to bury him so far down he'd never even be able to turn in his hole.'

'And when you had done all these things, what would you do if you had two marvellous wives waiting for you?'

'I'd ride back on a horse.'

'That's what I shall do, and that's dead certain.'

'And what if I'm old and ugly when you come back?'

'I'll be back long before you're old and ugly.'

'Yes: you let water run from your eyes. You could never have done that on purpose. So you may leave when you want; but you must go in broad daylight, in front of everybody, not like a thief. You must go just as you came, at the same time in the afternoon, properly dressed like a white man. You must say who is to watch over us night and day. Zato is the chief, but there must be another man to look after us. You must say that the house is still your house and that not a single man except for your son – if it is a man Zoraïma has in her womb – not a single man must ever come into it. Zorrillo must come the day you go. So that he can repeat all you have to say.'

We slept at Zorrillo's. It was a wonderfully soft, warm night. The murmuring and whispering of those two daughters of nature had such moving, loving tones that I was deeply stirred. We rode back all three, going slowly because of Zoraïma. I was to leave a week after the new moon, for Lali wanted to let me know whether it was certain she was pregnant. She had seen no blood the moon before. She was afraid she might be mistaken, but if she still saw none this month it would mean she was with child. Zorrillo was to bring all the things I was to wear: I was to dress there in the village, after I had spoken like a Goajira, that is to say, naked. The day before we were all three to go and see the medicine-man. There was nothing sad about this slow return. They preferred knowing to staying there, abandoned and mocked by the men and women of the village. When Zoraïma had had her child, she would take a fisherman to go out and bring up a great many pearls, which she would keep for me. Lali too would fish longer every day, so as to keep occupied. I was sorry I had not learnt to speak more than a dozen words of Goajira. There were so many things I wanted to tell them that could not be said through an interpreter. We reached the village. The first thing to be done was to see Zato and tell him I was sorry I had gone off without saying anything to him. Zato was as noble-minded as his father. Before I could speak he put his hand upon my throat and said, '*Uilu* (be quiet).' The new moon would be in about twelve days. Together with the eight I was to wait afterwards, that would make twenty before I left.

While I was looking at the map again, altering various details about getting round the villages, I thought over what Justo had said to me. Where could I be happier than here, where everybody loved me? Wasn't I bringing misfortune on myself, going back to civilization? The future would show.

These three weeks flashed by. Lali knew for sure she was pregnant, and it would be two or three children that would be waiting for me to return. Why three? She told me her mother had twice had twins. We went to see the medicine-man. No, my door was not to be shut up. There was to be nothing more than a branch set across it. The hammock in which we all three lay was to be slung from the roof of the hut. They must always go to bed in it together, because now they were only one being. Then he made us sit close to the fire, put on some green leaves and surrounded us with smoke for more than ten minutes. We went home and waited for Zorrillo, who arrived that same evening. We spent the whole of that night talking round a fire in front of my hut. By means of Zorrillo I said something friendly to each man of the village and they all answered with something of the same kind. At sunrise I went in with Lali and Zoraïma. We made love all day long. Zoraïma got on top of me to feel me in her better and Lali wrapped herself round me like a creeper, holding me tight inside her pulsating body – it beat like a heart. The afternoon brought the time for my going. With Zorrillo translating I said, 'Zato, great chief of this tribe that took me in and that gave me everything, I have to say that you must let me leave you for many moons.'

'Why do you want to leave your friends?'

'Because I must go and punish those who have hunted me like a beast. Thanks to you I have been sheltered here in your village, I have lived happy, eaten well, made greathearted friends and had wives who have made the sun shine in my bosom. But all this must not change a man like me into an animal that once it has found a warm dry refuge stays there all its life because it is afraid of fighting and suffering. I am going to face my enemies; I am going to my father, who needs me. I leave my heart here, inside my wives Lali and Zoraïma – the children who are the fruit of our marriage. My hut belongs to them and to my children yet to be born. If any man should forget it, I hope that you, Zato, will remind him. I ask that as well as your eyes, a man whose name is Usli should watch over my family day and night. I have loved you all deeply and I shall love you for ever. I shall do my very best to come back quickly. If I die, carrying out my duty, my thoughts will fly to you, Lali, Zoraïma and my children, and to you, Indians of the Goajira nation, who are my own people.'

I went into my hut, followed by Lali and Zoraïma. I put on a shirt and khaki trousers, with socks and boots.

For a long while I kept my head turned to see every part of this idyllic village in which I had just spent six months. This Goajira tribe, so dreaded both by the other Indians and by the whites, had been a sanctuary for me, a place where I could get my breath, an incomparable refuge against the wickedness of mankind. There I had found love, peace, quietness of mind and greatness of soul. Farewell, Goajiras, wild Indians of the Colombian-Venezuelan peninsula. Your territory is very large, and fortunately its ownership is disputed so that it is free from the interference of the two civilized countries that surround you. Your wild, savage way of living and protecting yourselves taught me something very important for the future – that it was better to be an untamed Indian than a legal official with a degree.

Farewell, Lali and Zoraïma, you incomparable women, so spontaneous and uncalculating, with your reactions so close to nature – at the moment of parting they simply swept all the pearls in the hut into the little linen bag for me. I shall come back, that's dead certain. When? How? I can't tell, but I promise to come back.

Towards the end of the afternoon Zorrillo mounted and we set off for Colombia. I had on a straw hat. I walked along, holding my horse by the bridle. All the Indians in the tribe, every single one, hid his face with his left arm and stretched the right out towards me. This meant they didn't want to see me go because it hurt them too much; and holding out their arms with the hand in the air was a gesture to hold me back. Lali and Zoraïma went with me for a hundred yards. I thought they were going to kiss me when suddenly they turned, and shrieking they ran to our house, never looking back.

Santa Marta Prison

There was no difficulty in leaving the Indian territory of Goajira, and we crossed the La Vela frontier posts without any trouble. On horseback we could make the journey which had taken me so long with Antonio in no more than two days. But it was not only these frontier posts that were extremely dangerous; there was also a seventy-five mile zone as far as Rio Hacha, the village I had escaped from.

In a kind of inn where you could eat and drink I carried out my first experiment in conversation with a Colombian civilian, Zorrillo at my side. I brought it off fairly well; and as Zorrillo had said, a strong stammer did a great deal to disguise accent and manner of speaking.

We set off again in the direction of Santa Marta. Zorrillo was to leave me when we got half way and go back that morning.

Zorrillo left me. We decided he should take the horse back with him. For after all, owning a horse meant having an address, belonging to some given village or other and so running the risk of being forced to answer awkward questions. 'You know So-and-So? What's the name of the mayor? What does Madame X do? Who keeps the fonda?'

No: it was better I should carry on on foot, travelling by lorry or bus, and then after Santa Marta by train. I was to be a *forastero* (stranger) in those parts saying I had just any sort of a job and place of work. Zorrillo changed three of the hundred-peso gold pieces for me. He gave me a thousand pesos. A good workman made eight or ten a day, so just with that alone I had plenty to keep myself for quite a time. I got abroad a lorry that was going very close to Santa Marta, quite a considerable port about seventy-five miles from the place where Zorrillo left me. The lorry was going to fetch goats or kids – I couldn't quite make out what.

Every six or seven miles there was a tavern. The driver got

out and asked me to have a drink. He asked me, but I was the one who paid. And every time he drank five or six glasses of fiery spirits. I pretended to drink just one. By the time we had gone thirty miles he was as drunk as Davy's sow. He was so pissed he took the wrong direction and got into a muddy side road where the lorry bogged down and could not get out. The Colombian didn't worry. He lay down in the back and told me to sleep in the cab. I didn't know what I ought to do. It must still be twenty-five miles to Santa Marta. Being with him meant that I was not questioned by people we met, and in spite of all these stops, I still got along quicker than on foot.

So towards the morning I made up my mind to go to sleep. Day was breaking so it must have been about seven o'clock. And here was a cart pulled by two horses. The lorry prevented it from getting by. Since I was sleeping in the cab they thought I was the driver, and they woke me up. I stammered and put on the look of a man started out of his sleep not rightly knowing which way up he is.

The real driver woke and argued with the man of the cart. After several tries we still could not manage to get the lorry out of the mud. It was in it up to its axles: nothing to be done. There were two black-dressed nuns in the cart, with coifs, and they had three little girls with them. After a great deal of talk the two men agreed to cut a clear space in the bush so the cart could get round, one wheel on the road and the other on the cleared part, thus avoiding the twenty yards of mud.

Each had a machete – a knife for cutting sugar-cane: a tool carried by every man travelling the roads – and they cut everything that stood in the way while I laid it on the road to make it less deep and also to prevent the cart sinking in. In two hours or so the path was ready. It was then that one of the nuns, having thanked me, asked me where I was going. I said, 'Santa Marta.'

'But you're not going in the right direction. You must turn back with us. We'll take you very close to Santa Marta – only five miles from it.'

It was impossible for me to refuse: it would have made me look conspicuous. I should have liked to be able to say I was staying with the driver to give him a hand, but faced with the difficulty of bringing all that out, I preferred saying, '*Gracias, Gracias.*'

And there I was in the back of the cart with the three little girls: the two nuns sat on the seat next to the driver.

We set off and quite quickly covered the three or four miles the lorry had taken by mistake. Once we reached the good road we trotted along, and about noon we stopped at an inn to eat. The three little girls and the carter were at one table and the nuns and I ate at another. The nuns were young, between twenty-five and thirty. Very white skinned. One was Spanish, the other Irish. Gently the Irish one questioned me. 'You're not from here, are you?'

'Oh yes, I come from Baranquilla.'

'No, you're not a Colombian: your hair is too fair and your skin is only dark because it's sunburnt. Where do you come from?'

'Rio Hacha.'

'What did you do there?'

'Electrician.'

'Oh? I've a friend in the electricity company. His name's Perez: he's a Spaniard. Do you know him?'

'Yes.'

'I'm glad.'

At the end of the meal they got up to go and wash their hands and the Irish nun came back alone. She looked at me and then in French she said, 'I shan't betray you but my companion says she's seen your picture in the paper. You're the Frenchman who escaped from the Rio Hacha prison, aren't you?'

Denying it would have been even worse. 'Yes, Sister. I beg you not to give me away. I'm not the wicked type they said. I love God and respect Him.'

The Spanish nun appeared: speaking to her the Irishwoman said, 'Yes.' There was a very quick reply that I didn't understand. They looked as if they were thinking; then they got up and went to the lavatory again. I thought fast during the five minutes of their absence. Should I get out before they came back? Should I stay? It would come to the same thing if they betrayed me, because if I left I'd soon be found. These parts had no really thick bush, and it would take no time to put a watch on the roads leading to the towns. I decided to trust to fate, which so far had not been unkind to me.

They came back smiling all over their faces and the Irish one asked me my name.

'Enrique.'

'Very well, Enrique: you must come with us as far as the convent we're going to, which is five miles from Santa Marta. You needn't be afraid of anything, travelling with us in the cart. Don't speak, and everybody will think you're a workman belonging to the convent.'

The sisters paid for everybody. I bought a tinder-lighter and twelve packets of cigarettes. We set off. All the time we travelled the nuns never spoke to me, which I was grateful for. This way the driver never realized I spoke badly. Towards the end of the afternoon we pulled up at a large inn. A bus was standing there and on it I read Rio Hacha – Santa Marta. I felt like taking it. I went up to the Irish nun and told her I was going to make use of this bus.

'That would be very dangerous,' said she, 'because before we get to Santa Marta there are at least two police posts where they ask passengers for their *cédula* (identity card); and that wouldn't happen in the cart.'

I thanked her heartily, and now the anxiety I'd felt ever since they discovered me vanished entirely. On the contrary, it was a stroke of wonderful luck for me, meeting these nuns. Just as they said, at nightfall we reached a police post (*alcabale* in Spanish). A bus, coming from Santa Marta and going to Rio Hacha, was being inspected by the police. I was lying on my back in the cart with my straw hat over my face, pretending to be asleep. A little girl of about eight had her head on my shoulder, and she really was asleep. When the cart went through the driver stopped his horses just between the bus and the post.

'*Cómo estan por aqui?* (how are you all here?)' asked the Spanish nun.

'*Muy bien, Hermana* (Very well, Sister).'

'*Me alegro, vamos, muchachos.* (I'm glad to hear it; let's go on, children).' And we drove quietly on.

At ten at night, another post, very brightly lit. Two lines of cars of all kinds waiting. One line coming from the right and ours from the left. The boots of the cars were opened and the police looked inside. I saw one woman made to get out; she was scrabbling in her handbag. She was taken off to the police post. She probably had no *cédula*. In that case there was nothing to be done. The cars went by one at a time. As there were two lines there was no possibility of being let through as a favour: there was no space, and so we had to resign ourselves to waiting. As far as I could see I was lost. In front of us there was a little bus crammed with people; on top, luggage and cases, and behind a kind of big net full of all sorts of bundles. Four police made all the passengers get out. The bus had only one door, in front. The men and women all filed through it. Some women carrying babies. And one by one they all got in again. '*Cédula! Cédula!*' And they all brought out a card with a photograph on and showed it.

Zorrillo had never told me about this. If I'd known, maybe I could have tried to get myself a forged one. I said to myself that if only I could get past this post I'd pay any money at all and somehow get hold of a *cédula* before travelling from Santa Marta to Baranquilla, a very large town on the Atlantic coast – two hundred and fifty thousand inhabitants, said my book.

Christ, this bus business was taking a long time. The Irish nun turned round. 'Rest easy, now, Enrique,' she said. Straight away I was furious with her for this incautions word – the driver must surely have heard.

Our turn came and the cart moved forward into the brilliant light. I had decided to sit up. It seemed to me it might look as though I were trying to hide, lying down like that. I leant my back against the slatted tail-board of the cart, facing towards the nuns' backs. I could only be seen from the side and my hat was pretty low down, but not exaggeratedly so.

'*Cómo estan todos por aqui?* (How is everybody here?)' said the Spanish nun again.

'*Muy bien, Hermanas. Y cómo víajan tan tarde?* (Very well, Sisters. Why are you travelling so late?)'

'*Por una urgencia, por eso no me detengo. Somos muy apuradas.* (Because of an emergency, so do not keep us. We are in a great hurry.)'

'*Vayanse con Dios, Hermanas* (Go with God, Sisters).'

'*Gracias, hijos. Que Dios les protege.* (Thank you, my sons. May God protect you.)'

'*Amén* (Amen),' said the police. And we passed quietly on, without anyone asking us anything. A hundred yards farther on the nuns made the cart stop and disappeared into the bush for a while. I was so moved that when the Irish nun got in again I said to her, 'Thank you, Sister.'

She said, 'It was nothing: but we were so frightened it upset our stomachs.'

191

About midnight we reached the convent. A high wall, a great door. The driver went off to stable the horses and cart and the three little girls were led into the convent. On the steps of the courtyard a heated discussion began between the two nuns and the sister in charge of the gate. The Irishwoman told me that she wouldn't wake the Mother Superior to ask her permission for me to sleep in the convent. At this point I was stupid – I didn't make my mind up quickly enough. I ought to have made the most of this incident to get out and leave for Santa Marta – I knew there was only five miles to go.

It was a mistake that cost me seven years of penal servitude.

At last the Mother Superior was woken and they gave me a room on the second floor. I could see the lights of the town from the window: I could make out the lighthouse and the markers in the channel. A big vessel was moving out of the harbour.

I went to sleep, and the sun was up when they knocked on my door. I had had a hideous dream. Lali ripped her belly open in front of me and our child came out in little pieces.

I shaved and washed very quickly. I went downstairs. At the bottom the Irish nun greeted me with a faint smile. 'Good morning, Henri. Did you sleep well?'

'Yes, Sister.'

'Please come along to the Mother Superior's office: she wants to see you.'

We walked in. There was a woman sitting behind a desk. A woman of about fifty or even more with a very severe face: her black eyes looked at me without the least tenderness. '*Señor, sabe usted hablar español?* (Do you speak Spanish?)'

'*Muy poco* (Very little).'

'*Bueno, la Hermana va servir de interprete* (Very well, the Sister will interpret for us). They tell me you are French?'

'Yes, Mother.'

'Did you escape from prison at Rio Hacha?'

'Yes, Mother.'

'How long ago?'

'About seven months.'

'What have you been doing meanwhile?'

'I was with the Indians.'

'What? You with the Indians? I can't accept that. Those savages have never allowed anyone into their territory. Not even one single missionary has been able to get in – just

192

imagine that. I cannot have that answer. Where were you? Tell me the truth.'

'I was with the Indians, Mother, and I can prove it.'

'How?'

'With these pearls they fished up.' My bag was pinned to the back of my jacket: I undid it and passed it over. She opened it and a handful of pearls spilled out.

'How many pearls are there here?'

'I don't know: maybe five or six hundred. About that.'

'This is no proof. You might have stolen them somewhere else.'

'To set your mind at rest, Mother, I'll stay here until you can find out whether there have been any pearls stolen, if you like. I've got some money. I can pay for my keep. I promise I won't stir from my room until you say.'

She looked at me very hard. At the same moment it occurred to me she would be saying to herself, 'And what if you escape? You've already escaped from prison; you'd find it easier from here.'

'I'll leave you my bag of pearls – my whole fortune. I know they're in good hands.'

'Very well, then. But you don't have to stay shut up in your room. You may come down into the garden in the morning and afternoon when my daughters are in chapel. You can eat in the kitchen with the staff.'

I came away from this interview more or less at ease. I was about to go up to my room again, but the Irish nun led me to the kitchen. A big bowl of café au lait, very new black bread, and butter. The nun watched me breakfast, standing there in front of me. She looked anxious. I said, 'Thank you, Sister, for all you have done for me.'

'I'd like to do more, but I can't – nothing more at all, friend Henri,' and with this she left the kitchen.

I sat at the window and I gazed at the town and the port and the sea. The countryside all round was well cultivated. I could not get rid of the notion that I was in danger. So much so that I made up my mind to escape the coming night. Never mind about the pearls: let the Mother Superior keep them for her convent or for herself if she liked! I didn't trust her, and it wasn't likely I was wrong, for how come she, a Catalan, the Mother Superior of a convent and therefore an educated woman, didn't speak French? It wasn't believable. Conclusion:

I'd be off that night. Yes, in the afternoon I'd go down into the courtyard and find out where I could get over the wall. At about one o'clock there was a knock on my door. 'Please come down for your meal, Henri.'

'Yes, I'm coming. Thank you.'

I was sitting at the kitchen table and I had hardly begun to help myself to a dish of meat and boiled potatoes when the door opened and in came four white-uniformed police with rifles and an officer with a revolver.

'*No te mueve, o te mato* (Don't move or I kill you).' He handcuffed me. The Irish nun uttered a great shriek and fainted. Two kitchen-sisters picked her up.

'*Vamos* (Let's go),' said the chief. He took me up to my room. They searched my bundle and straight away they found the thirty-six hundred-peso gold coins I still had, but they put the case with poisoned arrows aside without looking at it – no doubt they thought it was pencils. With a satisfaction he didn't attempt to hide the chief put the gold coins into his pocket. We left. An old crock of a car in the courtyard.

The five police and I crammed ourselves into this contraption and set off at full speed, driven by a chauffeur in police uniform, as black as coal. I was completely overwhelmed and I made no sort of a protest. I was doing all I could to hold myself together: this was no time to be asking for pity or forgiveness – be a man and remember you must never give up hope. All this flashed through my mind. And when I got out of the car I was so determined to look like a man and not like a mouse, and I succeeded so well that the first thing the officer who interrogated me said was, 'This Frenchman is tough all right: he doesn't seem to give a damn about being caught.' I walked into his office. I took off my hat and I sat down without being asked, my bundle between my feet.

'*Tu sabes hablar español*? (Can you speak Spanish, man?)'

'No.'

'*Llame el zapatero* (Call the cobbler).' A few minutes later there appeared a little man in a blue apron, carrying a shoemaker's hammer in his hand.

'Are you the Frenchman who escaped from Rio Hacha a year ago?'

'No.'

'You're lying.'

'I'm not lying. I am not the Frenchman who escaped from Rio Hacha a year ago.'

'Undo his handcuffs. Take off your jacket and shirt, man.' (He took up a paper and looked at it. All the tattooings were described.) 'You lack the thumb of your left hand. Yes. So it's you, then.'

'No it's not me, because it's not a year ago that I left. I left seven months back.'

'It's all one.'

'Maybe it is for you, man. Not for me.'

'I get it: you're the typical killer. French or Colombian, you killers (*matadores*) are all the same — untameable. I'm only the deputy-governor of this prison. I don't know what they'll do with you. For the moment I'll put you in with your companions.'

'What companions?'

'The Frenchmen you brought to Colombia.'

I followed the police, who took me to a cell whose barred windows looked out on to the courtyard. Here were all five of my friends again. We embraced. 'We thought you were out and away for good, mate,' said Clousiot. Maturette wept like the child he was. And the three others were thunderstruck too. The sight of them all gave me back my strength.

'Tell us all about it,' they said.

'Later. What about you?'

'We've been here these three months past.'

'Do they treat you good?'

'Neither good nor bad. We're waiting to be transferred to Baranquilla, where they're going to hand us over to the French authorities, it seems.'

'What a set of swine! And what about making a break?'

'You've hardly got here before you're thinking of getting out!'

'What's so bleeding odd about that? Do you think I'm giving in just like that? Are you very strictly watched?'

'Not all that much by day, but at night there's a special guard for us.'

'How many?'

'Three warders.'

'How's your leg?'

'OK. I don't even limp.'

'Are you always shut in?'

'No, we can take the sun in the yard, two hours in the morning and three in the afternoon.'

'What are the other Colombian prisoners like?'

'It seems there are some very dangerous types, the thieves as bad as the killers.'

I was in the yard that afternoon, talking to Clousiot privately, when I was sent for. I followed the cop into the same office as that morning. There I found the governor of the prison together with the one who'd already questioned me. It was a very dark man who was sitting in the place of honour – he was almost black. From his colour you would have said more black than Indian, and his short curly hair was that of a Negro. He was about fifty: black, wicked eyes. A very short-clipped moustache over the thick lips of a violent, angry mouth. His collar was open – no tie. On the left-hand side the green and white ribbon of some decoration or other. The cobbler was there too.

'Frenchman, you have been retaken after an escape of seven months. What did you do during that time?'

'I was with the Goajiras.'

'Don't you presume to make game of me or I'll have you punished.'

'It's true.'

'No one's ever lived with the Indians. This year alone they've killed more than twenty-five coastguards.'

'No, the coastguards were killed by smugglers.'

'How do you know?'

'I lived there seven months. The Goajiras never leave their own country.'

'All right, maybe it's true. Where did you steal these thirty-six hundred-peso pieces?'

'They're mine. It was the chief of a mountain tribe called Justo who gave them to me.'

'How could an Indian possess a fortune like this and then give it to you?'

'Well, Chief, has there been any robbery with gold hundred-peso pieces in it?'

'No: that's true. There's been no such theft in the reports. But that doesn't mean we shan't make inquiries.'

'Do. It's to my advantage.'

'Frenchman, you committed a serious crime by escaping from the Rio Hacha gaol, and a still more serious one in helping such a man as Antonio to escape be shot for having killed several coastguards. that you are wanted by the French and that you sentence waiting for you. You're a dangerous killer not going to leave you with the other Frenchmen and risk of having you escape again. You're going to be put the black-hole until you leave for Baranquilla. The gold coins will be given back if it is found there's been no such robbery.'

I left the office and they took me to a staircase that led underground. After we had gone down more than twenty-five steps we reached a very dimly-lit corridor with cages to the right and the left. One of the cells was opened and I was shoved in. When the door on to the passage closed a smell of decay rose from the slimy earth floor. I was hailed from all sides. Each barred hole had one, two or three prisoners.

'*Francés, Francés! Que has hecho? Por que esta aqui?*

(What did you do? What are you in for?) Do you know these are the death cells?'

'You shut up! Let him speak,' shouted a voice.

'Yes, I'm French. I'm here because I escaped from the prison at Rio Hacha.' They understood my pidgin-Spanish perfectly well.

'Listen to this, Frenchman: I'll tell you something. There's a plank at the back of your cell. That's to lie down on. On the right you'll find a tin with water in it. Don't waste any, because they only give you a very little in the morning and you can't ask for any more. On the left there's a latrine bucket. Cover it over with your jacket. You won't need a coat because it's so hot, so cover your bucket so it won't smell so bad. We all cover our buckets with our clothes, we do.'

I went to the bars and tried to make out their faces. I could only see the two opposite, right up against the bars with their legs out into the corridor. One was the Spanish-Indian type, like those first police who arrested me at Rio Hacha: the other was a very light-coloured Negro, a handsome young fellow. The Negro warned me that the water rose in the cells at each high tide. I was not to be frightened, because the water never came up higher than your middle. I was not to catch hold of the rats that might climb on to me; I was to hit them. Never catch hold of them if you don't want to be bitten. I said. 'How long have you been in this black-hole?'

'Two months.'

months. If they don't take you out
...ans you're meant to die down here.'
...ere longest – how long has he had?'
...won't last much longer now. This
...en able to get up on to his knees. He
...gh tide and he'll drown.'
...en, in this country of yours?'
...re civilized, did I? Yours is no more
civ... ...ou've got a life sentence. Here in Colombia it's ei... ...ty years or death. But never life.'

'Well, there you are, then. It's much the same everywhere.'

'Did you kill many people?'

'No. Only one.'

'That's not possible. For just one man you never get a sentence like that.'

'I give you my word it's true.'

'Well, then, your country's as savage as mine, don't you see?'

'OK, we won't argue about our countries. You're right. The police are shits everywhere. And what did you do?'

'I killed a man, his son and his wife.'

'Why?'

'They'd given my little brother to a sow to eat.'

'Christ above! It's not possible!'

'My little brother – he was five – used to throw stones at their boy every day, and he'd hit him on the head a good many times.'

'Still, that's no reason.'

'That's what I said when I found out.'

'How did you find out?'

'My little brother had been gone, missing for three days, and when I was searching for him I found one of his sandals in the dunghill. This dung came from the sow's stye. I raked through the muck and I found a bloodstained white sock. I knew what that meant. The woman confessed before I killed them. I made them say their prayers before I shot them. With the first shot I broke the father's legs.'

'You were quite right to kill them. What are you going to get?'

'Twenty years at the outside.'

'Why are you in the black-hole?'

'I hit a policeman belonging to their family. He was here in this prison. They've taken him away. He's not here any more, so I'm easy in my mind.'

The passage door opened. A warder came in with two prisoners who were carrying a wooden tub on two wooden poles. Behind them, right at the back, you could just see the shape of two more warders with rifles. They went along cell by cell, emptying the buckets into the tub. The stench of excrement and urine filled the air until you choked. No one spoke. When they reached me the one who took my bucket dropped a little packet on the ground. Quickly I shoved it farther into the darkness with my foot. When they had gone I found two packets of cigarettes in the parcel, a tinder-lighter and a note in French. First I lit two cigarettes and tossed them to the guys opposite. Then I called my neighbour, who held out his hand and caught cigarettes and passed them on to the others. When I'd handed them out I lit my own and tried to read the note by the corridor light. But I couldn't manage. So then I made a roll of the wrapping paper, and after a good many tries I got it to light. Quickly I read, 'Keep your heart up, Papillon. Rely on us. Look out for yourself. Tomorrow we'll send you paper and pencil so you can write. We're with you to the death.' How that note comforted me and warmed my heart! I was not alone any more, since my friends were there and I could count on them.

No one spoke. Everybody was smoking. Handing out these cigarettes showed me there were nineteen of us in these death cells. Well, here I was on the way down the drain again; and this time I was up to the neck in it. These Little Sisters of the Lord were rather sisters to the Devil. And yet it couldn't possibly have been the Irishwoman or the Spanish nun who betrayed me. Oh what a God-damned fool I had been to believe in those nuns! No, not them. Maybe the carter? Two or three times we had been careless, talking French. Might he have heard? What did it matter? You've copped it this time cock; and you've copped it good and proper. Nuns, driver, Mother Superior – it all comes to the same thing in the end.

Fucked is what I am, down here in this stinking cell that floods twice a day, it seems. The heat was so stiffing I first took off my shirt and then my trousers. And my shoes, and I hung everything on the bars.

And to think I had gone fifteen hundred miles just to end

up here! What a very brilliant success. Dear God. Are You going to abandon me now, You who have been so open-handed with me? Maybe You're angry: for after all You did give me freedom – the most certain, the most beautiful kind of freedom. You had given me a community that took me to its heart. You gave me not just one but two splendid wives. And You gave me the sun, and the sea. A hut where I was the unquestioned master. That primitive, natural life – very simple, but Lord how sweet and gentle. What an unrivalled gift You gave me – freedom, with no police, no judges, no back-biters or evil men around me! And I didn't know how to value it at its true worth. The sea so blue that it was almost green or black; those sunrises and sunsets that made everything swim in such gentle, peaceful serenity; that way of living without money, where I lacked nothing a man really wants – I had despised it all: I had trampled it underfoot. And all for what? For a society that wanted nothing to do with me. For people who would not even trouble to find out whether there was some good in me. For a world that rejected me – that would not even give me the smallest hope. For a community that only thought of one thing: wiping me out at any price.

When they heard of my recapture, how they'd laugh, those twelve bastards on the jury, that lousy Polein, the cops and the prosecuting counsel. For there'd certainly be some journalist who'd send the news to France.

And what about my family? They must have been so happy when the gendarmes came to tell them their son or brother had escaped from his gaolers! Now they would have to suffer all over again at the news that I was retaken.

I'd been wrong to abandon my tribe. Yes, I could certainly say 'my tribe', because they had all adopted me. I have done wrong and I deserve what is happening to me. But still . . . I'd not escaped just so as to increase the Indian population of South America. Dear Lord, You must understand that I just have to live in an ordinary civilized society once more and prove that I can be a harmless member of it. That's my real destiny – with Your help or without it.

I must manage to prove that I can be – that I am and shall be – an ordinary human being, if indeed not a better one than the other members of some given community or some given country.

I was smoking. The water began to rise. It was almost up to my ankles. I called, 'Black, how long does the water stay in the cell?'

'That depends on the strength of the tide. One hour: two at the most.'

I heard several prisoners saying, '*Está llegando* (Here it comes)!'

Very, very gradually the water rose. The half-caste and the Negro had climbed up on their bars: their legs were hanging out into the passage and their arms were round the uprights. I heard a noise in the water: it was a sewer-rat as big as a cat splashing about. It tried to get up the bars. I took hold of one of my shoes and when it came towards me I fetched it a great swipe on the head. It ran off down the corridor, squealing.

The Negro said to me, 'You've started hunting already, Francés. You've got a lot on your plate if you want to kill them all. Climb on to the bars, drape yourself round them and take it easy.'

I took his advice, but the bars cut into my thighs: I couldn't stand the position for long. I uncovered my bucket-latrine, tied my jacket to the irons and then sat on it. It formed a kind of seat that made the position more bearable, because now I was almost sitting down.

This coming in of the water, the rats, the centipedes and the tiny waterborne crabs, was the most revolting, the most depressing thing a human being could possibly have to bear. A good hour later, when the water ebbed away, it left half an inch of slimy mud. I put on my shoes, so as not to have to paddle in this filth. The black chucked me a four-inch piece of wood, telling me to sweep the mud out into the passage, starting first by the plank I was to sleep on and then at the back of the cell. This took me quite half an hour, and it forced me to think of what I was doing and nothing else. That was already something. There'd be no more water until the next tide, that is to say I'd have just eleven hours, since it was only during the last hour that it came in. Before we had it again I should have to reckon the six hours of the ebb and the five of the flood. A thought came to me – a rather absurd idea. 'Papillon, it's your fate to be linked to the tides. The moon is very important for you and your life, whether you like it or not. It was the flood and the ebb tides that let you get down the Maroni so easily when you escaped from penal. It was by working out the time of the tide that you left Trinidad and Curaçao. And the reason why you were arrested at Rio Hacha was that the tide wasn't strong enough to sweep you out quick enough: and now here you are, at the mercy of this tide for good and all.'

If one day these pages are printed, maybe some of their readers will feel a little pity for me when they learn what I had to bear in the Colombian black-hole. Those people are the good ones. The others, first cousins to the twelve bastards who found me guilty, or the prosecuting counsel's brothers, will say, 'It serves him right: he only had to stay in penal and it'd never have happened.' Well, whether you're one of the good guys or whether you're one of the bastards, would you like me to tell you something? I was not in despair, not at all: indeed I'll go farther and say I'd rather have been in the cells of that old Colombian fortress, built by the Spanish Inquisition, than in the Iles du Salut, where I ought to have been. Here there was a good deal still that I could try for carrying on with my break; and even in this rotting hole I was still at least fifteen hundred miles from the penal settlement. They were really going to have to take remarkable precautions to make me go all those fifteen hundred miles in reverse. There was only one thing I regretted – my Goajira tribe, Lali and Zoraïma, and that freedom in a life of nature. Without the comfort a civilized man looks for to be sure, but without police or prisons either, still less black-holes. I reflected that it would never occur to my savages to inflict a punishment of this kind on an enemy, far less to someone like me, who had never done the Colombians the slightest harm.

I lay down on the plank and I smoked two or three cigarettes at the back of my cell so the others shouldn't see. When I gave the black back his piece of wood I also tossed him a lighted cigarette and he, feeling awkward because of the others, did the same. These details may seem to have no sort of importance at all, but as I see it they meant a great deal. It proved that we, the outcasts of society, did at least possess the remains of a sense of right behaviour and consideration for others.

This place wasn't like the Conciergerie. Here I could dream and let my mind wander without having to put a handkerchief over my eyes to protect them from the glare.

Who could it have been who told the police I was in the

convent? Oh, if I were to find out one day, it'd cost him a packet. And then I said to myself, 'Don't talk balls, Papillon. What with all you've got to do in France by way of revenge, you've not come to this country in the back of beyond to do harm to anyone! Life itself will certainly punish the informer, and if one day you do come back it won't be for revenge but to bring happiness to Lali and Zoraïma and perhaps the children they'll have had by you. If you do come back to this God-forsaken place it'll be for them and for all the Goajiras who did you the honour of accepting you as one of themselves. I'm still on the way down the drain, but even right down in an underwater black-hole I'm still on the run, whether they like it or not – on the way to freedom. That's something that can't possibly be denied.'

I was brought paper, a pencil, two packets of cigarettes. Three days I had been here now. Or rather three nights, because down here it was night all the time. As I lit a Piel Roja cigarette I couldn't but admire the solidarity between the prisoners. The Colombian who gave me the packet was running a hell of a risk. If he was caught, it would be a spell in these same punishment cells for him, that was for sure. He certainly knew it, and agreeing to help me in my martyrdom was not only brave but it showed rare nobility of mind. Lighting the paper as I had done before, I read 'Papillon, we know you're bearing up well. Bravo! Send us news. Much the same with us. A nun who spoke French came to see you, they didn't let her talk to us, but a Colombian says he had time to tell her the Frenchman was in the death cells. She said: I'll come back. That's all. Love from your friends.'

It was not easy to answer, but still I managed to write, 'Thanks for everything. I'm bearing up OK. Write to the French consul – you never know. Let the same one always handle the messages so in case of accident only one's punished. Don't touch the points of the arrows. Long live the break!'

It was not until twenty-eight days later that I was brought out of that loathsome hole, and then it was because of the intervention of the Belgian consul at Santa Marta, a man named Klausen. The black, whose name was Palacios and who got out three weeks after I first came, had the idea of telling his mother, when she came to see him, that she was to warn the Belgian consul that there was a Belgian in the black-hole. The notion came to him one Sunday when he had seen a Belgian prisoner being visited by the consul.

So one day I was taken up to the governor's office, and he said to me, 'You're French, so why do you appeal to the Belgian consul?'

Sitting there in an armchair with a briefcase on his knee there was a gentleman of about fifty: dressed in white, fair, almost white hair; round, fresh, pink face. I grasped the position at once. 'You're the one who says I'm French. I admit I escaped from a French prison, but for all that I'm Belgian.'

'There, you see!' said the little man with a face like a priest.

'Why didn't you say so, then?'

'As far as I could see it had nothing to do with you, because I've not really committed any serious crime on your territory, apart from escaping, which is natural for any prisoner.'

'Bueno. I'll put you with your friends. But, Señor Consul, I warn you that at the first hint of an escape I put him back where he comes from. Take him to the barber and then put him in with his friends.'

'Thank you, Monsieur le Consul,' I said in French, 'thank you very much for having taken this trouble for me.'

'God above! How you must have suffered in that horrible black-hole. Go quickly before this brute changes his mind. I'll come again and see you. Good-bye.'

The barber wasn't there and they took me straight to my friends. I must have looked rather old-fashioned because they never stopped saying, 'Is it really you? It's not possible. What have those swine done to make you look like this? Speak – say something. Are you blind? What's wrong with your eyes? Why do you keep blinking them like that?'

'Because I can't get used to this light. It's too bright for me. My eyes are used to the dark.' I sat down, looking towards the inner part of the cell. 'It's better this way.'

'You smell of rot. It's unbelievable. Even your body smells rotten.'

I stripped and they put my things over by the door. My arms, back, legs and thighs were covered with red bites, like the bites of our bugs at home, and with the places where the tiny crabs that came in with the tide had nipped me. I was horrible: I didn't need a mirror to realize that. These five convicts had seen a good deal, but now they stopped talking, shocked at the state I was in. Clousiot called a warder and said although the barber wasn't there, there was water in the yard. The other told him to wait until it was time to go out.

I went out stark naked. Clousiot brought the clean clothes I was going to put on. With Maturette helping me, I washed and rewashed myself with the black soap of those parts. The more I washed, the more filth came off. At last, after several soapings and rinsings, I felt clean. The sun dried me in five minutes and I put on my clothes. The barber came. He wanted to crop my head: I said, 'No. Cut my hair in the ordinary way and shave me. I'll pay.'

'How much?'

'A peso.'

'Do it well,' said Clousiot, 'and I'll give you two.'

Washed, shaved, with properly cut hair and clean clothes, I felt myself coming to life again. My friends never stopped questioning me – 'And how high did the water come? What about the rats? What about the centipedes? And the mud? And the crabs? And the shit in the pails and the corpses they took out? Were they natural deaths or guys who'd hanged themselves? Or were they police suicides?'

The questions never stopped and so much talking made me thirsty. There was a coffee-seller in the yard. During the three hours we stayed there I drank at least ten strong coffees, sweetened with papelon (brown sugar). This coffee seemed to me the world's finest drink. The Negro of the black-hole opposite came and talked to me. In an undertone he told me about the business of his mother and the Belgian consul. I shook him by the hand. He was very proud of having been at the bottom of my getting out. He went off as happy as can be, saying, 'We'll have another talk tomorrow. That's enough for today.'

My friends' cell looked to me like a palace. Clousiot had a hammock he'd bought with his own money. He made me lie in it. I stretched out crossways. He was amazed, and I told him that the reason he lay longways was that he just didn't know how to use a hammock.

Our days and part of our nights were filled with eating, drinking, playing draughts, playing cards with a Spanish pack, talking Spanish between ourselves and with the Colombian police and prisoners so as to learn the language well. Having to go to bed at nine was not so good. As I lay there all the details of the break right the way from the hospital at Saint-Laurent to Santa Marta came crowding before my eyes; and they called for a continuation. The film couldn't stop there; it had to go on. It'll go on all right. Just let me get my strength back and believe me there'll be more of the story. I found my little arrows and two coca leaves, one completely dry and the other with still a little green. I chewed the green one. They all watched me, astonished. I explained that these were the leaves cocaine was made of.

'You're kidding.'

'Taste.'

'Well, yes: it does numb your lips and tongue.'

'Do they sell it here?'

'Don't know. How do you manage to produce cash, Clousiot?'

'I changed some in Rio Hacha, and since then I've always had it openly.'

'As far as I'm concerned,' I said, 'I've got thirty-six hundred-peso gold pieces with the governor, and each coin's worth three hundred pesos. One of these days. I'll bring the matter up.'

'Why not offer him a deal? They're all broke.'

'You may have something there.'

On Sunday I talked to the Belgian consul and the Belgian prisoner. The prisoner had swindled an American banana firm. The consul said he'd do all he could to protect us. He filled in a form saying I was born of Belgian parents in Brussels. I told him about the nuns and the pearls. But he was a Protestant and he knew nothing about priests or nuns: he was very slightly acquainted with the bishop. As for the coins, he advised me not to ask for them. It was too dangerous. He would have to be told twenty-four hours before we left for Baranquilla 'and

206

then you might claim them in my presence,' he said, 'since there were witnesses, if I have understood you properly.'

'Yes.'

'But at this point don't you claim anything: he might put you back into those horrible punishment cells or maybe even have you killed. These gold hundred-peso pieces are a little fortune. It's not three hundred pesos they're worth, as you think, but five hundred and fifty apiece. So it is an important sum. You mustn't lead the Devil into temptation. As for the pearls, that's something else again. Give me time to think it over.'

I asked the Negro whether he'd like to escape with me, and how, in his opinion, we ought to set about it. His skin turned grey at the mere sound of the word.

'Please, please, man. Don't you even think of such a thing. You put a foot wrong, and what's waiting for you is the most hideous slow death in the world. You've had just a taste of it. Wait until you're somewhere else – Baranquilla, say. But here it'd be suicide. Do you want to die? Keep quiet, then. There's not another black-hole in the whole of Colombia like the one you've been in. So why risk it here?'

'Yes, but it must be fairly easy in this place, with the wall no great height.'

'Hombre, facil o no, don't you count on me. Neither to escape nor even to help you. Not even to talk about it.' And he left me, terror-stricken, saying, 'Frenchman, you're not normal: you're mad to think of such things here at Santa Marta.'

Every morning and every afternoon I watched the Colombian prisoners who were inside for important jobs. They all had murderers' faces, but you felt they were tamed. The fear of being sent to those punishment cells completely paralysed them. Four or five days ago a man was brought out of the black-hole; he was a big guy, a head taller than me, and they called him El Caimán. He had the reputation of being extremely dangerous. I talked to him, and then, after we had walked about in the yard together three or four times, I said, 'Caimán, quieres fugarte conmigo? (Do you want to escape with me?)'

He looked at me as though I was the Devil and said, 'And go back where we came from if we fail? No thank you very much. I'd rather kill my mother than go back there.'

That was my last try. I was never going to talk to anyone about escaping again.

That afternoon I saw the prison governor passing by. He stopped, looked at me, and said, 'How are you?'

'I'm all right: but I'd be better if I had my gold pieces.'

'Why?'

'Because then I could afford to pay a lawyer.'

'Come with me.' And he took me into his office. We were alone. He gave me a cigar – so far so good – and lit it for me – better and better. 'Can you speak Spanish well enough to understand and answer properly if I speak slow?'

'Yes.'

'Good. So you tell me you'd like to sell your twenty-six coins?'

'No, my *thirty*-six coins.'

'Ah, yes, yes. And to pay a lawyer with the money? But there are only the two of us who know you possess these coins.'

'No, there's the sergeant and the five men who arrested me and the deputy-governor who received them before handing them over to you. And then there's my consul.'

'Ha, ha! Bueno. It's really better that plenty of people should know about it – that way we can act right out in the open. You know, man, I've done you a great favour. I've kept quiet. I didn't pass on the requests to the other police chiefs asking whether they knew of any theft of gold coins.'

'But you should have.'

'No. From your point of view it was better not to.'

'Thank you, Governor.'

'You want me to sell them for you?'

'For how much?'

'Why, at the price you told me you'd sold three for – three hundred pesos. You can give me one hundred pesos each for doing you this service. What do you say to that?'

'No. You give me back the coins in lots of ten and I'll give you not a hundred pesos apiece, but two hundred. That'll pay back all you've done for me.'

'Frenchman, you're too sharp. As for me, I'm just a poor Colombian officer, too trusting and not very bright; but you're really intelligent. And too sharp, as I've already said.'

'OK, mate. What reasonable kind of an offer have you got to make, then?'

'Tomorrow I'll send for the buyer, here in my office. He'll look at the coins, make an offer, and we split fifty-fifty. That or nothing. Otherwise I send you to Baranquilla with the coins; unless I keep them here for inquiries.'

'No. Here's my last suggestion. Let the man come here and look at the coins: and then anything over three hundred and fifty pesos each is for you.'

'*Está bien* (All right); *tu tienes mi palabra* (you have my word). But where are you going to put such a lot of money?'

'You'll send for the Belgian consul at the time of payment and I'll give it to him to pay for my lawyer.'

'No. I don't want any witnesses.'

'There's no danger for you. I'll sign a paper saying you've handed me back my thirty-six pieces. Agree to this, and if you act straight with me I'll put you on to another deal.'

'What?'

'Just you trust me. It's as good as the first deal, and in the second we'll split fifty-fifty.'

'*Cual es?* (What is it?) Tell me.'

'Get moving quickly tomorrow, and at five in the afternoon, when my money's safe with the consul, I'll tell you about the other business.'

We had been talking for a long while. By the time I went back to the yard, very pleased with myself, my friends were already shut up in their cell.

'Well, what happened?'

I told them everything word for word. We howled with laughter, in spite of the position we were in.

'What a quick worker, that guy! But you were quicker. Do you think he'll fall for it?'

'I'll lay two to one he's in the bag. Anyone take the bet?'

'No. I think you've got him all right.'

All that night I thought it over. The first deal was as good as through. The second too – he would be absolutely delighted to go and get the pearls back. There remained the third. The third . . . that was going to be when I offered him the whole of my share to let me get a boat from the harbour. I could buy it with the money I had in my charger. Would he resist the temptation? What did I risk? He couldn't even punish me, not after the first two deals. We'd see. Don't sell the bear's skin, etc. You might wait until Baranquilla, Papillon. Why? Bigger town, bigger prison: and therefore better watched, with higher walls. I ought to go back and live with Lali and Zoraïma. I'd escape right away, spend some years there, go to the mountains with the cattle-owning tribe, and then get into touch with the Venezuelans. I must at all costs succeed in this break. All night I worked out how I could carry the third deal through successfully.

The next day things moved quickly. At nine in the morning I was sent for to see a gentleman who was waiting for me at the governor's. When I got there the warder stayed outside: in the office I found a man of about sixty wearing a light grey suit and a grey tie. In his tie there was a big grey and silver-blue pearl, sticking out as though in a jewel case. This lean, dry man was not without a certain style.

'Good morning, Monsieur.'

'You speak French?'

'Yes, Monsieur, I come from the Lebanon. I see that you have some gold hundred-peso pieces. That interests me. Will you take five hundred each?'

'No. Six hundred and fifty.'

'You have been misinformed, Monsieur! The top price is five hundred and fifty.'

'Look, since you're taking the lot, I'll let you have them for six hundred.'

'No, five hundred and fifty.'

To cut it short, we agreed on five hundred and eighty. The deal was through.

'*Qué han dicho*? (What have you been saying?)'

'The deal's through, Governor: five hundred and eighty apiece. The sale goes through just after twelve o'clock this afternoon.'

The dealer left. The governor stood up and said to me, 'Fine. And what is there in it for me?'

'Two hundred and fifty on each coin. You had wanted to make a hundred pesos on each, but I'm giving you two and a half times as much, as you see.'

He smiled and said, 'What's the other business?'

'In the first place let the consul be here after twelve to receive the money. When he's left I'll tell you about the other deal.'

'So it's true there is another?'

'You've got my word.'

'Fine. *Ojalá* (Let it be true).'

At two o'clock the consul and the Lebanese were there. The dealer gave me twenty thousand eight hundred and eighty pesos. I handed over twelve thousand six hundred to the consul and eight thousand two hundred and eighty to the governor. I signed a receipt according to which the governor had given me back my thirty-six gold hundred-peso pieces. When the governor and I were alone again I told him about the incident with the Mother Superior.

'How many pearls?'

'Five to six hundred.'

'She's a bandit, that Mother Superior. She ought to have brought them or sent them back to you, or she ought to have handed them over to the police. I'll denounce her.'

'No. You must go and see her and give her a letter from me, in French. Before mentioning the letter, ask her to send for the Irish nun.'

'I get you. It's the Irish one who must read the French letter and translate it to her. Fine. I'll go.'

'Wait for the letter.'

'Why, that's true! José,' he called through the half-open door, 'get the car ready, with two men.'

I sat there at the governor's desk, and on official prison paper I wrote this letter;

Madame the Mother Superior of the convent,
    c/o the kind and charitable Irish nun,

When God brought me to your house, where I believed I was to receive the help that the Christian faith requires to be given to every fugitive, I entrusted you with a bag of pearls belonging to me, as a gesture to persuade you that I should not steal away from beneath your roof – a roof that shelters a house of God. Some infamous being thought proper to denounce me to the police, who at once came and arrested me in your house. I hope the crawling soul that was guilty of this does not belong to one of the nuns of your convent. I cannot tell you I forgive that vile man or woman, for it would be a lie. On the contrary, I most heartily beg that God or one of His saints will mercilessly punish the person (male or female) who has been guilty of such a shocking crime. I beg you, Madame la Supérieure, to deliver the bag of pearls I entrusted you with to Governor Cesario.

211

I am sure he will most scrupulously pass them on to me. This letter will be a sufficient receipt.

Yours, etc.

As the convent was five miles from Santa Marta the car was back in an hour and a half. The governor sent for me.

'Here we are. Count them and see if any are missing.'

I counted them. Not to see if any were missing, because I didn't know how many there had been in the first place, but to know how many there were now, in the hands of this brute. Five hundred and seventy-two.

'Right?'

'Yes.'

'*No falta?* (None missing?)'

'No. Now tell me what happened.'

'When I got to the convent, there was the Mother Superior in the courtyard. With a policeman on either side of me I said, "Madame, I must speak to the Irish nun in your presence about a very serious matter whose nature you will guess, no doubt."'

'What then?'

'The nun trembled as she read the letter to the Mother Superior. The Superior said nothing. She bowed her head, opened the drawer of her desk and said to me, "Here's the bag and its pearls, untouched. May God forgive the person who was guilty of such a crime against that man. Tell him we pray for him." So there you are, hombre!' ended the governor, beaming.

'When do we sell the pearls?'

'*Mañana* (tomorrow). I don't ask you where they come from: I know you're a dangerous *matador* (killer), but now I also know you're a man of your word and that you're straight. Here, take this ham and wine and French bread with you and drink to this memorable day with your friends.'

'Good night.'

And I came back with a two-litre bottle of Chianti, a seven-pound smoked ham and four long French loaves. It was a banquet. The ham, bread and wine shrank fast. Everybody ate and drank heartily.

'Do you think the lawyer will be able to do something for us?'

I burst out laughing. Poor souls – even they had fallen for

212

that crap about the lawyer. 'I don't know. We must think it over and consider before paying.'

'The best would be to pay only if it works,' said Clousiot.

'That's right. We must find a lawyer who'll agree to that.' And I didn't talk about it any more. I was slightly ashamed.

The next day the Lebanese came back. 'It's very complicated,' he said. 'To begin with the pearls have to be sorted according to size, then by colour, and then by shape – according to whether they're round or baroque.' In short it was not only complicated, but into the bargain the Lebanese said he'd have to bring another possible buyer who knew more about it than he did. In four days the business was finished. He paid thirty thousand pesos. At the last moment I withdrew one pink and two black pearls as a present for the Belgian consul's wife. As good businessmen they at once said that those three pearls alone were worth five thousand pesos. I kept them nevertheless.

The Belgian consul made a fuss about taking the pearls: but he was quite willing to keep the fifteen thousand pesos for me. So there I was in possession of twenty-seven thousand pesos. Now it was a question of carrying the third deal through.

How was I to set about it? What was the right angle? In Colombia a good workman earned between eight and ten pesos a day. So twenty-seven thousand was a lot of money. I must strike while the iron was hot. The governor had had twenty-three thousand pesos. With this twenty-seven thousand on top of it, he'd have fifty thousand.

'Governor, think of a business that would let a man live better than you do – what would it cost?'

'A good business, money down, would cost forty-five to sixty thousand pesos.'

'And what would it bring in? Three times what you get? Four times?'

'More. It'd bring in five or six times my pay.'

'Then why don't you become a businessman?'

'I'd need twice as much capital as I've got now.'

'Listen, Governor, I can suggest a third deal.'

'Don't play the fool with me.'

'No: I'm serious. Do you want my twenty-seven thousand pesos? They're yours whenever you like.'

'What do you mean?'

'Let me go.'

'Look, Frenchman, I know you don't trust me. Before, maybe you were right. But now I've escaped from poverty, or close on; and now I can buy a house and send my children to a paying school. And it's all thanks to you, so now I'm your friend. I don't want to rob you and I don't want you to be killed: I can't do anything for you here, not even for a fortune. I can't help you make a break with any chance of success whatsoever.'

'And what if I prove that that's not true?'

'Why, then we'll see: but think about it thoroughly first.'

'Governor, have you a friend who's a fisherman?'

'Yes.'

'Maybe he could take me out to sea and sell me his boat?'

'I don't know.'

'What would his boat be worth, roughly?'

'Two thousand pesos.'

'Suppose I give him seven thousand and you twenty thousand, would that be all right?'

'Frenchman, ten thousand's enough for me. Keep something for yourself.'

'You go ahead and fix it.'

'You going alone?'

'No.'

'How many?'

'Three altogether.'

'Let me talk to my fisherman friend.'

I was astonished at this character's change towards me. He had a villainous murdering face, but there were some fine things hidden far down in his heart.

In the yard I spoke to Clousiot and Maturette. They said for me to do as I thought best: they were ready to follow. This way of putting their lives into my hands gave me an immense satisfaction. I'd never let them down. I'd be extraordinarily cautious, for I'd taken a great responsibility on my shoulders. But I had to tell our other friends. We'd just finished a domino tournament. It was close on nine o'clock at night. It was the last moment we could still get any coffee. I called 'Cafetero!' and ordered six piping hot coffees.

'There's something I've got to say to you. I think I'm going to be able to make a break again. Unfortunately only three of us can go. It's natural I should take Clousiot and Maturette, the ones I escaped from penal with. If any of you have anything to say against it, let him speak out. I'll listen.'

'No,' said the Breton. 'It's fair enough, whichever way you look at it. To begin with because you all set off from penal together. And then because you'd never have been in this hole if we hadn't wanted to land in Colombia. But still thanks for asking what we think about it, Papillon. Of course you've got the right to do what you say; and I truly hope to God you bring it off, because if you don't it's certain death. And with very fancy trimmings, too.'

'We know that,' said Clousiot and Maturette together.

The governor spoke to me that afternoon. His friend was all right. He asked what we wanted to take with us in the boat.

'A ten-gallon keg of fresh water, fifty pounds of maize flour and ten pints of oil. That's all.'

'Carajo!' exclaimed the governor. 'You'll take to the sea with no more than that?'

'Yes.'

'You're brave, really brave.'

It was in the bag. He was determined to go through with this third deal. Quietly he added, 'Whether you believe it or not, friend, I'm doing this for my children in the first place, and then for you. You deserve it for your bravery.'

I knew it was true, and I thanked him.

'How are you going to manage so that my help doesn't show too much?'

'You won't be involved. I'll leave at night, when the deputy-governor's on duty.'

'What's your plan?'

'You must begin by reducing the night-guard by one man. Then three days later you take off another. When there's only one left you set up a sentry-box opposite the cell door. The first rainy night he'll take shelter in the box and I'll get out by the window behind. As for the lights round the wall, you'll have to find some way of short-circuiting them yourself. That's all I ask you to do. You can do it by tying two stones to a length of copper wire and tossing it over the two electric wires that run from the pole to the row of lights on the top of the wall. As for the fisherman, he must moor the boat by a pad-locked chain, with the padlock already forced so I shan't lose any time, the sails ready to be hoisted and three big paddles to get us out into the wind.'

'But there's a little motor,' said the governor.

'Ah? So much the better. Let him have it ticking over as though he was warming it up and go to the nearest café for a drink. When he sees us coming, he's to stand by the boat in a black oilskin.'

'What about the money?'

'I'll cut your twenty thousand pesos in two – dividing each note. I'll pay the fisherman his seven thousand in advance. I'll give you half the twenty thousand beforehand, and one of the Frenchmen that stays behind – I'll tell you which – will give you the other half.'

'You don't trust me then? That's bad.'

'No, it's not that I don't trust you; but you might muck up the short-circuiting, and then I shan't pay, because without the short-circuit there's no getting out.'

'OK.'

Everything was ready. Through the governor I had given the fisherman his seven thousand pesos. For the last five days there had been no more than a single man on guard. The sentry-box was there and we were only waiting for the rain, which did not come. The bar had been sawn through with blades the governor had supplied and the cut well camouflaged: what's more, it was completely hidden by a cage with a parrot in it – a bird that was just beginning to say 'Shit' in French. We were all on hot bricks. The governor had been given the half notes. Every night there we were, waiting. It would not rain. One hour after the start of a downpour the governor was supposed to short-circuit the current from the outside. Not a single drop: at this time of year it was utterly unbelievable. The smallest cloud seen through our bars at about the right time filled us with hope: but then nothing ever came. It was enough to drive you crazy. For sixteen days now everything had been ready – sixteen nights of waiting up, our hearts in our mouths. One Sunday morning the governor himself came into the yard to fetch me. He took me to his office: there he handed me back the bundle of half notes and three thousand uncut pesos.

'What's the matter?'

'Frenchman, my friend, you've only got tonight. At six o'clock tomorrow you leave for Baranquilla. I'm only giving you back three thousand of the fisherman's pesos because he spent the rest. If God sends rain tonight the fisherman will be waiting for you and you can give him the money when you take the boat. I trust you: I know there's nothing to be afraid of.'

It did not rain.

Breaks at Baranquilla

At six o'clock in the morning eight soldiers and two corporals, commanded by a lieutenant, put handcuffs on us and loaded us into an army lorry for Baranquilla. We did the hundred and twenty-five miles in three and a half hours. By ten we were at the prison they call 'Eighty', in the Calle Medellin at Baranquilla. Such a great deal of effort not to go to Baranquilla, and yet for all that here we were! It was a big town. The chief Atlantic port in Colombia, but lying high up in the estuary of the Rio Magdalena. As for the prison, it was a big one too: four hundred prisoners and close on a hundred warders. It was run just like any European gaol. Two surrounding walls, twenty-five feet high and more.

The top men of the prison welcomed us, with Don Gregorio, the governor, at their head. The prison was organized round four courtyards, two one side and two the other. They were separated by a long chapel where they had services and which also acted as a visiting-room. They put us into the 'highly dangerous' yard. When we were searched they found the twenty-three thousand pesos and the little arrows. I thought it my duty to warn the governor they were poisoned, which hardly made us look like model citizens.

'These Frenchmen even go so far as to carry poisoned arrows!'

For us, being in the Baranquilla prison was the most dangerous point in our whole break. Here we were to be handed over to the French authorities. Yes, Baranquilla (and for us that just meant its huge prison) was the turning point. We must escape whatever it cost – we must stake everything.

Our cell stood in the middle of the yard. It wasn't a cell in any case, but a cage – a concrete roof sitting on top of thick iron bars, with the lavatory in one of the corners. There were about a hundred other prisoners; they were housed in cells built in the four walls surrounding this court, which was about twenty yards by forty; and they could see into the court through their bars. Each set of bars had a kind of metal eave to stop the rain coming into the cell. We six Frenchmen were the only ones to be lodged in this central cage, open day and night to the gaze of the prisoners and, even more, of the warders. We spent the daytime in the yard, from six in the morning until six at night. We could walk in and out of the cells as we liked. We could talk, walk and even eat in the yard.

Two days after we got there we were all six taken into the chapel, where we found the governor, a few police and seven or eight newspaper photographers.

'You escaped from the French penal settlement in Guiana?'

'We've never denied it.'

'What crime led each of you to be punished so severely?'

'That doesn't matter. What does matter is that we've committed no crime on Colombian territory and that your nation is not only refusing us the right to remake our lives but is acting the part of man-hunters or gendarmes for the French government.'

'Colombia feels that she should not accept you on her territory.'

'But I myself and two other comrades were and still are perfectly determined not to live in this country. We were all three arrested far out at sea, not trying to land here at all. On the contrary, we were doing everything we possibly could to get away.'

'The French,' said the journalist belonging to a Catholic paper, 'are almost all Catholics, like us Colombians.'

'It may well be that you people are baptized Catholics, but your way of carrying on is very far from Christian.'

'What do you have against us?'

'You collaborate with the gaolers who are hunting us down. Even worse, you're doing their work for them. You've taken away our boat and everything in it – it all belonged to us, being a present from the Catholics of the island of Curaçao, so magnificently represented by Bishop Irénée de Bruyne. We can't think it right that you should refuse us a chance of redeeming ourselves; and even more than that, you stop us going to some other country at no expense to anyone else – some other country that might perhaps take the risk. That we think is really very wrong.'

'So you're angry with us – you're angry with the Colombians?'

'Not with the Colombians as such, but with their police and legal system.'

'What do you mean?'

'I mean that any mistake can be put right with good will. Allow us to set off by sea for some other country.'

'We'll try to get you permission.'

When we were back in the yard Maturette said to me, 'Well, did you get that? No kidding ourselves this time, man. We're in a hell of a tight corner, and it's not going to be easy to get out of it.'

'Listen,' I said, 'I don't know whether we'd be stronger if we were united, but what I have to say is each can do what he thinks best. As for me, I just have to break out of this Eighty of theirs.'

On Thursday I was called into the visiting-room and there I saw a well-dressed man of about forty-five. I looked at him hard. He was curiously like Louis Dega.

'You're Papillon?'

'Yes.'

'I'm Joseph, Louis Dega's brother. I've seen the papers and I've come to visit you.'

'Thanks.'

'Did you see my brother in Guiana? Did you know him at all?'

I told him exactly what had happened to Dega up until the day we parted in the hospital. He told me his brother was now on the Iles du Salut, a piece of news that had reached him from Marseilles. Visits took place in the chapel, on Thursdays and Sundays. He told me that in Baranquilla there were a dozen Frenchmen who had come to seek their fortune with their women. They were all ponces. There was a special district in the town, where some eighteen whores kept up the best French traditions of refined and skilful prostitution. It was always the same kind of men and the same kind of women from Cairo to the Lebanon, from England to Australia, from Buenos Aires to Caracas, Saigon to Brazzaville, who peddled their ancient speciality, the oldest in the world, prostitution and how to live off it handsomely.

Joseph Dega told me something pretty quaint: Baranquilla's French ponces were troubled in their minds. They were afraid our coming to the prison here might disturb their peace and damage their prosperous trade. And in fact, if one of us got out, or several of us, the police would go and look for them in the French girls' casetas, even if the escaped man had never been there to ask for help. And that might lead indirectly to the police finding out plenty – phony papers, out-of-date or cancelled residence permits, and so on. If they were looking for us they would also check identity-cards and permits. And if some of the women, and even some of the men, were found, it might be very bad for them.

So now I knew just where I was. He added that as far as he was concerned he'd do absolutely anything I asked and he'd come and see me on Thursdays and Sundays. I thanked him: he was a decent fellow and subsequent events showed he really meant what he said. He also told me that according to the papers France had been granted our extradition.

'Well, gents, I've plenty of news for you.'

'What?' cried all five of them in chorus.

'No illusions for us, to begin with. Our extradition is fixed. A special boat is coming from French Guiana to take us back where we came from. Next, our being here is worrying the ponces – French ponces who have settled comfortably in this town. Not the one who came to see me. He doesn't give a damn for what happens, but the other members of the union are afraid that if one of us escapes it may make things awkward for them.'

They all burst out laughing: they thought I meant to be funny. Clousiot said, 'Please, Monsieur Poncio Pilate, may I have your permission to escape?'

'It's not a joke. If any of the tarts come and visit us we must tell them not to come any more. Right?'

'Right.'

As I've said, there were about a hundred Colombian prisoners in our yard. They were by no means fools. There were some really skilful thieves, some elegant forgers, really bright confidence-men, hold-up specialists, drug peddlars and a few highly trained killers – it is a very commonplace calling in America, but these were really practised types. In those parts wealthy men and successful adventurers hire them to act on their account.

There were skins of every colour. From the African black of the Senegalese to the tea-colour of our Martinique Creoles, and from Indian red with blue-black hair to pure white. I made contacts. I tried to gauge the powers and the will to escape of some few picked men. Most were like me – they either feared a long sentence or already had one, and they lived in a continual state of readiness for a break.

Along the top of the four walls of this rectangular court there ran a sentinel's walk that was brilliantly lit by night and that had a little tower at each corner to hold a sentry. So there were four of them on duty day and night, with an extra man in the yard, by the chapel door. This one had no weapons. The food was quite good and many of the prisoners sold things to eat or drink – coffee or fruit-juice – orange, pineapple, pawpaw, etc. – that came in from outside. Every now and then one of these traders would be the victim of an astonishingly rapid attack. Before he knew what was happening there he would be with a big towel wrapped tight round his face to stop him crying out and a blade in his back or at his throat that was ready to go in deep at the slightest resistance. The victim's takings would be gone before he could say knife. As the towel came off so he'd get a crack on the back of the neck. Nobody ever said a word, whatever happened. Sometimes the trader would put his things away – shutting up shop, as it were – and try to find who it was who'd done it. If he did, then there was a fight: with the knife, always.

Two Colombian thieves came to me with a suggestion. I listened very closely. It seemed that in the town there were some police who were also thieves. When they were on duty in a given district, they would tell their accomplices so they could come out and do business there.

My two visitors knew them all, and they told me it would be very unlucky if one of these men didn't come during that week to stand guard at the chapel door. I'd have to get a revolver brought in to me at visiting time. The police-thief wouldn't mind being what he'd call forced to knock on the door leading out of the chapel: this gave on to a little guard-room with four or at the most six men in it. Surprised by us, threatened with the revolver, they couldn't stop us getting out into the street. And then all you'd have to do would be to lose yourself in the traffic, which was pretty dense just there.

I didn't much care for the scheme. If the revolver had to be hidden, it couldn't be a very big one – a 6.35 at the most. With a gun like that there was the danger the guards wouldn't be frightened enough. Or one of them might turn awkward and you'd have to kill him. I said no.

I wasn't the only one to be on fire to do something: there were my friends too. But there was this difference. After a few days of being very low they came round to accepting the idea that the boat coming for us should find us here in the prison. There was no great distance between that and accepting defeat. They even talked about what we might get in the way of punishment back in Guiana, and how we'd be treated there.

'The very sound of all this crap makes me sick,' I said. 'If you want to talk about that sort of future, do it without me: go and discuss it somewhere where I'm not. Only a eunuch would put up with what you call our fate. Are you eunuchs? Is there one of us who's had his balls cut off? If so, just let me know, will you? Because I'll tell you what, mates: when I think of a break out of here, I think of a break for us all. If my brain's bursting with trying to work out just how to set about getting out, it's because I mean us all to get out. And six men – it's not so easy. And I'll tell you something more: as far as I'm concerned – just me – it's easy. If I see the date coming too close and nothing done, I kill a Colombian cop to gain time. They won't hand me back to France if I've killed one of their cops for them. Then I'll have time and to spare. And as I'll be alone, a break will be all the easier.'

The Colombians worked out another scheme, not at all badly put together. At mass on Sunday morning the chapel was always full of visitors and prisoners. First everybody heard mass together, and then when the service was over the prisoners who had visitors stayed on in the chapel. The Colombians asked me to go to mass on Sunday to get a thorough idea of how it was run, so that we could plan our action for the following week. They asked me to lead the revolt. But I refused the honour: I didn't know the men who were to take part well enough.

I said that of the four Frenchmen, the Breton and the flat-iron man didn't want to join. No difficulty there. All they had to do was not to go to church. On Sunday the four of us who were in the plot would go to mass. The chapel was rectangular:

the choir at the far end: a door at either side giving on to the two yards. The main door opened into the guard-room: it had bars, and behind the bars there were a score of warders. And lastly, behind them, there was the gate into the street. As the chapel was crammed, the warders left the barred door open, and while the service was going on they stood there in a tight-packed line. Two men were to come in with the visitors; and weapons were to be brought in at the same time. They were to be brought by women, carrying them between their legs: they would pass them on to the men once everybody was inside. Two heavy revolvers – 38 or 45. A woman would give one to the leader of the plot and then get out right away. The moment the choir boy tinkled his little bell the second time we were all to attack together. I was to put a huge knife to the governor's throat and say, '*Don Gregorio, da la orden de nos dejar pasar, si no, te mato* (give the order to let us pass or I will kill you).'

Another man was to do the same to the priest. From different angles the three others were to train their guns on the warders standing at the barred main door of the chapel. Orders to shoot the first screw who wouldn't throw down his weapons. The unarmed men were to get out first. The priest and the governor would act as a shield for the rearguard. If all went well, the warders' rifles would be on the ground. The men with guns were to make the warders go into the chapel. We'd get out, first closing the barred door and then the wooden one. The guard-room would be empty, because all the men were required to be standing there in the chapel, hearing mass. Fifty yards from the entrance there would be a lorry waiting, with a little ladder behind to get in quicker. It would set off only when the leader had got in. He was to be the last. When I had seen how the mass went, I agreed. Everything had happened just as Fernando had told me.

Joseph Dega was not to come and see me on Sunday. He knew why. He was to get us a car disguised as a taxi so we shouldn't have to get into the lorry, and it would take us to a hide-out that he was also going to get ready. I was all keyed up the whole week, impatient to get moving. Fernando managed to get a revolver in by another route. It was a Colombian Civil Guard 45, a really formidable weapon. On Thursday one of Joseph's women came to see me. She was very sweet; she told me the taxi would be yellow – we couldn't miss it.

'OK. Thanks.'

'Good luck.' She kissed me prettily on both cheeks and it seemed to me she was quite moved.

'*Entra, entra.* Come in and fill this chapel, to hear God's word,' said the priest.

Clousiot could scarcely hold himself in. Maturette's eyes were sparkling and the other man kept right there by me, not an inch away. I was perfectly calm as I went to my place. Don Gregorio, the governor, was there, sitting on a chair next to a fat woman. I was standing against the wall. Clousiot on my right: the two others on my left, dressed so that people wouldn't notice us if we managed to get out into the street. My knife was open and ready, lying along my right forearm. It was held by a strong rubber band and hidden by the sleeve of my khaki shirt, carefully buttoned at the wrist. It is at the moment of the elevation, when everyone bends his head as though he were looking for something, that the choir-boy, having in the first place jangled his little bell, then clinks it three distinct times. The second of these was to be our signal. Each of us knew just what he was to do.

First clink: second . . . I flung myself upon Don Gregorio and clapped the big knife to his long, wrinkled neck. The priest shrieked, '*Misericordia, no me mata* (Don't kill me, for pity's sake).' Without seeing them, I could hear the three others ordering the warders to throw down their rifles. Everything was going well. I took Don Gregorio by the collar of his fine suit and said, '*Sigua y no tengas miedo, no te haré daño* (Follow me and don't be afraid: I'll do you no harm).'

The priest was held there with a razor to his throat, close to my group. Fernando said, '*Vamos, Francés, vamos a la salida* (Let's go, Frenchman. Let's get out).'

Full of triumph and the joy of success I was shoving all my people towards the gate giving on to the street when two rifles went off at once. Fernando fell and so did one of the other armed men. I still pushed on for another yard, but the warders had recovered and they barred our way with their rifles. Fortunately there were some women between them and us – that prevented them from firing. Two other rifle shots, followed by one from a revolver. Our third armed man had been killed, having just had time to fire once, more or less at random, for it was a girl he wounded. Pale as death, Don Gregorio said to me, 'Give me the knife'. I handed it to him. There was no point in going on. In under thirty seconds the whole situation had been reversed.

More than a week later I learnt that the revolt failed because of a prisoner from the other yard who had been watching the mass from outside. The moment things began he told the sentries on the high walk. They jumped down from the twenty-foot wall into the yard, one this side of the chapel and one the other, and through the bars of the side doors they shot the two men standing on a bench and covering the warders. Then a few seconds later they shot the third as he moved through their field of fire. After that there was a terrific hulla-balloo. For my part I stayed beside the governor, who was shouting orders. Sixteen of us, including the four Frenchmen, ended up in irons in the black-hole, on bread and water.

Joseph went to see Don Gregorio. The governor sent for me and said that as a favour to him he was going to put me back in the yard with my friends. Thanks to Joseph we were all of us, including the Colombians, in the yard once more after ten days, and in the same cell. When we got there I asked everyone to pay Fernando and his two dead friends the tribute of a few moments' silence. When Joseph came to see me, he told me he had passed the hat round among all the ponces, who contributed the five thousand pesos he had managed to persuade Don Gregorio with. This gesture raised the ponces in our esteem.

What was to be done now? What fresh ideas were there? For after all I was not going to give in and just wait for the coming of the boat without trying to do something about it.

Lying there in the wash-house, sheltering from the blazing sun, I could watch the sentries on their beat without being noticed. At night, every ten minutes, each one in turn called out 'Sentries, keep watch!' In this way the man in command could check if any one of the four was asleep. If one didn't answer, the other went on with his shout until he did.

I thought I'd found a crack in the system. At each of the boxes that stood at the four corners of the high walk, a tin hung by a string. When the sentry wanted some coffee he would call the cafetero, who would pour two or three cups into the can. All the sentry had to do was to pull it up by the string. Now the box on the far right had a kind of little tower that jutted out somewhat over the yard. It occurred to me that

225

if I could make a fair-sized grapnel and fix it to a plaited rope, it should catch there easily. In a few seconds I could get over the wall and into the street. Just one problem – coping with the sentry. How?

I saw him get up and take a few steps on the high wall. He looked as though he was overcome by the heat – struggling to keep awake. God above, that was it! He'd have to be put to sleep. First I'd make my rope, and then, if I could find a safe hook, I'd dope him and make a dash for it. Two days later I had about twenty feet of rope, made from all the strong linen shirts we could find, particularly the khaki ones. The hook had been fairly easy to come by. It was the thing that held up one of the metal eaves sheltering the cell doors from the rain. Joseph Dega brought me a bottle of a very strong sleeping-draught. The instructions said you were only to take ten drops at a time. The bottle held about six big spoonfuls. I got the sentry used to me giving him coffee. He would lower the can and I would send him up three coffees every time. As all Colombians love spirits and as the sleeping-draught tasted something like anis, I had a bottle of anis sent in.

I said to the sentry, 'Would you like a French coffee?'

'What's it like?'

'It's got anis in it.'

'I'll try. Let's taste it first.'

Several of them tasted my coffee with anis in it and now, when I offered them a cup, they'd say, 'French coffee!'

'All right,' and slosh, I'd pour in the anis.

Zero-hour came round. Noon, on a Saturday. A terrible heat was beating down. My friends knew it would be impossible for two to get over in time, but a Colombian with an Arabic name, Ali, said he'd come up behind me. I agreed. That would prevent any Frenchman from looking like an accomplice and therefore being punished. On the other hand, I couldn't have the rope and the hook on me, because the sentry would have plenty of time to inspect me while I was sending him up the coffee. We reckoned he'd be knocked out in five minutes.

Zero-hour less five minutes. I hailed the sentry. 'OK?'

'Yes.'

'Like a coffee?'

'Yes. French coffee – it's better.'

'Just a minute. I'll fetch some.' I went over to the cafetero. 'Two coffees.' I'd already poured the whole bottle of sleeping-stuff into the can. That'd stretch him out pretty flat! I went to the wall just under him, and he saw me pouring the anis in with a flourish. 'You want it strong?'

'Yes.'

I put in a little more and poured the whole lot into his can: he hauled it up straight away.

Five minutes went by. Ten, fifteen, twenty minutes! And still he wasn't asleep. Worse still, instead of sitting down he took a few paces to and fro, holding his rifle. Yet he had drunk the lot. And at one o'clock the guard would be changed.

On tenterhooks, I watched his every movement. There was nothing to show he was drugged at all. Ha, he'd stumbled! He sat down in front of his sentry-box with his rifle between his legs. His head drooped on to his shoulder. My friends and the two or three Colombians who knew what was up watched his motions as intently as I did.

'Go ahead,' I said to the Colombian. 'The rope!'

He was getting ready to throw it when the guard stood up, dropped his rifle, stretched, and stamped as though he were marking time. The Colombian stopped just before he was seen. Eighteen minutes left before the changing of the guard. Now, in my mind, I began calling for God's help. 'I beg You to help me just once more. I beg You not to abandon me!' But it was in vain I called on this God of the Christians, so awkward sometimes, particularly for me, an atheist.

'It's unbelievable,' said Clousiot, coming close. 'It's unbelievable the bloody fool doesn't go to sleep!'

The sentry went to pick up his rifle, and just as he was bending over it he fell his full length on the walk, as though he had been struck down. The Colombian flung the hook, but it did not take and it fell back again. He threw it up a second time. It held. He tugged to see if it was firm. I checked it and just as I got my feet against the wall to take the first heave and start climbing Clousiot said, 'Hold it! Here's the new guard.'

I just had time to get away before I was seen. With the protective instinct and spirit of solidarity you find among prisoners, a dozen Colombians quickly surrounded me, mixing me in their crowd. We walked away along the wall, leaving the rope hanging there. A man in the new guard caught sight of the grapnel and at the same moment the unconscious sentry lying over his rifle. He ran two or three yards and pressed the alarm, convinced there'd been an escape.

They came for the unconscious man with a stretcher. There were more than twenty police up there on the walk. There was Don Gregorio with them, having the rope hauled up. He had the grapnel in his hand. A few moments later the yard was surrounded by police, their guns pointing. There was a roll-call. After answering to his name, each man had to go back into his cell. Surprise! No one missing! Everyone was locked in, each in his own cell.

Second roll-call and check, cell by cell. No. Nobody had disappeared. At about three o'clock we were let out into the yard again. We heard that the sentry was still snoring, flat out, and nothing they could do would wake him. My Colombian accomplice was as shattered as I was. He had been so sure it was going to work! He raged against everything American, for the sleeping-draught had come from the States.

'What's to be done?'

'Why, start again, hombre!' That's all I could find to say to him. He thought I meant 'start doping another sentry', whereas what I was thinking was, 'Let's find some other way'.

He said, 'Do you think these warders are such simpletons that you'll find another to drink your French coffee?'

Although this was a tragic moment, I could not help laughing. 'Sure, man, sure.'

The sentry slept three days and four nights. When at last he woke up, of course he said it was certainly me who had put him out with my French coffee. Don Gregorio sent for me and brought us face to face. The commander of the guard went to hit me with his sword. I leapt into a corner and defied him. He raised the sabre. Don Gregorio stepped between us, took the blow full on his shoulder and went down. His collarbone was broken. He screamed so loud the officer had no time for any one but him. He picked him up. Don Gregorio roared for help. All the civilian employees came racing in from the nearby offices. The commander, two other policemen and the sentry in question had a pitched battle against a dozen civilians who were trying to avenge their governor. Several men were slightly wounded in this tangana. The only one not to be hurt was me. The great thing was, this was no longer my business but one between the governor and the officer. The governor was carried off to hospital, and his substitute took me back to the yard. 'We'll see about you later, Francés.'

The next day the governor, with his shoulder in plaster, asked me for a written statement against the officer. I said everything he wanted, with pleasure. The story of the sleeping-draught was completely forgotten. They were no longer interested in it – a bit of luck for me.

A few days went by and then Joseph Dega suggested he should set up a break from the outside. I told him escaping at night was impossible because of the lighting-up of the top of the wall, so he looked for some way of shutting off the current. Thanks to an electrician, he found it – he could throw over a switch on a transformer outside the prison. All I had to do was to buy the sentry on the street side and the one in the yard, at the chapel door. There was more to it than we had thought. To begin with I had to persuade Don Gregorio to let me have ten thousand pesos – the pretext was I wanted to send them to my family by way of Joseph. And of course I had to 'force' him to accept two thousand pesos to buy a present for his wife. Then when I had put my finger on the man who arranged the guards' rota and their times, I had to buy him too. He had three thousand pesos, but he wouldn't take any part in the negotiations with the other two sentries. It was up to me to find them and arrange the deal with them. Then I was to tell him their names and he would give them the guard-duty I said.

The preparations for this fresh break took me more than a month. At last everything was fixed. Since we didn't have to worry about the sentry in the yard, we'd cut the bars with a hacksaw in its proper frame. I had three blades. I told the grapnel-Colombian. He was going to cut his bar by stages. The night of the break one of his friends, who had been acting mad for some time, would bang on a piece of zinc and howl as loud as ever he could. The Colombian knew the sentry had only consented to a deal for the escape of two Frenchmen and that he had said if a third man came up the wall, he'd fire. Nevertheless he wanted to have a go, and he said if we climbed up right close to one another in the darkness the sentry couldn't see whether it was one man or two. Clousiot and Maturette drew lots for which should go with me. It was Clousiot who won.

The dark of the moon came round. The sergeant and the

two sentries had received the halves of the note due to each. This time I didn't have to cut them – they were in two already. They were to go and fetch the other halves in the Barrio Chino, at the house where Joseph Dega's woman lived.

The lights went out. We set about the bar. It was sawn through in under ten minutes. We left the cell, wearing dark shirts and trousers. As we went the Colombian joined us. Apart from a black slip he was completely naked. Reaching the wall, I climbed the bars of the gate of the *calabozo* (cell or prison), got round the overhanging cave and threw the grapnel with its three yards of rope. In under three minutes I was up on the sentry's walk without having made a sound. Lying there flat I waited for Clousiot. The night was pitch dark. Suddenly I saw or rather sensed a hand reaching up; I caught hold and heaved. Instantly there was a terrifying noise. Clousiot had climbed between the cave and the wall and had got caught: it was the top of his trousers hooked up in the metal. At the sound I stopped pulling, of course. The metallic row stopped. Once more I heaved, thinking Clousiot must have got free, and in the midst of the shattering din of this zinc sheet I hoisted him up by main force on to the top of the wall.

Rifle-fire from the other sentries, but not from ours. Badly rattled by the shots we jumped in the wrong place, down into a street that was thirty feet below whereas to the right there was one with a drop of only fifteen. Result: Clousiot broke his right leg again. I couldn't get up either – both my feet were broken. Later I was told it was the heel bones. As for the Colombian, he put his knee out. The rifle fire brought the guard out into the street. We were surrounded with rifles pointing at us, under the light of a big electric torch. I wept with fury. To add to it all, the guards would not believe I couldn't get up. So it was on my knees, crawling as they banged me with their bayonets, that I went back into the prison. Clousiot hopped on one foot, and the Colombian did the same. My head was bleeding horribly from a blow with a rifle-butt.

The firing had woken Don Gregorio, who was sleeping in his office, being on duty that night, luckily for us. If it hadn't been for him they would have finished us off with their rifle-butts and bayonets. The one who battered me most savagely was that very sergeant I'd paid for laying on the two sentries. Don Gregorio put an end to this massacre. He threatened to bring them before the courts if they hurt us seriously. These magic words quite took away their strength.

The next day Clousiot's leg was put in plaster at the hospital. A bone-setter doing time with us put the Colombian's knee back and strapped it. During the night my feet swelled until they were the size of my head, all red and black with blood and extraordinarily puffy: the doctor had my feet bathed in luke-warm salt water and then put leeches to them three times a day. When they were full of blood the leeches dropped off of themselves and they were put into vinegar to make them bring it up again. The wound in my head needed six stitches.

A journalist who was short of news brought out an article about me. He said I was the leader of the rising in the church, that I had 'poisoned' a sentry, and that now I had organized a mass break, with outside accomplices, for sure, since the whole district's light had been cut off by someone tampering with the transformer. 'Let us hope that France will rid us of her number one gangster as soon as possible,' he ended.

Joseph came to see me, bringing his wife Annie. The sergeant and the three guards had all come separately for the other halves of their notes. Annie asked me what she ought to do. I said to pay, since they had kept their word. Our failure wasn't their fault.

For a week now they had been trundling me about the yard in an iron wheelbarrow – it acted as my bed. I lay there, with my feet high, resting on a band of cloth fixed to two uprights on the shafts. It was the only possible position, if I didn't want to suffer too much. My huge, swollen feet, stiff with clotted blood, could not bear their own weight, even when I was lying down. In my barrow I felt it somewhat less. A fortnight after I broke them they had come down to half their size and I was X-rayed. The two heel bones were broken. I'd be flat-footed for the rest of my days.

Today's paper said the boat that was coming for us would arrive at the end of the month, bringing an escort of French police. The paper said she was called the *Mana*. It was 12 October. We had eighteen days left and we had to play our last card. But what card could we play with my broken feet?

Joseph was in despair. When he came to see me he told me all the Frenchmen and all the women in the Barrio Chino were terribly upset at the idea that I was within a few days of being handed over to the French authorities, having struggled so for

231

my freedom. The whole colony was deeply concerned about my fate. It was a great comfort to me to know all these men and their women were spiritually with me.

I'd quite given up my plan of killing a Colombian cop. In fact I could not bring myself to do away with the life of a man who had not hurt me in any way. It occurred to me he might have a father or a mother to keep – a wife and children. I smiled at the idea of having to find an evil-natured policeman who also had no family. For example, I might have to ask, 'If I murder you, is there really nobody who will miss you?' That morning of 13 October I had the blues very badly. I stared at some crystallized picric acid that was supposed to give me jaundice if I ate it. If I were sent to hospital maybe I could get myself taken out of it by men in Joseph's pay. The next day, the fourteenth, I was yellower than a lemon. Don Gregorio came to see me in the yard: I was in the shade, half lying in my barrow with my feet in the air. Straight away, without any precautions, I went to the point. 'Have me sent to hospital and there's ten thousand pesos in it for you.'

'Frenchman, I'll try. No, not so much for the ten thousand pesos, but because it really grieves me to see you struggling so for your freedom, and all in vain. Only I don't think they'll keep you there, because of that article in the paper. They'll be afraid.'

One hour later the doctor sent me to the hospital. I didn't even touch the ground there. I was taken out of the ambulance on a stretcher, and after a very careful examination of my body and my urine I went right back to prison two hours later, without ever having got off my stretcher.

Now it was the nineteenth, a Thursday. Joseph's wife Annie came to see me, together with the wife of a Corsican. They brought cigarettes and some cakes and sweets. With their affectionate conversation these women did me an immense amount of good. The sight of their pure friendship, the loveliest of things, really turned this bitter day into a sunlit afternoon. I can never say how much good the solidarity of the underworld did me during my stay in the prison called Eighty. Nor how much I owe Joseph Dega, who went so far as to risk his freedom and his position to help me to escape.

But something Annie said gave me an idea. As we were talking she said. 'Papillon dear, you've done everything humanly possible to get free. Fate's been very hard on you.

The only thing you haven't done is to blow Eighty sky high!'

'And why not? Why shouldn't I blow up this old prison? It would be doing these Colombians a kindness. If I blow it up, perhaps they'll make up their minds to build a new, more sanitary place.'

I said farewell for ever to these charming young women, and as I embraced them I said to Annie, 'Tell Joseph to come and see me on Sunday.'

On Sunday the 22nd, Joseph was there. 'Look, you've got to move heaven and earth to get someone to bring me in a stick of dynamite, a detonator and a fuse on Thursday. On my side I'll do the necessary to get a drill and three brickpiercers.'

'What are you going to do?'

'I'm going to blow up the prison wall in full daylight. Promise the fake cab we talked about five thousand pesos. Let it be in the street behind the Calle Medellin every day from eight in the morning till six at night. He'll get five hundred pesos a day if nothing happens and five thousand if it does. I'll come with a strong Colombian carrying me on his back, through the hole the dynamite makes in the wall as far as the taxi – then it's up to him. If the fake cab is OK, send in the stick: if not, well that's the end – the very end, and no more hope.'

'Count on me,' said Joseph.

At five o'clock I had myself carried into the chapel. I said I wanted to pray alone. They took me there. I asked for Don Gregorio to come and see me. He came.

'Hombre, it's only a week now before you leave me.'

'That's why I asked you to come. You are holding fifteen thousand pesos of mine. I want to give them to my friend before I go so he can send them to my family. Please accept three thousand. I offer it to you sincerely, because you've always protected me from ill-treatment by the soldiers. And it would be kind if you gave me the money today, with a roll of sticky paper so I can fix them by Thursday and hand them over all in one piece.'

'Right.'

He came back and gave me twelve thousand pesos, still cut in halves. He kept three thousand. Back in my wheelbarrow I called the Colombian over into a quiet corner – the Colombian who'd gone with me last time. I told him my scheme and asked if he felt he was strong enough to carry me piggy-back the twenty or thirty yards to the taxi. He solemnly undertook to do so. So that was OK. I was carrying on as though I was sure Joseph would succeed. I stationed myself under the wash-house early on Monday morning, and Maturette (he and Clousiot always acted as chauffeurs for my barrow) went to fetch the sergeant I'd given the three thousand pesos to and who'd bashed me so savagely at the time of the last escape.

'Sergeant Lopez, I've got to talk to you.'

'What do you want?'

'For two thousand pesos I want a very strong three-speed drill and six brick piercers. Two quarter-inch, two half-inch and two three-quarter inch.'

'I've no money to buy them with.'

'Here's five hundred pesos.'

'You'll have them tomorrow, Tuesday, at the changing of the guard – one o'clock. Get two thousand pesos ready.'

At one o'clock on Tuesday I had the lot in an empty tin in the yard, a paper bin that was emptied at the changing of the guard. Pablo, the tough Colombian, collected them and hid them.

On Thursday the 26th, no Joseph. Just at the end of the visiting hour I was called. It was an old, deeply wrinkled Frenchman: Joseph's messenger. 'What you asked for is in this loaf of bread.'

'Here's the taxi's two thousand pesos. Five hundred for each day.'

'The driver's an old Peruvian, as game as a fighting-cock – you don't have to worry about *him*. Ciao.'

'Ciao.'

So that the loaf shouldn't attract notice, they'd put cigarettes, matches, smoked sausage, salami, butter and a bottle of black oil into the big paper bag. When it was being searched I gave the guard on the door a packet of cigarettes, some matches and two little sausages. He said, 'Let's have a bit of that bread.'

That really would have been the last straw. 'No. You'll have to buy bread. Look, here's five pesos – there wouldn't be enough here for all six of us.'

Christ, that was a near shave. What a fool to have thought of sausages! The wheelbarrow hurried away from that blundering ox of a guard at full speed. His asking for bread had so taken me aback I was still in a cold sweat.

'The fireworks are for tomorrow. Everything's here, Pablo.

The hole's got to be made just under the overhang of the little tower. Then the sentry up there won't be able to see you.'

'But he'll hear.'

'I've taken care of that. At ten o'clock tomorrow that side of the yard will be in the shade. One of the metal-workers must flatten a sheet of copper, hammering it against the wall a few yards from us, out in the open. If there are two of them, so much the better. I'll give them five hundred pesos each. Find me two men for the job.'

He found them. 'Two friends of mine are going to beat copper non-stop. The sentry won't be able to make out the sound of the drill. But you'll have to be there in your barrow just beyond the overhang, talking with the other Frenchmen. That'll hide me a little from the sentry in the opposite corner.'

In an hour's time the hole was made. Thanks to the hammering of the copper and the oil an assistant poured on to the drill, the sentry never suspected a thing. The stick of dynamite was rammed into the hole together with its detonator and nine inches of fuse. The rest of the hole was stuffed with clay. We stood back. If all went well the explosion would blow a hole in the wall. The sentry and his sentry-box would come down and I, riding Pablo, would get through the gap and reach the taxi. The others would do the best they could on their own. It was reasonable that even if they came out after us, Clousiot and Maturette would reach the taxi first.

Just before lighting the fuse Pablo said to a group of Colombians, 'If you want to make a break, there'll be a hole in the wall in a few moments.'

'Fine. Because the police'll come running and shoot the ones behind – the ones that stand out most.'

The fuse was lit. A shattering crash shook the whole district. The little tower came down with the sentry on top of it. There were great cracks all over the wall, so wide you could see the street through them: but not one was wide enough for a man. No real gap had been made, and it was then – only then – that I admitted I was beaten. It was clearly my fate to go back to Guiana.

An indescribable turmoil followed this explosion. There were more than fifty police in the yard. Don Gregorio knew very well who was responsible. 'Bueno, Francés. This time is the very last, I believe.'

The commander of the garrison was out of his mind with

fury. He couldn't give orders to strike a wounded man lying there in a wheelbarrow; and so as to prevent trouble for anyone else I called out that I'd done the whole thing myself, quite alone. Six warders in front of the shattered wall, six in the yard and six outside in the street: they stood guard there right round the clock until builders had repaired it. The sentry who came down with the tower had had the good luck not to be hurt.

Back to Guiana

Three days later, at eleven o'clock on the morning of 30 October, twelve French warders, dressed in white, came to take possession of us. Before we left there was a little official ceremony – each of us had to be checked and identified. They'd brought our measurements, finger-prints, photos and all the rest of it. Once the identification was over, the French consul came forward to sign a paper for the local judge – he being the person who was to officially hand us over to France. All the people there were astonished at the friendly way the screws treated us. No harshness, no rough words. The three who had been there longer than us knew several of them and talked and joked with them like old friends. Major Boural, the leader of the escort, inquired into my condition: he looked at my feet and said I'd be taken care of on board – there was a good medical orderly in the group that had come to fetch us.

We travelled right down in the hold, and the voyage in this old tub was made really unpleasant by the stifling heat and the awkwardness of being coupled two by two in leg-irons that went right back to the days of the Toulon prison-hulks. There was only one incident worth recording. The boat had to coal at Trinidad: when we were in the harbour an English officer insisted upon our irons being taken off. Apparently it was forbidden to have men chained on board a ship. I took advantage of this to slap another English inspector. I was hoping to be arrested and taken off the boat. The officer said, 'I shan't arrest you or put you on shore for the serious crime you've just committed. You'll be punished far worse by being taken back to Guiana.'

All that trouble for nothing. No: it was clear I was fated to go back to penal. It was sad, but these eleven months of escape, of whole-hearted effort of every kind, were coming to a miserable end. And yet in spite of everything, in spite of the resounding failure of all these adventures, this return to penal with all its bitter consequences could not wipe out the unforgettable moments I had lived through.

Not far from this port of Trinidad we had just left, only a few miles away, there lived the wonderful Bowen family. We sailed by at no great distance from Curaçao, the country of that great man who was the bishop of those parts, Irénée de Bruyne. And we must also have been very close to the Goajira Indians' territory, where I had come to know the purest, most passionate love in its most natural and spontaneous form. Among those Indian women, so full of spirit and so rich in understanding, uncomplicated love and purity, I had found all the clear-sightedness of children and the direct way of viewing things that marks that privileged age.

And then those lepers of Pigeon Island! Those wretched convicts, infected by that horrible disease, who had nevertheless been noble enough to help us – who had found such splendid strength in their hearts!

And then there was the Belgian consul, with his spontaneous kindness: and Joseph Dega, who, without being a friend of mine, had risked so much to help me! It was worth having made this break for the people, the human beings it had brought me into contact with. Although it had failed, my escape had been a victory, merely by having enriched my heart with the friendship of these wonderful people. No, I was not sorry I had done it.

Here was the Maroni and its muddy waters. We were on the *Mana*'s deck. The tropical sun had already begun to scorch the earth: it was nine in the morning. I saw the estuary again. We were slowly coming in again just where I had gone down so fast. My friends did not say a word. The warders were glad to be back. During the voyage the sea had been rough and now many of them were happy to get away from it.

An extraordinarily dense crowd at the landing-stage. You could feel they were full of curiosity to see these men who had not been afraid of going such a distance. And as the day of our arrival was a Sunday, it also provided a diversion for this community that didn't have so very much in that line. I heard people say, 'The wounded one is Papillon. There's Clousiot. The one behind is Maturette . . .' And so on.

Inside the prison enclosure, six hundred men were lined up in groups in front of their huts. Warders next to each group. The first man I recognized was François Sierra. He was weeping openly, without attempting to hide his tears. He was perched up at one of the windows of the infirmary, watching me. You could feel that his sorrow was genuine. We stopped in the middle of the square. The governor took a megaphone. 'Transportees, you see how pointless it is to escape. Every country arrests you and hands you back to France. Nobody wants you. So it's better to stay quietly here and behave properly. What have these five men in store for them? A heavy sentence that they'll have to serve in the solitary-confinement prison on the Ile Saint-Joseph and then, for the rest of their time, life internment on the islands. That's what they have gained by escaping. I hope you get the point. Warders, take these men to the punishment block.'

A few minutes later there we were in a special cell in the high-security wing. As soon as we got there I asked for my feet to be attended to – they were still very bruised and swollen. Clousiot said the plaster on his leg was hurting. We were trying it on . . . if only they'd send us to hospital! François Sierra appeared with his warder.

'Here's the orderly,' said the screw.

'How are you, Papi?'

'I'm sick: I want to go to hospital.'

'I'll try and get you in, but after what you did when you were there last, I'm afraid it's almost impossible. The same goes for Clousiot.' He massaged my feet and put on ointment: he checked Clousiot's plaster and then went away. We couldn't say anything because the screws were there, but his eyes expressed such good will that I was deeply moved.

'No, there's nothing to be done,' he told me the next day as he was massaging me again. 'Do you want me to get you into the big room? Are you put in irons at night?'

'Yes.'

'Then it's better you should go into the big room. You'll have the irons on still, but at least you won't be alone. And just now being alone must be horrible for you.'

'Right.'

Yes, at this moment loneliness was even harder to stand than before. I was in such a state of mind that I didn't even have to close my eyes to fly away and wander both in the past and the present. And as I couldn't walk, the punishment cell was even worse for me than it had been formerly.

Oh, here I was back on the road down the drain all right! And yet I had been able to get shot of it quick enough, and there I had been, flying over the sea towards freedom, towards the delight of being a new man, and towards my revenge, too. The debt those three owed me – Polein, police and prosecutor: I mustn't forget that. As for the trunk, there'd be no need to hand it to the flats on the gate at the Police Judiciaire. I'd go as a Cook's man with the company's elegant cap on my head. A big label on the trunk: Commissionaire Divisionnaire Benoit, 36, quai des Orfèvres à Paris (Seine). I'd carry the trunk up to the orderly-room myself, and as I should have worked out that the alarm-clock wouldn't go off till I had left, it could not miss. The finding of this solution took a great weight off my mind. As for the prosecuting counsel, I had time and to spare to rip out his tongue. I had not decided quite how I should do it; but it was as good as done. That prostituted tongue, I'd tear it out bit by bit.

The very first thing to be done was to get my feet right. I must be able to walk as soon as possible. It would be three months before I came up for trial, and lots of things could happen in three months. One month to be able to walk again, one month to fix things, and then farewell, gentlemen. All aboard for British Honduras. But this time no one would be able to get their hands on me.

Yesterday, three days after our coming back, I was carried into the big room. There were forty men there, all waiting to be court-martialled. Some accused of theft, some of robbery, arson, manslaughter, attempted manslaughter, murder, attempted escape, escape and even cannibalism. There were twenty of us on either side of the wooden sleeping platform, and we were all fastened to the same iron bar, more than fifteen yards long. At six in the evening, each man's left foot was attached to the bar by an iron shackle. At six in the morning these big rings were taken off and all day long we were allowed to sit about, play draughts, walk and talk in what they called the alley, a kind of passage two yards wide that ran the whole length of the room. During the day I had no time to get bored. Everybody came to see me, in little groups, so as to hear about the break. They all cried out that I was crazy, when I told them how I had left my Goajira tribe and Lali and Zoraïma, of my own free will.

'What was it you were after, mate?' asked a Parisian as he listened to the story. 'Trams? Lifts? Cinemas? Electric light and high tension current to work an electric chair? Or did you want to have a bathe in the Place Pigalle fountain? You get yourself two broads, each better turned than the other, you live with nothing on right out on the edge of the sea with a crowd of nudists, you've got grub, you've got drink, and you can hunt; you've got the sea, the sun and the warm sand; even the pearls in the oysters are yours just for the asking, and you can't find anything better to do than to give it all up – for what? Tell me that. So as to have to cross the street at a run, not to be knocked down by the cars, to have to pay rent, pay a tailor, pay electricity and telephone bills, and push a barrow if you want a car or work like a square for some boss to make just enough not to die of starvation? I don't understand you, man. You're in heaven, and you come back to hell, where you've not only got all the ordinary bleeding worries of life but you've also got to watch out for all the cops in creation, they being right after you? Fair enough, you're fresh out from France and you haven't had time to see your brains and guts all leak away: with my ten years of penal, I can't understand you any more. But still, you're welcome here with us, and as you'll certainly mean to have another go, you can count on all of us to help you. Isn't that right, mates? You all agree?'

Every guy there agreed, and I thanked them all.

They were formidable characters; I could see that right away. Since we lived together so closely it was difficult for anyone not to let it be known whether he had a charger or not. And at night, when everyone was fixed to the same bar, it was not hard to kill a man without danger. All you had to

240

do was to fix it so that, for a certain amount of cash, the Arab turnkey agreed not to close the shackle properly. So you could get up in the darkness, do what you intended to do, and then go quietly back and lie down in your place, taking care to lock the shackle thoroughly. As the Arab was in some degree an accomplice, he'd keep his trap shut.

It was three weeks now since I had been back. They had passed pretty briskly. I was starting to walk a little, holding the bar in the passage that separated the two lines of sleeping platforms. I was coming on. Last week, at the official inquiry, I saw the three hospital screws we knocked out and disarmed. They were very pleased we had come back and they had great hopes that some day we'd land up where they were on duty. Because after our break they'd all three been severely punished – their six months' leave in Europe withheld and a year's colonial allowance on top of their pay withheld too. So ours was not the friendliest of meetings. We repeated their threats at the inquiry, so that they should be on the record.

The Arab behaved better. He just told the truth without any exaggeration, leaving out the part played by Maturette. The captain in charge of the inquiry pressed us very hard to find out who had provided the boat. We got into his bad books by telling unlikely tales, such as we made rafts ourselves, etc.

He told us that because of the attack on the warders, he'd do his very best to get Clousiot and me five years, and Maturette three. 'And since they call you Papillon,' he said, 'I'll trim your wings for you – you can rely on that. You're not likely to fly again for some time.'

I was very much afraid he was right. More than two months to wait before coming up in front of the court. I was vexed with myself for not having put one or two poisoned arrow-tips into my charger. If I'd had them I might perhaps have been able to make a last dash for it in the punishment wing. I was making progress every day now: I was walking better and better. François Sierra never failed to come and massage my feet with camphorated oil morning and night. These massage-visits did an enormous amount of good, both to my feet and my spirit. How good it is to have a friend in life!

I noticed that such a long break as this gave us real standing with all the convicts. I was certain we were quite safe there among them. There was no danger of our being murdered for what we had. The great majority would not put up with it and it was certain that the guilty men would be killed. Everyone, without exception, respected us, and they even had a very real admiration for what we had done. And then again, our having knocked out the screws classed us as men who would stop at nothing. It's pleasant to feel quite safe.

Every day I walked a little farther; and the other men would often offer to massage not only my feet with the oil in a little bottle Sierra left me, but also the muscles of my legs, which were atrophying with such long disuse.

The Arab and the Ants

In this room there were two silent men who never spoke to anyone. They always kept very close together and they only talked between themselves, and even then in a low voice no one could hear. One day I offered one of them an American cigarette from a packet Sierra had brought me. He thanked me and then said, 'François Sierra's a friend of yours?'

'Yes. The best I have.'

'Maybe one day, if things go badly, we'll send you our legacy through him.'

'What legacy?'

'My friend and I have made up our minds that if they guillotine us, we'll send you our charger so you can use it to make another break. So we'll give it to Sierra to pass it on to you.'

'You think you'll get death?'

'It's pretty nearly sure: there's very little chance of our getting off.'

'If it's so certain you're going to be condemned to death, why are you in this big room?'

'I think they're afraid we'll commit suicide if either of us is alone in a cell.'

'Yes. Yes, that's possible. What did you do?'

'We gave an Arab to the flesh-eating ants. I tell you this,

because unfortunately they've got certain proof. We were caught in the act.'

'And where did it happen?'

'At Kilometre Forty-Two, the death camp after Sparouine Creek.' His friend had come over to us: he was a man from Toulouse. I gave him a cigarette. He sat down next to his friend, opposite me.

'We've never asked anybody's opinion on the matter,' said the newcomer. 'But I'd rather like to know what you think of us.'

'Without knowing anything about you, how do you expect me to say whether you were right or wrong to give a living man, even if he was only an Arab, to the ants to eat? To tell you my opinion, I'd have to know the whole business from A to Z.'

'I'll tell you about it,' said the Toulousian. 'Kilometre Forty-Two is a logging camp forty-two kilometres from Saint-Laurent. The convicts there are forced to cut a cubic yard of hard-wood a day. You have to be there every evening in the bush, standing by the wood you have cut, neatly piled up. The warders, with Arab turnkeys with them, come and check that you've done your stint. When it's accepted, every cubic yard is marked with red, green or yellow paint. It's according to the day of the week. They'll pass the work if every bit is hard-wood. To manage it better, we two teamed up together. Pretty often, we couldn't reach the cubic yard. So then in the evening they'd put us in the punishment cell without anything to eat, and the next day, still without anything to eat they made us go back to work – we had to make up what was short the day before as well as cut this day's yard. We were being worked to death – they were treating us like dogs.

'The longer it went on, the weaker we got and the less we could manage the work. On top of that, they'd given us a special guard who wasn't a warder but an Arab. He came to the place we were working, sat there at his ease with his bull's pizzle between his legs and insulted us all the time. He ate, smacking his lips so as to make us feel really hungry. To put it in a word, it was non-stop hell. We had two chargers with three thousand francs in each, put by for our escape. One day we made up our minds to buy the Arab. That made the position even worse. Fortunately he always believed we only had one charger. His system was easy: for fifty francs, say, he'd let us go and steal from the heaps that had already been accepted the day before – we took the pieces that hadn't been painted and we made up our daily yard. This way he got nearly two thousand francs out of us, in goes of fifty or a hundred at a time.

'When we'd got up to date with our work, they took the Arab away. And then, thinking he wouldn't inform since he'd robbed us of so much money, we went into the bush to find the piles that had been accepted, so as to go on with the same manoeuvre. One day the Arab followed us very close, but hidden, to see if we really were stealing wood. Then he came out into the open. "Ha, ha! You still steal 'em wood and no pay! If you no give five hundred francs, me inform."

'Thinking it was only a threat, we refused. The next day he was back again. "You pay, or you in black-hole tonight." We refused again. In the afternoon he came back with the screws. It was horrible, Papillon! When they'd stripped us, they took us to the heaps where we'd taken wood, and with these savages behind us and the Arab flogging us with his pizzle, they forced us to undo our heaps at the double and make up each one we had stolen from. This corrida lasted two days, with nothing to eat or drink. Often we fell down. The Arab got us up with a kick or with his whip. Finally we just lay there on the ground – we couldn't go on. Do you know how he made us get up? He took one of those sort of wasps' nests, the kind the red stingers live in. He cut the branch the nest was hanging from and crushed it down on us. The pain was so terrible we not only got up, but we tore around as if we were mad. There's just no telling you how agonizing it was. You know how a wasp sting hurts? Well, imagine fifty or sixty of them. Those red stingers sting far, far worse than wasps.

'We were still in the black-hole for ten days on bread and water, and they never treated us at all. Even though we rubbed urine on the stings, they burnt terribly for three days on end. I lost my left eye – a dozen had attacked it all together. When we were sent back to the camp, the other prisoners decided to help us. They each gave us a bit of hard-wood cut to the same size. That provided us with close on a yard, and it helped us a very great deal, because then we only had about one yard to cut between us. It was hard, but we just managed it. Little by little our strength came back. We ate a great deal. And it was just by chance that we had the notion of using the ants for our revenge against the Arab. We were looking for hard-wood and we came across a huge nest of flesh-eating ants in a thicket – they were actually eating a deer the size of a goat.

'The Arab was still making his rounds, inspecting the work, and one fine day we knocked him out with the handle of an axe and dragged him to the ants' nest. We stripped him and tied him to a tree, bent backwards on the ground, his hands and feet tied with the thick ropes we used for the logs. We made a few cuts here and there on his body with the axe. We stuffed his mouth with grass, held in by a gag, so he couldn't shout; and we waited. The ants didn't go for him till we'd stirred their nest with a stick and sprinkled them on to him. Then it didn't take long. Half an hour later there were thousands and thousands of ants at work. Have you seen flesh-eating ants, Papillon?'

'No, never. I've seen the big black ones.'

'These ones are tiny, and as red as blood. They tear out microscopic bits of flesh and carry them to their nest. We'd suffered from the wasps, all right; but just imagine what he must have gone through, flayed alive by these thousands of ants. He took two whole days and one morning to die. In twenty-four hours he had no eyes left.

'I admit we had no mercy in our revenge, but then you have to think what he did to us. It was a miracle we survived. Of course they looked for the Arab everywhere; and the other Arab turnkeys, as well as the screws, suspected we had something to do with his disappearance.

'In another thicket we made a hole for what was left of him, deepening it a little every day. They'd still not found any trace of him when a screw saw this hole was being dug. When we went off to work, he followed to see what was up. That was what finished us.

'One morning, as soon as we had reached our place, we untied the Arab: he was still covered with ants although he was almost a skeleton. And just as we were dragging him to the hole (you couldn't carry him without the ants biting till the blood came) three Arab turnkeys and two warders came out. They had been waiting patiently, well hidden, for us to do just that – to bury him.

'Well, there you are. Our official version is that we killed him first and then gave him to the ants. The prosecution, backed by the medical evidence, says there was no mortal wound – they say we had him eaten alive. Our defending screw [warders there will act as counsel] says we might save our heads if they believe what we say. Otherwise we're for it. To tell you the truth, we haven't much hope. That's why my friend and me chose you as our heir, without saying.'

'Let's hope I don't inherit from you: I say that in all sincerity.' We had a cigarette and I saw they were looking at me as much as to say, 'Well, aren't you going to say something?'

'Look, brothers, I can see you're waiting for what you asked to begin with – what I think of your case, judging it as a man. One last question – it won't have any influence on what I'm going to say. What do most of the men in this room think of it, and why don't you speak to anybody?'

'Most of them think we ought to have killed him, but not to have had him eaten alive. As for our keeping quiet, we don't talk to anyone because one day we had a chance of rioting and making a break, and they wouldn't take it.'

'Well, mates, I'll tell you how I see it. You did right to pay him back a hundred times over for what he did to you: the caper with the wasps or red stingers was something that can't be forgiven. If they do guillotine you, at the last moment think as hard as ever you can just this one thing, "They're cutting off my head: from the moment of tying me down and shoving me into the hole to the dropping of the knife, it'll last thirty seconds. *His* death agony lasted sixty hours. I come out the winner." As for the other men in the room, I don't know whether you're right: you might have thought a riot that day would have made a mass break possible; and the rest might have thought otherwise. Besides, in a rising like that, you might always have to kill someone without having meant it beforehand. Now of all the people in here, I believe the only ones whose heads are in danger are you two and the Graville brothers. Friends, it all necessarily depends on where you sit.'

The two poor souls were pleased with our talk: they went off, going back to the life of silence they had broken to speak to me.

'Where's the wooden leg? They ate it.' 'One portion of peg-leg stew, hot.' Or a voice pretending to be a woman's and calling out, 'Just a slice of well-grilled gent, chef, with no pepper, please.'

In the silent darkness of the night it was rare we didn't hear one of these shouts, if not all three. Clousiot and I wondered what they meant, and who they were meant for.

This afternoon I had the key of the mystery. It was one of the chief actors that told me about it, Marius from La Ciotat, a specialist in safe-breaking. When he learnt that I'd known his father, Titin, he wasn't afraid of talking to me.

When I'd told him part of my break, I naturally said to him, 'And what about you?'

'Oh, me,' he said, 'I'm in a hell of a jam. I'm very much afraid I may cop five years, just for an ordinary escape. I belonged to the one they called the cannibals' break. When you hear them call out "Where's the wooden leg, etc.?" and "One stew, etc.," in the night, that's meant for the Graville brothers.

'Six of us left from Kilometre Forty-Two. In the break there were Dédé and Jean Graville, two brothers of thirty and thirty-five from Lyons; a Neapolitan from Marseilles and me from La Ciotat; and then a wooden-legged guy from Angers and a kid of twenty-three who acted as his wife. We got out of the Maroni well enough, but at sea we could never make our offing, and in a few hours we were forced back on to the shore of Dutch Guiana.

'There was nothing we could save from the wreck, no food, no stores, nor anything else. So there we were again in the bush – luckily we had our clothes. I ought to have said that in this part there's no beach at all and the sea comes right into the virgin forest. What with the fallen trees, broken off short at the bottom or undermined by the sea and all tangled with one another, it's impossible to get through.

'When we had walked for a whole day we reached dry land. We split into three groups, the Gravilles, Giuseppe and me, and peg-leg and his boy-friend. To cut it short, we set off in different directions and then twelve days later the Gravilles,

Marius and I met again almost at the place where we'd separated. It was surrounded with mud you sank down in and we hadn't found any way through. I don't have to tell you how browned off we were. We'd been living thirteen days with no grub apart from a few roots and the ends of twigs. We were dead-beat, dying of hunger – completely done. We decided that Marius and me should use what strength we had left to go back to the edge of the sea. There we should tie a shirt as high as we could in a tree and so give ourselves up to the first Dutch coast-guard boat – one would certainly be coming by. When the Gravilles had rested a few hours, they were supposed to try and find the track of the other two. It ought to be easy enough, because on setting out we'd agreed that each group should mark where it had gone with broken branches.

'But a few hours later, what did they see but peg-leg coming their way, all alone.

' "Where's the kid?"

' "I left him far behind: he couldn't walk any more."

' "You're a sod for having left him."

' "He was the one who wanted me to go back to where we'd started from."

'At that moment Déde noticed that on his solitary foot he was wearing one of the kid's shoes. "And you left him barefoot into the bargain, so you could put on his shoe? Congratulations! And you seem pretty fit: you aren't in the same state as us. Anyone can see you've had plenty to eat."

' "Yes, I found a big monkey that had been wounded."

' "How lucky for you." And with this Dédé got up, his knife in his hand. Seeing peg-leg's haversack full, he thought he knew what had happened. "Open your sack. What's it got inside?"

'He opened the bag and a piece of flesh appeared.

' "What's that?"

' "A bit of monkey."

' "You sod, you killed the boy to eat him!"

' "No, Dédé, I swear I didn't. He was so worn out he died, and I only ate a little bit of him. Forgive me."

'He hadn't time to finish before the knife was in his guts. And it was then, when they searched him, that they found a leather bag with matches and a striker. What with fury because peg-leg hadn't shared the matches before parting, and what with hunger – to cut it short, they lit a fire and started in on the type.

'Giuseppe arrived in the middle of the banquet. They asked him to join in. Giuseppe wouldn't. On the shore he'd eaten crabs and raw fish. So without joining in he watched the Gravilles arranging other pieces of flesh on the embers and even making use of the wooden leg to keep up the fire. That day and the next, then, he watched the Gravilles eat the man; and he even noticed what pieces they ate – the skin, the thigh, and both buttocks.

'As for me,' went on Marius, 'I was still there by the sea when Giuseppe came to fetch me. We filled a hat with little fishes and crabs and we went and cooked them at the Gravilles' fire. But I did see a good many pieces of meat left, lying on the ashes to one side of the fire.

'Three days later the coast-guards picked us up and handed us back to the authorities at Saint-Laurent-du-Maroni. Giuseppe couldn't keep quiet. Everyone in this room knows all about it, even the screws. And it's because everybody knows it that I'm telling you. And so – the Gravilles being bad characters – that's why you hear this nonsense in the night.

'We're officially accused of escape aggravated by cannibalism. The worst of it is, I can only defend myself by accusing others; and that's just not possible. Everybody, including Giuseppe, denied everything at the inquiry. We said they'd vanished in the bush. So that's how I stand, Papillon.'

'I pity you, brother: for you can't defend yourself by blaming others, and that's a fact.'

A month later Giuseppe was murdered, stabbed right in the heart by night. There was no sort of question who did it.

And that is the genuine story of the cannibals who ate the man, roasting him over his own wooden leg – the man who had himself eaten the kid who went along with him.

That night I lay farther along the iron bar. I took the place of a man who had gone, and Clousiot, having asked everybody to move up one, was next to me now. From this place, even with my left foot shackled to the bar, I could sit up and watch what went on in the yard. The security was so tight there was no rhythm in the patrols. They came one after another continuously; and different patrols might appear from the other direction at any moment.

My feet were carrying me very well now, and they didn't

hurt unless it rained. So I was all set up for fresh action: but what was to be done? This room had no windows, only a huge set of bars running in one sweep its whole length and going up to the roof. It was so placed that the north-east wind (but only the wind) could pass freely. I kept watch for a week, but even so I couldn't find the least opening in the warders' security. For the first time I was close to admitting that they might manage to shut me up in the solitary-confinement prison on the Ile Saint-Joseph. I was told it was horrible: they called it the man-eater. Another piece of information – in the eighty years it had been in existence, not a single man had ever managed to escape from it.

Of course this half-acceptance of having lost the game forced me to look towards the future. I was twenty-eight and the prosecuting captain was going to ask for five years of solitary. It would be hard to get off with less. So I'd be thirty-three when I came out.

I still had plenty of money in my charger. So if I couldn't escape, which, from what I knew, seemed likely, at least I should have to keep myself fit. It's hard to take five years solitary without going mad. So I should have to eat well, and from the first day of my sentence discipline my mind according to a carefully laid down and varied programme. Avoid day-dreaming about castles in Spain as much as possible; and even more day-dreaming about revenge. So from now on I prepare myself for the terrible punishment ahead, and come through a winner. Yes, their malice would get them nowhere. I'd come out of solitary physically strong and still in full possession of my bodily and mental powers.

It did me good to lay down this plan of conduct and to accept what was coming to me with a calm mind. The gentle wind that made its way into the room reached me before anybody else, and it was really soothing.

Clousiot knew when I didn't want to talk. So he didn't disturb my silence: he just smoked a great deal, that's all. There were a few stars showing. I said to him, 'Can you see the stars from where you are?'

'Yes,' he said, leaning over a little. 'But I'd rather not look at them; they remind me too much of the stars during our break.'

'Don't worry – we'll see thousands more in our next one.'

'When? In five years time?'

'Clousiot, don't you think the year we've just lived through and all the adventures we've had and all the people we've known are worth five years' solitary? Would you rather have been on the islands from the beginning and not have gone on this break? What's waiting for us is not all jam; but does it make you regret you ever came on the break? Tell me straight, do you regret it, yes or no?'

'Papi, you're forgetting one thing I didn't have – the seven months you spent with the Indians. If I'd been with you, I'd think the same: but I was in prison.'

'Forgive me. I'd forgotten – I'm wandering in my mind.'

'No, you're not wandering at all; and in spite of everything I'm glad we made our break, because I had some unforgettable moments too. Only I do feel rather anxious about what's waiting for me in the man-eater. Five years – it's next to impossible to come through.'

Then I told him just what I'd determined to do and I felt him respond very positively. It made me happy, seeing my friend's morale coming right back. In a fortnight's time we were to come up before the court. According to certain rumours the major who was coming to preside over the court-martial was a hard man, but very just, it seemed. He wouldn't swallow the Administration's nonsense too easily. So the news was good rather than bad.

Maturette had been in a cell ever since we got back. But Clousiot and I refused to have a warder to act as counsel: we decided that I should speak for all three and that I should put forward our defence myself.

The Trial

That morning, freshly shaved and clipped, dressed in new red-striped dungarees and wearing shoes, we were waiting in the yard until we should be called before the court. Clousiot

251

had had his plaster off a fortnight before. He could walk normally; it had not left him with a limp.

The court-martial had begun on Monday. Now it was Saturday morning, and so there had been five days taken up with the various trials – the business of the fellows with the ants had taken up a whole day. They were both sentenced to death, and I never saw them again. The Graville brothers only copped four years (no proof of the act of cannibalism). Their trial lasted more than half a day. The other killings got four or five years. Looking at the fourteen defendants as a whole, the sentences were rather on the severe side, but reasonable – not exaggerated. The sittings began at half past seven. We were there when a major in the Camel Corps uniform came in, accompanied by an elderly infantry captain and a lieutenant – his two assessors.

To the right of the court a sergeant warder and a captain – the prosecutor representing the Administration.

'Case of Charrière, Clousiot, Maturette.'

We were about four yards from the judges. I had time to look very attentively at the major: he was about forty or forty-five; the desert had lined his face, and the hair at his temples was silver. Thick eyebrows over splendid black eyes that looked straight into our faces. A genuine soldier. There was nothing wicked in his gaze. He looked searchingly at us and weighed us up in a few seconds. My eyes met his and then I lowered them of my own free will.

The Administration captain knocked us about altogether too hard and that was what lost him the game. He called the stunning of the warders attempted murder. He would have it that it was a miracle the Arab had not died under our repeated blows. He made another error when he said that we were the convicts who had carried France's dishonour farthest afield since the penal settlement was founded. 'As far as Colombia! Monsieur le Président, these men traversed one thousand five hundred miles and more. Trinidad, Curaçao and Colombia – all these countries will certainly have heard the vilest calumnies about the French penal administration. I ask for two consecutive sentences, that is to say a total of eight years – five for attempted manslaughter on the one hand, and on the other three for escaping. This applies to Charrière and Clousiot. As far as Maturette is concerned, I only ask three years for escap-

252

ing; because at the inquiry it came out that he took no part in the attempted murder.'

The president: 'The court would like to hear the shortest possible account of this very long odyssey.'

Leaving out the Maroni part, I told them about our sea voyage as far as Trinidad. I described the Bowens and their kindness. I quoted the remark of the Trinidad chief of police, 'We are not here to pass judgment on the French legal system, but there's one thing we don't agree with, and that's the sending of criminals to French Guiana; which is the reason why we are helping you.' I told them about Curaçao, Father Irénée de Bruyne, the incident of the bag of florins, and then about Colombia – how and why we went there. Then, in very few words, a short account of my life with the Indians. The major listened without interrupting. He only asked for a few further details about my time with the Indians, which interested him immensely. Then I spoke of the Colombian prisons, especially the under-water black-hole at Santa Marta.

'Thank you: your account has enlightened and at the same time interested the court. Now there will be a break for fifteen minutes. I do not see your defending counsel; where are they?'

'We haven't got any. I'm going to ask your permission to put forward my friends' defence and my own.'

'You may do so: it is allowed by the regulations.'

'Thank you.'

A quarter of an hour later the sitting began again. The president: 'Charrière, the court allows you to put forward your friends' defence and your own. Nevertheless we warn you that the court will reduce you to silence if you speak disrespectfully to the representative of the Administration. You are quite free to defend yourself, but you must use proper language. You may begin.'

'I ask the court to simply ignore the accusation of attempted murder – to set it aside. It is completely unbelievable, and I'll show why: I was twenty-seven last year and Clousiot thirty; we were just out from France and we were fit and strong. One of us is five foot seven and the other five foot eight. We hit the Arab and the warders with our iron bed-legs. Not one of the four was seriously hurt. We had not meant to harm them and we hit very carefully, just so as to knock them out, and that's exactly what we managed to do. The prosecuting warder forgot to mention – or perhaps he didn't know it – that the lengths of iron were wrapped in cloth so there'd be no danger of killing anyone. The court, made up of regular soldiers, is very well aware of what a strong man can do when he hits anyone on the head, even if it's only with the flat of a bayonet. So just imagine what could be done with an iron bed-leg. I'd like to point out to the court that not one of the four men who were attacked had to go to hospital.

'Seeing we've got life sentences, it seems to me that the crime of escaping is less serious than it would be for men with a short time to serve. At our age it's very hard to bear the thought of never going back into real life again. I ask the court's indulgence for all three of us.'

The major whispered with his two colleagues, then he tapped his desk with a mallet. 'Defendants, stand up.'

We stood there waiting, as stiff as ramrods.

The president: 'The court sets aside the accusations of attempted murder: it therefore has not to pronounce sentence, even of acquittal, upon that subject. You are found guilty of the crime of escaping, guilty in the second degree. For this crime, the court sentences you to two years of solitary confinement.'

Speaking all together, we said, 'Thank you, Major.' And I added, 'We thank the court.'

The screws who were listening to the trial at the back of the room were absolutely thunderstruck. When we went back to our companions, everybody was happy about the news – not the least jealousy. On the contrary. Even those who had copped it hard whole-heartedly congratulated us on our luck. François Sierra came and embraced me. He was wild with delight.

Our Arrival at the Islands

The next day we were to take ship for the Iles du Salut. This time, in spite of all my struggles, here I was within not much more than a few hours of life internment. In the first place I'd have to do two years of solitary on the Ile Saint-Joseph. The convicts called that prison the man-eater: I hoped I'd be able to prove the nickname false.

I'd lost the game; but my heart wasn't that of a loser.

I ought to be very happy at having only two years to do in this prison within a prison. As I'd sworn to myself, I shouldn't allow my mind to go wandering the way it so easily does in complete isolation. I had a remedy to keep me away from that. From this very moment I must consider myself as a free man, already free, healthy and well, like any other ordinary convict on the islands. I should be thirty when I came out.

I knew that escapes from the islands were very rare. They could be counted on your fingers; but even so, men *had* got away. Well, I'd get away too: that was for sure. In two years I'd escape from the islands: I repeated this to Clousiot, who was sitting there next to me.

'It's hard to get you down, Papillon, my old mate; and I wish I had your faith in being free one of these days. For a year now you've been making break after break, and you've never once given up. No sooner has one gone bad on you but you're preparing another. It astonishes me you've tried nothing here.'

'Here there's only one possible way of setting about it, mate, and that's starting a riot. But that means taking all these extremely difficult men in hand and I just haven't got the time that it needs. I very nearly started one, but I was afraid it'd get out of control. All the forty men in here are old lags. They've gone pretty well down the drain and they don't react the same as us. Look at the cannibals, for example, and the characters with the ants; and then the character who wanted to kill a man and didn't hesitate to put poison in the soup, finishing off seven others who'd never done him any harm.'

'But on the islands it's going to be the same kind of men.'

'Yes, but I'll escape from the islands without needing anybody's help. I'll make my break alone, or with one companion at the most. What are you smiling about, Clousiot?'

'I'm smiling because you never give up. You're on fire to be in Paris, handing the bill to your three friends there, and that keeps you going at such a pitch you just won't admit that what you long for may never happen.'

'Good-night, Clousiot. See you tomorrow. Yes, so we're going to have a look at these bleeding Iles du Salut after all. The first thing I'll ask is why they call that fag-end of hell the Islands of Salvation.' I turned my back on Clousiot and leant out a little more to the night-wind.

Very early the next day we embarked for the islands. Twenty-six men on board a four hundred-ton tub called the *Tanon*, a coaster that made the round trip Cayenne – the Islands – Saint-Laurent and back again. We were shackled two by two to a chain; and we were handcuffed as well. There were two groups of eight men each on the fo'c'sle, guarded by four screws holding rifles. Ten aft, with six screws and the two leaders of the escort. Everybody was on the deck of this old tramp: she was obviously longing to plunge to the bottom at the first hint of a heavy sea.

I'd made up my mind not to think during the crossing, and I looked round for some way of amusing myself. So speaking loud and clear to a glum-faced warder next to me, I said, just by way of putting him out, 'What with all these chains you've loaded us with, we shan't have much chance of escaping if this staggering old wreck sinks, which seems very likely, seeing her condition and how rough the sea is.'

The screw wasn't all that bright and he reacted just as I had foreseen. 'Whether you people drown or not is all one to us. We've had orders to chain you and that's all there is to it. The people who gave the orders are responsible. In any event, we're covered.'

'Why, you're quite right, Monsieur le Surveillant, whichever way you look at it: because if this floating coffin falls apart at sea, we all go to the bottom, chains or no chains.'

'Oh, she's been doing this round for a long time now, you

256

know,' said the half-wit, 'and nothing's ever happened to her.'

'Sure: but it's just for that reason — just because this boat's been going the round *too long* that she's ready to fall to pieces at any moment now.' I had succeeded in doing what I had set out to do — I'd stirred the general silence that was getting on my nerves. The warders and the convicts at once seized upon the subject. 'Yes, this old tub is dangerous: and on top of that, we're in chains. With no chains, at least we'd stand a chance.' 'Oh, that doesn't make any difference. With our uniform, boots and rifle, we're not so light, either.' 'The rifle doesn't count, because in case of shipwreck you can chuck it away at once,' said another.

Seeing the thing had caught on, I tossed off another remark. 'Where are the life-boats? I can only see one very small job, just big enough for eight at the outside. What with the captain and the crew, it would be crammed. As for everybody else — kiss my hand, farewell.'

Now it really got going, and the tone of the discussion rose. 'It's quite true, there's nothing at all; and this boat's in such a state — it's a wicked piece of irresponsibility to make family men run such a risk, escorting these scum.'

As I formed a part of the group aft, the two leaders of the convoy were near at hand. One of them looked at me and said, 'Are you the one they call Papillon? The man they brought back from Colombia?'

'Yes.'

'It doesn't surprise me you went so far: you look as though you understood the sea.'

Ostentatiously I replied, 'Yes, I do. Thoroughly.' That cast a damp, all right. What's more the captain was on deck: he'd come down from the bridge to take the wheel as we left the estuary of the Maroni, that being the most dangerous place, and now he'd handed it over to someone else. This captain, then — a very small, fat, coal-black Negro with quite a youthful face — asked which were the men who'd sailed as far as Colombia on a bit of driftwood.

'This one here, and him, and the other one over there,' said the head of the convoy.

'Which was the captain?' asked the dwarf.

'I was, Monsieur.'

'Well, shipmate, as a sailor I congratulate you. You're no ordinary man. Here.' He put his hand in his jacket pocket.

'Take this tobacco and these cigarette papers. Smoke it and wish me good luck.'

'Thanks, Captain. But I must congratulate you too, for having the courage to sail in this death-trap: and to do so once or even twice a week, they tell me.'

He roared with laughter, terrifying the people I had wanted to upset. 'Oh, you're right,' he said. 'This tub ought to have been sent to the breaker's yard years and years ago, but the company's waiting for it to sink so as to get the insurance.'

Then I ended up with a splendid stroke. 'Luckily there's a life boat for you and the crew.'

'Yes, isn't it lucky?' said the captain without thinking as he went down the ladder.

I'd started this subject of conversation on purpose, and it filled more than four hours of my journey. Everyone had his bit to say, and somehow – I don't know how – the argument spread as far as the fo'c'sle.

Towards ten o'clock that morning there wasn't much of a sea, but the wind was unfavourable. We steered north-east, that is to say against the sea and against the breeze; so of course we rolled and pitched more than usual. Many warders and convicts were seasick. Fortunately the one chained to me had his sea-legs, because there's nothing so unpleasant as seeing someone throw up right next to you. This character was a genuine Parisian *titi* – a tough, a wide-boy. He'd come to Guiana in 1927. So it was seven years now that he'd been on the islands. He was comparatively young – thirty-eight. 'They call me Titi la Belote, because I must admit I'm a wonderful player of belote. In any case, that's what I make my living at, on the islands. Belote all night long at two francs the point. If you bid, you can go a long way. If you win with the jack at two hundred, the type pays out four hundred francs plus the small charge for the other points.'

'But do you mean there's that kind of money on the islands?'

'Why, of course there is, my poor Papillon! The islands are full of chargers stuffed with cash. Some come across with them: others get it in through bent warders, paying fifty per cent. Anyone can tell you're green, mate. You sound as though you didn't know the first thing about it.'

'No, I know absolutely nothing about the islands. All I know is it's very hard to escape from them.'

'Escape?' said Titi. 'It's not even worth wasting your breath,

258

talking about it. I've been on the islands seven years now, and in that time there've been two breaks. And how did they end up? Three dead and two retaken: that's how they ended up, brother. Nobody's succeeded. That's the reason why there aren't many who want to have a go.'

'Why did you go to the mainland?'

'To be X-rayed to see if I had an ulcer or not.'

'And you didn't try to escape from the hospital?'

'You're dead right I didn't try to escape from the hospital! You're the one who mucked all that up, Papillon. And on top of that, it was just my luck to be shoved into the very ward you escaped from. So just try and imagine the security, will you? Every time you went anywhere near a window to get a breath of air, they made you stand back. And when you asked why they said, "It's in case you might have the idea of carrying on like Papillon."'

'Tell me, Titi, who's the big guy sitting next to the convoy leader? An informer?'

'Are you crazy? That guy, everybody thinks the world of him. He's a square, but he knows how to behave like a genuine crook – no matinees with the warders, no privileges accepted. Knows his place as a convict and keeps to it properly. Can give you sound advice: a good sidekick: cold and distant with the cops. Not even the priest or the doctor can get him to work for them. And this square who behaves like a right tough guy, as you see, is a descendant of Louis XV. He's a count, the genuine article: his name's Comte Jean de Bérac. But still, when he first came it took a very long while for the men to come to think anything of him, on account of what sent him to penal was a very dirty, messy job indeed.'

'What did he do?'

'Well, he went and tossed his own baby off a bridge into a stream, and as the kid fell in where it was very shallow, he found it in his heart to go down and chuck it into a deeper place.'

'Really? It's as though he went and killed his own kid twice over.'

'According to a friend of mine who's a clerk and who's seen his file, this character was terrorized by all his grand people. The girl who had had the baby was a servant in the big house, and the character's mother flung her out like a dog. According to my friend, this young fellow was under his proud old shrew of a mother's thumb, and she'd so ground him down because he, a count, had had an affair with a servant-girl, that when he tossed the kid into the water, having told the girl he was taking it to the Public Assistance, he didn't know which way up he was.'

'What did he get?'

'Only ten years. You must realize, Papillon, he's not an ordinary type like us. The countess, the guardian of the family's honour, must have made the judges understand that killing a servant's baby wasn't such a very serious crime when it was committed by a count – a guy that only wanted to preserve the glory of his house.'

'Moral?'

'Well, as I see it – but I'm just a humble Parisian wide-boy – as I see it, the moral is this: by and large, this Comte Jean de Bérac was a gent who'd been brought up in such a way that nothing counted except blue blood – everything else was unimportant, just not worth bothering about. Maybe they weren't serfs in the full meaning of the word, but at all events they were people who didn't amount to anything at all. His mother, that monster of pomp and selfishness, had so put him through the mangle that he was like the rest of them – he thought he had the hereditary right to any of the girls in the neighbourhood. It was only in penal that he became a real noble in the right sense of the word. It may sound crazy, but it's only now that he's the genuine Comte Jean de Bérac.'

The Iles du Salut, that unknown quantity for me, were not going to remain unknown for more than a few hours now. What I did know was that it was very hard to escape. But not impossible. And as I drew in delightful breaths of the sea wind I said to myself, 'When will this head-wind be turned into a full following breeze for an escape?'

We were coming in. Here were the islands! They made a triangle with Royale and Saint-Joseph forming the base and Devil's Island the apex. The sun was already low in the sky, and it lit them up with that extreme brilliance you only see in the tropics. So we had plenty of time to make out all the details. To begin with there was Royale, with a flat ledge running right round a hill about seven hundred feet high. The very top was flat too. The whole thing looked just like a Mexican hat set down on the sea, with its top cut off. Very tall coconut palms everywhere: very green, too. The little red-

260

roofed houses made the island look particularly attractive, and anyone who didn't know what was on shore might have wanted to spend his life there. There was a lighthouse on the plateau, and no doubt they lit it up at night in bad weather, so that ships shouldn't run on the rocks. Now that we were close in I could make out five long buildings. Titi told me the first two were huge barracks with four hundred convicts living in them. Then the disciplinary block, with its punishment cells, all surrounded by a high white wall. The fourth building was the hospital and the fifth housed the warders. And scattered all over the slopes there were these little red-roofed houses where other warders lived. Farther away, but quite close to the tip of Royale, there was Saint-Joseph. Fewer palms, less foliage: and then, right up on top of the plateau, a huge construction that could be seen quite clearly from the sea. I knew what it was at once – the solitary-confinement prison. Titi la Belote confirmed this. He pointed out the barracks of the camp where the prisoners doing ordinary sentences lived. They were lower down, near the sea. You could see the watch-towers and their crenellations standing out quite clearly. And then there were other pretty little houses, with their white walls and red roofs.

As the ship was going into Royale by the southern channel we could now no longer see Devil's Island. In the glimpse I had had of it earlier, it had looked like one enormous palm-covered rock, with no considerable buildings on it. A few yellow houses along the edge of the sea, with black roofs. I learnt later that these were the houses where the political prisoners lived.

We were running into the harbour of Royale, well sheltered behind an immense breakwater made of huge blocks. A work that must have cost a good many convicts their lives in the building.

Three hoots on the siren, and the *Tanon* dropped anchor about two hundred and fifty yards from the quay. This very long jetty, well built of rounded stones and cement, rose about ten feet from sea-level. White-painted buildings ran parallel with it, some way back. I read *Guard-Room, Boat Office, Bakery* and *Harbour-Master's Office* painted in black on the white background.

I could see convicts staring at the boat. They were not dressed in the striped uniform: they were all wearing trousers and a kind of white jacket. Titi la Belote told me that on the islands the men with money had comfortable and even quite decent-looking uniforms made to measure by the tailors, who used flour sacks with the lettering removed. He said almost no one wore convict's clothes.

A boat came towards the *Tanon*. One warder at the tiller, two warders with rifles to the right and the left of him: close to the steersman, aft, six convicts. They stood there, bare to the waist, in white trousers, and they rowed along, plying huge oars. They covered the distance in no time. Behind they towed a large craft rather like a ship's lifeboat; it was empty. They came alongside. First the leaders of the convoy got into the stern. Then two armed warders moved into the bows. Our legs were unchained but our handcuffs were left on, and two by two we went down into the boat, first the ten in my group and then eight from the fo'c'sle. The rowers gave way. They'd make another trip for the rest. We got out at the quay, and there, lined up in front of the harbour-master's office, we waited. None of us had any baggage. The transportees, taking no notice of the screws, talked to us openly, at a prudent distance of five or six yards. Several of the men who had been in my convoy called out friendly greetings to me. Cesari and Essari, two Corsican strong-arm men I'd known at Saint-Martin, told me they were boatmen, working in the harbour. At this point there appeared Chapar, of the Marseilles stock-exchange business, whom I'd known in Paris, quite apart from prison. Without taking any notice at all of the screws he called out, 'Don't you worry, Papillon! You can count on your friends – you'll lack for nothing in solitary. What did you get?'

'Two years.'

'Fine: that's soon over. Then you'll come in with us, and you'll see life's not too bad here.'

'Thanks, Chapar. How's Dega?'

'He's a clerk up there. I'm surprised he hasn't come. He'll be sorry not to have seen you.'

Now here was Galgani. He came towards me, and when the guard tried to stop him he pushed past, saying, 'You're not going to stop me embracing my own brother, are you? What the bloody hell?' And as he embraced me he said, 'You can count on me.'

He was about to go when I said, 'What are you doing?'

'I'm a postman – I look after the letters.'

'You OK?'

'It's a quiet life.'

The remaining men had been brought ashore and now they joined us. We were all unhandcuffed. Titi la Belote, de Bérac and some men I didn't know moved away from the group. A warder said to them, 'Come on: up to the camp.' All of them had their kitbags with the prison outfit: each swung his bag on to his shoulder, and they set off for a road that must lead to the top of the island. The governor of the islands appeared, accompanied by six warders. There was a roll-call. We were all there, and he took delivery of us. The escort withdrew.

'Where's the clerk?' asked the governor.

'He's coming, sir.'

I saw Dega appear, in good white clothes and a buttoned jacket; and with him there came a warder. Each had a big book under his arm, they brought the men out of the ranks one by one, giving each his new number. 'You, prisoner So-and-so, transportee number x, you'll now be confinee number z.'

'What sentence?'

'X years.'

When it came to my turn, Dega embraced me again and again. The governor came over. 'Is this Papillon?'

'Yes, sir,' said Dega.

'Take care of yourself in solitary. Two years soon pass.'

Solitary Confinement

A boat was ready. Out of the nineteen for solitary, ten were going in this first one. My name was called. Calmly Dega said, 'No. This man's going on the last trip.'

Ever since I'd arrived I'd been astonished at the way the convicts spoke. There was no feeling of discipline and they looked as though they didn't give a damn for the screws. Dega came and stood next to me, and we talked. He already knew all about me and about my break. Men who had been with me at Saint-Laurent had come to the islands and had told him everything. He was too delicate to say he was sorry for me. He said just one thing, but very sincerely – 'You deserved to bring it off, boy. It'll be for the next time.' He didn't even tell me to keep my heart up: he knew there was no need.

'I'm the chief accountant and I'm in with the governor. Look after yourself in solitary. I'll send you in tobacco and enough to eat. You won't go short of anything.'

'Papillon, on your way!'

It was my turn. 'Be seeing you all. Thanks for everything.'

And I stepped into the boat. Twenty minutes later we came alongside at Saint-Joseph. I had time to notice that there were only three armed warders aboard for the six convict-boatmen who were rowing and the ten men on their way to solitary. Working out the taking of this boat would have been a piece of cake. Welcoming committee at Saint-Joseph. Two governors introduced themselves to us – the governor of the island's ordinary prison establishment and the governor of the Réclusion – the solitary-confinement prison. With an escort, we were marched up the road leading to solitary. Not a single convict on our path. As we went in through the big iron gates with the words *Réclusion Disciplinaire* over them I at once grasped just how grimly efficient this prison was. Behind the iron gate and the four high walls there was a little building with the words Administrative Block on it, and three other larger ones labelled A, B and C. We were taken into the administration block. A cold great room. The nineteen of us lined up in two ranks. The governor of the Réclusion said to us, 'Prisoners, as you know, this establishment is a place for the punishment of crimes committed by men who have already been sentenced to penal servitude and transportation. Here we don't try to make you mend your ways. We know it's useless. But we do try to bring you to heel. There's just one rule here – keep your mouth shut. Total silence. It's dangerous to telephone: if you're caught, a very severe punishment. If you're not seriously ill, don't go sick. Because if you do, and you're found to be swinging the lead, that's another punishment. That's all I have to say to you. Oh, and by the way, smoking is strictly forbidden. Right, warders: search them thoroughly and put each into his cell. Charrière, Clousiot and Maturette are not to be in the same building. See to it yourself, Monsieur Santori.'

264

Ten minutes later I was shut up in cell 234 in block A. Clousiot was in B and Maturette in C. We said good-bye with a silent look. The moment we came in, we had all grasped that if we wanted to come out alive we should have to obey these inhuman rules. I saw my companions go, companions of this long, long break, proud, brave comrades who'd gone along with me so courageously, never complaining, never regretting what we had done together. There was a lump in my throat, for these fourteen months of fighting side by side for our liberty had bound us together in a friendship that had no limits.

I looked closely at the cell they had put me into. I should never have imagined or believed that a country like mine, a country like France, the mother of freedom throughout the world, a country that had brought forth the Rights of Man and of the citizen, could possibly possess an establishment of such barbarous repression as the Saint-Joseph solitary-confinement prison – not even in French Guiana, not even in a pocket-handkerchief-sized island lost in the Atlantic. Imagine a hundred and fifty cells in a line, each one backing on to another, and each with no opening whatever in its four thick walls except a small iron door with a little trap in it. Painted on the door over each trap *It is forbidden to open this door without administrative order*. To the left there was a sleeping-plank with a wooden pillow – the same system as at Beaulieu – the plank was on hinges and it hooked up against the wall. One blanket; a block of cement in the far corner, to sit on; a brush; an army mug; a wooden spoon; an upright iron plate concealing a metal chamber-pot that was fixed to it by a chain. (It could be moved outwards into the corridor for emptying and inwards, into the cell, when you wanted to use it.) The cell was ten feet high. By way of a ceiling, huge iron bars as thick as tram-rails running criss-cross so that nothing of any size could come through. Then higher still the real roof of the building, perhaps twenty feet above the ground. A sentry-walk, about a yard wide, with an iron hand-rail, ran high over the back-to-back cells. Two warders continuously paced half the length of this walk, meeting in the middle and turning about. The impression was hideous. A fair amount of daylight came in as far as the sentry-walk. But even at midday you could hardly see at all right down in the cell. Straight away I began walking, waiting for them to blow the whistle or whatever they did to say the plank could be let down. So that there shouldn't be the slightest sound, both prisoners and warders were in soft slippers. At once there came to me the thought, 'Here, in cell 234, Charrière, nicknamed Papillon, is going to try and live through a sentence of two years, or seven hundred and thirty days, without going mad, It's up to him to show that this prison's name of man-eater is not entirely true.'

One, two, three, four, five, about-turn. One, two, three, four, five, about-turn. The screw's just gone by over my roof. I didn't hear him come – just saw him. Clack! The light was on: but it was very high up, hanging from the upper roof, twenty feet above. The sentry-walk was lit up, but the cells were in the twilight. I walked: the pendulum was swinging once more. Sleep in peace, you bastards of jurymen who sent me down, sleep in peace: because I believe that if you knew what you'd sent me to, you'd refuse to be party to the infliction of such a punishment – refuse with horror. It's going to be very hard to stop my imagination wandering. Almost impossible. The best thing to do is to direct it towards ideas that aren't too discouraging – better that than trying to suppress it altogether.

Yes, it was in fact a whistle that said it was time to lower the plank. I heard a loud voice saying, 'New men, this is to tell you that from now on you can lower your beds and lie down if you want to.' The only part I took notice of was 'if you want to'. So I went on walking: this was too grave a time for sleep. I'd have to get used to this cage open at the top. One, two, three, four, five: I'd got the pendulum rhythm right away: head down, hands behind my back, steps exactly the right length – to and fro like a pendulum, as though I were walking in my sleep. At the end of the five paces I didn't even see the wall, I just brushed against it in this tireless marathon that had neither finishing-post nor any given time in which it had to be run.

Yes, Papi, this man-eater is no sort of a joke: no sort of joke at all. And the shadow of the screw on the wall has a pretty quaint effect, too. If you looked up, raising your head, it was even more discouraging: you were like a leopard in a pit, watched from above by the hunter who'd just caught it. It was a horrible feeling, and it took months before I could get used to it.

Three hundred and sixty-five days in each year: seven hundred and thirty in two, unless there was a leap-year. I smiled at the notion. Seven hundred and thirty or seven hundred and thirty-one, it's all one, you know. What do you mean, it's all one? It's not the same thing at all. One day more is twenty-four hours more. And twenty-four hours, that's a long time. Seven hundred and thirty days of twenty-four hours each is a good deal longer. How many hours would that make? Could I work it out in my head? How could I tackle such a sum? Impossible. But why not? It can be done all right. Let's have a bash. A hundred days, that makes two thousand four hundred hours. Multiplying by seven is easy; it gives sixteen thousand eight hundred to begin with plus the remaining thirty days at twenty-four hours apiece, which gives seven hundred and twenty. Sixteen thousand eight hundred plus seven hundred and twenty, if I'm not mistaken, ought to give an answer of seventeen thousand five hundred and twenty hours. My dear Monsieur Papillon, you've got seventeen thousand five hundred and twenty hours to kill in this cage – a cage carefully designed for wild beasts, with its smooth walls. How many minutes have I got to spend here? That's of no consequence: hours, fair enough: but minutes, no. Let's not exaggerate. If minutes, why not seconds? But whether they signify or not, it's not that I'm interested in. What I really have to do is to fill these days, hours, minutes by myself, out of myself! Who can there be to the right of me? And to the left? And behind? If these three cells are filled those three men must also be wondering who's just arrived in 234.

There was the plop of something falling behind me, inside my cell. What could it be? Had my neighbour been skilful enough to toss something in through the bars? I tried to make out what it was. I could just distinguish something long and thin – I sensed it rather than saw it. Just as I was about to pick it up it moved and began to hurry towards the wall. At its first movement I recoiled. When it reached the wall it climbed a little way up and then fell back to the ground. The surface was too smooth for it to get a footing. I let it try to make its way up the wall three times and then the fourth time, as it fell, I squashed it with my foot. It was soft under my slipper. What could it be? Going down on my knees I looked as close as I could and at last I made it out – it was a huge centipede, a good nine inches long and two fingers thick. I was filled with such disgust that I could not pick it up and put it in the chamber-pot. I kicked it under the bed. I'd look at it tomorrow, by daylight. As it happened I had plenty of time to see centipedes: they used to fall from the main roof high above. I learnt to let them walk about on my naked body, without catching hold of them or disturbing them as I lay there. I also had occasion to find out just how much a tactical error could cost in the way of pain. A sting from one of these revolting creatures could give you a raging fever for more than twelve hours, and it burnt terribly for close on six.

However, it was an amusement, too – something to divert my thoughts. When a centipede fell into my cell and I was awake, I would torture it as long as possible with the brush; or else I'd play with it, letting it hide and then trying to find it a few moments later.

One, two, three, four, five . . . Dead silence everywhere. Was there nobody here who snored? Nobody who coughed? The heat was stifling, true enough. And this was night-time! What was it going to be like during the day? I was fated to live with centipedes. When the tide rose in the under-water black-hole of Santa Marta, great numbers of them used to come in: they were smaller, but they were of the same family as these. At Santa Marta, to be sure, there was the daily flooding; but we could talk and call out, we could listen to the others singing or the lunatics (temporary or permanent) shouting and raving. It wasn't the same thing at all. If I had the choice, I'd take Santa Marta. What you're saying now doesn't make sense, Papillon. At Santa Marta everyone agreed that the very most any man could stand was six months. Whereas here there are plenty who have four or five years to do, or even more. Sentencing them to do it is one thing: but the actual doing of it is something else again. How many kill themselves? I don't see how they could manage it. But it is possible, though. It wouldn't be easy, but you could just hang yourself. You make a rope with your trousers. You tie one end to the brush, stand on the sleeping-plank and push the rope round a bar. If you do it right up against the sentry-walk, it's probable the screw won't notice the rope. And just when he's gone by, you launch yourself into the empty air. By the time he comes back, you've already had it. In any case, he'd be in no hurry to come and open your cell to cut you down. Open the cell? He couldn't. On the door it's written *It is forbidden to open this door without administrative order*. So don't you worry: the man who wants to commit suicide will have plenty of time before they unhook him 'by administrative order'.

All this I am writing about is perhaps neither very exciting nor very interesting for people who like action and movement. They can skip these pages if they find them dull. Yet it seems to me I ought to record these first impressions, these reactions during the first hours I was laid in the grave and these first thoughts that came flooding in upon me as I came into contact with my new cell – it seems to me I ought to describe them as exactly as I can.

I had been walking for a very long time now. I could hear a murmur in the darkness – the guards changing. The first had been a big, thin fellow: this one was small and fat. He dragged his slippers. You could hear them scuffing along two cells before and two cells after. He wasn't a hundred per cent silent like his mate. I went on walking. It must be late. What time could it be? Tomorrow I should have something to measure the time by. The trap in the door would open four times every day, and thanks to that I'd know roughly what o'clock it was. And at night, knowing the time the first patrol came on and how long it lasted, I'd have a fixed standard to live with – first, second, third patrol, etc.

One, two, three, four, five . . . Mechanically I returned to this endless walk, and with tiredness helping, I took off easily and travelled back into the past. It must certainly have been by way of contrast to the darkness of my cell, but there I was in the full sunlight, sitting on the beach belonging to my tribe. The canoe with Lali fishing in it rose and fell on that matchless opal-green sea, two hundred yards away. The sand was rough under my feet. Zoraïma brought me a good-sized fish, cooked over the embers and carefully kept hot in a banana leaf. I ate with my fingers, of course, and she sat there cross-legged opposite me. She was very pleased with the way the flakes came away from the bone; and my face showed her how delighted I was with her dish.

I was no longer in my cell. I did not yet know anything about the Réclusion, nor Saint-Joseph, nor the islands. I rolled on the beach, cleaning my hands by rubbing them in the coral sand, as fine as flour. Then I went down to the sea to rinse my mouth in that brilliantly clear and salty water. I scooped it up and splashed my face. As I rubbed it on my neck I noticed how long my hair had grown. When Lali came back I'd ask her to shave the back of my neck. I spent all that night with my tribe. I undid Zoraïma's loin-cloth, and there on the beach, under the hot sun, with the sea breeze wafting over us, I had her. She uttered amorous groans, as she did when she was taking delight in it. Perhaps it was the wind that carried this music as far as Lali. In any case she saw us clearly enough, and she knew quite well we were fast together – she was too near not to be sure we were making love. She must certainly have seen us, for the boat came back to the land. Smiling, she jumped out. On the way she had undone her plaits and combed out her wet hair with her long fingers – the wind and the sun of that wonderful day were already drying it. I went over to her. She put her right arm round my waist and urged me up the beach in the direction of our hut. All the way she kept making me understand – 'Me too, me too'. When we were indoors she pushed me on to a hammock folded on the ground by way of a blanket; and interlaced with her I forgot the existence of the world. Zoraïma was very bright, and she took care not to come back until our play was over. When she appeared we were still lying there naked on the hammock, destroyed with love. She came and sat next to us, patting her sister's cheek and repeating a word that must certainly have meant something like *greedy Lali*. Then, with movements full of modest affection, she fixed my loin-cloth and then her sister's. I spent the whole of that night with the Goajiras. I didn't sleep at any time whatsoever. I did not even lie down so that behind my closed eyelids I might see the scenes I had lived through. It was during this continual pacing up and down in a kind of hypnosis that I was taken back, without any effort on my part, and set down once more in that extraordinarily beautiful day I had experienced nearly six months before.

The light went out and I could see that daybreak was flooding into the twilight of my cell, dispelling the kind of drifting dimness that enveloped everything below, everything around me. A blast on a whistle. I heard the planks banging up and I even distinguished the sound of my right-hand neighbour fastening his with the ring fixed in the wall. My neighbour coughed, and I heard the splash of water. How did you wash here?

'Monsieur le Surveillant, how do you wash here?'

'Confinee, I forgive you for not knowing, but here you're not allowed to speak to a warder on duty without being severely punished. To wash, you stand over the pot and pour from the jug with one hand. You wash yourself with the other. Haven't you unfolded your blanket?'

'No.'

'There'll certainly be a canvas towel inside it.'

Can you just imagine that? So you aren't allowed to speak to the warder on duty. Not for any reason at all? And what about if you're in too much pain from some illness? What if you're dying? Heart disease, appendicitis, a mortal go of asthma? Are you forbidden to call for help here, even though you're dying? That crowns everything! No: not really. It's quite natural. It would be too easy to kick up a row when you reach the end of your tether and your nerves give way. Just to hear voices, just to be spoken to, even if you were only to hear 'Die then; but shut up.' Twenty times a day a score out of the two hundred and fifty characters there might be here would start something so as to get rid of the gas building up its pressure inside their heads – get rid of it through a safety-valve, as it were.

It couldn't have been a psychiatrist who had the notion of building these lion cages: no doctor would lower himself so far. It wasn't a doctor who worked out the rules, either. But both the architect and the civil servant who did create this establishment, the two who laid down the smallest details of the carrying out of the sentences, were both of them revolting monsters, vicious, evil psychologists full of sadistical hatred for the convicts.

The black-hole of the central prison at Beaulieu, near Caen, might be very deep – two storeys beneath the ground – but even so, some echo of the tortures and ill-treatment handed out to a prisoner might in time make its way up to the rest of the world. That's proved by the fact that when they took off my handcuffs and thumb-pieces I really saw fear on the warders' faces – fear they might get into trouble, of that there is no doubt.

But here, in the settlement's solitary-confinement prison, where only people belonging to the service could come in, they were perfectly easy in their minds. Nothing could ever happen to them.

Clack, clack, clack, clack: all the traps were being opened. I went to mine, took the risk of peeping out, then leant through a little, and then pushed my whole head through into the corridor: to the left and right I saw a crowd of heads. Straight away I grasped that the moment the hatches were opened everyone darted his head out. The man on my right looked at me with absolutely no expression whatsoever. His brain numbed with masturbation, no doubt. His poor dim idiot face was pale and greasy. The one on the left quickly said, 'How long?'

'Two years.'

'I got four. Served one. What's your name?'

'Papillon.'

'I'm Georges. Jojo l'Auvergnat. Where were you copped?'

'Paris. And you?'

He had no time to answer. The coffee, with the hunk of bread coming after it, was only two cells away. He pulled in his head, and I did the same. I held out my mug, which was filled with coffee; then they gave me a piece of bread. As I didn't take it quick enough the hatch came down and my bread fell to the ground. In less than a quarter of an hour the silence had returned. There must be two separate distributions – a party for each corridor. Otherwise it was too quick. At noon, soup with a bit of boiled meat in it. In the evening, a dish of lentils. During two years this bill of fare never changed except at night, when it might be lentils, red beans, split peas, chickpeas, haricots or fried rice. Midday was always the same.

And then every fortnight you put your head out through the hatch and a convict took off your beard with fine barber's clippers.

Now I had been there three days. There was one thing that preyed on my mind. On Royale my friends had said they'd send me in things to smoke and eat. I'd still had nothing and in any case I wondered how they'd ever manage to bring off a miracle like that. So I was not absolutely amazed at having received nothing. Smoking must be very dangerous; and anyhow it was a luxury. Food, yes, that was going to be of the first importance, because the midday soup was just hot water with two or three bits of greenery in it and a little scrap of boiled meat – three or four ounces, maybe. In the evening it was a ladle of water with a few haricots or other dried vegetables floating about in it. To speak plainly, I didn't so much suspect the administration of not giving us proper rations as the other prisoners, who handed out the food or prepared it. This idea came to me because it was a little guy from Marseilles who dealt out the vegetables in the evening. His ladle went right down to the bottom of the pail, and when he was on duty I had more vegetables than water. With the rest it was the other way about: they didn't push the ladle far in but skimmed the top, having stirred a little. So what did you get? Plenty of wet, precious few vegetables. This underfeeding was very dangerous. To have willpower you need a certain bodily strength too.

The corridor was being swept: it seemed to me the broom kept going a long while outside my cell. The bristles swished again and again against my door. I looked closely and I saw a scrap of white paper showing underneath. I instantly understood that something was being slipped through for me, but it couldn't be pushed farther. He was waiting for me to pull it out before going on to sweep somewhere else. I pulled the paper in and unfolded it. It was a note written in phosphorescent ink. I waited for the screw to go by and then quickly I read, 'Papi, from tomorrow there'll be five cigarettes and a coconut in your pot every day. Chew the coconut well when you eat it if you want it to do you good. Swallow the chewed meat. Smoke in the morning when the pots are being emptied. *Never after coffee in the morning*: after soup at twelve the minute you've finished: and after supper. Enclosed there's a bit of pencil lead. Any time you want anything, ask for it on the enclosed scrap of paper. When the sweeper rubs his broom against the door, scratch with your fingers. If he scratches, shove your paper under. Never pass the note unless he's answered your scratching. Put the bit of paper in your ear so as not to have to take your charger out, and your pencil lead anywhere at the bottom of your cell wall. Thumbs up. Love. Ignace, Louis.'

Galgani and Dega had sent me this message. A glow rose in my heart: having such faithful, loving friends gave me a feeling of warmth. And now I returned to my pacing with a cheerful, lively step, with even more faith in the future and a certainty of coming out of this living grave on my feet – one, two, three, four, five, about-turn, etc. And as I walked I thought 'What noble hearts those two have, what strength in doing good. They must certainly be running a very serious risk: maybe even the risk of losing their jobs as clerk and postman. It's really magnificent, what they're doing for me, quite apart from the fact that it must cost them a packet. What quantities of people they must have to buy to reach out from Royale as far as me in my cell in the man-eater.'

Reader, you must know that a dry coconut is full of oil. Its hard white flesh is so full of it that you only have to grate six nuts and put them to soak in hot water to be able to skim off nearly two pints of oil from the surface next morning. The thing we missed worst in this diet of ours was oil: and coconut is crammed with vitamins, too. A nut a day was an almost certain guarantee of health. To put it at the lowest, with that to eat you couldn't dry out or die of mere want. Today it is more than two months that I have been getting food and tobacco without anything going wrong. I take a Red Indian's precautions when I smoke, inhaling deeply and then letting it out little by little, fanning it away with my right hand.

An odd thing happened yesterday. I don't know whether I behaved rightly or wrongly. A warder on duty on the sentry walk leant on the rail and looked down into my cell. He lit a cigarette, took a few drags and then let it drop into my cell. When he had done so he moved off. I waited for him to cross over again and then I ostentatiously crushed the cigarette with my foot. He made a very slight pause: as soon as he realized what I had done he went straight on. Had he been sorry for me? Was he ashamed of the service he belonged to? Or was it a trap? I don't know and it gets me down. When you're having a very bad time, you grow over-sensitive. If that warder meant to be a decent man for the space of a few seconds I shouldn't have wanted to hurt him by my gesture of contempt.

Yes, it was in fact more than two months that I'd been here. As I saw it, this prison was the only one in which there was nothing to be learnt. Because there was no possible line of approach. I was thoroughly used to getting out of myself, and I had a sure-fire way of taking off for a journey among the stars or for an effortless vision of the various stages in my life as a child or a man on the run or for a session of building wonderfully real castles in Spain. What I had to do was to get very tired in the first place. I had to walk for hours without sitting down, without stopping, and thinking of ordinary subjects in the usual sort of way. Then when I was absolutely all in I'd lie down on my plank, rest my head on one half of my blanket, and cover my face with the other. Then the already stale air of the cell would filter slowly through to my mouth and nose. This started off a kind of smothering in my lungs and my head would begin to burn. I'd stifle with heat and lack of air and then suddenly I'd take off. Oh, what indescribable journeys my spirit made and what sensations I had during these voyages! Nights of love truly more vivid and moving than when I was free, even more stirring than the real ones, the nights I'd actually experienced. Yes: and this power of moving through space and time allowed me to sit there with my mother, who had died seventeen years before. I played with her dress and she fondled my curly hair, which she let grow very long when I was about five, as though I was a little girl. I stroked her long, delicate fingers, their skin as soft as silk. She and I laughed about my daring notion of diving into the stream as I'd seen the big boys do, when we were out for a walk. The smallest details of the way her hair was done, the glowing affection of her brilliant eyes, her gentle, unforgettable voice: 'Riri, dear, be good, be very good so that Maman can love you very much. When you're a little bigger you'll be able to dive into the river from high, high up. Just now you're still too small, darling. But never mind, soon you'll be quite a big boy – all too soon, perhaps.' And hand in hand we walked home along the stream. And now there I was, really there in my childhood home. So thoroughly was I there that I placed my hand over Maman's eyes so that she could not see the music but would still go on playing to me. I was actually there: it wasn't just imagination. I was there with her, standing on a chair behind the music stool she was sitting on, and I closed her great eyes firmly with my little hands. Her nimble fingers ran on over the notes, and I heard the *Merry Widow* right through to the end.

Nobody, neither the merciless prosecutor, nor the shady police, nor that vile Polein, who bought his freedom with perjured evidence, nor the twelve bastards who were such fools as to accept the prosecutor's line and his way of seeing things, nor the Réclusion screws, those worthy associates of the man-eater – absolutely no person and no thing, not even these thick walls or the remoteness of this island lost in the Atlantic Ocean, could prevent my exquisitely happy rose-pink journeys, when I took off for the stars.

I got it wrong when I was working out the time that I should have to be by myself: I only talked about time in hours. That was a mistake. There are periods you have to measure in minutes. For example, the emptying of the pots took place after the handing out of the coffee and bread, about an hour after. It was when the empty pot came back that I found the coconut, the five cigarettes and sometimes a note in phosphorescent ink. At those times I would count the minutes. Not always, but pretty often. It was easy enough, because I regulated each pace so that it took one second, and as I went to and fro in my pendulum swing I made a mental reckoning at each turn. One, I would say. So twelve made a minute. Above all you mustn't think I was worried about whether I'd get that coconut (which was really much the same as my life) nor whether I'd get cigarettes and the indescribable pleasure of smoking ten times during the next twenty-four hours in this tomb – for I smoked each cigarette in two goes. No: sometimes when the coffee came round I was seized with a kind of distress, and for no particular reason I'd be afraid that something had happened to the men who were helping me so generously, at the risk of their own peace and quiet. So I'd wait, and I was never relieved from my anxiety until I saw the coconut. There it would be, and so everything was all right *for them.*

Slowly, very slowly, the hours, days, weeks, months went by. Now it was almost a year that I had been here. It was exactly eleven months and twenty days that I had not spoken to anyone for more than forty seconds, and that in quick, muttered rather than spoken words. Though I did have one proper conversation aloud. I'd caught a cold and I was coughing a great deal. I thought it was enough to justify going to see the doctor, so I reported sick.

Here was the doctor. To my great astonishment the trap opened. A head appeared in the opening. 'What's the matter with you? What are you complaining of? Lungs? Turn round. Cough.'

God above! What was this – a joke? And yet it is the strict and literal truth. There did exist a doctor in the colonial service who would consent to examine me through a trap and make me turn round a yard away from the door so that he, clapping his ear to the hole, could listen to my chest. Then he said, 'Put your arm out.' I was about to put it out without thinking, but then a kind of self-respect stopping me, I said to this curious medico, 'Thank you, Doctor, but don't you bother. It's not worth troubling.' And at least I did have the strength of mind to make him see I didn't take his examination seriously.

He was brazen enough to say, 'As you like,' and then he walked off. Just as well, for I was on the point of bursting with indignation.

One, two, three, four, five, about-turn. One, two, three, four, five, about-turn. Tirelessly on and on, without stopping: today I walked furiously, my legs all tense: usually they were quite relaxed. It was as though I had to trample something underfoot, after what had just happened. What was there I could trample underfoot? There was only cement down here. No, there were plenty of things I could trample in my pacing. I trampled the spinelessness of that medico who would lend himself to such disgusting conduct merely to be in with the authorities. I trampled the total want of feeling of one class of men for the sufferings and unhappiness of another class of men. I trampled the ignorance of the French nation and its want of interest or curiosity about what happened to the human cargoes that set off from Saint-Martin-de-Ré every two years, or where they went. I trampled the criminal court journalists who'd write a scandalous article about a man over some given crime and then a few months later would not even remember his existence. I trampled the Catholic priests who heard confession and knew what happened in the French penal settlements but nevertheless kept their mouths shut. I trampled the organization of the Ligue des Droits de l'Homme et du Citoyen that never spoke out and said, 'Stop killing people as surely as if they were guillotined: abolish the mass sadism among the employees of the prison service.' I trampled the fact that not a single organization or association ever questioned the top men of this system to find out how and why eighty per cent of the people who were sent away every two years vanished. I trampled on the official doctors' death certificates – suicide, general debility, death from prolonged under-nourishment, scurvy, tuberculosis, raving madness, senile decay. What else did I trample upon? I don't know, but in any case, after what had just happened I certainly wasn't walking ordinarily – I was crushing something at every step.

One, two, three, four, five . . . and the weariness of the slow flowing hours calmed my silent rebellion. Ten days more and I should have served just half my time of solitary confinement. This really was an anniversary worth celebrating, for apart from my heavy cold I was in good health. I was neither mad nor anywhere near going mad. I was sure, a hundred per cent sure, that I'd come out at the end of this coming year alive and in my right mind.

I was woken up by hushed voices. One said, 'He's completely mummified, Monsieur Durand. How can it be you didn't notice earlier?'

'I don't know. As he hanged himself in the corner of the sentry-walk side, I must have gone by many a time without seeing him.'

'Well, it doesn't matter: but you must admit it makes no sense that you didn't notice him.'

My neighbour on the left had killed himself. That's what I gathered. They carried him away. The door closed. The rules had been strictly obeyed, since the door had been opened and closed in the presence of an 'administrative authority', in this case the governor of the prison – I had recognized his voice. This was the fifth man round me who had vanished in ten weeks.

The day of the celebration came round. I found a tin of Nestlé's milk in the pot. My friends were out of their wits. A fortune to buy it and very serious risks in getting it to me. For me this was a day of triumph over the enemy. So I promised not to take off for somewhere else. Here I was in the Réclusion. A year had gone by since I came in and I was fit to make a break and go off tomorrow if the occasion turned up. This was a fine positive thing to be able to state and I was proud of it.

Something out of the ordinary happened: the afternoon sweeper brought me a note from my friends. 'Keep your heart up. You've only got a year left to do. We know your health's OK. We're pretty well too. Love, Louis, Ignace. If you can, send a line back at once by the person who gives you this.'

On the scrap of blank paper that came with the note I wrote, 'Thanks for everything. I'm strong and hope to be the same in a year's time, thanks to you. Can you give me news of Clousiot, Maturette?' And now here was the sweeper, scratching at my door. Quickly I slipped out the paper, which disappeared at once. All that day and part of the night there I was, with my feet firmly on the ground and as fit as I had often promised myself I should be. In a year's time I was going to be sent to one of the islands. Royale or Saint-Joseph? I'd fill myself to overflowing with talk, tobacco and schemes for another break right away.

278

The next day I set about the first of the three hundred and sixty-five that I still had to do, and I did so feeling happy about my fate. I was right for the eight months that followed. But the ninth, things went bad. That morning, when the pots were being emptied, the man carrying the coconut was caught red-handed just as he was shoving my pot back, with the nut and the five cigarettes already in it.

This was so serious an incident that for some minutes the rule of silence was forgotten. You could very distinctly hear the blows the unfortunate prisoner received. Then the gasping cry like a man given a mortal wound. My flap opened and a warder's furious face bawled at me, 'You'll lose nothing of what's coming to you by waiting!'

'Whenever you like, you fat sod!' I cried, ready to burst at what I'd heard of the way they'd treated the poor bastard.

This happened at seven o'clock. It was only at eleven that a group led by the deputy-governor came for me. They opened this door that had been closed on me twenty months before and had never been opened in all that time. I was at the back of my cell, grasping my mug, ready to defend myself and perfectly determined to hit as hard and as often as I could. This was for two reasons: first, so that a handful of warders shouldn't beat me up and get away with it; and secondly, so as to be knocked out the quicker. Nothing of the kind happened. 'Confinee, come out.'

'If I'm to come out to be beaten up, you can expect me to defend myself. I'm not coming out to be attacked on all sides. I'm better placed here to bash the first man that touches me.'

'You're not going to be hit, Charrière.'

'Who says so?'

'I do. The deputy-governor.'

'Are you to be trusted?'

'Don't be rude: it'll get you nowhere. I give you my word you won't be hit. Come on, now, out of it.' I held on to my mug. 'You can keep that. You won't have to use it.'

'OK.' I came out, and with the deputy-governor and six warders round me I went right along the corridor. The moment I reached the courtyard my head spun and my eyes closed, stabbed by the light. At last I made out the little building where we'd been received. There were a dozen warders there. Without pushing me they took me to the administrative office. A man, covered with blood, was lying there on the ground, groaning. A clock on the wall said eleven and I thought, 'They've been torturing the poor sod for four hours.' The governor was sitting behind his desk: the deputy took a chair next to him.

'Charrière, how long have you been receiving food and cigarettes?'

'He must have told you.'

'I'm asking you.'

'As for me, I've got amnesia. I don't even know what happened yesterday.'

'Are you trying to make game of me?'

'No. I'm astonished it's not in my file. A blow on the head and I lost my memory.'

The governor was so surprised by this answer that he said, 'Ask Royale whether there is any such thing on his record.' While they were telephoning he went on, 'You remember you're called Charrière all right?'

'Oh yes.' And quickly, so as to unsettle him all the more, I said in a mechanical voice, 'My name's Charrière, I was born in 1906 in the Ardèche and I was sentenced to life in Paris, Seine.' His eyes were as round as saucers, and I sensed I had shaken him.

'Did you have your coffee and your bread this morning?'

'Yes.'

'What vegetable did you have last night?'

'Don't know.'

'So according to what you say, you've no memory at all?'

'None at all for things that happen. Faces, yes: I remember them. For example I know it was you that received me one time. When? I can't tell.'

'So you don't know how much longer you've got to serve?'

'Out of my lifer? Why, until I die, I suppose.'

'No, no. Out of your solitary.'

'They've given me solitary? What for?'

'Come, this really is the limit! God above! Don't put me into a rage. You're not going to tell me you don't remember you're doing two years for an escape. Don't you try it on to that extent!'

Then I finished him off completely. 'What, me escape? Governor, I'm a responsible man and I can answer for all my doings. Come with me and have a look at my cell: you'll soon see whether I've escaped or not.'

At this moment a screw said, 'Royale on the line, sir.'

He took the telephone. 'Nothing? Odd: he claims he has amnesia. What gave it him? A blow on the head ... Right, I understand. He's swinging the lead. I'll find out ... I'm sorry I troubled you, Governor. I'll check on it. Good-bye. Yes, I'll let you know how it goes. Now then, Charlie Chaplin, just let's have a look at your head. Well, yes; there is quite a long scar. How come you remember that you've had no memory since they gave you this bang, eh? Answer me that one, will you?'

'I can't explain it. I just know I remember the blow, that my name is Charrière, and a few other things.'

'What are you driving at, when all's said and done?'

'That's just the question. You ask me how long I've been having food and tobacco. And this is what I say: I don't know whether it's the first time or the thousandth. What with my loss of memory, I just can't tell you. That's all: do what you like about it.'

'What I like is easy enough. You've been eating too much for a long while: well, now you can lose a little weight. No supper till the end of his sentence.'

That same day I had a note at the time of the second sweeping. Unfortunately I couldn't read it, it not being phosphorescent. At night I lit a cigarette that I still had from the day before and that had been so well hidden in the plank they had not found it when they searched. Drawing on it, I managed to read, 'Cleaner didn't blab. He said it was only second time he gave you anything to eat. Did it by himself. Because he knew you in France. Nobody on Royale will get into trouble. Courage.'

So there I was, deprived of my coconut and cigarettes, and cut off from news of my friends on Royale. As well as that, they'd done away with my evening meal. I'd got used to not having to feel hungry; and what's more, those ten periods when I could smoke helped fill the day for me and part of the night. I wasn't only thinking of myself, either, but also of the poor bastard they'd beaten up. I hoped he wouldn't be too severely punished.

One, two, three, four, five, about-turn ... one, two, three, four, five, about-turn. You're not going to be able to stand this starvation-diet as easily as all that, cock; and since you're going to eat so little, maybe you'd better change your tactics.

Lying down as long as possible, for example, so as not to waste any strength. The less I move about, the fewer calories I burn up. Sit for hours and hours during the daytime. It was quite another kind of life I was going to have to learn. Four months: that was one hundred and twenty days to get through. With the diet they'd just put me on, how many days would it take before I became thoroughly anaemic? Two months at least. So the two vital months lay ahead of me. If I grew too weak, every kind of illness would have a perfect breeding-place in my body. I made up my mind to stay lying down from six in the evening until six in the morning. I'd walk between coffee and the emptying of the pots, or roughly two hours. After the midday soup, about two hours more. Four hours walking altogether. All the rest of the time, sitting or lying down. It would be hard to take off without being physically tired. Still, I'd try to do it.

Today, after I'd spent a long while thinking about my friends and the poor bastard who'd been so brutally ill-treated, I began to follow this new routine. I did fairly well, although the hours seemed to me to take longer to go by and although my legs, which hadn't been in action now for hours on end, kept tingling with a desire to move.

This way of life had been going on for ten days now. Now I was hungry all the time, right round the clock. A continual weariness had hold of me and it never let go. I missed my coconut terribly; and to some extent the cigarettes. I went to bed very early and as quickly as I could I took off from my cell. Yesterday I was in Paris, at the Rat Mort, drinking champagne with friends: London Antonio was there – he came from the Balearics in the first place, but he spoke French like a Parisian and English like a genuine rosbif. The next day, at the Maronnier in the boulevard de Clichy, he put five revolver bullets into a friend of his, killing him. In the underworld friendship can change into mortal hatred very quickly. Yes, I was in Paris yesterday, dancing to an accordion at the Petit Jardin in the Avenue de Saint-Ouen, where the customers were Corsicans or Marseillais to a man. The friends who passed before my eyes during this imaginary journey were so utterly convincing that I had no doubt they were really there, any more than I doubted my presence in all those night-spots where I'd had such fun.

So with this very low diet, and without much walking, I

reached the same result that I used to get from fatigue. These pictures of my former life had such a power of taking me out of my cell that I really spent more hours a free man than a convict in solitary confinement.

Only a month to do now. For the last three all I'd had to eat was a hunk of bread in the morning and at noon hot thin soup with its scrap of boiled meat. I was so continually hungry that the moment it was given to me I examined the little lump to see whether it was just a bit of skin – and often enough it was.

I'd lost a great deal of weight, and I realized just how important the coconut had been in keeping me healthy and sane in this terrible exclusion from life – the coconut I'd been lucky to have for twenty months.

I was all on edge this morning, after I'd drunk my coffee. I allowed myself to eat half my bread, which was something I never did. Ordinarily I broke it into four more or less equal pieces and ate them at six o'clock, noon, six again and then a little bit during the night. 'Why did you do that, man?' I asked myself angrily. 'Is it now, near the end, that you're going to let yourself fall to pieces?' 'I'm hungry, and I've no strength left.' 'Don't be such a fool. How could you have any strength left, eating what you eat? You're weak, fair enough, but you're not ill, and that's the whole point – you win. Looking at it reasonably, and with a little luck, the man-eater ought to lose.' I was sitting there on my concrete block of a stool, after my two hours of walking. Thirty more days, or seven hundred and twenty hours, and the door would open and they'd say to me, 'Confinee Charrière, come out. You've finished your two years of solitary.' And what should I say? This. 'Yes, I've finished my two years of martyrdom.' Come, no! That wouldn't do. If it's the governor you tried the loss-of-memory caper with, you must go on with it: quite calmly. You must say, 'What, am I pardoned? Am I going back to France? Is my lifer over?' just so as to see his expression and to convince him that the hunger he condemned you to was unjust. 'Man, what's wrong with you?' Just or unjust, the governor doesn't give a damn whether he was wrong. What importance could it have for a mind like that? You're not such a fool as to believe he's going to feel remorse just for having punished you unjustly? I forbid you to suppose, now or at any other time, that a gaoler can be a normal human being. No man worthy of the name could possibly belong to that body. In life you get used to everything, even to being a wicked old sod throughout your career. Maybe when he's close to the grave, but only then, the fear of God (if he has any religion) may make him anxious and repentant. No, not out of real remorse for the stinking things he's been guilty of, but out of dread that his God may send him down too, in his turn. So when you come out and you're sent to one of the islands – it doesn't matter which – you're never to have any dealings with that tribe. Each is on his own side of a clearly marked boundary. On the one side mean flabbiness, pettifogging heartless authority, instinctive and automatic sadism: and on the other, me and men like me, who have committed serious crimes, to be sure, but in whom suffering has brought out marvellous qualities – compassion, kindness, self-sacrifice, magnanimity, courage. In all sincerity, I'd rather be a convict than a gaoler.

Only twenty days to go. I was really weak now. I'd noticed that my hunk of bread was always among the smaller bits. Who could have sunk so low as to pick out a special piece for me? For some days my soup had been nothing but hot water, and the meat was always a bone with very little on it, or else it was a bit of skin. I was afraid I'd fall sick. This haunted me all the time. I was so weak that without any effort I could go into dreams of every kind, wide awake. This deep weariness and the really serious depression that came with it worried me badly. I tried to stand up to it and I managed to get through the twenty-four hours of every day; but it was hard.

There was a scratching at my door. I snatched in the note. It was phosphorescent and it came from Dega and Galgani. 'Send a line. Very anxious about your health. Only nineteen days left: keep your heart up. Louis, Ignace.'

There was a scrap of paper and a bit of lead. I wrote, 'Holding out: very weak. Thanks. Papi.' And when the broom scraped against my door again I pushed back the note. No cigarettes, no coconut, but this note meant more than all those things. The proof of this wonderful, lasting friendship gave me the sudden lift I needed. They knew what state I was in outside, and if I fell ill my friends would certainly go and see the doctor and urge him to look after me properly. They were right: only nineteen days to go. I was coming towards the end of this exhausting race against death and madness. I must not fall ill. It was up to me to move as little as possible so as to use up only the essential calories. I'd do away with the morning walk and the one in the afternoon – two hours each. That was the only way of holding out. So all night, for twelve hours on end, I lay down; and the other twelve hours I sat on my stone bench, never stirring. From time to time I got up and did a few knee-bends and arm movements; then I sat down again. Only ten days left.

I was walking about in Trinidad, lulled by the one-stringed Javanese fiddles with their plaintive tunes when a hideous, inhuman roar brought me back to earth. The shout came from the cell behind mine or from another very near to it. I heard, 'Come down here into my pit, you bleeding sod. Aren't you tired of watching me from above? Don't you understand you lose half the fun – you can't see down into this dark hole.'

'Shut up, or you'll cop it really hard.'

'Ha, ha! Just hear me laugh, you silly bastard. Do you think you can find anything worse than this silence? Punish me as much as you like: knock me about if you feel like it, you ugly son of a bitch: but you'll never find anything to come up to this silence that you force me to live in. No, no, no! I can't stand it any more, I can't stand never hearing a word! It was three years ago I ought to have said "Shit to you, you bleeding sod!" And I've been such a bloody fool that I've waited thirty-six months before telling you what I think of you, because I was afraid of being punished. What I think of you and everybody like you, you lousy rotten set of screws.'

A few moments later the door opened and I heard, 'No, not like that! Put it on him backwards – it works better that way.'

And the poor bastard roared out, 'Put your stinking strait-jacket on whichever way you like, you shit! Put it on backwards and tighten it till I can't breathe. Put your knee in and pull hard on the laces. That won't stop me telling you your mother was a bitch and that's why you're a heap of shit yourself.'

They must have gagged him, because I heard nothing more. The door closed again. This scene must have shaken the young warder, for a few minutes later he stopped in front of my cell and said, 'He must have gone mad.'

'You think so? Yet everything he said made very good sense.'

That knocked the screw flat. He went off, saying, 'Well, I never expected that from you!'

All this had snatched me away from that island full of kind people and from the fiddles, the Hindu girls' tits, and Port of Spain harbour, and it had dumped me down again in the grim reality of the Réclusion.

Ten days more: that meant two hundred and forty hours to get through. These days were passing by more easily: either it was the idea of keeping still that was bearing fruit, or it was the lift my friends' letter had given me. Or more likely I felt stronger because of the idea of comparison that forced itself upon my mind: here I was within two hundred and forty hours of being let out of solitary; I was weak, but my brain was all right and my energy only wanted a little more bodily strength behind it to be restored. Whereas a couple of yards behind me, the other side of the wall, there was a poor type who was moving into the first stage of madness by what was probably the worst possible door – the one of violence. He'd not live long, because his mutiny would provide them with the opportunity of giving him the whole satisfying range of treatment they'd carefully worked out so as to kill him in the most scientific manner possible. I blamed myself for feeling stronger just because the other chap was beaten. I wondered whether I was one of those selfish brutes who go out in the winter wearing good shoes, good gloves and a fur-lined coat and who watch the ordinary people going to work, badly dressed and frozen with cold or at least with their hands blue from the morning frost – watch them running for the underground or the first bus and feel warmer than before and take a much livelier pleasure in their fur lining. Quite often in life everything is a matter of comparison. True enough, I've got ten years: but Papillon, he's got life. True enough, I've got a lifer: but I'm twenty-eight, whereas he's fifty, even if he has only got fifteen years.

Right, here I was coming to the end of it, and I was confident I should be quite fit from every point of view – health, spirit and energy – for a truly outstanding break. The first one had been talked about: the second would be carved in the stone of one of the prison walls. There was no question about it. I'd be off before six months were over, and that was for sure.

This was the last night I was to spend in solitary. Seventeen thousand five hundred and eight hours had passed since I walked into cell 234. My door had been opened once, for me to be taken to the governor for punishment. Apart from my neighbour, with whom I exchanged a few monosyllables a few seconds every day, I had been spoken to four times. Once to tell me that at the whistle you had to lower your plank: that was the first day. Once the doctor had said, 'Turn round. Cough.' There had been a longer, livelier conversation with the governor. And then the other day a few words with the warder who had been shocked by the poor type going mad. It didn't amount to a very great deal by way of light relief. I went calmly to sleep, with just this single thought – tomorrow they'll open my door for good. Tomorrow I'll see the sun, and if they send me to Royale I'll breathe the sea air. Tomorrow I'll be free. I burst out laughing. Free? What do you mean? Tomorrow you'll officially begin on your sentence of hard labour for life. Is that what you call free? I know, I know: but there's no comparison between that and the life I've had to bear. What state will I find Clousiot and Maturette in?

At six o'clock they gave me coffee and bread. I felt like saying, 'But I go out today. You've got it wrong.' Then I quickly remembered I'd lost my memory, and if I was to go and acknowledge I'd been stuffing the governor up like this, who knows but he might give me thirty days black-hole to be served right away. For whatever happened the law stated that I had to leave the solitary confinement prison of Saint-Joseph today, 26 June 1936. In four months time I would be thirty.

Eight o'clock. I'd eaten my whole hunk of bread. I'd get something to eat in the camp. The door opened. The deputy-governor and two warders appeared.

'Charrière, your sentence is finished. This is 26 June 1936. Follow us.'

I walked out. In the courtyard the sun was already bright enough to dazzle me. A kind of general weakness came over me. My legs went soft and black spots danced in front of my eyes. Yet I'd not gone more than fifty yards; and of them only thirty were in the sun.

When I reached the administration block I saw Maturette and Clousiot. Maturette was skin and bone – hollow cheeks, sunken eyes. Clousiot was lying on a stretcher. He was grey and already he smelt of death. I thought, 'Brothers, you aren't very pretty. Do I look like that?' I longed to see myself in a mirror. I said to them, 'You OK, mates?'

They made no reply. Once more I said, 'You OK?'

'Yes,' said Maturette softly.

I wanted to tell them that now solitary was over we were allowed to talk. I kissed Clousiot on the cheek. He looked at me with his shining eyes and smiled. 'Good-bye, Papillon,' he said.

'No, no. Don't say that!

'I've had it: done for.'

He died a few days later in the hospital on Royale. He was thirty-two and he had been sent down for twenty years for a bicycle theft he hadn't committed. But here was the governor coming.

'Bring them in. Maturette and Clousiot, you've behaved well. So I'll put *Conduct good* on your file. As for you, Charrière, you committed a serious crime, so I'll put what you deserve – *Conduct bad*.'

'Excuse me, Governor, but what crime did I commit?'

'You really don't remember the finding of the cigarettes and the coconut?'

'No. Quite honestly I don't.'

'Come now, what diet have you been on these last four months?'

'How do you mean? You mean the food? Always the same ever since I came in.'

'Well, that crowns everything! What did you eat yesterday evening?'

'As usual – whatever they gave me. What do I know about it? I don't remember. Maybe beans or fried rice: or some other vegetable.'

'So you do have supper then?'

'I should bloody think I do! You don't imagine I throw my bowl out, do you?'

'No: it's no good. I give it up. All right, I'll withdraw the *conduct bad*. Monsieur X, make out another discharge ticket. I'll give you *conduct good*. All right?'

'It's only fair. I've done nothing to deserve anything else.' And it was with these last words that we left the office.

The great gate of the Réclusion opened to let us through. With just one warder as an escort we walked slowly down the road leading to the camp. We were high over the sea – white foam, brilliant light. Opposite there was Royale, covered with green trees and red roofs. Devil's Island, grim and harsh. I asked the warder for us to be allowed to sit down for a few minutes. He said yes. We sat there, one on Clousiot's right and the other on his left, and without even noticing it we held hands. This contact moved us strangely and without a word we embraced. The warder said, 'Come on, boys. We must get moving.'

And slowly, very slowly, we went down to the camp; there we went in side by side, still holding hands, followed by the two stretcher-bearers carrying our dying friend.

Life on Royale

The moment we were in the yard we were surrounded by the convicts, all full of kindness for us. Once again I saw Pierrot le Fou, Jean Sartron, Colondini and Chissilia. The warder told us we were all three to go to the infirmary, and as we crossed the yard at least twenty men went with us. In a few minutes Maturette and I had a dozen packets of cigarettes and tobacco there in front of us, with piping hot café au lait and the best chocolate. Everybody wanted to give us something. The orderly gave Clousiot a camphor injection and some adrenalin for his heart. A very thin Negro said, 'Orderly, give him my vitamin tablets: he needs them more than me.' This display of solidarity and kindness was deeply moving.

Pierre le Bordelais asked me, 'Would you like some dough? I've got time to pass the hat round before you leave for Royale.'

'No, thanks very much: I have some. But you know I'm going to Royale, then?'

'Yes, the clerk told us. All three of you. Indeed, I think you're all going to hospital.'

The orderly was a Corsican strong-arm man from the mountains. His name was Essari. I knew him very well later on: one day I'll tell his whole fascinating story. These two hours in the infirmary went by very fast. We ate well and we drank well. Full and happy, we set off for Royale. Nearly all the time Clousiot kept his eyes shut, except when I went over and put my hand on his forehead. Then he opened them – they were already clouded – and said to me, 'Friend Papi, you and I are what you call real friends.'

'We're more than that; we're brothers,' I replied.

Still with just one warder we went down to the shore. Clousiot's stretcher in the middle, Maturette and I on each side. At the camp gate all the convicts wished us good-bye and good luck. We thanked them, in spite of their protests, Pierrot le Fou hung a knapsack round my neck: it was full of tobacco, cigarettes, chocolate and tins of Nestlé's milk. Maturette had one too. He didn't know who had given it to him.

Fernandez, the medical orderly, and the warder were the only ones to go down to the quay with us. He handed us each a paper for the hospital on Royale. I gathered that it was the convict orderlies Essari and Fernandez who were sending us to hospital, without consulting the medicos. Here was the boat. Six rowers, two armed warders in the stern-sheets and another at the tiller. One of the boatmen was Chapar, of the Marseilles stock-exchange business. All right, let's go. The oars dipped into the sea, and as he rowed Chapar said to me, 'OK, Papi? Did you get the coconut all the time?'

'No, not the last four months.'

'I know. There was an accident. The chap behaved well though. I was the only one he knew, but he didn't grass.'

'What happened to him?'

'He's dead.'

'You don't say so! What of?'

'According to an orderly, it seems they burst his liver, kicking him.'

We landed at the wharf on Royale, the biggest of the three islands. The bakery clock said three. The afternoon sun was really hot: it dazzled me and warmed me more than I cared for. A warder called for two stretcher-bearers. Two strongly built convicts, immaculately dressed in white and each wearing a black leather wrist-band, picked Clousiot up as though he weighed no more than a feather: Maturette and I followed behind. A warder came along after us, carrying some papers.

A cobbled road, about four yards wide: heavy going. Fortunately the two stretcher-bearers stopped every now and then for us to catch up. When we did so I sat down on the shaft of the stretcher, just by Clousiot's head, and I put my hand gently on his forehead. Each time he smiled, opened his eyes and said, 'Good old Papi.'

Maturette took his hand. 'Is that you, boy?' whispered Clousiot. He seemed unspeakably happy, having us close to him. During one of the last halts, we met a fatigue-party going off to work: they were almost all convicts belonging to my convoy. All of them, as they went by, said something friendly. We reached the plateau, and there we saw the island's highest authorities sitting in the shade in front of a square white building. We went up to Major Barrot, nicknamed Coco sec, and the other heads of the establishment. Without getting up and without any formalities the major said to us, 'So it wasn't too tough in solitary, then? Who's the man on the stretcher?'

'It's Clousiot.'

He had a look at him and then said, 'Take them to hospital. When they come out, let me know, so I can see them before they're sent to the camp.'

At the hospital they put us to bed – very clean beds with sheets and pillows – in a big, well-lit ward. The first orderly I saw was Chatal, who had been in the high-security ward at Saint-Laurent-du-Maroni. He attended to Clousiot right away and told a warder to call the doctor. The doctor came at about five o'clock. After a long, careful examination, I saw him shake his head, looking concerned. He wrote out a prescription and then came over to me. He said to Chatal, 'Papillon and I are not very good friends.'

'Well, that's surprising, Doctor, because he's a decent type.'

'Maybe. But he doesn't care for me.'

'How come?'

'Because of an examination I carried out in the Réclusion.'

'Doctor,' I said, 'do you call listening to my chest through a trap an examination?'

'The service lays down that a convict's door cannot be opened.'

'Fine, Doctor: but I hope for your sake you're only lent to the service and not a part of it.'

'We'll talk about that some other time. I'll try to set you on your feet again, you and your friend. As for the other one, I'm afraid it may be too late.'

Chatal told me he'd been interned on the islands, under

291

suspicion of preparing a break. He also said that Jesus, the character who had swindled me during my escape, had been murdered by a leper. He didn't know the leper's name, and I wondered whether it might have been one of those who had helped us so generously.

The life of the convicts on the Iles du Salut was completely different from what you might suppose. Most of the men were extremely dangerous, dangerous for various reasons. In the first place, everybody was well fed, because everything was the subject of some racket – spirits, cigarettes, coffee, chocolate, sugar, meat, fish, fresh vegetables, coconuts, cray-fish, etc. So they were all perfectly fit and the climate was very healthy. The men with limited sentences were the only ones with any chance of being let out: those with life, those with no hope at all, were all dangerous. Everybody, prisoners and warders, were involved in the rackets that were going on all the time. It was not easy to see the pattern at first. The warders' wives looked out for young convicts to do their housework, and quite often took them as lovers, too. These ones were called houseboys. Some were gardeners, others cooks. It was this class of transportee that acted as the link between the convict camp and the warders. The other convicts didn't look upon the houseboys with disfavour, because it was thanks to them that any racket was possible at all. But they were not considered altogether clean – not pure. No real member of the underworld would lower himself to do jobs of this sort. Nor to be a turnkey: nor to work in the warders' mess. On the other hand, they would pay a great deal for jobs that had nothing to do with the screws – cleaners, sweepers, buffalo-drivers, hospital orderlies, prison gardeners, butchers, bakers, boatmen, postmen, lighthouse keepers. The real hard men would accept any of these jobs. A hard man would never work on the fatigues of repairing walls or roads or flights of steps, nor at planting coconut palms – that is to say, work in the full sun or under the supervision of the screws. Working hours were from seven until noon and from two o'clock till six. This may give you some idea of the atmosphere with all these different people living together, prisoners and warders making up a positive little town in which everything was discussed and commented upon, and where everybody's activities were known to everybody else.

Dega and Galgani came to spend Sunday with me in the

hospital. We had ailloli with fish, fish soup, potatoes, cheese, coffee and white wine. We all of us, Chatal, Dega, Galgani, Maturette, Grandet and I, ate this meal in Chatal's room. They asked me to tell them about my break in all its smallest details. Dega had decided not to make any further attempt at escape. He was expecting a pardon from France that would shorten his sentence by five years. Counting the three years he'd served in France and the three here, that would only leave him four to do. He had resigned himself to serving that long. As for Galgani, he said a Corsican senator was looking after him.

Now it was my turn. I asked them what were the best places here for an escape. There was a general outcry. For his part, Dega had never even thought of the idea; nor had Galgani. Chatal was of the opinion that a garden might be a useful place for preparing a raft. Grandet told me he was a blacksmith in the Public Works. This was a workshop that had everything, he said – painters, carpenters, smiths, builders, plumbers: close on a hundred and twenty men. Its job was looking after the establishment's buildings. Dega was the head accountant and he would put me into any job I wanted. The choice was up to me. Grandet offered me half his place as head of a gambling table, so that with what I got from the men who played I could live decently without having to spend what I had in my charger. Later I found that this was a very profitable job, but exceedingly dangerous.

Sunday flashed by. 'Five o'clock already,' said Dega, who was wearing a handsome watch. 'We must get back to the camp.' As he left, Dega gave me five hundred francs to play poker with, because now and then there were very good games in our ward. Grandet gave me a splendid lock-back knife that he had tempered himself. It was a formidable weapon. 'Keep it on you, day and night.'

'What about the searches?'

'Most of the screws who carry them out are Arab turnkeys. When a man is listed dangerous, they never find any weapon, even if they actually put their hands on it.'

'We'll meet again in the camp,' said Grandet.

Before he left, Galgani told me he'd already reserved me a place in his corner and that we'd be in the same gourbi (the members of a gourbi all eat together and money that belongs to one belongs to all). As for Dega, he did not sleep in the camp but in a bedroom in the administration block.

We had been here three days now, but as I spent my nights at Clousiot's side I had not really gathered how life went on in this ward of about sixty men. But then Clousiot took a bad turn and he was moved into a room where there was already another very sick man. Chatal crammed him with morphia. He was afraid he wouldn't live through the night.

Thirty beds on each side of a ten-foot passage running down the middle of the big ward: almost all the beds occupied. The whole room lit by two paraffin lamps. Maturette said to me, 'They're playing poker down there.' I went over to the players. There were four of them.

'Can I make the fifth?'

'Yes. Sit down. A hundred francs is the minimum raise. Three hundred to come in. Here's three hundred francs' worth of chips.'

I gave two hundred to Maturette to keep. A Parisian named Dupont said to me, 'We play the English game, with no joker. You know it?'

'Yes.'

'Your deal, then.'

The speed these men played at was unbelievable. The raises had to be very quick or the head of the table would say, 'Slow raise' and you had to hold everything. It was here I discovered a fresh class of convicts – the gamblers. They lived on gambling, amidst gambling. Nothing apart from gambling interested them. They forgot everything, what they had been, the length of their sentences, all the things they might do to change their lives. Whether their opponent was a decent guy or not, only one thing interested them – gambling.

We played all night long. We stopped when the coffee came round. I won one thousand three hundred francs. I was going towards my bed when Paulo caught me up and asked me to lend him two hundred to go on playing double-handed belote. He needed two hundred and he only had one. 'Here's three hundred. We'll go splits,' I said.

'Thanks, Papillon: you're certainly the guy they said you were. We'll be friends.' He held out his hand, I shook it, and he went off beaming with delight.

Clousiot died that morning. In a moment of clear-mindedness the evening before he had told Chatal not to give him any more morphia. 'I want to die in my right senses, sitting up in my bed with my friends beside me,' he said.

It was strictly forbidden to go into the isolation rooms, but Chatal took the responsibility and our friend was able to die in our arms. I closed his eyes. Maturette was quite shattered with grief.

'Clousiot's gone, the friend we went right through our splendid break with. They've thrown him to the sharks.'

When I heard the words, 'They've thrown him to the sharks,' my blood ran cold. On the islands there was in fact no graveyard for the convicts. When a prisoner died they went out to sea at six o'clock, the time of sunset, and threw him in between Saint-Joseph and Royale, in a place infested by sharks.

My friend's death made the hospital unbearable for me. I sent to tell Dega I would be going out in two days' time. He sent a note saying, 'Ask Chatal to get you a fortnight's rest in the camp: that way you'll have time to pick a job you like.' Maturette was going to stay in a little longer. Chatal might be able to take him on as an assistant orderly.

As soon as I left the hospital I was taken up before Major Barrot, Coco sec, in the administration block. 'Papillon,' he said, 'I wanted to see you before you were sent to the camp. You have a very valuable friend here, my chief accountant, Louis Dega. He says you don't deserve the reports that they have sent us from France, and that as you look upon yourself as an innocent man unjustly condemned, it is natural you should be in a state of perpetual revolt. I must tell you I don't altogether agree with him on that point. But what I'd like to know is what state of mind you're in at present.'

'In the first place, sir, and so I can give you an answer, could you let me know what the notes on my file actually say?'

'Look for yourself.' And he passed me a yellow folder in which I read roughly this –

'Henri Charrière, nicknamed Papillon, born 16 November 1906 at – in the Ardèche, condemned at the Seine Assizes to transportation with hard labour for life for wilful homicide. Dangerous from every point of view: to be carefully watched. Not to benefit from privileged employment.

'Caen Prison: Incorrigible prisoner. Capable of rousing and directing a mutiny. To be kept under constant watch.

'Saint-Martin-de-Ré: Amenable to discipline but undoubtedly has great influence over his companions. Will attempt to escape from any place of confinement whatsoever.

'*Saint-Laurent-du-Maroni:* Committed a violent assault upon three warders and a turnkey to escape from the hospital. Brought back from Colombia. Good conduct during inquiry period. Given light sentence of two years solitary confinement.

'*Réclusion de Saint-Joseph:* Conduct good until release.'

'What with all this, my dear Papillon,' said the governor as I handed him back the file, 'we don't feel altogether comfortable about having you as a boarder. Would you like to come to an agreement with me?'

'Why not? It depends on the agreement, though.'

'There's no sort of doubt that you're a man who'll do everything possible to escape from the islands in spite of every difficulty. You may even succeed. Now from my point of view, I still have five months of governing this island. Do you know what an escape costs a governor here? One year's ordinary pay. That is to say, the total loss of the colonial bonus. As well as leave delayed for six months and reduced by three. And if the inquiry shows there was negligence on the governor's part, he may lose a stripe. It's serious, as you see. Now if I want to do my job properly I have no right to shut you up in a cell or a black-hole just because it's possible you might escape. Unless I think up some imaginary crime. And that's something I don't choose to do. So I'd like you to give me your word not to try to escape until I leave the islands. Five months.'

'Governor, I give you my word of honour that I shan't leave while you're here, so long as it doesn't exceed six months.'

'I'm leaving in rather under five: that's certain.'

'All right. You ask Dega, and he'll tell you I keep my word.'

'I'm sure you do.'

'But in return, I'll ask you for something.'

'What?'

'That during the five months I must spend here, I should be allowed to have the jobs now that I might have had later, and even perhaps be allowed to change islands.'

'All right. Agreed. But this must remain strictly between ourselves.'

'Yes, Governor.'

He sent for Dega, who persuaded him that my place was not with the good conducts, but with the crooks in the 'dangerous' building, where all my friends were lodged. I was given my full issue of convict's equipment, and the governor added some white trousers and jackets that had been confiscated in the tailors' shop.

So I was carrying two pairs of brand new, perfectly white trousers, three jackets and a straw hat as I made my way to the central camp, accompanied by a screw. To get there from the little administrative block we had to cross the whole plateau. We went past the warders' hospital, going along the outside of the thirteen-foot wall that surrounded the entire establishment. When we had got almost right round the huge rectangle we reached the main gate. *Penal Settlement. Ile Royale Section.* The enormous door was made of wood, and it stood wide open. It must have been nearly twenty feet high. Two guard-rooms with four warders in each. A sergeant sitting on a chair. No rifles: everybody had revolvers. I also saw five or six Arab turnkeys.

When I appeared in the gateway all the warders came out. The chief warder, a Corsican, said, 'Here's a new one: a big boy.' The turnkeys were preparing to search me, but he stopped them. 'Don't bugger about, making him show all his kit. Go on inside, Papillon. You've got lots of friends waiting for you in the special block, I'm sure. My name's Soffrani. Good luck here on the islands.'

'Thanks, Chief.' And I walked into a huge yard in which there stood three great buildings. I followed the warder to one of them. Over the door it said *Block A: Special Category.* Standing in front of the wide-open door the warder shouted, 'Leader!' An aged convict appeared. 'Here's a new one,' said the warder, and walked off.

I made my way into a very large rectangular hall in which there lived a hundred and twenty men. An iron bar, like the one in that first building at Saint-Laurent, ran down each of its longer sides, broken only by the gaps for the door: this door was an iron grill, only closed at night. Between the wall and the bar were stretched the pieces of very taut canvas that were falsely called hammocks and that served as beds. These so-called hammocks were very comfortable and hygienic. Each had two shelves fixed over it, and on these you could put your things: there was one for clothes and one for your food, mug, etc. Between the lines of hammocks ran the alley, a passage ten feet wide. Here too the men lived in little groups – gourbis. Some of these messes had only two men, but in some there were as many as ten.

I was scarcely inside before convicts dressed in white came hurrying from all round. 'Papi, come over here.' 'No, come along with us.' Grandet took my bag and said, 'He's going to gourbi with me.' I followed him. They set up the canvas I was to lie on and stretched it tight. 'Catch. Here's a feather pillow, brother,' said Grandet, I found many friends. A great many Corsicans and types from Marseilles, and a few Parisians: all acquaintances from back in France or men I'd known in the Santé, the Conciergerie or in the convoy. But I was astonished at seeing them and I asked, 'How come you're not at work, this time of day?' Everyone laughed very heartily. 'Oh, you can write that one out in capitals! The characters in this block who work never do more than an hour a day. Then we come back to the gourbi.' This really was a warm welcome. I hoped it would last. But there was one thing I noticed in no time at all – a thing I had never expected: in spite of these few days spent in hospital I was going to have to learn how to live in a group all over again.

Then something quite extraordinary happened. A fellow came in, dressed in white and carrying a tray covered with a spotless cloth: he called out, 'Steak, steak, who wants beef-steak?' Gradually he reached our corner, stopped, lifted the linen, and there, in neat rows just like you see them in a French butcher's shop, there was a whole trayful of steaks. It was clear that Grandet was a daily customer, because the type didn't ask *whether* he wanted any but *how many* he should pick out.

'Five.'

'Rump or butt?'

'Rump. What do I owe you? Make out the bill, because now there's one more of us it won't be the same.'

The steak-seller brought out a notebook and began doing sums. 'That makes one hundred and thirty-five francs in all.'

'Take it out of this and then start a clean sheet.'

When the man had gone Grandet said to me, 'You die like a dog here if you've got no cash. But there's one way you can get it all the time – a racket.'

In penal, a racket meant the way each man sets about getting hold of money. The camp cook sold the meat meant for the prisoners – sold it as steaks. When it was issued to him at the kitchen he cut off round about half. According to the pieces, he prepared joints, steaks or stewing beef. Some was sold to the warders through their wives and some to the convicts who had the money to pay for it. Of course the cook handed over part of what he made this way to the screw in charge of the kitchen. The first block where he peddled his wares was always Block A, Special Category – our building.

So a racket meant the cook who sold meat and dripping; the baker who sold fancy bread and the long thin white loaves meant for the warders; the butcher who sold meat too; the medical orderly who sold injections; the clerk who was paid for getting you any particular job or just for having you let off a fatigue; the gardener who sold fresh vegetables and fruit; the convict laboratory assistant who sold the results of analyses and even went so far as to manufacture phony consumptives, phony lepers and phony cases of enteritis; the men who specialized in stealing from the yards of the warders' houses and who sold eggs, chickens and soap; the houseboys who traded with the women they worked for and who brought anything they were asked to bring – butter, condensed milk, powdered milk, tins of tunny or sardines, cheese, and of course wine and spirits (in this way there was always a bottle of Ricard in our gourbi, as well as English and American cigarettes); and also those who were allowed to go fishing and who sold what they caught.

But the best racket, and the most dangerous, was keeping a gambling table. The rule was that there could never be more than three or four heads of table in each block of a hundred and twenty men. The man who wanted to take a table would turn up one night as the game began and say, 'I want a place as a banker.'

'No,' they would say.

'Everybody says no?'

'Everybody.'

'Well then, I name So-and-so: I'll take his place.'

The man whose name he said knew what had to be done. He would get up, walk to the middle of the room, and there they would fight it out with the knife. The winner took the table. The bankers had five per cent of all winnings.

Gambling provided the occasion for other little rackets or at least ways of earning money. There was the character who spread the smoothed blankets on the floor; the one who hired out small stools for the players who couldn't sit cross-legged; and the cigarette seller. He spread out several empty cigar boxes on a blanket, with cigarettes in them – French, English, American or even hand-made. Each had its price showing, and the card-player helped himself, scrupulously putting the money in the box. And then there was the man who looked after the paraffin lamps and saw to it they didn't smoke too much. These lamps were made out of condensed milk tins with a hole in the top for the wick, which had to be snuffed frequently. For the ones who didn't smoke, there were sweets and cakes – making them was a separate racket. And each block had one or two coffee sellers: they made their coffee in the Arab way, and kept it hot all night under two jute sacks. From time to time they would go up and down the room peddling coffee or chocolate kept hot in a kind of home-made haybox.

Then lastly there was the stuff they made to sell – the junk. This was a kind of handyman's racket. Some worked the tortoiseshell the fishermen brought in: the right sort of turtle's shell has thirteen scales, and they can weigh as much as five pounds apiece. Craftsmen turned them into bracelets, earrings, necklaces, cigarette-holders, combs and brush backs. I even saw a jewel box made of a blond tortoiseshell, a beautiful piece of work. Others carved coconut shells and cow or buffalo horn, or made snakes out of a local hard-wood or of ebony. Still others went in for very perfect cabinet-making, all put together without a single nail. The most skilful of the lot worked in bronze. And of course there were the painters.

Sometimes several craftsmen would combine to carry out a single project. For example, a fisherman would catch a shark. He'd prepare its jaws, wide open and with all the teeth properly arranged and brightly polished. Then a cabinet-maker would make a small-scale anchor out of a hard, cross-grained wood, wide enough in the middle for a painting. The anchor would be wedged into the open jaws, and a painter would paint the Iles du Salut with the sea all round. The most usual subject was this: the headland of Ile Royale, Saint-Joseph beyond and the strait between the two; the setting sun, with its rays spreading over the blue sea; on the water a boat, with six convicts, bare to the waist, standing and holding their oars straight up in the air; in the stern, three warders with sub-machine-guns. In the bows two men tilting a coffin with the body of a dead convict, swathed in flour sacks, sliding out of it: sharks on the surface, waiting open-mouthed for the corpse. In the bottom right-hand corner the words *Funeral at Royale*, and the date.

All these different kinds of junk were sold to the warders' houses. The finest pieces were often bought in advance or made to order. The others were sold on board the ships that touched at the islands. This was the boatmen's province. And then there were the jokers who'd take an old battered mug and engrave on it *This mug belonged to Dreyfus – Ile du Diable* and the date. And the same with spoons and bowls. There was a sure-fire piece of junk for the Breton sailors – anything at all that had the name Sezenac on it.

This non-stop racketing meant that a great deal of money came into the islands, and it was in the warders' interest to let it come. The men were completely absorbed in their schemes – they were easier to handle and they settled down in their new lives.

Homosexuality was officially recognized, or close on. Everybody, from the governor downwards, knew that So-and-so was So-and-so's wife, and if one was sent to another island the other was soon sent after him – if, indeed, they weren't sent together.

Out of all these men, there weren't three in a hundred who thought of escaping from the islands. Even those serving life sentences. The only way of setting about it was to use every possible means of being un-interned and sent to the mainland – to Saint-Laurent, Kourou or Cayenne. But this would only work for those with a set number of years. For the lifers, it was impossible except in the case of manslaughter: if you killed someone you were sent to Saint-Laurent to be tried. But to get there you had to confess; and that meant the risk of five years solitary for manslaughter, without any certainty of being able to use the short stay in the punishment block at Saint-Laurent – three months at the most – for an escape.

You could also try to be un-interned for health reasons. If you were certified tubercular they would send you to the place for consumptives called the Nouveau Camp, fifty miles from Saint-Laurent.

Leprosy would work too, or chronic enteritis with dysentery. It was fairly easy to get the certificate, but it involved running a hideous risk – that of living for close on two years in a special isolation wing with the patients suffering from the disease you had chosen. It was only a step between wanting to pass for a leper and actually catching the disease, or going in with lungs like a first-rate pair of bellows and coming out a consumptive: and the step was quite often made. As for dysentery, it was even harder to escape the infection.

So here I was, settling down in Block A with my hundred and twenty companions. I had to learn how to live in this society: it was one in which you were very quickly classified. In the first place everybody had to know you couldn't be shoved around. And then once you were feared you had to earn respect by the way you behaved with the screws, by never accepting certain jobs, by refusing certain fatigues, by never acknowledging the turnkeys' authority and by never obeying them, even if it meant a row with a warder. If you had been gambling all night, you mustn't even get up for the roll-call. The leader, or man in charge of the block, would call out, 'Sick: in bed.' In the two other blocks the warders would sometimes go in, have a look at the so-called invalid and make him come out for the roll-call. Never in the tough boys' block. When all was said and done, what they were all of them looking for, whether they were big or small, was a quiet life in this penal settlement.

My friend Grandet, my messmate, came from Marseilles. He was thirty-five, tall and as thin as a rail, but very strong indeed. We had been friends in France. We had gone around together at Toulon, as well as in Marseilles and Paris. He was a well-known safe-breaker. He was good-natured, but he could be an exceedingly ugly customer.

This particular day I was almost alone in the huge room. The leader was sweeping and mopping the cement floor. I noticed a man busy repairing a watch, with one of those wooden things screwed into his left eye. Over his hammock there was a shelf with perhaps thirty watches hanging on it. His face was that of a man of thirty, but his hair was completely white. I went over, watched him working, and then tried to get into conversation with him. He never even looked up – remained silent. I went off, rather irritated, and walked out into the yard. I sat in the wash-house, and there I found Titi la Belote practising with a brand-new pack. His nimble fingers shuffled and reshuffled the thirty-two cards with incredible speed. His conjuror's hands went on without a pause, as he said to me, 'Well, brother, how are you getting along? You like it on Royale?'

'Yes, but today I'm fed up. I'm going to get myself a little job of some sort: that way I'll get out a bit. Just now I felt like having a natter with a guy that was mending a watch, and he wouldn't even answer.'

'You're telling me he didn't, Papi. That character doesn't give a fuck for anyone on God's earth. His watches, and the rest can go to hell. It's true he has the right to be mental, after what happened to him. It would certainly have driven me round the bend. Listen: this young chap – you can say young, because he's not thirty – was condemned to death last year for the so-called rape of a warder's wife. All genuine guaranteed crap. He'd been stuffing the woman he worked for, a Breton chief warder's certificated wife, time out of mind. He worked there as houseboy, so every time the Breton was on day-duty, the watchmaker stuffed the bird. But they made one error: the broad wouldn't let him wash and iron the clothes any more. She did it herself, and her cuckold of a husband, who knew she was bone-idle, found that very quaint indeed and began to have his doubts. But he had no proof of his horns. So he worked out a scheme to catch them actually at it and kill them both. He reckoned without the woman's presence of mind. One day he left duty two hours after having come on and he asked a warder to go back to his house with him, saying he'd give him a ham they'd sent him from his village. He walked in through the garden gate without making a sound, but the moment he opened the front door of the cottage a parrot started bawling out "Here's the boss!" as it always did when the screw came home. The same second the woman screeched, "Rape! Rape! Help, help!" The two screws came into the bedroom just as the woman disentangled herself from the convict: he jumped out of the window as the cuckold fired at him. He got the bullet in his shoulder and at the same time the broad scratched her tits and cheek and tore her dressing-gown. The watchmaker fell, and just as the Breton was going to finish him off the other screw took his gun away. I must tell you this other screw was a Corsican and right away he'd understood his chief's story was so much cock and it was no more a question of rape than it was of butter up her arse. But the Corsican couldn't very well open his mind to the Breton on the subject, so he behaved like he believed in the rape. The watchmaker was condemned to death. Well, brother, nothing surprising so far. It was afterwards it turned interesting.

'Now here on Royale, in the punishment block, there's a guillotine, with each part carefully put away in a special place.

In the yard there are the five paving slabs they set it up on, all carefully cemented down and levelled. Every week the executioner and his assistants, a couple of convicts, set it up with its knife and all the other fixings, and they slice through two banana stems. That way, they know it's always working properly.

'So there was this Savoyard, the watchmaker, in a condemned cell with four others who were for it too – three Arabs and a Sicilian. All five were waiting for the result of the petition for reprieve their defending warders had put in.

'One morning the guillotine was set up and suddenly the Savoyard's door burst open. The executioners darted at him and hobbled his feet. Then they tied his hands with the same line, so it ran down to the hobble. They cut his collar open with scissors, and then with little hobbled steps in the dawn twilight he walked the twenty yards. As you know, Papillon, when you reach a guillotine, you are brought face to face with an upright plank, and they tie you to it with the straps fixed along the edge. So they strapped him on, and they were just going to swing him level, with his head over the edge for the knife, when Coco sec, the one who's governor now, turned up – he has to be present at all executions. He was carrying a big hurricane-lamp and the moment he lit up the scene he saw these bastards of screws had got it wrong – they were going to cut off the watchmaker's head, and that particular day, the watchmaker had just not been invited to the party.

' "Stop! Stop!" shouts Barrot. He was so shook, it seems he couldn't speak properly. He dropped his hurricane-lamp, shoved them aside, screws and executioners, and undid the Savoyard himself. At last he managed to give some orders. "Take him back to his cell, orderly. Take care of him – give him some rum and stay with him. And you, you bloody fools, go and get hold of Rencasseu as quick as you like – he's the one that's being executed today and not anybody else!"

'The next day the Savoyard's hair was snowy white, just like you saw it today. His defender, a screw from Calvi, wrote another petition to the minister of justice, telling him about what had happened. The watchmaker was pardoned and given life instead. Ever since, he's spent his time mending the screws' watches. That's his one passion. He goes on and on checking the time they keep; that's why there are so many hanging on his shelf. So now you understand the guy has a right to be a little old-fashioned, am I right or am I wrong?'

'Right, Titi: after something like that, he's certainly allowed to be what you might call unsociable. I'm genuinely sorry for him.'

Every day I learnt something more about this new kind of life. Block A did indeed contain a rich mixture of formidable men – formidable both where their past was concerned and in the way they behaved in everyday life. I was still not working: I was waiting for a cleaner's job that would leave me free to wander about the island after three quarters of an hour of work; and I should have the right to go fishing.

That morning, at the roll-call for the coconut planting fatigue, Jean Castelli's name was called. He stepped from the ranks and said, 'What's all this. You mean I'm being sent to work? Me?'

'Yes, you,' said the screw in charge of the fatigue. 'Here, take hold of this mattock.'

Castelli stared at him coldly. 'Man, get this: you have to come from some remote hole in the country to know how to handle this sort of an object. You have to be a provincial, like you. I'm a Marseilles Corsican. In Corsica we throw picks and spades and such a great way off; and in Marseilles we don't even know they exist. Keep your mattock and leave me in peace.'

The young screw who, as I learnt later, didn't know how things worked here yet, threatened Castelli with the mattock handle. All together the hundred and twenty men roared, 'Touch him, you scum, and you're a dead man!'

'Fall out,' shouted Grandet, and without bothering about the offensive positions the screws had taken up, we all went back indoors.

Block B marched off to work. Block C too. A dozen screws came back and closed the barred door – this rarely happened. An hour later there were forty screws either side of the door, sub-machine-guns at the ready. Deputy governor, head warder, chief warder, ordinary warders: they were all there except for the governor himself, who had gone off at six to inspect Devil's Island, before the incident. The deputy governor said, 'Dacelli, call the names, one by one.'

'Grandet?'

'Here.'

'Come out.'

He went out into the middle of the forty screws. Dacelli said, 'Go to your work.'

'I can't.'

'You're refusing?'

'No, I'm not refusing. I'm ill.'

'Since when? You didn't report sick at the first roll-call.'

'This morning I wasn't ill: now I am.'

The first sixty men called up made exactly the same reply, one after the other. Only one went so far as to refuse to obey. No doubt he did so in order to get himself sent back to Saint-Laurent and be brought up in front of a court-martial. When they said, 'You're refusing?' he answered, 'Yes, I'm refusing: three times over.'

'Three times over? Why?'

'Because you make me throw up. I flatly refuse to work for such a bleeding set of bastards as you.'

The tension was very, very great. The screws, particularly the young screws, could not bear being humiliated in this way by the convicts. They were waiting for just one thing – a threatening movement that would allow them to go into action with their guns, now pointing at the ground.

'All the men who've been called out, strip! Quick march to the cells.' As the clothes came off so every now and then you heard the clash of a knife ringing on the macadam of the yard. At this moment the doctor appeared. 'Right. Halt! Here's the doctor. Doctor, please would you examine these men? Those who are not found to be sick, straight to the black-hole. The others can stay in their block.'

'Are there sixty reporting sick?'

'Yes, Doctor: all except for that man over there – he refused to work.'

'First man,' said the doctor. 'Grandet, what's wrong with you?'

'A stomach turned by gaolers, Doctor. We're all of us men sent down for long sentences and most of us for life, Doctor. No hope of escape on the islands. So we can only bear this life if there's a certain amount of give and take in the application of the rules. But this morning a warder went so far as to try and knock out a comrade we all think highly of – knock him out with a mattock handle there in front of us all. It wasn't in self-defence, because the man hadn't threatened anyone. All he'd said was he didn't want to use a mattock. That's the real reason for our epidemic. I leave it to you.'

The doctor bowed his head, thought for a good minute, and then said, 'Orderly, write this: "On account of a mass food-poisoning, medical warder So-and-so will take the necessary steps to purge the transportees who have reported sick today: he will give them each twenty grammes of sodium sulphate. As for transportee X, please have him placed under observation in the hospital so that we can judge whether he was in full possession of his faculties when he refused to work.'

He turned his back on the group and walked off.

'Everyone inside!' shouted the deputy governor. 'Pick up your things, and don't forget your knives.'

That day everybody stayed indoors. No one was allowed out, not even the man who fetched the bread. At about noon, instead of soup, the medical warder and two convict orderlies brought in a wooden pail full of sodium sulphate. Only three men were obliged to swallow the purge. The fourth fell on the pail in a wonderfully imitated epileptic fit, and flung the purge, the bucket and the spoon in every direction. With this the whole incident was closed, except that the block leader had the trouble of mopping up the mess.

I spent the afternoon talking to Jean Castelli. He had come to eat with us. He ordinarily messed with a man from Toulon, Louis Gravon, who had been sent down for stealing furs. When I spoke to him of escaping, his eyes gleamed. He said, 'Last year I very nearly made a break, but it went sour on me. I was pretty sure you weren't the kind of man who would sit quietly here. The only thing is, you might as well talk Greek as talk about a break here on the islands. What's more, I see you haven't yet understood what kind of men they are, these island convicts. Ninety per cent of the characters you see are fairly happy here. No one will ever inform on you, whatever you do. You kill somebody, and there's never any witness: you steal – the same thing. Whatever a man may have done, the ranks close to protect him. There's only one thing the convicts on the islands are afraid of, and that is that a break should succeed. For if that happens, good-bye to their comparatively peaceful existence – continual searches, no cards any more, no music – the instruments are smashed during the searches – no more chess or draughts, no more books, no nothing. No junk, either. Everything, absolutely everything, is done away with. Non-stop searches. Everything disappears – sugar, oil, steak, butter, everything. Every time a man has made a break from the islands he's been picked up on the mainland, round about Kourou. But as far as the islands are concerned, the break has succeeded – the guys have managed to get off the island. And so the screws are punished and then they take it out on everybody else.'

I listened with all my ears. I was astonished – amazed. I'd never seen the question in that light at all.

'The moral,' said Castelli, 'the moral is, that when you make up your mind to escape, set about it with the utmost caution. Before talking to a guy who's not a very close friend already, think it over ten times.'

Jean Castelli was a professional burglar: he possessed most unusual willpower and intelligence. He loathed violence. His nickname was l'Antique. For example, he would only wash with common soap; and if I washed with Palmolive he'd say, 'Lord, it smells of buggery here! You've been washing with tart's soap.' He was fifty-two, alas; but it was a pleasure to see his terrific energy. He said, 'Papillon, anyone would think you were my son. Life here doesn't interest you. You eat well because you have to keep fit; but you'd never settle down to live your life here in the islands. I congratulate you. There are only half a dozen of us out of all the convicts who think that way. Above all, about escaping. Sure, there are quantities of men who'd pay a fortune to get themselves un-interned and so go to the mainland to make a break there. But here nobody believes in escaping.'

Old Castelli advised me to learn English and to talk Spanish with Spaniards whenever I could. He lent me a book to learn Spanish in twenty-four lessons. And a French-English dictionary. He was close friends with a Marseillais called Gardès, who knew a great deal about escaping. He had made two breaks himself. The first was from the Portuguese penal settlement; the second from the mainland. He had his own ideas about escaping from the islands: so had Castelli. Gravon, the Toulonnais, had his opinions too. None of these ideas coincided. From that day on, I made up my mind to take my own decisions and not to talk about escaping any more.

It was rough, but that was how it was. The only thing they agreed upon was that there was no sort of point in gambling except to make money; and that it was very dangerous. At any time you might be called upon to tackle any tough guy that challenged you to come out with a knife. They were all three men of action and for their age they were really terrific: Louis Gravon was forty-five and Gardès close on fifty.

Yesterday evening it so happened that I let almost every man in our block know my point of view and my idea of right behaviour. A little guy from Toulouse was challenged to fight – with knives of course – by a Nîmois. The little guy from Toulouse was nicknamed Sardine and the big tough from Nîmes, Mouton. 'Either you pay me twenty-five francs every poker game, or you don't play.'

Sardine said, 'Nobody's ever paid anybody anything for playing poker. Why pick on me? Why don't you go for the men at the Marseilles game?'

'That's none of your business. Either you pay or you don't play: or you fight.'

'No, I shan't fight.'

'You climb down, then?'

'Yes. Because I'm not going to risk getting a stab or being killed by a gorilla like you that's never gone off on a break. I'm here to make a break: I'm not here to kill or get myself killed.'

We were all tense to see what would happen. Grandet said to me, 'The little one is a good guy, that's for sure; and he's a right escaper. What a pity we can't say anything.'

I opened my knife and laid it under my thigh. I was sitting in Grandet's hammock.

'Well then, yellow-boy, are you going to pay or are you going to stop playing? Speak up.' He took a step towards Sardine.

Then I called out, 'You shut your bloody trap, Mouton, and leave the guy alone.'

'Are you crazy, Papillon?' said Grandet.

Still sitting there motionless with my open knife under my thigh and my hand on its hilt, I said, 'No, I'm not crazy, and you can all of you listen to what I've got to say. Mouton, before I fight with you, which I'll certainly do if you insist upon it even after you've heard my piece, just let me tell you and all the others that since I've been in this block, where there are more than a hundred of us, and all genuine crooks, I have been ashamed to see that the one right thing – the

309

finest, most worthwhile, the one pure thing – the break, is not respected. Now any man who has proved he is a genuine escaper, any man with guts enough to risk his life in a break, ought to be respected by one and all, quite apart from anything else. Does any man contradict me?' Silence. 'You got laws all right, but you lack the most important one of all, the one that says everybody must not only respect an escaper but must also help him and back him up. Nobody's required to go off on a break and I quite admit it's reasonable most of you should make up your minds to live your lives here. But if you don't possess the spirit to try and make another life for yourselves, do at least pay the breakers the respect they deserve. If anyone forgets this natural law, let him expect serious consequences. And now, Mouton, if you still want a fight, let's go!' And I leapt into the middle of the room, knife in hand. Mouton threw his down and said, 'You're right, Papillon: so I won't fight you with a knife. But I will with fists, to show you I'm not yellow.'

I left my knife with Grandet. We went for one another like wild cats for about twenty minutes. At last, with a lucky butt, I just managed to win. We went off to the latrine together to wash the blood off our faces. Mouton said, 'You're right: we grow dull and stupid on the islands. Here I have been these fifteen years now, and I haven't even spent so much as a thousand francs on trying to get myself un-interned. It's shameful.'

When I went back to the gourbi Grandet and Galgani bawled me out. 'Are you mental, insulting everybody like that? It was a bleeding miracle no one jumped out into the alley to have a go at you with the knife.'

'No, brothers, there's nothing surprising about it. Every man belonging to our world admits it when somebody else is absolutely dead right.'

'Well, maybe so,' said Galgani. 'But you'd be wise not to arse about with dynamite too much.'

All that evening men came and spoke to me. They came over as if by chance and talked about just anything at all; then, before they went, they'd say, 'I agree with what you said, Papi.' This incident placed me exactly.

From that time on my companions certainly looked upon me as a man belonging to their world, but as one who would not bow to accepted notions without analysing them and arguing about them. I noticed that when I was the one in charge of the table there were fewer wrangles; and when I gave an order it was obeyed right away.

The head of the table, as I said, took five per cent on every winning bet. He sat on a bench with his back to the wall as a protection against murder – a possibility that was always there. A rug over his knees hid a wide-open knife. In a circle round him, thirty, forty, and even sometimes fifty gamblers from every part of France as well as many foreigners, including Arabs. The game was very simple. There was the banker and the cutter: every time the banker lost he passed the cards on to his neighbour. They played with fifty-two cards. The cutter cut the pack and left one card face down. The banker dealt a card face up on the blanket. Then the bets were made. They laid their money either on the cut or on the banker. When the bets were all in little heaps on the table, the cards were dealt one by one. Any card of the same value as one of the two on the table lost. For example, the cutter would have a queen hidden and the banker would have turned up a five. If a queen came up before a five, then the cut was the loser. If it was the other way about and a five came up, then it was the bank that lost. The head of the table had to know the amount of each stake and remember which was the cutter and which the banker so as to know which way the money was to go. This was not easy. You had to defend the weak against the strong, who were always trying to throw their weight about. When the head of the table made a decision in a tricky case, that decision had to be accepted without a murmur.

Last night an Italian named Carlino was murdered. He lived with a boy who acted as his wife. They both worked in a garden. He must have known his life was in danger, because when he slept the boy kept watch: and the other way about. They'd put empty tins under their hammock so that no one could slip under it without making a noise. And yet he was murdered, and from below. Immediately after his shriek there was a terrible clatter of tins as the killer scattered them.

Grandet was running the Marseilles game with more than thirty players all round him. I was standing near, talking. The shriek and the noise of the empty tins stopped the game. Everyone sprang up, asking what had happened. Carlino's boy-friend had seen nothing, and Carlino was no longer breathing. The block leader asked if he should tell the warders. No.

It would be time to tell them tomorrow, at the roll-call: since he was dead, there was nothing to be done for him.

Grandet spoke up. 'Nobody heard anything. You didn't hear anything, either, boy,' he said to Carlino's friend. 'When they wake us tomorrow, you'll notice he's dead.'

And before you could say knife the game had begun again. As if nothing had happened the players went back to their cry of 'Cutter! No, banker!' etc.

I waited impatiently to see what would happen when the warders discovered there'd been a killing. Half past five, first bell. Six o'clock, second bell and coffee. Half past six, third bell and we went out for the roll-call in the usual way. But this time it was different. At the second bell the block leader said to the screw who came round with the coffee-man, 'Chief, a man's been killed.'

'Who?'

'Carlino.'

'OK.'

Ten minutes later six screws appeared. 'Where's the corpse?'

'Over there.' They saw the dagger driven into Carlino's back through the canvas. They pulled it out.

'Stretcher-bearers, take him away.' Two men carried him off. The sun rose. The third bell rang. Still holding the bloody knife, the head warder gave the order. 'Everyone outside, lined up for roll-call. No sick men allowed to stay in bed today.'

Everyone went outside. The governors and the chief warders were always there for the morning roll-call. The names were called. When they reached Carlino's, the block leader replied, 'Died during the night: has been taken to the morgue.'

'Right,' said the screw who was calling the roll.

When everybody had answered present, the head of the camp held up the knife and said, 'Does anyone recognize this knife?' Nobody replied. 'Did anyone see the murderer?' Dead silence. 'So as usual nobody knows anything at all. March past in front of me one by one with your hands stretched out: then each man to his work. It's always the same, Major: there's no way of finding out who did it.'

'Inquiry closed,' said the governor. 'Keep the knife: tie a label on stating it was the one used to kill Carlino.'

That was all. I went back indoors and I lay on my hammock to get a little sleep, for I had not had a wink all night. Just as

312

I was going off I reflected that a convict didn't amount to much. Even if he was murdered in the most cowardly way, they wouldn't bother to find out who did it. As far as the administration was concerned a convict didn't count at all. Less than a dog.

I decided to begin work as a cesspitman on Monday. At half past four I'd go out with another man and empty the pots in Block A – our pots. The rules said you had to take them right down to the sea to empty them. But if he was paid, the buffalo-driver would wait for us on the plateau at a place where a narrow cemented channel ran down to the water. Then quickly, in less than twenty minutes, we emptied all the tubs into this channel and poured six hundred gallons of sea water to carry it all down. This sea water came in a huge barrel and we gave the driver, a pleasant Martinique Negro, twenty francs a go. We helped the whole lot on its way with a stiff broom. As this was my first day of work, carrying the tubs on their two wooden handles tired my wrists. But I soon got used to it.

My new mate was a very kindly, helpful type; yet Galgani told me he was an exceedingly dangerous man. It seemed he had committed seven murders on the islands. His own particular racket was selling shit. After all, every gardener had to have manure. For this, he would dig a pit, and put dried leaves and grass into it; then my black man would secretly take one or two tubs of the cess to the garden we pointed out to him. Of course, this could not be done alone, so I had to help him. But I knew it was very wrong, because by contaminating the vegetables it might spread dysentery not only among the warders but also among the convicts. I made up my mind that one day, when I knew him better, I'd stop him. Of course I'd pay him so that he wouldn't be a loser by giving up his racket. Apart from this, he also made ornaments out of horn. As far as fishing was concerned, he said he couldn't tell me anything; but down on the wharf Chapar or someone else might be able to help me.

So there I was – a cesspit man. Every day when work was over I had a good shower, put on a pair of shorts, and went fishing wherever I chose. There was only one thing I was required to do – be in the camp at noon. Thanks to Chapar I was well supplied with rods and hooks. When I went up the road carrying red mullet threaded through their gills on a wire, the warders' wives would often call out from their cottages. They all knew my name. 'Papillon, sell me five pounds of mullet.'

'Are you sick?'

'Have you got a sick child?'

'No.'

'Then I shan't sell you my fish.'

I made quite large catches and I gave them to friends in the camp. I swapped fish for long thin loaves, vegetables or fruit. In my gourbi we ate fish at least once a day. I was on my way up with a dozen big crayfish and about fifteen pounds of mullet one day, and as I passed in front of Major Barrot's house a rather fat woman said to me, 'You've had a good catch, Papillon. Yet the sea's rough and nobody else has caught any. It's at least a fortnight since I've eaten any fish. What a pity you don't sell them. My husband tells me you won't let the warders' wives buy any.'

'That's true, Madame. But maybe it's different with you.'

'Why?'

'Because you're fat, and perhaps meat is not good for you.'

'That's quite true. I've been told I should only eat vegetables and simply-prepared fish. But here it's not possible.'

'Here, Madame, take these crayfish and mullet.' And I gave her about five pounds of fish.

From that day on, every time I made a good catch, I gave her what was needed for a proper diet. She knew very well that on the islands everything was bought and sold, and yet she never said anything to me but 'Thank you.' She was right, because she sensed I would take it amiss if she offered me money. But she often asked me in. She herself would pour me out a pastis or a glass of white wine. If she was sent figatelli from Corsica, she gave me some. Madame Barrot never asked me a single question about my past. She only let out one thing, when we were speaking about the penal settlement one day – 'It's true you can't escape from the islands; but it's better to be here in a healthy climate than rotting on the mainland.'

It was she who told me about the origin of the name of these islands: once when there was an epidemic of yellow fever at Cayenne, the White Fathers and the nuns of a convent took refuge there and they were all saved. Hence the name Iles du Salut.

Thanks to my fishing, I could go everywhere. It was three months now that I had been cesspit man and I knew the island better than anyone. I went and looked at the gardens under the pretext of trading my fish for vegetables and fruit. The gardener of one that lay at the edge of the warders' graveyard was Matthieu Carbonieri; he belonged to my gourbi. He worked there by himself and it occurred to me that later on a raft could be made or buried in his garden. Two months more and the governor would be gone. I should be free to act.

I got things organized: I was officially the cesspit man and so I went out as if I were going about my work, but in fact it was the Martiniquais who did it for me – being paid for his trouble, of course. I began to make friends with two brothers-in-law who were serving life sentences, Narric and Quenier. They were called the pram boys. I was told they'd been accused of turning a debt-collector they'd murdered into a block of concrete. It was said that witnesses had seen them pushing this block in a pram; and they were supposed to have tossed it into the Marne or the Seine. The investigation proved that the collector had gone to their place to get the money for a bill and that he'd never been seen since. They denied it all their lives long. Even in penal they swore they were innocent. But although the police never found the body, they did find the head, wrapped up in a handkerchief. Now in the brothers' house there were handkerchiefs that 'according to the experts' were of the same weave and the same thread. But they and their lawyers showed that thousands and thousands of yards of this same cloth had been turned into handkerchiefs. Everybody had them. In the end the two brothers-in-law got life and the wife of one, who was the sister of the other, got twenty years solitary.

I managed to get to know them well. They were builders, so they could go in and out of the Public Works yard. Maybe little by little they would be able to bring me out what was needed to make a raft. I'd have to persuade them.

Yesterday I met the doctor. I was carrying a forty-pound fish called a mérou – very good eating. We walked up towards the plateau together. Half way we rested on a low wall. He told me you could make a delicious soup with a mérou's head.

315

I gave it to him, together with a big lump of its flesh. This astonished him, and he said, 'You're not one for bearing a grudge, Papillon.'

'Well, Doctor, this wasn't really for me. I owed it to you because you did everything you possibly could for my friend Clousiot.'

We talked for a while, and then he said, 'You really would like to escape, wouldn't you? You're not an ordinary convict. You give me the feeling of being quite a different sort of person.'

'You're right, Doctor. I don't belong in penal. I'm only here on a passing visit.'

He began to laugh, but then I tackled him. 'Doctor, do you believe a man can make himself a new life?'

'Why, yes.'

'Would you be prepared to say that I might live in society without being a danger to it, and that I might turn myself into a respectable member of the community?'

'I do sincerely believe that that is so.'

'Then why don't you help me bring it about?'

'How?'

'By getting me un-interned as a consumptive.'

Now he confirmed something I'd heard before. 'It's not possible, and I advise you never to do it. It's too dangerous. The Administration only un-interns a man for health reasons after he's spent at least a year in the wing set apart for that particular disease.'

'Why?'

'It's rather shameful, but I believe it's so that if the man in question is malingering, he shall know he's got a very fair chance of being genuinely infected by being in with the other patients, and indeed so that he may catch the disease. So I can't do anything for you.'

From that day on the medico and I were quite friendly. Up until the time he nearly killed my friend Carbonieri. Now Matthieu Carbonieri, in agreement with me, had accepted the job of cook-storekeeper in the head warders' mess. It was to see whether it would be possible, what with the wine, the oil and the vinegar, to steal three barrels that we could fix together in order to get out to sea. There were great difficulties, because in the course of the same night we'd have to steal the barrels, get them down to the sea without being heard or seen and lash them together with cables. The only chance would be a stormy night with wind and rain. But with wind and rain the hardest thing would be launching the raft into the sea, which would necessarily be very rough.

So Carbonieri was cook. The head of the mess gave him three rabbits to prepare for the next day, a Sunday. Luckily Carbonieri skinned them before sending one to his brother down on the wharf and two to us. Then he killed three fat cats and made a splendid dish.

Unfortunately for Carbonieri, the doctor was invited the next day, and as he was tasting the rabbit he said, 'Monsieur Filidori, I congratulate you on your cooking: this cat is delicious.'

'Don't you make game of me, Doctor: these are three fine plump rabbits we're eating.'

'No,' said the doctor, as obstinate as a mule. 'This is cat. Do you see these ribs I'm eating now? They're flat. Rabbits have rounded ribs. So there's no mistake possible: what we're eating is cat.'

'Almighty God in heaven, Cristacho!' cried the Corsican. 'There's cat in my stomach!' He tore into the kitchen, clapped his revolver to Matthieu's nose and said, 'You may be a Napoleonist like me, but I'm going to kill you for having made me eat cat.'

He was glaring like a maniac. Carbonieri couldn't understand how he knew: but he said, 'If you choose to call the things you gave me cats, that's not my fault.'

'I gave you rabbits, man.'

'Well, that's what I cooked. Look, the heads and skins are still here.'

The screw saw the rabbits' heads and skins and he was completely taken aback. 'So the doctor doesn't know what he's talking about?'

'Was it the doctor who said it?' asked Carbonieri, breathing once more. 'He's pulling your leg. Tell him that kind of joke's not funny.'

Quite happy, Filidori went back to the dining-room and said to the doctor, 'Talk away as much as you like, Doc. The wine has gone to your head. Round ribs or flat, I know it's rabbit I've been eating. I've just seen their three jackets and their three heads.' Matthieu had had a narrow squeak. Still, a few days later he thought it better to resign his post as a cook.

*

The time when I should be free to act was coming nearer. Only a few weeks now and Barrot would be off. Yesterday I went to see his fat wife, who, by the way, had grown much thinner on her diet of plain fish and vegetables. The kind woman asked me in to give me a bottle of Quinquina. The room was full of half-packed cabin trunks. They were getting ready to go. The major's wife said, 'Papillon, I don't know how to thank you for your kindness to me during these last months. I know that some days when you didn't catch many fish you gave me all you had. I thank you most sincerely. Thanks to you I feel very much better – I've lost thirty pounds. What can I do to show you my gratitude?'

'Something you'll find hard, Madame. I need a good compass. Accurate, but small.'

'What you're asking is not much, Papillon, and yet at the same time it's a great deal. And with only three weeks left, it's going to be difficult.'

A week before their departure, this great-hearted woman had still not been able to get hold of a good compass, so she took the boat and went to Cayenne. Four days later she was back with a magnificent antimagnetic compass.

Major Barrot and his wife left this morning. Yesterday he handed over the command to an official of the same rank, a man called Prouillet, who came from Tunisia. One piece of good news: the new governor had confirmed Dega in his place as chief accountant. This was very important for everybody, above all for me. The new governor addressed the body of convicts lined up in the main courtyard, and he gave the impression of being a very intelligent, very energetic man. Among other things, he said to us, 'From today I take over command of the Iles du Salut. Having observed that my predecessor's methods have produced positive results, I see no reason to alter the existing state of affairs. Unless your behaviour forces me to do so, there doesn't seem to me any necessity for changing your way of life.'

It was with a very understandable delight that I saw the major and his wife sail away, although these five months of obligatory waiting had passed with extraordinary speed. What with this false liberty almost all the convicts on the islands enjoyed, and the gambling, the fishing, the talk, the new acquaintances, the arguments and the fights, I had not had time to get bored – they were all very strong distractions.

318

Yet I'd not really let myself be entrapped by this atmosphere. Every time I made a new friend I wondered, 'Might he be the man for a break? Even if he doesn't want to escape, might he help another man to do so?'

That's all I lived for – escape, escape, by myself or with others: but in any case to escape, to have it away, to make a break. It was an obsession: following Jean Castelli's advice I never talked about it, but it haunted me. And I'd accomplish my ideal without weakening: I'd break out and away.

A Raft in a Grave

By the end of five months. I'd come to know every nook and cranny on the island. At present it seemed to me that the best place for making a raft was the garden my friend Carbonieri had near the graveyard – he was no longer there. So I asked him to take his garden back but with nobody to help him. He agreed. Thanks to Dega he was given it.

As I was passing by the new governor's house this morning with a fine catch of red mullet hanging on my wire I heard a convict houseboy tell a young woman, 'Madame, there's the man who used to bring Madame Barrot fish every day.' And then I heard the good-looking, dark, sunburnt woman – rather the Algerian type – say to him, 'So that's Papillon?' And calling out to me she said, 'I've had delicious crayfish caught by you at Madame Barrot's. Come in. I'm sure you'd like a glass of wine and a little of the goat cheese I've just received from France.'

'No thank you, Madame.'

'Why not? You came all right for Madame Barrot, so why not for me?'

'Because her husband said I could.'

'Listen, Papillon: my husband's in command of the camp, and I'm in command of the house. Walk in and don't be afraid.' I felt that this self-willed, pretty woman might either be useful or dangerous. I walked in.

In the dining-room she gave me some smoked ham and some cheese. Without any ceremony she sat down opposite me and poured me out wine, then some coffee and excellent Jamaica rum. 'Papillon,' she said, 'in spite of all the fuss of her going and us arriving, Madame Barrot had time to tell me about you. I know she was the only woman on the islands who had fish from you. I hope you'll do me the same favour.'

'That's was because she was ill; but as far as I can see, you're perfectly fit.'

'I can't lie, Papillon. Yes, I'm quite well, but I come from a seaport and I just love fish. I'm from Oran. There's only one thing that worries me – I also know you don't sell your fish. That really is awkward.'

To cut it short, we agreed that I should bring her fish. I was just smoking a cigarette, having given her a good seven pounds of mullet and six langoustines, when the governor appeared.

He saw me and said, 'Juliette, I've told you that apart from the houseboy no transportee is to come into the house.'

I stood up, but she said, 'Sit down. This transportee is the man Madame Barrot told me about before she left. So it's nothing to do with you. No one will come in except for him. Besides, he's going to bring me fish whenever I need it.'

'All right,' said the governor. 'What's your name?'

I was going to stand up to reply when Juliette put her hand on my shoulder and made me sit down again. 'This is *my* house,' she said. 'The governor's not the governor here: he's my husband, Monsieur Prouillet.'

'Thank you, Madame. My name's Papillon.'

'Ha! I've heard about you and your escape from the hospital at Saint-Laurent-du-Maroni three years ago and more. And it so happens that one of the warders you stunned was none other than our nephew.' At this Juliette laughed – fresh, young laughter – and said, 'So you're the one who knocked Gaston out? That won't change our relations in the least.'

The governor was still standing: he said to me, 'The number of killings and murders committed every year on the islands is unbelievable. Many more than on the mainland. How do you account for this, Papillon?'

'Why, Governor, here the men can't escape, so they're full of ill-temper. They live on top of one another for years on end, and it's natural their friendships and enmities should be very, very strong. Besides, less than five per cent of the man-slaughters or murders are solved, so the killer is pretty well sure of getting away with it.'

'That's a reasonable explanation. Since when have you been fishing, and what job do you do so that you can fish?'

'I'm a cesspitman. I finish my work by six in the morning, and that allows me to go off with my rod.'

'All the rest of the day?' asked Juliette.

'No. I have to be back in camp at noon, and then I'm allowed out again from three to six. It's a nuisance, because what with the change of the tide, I sometimes lose the right time for fishing.'

'You'll give him a special pass, won't you, darling?' said Juliette, turning to her husband. 'From six in the morning till six at night: that way he'll be able to fish whenever he likes.'

'All right,' he said.

I left the house, pleased with myself for having behaved like this, because these three hours from noon till three o'clock were of the greatest value. This was the time of the siesta, and as almost all the warders were asleep it meant that security was much less tight.

Juliette took me and my fishing over almost entirely. She even went so far as to send the young houseboy to see where I was so he could come and fetch my catch. He often turned up and said, 'The governor's wife sent me for everything you've caught, because she's got guests coming and she wants to make a bouillabaisse,' or something else of that kind. In short, she owned my fishing and she'd even ask me to try to catch some particular fish or other, or to dive for langoustines. This was quite a serious nuisance from the point of view of the gourbi's menu, but on the other hand I did have a marvellous friend at court. She was civil, too. 'Papillon, high tide's at one o'clock, isn't it?' 'Yes, Madame.' 'Come and eat at the house, then, so you won't have to go back to the camp.' And I would eat at her place, never in the kitchen, but always in the dining-room. She'd sit there opposite me, helping me to food and pouring out the wine. She was not as delicate as Madame Barrot. She would often question me rather artfully about my past. I always avoided my life in Montmartre, which was the thing that interested her most, and told her about my childhood and youth. At these times the governor would be asleep in his bedroom.

One morning when I'd made a very good catch early in the day, I called at her house at ten o'clock, carrying close on sixty langoustines. I found her sitting there in a white dressing-gown, with a young woman standing behind curling her hair. I said good-morning and offered her a dozen langoustines.

'No, give me the lot,' says she, using the very intimate *tu*. 'How many are there?'

'Sixty.'

'That's fine. Just leave them there, will you? How many fish do you and your friends need?'

'Eight.'

'Then you take your eight and give the rest to the houseboy to put in the refrigerator.'

I didn't know what to say. She'd never said *tu* to me before, above all not in front of another woman who was certainly going to talk about it. I was about to go, feeling horribly awkward, when she said, 'Sit still: stay where you are and have a pastis. You must be hot.'

I was so taken aback by her authoritarian attitude I sat down. Slowly I drank my pastis, smoking and watching the young woman who was combing the governor's wife's hair, glancing at me from time to time as she did so. The governor's wife had a glass in her hand and she noticed this. She said, 'My boy-friend's handsome, isn't he, Simone? All you other women are jealous of me, aren't you?' And they giggled together. I didn't know which way to look. Stupidly I blurted out, 'Fortunately your boy-friend, as you call him, can't be very dangerous: the position he's in, he can't be anyone's boy-friend.'

'You're not going to tell me you don't want to be my boy-friend,' said Juliette. 'You're one of these lions nobody's been able to tame, and yet I can twist you round my little finger. There must be some reason for that, don't you think, Simone?'

'I don't know what reason there can be,' said Simone. 'But you're a proper old bear for everybody except the governor's wife, Papillon, and that's a fact. Such a bear that the chief warder's wife told me that last week when you were going by with more than thirty pounds of fish you wouldn't let her have the two miserable objects she so longed for, there being no meat at the butcher's.'

'Ha, ha! That's a new one to me, Simone!' said Juliette.

'Do you know what he said to Madame Kargueret the other day?' went on Simone. 'She saw him going along with some langoustines and a great big moray eel. ''Sell me that moray. Papillon, or at least half of it,'' she says. ''You know we Bretons cook moray very well.'' ''It's not only the Bretons that appreciate it,'' says he. ''Plenty of people, including those from the Ardèche, have known it was a prime dish since the days of the Romans.'' And he walked on without selling her anything at all.' They laughed and laughed.

I went back to the camp in a rage and that evening I told

the gourbi the whole story. 'It's very serious,' said Carbonieri. 'That bitch is putting you in a dangerous position. Go there as little as you possibly can and only when you know the governor's at home.' Everybody was of the same opinion. I made up my mind to do just that.

I'd chanced upon a joiner from Valence. He was almost a fellow-countryman of mine. He'd killed a government game-keeper. He was a furious gambler, always in debt: by day he worked like mad at making junk and at night he'd lose all he'd earned. He often had to provide some particular object or other to satisfy a creditor; and when he had to do this they took advantage of him, and for a rosewood box worth three hundred francs they'd give him a hundred and fifty or two hundred. I decided to tackle him.

In the wash-house one day I said, 'I want to talk to you tonight. I'll wait for you in the latrines. I'll give you the nod.' That night there we were alone, where we could talk in peace. I said, 'Do you know we're from the same part, Bourset?'

'No! How come?'

'Aren't you from Valence?'

'That's right.'

'Well, I'm from the Ardèche. So we're countrymen.'

'What of it?'

'Just this – I don't like seeing them exploit you when you owe money and they give you only half the value of something you've made. Bring it to me, and I'll give you the full price. That's all.'

'Thanks,' said Bourset.

I stepped in again and again to help him. He was perpetually at cross-purposes with the men he owed money to. Everything went well until the day he contracted a debt to Vicioli, a Corsican hill-bandit and a good friend of mine. It was Bourset who told me; furthermore he said Vicioli was threatening him if he couldn't produce the seven hundred francs he owed. He had a little writing-desk almost ready but he couldn't say when it would be finished because he had to work on it in secret – no one was allowed to make furniture of any size because of the amount of wood it needed. I told him I'd see what I could do. And I made an agreement with Vicioli to put on a little act.

Vicioli was to bring pressure to bear on Bourset and threaten him very seriously indeed. I'd come in and save the situation. That's just what happened. Ever after this business that had supposedly been cleared up by me, I had Bourset right there in my pocket, where I wanted him to be – he trusted me absolutely. For the first time in his life as a convict he could breathe easy. At this point I decided to risk it.

One evening I said to him, 'I've got two thousand francs for you if you'll make the thing I want – a raft big enough for two, in sections that'll fit together.'

'Listen, Papillon, there's no one else I'd do that for. But for you I'm ready to run the risk of two years solitary if I'm caught. There's only one snag – I can't take wood of any size out of the yard.'

'I've got someone who can.'

'Who?'

'The pram boys, Naric and Quenier. How are you going to set about it?'

'We must draw a scale plan to begin with and then make the pieces one by one, with mortises so that everything'll fit together perfectly. The difficulty will be to find wood that floats, because here on the islands everything's hardwood and sinks.'

'When can you let me know?'

'In three days.'

'Would you like to go with me?'

'No.'

'Why not?'

'I'm afraid of the sharks and of drowning.'

'Will you promise to help me right through to the end?'

'I swear it on the heads of my children. The only thing is, it's going to take a long time.'

'Listen carefully: this very day I'll set you up a defence in case of anything going wrong. I'll copy the plan of the raft on exercise-book paper myself. Underneath I'll write, *Bourset, if you don't want to be murdered, just you make the raft shown above*. Later on I'll give you written orders for the making of each section. When each one is finished, you'll put it in a certain place. It'll be taken away. Don't try to find out who by or when' (this idea seemed to relieve his mind). 'In this way I prevent you being tortured if you're taken, and you only risk six months at the most.'

'And what if you're the one that's caught?'

'In that case it'll be the other way around. I'll admit I wrote the notes. You've got to keep these written orders, of course. Is it a deal?'

'Yes.'

'You're not frightened?'

'No, I'm not afraid any more; it'll make me happy to help you.'

I did not tell anyone. I was waiting for Bourset's definitive answer first. It was not until a tedious, endless week had gone by that I was able to talk to him alone, in the library. There was no one else there. It was a Sunday morning. In the yard, under the wash-house, the gambling was in full swing. Close on eighty players and the same number of men watching.

Straight away he filled my heart with sunshine. 'The hardest thing was to make sure of having enough light, dry wood. I got round that by thinking up a kind of wooden frame to be filled with dry coconuts – the nuts still in their husks, of course. There's nothing lighter than that fibre, and the water can't get into it. When the raft's ready, it'll be up to you to get enough coconuts to fill it. So tomorrow I'll start on the first section. It'll take me about three days. Any time after Thursday one of the pram boys can take it away during the first lull. I'll never begin another piece before the last has left the yard. Here's the plan I made: you copy it and write me the letter you promised. Have you spoken to the pram boys?'

'No, not yet: I was waiting for your answer.'

'Well, now you've had it. It's yes.'

'Thanks, Bourset. I don't know how to thank you. Look, here's five hundred francs.'

Looking me straight in the eye, he said, 'No, keep your money. If you get to the mainland you'll need it for the next part of the break. From today on I shan't gamble until you've gone. I can always make enough with a few little jobs to earn my cigarettes and my steak.'

'Why won't you take it?'

'Because I wouldn't do this even for ten thousand francs. The risk is too great, even with all your precautions. But for free, that's something else again. You've helped me: you've been the only one to stand up for me. Although I'm frightened, I'm still happy to help you to be free again.'

As I sat there, copying the plan on a sheet torn from an exercise-book, Bourset's simple, direct greatness of heart filled me with shame. It had never even occurred to him that my behaviour might have been calculated or insincere. To rise a little in my own esteem, I had to tell myself that I *had* to escape, at any cost at all, even if necessary at the price of trickery and not always very pretty situations. That night I spoke to Naric, whom they called Bonne Bouille, and who was to tell his brother-in-law later. Without any hesitation he said, 'You can rely on me to get the sections out of the yard for you. Only don't be in too much of a hurry, because we can only get them out when we're taking a good deal of stuff for some building job on the island. In any case, I promise we'll not let any chance slip by.'

Good. Now I only had to talk to Matthieu Carbonieri, for he was the man I wanted to make the break with. He agreed one hundred per cent.

'Matthieu, I've found a man who'll make me the raft: I've found a man who'll get the sections out of the yard for me. It's up to you to find a place in your garden to bury it in.'

'No, a kitchen-garden would be too dangerous, because there are screws that go stealing vegetables at night, and if they were to walk on the bed and notice it was hollow underneath, we'd have had it. I'll hollow out a place in a retaining wall – I'll take out a big stone and make a kind of little cave. That way, when a section comes along, I'll only have to lift the stone, hide the wood, and put it back again.'

'Should the sections be taken straight to your garden?'

'No, that would be too risky. The pram boys couldn't say what they were doing in my garden. The best thing is to work out a scheme for them to leave each piece in some different place, not too far from the garden.'

'Right.'

Everything seemed to be running smoothly. There were still the coconuts. I'd have to find out how I could get a sufficient number together without drawing attention to myself.

And now I began to feel as if I were coming to life again. All there was left to do was to speak to Galgani and Grandet. I had no right to keep quiet, because they might be accused of complicity. The normal thing would be to make an open breach with them and go and live by myself. When I told them I was going to make preparations for an escape and so I ought to live apart from them, they bawled me out and flatly refused.

'You go off as soon as ever you can. As for us, we'll manage. Meanwhile, stay with us – we can cope, all right.'

It was a month now that plans for the break had been on the go. I'd already received seven pieces of the raft, two of them big ones. I'd been to see the retaining wall in which Matthieu had hollowed out the hiding-place. You couldn't see the stone had been moved, because he'd taken care to put moss all round it. The hiding-place was perfect, but the hollow seemed to me too small to hold everything. Still, it was big enough for the moment.

The fact that I was getting ready for a break put me in terrific spirits. I was eating better than I'd ever eaten before, and fishing kept me wonderfully fit. On top of that, I did more than two hours of physical training on the rocks every morning. It was my legs I concentrated on, because fishing already looked after my arms. I discovered a splendid exercise for my legs: I waded in deeper than I would for ordinary fishing and the waves came breaking against my thighs. To withstand their force I kept all my muscles taut. The result was excellent.

Juliette, the governor's wife, was still very pleasant with me, but she'd noticed that I only went to her house when her husband was there. She told me so frankly, and to make me easy in my mind she said she had only been joking, that day when her hair was being done. Still, the young woman who had acted as hairdresser watched for me often enough when I was coming back from fishing, and she always had something kind to say – was I well? How was I getting along? So everything was fine. Bourset never lost a chance to make me a section. It was two and a half months now since we had begun.

The hiding-place was full, as I had foreseen. There were only two sections to come now, the longest ones – the first over six feet and the other about five. These sections would not be able to get into the hiding-place.

I noticed a fresh grave over in the cemetery: it belonged to the wife of one of the warders – she had died last week. A miserable withered bunch of flowers lay upon it. The keeper of the graveyard was an old, half-blind convict they called Papa. He spent all day sitting in the shade of a coconut palm in the opposite corner of the cemetery, and from where he was, he couldn't see the grave nor if anyone was going towards it. So I had the idea of making use of this grave for putting the raft together and filling the frame with as many coconuts as possible. Between thirty and thirty-four – many fewer than we had thought. I had more than fifty stored in different places. In Juliette's yard alone there were twelve. The houseboy thought I'd left them there meaning to extract the oil one day.

When I heard that the dead woman's husband had left for the mainland, I made up my mind to scoop out some of the earth from the tomb, going down as far as the coffin.

Sitting there on his wall, Matthieu Carbonieri kept watch. He had a white handkerchief on his head, tied at the four corners. Just by him, there was another handkerchief, also tied at the corners, but red this time. So long as there was no danger, he kept the white one on. If anyone appeared, whoever it might be, Matthieu put on the red handkerchief.

This very dangerous work took me one afternoon and one night: no more. I had to widen the hole to the breadth of the raft – four feet plus a little room for play – so it was not necessary to take the earth away as far down as the coffin. The hours seemed endless, and the red handkerchief appeared several times. At last this morning it was finished. The hole was covered over with plaited palm fronds, making a fairly solid kind of floor. Earth scattered over the whole, with a little border. It could scarcely be seen. I was at the very end of my tether.

It was three months now that the preparations for this break had been going on. We had taken all the sections, numbered and assembled, out of the hiding-place and now they lay upon the good lady's coffin, well hidden by the earth which covered the mats. In the place in the wall we put three flour-sacks and two yards of rope for the sail, a bottle full of matches and strikers, and a dozen tins of milk: that was all.

Bourset grew more and more worked up. You would have thought it was him who was going rather than me. Naric was sorry now that he had not said yes to begin with. We'd have worked on a raft for three rather than two.

It was the rainy season and rain fell every day; this was an advantage when I went to the hiding-place, where I had almost finished setting up the raft. The only parts unfixed were two side pieces in the frame. I had brought all the coconuts nearer and nearer to my friend's garden. They were in the open buffalo-stable, where they could be taken easily and without risk. My friends never asked what stage I had reached. From time to time they'd just say, 'OK?' 'Yes, fine.' 'It's taking rather a long time, isn't it?' 'We can't go faster without its being too risky.' That was all. When I was taking away the coconuts I had stored at Juliette's she saw me and gave me a most horrible fright.

'Why, Papillon, so you're going to make that coconut oil. Why don't you do it here in the yard? There's a mallet here to open them with and I'll lend you a big saucepan.'

'I'd rather do it at the camp.'

'How odd: it can't be very convenient there.' She thought for a moment and then said, 'Do you know what? I don't believe you're going to make coconut oil at all.' My blood ran cold. She went on. 'In the first place, what would you do with it, since you can get all the olive oil you want from me? Those nuts are for something else, aren't they?'

The sweat was dripping off me: right from the start I'd been expecting the word *escape*. My breath came short. I said, 'Madame, it's a secret: but as you are so curious – you want to know about it so much that you'll spoil the surprise. All I'll tell you is that these big nuts were chosen so that I could make you something really pretty out of the shells. That's the truth of it.'

I'd won, for she replied, 'Papillon, don't put yourself out for me: and I absolutely forbid you to spend any money on making me anything. I'm truly grateful, I really am, but I ask you not to do it.'

'All right: we'll see.' Relief, relief. Straight away I asked her to give me a pastis, which was something I never did. Luckily, she didn't notice my shattered state. The Lord was with me.

It rained every day, particularly in the afternoon and at night. I was afraid the water would wash away the sprinkling of earth and uncover the palm-frond mats. Matthieu continually kept replacing the earth that was carried away. Underneath, everything must be quite soaked. With Matthieu's help I pulled the mats off – the water was almost over the top of the coffin. Things were growing critical. Not far away there was a vault with two children who had died long ago. One day we forced off the cover: I got in and with a short crowbar I set about the cement, going to work as low as possible on the side where the grave with the raft was. Once I was through the cement, I had hardly driven the bar any distance into the earth before a great jet shot in. It was the water from the grave pouring into the vault. I came out when it reached my knees. We put the slab back and ran the white putty Naric had given me round the edge. This operation drained off half the water in our grave-hiding-place. That evening Carbonieri said, 'There'll never be an end to the things that go wrong with this break.'

'We're almost there, Matthieu.'

'Almost: let's hope so. We were both on hot bricks – very hot bricks.'

That morning I went down to the harbour. I asked Chapar to buy me five pounds of fish – I'd come and fetch it at noon. Right. I went up again to Carbonieri's garden. As I got nearer I saw three white caps. Why three screws in the garden? Were they making a search? It wasn't usual. I'd never seen three screws all at once at Carbonieri's place. I waited for more than an hour and then I couldn't bear it any longer. I made up my mind to push on and see what was happening. Quite openly I walked up the path leading to the garden. The screws watched me coming. When I was about twenty yards from them I was exceedingly interested to see Matthieu putting on his white handkerchief. I could breathe easy now, and I had time to collect myself before I reached them.

'Good morning, Messieurs les Surveillants. Good morning, Matthieu. I've come for the pawpaw you promised me.'

'I'm sorry, Papillon, but it was stolen this morning when I went to get sticks for my runner beans. But there'll be some others ripe in four or five days; they are beginning to turn yellow already. Well, now, warders, wouldn't you like a few lettuces and tomatoes and radishes for your wives?'

'Your garden's very well kept, Carbonieri,' said one of them. 'I congratulate you.'

They took the tomatoes, lettuces and radishes, and went off. I left ostentatiously some little time before them, carrying two lettuces. I went by the graveyard. The rain had washed half the earth off the grave. Ten yards off I could see the mats. If we hadn't been discovered, the Lord really was with us.

Every night the wind blew like fury, howling madly and roaring over the plateau: and often it brought rain with it. Let's hope it would last. It was the ideal time for getting away; but not for the grave.

The biggest piece of wood, the six-footer, had been delivered safely. It had gone to join the other sections of the raft. I'd even placed it: it fitted into the mortises exactly, to a hair's breadth, without any force. Bourset ran all the way to the camp to find out whether I had received it – the long piece of wood was of the very first importance, but it was most uncommonly awkward and bulky. He was delighted to know that everything had passed off well. You would have thought he wasn't sure of its getting there. I questioned him. 'Were you in doubt? Do you think someone knows what's up? Have you told anyone in private? Tell me.'

'No. Absolutely no.'

'Yet it seems to me something's worrying you. Tell.'

'I had a nasty feeling because of the way a guy called Bébert Celier watched – curiously interested, he was. I felt he'd seen Naric take the piece of wood from under the workbench, put it in the lime barrel and then carry it off. He watched Naric as far as the gate of the yard. The brothers were going to whitewash a building. That's why I was worried.'

I said to Grandet, 'This Bébert Celier is in our block: so he's not an informer.'

He said, 'That man goes in and out of the Public Works as he likes. It's quite obvious the sort of guy he is – penal battalion, one of those bad bargains of the Army who's been through all the military prisons of Algeria and Morocco, quarrelsome, dangerous with a knife, red-hot after boys, and a gambler. He's never had any life as a civilian. In a word – no bloody good and extremely dangerous. Prison is his life. If you feel suspicious, get in first – kill him tonight, and then if he means to shop you, he won't have time for it.'

'There's nothing to prove he's an informer.'

'That's true,' said Galgani. 'But there's nothing to prove he's a decent type, either. Convicts of that kind don't like breaks, as you know. Breaks upset their quiet little well-organized lives. There's nothing else on earth they'd inform about, but for a break – who can tell?'

I asked Matthieu Carbonieri's advice. He was in favour of killing him that night. He wanted to do it himself. I was fool enough to stop him. I hated the idea of killing someone on mere appearances, or letting him be killed. What if Bourset had only imagined it all? Fear might have made him see things that weren't there. I questioned Naric. 'Bonne Bouille, did you notice anything about Bébert Celier?'

'No: I didn't. I carried the barrel out on my shoulder so the turnkey on the gate shouldn't see into it. We'd agreed I should stand there just in front of him, without putting the barrel down, and wait for my brother to catch me up. That was so the Arab should see I was in no hurry, and not bother to look into the barrel. But afterwards my brother told me that he thought he saw Bébert Celier watching us closely.'

'What do you think yourself?'

'I think my brother was on edge because this piece is so big and because you can see straight away it's meant for a raft: and he was afraid, too. He thought he saw more than he really did see.'

'That's what I think too. Let's leave it at that. For the last section, find out just where Bébert Celier is before you make a move. Take the same precautions with him as you would for a screw.'

All that night I played the Marseilles game like crazy. I won seven thousand francs. The wilder I played the more I won. At half past four I went out for my so-called fatigue. I let the Martiniquais do my work. The rain had stopped and I went, though it was still quite dark, to the graveyard. I couldn't find the spade, but I scuffed the earth over the grave with my feet: this did the job fairly well. By seven o'clock, when I went down to go fishing, a splendid sun was already shining. I went in the direction of the southern tip of Royale, the place where I meant to launch the raft. A rough cross-sea was running. I couldn't be sure, but I had the feeling that it was not going to be so easy to get away from the islands without being picked up by a wave and flung on to the rocks. I began fishing and straight away I caught a great many mullet. In no time at all I had over ten pounds. When I'd cleaned them in sea water I stopped. I was uneasy in my mind and tired after that night of wild gambling. I rested, sitting in the shade of a rock, and I told myself that this tension I'd been living in for three months and more was reaching its end: and when I reflected on this business of Celier, I once more came to the conclusion that I had no right to kill him.

I went to see Matthieu. You could see the grave very well from his garden wall. Earth had drifted along the path. Carbonieri was going to go and sweep it off at midday. I called in at Juliette's and gave her half my fish. She said, 'Papillon, I had a bad dream about you: I saw you covered with blood and then chained up. Don't do anything stupid – if anything were

333

to happen to you I'd suffer dreadfully. That dream up set me so, I've neither washed nor done my hair. I took the binoculars and tried to see where you were fishing, but I couldn't find you. Where did you catch these?'

'The other side of the island. That's why you didn't see me.'

'Why do you go and fish so far away, where I can't see you even with the binoculars? What if you were swept off by a wave? There'd be no one to see you or help you escape from the sharks.'

'Oh come, don't exaggerate.'

'You think that's exaggerating? I forbid you to go fishing on the other side of the island, and if you don't obey, I'll have your pass taken away from you.'

'Let's be reasonable, Madame. To please you, I'll let your houseboy know where I'm going to fish.'

'All right. But you look tired.'

'Yes, Madame. I'm on my way up to the camp to lie down.'

'Very well. I'll expect you at four o'clock for a cup of coffee. You'll come?'

'All right, Madame. I'll be seeing you.'

This dream of Juliette's was just the very thing to make me feel perfectly calm, of course! As if I hadn't enough solid difficulties, dreams had to be added to make up the weight.

Bourset said he really did feel he was being watched. It was a fortnight now that we had been waiting for the last four-foot section. Naric and Quenier said they noticed nothing out of the way, but still Bourset would keep holding up the work on this plank. If it hadn't been for the five mortises that had to fit exactly, Matthieu would have made it in the garden: but these slots had to take all five ribs. Naric and Quenier were repairing the chapel, and so they could move a good deal of stuff in and out of the yard quite easily. Even more, they sometimes had the use of a cart pulled by a little buffalo. This was something we just had to take advantage of.

Urged on by us, Bourset made the piece, but against his better judgment. One day he said he was sure that when he wasn't there someone moved the plank and then put it back. There was still one mortise to be cut at the far end. We decided he should make it and then hide the wood under the top of his workbench. He was to lay a hair on it to see whether

334

anyone touched it. He cut the mortise and at six o'clock he left the workshop, the last man to go – he had checked to see that there was no one there except for the screw. The section was there in its place, with the hair over it. At noon I was at the camp, waiting for the building yard men, eighty of them, to turn up. Naric and Quenier were there, but not Bourset. A German came up to me and gave me a carefully closed, stuck-down note. I could see it hadn't been opened. It read, 'The hair's no longer there, so someone has touched the section. I've asked the screw to let me stay during the siesta to finish the little rosewood chest I'm working on. I'm going to take the section and put it with Naric's tools. Tell them. At three o'clock they must take it out of the yard at once. Maybe we can move faster than the bastard who's watching.'

Naric and Quenier agreed. They would get into the front rank of the building yard workmen. Just before the column went in, two men would have a fight some way outside the gate. We asked a couple of Carbonieri's countrymen to do us this favour – two Montmartre Corsicans, Massani and Santini. They didn't ask for any reason: quite the right way to behave. Naric and Quenier were to take advantage of this to hurry out with building material, as though they wanted to get to their work fast and the quarrel didn't interest them. We all thought we still had a chance. If we brought it off, then I wouldn't stir for a month or two, because it was quite certain that at least one man if not more knew a raft was being prepared. It was up to them to find out who was doing it, and where the hiding-place was.

At last half past two came round and the men began to get ready. It took thirty minutes from the roll-call to marching off to work. They set out. Bébert Celier was in the middle of the column of eighty men marching in fours.

Naric and Quenier were in the front rank; Massani and Santini in the twelfth; Bébert Celier in the tenth. It seemed to me a good arrangement, because when Naric got hold of his material and scaffolding and the piece of raft, a good deal of the column wouldn't yet be inside. Bébert would be nearly at the gate or perhaps some way short of it. As the Corsicans were going to roar at one another like a couple of maniacs everyone, including Bébert, would naturally turn round to see what was going on.

Four o'clock. Everything had gone off perfectly and the

section was lying under a heap of builder's material in the church. They hadn't been able to take it further, but it was perfect there.

I went to see Juliette. She wasn't at home. Going up again. I passed the administration block. Massani and Jean Santini were standing there in the shade, waiting to be taken to the punishment cells. Everyone had known that was bound to happen. I went by close to them and said, 'How long?'

'A week,' replied Santini.

A Corsican screw said, 'What a bleeding shame to see men from the same country fighting one another.'

I went back to the camp. Six o'clock: Bourset came back delighted. He said, 'It was as if I'd had cancer and then the doctor told me he'd got it wrong – there was nothing the matter with me.' Carbonieri and my other friends exulted and they congratulated me on the way I'd organized the scheme. Naric and Quenier were pleased, too. Everything was fine. I slept all through that night, although in the evening the gamblers came and asked me to join their game. I pretended to have a bad headache. I was in fact dying on my feet: but I was satisfied, and I was happy at being on the very edge of success. The hardest part was over.

This morning Matthieu put the section in the hollow of the wall just for the time being, because the man who looked after the graveyard was sweeping the paths over by the tomb hiding-place. It wouldn't be wise to go to it at present. At dawn every morning I hurried there with a wooden shovel and tidied the earth on the grave. I swept the path and then, still at the double. I went back to my pot-emptying, leaving the shovel and the broom in a corner belonging to my job.

It was four months to the day since the preparations for the break had begun and nine days since we had at last received the final section of the raft. Now the rain was no longer falling every day and sometimes all night long too. All my senses were on the stretch for the two D-days – the first when this last piece was to be taken out of Matthieu's garden and fixed in its place on the raft, holding all the ribs. This was something that could only be done in daylight. And the second D-day would be that of our escape. It could not be directly after the first, because once the raft was taken out, the coconuts and the stores still had to be fitted into it.

Yesterday I told Jean Castelli all about it: and I told him

just what point I'd reached. He was happy for me that I was so near my goal. He said, 'The moon's in its first quarter.'

'I know; and so it won't worry us at midnight. Low tide's at ten, and therefore the right moment for the launch will be two in the morning.'

Carbonieri and I had decided to hurry things. Tomorrow morning at nine, the last section to be fitted. And the same night, the break.

The next morning, having carefully planned our movements, I went from the garden to the graveyard and I jumped over the wall with a spade. While I was scooping the earth from over the plaited fronds, Matthieu raised his stone and brought me the last section. Together we lifted off the mats and put them to one side. There was the raft, perfectly preserved. A little earth sticking to it, but perfectly sound. We lifted it out, because we needed side-room to fit the last section. We settled the five ribs in their places: to get them right home we had to hammer them with a stone. Just as we had finished and were in the act of putting it back, we looked up and saw a warder, holding a gun.

'Don't move, or you're dead men!'

We dropped the raft and raised our hands. I recognized the screw: he was the building yard chief warder.

'Don't be such bloody fools as to resist. You're caught. Give in and maybe you'll save your skins at least: but I feel so like filling you full of lead it's not all that sure. On your way, now: keeping your hands right up in the air. Get along to the administration block.'

As we went past the cemetery gate we met an Arab turnkey. The screw said, 'Mohamed, thanks for this bit of work. Come and see me tomorrow morning and I'll give you what I promised.'

'Thanks,' said the Arab. 'I'll come for sure. But chief, Bébert Celier has to pay me too, doesn't he?'

'You fix that with him yourself,' said the screw.

Then I said, 'So it was Bébert Celier that shopped us, Chief?'

'It's not me that said so.'

'That's all one. I just like to know.'

Still covering us with his rifle, the screw said, 'Mohamed, search them.'

The Arab took the knife out of my belt; and he found

Matthieu's. I said, 'You're a sharp lad, Mohamed. How did you find out?'

'I climbed up a coconut palm every day to see where you were hiding the raft.'

'Who told you to do that?'

'It was Bébert Celier first, then Monsieur Bruet, the warder.'

'Too much chat,' said the screw. 'Get going. You can lower your hands now, and walk quicker.'

The four hundred yards we had to cover to reach the administration block seemed to me the longest road I'd ever travelled in all my life. I was utterly crushed. All that effort just to be caught like a couple of twits. God, how cruel You are to me!

Our arrival at the block made quite a stir. For going along we had met other warders, and they had joined the first, who was still covering us with his rifle. By the time we got there we had seven or eight screws behind us.

The governor had been told by the Arab, who had run ahead, and he was there on the steps of the administration block, together with Dega and five head warders.

'What's happened, Monsieur Bruet?' asked the governor.

'What's happened is that I've caught these two men redhanded, busy hiding a raft – a finished raft, I think.'

'What have you to say, Papillon?'

'Nothing. I'll talk at the inquiry.'

'Put them in the black-hole.'

I was put into a black-hole whose bunged-up window gave on to the entrance by the governor's office. The cell was dark, but I could hear people talking in the street leading to the block.

Things moved fast. At three o'clock we were brought out and handcuffed. A kind of court was sitting there in the big room: governor, deputy-governor, chief warder. Dega, sitting to one side at a little table, was obviously there to take the statements as they were made.

'Charrière and Carbonieri, listen to Monsieur Bruet's report concerning you. "I, Bruet Auguste, head warder in charge of the building yard on the Iles du Salut, accuse the two convicts Charrière and Carbonieri of theft and misappropriation of material belonging to the State. I accuse the joiner Bourset of complicity. I believe Naric and Quenier are also to be considered guilty of complicity. I further state that I discovered

Charrière and Carbonieri in the very act of violating the grave of Madame Privat, which they used as a hiding-place to conceal their raft." '

'What have you to say?' asked the governor.

'In the first place Carbonieri has nothing to do with it. The raft is planned to carry one man only – me. I merely forced him to help take the mats off the grave, a job I couldn't do alone. So Carbonieri's not guilty of misappropriation and theft of State material; nor of complicity in an escape, seeing the escape never came off. Bourset is just a poor devil who was threatened with death if he didn't do what he was told. As for Naric and Quenier, I scarcely even know them. I assert that they have nothing whatsoever to do with the matter.'

'That's not what my informer says,' said the screw.

'This Bébert Celier, your informer, may very well be taking his revenge by falsely mixing other men up with this business. Who can trust what an informer says?'

'In short,' said the governor, 'you are officially accused of theft and misappropriation of State material, profanation of a grave and attempting to escape. Be so good as to sign the record.'

'I shan't sign unless my statement about Carbonieri, Bourset and the brothers-in-law Naric and Quenier is added.'

'I grant that. Draw it up.'

I signed. I just can't express what had been going on inside me since this last-moment failure. In the black-hole it was as though I was out of my mind: I scarcely ate and I didn't walk; but I smoked on and on, one cigarette after another. Luckily I was well supplied with tobacco by Dega. Every morning there was an hour's exercise in the punishment cell yard, in the sun.

This morning the governor came and talked to me. There was one odd thing – if the escape had come off, he would have been the one to suffer most; and yet it was he who was the least angry with me.

Smiling, he said his wife had told him it was natural for a man to try to escape, unless he had become utterly demoralized. He very cleverly tried to get me to incriminate Carbonieri. I had the feeling that I'd persuaded him of the contrary, explaining how impossible it was for Carbonieri to refuse to give me a hand for a few moments, pulling off the mats.

Bourset had shown the threatening note and the plans drawn by me. As far as he was concerned the governor was quite convinced that that was how things were. I asked him what he thought this charge of stealing material might come to. He said, 'Not more than eighteen months.'

To cut things short, I gradually began to come up out of the abyss I'd plunged into. I had a note from Chatal, the medical orderly. He told me Bébert Celier was in a ward by himself in the hospital, waiting to be un-interned – a rare disease had been diagnosed: abscess on the liver. This must be something cooked up between the administration and the doctor to protect him from reprisals.

They never searched me or my cell. I took advantage of this to get a knife sent in. I told Naric and Quenier they must ask for the yard warder, Bébert Celier, the joiner and me to be brought face to face with them: they were to ask the governor to take whatever decision about them he thought right after this confrontation – inquiry, disciplinary punishment or a return to freedom in the camp.

At today's exercise Naric told me the governor had agreed. The confrontation would take place tomorrow at ten in the morning. A head warder would be there to conduct the proceedings. All night long I tried to reason with myself; for I meant to kill Bébert Celier. I could not force my mind to alter. No, it would be too unfair if the fellow were to be un-interned for this piece of work and that then on the mainland he should make a break – a reward, as it were, for having prevented one. Yes, but they might condemn you to death, man, because they could accuse you of malice aforethought. I don't give a fuck. That was the conclusion I came to – I had truly lost all hope. Four months of expectation and joy, fear of being caught, intelligent effort: and then, when everything was just coming off, the whole thing pitifully wrecked by the tongue of an informer. Come what may, tomorrow I'd try and kill Celier!

The only way of avoiding a death-sentence was to make him bring out his knife. To do that, I'd have to let him see quite clearly that I had mine open. Then he'd certainly whip out his. It would have to be done a little before or just after the confrontation. I couldn't kill him during it, because that would mean the risk of a screw shooting me. I relied on the proverbial carelessness of warders.

All night long I struggled against this idea. I could not

overcome it. In life there really are some things that can't be forgiven. I know you haven't the right to take the law into your own hands: but that's for people belonging to another social class. It's inconceivable that you shouldn't be allowed to think of punishing – mercilessly punishing – such a crawling, base creature as this. I'd never done this barrack-bird the least harm in the world: he didn't even know me. So he was sending me down for X years of solitary without having the least thing against me. He was trying to bury me alive so that he could live again. Was I going to put up with that? No: I was not. It was inconceivable that I should allow him to profit by his sewer rat's action. Inconceivable. I felt that I was done for. Done for: so let him be done for too, and even more so than me. And what if you're sentenced to death, man? It would be a fool's game to die for such a louse. I reached the point of promising myself just this one thing – if he didn't bring out his knife, I shouldn't kill him.

I didn't sleep at all the whole night, and I smoked right through a packet of tobacco. I only had two cigarettes left when the coffee came round at six in the morning. I was so on edge that although it was forbidden I said to the coffee man, with the screw there, 'Could you let me have a few cigarettes or a little tobacco, with the chief's permission? I'm all in, Monsieur Antartaglia.'

'Yes, give it to him if you've got any. I don't smoke myself. I'm really sorry for you, Papillon. I'm a Corsican, so I like men who are men, and I loathe scum.'

At a quarter to ten I was in the yard, waiting to go into the main room. Naric, Quenier, Bourset and Carbonieri were there too. The screw in charge of us was Antartaglia, the one who'd been there at coffee time. He was talking to Carbonieri in Corsican. I gathered he was saying it was a pity for Carbonieri that this had happened and that he ran the risk of three years' solitary. At this moment the gate opened and into the yard came the Arab who had climbed the palm tree, the Arab in charge of the building yard gate, and Bébert Celier. When he saw me he started back, but the warder with them said to him, 'Go on and keep away from the others – stand over there on the right. Antartaglia, don't let there be any communication between them.'

Here we were not two yards from one another. Antartaglia said, 'No talking between the two groups.'

Carbonieri went on talking Corsican with his fellow-countryman, who was watching both sets of men. The screw bent to tie his shoelace: I motioned to Matthieu to move forward a little. He understood at once, looked towards Bébert Celier and spat in his direction. When the screw was upright again Carbonieri talked on without a pause and took up his attention so much that I was able to take a step without his noticing it. I let my knife slide down into my hand. Only Celier could see it, and with unexpected speed – for he had his knife right there open in his trousers – he stabbed me deep in the muscle of my right arm. I'm a left-handed man, and in a single lunge I thrust my knife into his chest up to the hilt. An animal cry, 'A – a – ah!' He went down in a heap.

With his revolver in his hand, Antartaglia said, 'Get back, boy. Don't stab him on the ground or I'll be forced to shoot you, and I don't want to do that.'

Carbonieri went over to Celier and pushed his head with his foot. He said a couple of words in Corsican. I understood he meant, 'He's dead.'

The warder said, 'Give me your knife, boy.'

I gave it to him; he put his gun back in its holster, went to the iron door and knocked. A screw opened and he said to him, 'Send the stretcher-bearers to pick up a corpse.'

'Who's dead?' asked the screw.

'Bébert Celier.'

'Oh! I thought it was Papillon.'

They put us back in the black-hole. The confrontation was suspended. Before going into the corridor Carbonieri said, 'My poor old Papi, you're for it this time.'

'Yes, but I'm alive and he's dead.'

The screw came back alone, very quietly opened the door and said, 'Knock and say you're wounded. He was the one who struck first; I saw him.' And he closed it again quietly: he was still really upset.

These Corsican screws are terrific – they're either completely bad or completely good. I beat on the door and shouted, 'I'm wounded. I want to be taken to hospital to have my wound dressed.'

The screw came back with the head warder of the punishment block. 'What's wrong with you? What's all this noise about?'

'I'm wounded, Chief.'

'Oh, you're wounded? I thought he didn't get home when he went for you.'

'The muscle of my right arm's sliced through.'

'Open up,' said the other screw.

The door opened. I stepped out. And indeed the muscle was deeply cut.

'Put the handcuffs on him and take him to hospital. Don't leave him there on any pretext whatsoever. Bring him back here as soon as he's been treated.'

When we went out there were more than ten screws with the governor. The building yard screw said to me, 'Murderer!'

Before I could reply the governor said, 'Be quiet, Warder Bruet. The man went for Papillon.'

'That's not very likely,' said Bruet.

'I saw it and I'll bear witness,' said Antartaglia. 'And get this, Monsieur Bruet: Corsicans don't lie.'

When we reached the hospital, Chatal sent for the doctor. He sewed me up without gas or a local anaesthetic; then, still without speaking to me, he put on eight clips. I let him do it without a murmur. When it was done he said, 'I couldn't give you a local anaesthetic: I've none left.' Then he added, 'It wasn't right, what you've just done.'

'Oh, in any case he wasn't going to live much longer, you know, not with that abscess on his liver.' This unexpected answer left the medico gaping.

The inquiry was resumed. Bourset was dismissed from the case as having no responsibility whatsoever: it was admitted that he was terrorized, and I did all I could to help this point of view. Naric and Quenier were set aside too, for want of proof. That left Carbonieri and me. The accusations of theft and misappropriation against him were withdrawn, leaving only complicity in attempted escape. The most he could get for this was six months. But as far as I was concerned, things became more complicated. In spite of all the evidence in my favour the man in charge of the inquiry would not accept that I'd acted in self-defence. Dega saw the whole file, and he told me that in spite of the investigator's zeal I couldn't possibly be condemned to death because of my having been wounded. One thing the prosecution used against me was that the two Arabs said they'd seen me draw my knife first.

The inquiry was over. I was waiting to go over to Saint-Laurent to appear before a court-martial. I did nothing but smoke: I hardly walked at all. They granted me an extra hour's exercise in the afternoon. At no time did the governor or any of the warders – apart from the building yard screw and the one in charge of the inquiry – show any hostility towards me. They all talked to me without any kind of enmity and they let me have all the tobacco I wanted sent in.

I was to leave on Friday: and this was Tuesday. At ten on Wednesday morning I had been in the yard for close on two hours when the governor sent for me and said, 'Come with me.' I went along with him, unescorted. I asked where we were going: he led the way down the path towards his house. As we went along he said, 'My wife would like to see you before you go. I didn't want to upset her by having an armed warder behind you. I'm sure you'll behave properly.'

'Yes, Governor.'

We reached his house, 'Juliette, I've done what I promised and I've brought your protégé. I have to take him back again before twelve, as you know. You've got nearly an hour to talk to him.' And with this he left us.

Juliette came over to me and laid her hand on my shoulder, looking right into my face. Her black eyes shone all the more because they were swimming with the tears that fortunately she managed to hold back. 'You're out of your mind, friend Papillon. If you'd told me you wanted to go, I think I might have been able to make things easier for you. I've asked my husband to help you all he can, but he tells me that unluckily it doesn't depend on him. I sent for you to see how you were, in the first place. I congratulate you on your spirit – you look much better than I thought you would. And then in the second place to tell you I want to pay you for the fish you've been giving me so generously all these months. Look, here's a thousand francs – it's all I can produce. I'm sorry it's not more.'

'Listen, Madame, I don't need money. Please understand that I can't take it: as I see things it would spoil our friendship.' And I pushed back the money she had so handsomely offered me – two five-hundred franc notes. 'Don't press me, please.'

'As you like,' she said. 'Will you have a drop of pastis?' And for an hour and more this splendid woman talked to me charmingly. She thought that I should certainly be acquitted for the murder of that swine and that I might get perhaps eighteen months to two years for the rest.

When I left she took my hand in both of hers and pressed it for a long while. She said, 'Au revoir. Good luck,' and burst into tears.

The governor took me back to the punishment block. On the way I said to him, 'Governor, you have the noblest wife on earth.'

'I know it, Papillon: she's not made for this kind of life here – it's too cruel for her. And yet what can I do about it? Still, only four more years and I retire.'

'I'd like to take advantage of our being by ourselves, Governor, to thank you for having me treated as well as possible, in spite of the difficulties you would have had if I'd brought it off.'

'Yes, you might have caused me some very nasty headaches. But for all that, I'll tell you something – you did deserve to succeed.' And as we reached the gate of the punishment block he said, 'Good-bye, Papillon. May God help you: you'll need it.'

'Good-bye, Governor.'

Yes, I was certainly going to need God's help, for the court-martial, with a four-ring Gendarmerie major presiding, was merciless. Three years for theft, misappropriation, violation of a grave and attempted escape: and on top of that five years for the manslaughter of Celier, to run consecutively. Eight years solitary in all. If I'd not been wounded, they'd have condemned me to death for sure.

This court that was so hard on me was more lenient to a Pole named Dandosky, who had killed two men. They only gave him five years, and yet there was premeditation, without a shadow of a doubt.

Dandosky was a baker who made yeast and nothing else. He only worked between three and four in the morning. As the bakery was on the wharf, facing the sea, he spent all his free time fishing. He was a quiet man and he couldn't speak French well: he made close friends with nobody. This lifer kept all his affection for a splendid black cat with green eyes that lived with him. They slept in the same bed; it followed him like a dog and kept him company when he was at work. In short, the man and the cat were devoted to one another. The cat used to go fishing with him, but if the day was too hot and there was no shade, it would walk back by itself to the bakery and lie in its friend's hammock. When the bell

345

went for midday, it would go and meet the Pole, who would give it little fish, dangling them until the cat jumped up and caught them.

All the bakers lived together in a room next to the bakery. One day two convicts by the name of Corrazi and Angelo invited Dandosky to come and eat a rabbit Corrazi had stewed – a dish he made at least once a week. Dandosky sat down and ate with them, bringing a bottle of wine to go with the meal. That evening the cat did not come home. The Pole searched for it everywhere, but in vain. A week went by: no cat. The Pole was so wretched at the loss of his friend that he no longer took any pleasure in life. It was really sad that the one creature he loved and that returned his love so well should have vanished in this mysterious way. A warder's wife, hearing of his great unhappiness, gave him a kitten. Dandosky drove it away and indignantly asked the woman how she could possibly imagine he could love any cat but his own: it would be a gross insult to the memory of the dear departed, he said.

One day Corrazi hit a baker's apprentice who was also a delivery boy, one who didn't sleep with the bakers but belonged to the camp. Full of resentment, the apprentice looked for Dandosky, found him, and said, 'You know, the rabbit Corrazi and Angelo invited you to share was your cat.'

'Where's your proof?' cried the Pole, grasping the boy by the throat.

'I saw Corrazi burying the skin of your cat under the mango tree that stands rather back, behind the boatmen's place.'

The Pole rushed off like a madman, and there indeed he did find the skin. He dug it up, half rotted and the head almost gone. He washed it in sea-water, dried it in the sun, wrapped it in perfectly clean linen and buried it deep in a dry place, so the ants shouldn't get at it. That's what he told me.

That night Corrazi and Angelo were sitting side by side on a massive bench in the baker's room, playing four-handed belote by the light of a paraffin lamp. Dandosky was a man of about forty, medium-sized, thickset and with broad shoulders: he was very strong. He had prepared a thick ironwood club, as heavy as iron itself: he came up behind them and without a word he brought the club down on the head of each. Their skulls opened like two pomegranates and their brains spilt on the ground. He was quite mad with fury and just killing them was not enough – he scooped up the brains and

346

flung them against the wall. The whole place was spattered with blood and brains.

Although the Gendarmerie major, the president of the court-martial, did not feel much sympathy for me, he did for Dandosky, who was lucky enough to get away with no more than five years for two premeditated murders.

Second Term of Solitary

I went back to the islands chained to this Pole. They hadn't kept us hanging about in the punishment cells of Saint-Laurent! It was on a Monday we got there; we were court-martialled on the Thursday, and on Friday morning they put us on the boat for the islands again.

So we were on our way back, sixteen of us: and of the sixteen twelve were for solitary. During the crossing the sea was very rough, and quite often a larger wave than usual swept along the deck. My despair reached the point of hoping the old tub would sink. I spoke to no one, and the sea-laden wind that stung my face closed me in upon myself. I didn't shelter from it at all. I deliberately let my hat blow off – in eight years of solitary I shouldn't have much need of hats. I faced into the lashing wind and breathed it in so deep it almost choked me. When I'd thought of the ship going down I checked myself, saying, 'The sharks have eaten Bébert Celier: you're thirty, and you've got eight years to serve.' But was it possible to do eight years inside the walls of the man-eater?

As far as my experience went, I thought it was *not* possible. Four or five must be the limit of any man's resistance. If I'd not killed Celier I'd only have had three years to serve, perhaps only two: because the killing had made everything seem worse, including the escape. I shouldn't have killed the rat. My duty as a man, my duty towards myself, was not to take the law into my own hands, but in the very first place and above all, to live – to live in order to escape. How did I come to make

347

such a mistake? Quite apart from the fact that it was a very close thing whether it was me or that bastard who got killed. Live, live, live: that ought to have been and now must be my one religion.

Among the warders escorting the convoy there was one I'd known in solitary. I didn't know his name, but I had a great longing to ask him a question. 'Chief, I'd like to ask you something.'

Astonished, he came over and said, 'What?'

'Have you ever known a man who managed to do eight years solitary?'

He thought, and then said, 'No. But I've known a good many who've done five; and there was even one – I remember him very well – who came out quite fit and right in the head after six years. I was there at the Réclusion when they set him free.'

'Thanks.'

'That's all right,' said the screw. 'You've got eight, I believe?'

'Yes, Chief.'

'You'll only manage it if you're never punished.' And he moved away.

That observation was very important. Yes: I should only come out alive if I was never punished. For the punishments were all based on the temporary stopping of rations; and even when you returned to normal diet you could never really get your strength back. A few fairly rigorous punishments would mean you couldn't hold out to the end – you'd kick the bucket first. Moral: I must never take coconuts or cigarettes; never even write or receive messages.

I chewed over this decision all the rest of the trip. Nothing, absolutely nothing either from the outside or from inside. I had an idea: the only way of being helped in the matter of food without danger was for someone outside to pay the soup-carriers so that they should pick me out one of the biggest and best pieces of meat at midday. It would be easy, because one ladled out the broth while another coming behind with a tray put a lump of meat in the bowl. He'd have to scrape the bottom of the pail and give me as many vegetables as possible in my share. Hitting upon this idea was a comfort. For that way I could quite well eat enough not to be hungry – I could almost eat as much as I wanted if this scheme was properly carried

348

out. Then it would be up to me to take off and dream as much as possible, pitching upon cheerful subjects so as not to go mad.

We reached the islands. It was three in the afternoon. I was scarcely ashore before I saw Juliette's pale yellow dress, at her husband's side. The governor came quickly over to me, even before we had time to line up, and he said, 'How long?'

'Eight years.'

He went back to his wife and spoke to her. She sat down on a stone, no doubt badly upset. Almost entirely overcome. Her husband took her arm, she stood up, cast me a meaning, sorrowful look from her huge black eyes, and they both moved away without turning back.

'Papillon,' said Dega, 'how long?'

'Eight years solitary.' He said nothing and he didn't even like to look at me. Galgani came up but before he could speak I said to him, 'Don't send me anything: don't write, either. With a sentence this long I can't risk any punishment.'

'I get you.'

In a low voice I quickly added, 'Fix it so they give me as much food as possible at noon and evening. If you can manage that maybe we'll see one another again some day. Goodbye.'

I deliberately walked towards the first boat of those that were to take us across to Saint-Joseph. They all watched me as people watch a coffin being lowered into a grave. No one spoke. During the short crossing I repeated what I'd said to Galgani to Chapar.

'That should be possible. Keep your heart up, Papi.' Then he said, 'And what about Matthieu Carbonieri?'

'I'm sorry I forgot him. The president of the court-martial wanted further inquiries to be made into his case before coming to a decision: is that good or bad?'

'Good, I think.'

I was in the first rank of the little column of twelve climbing the hill to reach the Réclusion. I went up fast: it was odd, but I was in a hurry to be alone in my cell. I stepped out so that the screw said, 'Not so fast, Papillon. Anyone would think you couldn't wait to get back to the place you left such a little while ago.'

We were there.

'Strip! Here's the governor of the Réclusion.'

'I'm sorry you're back, Papillon,' he said. Then, 'Confinees, etc.' – his usual piece. 'Block A, cell 127. It's the best, Papillon, because you're opposite the door of the passage and that gives you more light – and you're never short of air. I hope you'll behave well. Eight years is a long time: but who knows, maybe excellent conduct will earn you one or two years remission. I hope so, because you're a brave man.'

So here I was in 127. It was, as he'd said, just opposite a big barred gate that opened on to the passage. I could still see quite clearly, although by now it was nearly six in the evening. And this cell didn't have the smell and taste of decay that had filled my other one. My spirits rose a little. 'Friend Papillon, here are the four walls that are going to watch you live for the next eight years. Don't count months and hours – there's no point. If you want a proper yardstick you must count by units of six months. Sixteen times six months and you're free again. In any case there's one good thing about it. If you die here – at least, if you do it during the day – you'll have the satisfaction of dying in the light. That's very important. It can't be much fun to die in the dark. If you're ill, at least here the doctor can see your face. You don't have to blame yourself for having wanted to escape and make a new life; hell, nor for having killed Celier, either. Imagine how you would have suffered thinking that while you were in here, he was off, making a break! Time will tell. Maybe there'll be an amnesty, a war, or an earthquake or typhoon that will destroy this place. Why not? Maybe there'll be an upright, decent man who'll go back to France and manage to stir up French public opinion so that it will force the prison service to do away with this manner of guillotining people without a guillotine. Maybe a doctor, sickened by it all, will tell some journalist or priest all about it – something of that kind. At all events, the sharks have digested Celier long ago. I'm here: and if I'm up to my own standards, I ought to come out of this living grave on my feet.'

One, two, three, four, five, about-turn; one, two, three, four, five, about-turn. I began walking, going straight back to the right position of head and arms and the exact length of pace for the pendulum to work perfectly. I determined only to walk two hours in the morning and two in the afternoon until I should know whether I could rely on more than the regulation amount of food. Don't let these first edgy days fool you into wasting energy.

Yes, it was pitiful to have failed at the very end. To be sure, it was only the first part of the break, and I should still have had to bring off a crossing of more than ninety miles on that frail raft. And then, according to where we touched the mainland, to have started another escape all over again. If the launching had worked well, the flour-sack sail would have carried the raft along at a good six miles an hour. We'd have reached the mainland in under fifteen hours, perhaps in twelve. That is to say if it rained during the daytime, of course; since it was only with rain falling that we would have dared set the sail. I seemed to remember that it had rained the day after I was put into the black-hole. I couldn't be sure. I tried to see what mistakes or errors I had made. I could only discover two. The joiner had insisted on making too good, too solid a raft; and then, to hold the coconuts, he had had to make a framework that amounted to much the same as two rafts one on top of the other. Hence too many pieces to work up and too much time needed to be able to work on them without danger.

The second, far more serious fault was this: when we had the first hard suspicion about Celier, I ought to have killed him that same night. If I'd done that, who could tell where I'd be now? Even if things had gone sour on the mainland or if I'd been arrested at the moment of the launch, I'd only have copped three years instead of eight, and I'd have had the satisfaction of having done something. And if everything had gone smoothly, where should I be, on the islands or on the mainland? No telling. Maybe talking to Bowen in Trinidad: maybe in Curaçao, under the protection of Bishop Irénée de Bruyne. And we'd only have gone off from Curaçao if we had been certain that some nation or another would allow us in. If they wouldn't, it would have been easy enough to go back alone, sailing a little boat straight to the Goajira and my tribe.

I went to sleep very late, and I rested quite normally. This first night wasn't so very depressing after all. Live, live, live. Every time I was on the point of giving up from despair, I was to repeat 'While there's life there's hope' three times over.

A week had gone by. Since yesterday I had noticed a change in my rations. A splendid lump of boiled meat at midday, and in the evening a bowl crammed with lentils – hardly any water at all. Like a child I said, 'Lentils have iron in them; they are very good for the health.'

If this went on, I was going to be able to walk ten or twelve hours a day; and then, tired out, I'd be ready to take off for the stars. No, I was not wandering; I was here on earth, firmly on this earth. I thought about all the convicts I'd known on the islands: each had his own story, his past and his present. And I thought of the legends they told on the islands, too. There was one that I swore I should check if ever I was on the island again – it was the story of the bell.

As I said earlier, the convicts were not buried but thrown into the sea in a shark-infested place between Saint-Joseph and Royale. The dead man was wrapped in flour sacks with a big stone tied to his feet. A rectangular chest – always the same chest – was fixed level in the bows. When the boat reached the right place the six rowers, all convicts, lay on their oars. One man opened a kind of trap-door and another tilted the chest. The corpse slid into the water. There was not the least doubt about it – it was certain that the sharks bit through the rope immediately. No dead man ever had the time to sink to any depth. He came up to the surface and the sharks began fighting over this particular treat of theirs. According to those who had been there, the sight of a man being eaten was very striking indeed, for when there were a great many sharks they managed to thrust the shroud and its contents right up out of the water, tear the flour sacks off, and carry away great lumps of the body.

All this did happen just as I have said, but there was one thing I had been unable to check. Every convict without exception said that what attracted the sharks to this place was the sound of the bell that tolled in the chapel when there was a death. It seems that if you were on the end of the jetty at Royale at six in the evening, some days you wouldn't see a single shark. When the bell began ringing in the little chapel, the place would be stiff with them in no time at all – sharks waiting for the dead man; for there was nothing else to explain their presence there at just that particular moment. Let's hope I shan't be served up to the sharks of Royale like that: if they eat me during a break, well that's just too bad: but at least it would be while I was trying to win my freedom. But not when I'd died of some disease in my cell: no, that just mustn't happen.

Thanks to my friends' arrangements I was eating as much as I needed, and I felt perfectly fit. I walked without stopping from seven in the morning until six in the evening. So the evening bowl full of dried vegetables, beans, lentils, split peas or fried rice, went down very easily. I always ate the lot without any effort. Walking did me good; the tiredness it produced was healthy, and I even managed to take off while I was still going to and fro. Yesterday, for example, I spent the whole day in the meadows of a little district in the Ardèche by the name of Favras. When Maman died I often used to go there and spend a few weeks with my aunt, my mother's sister, who was a schoolteacher in the village. Well, yesterday I was as good as there, walking about in the chestnut woods, finding mushrooms; and then I heard a little friend of mine, a shepherd, calling out orders to his dog – orders that the dog carried out perfectly, bringing back a lost sheep or punishing a straying goat. Even better, there in my mouth was the coolness of the iron-bearing spring, and its tiny bubbles tickled my nose. This total recall of a time more than fifteen years in the past and this power of experiencing it again with such vividness is possible only in a cell, far from all noise, in the most profound silence.

I could even see the yellow of Auntie Outine's dress. I heard the wind whispering through the chestnut trees, the sound of a falling chestnut, sharp when it dropped on dry earth and muffled when it came down into a bed of leaves. A huge wild boar came out of the tall broom and frightened me so dreadfully that I tore away, losing most of the mushrooms I had gathered, in my panic. Yes, pacing there in my cell, I spent the whole day at Favras with auntie and my little friend Julien, the shepherd, a child from the Public Assistance. There was no one who could prevent me from delighting in these tender memories, so clear and sharp; and no one could prevent them from giving me the peace my wounded heart so called for.

As far as society was concerned, I was in one of the many punishment cells of the man-eater. In fact I had stolen a whole day from them: I had spent it at Favras, in the meadows and under the chestnut trees; and I had even drunk at the place they called the Peach-tree Spring.

Now the first six months had gone by. I had said I should count by units of six months, and so I had kept my promise. It was only this morning that I reduced the sixteen to fifteen . . . Only fifteen lengths of six months left.

Let's see how things stand. No outstanding personal event

during these six months. Always the same food, but always a perfectly adequate amount of it, a ration that meant my health didn't suffer. A great many suicides and men going raving mad around me, carried off quite soon, thank God. It is depressing to hear men shouting, weeping or moaning for hours or even days on end. I had found quite a good dodge, but one that was bad for the ears. I cut off a bit of soap and stuffed it into my ears so that I should no longer hear the awful shrieks. Unfortunately the soap did harm and after a day or two both my ears were running.

For the first time since I'd been in penal I lowered myself to ask a screw for something. One of the soup warders came from Montélimar, which was near to my part. I had known him on Royale and I asked him to bring me a ball of wax to help me put up with the row of the maniacs before they were taken off. The next day he brought me a piece the size of a walnut. The relief of not hearing those wretched men any more was quite unbelievable.

I was kept in good training by the big centipedes. I had only been bitten once during these six months. I had learnt to bear it calmly when I woke up and found one of them wandering about on my naked body. You can get used to anything. It's a question of self-control, for the tickling of all those legs and feelers is very unpleasant. But if you catch hold of it the wrong way, you're stung. It's better to wait until it goes of its own accord, then find it and squash it. There were always two or three little bits of today's bread on my concrete stool. Naturally, the smell of the bread attracted the centipedes and they would go in that direction. Then I'd kill them.

I had to get rid of an idea that haunted me all the time. Why didn't I kill Bébert Celier the very day we had doubts about the ugly game he was playing? Starting from that point, I argued with myself — when do you have the right to kill? My conclusion was, that the end justifies the means. My end was to make a successful break: I'd had the good luck to finish making a well-made raft and hide it in a safe place. It was only a matter of days before I was to set off. Since I knew how dangerous Celier was in the matter of the last section but one, which reached the right place by something like a miracle. I ought to have killed him without hesitation. But what if I had been wrong? What if it had only looked as if he was guilty? I should have killed an innocent man. How terrible!

But it's unreasonable for you to worry about scruples, you a convict with a lifer – worse, a convict whose lifer includes eight years of solitary.

Who do you think you are, you drop-out that the community treats like so much dirt? I'd like to know whether the twelve bastards on the jury have ever once troubled their consciences with wondering if they did right in sending you down for so long. And whether the prosecutor (I'd still not made up my mind how I'd tear out his tongue) had ever wondered if he hadn't come it a little strong in his indictment. I was sure that even my own lawyers didn't remember me. They no doubt talked in general terms about 'that unfortunate Papillon business' at the 1932 assizes. 'That particular day I was not on top of my form, you know, whereas it so happened that Pradel, for the prosecution, was at his very best. He swung the trial in his own favour in the most masterly fashion. He really is an opponent who keeps you on your toes.' I could hear it as though I were next to Maître Raymond Hubert as he was talking to other lawyers, or at some party, or in the corridors of the law-courts.

There was certainly one man who might be set up as a straight-dealing, honest judge, and that was Bevin, the president of the court. That fair-minded man, in professional conversation or at a dinner, might very well speak about the danger of having a man judged by a jury. In proper words, of course, he might very well say that the twelve bastards, the jurymen, were not prepared for a responsibility of that kind, that they might be too easily swayed by the charm either of the prosecution or the defence, whichever happened to be getting the better of the rhetorical contest – that they acquitted too quickly or condemned scarcely knowing why, all according to the positive or negative atmosphere that the stronger counsel had managed to create.

The president, and my family too: yes, but perhaps my family was rather against me because of the disgrace I'd quite certainly brought upon them. There was one, only one, who I was sure would never complain of the cross I had lain on his shoulders, and that was my poor old father. He would bear this heavy cross without crying out against his son and without blaming him; and this he'd do although as a schoolmaster, he respected the laws and even taught his pupils to understand and accept them. I was sure that deep inside his heart cried out, 'You swine, you've killed my boy – even worse you've condemned him, at twenty-five, to die inch by inch!' If he knew where his boy was now, and what they were doing to him, he might indeed turn anarchist.

Last night the man-eater earned its name even more than usual. I gathered that two men had hanged themselves and that another had choked to death by stuffing his mouth and nostrils with bits of cloth. Cell 127 was near the place where the screws changed guard and sometimes I heard scraps of their talk. This very morning, for instance, they didn't speak so quietly that I missed what they were saying about what had happened during the night.

Another six months had gone by. I took my bearings, and just now I scratched an elegant fourteen on the wood – I'd a nail that I only used every six months. Yes, I took my bearings, and I found that everything was in order from the point of view of health and that my spirits were in an excellent state.

Thanks to my wandering among the stars it was very rare that I ever had a lasting fit of despair. I got over them pretty fast and quickly invented a real or imaginary voyage that would dispel the black ideas. Celier's death was a great help to me in these serious fits of depression. I used to say to myself, I'm alive, alive; I'm still alive, and I must go on living, living, living so as to live a new free life one day. He tried to stop me escaping and now he's dead: he'll never be free as one day I'll be free – that's certain and for sure. In any case, if I'm thirty-eight when I come out, that's not old, and I'm quite sure the next break will be the right one.'

One, two, three, four, five, about-turn: one, two, three, four, five, about-turn again. For some days now my legs had been black and my gums oozed blood. Should I report sick? I pressed the lower part of my leg with my thumb and the mark stayed there, a dent. You'd have said I was full of water. For a week now I'd no longer been able to walk my ten or twelve hours a day: six hours, taken in two goes, tired me out. When I cleaned my teeth I could not rub them with the rough towel smeared with soap without its hurting and bleeding a great deal. There was even one tooth that came out all by itself yesterday – an upper incisor.

This third period of six months ended in a complete upheaval. Yesterday they made us all poke our heads out through the

356

hole and a doctor went by raising each man's lips. And this morning, when I'd done exactly eighteen months in this cell, the door opened and they said, 'Come out: stand against the wall and wait.'

I was the first at the gate end: about seventy men were brought out. 'About turn!' And now I was at the end of a line of men marching towards the other end of the building and out into the yard.

Nine o'clock. A young medico in a short-sleeved khaki shirt sitting at a little wooden table in the open air. Two convict orderlies next to him; one medical warder. I knew none of them, not even the medico. Ten screws with rifles kept the whole party covered. The governor and head warders stood there, watching silently.

'Everyone strip!' shouted the head warder. 'Clothes under your arms. First man, Name?'

'X.'

'Open your mouth and stand with your legs apart. Take these three teeth out for him. Tincture of iodine first, then methylene blue: syrup of cochlearia twice a day before meals.'

I was the last in the line.

'Name?'

'Charrière.'

'Why, you're the only one with a body that's something like. Have you just come in?'

'No.'

'How long have you been here?'

'Eighteen months today.'

'Why aren't you thin like the others?'

'I don't know.'

'All right, I'll tell you. Because you eat better than them; unless maybe you masturbate less. Mouth: legs. Two lemons a day, one in the morning, one at night. Suck the lemons and rub the juice on your gums: you've got scurvy.'

They cleaned my gums with iodine, then daubed them with methylene blue: they gave me a lemon. About turn. I went back to my cell, the last in the file.

What had just happened – this bringing the sick men right out into the yard, so they could see the sun and the doctor could see them close to – was a genuine revolution. Nothing of the kind had ever been known in the Réclusion. What was happening? Could it be that at last there was a doctor who would not be a mute accomplice – who would not apply these infamous rules? This medico, who later became my friend, was called Germain Guibert. He died in Indo-China. Many years after this particular day, his wife wrote to me at Maracaibo in Venezuela to tell me about it.

Every ten days, medical inspection in the sun. Always the same treatment – iodine, methylene blue, two lemons. My condition grew no worse, but it didn't get any better, either. Twice I asked for syrup of cochlearia and twice the doctor wouldn't let me have it: this began to irritate me, because I still couldn't walk for more than six hours a day and because the lower part of my legs was still black and swollen.

One day when I was waiting my turn to be looked at, I noticed that the spindly tree in whose meagre shade I was standing was a lemon tree with no lemons on it. I picked a leaf and chewed it; and then without thinking I broke off a twig with some leaves on it – I had no clear notion in my mind as I did so. When the medico called me I stuffed the twig up my arse and said, 'Doctor, I don't know whether it's the fault of all your lemons, but look what I've got growing behind.' And I turned round to show him the leafy twig.

The screws roared with laughter at first, but then the head warder said, 'Papillon, you'll be punished for disrespect to the doctor.'

'Not at all,' said the doctor. 'I make no complaint, so you can't punish him. Don't you want any more lemons? Is that what you're trying to say?'

'Yes, Doctor: I'm fed up with lemons. I'm not getting better: I want to try the cochlearia syrup.'

'I've not given you any because there's not much of it and I keep it for the very serious cases. Still, I'll let you have one spoonful a day, and we'll continue the lemons.'

'Doctor, I used to see the Indians eat seaweed: I noticed the same kind on Royale. There must be some on Saint-Joseph too.'

'That's a very valuable idea. I'll have a daily distribution of a certain seaweed I have seen growing round the coast myself. Did the Indians eat it cooked or raw?'

'Raw.'

'Very good: thank you. And Governor, I rely upon you to see that this man is not punished.'

'All right, Captain.'

It was a miracle that had been accomplished. Leaving your cell every week and standing in the sun for a couple of hours waiting your turn or waiting for the others to be seen to, seeing faces, whispering a few words – who would ever have dreamt that such a wonderful thing could happen? It made a fantastic difference to everybody. Dead men got up and walked about in the sun: these people who had been buried alive could at last speak to each other. It was oxygen, breathing fresh life into all of us.

Clack, clack, innumerable clacks as all the cell doors opened at nine o'clock one Thursday morning. Each man was to stand there on the threshold of his cell. 'Confinees,' shouted a voice, 'Governor's inspection.'

A tall, distinguished, grey-haired man walked slowly down the corridor, passing in front of each cell; with him there were five officers of the colonial service, all doctors, no doubt. I heard him being told the heavy sentences and the reasons for them. Before he reached me, a prisoner who had not been strong enough to stand so long was helped to his feet. This was Graville, one of the cannibals. An officer said, 'But this man's a walking corpse!'

The governor replied, 'They are all of them in a lamentable condition.'

The committee reached me. The local governor said, 'This man has the longest sentence in the prison.'

'What is your name?' asked the governor.

'Charrière.'

'Your sentence?'

'Eight years for stealing material belonging to the State, etc., manslaughter – three and five years consecutive.'

'How many have you done?'

'Eighteen months.'

'How has he behaved?'

'Well,' said the local governor.

'His health?'

'Fair,' said the medico.

'What have you to say?'

'That this system is inhuman and unworthy of a nation like France.'

'In what respect?'

'Total silence, no exercise and until these last few days, no medical care.'

359

'Behave yourself, and maybe, if I am still governor, you will get a remission.'

'Thank you.'

From that day on we were allowed an hour's exercise every day, bathing in a kind of artificial pool with great blocks of stone protecting the swimmers from the sharks: and all this by order of the governor and the top medico from Martinique and Cayenne.

Groups of a hundred men went down at nine every morning, walking stark naked from the Réclusion to the sea. The warders' wives and children had to stay in their houses so we could go down with nothing on.

This had been the system for a month now. The men's faces had completely changed. The prisoners in solitary, mentally and physically sick men, had been wholly transformed by this hour of .sunshine, this swimming in the salt water, and the possibility of talking for an hour every day.

One day we were going up from the sea towards the prison: I was among the men at the tail of the column when there was a woman's desperate shriek and two revolver shots. I heard, 'Help! My little girl is drowning!'

The cry came from the jetty, which was merely a cemented ramp going down into the water – a place where the boats landed. Other shouts – 'The sharks!' And two more revolver shots. Everybody had turned in the direction of these cries and the shots, and without thinking I shoved a warder aside and ran naked as I was towards the quay. When I got there I saw two women shrieking like maniacs, three warders and some Arabs.

'Jump in!' shrieked the woman. 'She's not gone far! I can't swim, or I'd do it. Oh you set of cowards!'

'The sharks!' cried a screw, and he fired at them again.

There was a little girl in a blue and white frock floating on the sea, drifting slowly away on the current. She was going straight for the place that was the convicts' graveyard; but she still had a long way to go. The screws never stopped firing and they must certainly have hit several sharks, for there were swirls in the water near the child.

'Stop shooting!' I cried. And without thinking I dived in. Helped by the current I swam as fast as I could towards the little girl, splashing my feet hard to keep the sharks off – she was still floating, buoyed up by her dress.

I was no more than thirty or forty yards from her when a boat came from Royale – they had seen what was happening from over there. It reached the child a little before I did, caught hold of her and pulled her to safety. I was weeping with rage, not even thinking of the sharks, when in my turn I was hauled aboard. I'd risked my life for nothing.

At least that's what I thought: but a month later, as a sort of reward, Dr. Germain Guibert obtained the suspension of my sentence of solitary confinement on medical grounds.

The Buffaloes

So there I was, miraculously back on Royale as an ordinary convict serving an ordinary sentence. I'd left, sent down for eight years; and because of the attempt at life-saving, here I was back in nineteen months.

I was with my friends again: Dega was still chief accountant and Galgani postman; Carbonieri too was there, having been acquitted on the escaping charge, and so were Grandet, Bourset the joiner, Chatal of the infirmary, and the pram boys, Naric and Quenier: and still on Royale as assistant medical orderly, Maturette, the partner of my first break.

The Corsican gangsters were all still there too – Essari, Vicioli, Césari, Razori, Fosco, Maucuer and Chapar, who had sent La Griffe to the guillotine over the Marseilles stock-exchange job. All the star turns of the criminal court reports from 1927 to 1935 were there.

Marsino, the man who murdered Dufrêne, died last week of general debility. The sharks had a very special dish that day – the most highly esteemed gem expert in Paris.

Barrat, whom they called the Actress, the millionaire tennis-champion from Limoges, who murdered a chauffeur and his boy-friend – his too friendly boy-friend – Barrat was head of the laboratory and dispenser in the Royale hospital. One of the doctors who was fond of his joke said that on the islands you were tubercular by *jus primae noctis.*

In a word, my arrival on Royale was a bombshell. It was a Saturday morning when I walked into the hard cases' building once more. Almost everyone was there, and all of them, without exception, welcomed me in the most friendly way you can imagine. Even the watch-mending character who had never spoken since that famous morning when they nearly guillotined him by mistake, came over and said hallo.

'Well, brothers, are you all OK?'

'Yes Papi: and you're very welcome back.'

'You've still got your place,' said Grandet. 'It's been kept empty ever since the day you left.'

'Thanks, everybody. What's new?'

'One good thing.'

'What's that?'

'Last night they found the Arab who informed on you killed in the hall opposite the good conducts – the Arab who climbed the palm tree and watched. It must have been some friend of yours who didn't want you to have to come across him alive, and who's spared you the trouble.'

'I'd very much like to know who it was, so as to thank him.'

'Maybe he'll tell you one day. They found the Arab at the roll-call with a knife in his heart. Nobody had seen or heard anything at all.'

'It's better that way. How's the gambling?'

'Fine. Your place is still open.'

'Good.' So now I was about to start living like a man with a life sentence again: who could tell how and when the story would end?

'Papi, we were really upset when we heard you'd copped an eight-year stretch. I don't think there's a single man on the islands now who'd refuse to help you, now you're back again, whatever the risk.'

'The governor wants you,' said an Arab.

I went out with him. Several screws in the guard-room spoke pleasantly as I went through: I followed the Arab, and there was Governor Prouillet.

'Are you all right, Papillon?'

'Yes, Governor.'

'I'm glad you've been pardoned, and I congratulate you on your brave attempt at saving my colleague's little girl.'

'Thanks.'

'I'm going to make you an ox-driver until you can be a cesspit man again with the right to go fishing.'

'If that doesn't compromise you too much, fine.'

'That's my business. The building yard chief is no longer here, and as for me, I'm off to France in three weeks. You start tomorrow.'

'I don't know how to thank you, Governor.'

'Perhaps by waiting a month before you try another break?' said Prouillet, laughing.

The men in our block were still the same men; their way of life was still the same as it had been before I went away. The gamblers, a class apart, thought of nothing and lived for nothing but cards. The men who had boys lived and ate and slept with them. They were genuine couples, with their thoughts taken up, day and night, by their passion and by homosexual love. Jealous scenes, unchecked furious emotions in which the 'wife' and the 'husband' each kept secret watch on the other and which inevitably set off killings when one got tired of the other and drifted away to other lovers.

Only last week the Negro Simplon killed a man by the name of Sidero, all for the sake of the lovely Charlie (Barrat). This was the third man Simplon had killed because of Charlie.

I had only been in the camp a few hours before two characters came to see me. 'Tell me, Papillon, I'd like to ask whether Maturette is your baby or not.'

'Why?'

'Personal reasons.'

'Listen. Maturette made a thousand-mile break with me and he behaved himself like a man: that's all I've got to say.'

'I wanted to know if he was sweet on you.'

'No. From the point of view of sex, I know nothing about Maturette. From the point of view of friendship, I think he's great: the rest's nothing to do with me, unless anyone does him harm.'

'And suppose one day he was my wife?'

'If he was willing, I'd never interfere in such matters. But if by any chance you were to threaten him so as to get him to be your boy-friend, then you'd have to reckon with me.'

It was the same, whether the homosexuals were active or passive; for both kinds settled down to live in their passion, thinking of nothing else at all.

I met the Italian with the gold charger, the one who had been in our convoy. He came and said hallo. I said, 'You still here?'

'I've done everything I can. My mother sent me twelve thousand francs: the screw took six thousand for his commission: I paid four thousand to get myself un-interned and I managed to be sent to Cayenne for an X-ray. But I couldn't do a thing there. Then after that I got myself accused of wounding a friend. You know him – Razori, the Corsican strong-arm man.'

'Yes: and what then?'

'We came to an agreement: he cut himself in the belly and he and I were taken over for a court-martial – he being the accuser and me the defendant. We never even got going at all. In a fortnight it was all over. I copped six months and I did them in the Réclusion last year. You didn't even know I was there. Papi, I can't bear it any more. I feel like killing myself.'

'It would be better to perish at sea, escaping: at least you'd die free.'

'You're right: I'm ready for anything. If you think something up, let me know.'

'OK.'

And so life on Royale began again. I was an ox-driver and I had a buffalo called Brutus. He weighed two tons and as far as the other buffaloes were concerned he was a killer. He had already put paid to two other males. 'This is his last chance,' said Agostini, the warder in charge of the job. 'If he kills another, he'll be slaughtered.'

This morning I had my first meeting with Brutus. The Martinique Negro who drove him was to stay for a week to teach me the job. I made friends with Brutus at once by pissing on his muzzle: he adored lapping the taste of salt. Then I gave him some green mangoes I'd picked up in the hospital garden. With Brutus yoked to the great pole of a roughly-made cart – it might have belonged to the Pharaohs – carrying a six hundred gallon barrel, I went down to the beach. It was my job, and friend Brutus's, to go down, fill the barrel, and then climb that terrible slope up to the plateau. There I opened the tap and the water ran down the channels, carrying away everything that was left from the morning's emptying. I began at six and by about nine I was through.

After four days the Martiniquais said I could get along by myself. There was only one snag – I had to swim in the pond at five in the morning, looking for Brutus, who did not care for work and used to hide there. He had very sensitive nostrils, and there was a ring through them with two feet of chain hanging there permanently. Whenever I found him, he would draw back, dive, and come up farther off. Sometimes it took me more than an hour to catch him in this revolting stagnant pool, full of creatures and water-lilies. All by myself there I'd fly into a gibbering rage. 'Swine! You slow-bellied obstinate bastard! Will you get the hell out of this water?' The only thing he minded was the chain when I caught him. The insults never wounded him in the least. But when at last he was brought out of the pond, then we were close friends again.

I had two old lard drums that I kept full of clean, fresh water. I started by taking a shower to get the slime off from the pool. Then when I was thoroughly soaped and rinsed I usually had more than half a drum left, and I'd wash Brutus, scrubbing him with the hairy husk of a coconut. I went carefully over his delicate parts and sprinkled him as I scrubbed. Brutus would rub his head against my hands and go and stand in front of the shafts all by himself. I never used the goad on him like the Martiniquais. He was grateful, and he'd walk quicker for me than he did for the Negro.

There was a pretty little buffalo cow who was in love with Brutus: she went along with us, walking at his side. I did not shoo her away as the other driver did – far from it. I let her kiss Brutus and come with us wherever we went. I never disturbed them when they were kissing, and Brutus showed his gratitude by carrying up his six hundred gallons at an extraordinary pace. He looked as though he were trying to make up for the time he had spent in his dallying with Marguerite – for Marguerite was the cow-buffalo's name.

Yesterday, at the six o'clock roll-call, there was a little scene on account of Marguerite. It seems that the Martiniquais used to get up on a little wall, and from this height he stuffed her every day. He was caught at it by a screw, and he got thirty days in the black-hole. Bestiality was the official charge. And yesterday, when the roll was being called, Marguerite appeared in the camp, walked along past more than sixty men and reached the Negro: there she turned about, presenting him with her bottom. Everybody howled with laughter, and the blackamoor went grey with shame and confusion.

I had to make three trips a day. The longest part was the filling of the barrel by the two men at the shore; but it was fairly quick. By nine I was through and I could go off fishing.

I made an ally of Marguerite so as to get Brutus out of the pond. When I scratched her ear in a certain way she uttered a sound very like the voice of a mare in season. At this Brutus would come out of his own accord. Although I no longer needed to wash myself, I went on grooming him, and better than before. Shining clean and free from the stench of the disgusting water he spent the night in, he was even more attractive to Marguerite, and that raised his spirits wonderfully.

Half way up the hill from the sea there was a flattish place where I kept a big stone. Brutus had the habit of drawing breath there for five minutes, and I wedged the wheel with the stone, so he could rest better. But this morning there was another buffalo called Danton, as big as Brutus, who was waiting for us hidden behind the little coconut palms that were nothing more than leaves, for this was the nursery garden. Danton rushed out and went for Brutus. Brutus dodged and avoided the charge: Danton hit the cart. One of his horns pierced the barrel. He made prodigious efforts to free himself, while I was unyoking Brutus. Once he was unharnessed, Brutus took his distance, a good thirty yards up the slope, and charged straight at Danton. Dread or despair made Danton wrench free, leaving the tip of his horn in the barrel, before my buffalo reached him; but Brutus couldn't stop and he smashed into the cart, turning it over.

Then one of the strangest things I've ever seen took place. Brutus and Danton touched their horns without thrusting; they just rubbed these huge weapons gently together. It looked as though they were talking, and yet they merely blew – uttered no sound. Then the cow buffalo walked slowly up the hill, followed by the two bulls, who stopped every now and then to rub horns again, entwining them gently. When they took too long over it Marguerite moaned languourously and set off again in the direction of the plateau. The two great monsters, still following the same line, moved after her. After three halts, with the same ceremonies each time, we reached the plateau. We came out on the flat in front of the lighthouse, a bare stretch of ground about three hundred yards long. At the far end, the convicts' camp: right and left, the two hospitals, the one for the prisoners and the other for the soldiers.

Danton and Brutus were still following, twenty yards behind. Marguerite paced calmly to the middle and stood there. The two rivals joined her. From time to time she uttered her wail, a long and markedly sexual cry. Once again they touched horns, but this time I had the feeling that they really were talking together, because in among their blowing there were sounds that no doubt meant something.

After this conversation the one walked off slowly to the left and the other to the right. They went as far as the limits of the flat stretch. So between them there lay three hundred yards. Marguerite waited, still standing there in the middle. I grasped what it was all about now: this was a proper formal duel, agreed to on either side, with the cow buffalo as the prize. She was quite willing, too; and she was as proud as a peacock that her two boy-friends were going to fight for her.

A cry from Marguerite and they launched themselves at one another. I don't have to say how their two tons increased in force with their speed as each covered his hundred and fifty yards. The crash of the two heads was so violent that for more than five minutes they were both stunned. Brutus was the first to recover, and this time he galloped back to his place. The battle lasted two hours. The screws wanted to kill Brutus, but I wouldn't let them: then, at a certain moment Danton broke a horn as they crashed together – the horn he'd damaged with the barrel. He fled, with Brutus after him. The chase and the fight went on until the next day. They smashed everything that stood in their way – gardens, graveyard, laundry.

They fought all night, and it was only at about seven the next morning that Brutus managed to get Danton up against the wall of the butchery down by the sea, and there he thrust a horn its whole depth into Danton's belly. To finish it off thoroughly Brutus rolled over twice, so that the horn, deep inside, should turn in Danton's belly. And Danton, in the midst of a flood of guts and blood, fell, conquered and destroyed.

This battle between giants had so weakened Brutus that I had to pull the horn out for him so that he could get to his feet again. He staggered off along the path by the sea, and there Marguerite joined him, walking by his side and supporting his huge neck with her hornless head.

I was unable to be present at their wedding night, because the screw in charge of the buffaloes accused me of having unharnessed Brutus, and I was sacked.

I asked to see the governor to talk to him about Brutus.

'What's been going on, Papillon? Brutus must be slaughtered: he's too dangerous. This makes three fine specimens he's killed now.'

'That's just what I came for – to ask you to save Brutus. The farm screw in charge of the buffaloes knows nothing about it. Please let me tell you how Brutus came to act in legitimate self-defence.'

The governor smiled. 'I'm listening.'

'. . . so you understand, Governor, my buffalo was the one who was attacked,' I ended, having told him all the details. 'What's more, if I hadn't unharnessed Brutus, Danton would have killed him when he was unable to stand up for himself, fastened to his yoke and the cart the way he was.'

'That's true,' said the governor.

At this point the farm screw appeared. 'Good morning, Governor. I've been looking for you, Papillon: this morning you walked out of the camp as though you were going to your job. But your job's gone – you've been sacked.'

'Monsieur Agostini, I went out to see whether I could stop the fight, but unfortunately they were absolutely mad with rage.'

'Well, that may be so. But you're not driving that buffalo any more, as I've already told you. In any case, he's going to be slaughtered on Sunday morning – he'll provide meat for the whole gaol.'

'You can't do that.'

'You're not the one who's going to stop me.'

'No, but the governor is. And if that's not enough, then Doctor Germain Guibert will – I'll ask him to step in and save Brutus.'

'What are you interfering for?'

'Because it's my business. I'm the buffalo's driver, and he's my friend.'

'Your friend? A buffalo? Are you trying to be funny?'

'Monsieur Agostini, will you listen to me for a minute?'

'Let him speak in his buffalo's defence,' said the governor.

'All right. Talk away.'

'Monsieur Agostini, do you think animals can speak to one another?'

'Why not, seeing they communicate?'

'Well, then, Brutus and Danton agreed to fight a duel.' And once again I explained the whole thing, from beginning to end.

'Cristacho!' said the Corsican. 'You're a proper old character, Papillon. Do what you like about Brutus, but the next time he breaks out, no one'll save him, not even the governor. You can be a driver again. See to it that Brutus starts work soon.'

Two days later Brutus returned to his daily sea-water fatigue, accompanied by his certificated mate Marguerite, and pulling the cart that the building yard craftsmen had repaired. When we reached our resting place, with the cart thoroughly wedged with the stone. I said, 'Where's Danton, Brutus?' And with a single heave the great monster set the cart in motion, finishing the whole journey without a pause, nimbly pacing along with a conqueror's tread.

Mutiny at Saint-Joseph

The islands were extremely dangerous because of the apparent freedom the men enjoyed. It irked me deeply to see everybody settling down comfortably to lead a trouble-free existence. Some waited for the end of their time; some did nothing at all but wallow in their vices.

Last night I was lying in my hammock: at the far end of the room the gambling was so hot that my two friends, Carbonieri and Grandet, had been obliged to join forces to keep control; one man would not have been enough. As for me, I was trying to revive my memories of the past. They wouldn't come: you would have thought the assizes had never existed. I tried to light up the dim figures of that day which had been so fatal for me, but in vain: I could not see a single person clearly. The only one to appear in all his harsh reality was the prosecuting counsel. Christ, I thought I'd overcome you for good and all when I was with the Bowens in Trinidad. What kind of ill luck have you put on me, you louse, for six breaks to go bad on me? When you heard I'd made the first, the one from penal, did you manage to sleep easy? I'd very much like to know if you were frightened or if all you felt was fury at the idea of your prey escaping from the way down the drain – the path you'd put him on forty-three days earlier. I'd broken out of the cage. Why was I fated to come back to prison eleven months later? Perhaps God was punishing me for despising the primitive but beautiful – oh so beautiful – life that I could have gone on living for ever, if I'd liked.

My two loves, Lali and Zoraïma; my tribe without a single

gendarme and no laws except for the closest understanding between its members – yes, it's my own fault I'm here, but I must think of one thing only. Only one thing – escape, escape, escape or die.

Prosecutor, when you learnt I had been retaken and sent back to the settlement, you certainly put on your conquering assizes smile, didn't you? You thought, 'Now everything's fine: he's back where I put him, on the way down the drain.' And you were wrong: my heart and soul will never belong to this degrading way of life. All you have a hold on is my body: twice every day your guards and your prison system take note that I am present, and that satisfies you. At six in the morning, 'Papillon?' 'Here.' Six in the evening, 'Papillon?' 'Here.' All's well. We've had our hands on him nearly six years now; he must be beginning to rot, and with a little luck one of these days the bell will toll for the sharks to come and receive him with all due honours – the daily feast provided for them by your system of getting rid of men by wearing them out.

You've got it wrong: your figures don't add up. My physical presence has nothing to do with my spiritual presence. Do you want me to tell you something? I don't belong in this prison: I've not adopted the ways of my fellow-prisoners in the smallest degree, not even of my closest friends. I'm on my toes for a break twenty-four hours a day.

I was arguing with the prosecutor when two men came up to my hammock.

'You asleep, Papillon?'

'No.'

'We'd like to talk to you.'

'Talk away. If you speak quietly, no one can hear.'

'Listen, we're getting ready for a mutiny.'

'What's your plan?'

'Kill all the Arabs, all the screws, all the screws' wives and all their children – bad seed, the whole lot. Me – my name's Arnaud – and my friend Hautin, together with four men who're with us, are going to attack the command-post arsenal. I work there keeping the weapons in order. There are twenty-three light machine-guns, more than eighty rifles and carbines. We'll set about it the . . .'

'Stop: don't go on. I'm not with you. I'll have nothing to do with it. Thanks for letting me into your secret, but I'm not with you.'

'We thought you'd agree to lead the rising. Just let me tell you the details we've worked out and you'll see it can't go wrong. We've been planning it these last five months. There are more than fifty men with us.'

'Don't you tell me a single name: I refuse to be the leader or to make the slightest move in this business.'

'Why? You owe us an explanation, after the way we've trusted you, telling you everything.'

'In the first place I never asked you to tell me your plans. And in the second, I do what I want to do in this life, and not what other people want me to do. And in the third I'm not a mass killer. I may kill a man I've got something serious against; but not women and children who've done me no harm. What's more, you don't seem to realize the worst side of it all, and I'll have to tell you – even if you bring this rising off, you necessarily fail.'

'How come?'

'Because the main thing, escaping, just isn't possible. Suppose a hundred men join in the mutiny, how are they going to get away? There are only two boats on the islands. At the very outside limit they can't carry more than forty convicts between them. What are you going to do about the other sixty?'

'We'll be among the forty who leave in the boats.'

'That's what you think: but the others aren't bloodier fools than you are. They'll be armed like you, and if each one's got the smallest scrap of brain, he's not going to put up with being wiped out like you say. You'll be shooting one another to get into the boats. And still worse, there's not a country on earth that'll allow these two boats to land, because telegrams will get to every possible country before you – particularly with the holocaust you mean to leave behind. Anywhere on earth you'll be arrested and handed back to France. As you know, I came back from Colombia: I know what I'm talking about. I give you my sacred word that after a job like that you'll be handed back from anywhere in the world.'

'Right. So you refuse?'

'Yes.'

'It's your last word?'

'I'm absolutely determined.'

'There's nothing left for us but to go.'

'One minute. I ask you not to speak to any of my friends about this plan.'

'Why not?'

'Because I know beforehand they'll refuse; so it's not worth it.'

'All right.'

'Do you feel you can't possibly give up this scheme?'

'Speaking straight, Papillon, no.'

'I can't understand what you're aiming at; because I tell you very seriously that even if you do bring the rising off, you'll never be free.'

'What we want above all is our revenge. And now you've shown us it's impossible to find any country that would let us stay, then we'll take to the bush – we'll live as a gang in the forest.'

'I give you my word I shan't speak about this even to my best friend.'

'We're quite certain of that.'

'OK. One last thing – give me the nod a week ahead so I can get across to Saint-Joseph and not be on Royale when it starts.'

'You'll be warned in time to change islands.'

'Isn't there anything I can do to make you change your minds? Wouldn't you like to work out some other scheme with me? Steal four carbines, for instance, and attack the guard on the boats without killing anyone. Then take a boat and go off together.'

'No. We've gone through too much. For us the great thing is revenge, even if it costs us our lives.'

'And the kids too? And the women?'

'It's all the same seed, the same blood: they must all die, every one of them.'

'Let's not talk about it any more.'

'You don't wish us good luck?'

'No. What I say to you is, give it up. There are better things to do than this bloody butchery.'

'You don't agree we've got the right to have our revenge?'

'Yes, but not on people who've done no wrong.'

'Good night.'

'Good night. Nothing's been said, right, Papi?'

'Right, brothers.'

And Hautin and Arnaud went away A hell of a caper this is! These guys are right off their heads: and what's more they say there are fifty or sixty others mixed up in it. By their

D-day there'll be more than a hundred. What a crazy scheme! Not a single one of my friends has given me the least hint of it, so these two can only have talked to the squares. It's just not possible any men belonging to our world should be in this plot. And that makes it all the worse, because your square murderers are the genuine murderers – your underworld character may kill, but just by way of manslaughter, which is not the same thing at all.

For a week I very quietly gathered information about Arnaud and Hautin. Arnaud had been sent down for life – unjustly it seemed – for a little job that didn't even deserve ten years. The reason why the jury had come down on him so heavy was that the year before his brother had been guillotined for killing a cop. So he'd been condemned to this hideous sentence just because the prosecutor, who'd talked more about his brother than about him, had managed to work up a very hostile atmosphere. He'd also been horribly tortured at the time of his arrest, because of what his brother had done.

Hautin had never known freedom: he'd been in prison since the age of nine. Just before leaving the reformatory school when he was nineteen he killed a guy: this was when he was on the point of going into the navy – he'd enlisted to get out of the school. He must have been a trifle crazy, because it seems his plan was to get to Venezuela, work in a gold-mine there, and blow off one of his legs for the compensation-money. This leg was stiff, on account of some chemical or other he'd injected into it at Saint-Martin-de-Ré.

Bombshell. At this morning's roll-call Arnaud, Hautin and Jean Carbonieri, my friend Matthieu's brother, were taken out of the ranks. Jean was a baker, and so he lived down on the quay, near the boats. They were sent to Saint-Joseph without any explanation or apparent reason. I tried to find out why. Not a word: yet Arnaud had been looking after the armoury for four years now, and Jean Carbonieri had been a baker for five. This couldn't be just chance. There must have been a leak; but just what kind of a leak; and how far had it gone?

I decided to talk to my three closest friends, Matthieu Carbonieri, Grandet and Galgani. None of them knew a thing. So Hautin and Arnaud could only have tackled the convicts who didn't belong to the underworld.

'Why did they speak to me, then?'

'Because everyone knows you want to escape at any price at all.'

'Not at that price, though.'

'They couldn't tell the odds.'

'And what about your brother Jean?'

'God knows how he ever came to be such a bloody fool as to get into a mess like this.'

'Maybe the guy that shopped him just *said* he was in it: maybe he's nothing to do with it at all.'

Things began to move faster and faster. Last night Birasolo was murdered as he was going into the latrine. Blood was found on the Martiniquais ox-driver's shirt. Two weeks after a much too hasty inquiry and a statement by another Negro they kept shut up by himself, the Martiniquais was condemned to death by a special court.

An old lag called Garvel or the Savoyard came and spoke to me by the wash-house in the yard. 'Papi, I'm in a hell of a fix; because it was me that killed Girasolo. I'd like to save the darkie, but I'm scared they'd guillotine me. And I'm not opening my mouth at that price. But if I could find a way of getting off with no more than three to five years, I'd confess.'

'What's your sentence?'

'Twenty years.'

'How many have you done?'

'Twelve.'

'Find some way of getting life, and then they won't put you in solitary.'

'How can I do that?'

'Give me time to think! I'll tell you tonight.' Night came. I said to Garvel, 'You can't fix it so that you're accused and then you confess.'

'Why not?'

'You're too likely to be condemned to death. The only way of avoiding solitary is to get life. Do the denouncing yourself. Say your conscience won't allow you to let an innocent man have his head chopped off. Pick a Corsican screw to defend you. I'll tell you his name when I've spoken to him. You've got to move fast. They mustn't top him too quick. Wait two or three days.'

I spoke to a warder named Collona and he gave me a wonderful idea. I was to take Garvel to the governor myself and say he had asked me to defend him and to come with him

375

to own up: and I was to say I'd promised him it was impossible he should be condemned to death after such a noble action, but that it was a very serious offence and he must expect to be given life.

It all ran perfectly. Garvel saved the darkie, who was let out straight away. The perjured witness was given a year in prison. Robert Garvel got life.

All this was two months ago. Now that it was over and done with, Garvel told me all about it. Girasolo had agreed to join in the rising; he had been told all the details; and he was the man who betrayed Arnaud, Hautin and Jean Carbonieri. Luckily he hadn't known any of the other names.

The denunciation was so huge, so prodigious, the screws didn't believe in it. Still, by way of precaution they did send the three convicts who'd been informed upon to Saint-Joseph, without saying anything to them or questioning them or anything.

'What did you give as a reason for killing him, Garvel?'

'I said he'd stolen my charger. I said he slept opposite me, which was true, and that at night I took my charger out and hid it under the blanket I use as a pillow. One night I went to the latrine and when I came back my charger had gone. And near my place there was only one man who wasn't asleep – Girasolo. The screws believed what I said: they didn't even tell me he'd informed about a mutiny that was likely to break out.'

'Papillon! Papillon!' they shouted from the yard. 'Roll-call! Come on!'

'Here,' I answered when my name was called.

'Pack your things. You're for Saint-Joseph.'

'Oh, hell.'

War had just broken out in France. It brought with it a new kind of discipline: the service chiefs who were answerable for an escape would henceforward be dismissed the service. Transportees arrested during an escape were to be sentenced to death. Escape was to be considered as proof of a desire to join the Free French, who were betraying France. Everything would be tolerated except for escape.

Governor Prouillet had left two months earlier. I didn't know the new man at all. Nothing to be done about it. I said good-bye to my friends. At eight o'clock I got into the boat for Saint-Joseph.

Lisette's father was no longer in the camp there. He had left for Cayenne with his family the week before. The present governor of Saint-Joseph was a man from Le Havre by the name of Dutain. It was he who received me. I was alone, as it happened, and the head warder in charge of the boat handed me over to the duty screw on the wharf together with some papers that went with me.

'You're the one they call Papillon?'

'Yes, Governor.'

'You're an odd character,' he observed, leafing through my papers.

'What's so odd about me?'

'Because on the one hand you're marked down as dangerous from every point of view, with a particular note in red saying "In a continual state of preparedness for escape". And then on the other, there's the remark, "Attempted to save the governor of Saint-Joseph's child from the sharks". I've two little girls myself, Papillon. Would you like to see them?'

He called, and two very fair-haired children of three and five came in, together with a young Arab dressed all in white and a very pretty dark-haired woman.

'You see this man, my dear? He was the one who tried to save your god-daughter Lisette.'

'Oh, let me shake you by the hand,' said the young woman.

Shaking a convict's hand is the greatest honour you can pay him. People never offer their hands to a man in prison. I found this spontaneous gesture very moving.

'Yes, I'm Lisette's godmother. We are very close friends of the Grandoits. What are you going to do for him, my dear?'

'He'll go to the camp first, and then,' he said, speaking to me, 'you'll let me know what job you'd like me to give you.'

'Thank you, Governor. Thank you, Madame. Please would you tell me why I've been sent to Saint-Joseph? It's almost a punishment.'

'There was no reason that I know of. I dare say the new governor was afraid you'd escape.'

'He's not wrong.'

'They've increased the penalties for the officials who have to answer for an escape. Before the war you might perhaps lose a stripe: now it's certain, quite apart from all the rest.

That's why he's sent you here. He'd rather you went to Saint-Joseph, where he has no responsibility, than stay on Royale, where he has.'

'How long do you have to stay here, Governor?'

'Eighteen months.'

'I can't wait that long; but I'll find some way of getting back to Royale so as not to do you any harm.'

'Thank you,' said the woman. 'I'm glad to know you're so great-hearted. If there's anything at all you need, don't hesitate to come here. Papa, you must tell the guard-room of the camp that Papillon is to be brought to see me whenever he asks.'

'Yes, my dear. Mohamed, take Papillon to the camp; and Papillon, you choose the block you want to be put into.'

'Oh, that's easy enough: put me in the "dangerous" block.'

'That won't be hard,' said the governor, laughing. And he wrote out a paper that he gave to Mohamed.

I left the house on the quay that served as the governor's residence and his office – once Lisette's house – and escorted by the young Arab, I reached the camp.

The man in charge of the guard-room was a very ferocious old Corsican, a well-known killer. His name was Filissari. 'So it's you, Papillon, is it? Now I'm all good or all bad, as you know. So don't you try and escape with me, because if you fail I'll kill you out of hand. I'm retiring in two years, so now's the time I hit really hard.'

'Well now, I like all Corsicans; so although I won't promise not to escape, if I do I'll fix it so it's a time when you're not on duty.'

'Fine, Papillon. That way we shan't be enemies. Young men can put up with all the trouble and fuss after an escape better than me. I couldn't stand it, not at my age and just before I retire. So it's a deal, then? Get along to the block you've been put down for.'

Here I was in the camp, in a block exactly like the one on Royale, with between a hundred and a hundred and twenty men in it. Pierrot le Fou, Hautin, Arnaud and Jean Carbonieri were all there. Rightly speaking, I ought to have joined Jean's gourbi, seeing he was Matthieu's brother; but he hadn't Matthieu's quality, and then again I didn't care for his friendship with Hautin and Arnaud. So I left him alone and settled down next to Carrier, the Bordelais they called Pierrot le Fou.

The Ile Saint-Joseph was wilder than Royale and rather smaller, though it seemed bigger because it ran more to length. The camp was half way up, for the island consisted of two plateaux one over the other. The first one had the camp on it, and the higher one the grim Réclusion. By the way, the men in solitary were still going down to bathe for an hour every day. Let's hope it would last.

Every dinner-time the Arab who worked in the governor's house brought me three mess-tins fitting into one another and held by a wooden handle. He left these three tins and carried off the ones I'd had the day before. Every day Lisette's god-mother sent me exactly the same dishes she cooked for her own family.

On Sunday I went to see her to say thank you. I spent the afternoon talking to her and playing with the children. As I stroked their blond heads I reflected that sometimes it was hard to know where one's duty lay. There was an appalling danger hanging over this family if those two maniacs still had the same ideas. The screws had only believed Girasolo's denunciation to the point of sending them to Saint-Joseph; not to the point of separating them. If I were to say they ought to be separated that would confirm the truth and seriousness of the first squeal. But how would the warders then react? It would be better to keep my mouth shut.

Arnaud and Hautin scarcely spoke to me in the hall. In any case I preferred to be on civil but not familiar terms with them. Jean Carbonieri didn't speak to me at all: he was angry because I hadn't joined his gourbi. Ours was made up of four men – Pierrot le Fou; Marquetti, who'd won the second prix de Rome for the violin and who often played for hours on end, which made me rather low; and Marsori, a Corsican from Sète.

I spoke to nobody about the abortive preparations for a mutiny on Royale, and I had the feeling that nobody here knew anything at all about it. Did they still have the same notions? They were all three working on a very disagreeable, laborious fatigue. They had to drag boulders along, hauling them with a kind of harness. These rocks were being used to make a swimming-pool in the sea. A boulder was well fastened with chains; another fifteen or twenty yards of chain was attached, and each convict, either to the right or the left, hooked on to this chain with an iron held in a harness round his chest and shoulders. Then, just like so many animals, they dragged the

379

rock straight off to the place it was meant to be in. It was a very arduous job in the full sun; even more, it was a very disheartening one.

Shots from over by the quay – rifle, carbine and revolver shots. I knew what it was – those maniacs had started. What was happening? Who was winning? Sitting there in the hall I never stirred. All the convicts said, 'It's the mutiny!'

'Mutiny? What mutiny?' I meant to make it perfectly clear I knew nothing about it.

Jean Carbonieri hadn't gone to work that day: he came over to me, as pale as a corpse in spite of his sunburn. In a very low voice he said, 'It's the mutiny, Papi.' Coldly I said, 'What mutiny? I'm not in on this.'

The rifle fire continued. Pierrot le Fou came running into the hall. 'It's the mutiny, but I think they've failed. What bloody maniacs! Papillon, get out your knife. At least let's kill as many as possible before we're done for.'

'Yes,' said Carbonieri, 'let's kill as many as we can!'

Chissilia brought out a razor. Everyone had an open knife in his hand. I said, 'Don't be bloody fools. How many of us are there?'

'Nine.'

'Throw down your knives, seven of you. I'll kill the first man that threatens a screw. I don't want to get shot down in this room like a rabbit. Are you in this job, you?'

'No.'

'And you?'

'Nor me, either.'

'And you?'

'I knew nothing about it.'

'Good. None of us knew anything about this squares' mutiny. Do you get me?'

'Yes.'

'Anyone who feels like talking had better understand that he'll be killed the moment he admits he knew anything. Just like that. So there's nothing to be gained by being such a bastard as to split. Toss your knives into the pot. It won't be long before they're here.'

'And what if it's the lags who've won?'

'If it's the lags, then let them fix it so that their victory ends in a break. At that price, I want no part of it. What about you?'

'We don't, either,' said the eight others, including Jean Carbonieri.

As for me, I hadn't given a hint of what I knew – that is, that as the firing had stopped the lags must have lost. For the massacre they had planned couldn't have been over by this time.

The screws rushed into the camp like madmen, driving the fatigue party before them with blows from their rifle butts and sticks, kicking them, and shoving them into the next-door block. The warders trampled, smashed and chucked out everything in the way of guitars, mandolines, chessmen and draughts, lamps, little benches, bottles of oil, sugar, coffee, white clothes – they took their revenge on everything that was outside the rules. We heard two shots: certainly fired from a revolver.

There were eight buildings in the camp: they went through the lot in the same way, every now and then dealing out furious blows with their rifle-butts. One man came out stark naked, running towards the punishment block, battered without a pause by the screws who were taking him there.

Now they were in the building just over the way from us – the seventh. Ours was the only one left. There we were, all nine of us, each in his place. Not a single man who'd been out to work had come back. Everyone sat motionless. No one said a word. My throat was dry: I was thinking, 'Let's hope no God-damned fool takes advantage of this caper to shoot me down and get away with it.'

'Here they come,' said Carbonieri, more dead than alive with fright.

They rushed in, more than twenty of them, all with carbines or revolvers at the ready. 'What the hell?' bawled Filissari, 'not stripped yet? What are you waiting for, you rats? We're going to shoot the lot of you. Strip. We don't want to have to take your clothes off when you're corpses.'

'Monsieur Filissari . . .'

'You shut your trap, Papillon. It's no good asking to be forgiven. What you planned was too wicked. And all of you in the tough block were part of it – that's for certain!' His eyes were starting out of his head; they were all bloodshot, and there was no mistaking the pure light of murder in them.

'We're for it,' said Pierrot.

I decided to stake everything on one throw. 'It astonishes

me that a Napoleonist like you is going to literally murder innocent men. You're going to shoot? Fine: we don't want any speeches about it. Fire away. But for Christ's sake get it over quick. I'd thought you were a real man, old Filissari, a genuine Napoleonist: well, I got it wrong. But what the hell. I don't even want to see you when you fire: I turn my back on you. Brothers, turn your backs on these screws, so they can't say we were going to attack them.'

And moving like one man they all turned their backs. My attitude flabbergasted the screws, all the more so because (as we learnt afterwards) Filissari had just shot two poor bastards in the other blocks.

'Got anything else to say, Papillon?'

Still with my back turned I said, 'I don't believe a word of all this balls about a mutiny. Mutiny for what? To kill the screws? Then make a break? Where could you go? I'm an escaper, and I've come back from a thousand miles away – from Colombia. What country's going to take in escaped murderers, I ask you? What's the country called? Don't be bloody fools – there's no man worthy of the name that could possibly join in a plot like that.'

'Maybe not you, but what about Carbonieri? He's in it, I'm sure, because this morning Arnaud and Hautin were surprised he reported sick so as not to go to work.'

'That's just conjecture, I promise you.' I turned round and faced him. 'I'll tell you why this minute. Carbonieri's my friend: he knows every last thing about my break and so he can't nourish any illusions – he knows how an escape after a mutiny will end up, all right.'

At this point the governor appeared. He stayed outside. Filissari went out and the governor called, 'Carbonieri.'

'Here.'

'Take him to the black-hole without knocking him about. Warder So-and-So, go with him. Everyone outside: only head warders to stay. Bring in all the transportees scattered about the island. Don't kill anyone: bring every single man back to the camp.'

The governor walked into the hall, together with the deputy, Filissari and four screws. 'Papillon, something very serious has just happened,' said the governor. 'As the governor of this gaol I must assume a very grave responsibility. Before making certain arrangements I want some information right away. I know that you would have refused to talk to me in private at such a critical moment and that's why I've come here myself. Warder Duclos has been murdered. There's been an attempt at seizing the weapons in my house. That means mutiny. I've only a few minutes. I trust you: tell me your opinion.'

'If there'd been a mutiny, how could we possibly not have known about it? Why should nobody have told us? How many people are supposed to be involved? I'll give you the answers to these three questions, Governor, but first you must tell me how many men broke out after they'd killed the screw and, I imagine, taken his gun.'

'Three.'

'Who were they?'

'Arnaud, Hautin and Marceau.'

'I get it. Whatever you may think about it, there's been no mutiny.'

'You're lying, Papillon,' said Filissari. 'This mutiny was supposed to come off on Royale. Girasolo split, and we didn't believe him. Now we see that all he said was true. So you're double-crossing us, are you, Papillon?'

'Well then, if you're right, I'm an informer and so are Pierrot le Fou and Carbonieri and Galgani and all the Corsican bandits on Royale and all the rest of us. In spite of what's happened, I don't believe it. If there'd been a mutiny, the leaders would have been us: not anybody else.'

'What are you saying? You mean nobody else is involved at all? That's impossible.'

'Where are all these other mutineers? Who else but these three maniacs has stirred? Was there even a hint of action to take the post here, with only four armed guards in it, apart from Monsieur Filissari? How many boats are there on Saint-Joseph? Just one. One boat for six hundred men – does that make any sense? We're not complete, utter morons, are we? And then killing to make an escape! Even supposing twenty men did manage to get away, it would only mean being arrested and handed back from any country on earth. Governor, I don't know how many men you or your screws have killed so far, but I'm very nearly sure they were all innocent. And then what sense does it make, smashing every little thing we possess? It's natural you should be furious; but don't you forget that the day you deprive the convicts of the last scrap of pleasure in life, there may really be a mutiny – a mutiny of desperate men, a mass suicide, to kill for the sake of killing and be damned if we're killed too – everybody killed, screws and lags together. Monsieur Dutain, I've spoken in all sincerity: I think you deserve it, for the simple reason you came and asked us before taking your decisions. Leave us alone.'

'And what about the men who were in the plot?' said Filissari again.

'It's up to you to find them. We know nothing about it at all: we can't be any use to you whatsoever. I say it again – this whole thing is a piece of madness on the part of just one or two squares. We've nothing to do with it.'

'Monsieur Filissari,' said the governor, 'when the men come back into the dangerous block, have the door closed until further orders. Two warders on the door: no beating-up of the men and no destruction of their property. Come on.' And he left with the other screws.

Relief, relief. That was a very close thing. As he shut the door Filissari called out to me, 'It was lucky for you I'm a Napoleonist!'

In under an hour almost all the men belonging to our block were back. There were eighteen missing: the screws found that in their blind rush they'd shut them up in other blocks. When they were in with us again we learnt what happened, because these men belonged to the fatigue party. In a low voice a thief from Saint-Etienne told me about it. 'We'd dragged a boulder weighing close on a ton for about four hundred yards, Papi. The road we dragged it along had no very steep places, and we reached the well about fifty yards from the governor's house. We always stop there. It's in the shade of the coconut palms and it's the half-way mark. So there we were, stopping as usual, and someone hauled up a big bucket of cold water from the well: some people had a drink and others wetted their handkerchiefs to put them on their heads. It's always a ten minute halt, so the screw sat down too, resting on the edge of the well. He took off his sun helmet and he was wiping his forehead and the top of his head with a big handkerchief when Arnaud came up behind him with a hoe in his hand. He didn't raise it and so nobody shouted out to warn the screw. It didn't take Arnaud a second to whip it up and bring the blade down right on the middle of the screw's skull. The screw went down without a sound, his head cut in two. Hautin had been standing there quite naturally in front of him, and the instant he fell Hautin snatched his carbine while Marceau took off his belt with the revolver in it. Holding the revolver, Marceau turned to the whole party and said, "This is a mutiny. Those who're with us come on!" Not one of the turnkeys moved or said a word: not one of the men on the fatigue gave a sign of following. Arnaud looked at us all and he said, "You lousy cowards, we'll show you what men are!" He took the carbine from Hautin, and they both of them ran towards the governor's house. Marceau moved a little to one side and stood still. He had the heavy revolver in his hand and he said, "Don't move, don't talk, don't shout. You Arabs, face down on the ground." From where I was I could see everything that happened. Arnaud was going up the steps to the governor's house when the Arab who works there opened the door. He had the two little girls with him; he was holding one by the hand and carrying the other. Both Arnaud and the Arab were caught completely unawares: the Arab let fly a kick, still holding the kid in his arms. Arnaud was going to shoot the Arab, but the Arab shielded himself with the child. Nobody uttered a sound. Neither the Arab nor the others. Four or five times there was, the carbine pointing at the Arab from different angles. Each time there was the kid held in front of the barrel. Without going up the steps, Hautin caught hold of the Arab's trousers from the side. As the Arab was just about to fall he flung the kid right on to Arnaud's carbine. Arnaud lost his balance, and he and the child and the Arab, thrown down by Hautin, all fell in a heap. Now there were the first cries – the children first, then the Arab, and then Arnaud and Hautin shouting insults. The Arab moved quickest and he snatched the fallen carbine, but he only got his left hand to the barrel. Hautin grabbed his leg again. Arnaud caught his right arm and twisted it. The Arab hurled the weapon a good ten yards from him.

'Just as all three were running to get it there came the first shot, fired by the screw in charge of the dry-leaf fatigue. The governor appeared at his window and fired shot after shot, but for fear of hitting the Arab he fired at the place where the carbine lay. Hautin and Arnaud ran in the direction of the camp, taking the sea road, followed by rifle shots. With his stiff leg, Hautin ran slower, and he was brought down before he reached the water. As for Arnaud, he went into the sea in the place between the pool we're building, and the screws' swimming-pool. It's always stiff with sharks there, you know.

Arnaud was surrounded with shots, for another warder had come to the help of the governor and the dry-leaf screw. He sheltered behind a big rock.

' "Surrender," shouted the screws. "Your life will be safe."

' "Never," says Arnaud. "I'd rather the sharks ate me than have to put up with you swine any more."

'And he walked into the sea, straight towards the sharks. He must have been hit, because at one moment he stopped. But still the screws went on firing. He set off again, walking – not swimming. He wasn't even chest deep before the sharks went for him. We saw him hit one that came half out of the water to attack him. Then he was literally quartered as the sharks pulled from all sides without biting through his arms and legs. In less than five minutes he'd vanished.

'The screw fired at least a hundred shots at the swirling mass of Arnaud and the sharks. Only one shark was killed – it was washed up on the beach, belly in the air. Now that screws were coming in from every side, Marceau thought he'd save his life by throwing the revolver down the well; but the Arabs had got up, and hitting him with their sticks and kicking and punching him they drove him towards the screws, saying he was in the plot. Although he was covered with blood and had his hands up, the screws killed him with their revolvers and carbines, and to finish him off one of them smashed in his head, holding his rifle by the barrel and using the butt as a club.

'All the screws fired their revolvers into Hautin. There were thirty of them and they had six rounds apiece, so they hit him, living or dead, about a hundred and fifty times. The guys Filissari killed were ones the Arabs pointed out as having made a move to follow Arnaud at first and then having lost heart. All bloody lies, because even if there were any accomplices, no one moved a finger.'

We'd been shut up for two days now in our respective blocks. No one went outside to work. The sentries at the door were relieved every two hours. Other sentries between the blocks. No speaking from one block to another. No standing at the windows. You could only see into the yard by looking through the grill from the alley between the two rows of hammocks. Screws from Royale had arrived to reinforce Saint-Joseph. Not a single transportee outside. Nor an Arab turnkey. Everybody shut up. Now and then we'd see a naked man going

386

to the punishment cells, followed by a warder – no shouts or blows. The screws often looked into the hall from the side windows. Two sentries on the door, one to the right and one to the left. Their turn of duty was short – only two hours – and they never sat down or slung their rifles: always had them at the ready.

We decided to play poker in little groups of five. No playing of the Marseilles game or any of the big, crowded versions – too much noise. Marquetti started playing a Beethoven sonata on his violin, but they made him stop.

'Stop that music: we screws are in mourning.'

There was a most unusual tension not only in the block but throughout the entire camp. No coffee: no soup. A hunk of bread in the morning, corned beef at noon and corned beef in the evening, one tin between four men. As nothing had been destroyed in our block, we had coffee and stores – butter, oil, flour, etc. The other blocks had nothing left. When the smoke rose up from the latrines, where there was a fire for our coffee, a screw shouted to us to put it out. It was an old guy from Marseilles, a lag called Niston, who was making the coffee in order to sell it. He had the guts to reply. 'If you want the fire to be put out, mate, just come in and do it yourself.'

Upon this the screw fired several shots through the window. The fire and the coffee were soon scattered.

Niston had a bullet in the leg. Everyone was so tense and on edge we thought they were about to shoot us down and we all flung ourselves flat on the ground. It was still Filissari who was in charge of the guard at this time of day. He came tearing up like a maniac, his four screws with him. The screw who'd fired explained why – he came from the Auvergne. Filissari insulted him in Corsican, which the Auvergnat couldn't understand. All he could say was, 'I don't follow you.'

We got back into our hammocks. Niston's leg was bleeding. 'Don't say I'm wounded: they might finish me off outside.'

Filissari came up to the bars. Marquetti spoke to him in Corsican. 'Make your coffee. This won't happen again.' And he went off.

Niston was lucky. The bullet hadn't stayed in his flesh: it had gone in low down the muscle and had come out again half way up his leg. We put on a tourniquet, which stopped the blood, and then dressed the wound with vinegar.

'Papillon, outside.' It was eight o'clock, that is to say dark-

ness had fallen. I didn't know the screw who was calling me
– he must have been a Breton.

'Why should I go out at this time of night? There's nothing
for me to do outside.'

'The governor wants to see you.'

'Then tell him to come here. I'm not going out.'

'You refuse?'

'Yes, I refuse.'

My friends stood round me, forming a circle. The screw
was talking from the other side of the closed door. Marquetti
went to the door and said, 'We shan't let Papillon out unless
the governor's here.'

'But it's the governor who's sending for him.'

'Tell him to come himself.'

An hour later two young screws appeared at the door. With
them came the Arab who worked at the governor's house –
the one who'd saved him and prevented the mutiny.

'Papillon, it's me, Mohamed. I've come to fetch you. The
governor wants to see you: he can't come here.'

Marquetti said, 'Papi, that guy's got a carbine.'

At this I left the circle of my friends and walked over to
the door. And in fact Mohamed did have a carbine under his
arm. Now, I thought, I've seen everything: a convict in penal,
officially armed with a carbine!

'Come on,' said the Arab. 'I'm here to protect you if need
be.' But I didn't believe him. 'Come on; come with us.'

I went out. Mohamed walked by my side and the two screws
came behind. I went to the command post. As I went through
the guard-room at the camp gate Filissari said, 'Papillon, I
hope you've nothing to say against me.'

'Neither me personally nor the others in the dangerous
block. I don't know about anywhere else.'

We went down to the command post. The house and the
quay were lit up with acetylene lamps that tried unsuccessfully
to dispel the darkness all round. As we went Mohamed gave
me a packet of Gauloises. We went into the brilliantly-lit room
– two acetylene lamps – and sitting there I saw the governor
of Royale, the deputy, the governor of Saint-Joseph, his deputy,
and the governor of the Réclusion. Outside I'd noticed four
Arabs, guarded by screws. Two of them I recognized as
belonging to the party in question.

'Here's Papillon,' said the Arab.

'Good evening, Papillon,' said the governor of Saint-Joseph.

'Good evening.'

'Sit down. Take that chair over there.'

I sat down facing them all. The door of the room opened on to the kitchen, and I saw Lisette's godmother – she gave me a friendly wave.

'Papillon,' said the governor of Royale, 'Governor Dutain looks upon you as a man worthy of confidence, one who has redeemed himself by the attempted rescue of his wife's godchild. As for me, I only know you by our official reports, which describe you as really dangerous from every point of view. I'd rather forget the reports and rely on my colleague Dutain. Now a commission will undoubtedly come over here to make an inquiry, and the transportees of all categories will have to state what they know. It's certain that you and a few others have a great deal of influence over all the prisoners and that they'll follow your instructions to the letter. We'd like to know your opinion on the mutiny and also whether, to a greater or lesser extent, you can foresee what your block will say – yours in the first place and then the other ones.'

'For my part, I've nothing to say, nor can I influence what the others may say. If the commission comes to make a genuine inquiry in the present atmosphere, you're all done for – sacked.'

'What are you talking about, Papillon? The mutiny has been stopped by me and my colleagues.'

'You may be able to save your own skin; but the chiefs on Royale won't.'

'What do you mean?' The two governors of Royale started up and then sat down again.

'If you go on talking about a mutiny *officially*, you're all lost. If you like to accept my conditions, I'll save the lot of you, except for Filissari.'

'What conditions?'

'First, that life should go back to normal at once, starting from tomorrow morning. It's only with free talk and movement that there's any possibility of influencing what people are to tell the inquiry. Am I right or wrong?'

'Right,' said Dutain. 'But why do we have to be saved?'

'You two from Royale, you're not only in charge of Royale but of the other islands too.'

'Yes.'

'Well, Girasolo squealed, telling you a mutiny was being prepared. With Hautin and Arnaud as the leaders.'

'Carbonieri too,' put in the screw.

'No, that's not true. Carbonieri was a personal enemy of Girasolo's from back in Marseilles: he was just compromising him out of revenge. *But you didn't believe in this mutiny.* Why not? Because he told you that its object was to kill all the women, children, Arabs and screws – it seemed unbelievable. And then again, two boats for eight hundred men on Royale and only one for the six hundred on Saint-Joseph. No level-headed man would agree to take part in a job of that kind.'

'How do you know all this?'

'That's my business. But if you go on talking about a mutiny all this will come out and be proved, even if you make me vanish – indeed, even more so if you try that on. So the responsibility lies with Royale, who sent these men to Saint-Joseph, but *without separating them*. The right decision was to send one to Devil's Island and the other to Saint-Joseph; although I admit the crazy story was difficult to believe: and that's why you can't escape heavy punishment if the inquiry finds out. I say it again: if you go on talking about a mutiny you're sunk – sunk by your own words. So if you accept my conditions – first, as I've already said, that life returns to normal from tomorrow morning: second, that all the men in the cells on suspicion of complicity are let out at once and that they aren't submitted to any interrogation about the part they played in the mutiny, *since it never existed*: and third, that Filissari is sent to Royale this minute, in the first place for his own safety, because if there was no mutiny, how can the killing of those three men be accounted for? And then because that warder is no better than a crawling murderer and at the time of the incident he was yellow with fright – he wanted to kill everybody including all of us in our block. If you accept these conditions, I'll fix it so that everyone says Arnaud, Hautin and Marceau behaved as they did so as to do the greatest possible amount of harm they could before being killed themselves. It was absolutely impossible to have fore-seen what they were going to do. They had no accomplices: they told no one. What everyone will say is that these guys had made up their minds to commit suicide this way – to kill as many as they could before they were knocked on the head. It's suicide they were after. Now, if you like, I'll step into the kitchen and let you think it over before giving me your answer.'

I went into the kitchen and closed the door. Madame Dutain grasped my hand and gave me some coffee and brandy. Mohamed said, 'You didn't put in a word for me?'

'That's the governor's business. He's given you a gun, so obviously he means to have you pardoned.'

Lisette's godmother murmured to me, 'Well, those men from Royale have had what was coming to them.'

'Ha, ha! It was just too easy for them to say there was a mutiny on Saint-Joseph, and everyone knew all about it except for your husband.'

'Papillon, I heard everything, and I understood right away that you meant to take our side.'

'That's true, Madame Dutain.'

The door opened. 'Come in, Papillon,' said a screw.

'Sit down, Papillon,' said the governor of Royale. 'We've talked it over and we've come to the unanimous decision that you're certainly right. *There was no mutiny.* These three transportees had made up their minds to commit suicide, killing as many as possible first. So from tomorrow life will be as it was before. Monsieur Filissari is posted to Royale this very night. His case is our business and as far as he's concerned we don't ask for your collaboration. We rely upon you to keep your word.'

'You can count on me. Good-bye.'

'Mohamed and you two warders, take Papillon back to his block. Bring Filissari in: he's going back to Royale with us.'

On the way I told Mohamed I hoped he'd leave the island a free man. he thanked me.

'Well, and what did the screws want with you?'

Speaking clearly in that total silence I gave an exact, word-by-word account of what had happened. 'If there's anyone who doesn't agree or who thinks he's got anything to say against this arrangement I made with the screws for all of us, let him speak up.'

They all said they agreed. 'Do you think they believed no one else was involved?'

'No, but unless they want to be torpedoed they just have to believe it. And if we don't want trouble, we have to believe it too.'

At seven o'clock the next morning all the punishment cells were emptied. There were more than a hundred and twenty in them. No one went off to work, but all the buildings were open and the yard was full of convicts walking around perfectly free, talking, smoking, and sitting either in the sun or the shade as they chose. Niston had gone off to hospital. Carbonieri told me they'd put a label 'Suspected of being involved in the mutiny' on between eighty and a hundred of the cell doors.

Now that we were all together again, we learnt what had really happened. Filissari had only killed one man: the two others had been killed by young screws who were threatened by convicts – the men were cornered and thought they were going to be killed, so they drew their knives and charged, hoping to account for at least one before they were done for. And so that was how a genuine mutiny (which luckily failed at the very beginning) was turned into a strange kind of suicide on the part of three convicts: for that was the explanation officially accepted by everybody – by the prison service and by the prisoners alike. It left behind it a legend or a true story. I'm not sure which – probably something between the two.

It seems that the funeral of the three men killed in the camp and of Hautin and Marceau was carried out like this: since there was only one box with a trap for throwing the bodies into the sea, the screws laid them all in the bottom of the boat and tossed all five to the sharks at the same moment. They'd worked out that the first would have time to sink, the stones on their feet taking them down, while their friends were being eaten by the sharks. I was told that not a single one of these corpses had gone down but that all five had jigged about on the surface just as the sun was setting, a shroud-white ballet, puppets jerked by the snouts and the tails of the sharks in a banquet worthy of Nebuchadnezzor. It was said that the horror of the sight was so great that the screws and lags fled before it.

A commission of inquiry came, staying nearly five days on Saint-Joseph and two on Royale. I wasn't singled out for questioning: I just went before it like the others. Through Governor Dutain I learnt that everything passed off well. Filissari was sent on leave until it should be time for him to retire: so he wouldn't be coming back. Mohamed was given a remission of the whole of his sentence. Governor Dutain was awarded an extra stripe.

There are always moaners, and yesterday a man from Bordeaux said to me, 'And what have we lags gained by fixing things for the screws?'

I looked at him and said, 'Not much. Just fifty or sixty convicts won't have to do five years solitary for complicity. Nothing much, is it, mate?'

The storm died away. There was a silent connivance between warders and prisoners that completely disoriented the inquiry: and maybe that was just what the commission wanted – everything to be settled peacefully.

As far as I myself was concerned I'd neither gained nor lost, apart from the fact that my friends were grateful to me for not having to undergo a severer discipline. Far from it – the authorities even did away with the dragging of boulders. That horrible fatigue was abolished. Now it was the buffaloes that did the pulling and the convicts that put the rocks into their places. Carbonieri went back to the bakery. For my part I too was trying to get back to Royale. For there was no workshop here on Saint-Joseph, and therefore it was impossible to make a raft.

Pétain's coming to power made the relations between the transportees and the warders worse. All the men belonging to the prison service said very loud and clear that they were Pétainists: so much so that one screw from Normandy said to me, 'Shall I tell you something, Papillon? I never really was a republican.'

No one had a radio on the islands and no one knew what was going on. What's more, it was said that we were providing supplies for German submarines at Martinique and Guadaloupe. There was no making head or tail of it. There were arguments and discussions all the time.

'Do you know what I think, Papi? This is the moment for us to have a mutiny, so as to hand over the islands to de Gaulle's Free French.'

'So you think Long Charlie wants a penal settlement? What for? Just tell me that, will you?'

'Why, to pick up two or three thousand men, of course.'

'Lepers, lunatics, consumptives, characters rotted with dysentery? You're a right comic, you are. That guy's not a bloody fool, cluttering himself up with convicts.'

'And what about the two thousand healthy men?'

'That's different. But just because they're men, does that mean they're any good as soldiers? Do you think war's the same as a hold-up? A hold-up lasts ten minutes: a war goes on for years and years. Patriotic fervour, that's what you need to be a good soldier. And whatever you may say, I don't see a single guy here who'd want to give his life for France.'

'And why should anybody, after what France has done for us?'

'There you are – you've admitted I was right. Fortunately Charlie has other people apart from you to carry on the war. But still and all, when I think of those lousy Germans in our country . . . ! And when you think there are Frenchmen who go along with the Huns! Every single screw here, every last one, says he's for Pétain.'

The Comte de Bérac said, 'It would be one way of redeeming oneself.' And now there happened something very extraordinary – there wasn't a soul among us who'd ever spoken of redeeming himself, but now all of a sudden everybody, crooks and squares, all these poor bloody convicts, saw a gleam of hope.

'What do you say to having this mutiny, Papillon, so de Gaulle should take us under his orders?'

'I'm very sorry, but I don't have to redeem myself in the eyes of anyone on God's earth. As for French justice and its piece about ''rehabilitation'' – my arse. I'll be the one to say when I'm rehabilitated. My duty is to go off on a break and then once I'm free, to be an ordinary citizen living in society without being a danger to it. I don't believe a guy can prove anything else any other way. Still, I'm ready for anything at all that'll lead to a break. Handing over the islands to Long Charlie doesn't interest me and I'm dead certain it doesn't interest him either. Anyhow, do you know what the characters in power will say if you bring off a stroke of that kind? They'll say you took the islands just to be free, not to strike a blow for Free France. And then again, do you guys really know which is right, de Gaulle or Pétain? I don't. I know absolutely nothing about it. I suffer like a poor miserable bastard at knowing that my country's invaded: I think about my people, my relatives, my sisters, my nieces.'

'We'd have to be a right set of twats, though, to worry ourselves sick about a society that's never had the least pity on us.'

'But it's natural that one should; because the cops and all the French legal machinery and these gendarmes and screws, that's not France. They're a class apart, made up of people with completely twisted minds. How many of them are ready to go into the service of the Germans at this minute? You can bet your bottom dollar the French police are arresting their own countrymen and handing them over to the German authorities. Right. I've said it once and I'll say it again, I'll have nothing to do with a mutiny, whatever it's for. Except for a break. But how and when?'

There were very serious arguments between the two sides. One lot were for de Gaulle and the others were for Pétain. When it came down to brass tacks nobody really knew anything, because as I've said there was no radio, either among the lags or among the screws. News reached us by the boats that called in, leaving us a little flour, dried vegetables and rice. The war, seen from such a great way off, was hard for us to understand.

It was said that a man had come to Saint-Laurent-du-Maroni, recruiting for the Free French. Here in penal we knew nothing, only that the Germans were all over France by now.

One amusing thing happened: a priest came to Royale and after mass he gave a sermon. He said, 'If the islands are attacked, you'll be given weapons to help the warders defend French soil.' That's perfectly true. He was a splendid man, that curé; and he must have had a wonderfully low opinion of us. Asking prisoners to defend their own cells! God above, we really had seen everything in penal!

As far as we were concerned, the war amounted to this – twice the number of screws, everything doubled, all the way from simple screw right up to governor and chief warder; a great many inspectors, some with a very strong German or Alsatian accent; very little bread – fourteen ounces; very little meat. In a word, there was only one thing that had gone up, and that was the penalty for a botched escape – death-sentence and execution. For added to the accusation of escape there was 'Attempted to join the enemies of France.'

I had been on Royale for nearly four months. I had made a great friend, Dr. Germain Guibert. His wife, a wonderful person, asked me to make her a kitchen garden to help them live on this wretched diet. I made her a plot with lettuces, radishes, haricots, tomatoes and aubergines. She was delighted and she treated me as a real friend.

This doctor had never shaken a warder's hand, whatever his

rank; but he often did so with me and some other convicts he'd come to know and respect.

When at last I had become a free man once more I got into touch with Dr. Germain Guibert again through Dr. Rosenberg. He sent me a photo of himself and his wife on the Canebière in Marseilles. He was coming back from Morocco, and he congratulated me on being free and happy. He was killed in Indo-China, trying to save a wounded man who had been left behind. He was an exceptional person and he had a wife worthy of him. When I was back in France in 1967 I wanted to go and see her. But I gave up the idea, because she had stopped writing to me after I'd asked for a testimonial. She had sent it, but since then I'd never heard from her. I don't know the reason for this silence, but in my heart I still have the utmost gratitude to both of them for the way they treated me in their home on Royale.

A few months later I was able to get back to Royale.

Carbonieri's Death

Yesterday my friend Matthieu Carbonieri was stabbed clean through the heart. This killing started off a series of others. He was in the wash-house, quite naked, having a shower; and it was when his face was covered with soap that he was stabbed. When you had a shower it was usual to open your knife and lay it under your things, so as to have just time to get it if anyone who looked like an enemy suddenly appeared. The neglect of this little precaution cost him his life. The man who'd killed my mate was an Armenian, a life-long ponce.

With the governor's permission. I carried my friend down to the quay myself, helped by another man. He was heavy and going down the hill I had to rest three times. I attached a big stone to his feet, using wire instead of rope. That way the sharks wouldn't be able to bite through it, and he'd go down without their eating him.

The bell tolled and we reached the wharf. It was six o'clock in the evening. We got into the boat. The sun was touching the horizon. There under the lid of the well-known box that was used for everybody lay Matthieu, sleeping for ever. For him everything was over.

'Right, give way,' said the screw at the tiller. In under ten minutes we reached the current formed by the run between Royale and Saint-Joseph. And then all at once there was a great lump in my throat. Dozens of shark-fins appeared above the surface, cruising swiftly in an area not more than four hundred yards wide. Here they were, the convicts' undertakers, at the rendezvous on time.

God willing they wouldn't have time to seize hold of my

friend. We raised our oars to say farewell. The box was tilted. Wrapped in flour sacks, Matthieu's body slid out, drawn by the weight of the heavy stone, and in a moment it was in the sea.

Horror! It had just touched and I thought it was vanishing when it was heaved right up in the air by God knows how many sharks – seven, ten, twenty – there was no telling. Before the boat could get away the flour sacks were ripped off: and then something incomprehensible happened. Matthieu showed there for two or three seconds, standing upright in the water. His right forearm had already gone. With half his body above the surface he came straight for the boat, and then, in the midst of a still stronger swirl, he disappeared for ever. The sharks passed under the boat, thumping the bottom so that one man lost his balance and nearly fell into the water.

All of us, including the screws, were horror-struck. For the first time in my life I wanted to die. I was very close to throwing myself to the sharks, so as to leave this hell for good and all.

Slowly I walked up from the wharf to the camp. No one with me. I put the stretcher over my shoulder and I reached the flat place where my buffalo Brutus went for Danton. I stopped and sat down. Night had fallen although it was only seven. In the west the sky was still faintly lit by a few gleams from the sunken sun. All the rest was black, with the beam of the light-house piercing the darkness every now and then: my heart was full.

What the hell, you wanted to see a funeral, and your best friend's funeral into the bargain? Well, you've seen it, all right, all right. You heard the bell. Have you had enough, brother? Is your unhealthy curiosity satisfied?

The guy who did it – you've still got him to take apart. When? Tonight. Why tonight? It's too early: the guy will be absolutely on tip-toe. They are ten in his gourbi. Still, you mustn't be beaten to the mark. How many men can I count on, now? Four, and then there's me: five. That's all right. Wipe this guy out. Yes: and if possible I'll get away to Devil's Island. No rafts there, no preparations, nothing: just two sacks of coconuts and I jump into the sea. The distance to the coast is fairly short – twenty-five miles as the crow flies. What with waves, winds and tides, that would probably turn into seventy-five. It would only be a question of holding out. I was strong, and two days at sea, astride my sack – why, I ought to be able to cope with that.

I shouldered the stretcher and went up to the camp. When I reached the gate a very extraordinary thing happened: I was searched. That never happened: not ever. The screw himself took my knife.

'Are you trying to get me killed? What am I being disarmed for? Don't you know you're sending me to my death, doing this? If I'm killed, it'll be your fault.' No one replied, neither the screws nor the Arab turnkeys. The door was opened and I walked into the hall. 'You can't see a thing in here. Why's there only one lamp instead of three?'

'Papi, come over here.' Grandet pulled me by the sleeve. There was not much noise in the room. You could feel something serious was just going to happen, or had just that moment happened.

'I've not got my knife any more. They searched me and took it away.'

'You won't need it tonight.'

'Why not?'

'The Armenian and his friend are in the latrines.'

'What are they doing there?'

'They're dead.'

'Who put the chill on them?'

'I did.'

'That was quick. What about the others?'

'There are four left in their gourbi. Paulo gave me his sacred word they wouldn't stir but would wait to know whether you agree that the business should stop here.'

'Give me a knife.'

'Here's mine. I'll stay in this corner: you go and speak to them.'

I walked towards their gourbi. My eyes were used to the dimness now. I could make them out quite clearly. There they stood, the four of them, close together, side by side in front of their hammocks.

'You want to talk to me, Paulo?'

'Yes.'

'Alone or with your friends here? What do you want with me?' I left a prudent five feet between us. I had the knife open in my left hand with its hilt right there in my palm.

'I wanted to tell you it seems to me your friend has been

399

properly revenged – that this is enough. You've lost your best friend: we've lost two of ours. As I see it, things ought to stop here. What do you think?'

'Paulo, I hear what you say. If you agree, what we might do would be for the two gourbis to promise not to make a move for a week. By then we'd know what ought to be done. Right?'

'Right.'

And I withdrew.

'Well, what did they say?'

'That they thought the death of the Armenian and Sans-Souci revenge enough for Matthieu.'

'No,' said Galgani. Grandet said nothing. Jean Castelli and Louis Gravon were in favour of a peace agreement. 'What about you, Papi?'

'In the first place, who killed Matthieu? The Armenian. Right. I've suggested an agreement. I've given my word and they've given theirs that none of us will stir for a week.'

'So you don't want to revenge Matthieu?' said Galgani.

'Matthieu's revenged already: two men have been killed for him. Why kill the others?'

'Were they even in on what was going to happen? That's what we ought to find out.'

'Good night, everyone. You must excuse me – I'm going to try to get some sleep.'

In any case I felt I had to be alone, and I stretched out on my hammock. I felt a hand gliding gently over me and taking the knife. A low voice in the darkness. 'Sleep if you can, Papi: sleep easy. We're going to keep watch, turn and turn about.'

There had been no real sound reason for my friend's sudden, violent, disgusting death. The Armenian had killed him just because during the gambling the night before Matthieu had compelled him to pay a bet of a hundred and seventy francs. The bleeding fool thought he'd lost face because he'd had to obey in front of the thirty or forty other men in the game. Wedged there between Matthieu and Grandet he'd had no choice about it.

In that back-handed, cowardly way he had killed a man who was the very best example of the pure adventurer, clean and straight in his own particular world. It wounded me deeply, and the only satisfaction I had was that the killers had survived their crime by no more than a few hours. A precious small satisfaction.

Grandet, moving like a tiger, had stabbed them in the throat, one after the other, before they had had time to defend themselves – he had thrust with the speed of an expert fencer. It occurred to me that the place where they had fallen must be swimming with blood. Stupidly I thought, 'I should like to ask who dragged them off to the latrine.' But I could not bring myself to speak. Behind my closed eyes I could see the tragic red and violet sunset, its last gleams lighting up the Dantesque scene of the sharks fighting over my friend . . . And that upright trunk, the right forearm already gone, advancing towards the boat! So it was true that the bell called the sharks and that the swine knew they were going to be fed when it began to toll . . . Once again I saw those scores of fins – the sombre gleam as they cruised, circling round and round like submarines. There were certainly more than a hundred of them . . . For my friend it was all over: the way down the drain had done its job right through to the end.

To be stabbed to death over a trifle at the age of forty! Poor Matthieu. I couldn't bear it any more. No. No. No. I was quite happy to have the sharks eat me, but alive, making a dash for freedom, with no flour sacks, stone and rope. No spectators, either screws or convicts. No bell. If I was to be eaten, fine; but let them get me down alive, struggling against the sea and sky to reach the mainland.

'It's over – finished. No more too-carefully-prepared escapes. Devil's Island, two sacks of coconuts and have it away – let everything rip and trust in God.'

After all, it would only be a question of my holding out. Forty-eight hours or sixty? Would such a long time in the water, together with the muscular effort of holding myself astride on the sacks, paralyse me at some point? If I was lucky enough to get to Devil's Island I'd try the experiment. The first thing to do was to get off Royale and be sent to Devil's Island. Then I'd see.

'Are you asleep, Papi?'

'No.'

'Like some coffee?'

'I don't mind if I do.' I sat up in my hammock and took the hot mug that Grandet was holding out, together with a Gauloise already lit.

'What's the time?'

'One in the morning. I took over the watch at midnight, but as I saw you were moving all the time it occurred to me you weren't asleep.'

'I wasn't, either. Matthieu's death knocked me flat: but his funeral there with the sharks was even worse. It was hideous. Do you know that?'

'Don't tell me, Papi; I can imagine what it must have been like. You should never have gone.'

'I thought the stuff about the bell was all balls. And then with the heavy stone held by wire I'd never have believed the sharks would have had time to catch him as he sank. Poor old Matthieu: I'll see that horrible sight as long as I live. And what about you – how did you manage to wipe out the Armenian and Sans-Souci so quickly?'

'I was at the far end of the island, fixing an iron door at the slaughterhouse when I heard they'd killed our friend. It was midday. Instead of going up to the camp I went back to work, saying I had to see to the lock. I managed to fit a two-edged blade into a tube a yard long. Both the tube and the handle of the knife were hollowed out. I went back to the camp at five, carrying the tube. The screw asked me what it was and I said the wooden bar of my hammock had broken, so for that night I was going to use this tube. It was still day-light when I went into the hall, but I left the tube in the washhouse. I picked it up before roll-call. It began to grow dark. With our friends standing round me I quickly fitted the blade on to the tube. The Armenian and Sans-Souci were standing in their part of the room, in front of their hammocks; Paulo was a little way behind them. Jean Castelli and Louis Gravon are very good guys, as you know: but they're old and they aren't quick enough for a set battle of this kind. I wanted to do it before you came back, so that you shouldn't be mixed up in it. If we were caught, with your record you'd have risked the maximum. Jean went down to the far end of the hall and put out one of the lights: Gravon did the same at the top end. With just the one in the middle, there was almost no light in the room. I had a big electric torch that Dega had given me. Jean walked in front, me behind him. When we reached them he raised his arm and shone the torch in their faces. The Armenian was dazzled and he lifted his left arm to his eyes: there was time to get him in the throat with my lance. Sans-

Souci was dazzled next and he stabbed out in the air in front of him. I hit him so hard with my blade I went right through and out the other side. Paulo flung himself flat on the ground and rolled under the hammocks. As Jean had turned off the torch I didn't go after him – that's what saved Paulo.'

'Who dragged them off to the latrines?'

'I don't know. I think it was the other men of their gourbi, so as to get the chargers out of their guts.'

'But there must have been a hell of a great pool of blood.'

'You're telling me there was a hell of a great pool of blood. Their throats were cut through and through, and they must have spilled every last drop of juice they had. I had the idea of the torch while I was getting the lance ready. In the workshop there was a screw, changing the batteries in his. That gave me the notion and I got into touch with Dega at once, making him let me have one. They can make a full-blown search if they like. The torch has been taken out and given back to Dega by an Arab turnkey: the knife, too. So no leaks as far as those things are concerned. I've no regrets. They killed our friend when he had his eyes full of soap: I helped them to commit suicide when their eyes were full of light. We're quits. What do you think about it, Papi?'

'You did splendidly, and I don't know how to thank you for having revenged our friend so soon: and for having had the idea of keeping me out of the whole business, too.'

'Think nothing of it. I did my duty: you've had such a bad time and you so desperately want to be free, I just had to do it.'

'Thank you, Grandet. Yes, I want to get out more than ever now. Will you help me to fix things so this business stops here? To tell you the truth, I'd be very surprised if the Armenian had told his gourbi before he killed Matthieu. Paulo would never have put up with such a cowardly murder. He would have known what it would lead to.'

'I'm of the same opinion. Only Galgani says they're all guilty.'

'We'll see what happens at six. I won't go out to work. I'll pretend to be ill so as to stay.'

Five in the morning. The block leader came over to us. 'Do you guys think I ought to call the guard? I've just found two stiffs in the latrine.' This chap, an old lag of seventy, was trying to make us, *us*, believe he hadn't noticed a thing since half-past six yesterday evening, the time the chill had been put on them. The hall must have been covered with blood, because as men walked to and fro they must necessarily have stepped in the pool, which was right there in the middle of the alley.

Grandet replied just as cunningly as the old boy. 'Really? Two stiffs in the latrine? Since when?'

'Search me,' said the old lag. 'I've been asleep since six. It was only just now, when I went to have a piss, that I slipped in the sticky mess. I lit my lighter, saw it was blood, and then I found the characters there in the latrine.'

'Call them, and we'll see what they say.'

'Warders! Warders!'

'What are you bawling for, you old brute? Is the block on fire?'

'No, Chief: there are two stiffs in the bogs.'

'Well, what do you want me to do about it? Bring them back to life? It's a quarter past five now: at six we'll have a look. Stop anyone going into the latrine.'

'That's just not possible. Now, just when everybody's getting up, everyone goes to have a piss or a shit.'

'True enough. Wait a minute – I'll tell the boss.'

They appeared: three screws, one chief warder and two others. We thought they were going to come in, but no, they stayed there at the barred door.

'You say there are two dead men in the latrine?'

'Yes, Chief.'

'Since when?'

'I don't know. I found them just now, when I went to have a piss.'

'Who are they?'

'I don't know.'

'Oh all right, you old lunatic, I'll tell you. One of them's the Armenian. Go and have a look.'

'You're quite right: it's the Armenian and Sans-Souci.'

'Good. We'll wait for the roll-call.' And they went off.

Six o'clock and the first bell. The door opened. The two coffee men hurried along, followed by the ones with the bread.

Half past six and the second bell. Day had broken and the alley was covered with the footprints of the men who'd walked in the blood during the night.

The two governors appeared. It was full daylight. Eight warders and the doctor with them.

'Everyone strip! Stand to attention in front of your hammocks. It's an absolute slaughter-house – there's blood everywhere!'

The deputy-governor was the first to go into the latrines. When he came out again he was as white as a sheet. 'Their throats have been literally ripped out. Nobody heard or saw anything, of course?'

Total silence.

'You're the block leader, old man: these men are stiff. Doctor, about how long have they been dead?'

'Eight to ten hours,' said the medico.

'And you only found them at five? You never saw or heard anything?'

'No. I'm hard of hearing and I can scarcely see: what's more I'm seventy years old – forty of them in penal. So I sleep a lot, you see. I was asleep by six, and it was only because I wanted to piss that I woke up at five. It was a bit of luck, because ordinarily I sleep until the bell.'

'You're right, it was a bit of luck,' said the governor ironically. 'It was a bit of luck for us, too, because this way everybody's slept peacefully all night through, both warders and prisoners. Stretcher-bearers, pick up these two corpses and carry them off to the operating room. I'd like you to do a postmortem, Doctor. And you people, get out one by one into the yard, naked.'

Each one of us filed past the governor and the doctor. The men were very closely examined all over. No one had a wound: several had splashes of blood. They said they'd slipped, going to the latrines. Grandet, Galgani and I were inspected more attentively than the others.

'Papillon, which is your place?' They searched all my possessions: 'Where's your knife?'

'The warder on the gate took it from me at seven yesterday evening.'

'That's true,' said the screw. 'He cut up very rough, saying we wanted him to be killed.'

'Grandet, is this knife yours?'

'Why, yes: it was in my place, so it must be mine.' He looked at the knife very carefully: it was as clean as a new pin – not a spot anywhere.

The medico came out of the latrine and said, 'It was a double-edged dagger that was used to cut these men's throats. They were killed standing up. It's incomprehensible. A convict doesn't just stand there like a rabbit, without defending himself, while his throat is cut. Someone must have been wounded.'

'And yet as you can see for yourself, Doctor, no man here has so much as a scratch.'

'Were these two men dangerous?'

'Very dangerous indeed, Doctor. The Armenian was certainly the man who killed Carbonieri in the wash-house at nine yesterday morning.'

'Investigation closed,' said the governor. 'Still, keep Grandet's knife. Everybody out to work, except for the invalids. Papillon, you reported sick?'

'Yes, Governor.'

'You lost no time in revenging your friend. I'm not taken in, you know. Unfortunately I've no proofs and I know I shan't get any. For the last time, has anyone any statement to make? If there is one of you who can shed any light on this double crime, I give my word he'll be un-interned and sent to the mainland.'

Dead silence.

The whole of the Armenian's gourbi reported sick. Seeing this, Grandet, Galgani, Jean Castelli and Louis Gravon also put themselves on the list at the last moment. The room was emptied of its hundred and twenty men. There remained the five of my gourbi and the four of the Armenian's, together with the watchmaker, the block leader, grumbling continually about all the cleaning he was going to have to do, and two or three other convicts, of whom one was an Alsatian called Big Sylvain.

This was a man who lived all by himself in penal: everyone liked him. He was a highly respected man of action, and it was a most uncommon feat that had sent him down for twenty years. Single-handed, he attacked the mail van on the Paris-Brussels express, knocked out the two men in charge and tossed the mail sacks on to the ballast; they were picked up by accomplices along the line and they brought in a handsome sum.

Sylvain saw the two gourbis whispering, each in a different corner, and as he didn't know we'd agreed not to make a move, he went so far as to take it upon himself to speak. 'I hope you're not going to fight a pitched battle – a Three Musketeers kind of job?'

'Not today,' said Galgani. 'That'll be for later.'

'How come later? Never put off for tomorrow what you can do today,' said Paulo. 'But for my part I can't see any reason why we should kill one another. What do you think, Papillon?'

'One single question: did you know what the Armenian was going to do?'

'On my word as a man, Papi, we knew nothing: and if you want to know, I'm not sure – if the Armenian wasn't dead – whether I should have put up with what he did.'

'Well, if that's how it is, why not let's stop the whole thing for good?' said Grandet.

'That's what we think. Let's shake hands and say no more about this wretched business.'

'OK.'

'I'm the witness,' said Sylvain. 'I'm truly glad it's over.'

'Let's say no more.'

At six that evening the bell began to toll. Hearing it, I could not prevent myself from seeing yesterday once again: my friend rushing towards the boat with half his body reared out of the water. The picture was so striking, so shocking, even twenty-four hours later, that not for a moment could I hope that the Armenian and Sans-Souci were being treated so by the sharks.

Galgani said not a word. He knew very well what had happened to Carbonieri. Swinging his legs as he sat astride his hammock, he stared into emptiness. Grandet was not back yet. The tolling had been over for a good ten minutes when, without looking at me, Galgani, still swinging his legs, said in an undertone, 'I hope none of the sharks that ate Matthieu got so much as a scrap of that Armenian sod. It would be too bloody silly for them to have been dead against one another in life and then to come together in a shark's belly.'

The loss of that true, great-hearted friend was going to mean a dreadful gap in my life. It would be better for me to get off Royale as soon as possible and start moving. That's what I said to myself over and over again every day.

'Since there's a war on and the punishment for a bungled escape is so much heavier, this isn't a time to muck up a break, Salvidia. Right?' The Italian with the gold charger and I were talking by the wash-house: we'd just re-read the poster that announced the new regulations in case of escape. I went on, 'Yet it's not the risk of being sentenced to death that'll stop me going. What about you?'

'As far as I'm concerned, Papillon, I just can't take it any more and I want to make a break. However it ends. I've asked to be taken on in the lunatic asylum as an attendant. I know there are two drums in the asylum dispensary; they hold fifty gallons apiece, so they are plenty big enough to make a raft. One's full of olive-oil and the other of vinegar. It seems to me that if we lashed them together so that they couldn't possibly come apart, there would be a very fair chance of reaching the mainland. There's no watch kept on the outside of the walls round the asylum. On the inside there's only one medical warder on guard at any time, with some convicts to help him keep watch on the lunatics. Why don't you join me up there?'

'As an attendant?'

'Impossible, Papillon. You know very well they'd never give you a job in the asylum. It's far from the camp; it's not heavily guarded – there's everything against sending you there. But you might get in as a patient.'

'That would be very tricky, Salvidia. When the doctor puts you down as cracked, what he's giving you is nothing more nor less than the right to do whatever you like without being held responsible. It's officially admitted that you aren't answerable. Do you realize the responsibility he takes upon himself when he signs that kind of a certificate? You can kill a convict, or even a screw or a screw's wife, or a child if you like. You can escape – you can commit any crime you can think of and the law has no hold on you. The very worst it can do is to put you into a padded cell with nothing on except a strait-jacket. And even that can only go on for a certain period: in time they have to let up. The result is that however serious your crime, escapes included, you don't pay the penalty.'

'Papillon, I believe in you: you're the man I'd really like

to make a break with. Do everything you possibly can to join me as a lunatic. Being an attendant I'll be able to help you bear it – I'll be able to give you a hand when things are tough. I admit it must be horrible to find yourself among all those very dangerous creatures when you're not mad yourself.'

'You go on up to the asylum, Romeo. I'll look thoroughly into the whole thing; and above all I'll find out about the first signs of madness so as to convince the doc. In any case, it's not at all a bad idea to get myself certified as irresponsible.'

I began studying the question seriously. There was no book on the subject in the prison library. Whenever I had an opportunity I talked about it with men who had been ill for quite a time and gradually I formed a fairly clear notion.

1. All lunatics have agonizing pains in the back of the head.
2. They often have a humming in their ears.
3. They are very much on edge, so can't stay lying in the same position for long without having a nervous explosion that wakes them up, their whole body jerking, tensed to the breaking-point.

So what I had to do was to have someone find out I had these symptoms, rather than me speaking of them directly. I was to be just mad enough to force the doctor to put me into the asylum, but not so mad, not so violently mad, as to justify ill-treatment by the warders – strait-jackets, beating-up, reduced diet, bromide injections, cold or boiling baths, etc. If I did the act well enough I ought to be able to come it over the doctor.

There was one thing in my favour – what reason could I possibly have for swinging the lead? As the doctor would find no answer to that question, it was likely that I should win the game. There was no other way out for me. They had refused to send me to Devil's Island. Now that my friend Matthieu had been murdered I could no longer bear the camp. To hell with hesitation! My mind was made up. I'd get myself on the sick-list on Monday. It would be better if someone else reported me sick, someone who would speak in good faith. I'd have to behave abnormally inside the block now and then. Then the block leader would speak to the screw and the screw himself would put me down on the list.

For three days now I had not slept: I no longer washed or shaved. I masturbated several times every night and I ate very little. Yesterday I asked my neighbour why he'd taken a non-existent photo from my place. That made him uneasy and he moved elsewhere. The soup often stood for a few minutes in the tub before it was distributed. I went over to the tub, and there in front of everybody I pissed into it. That cast something of a damper on the room, but I dare say my look discouraged them, because no one made any objection. Only my friend Grandet said, 'Papillon, what did you do that for?'

'Because they forgot to salt it.' And without paying any attention to the others I went and fetched my bowl, holding it out to the block leader to be filled. There was a dead silence, and they all watched me as I ate my soup.

These two happenings brought me up in front of the doctor this morning without any asking on my part.

'Well, Doctor, are you all right? Yes or no?' I repeated my question. The doctor looked at me, amazed. I fixed him with a studiedly natural stare.

'Yes, I'm all right,' said the doctor. 'But what about you? Are you sick?'

'No.'

'Then why are you on the list?'

'No reason at all: they told me you were ill. I'm glad to see it wasn't true. Good-bye.'

'Just a minute, Papillon. Sit down there, opposite me. Look into my face.' And the medico examined my eyes with a little torch that threw a narrow beam.

'Did you see any of the things you thought you were going to find, Doc? Your light isn't very strong, but even so I think you know what I mean. Tell me, did you see them?'

'See what?' said the medico.

'Don't be such a bloody fool. Are you a doctor or a vet? Don't you tell me you didn't have time to see them before they hid – either you don't want to tell me, or you take me for a genuine twat.' My eyes were shining with tiredness. I was unwashed and unshaved, and my appearance told in my favour. The screws were listening, fascinated; but I didn't make the slightest violent gesture that would let them step in. The doctor, soothing me and jollying me along so that I shouldn't get excited, stood up and put his hand on my shoulder. I was still sitting down.

'Yes, I didn't like to tell you, Papillon, but I did have time to see them.'

'You're lying, Doc, lying like a real member of the colonial. You didn't see anything at all! What I thought you were looking for was those three little black specks in my left eye. I can only see them when I look at nothing or when I'm reading. But when I take a mirror I can see my eye quite clearly, without the least trace of the three specks. They hide the second I get hold of the glass to look at them in.'

'Send him to hospital,' said the medico. 'Take him there at once: he's not to go back to the camp. You tell me you're not sick, Papillon? Maybe you're right, but I think you're very tired and so I'm going to give you a few days' rest in hospital. You'd like that?'

'I don't mind one way or another. Hospital or camp, it's still the islands.'

The first step had been taken. Half an hour later there I was in the hospital, lying in a clean, white-sheeted bed in a well-lit cell. On the door a label: 'Under observation'.

Gradually, self-hypnotized through and through, I turned myself into a looney. It was a dangerous game: I'd worked so carefully, practising that way of twisting my mouth and perpetually catching my lower lip with my teeth, I'd studied it so thoroughly in front of a hidden scrap of mirror, that I caught myself doing it without meaning to. You mustn't play this little game too long, Papi. If you go on forcing yourself to feel you're going crazy it may leave dangerous traces that you'll never lose. Yet I had to play the game all out if I wanted to win – that is to say, to get into the asylum, to be certified irresponsible and then to set off on a break with my mate. Break! That magic word filled me with wild delight, and I could already see myself sitting on the two barrels together with my friend the Italian attendant, making our way towards the mainland.

The doctor went his rounds every day. He examined me at length: we always talked civilly and pleasantly. The doc was worried, but he wasn't yet convinced. So the next thing was to tell him I had stabbing pains in the back of my head – the first symptom.

'How are you, Papillon? Slept well?'

'Thanks, Doctor, yes, I'm pretty well. And thank you for the *Match* you lent me. But as for sleeping, that's something else again. Because, do you see, behind my cell there's a pump. It's there for watering something or other, I dare say, but the thump-thump-thump all night gets into the back of my head, and it's just as though there was a thump-thump-thump echoing inside my skull. All night it goes on. Unbearable. So I'd be very grateful if you'd have my cell changed.'

The doctor turned towards the medical warder and quickly whispered, 'Is there a pump?' The warder shook his head. 'Change his cell, warder. Where do you want to go, Papillon?'

'As far as possible from that bloody pump – right to the end of the corridor. Thank you, Doctor.'

The door closed; I was alone in my cell again. I caught the very faintest hint of a sound – I was being watched through the judas. It was certainly the doctor, because I had not heard their steps going away after they left the cell. So I quickly shook my fist at the wall with the imaginary pump behind it and called out – but not too loud – 'Stop it, stop it, you drunken bastard! Are you going to go on watering your garden for ever, you ugly sod?' And I lay down in my bed with my head buried under the pillow.

I didn't catch the little sound of the brass lid closing over the judas, but I did hear footsteps going away. So the character at the spy-hole was certainly the doctor.

That afternoon they changed my cell. I must have made the right impression in the morning, because just to take me the few yards to the end of the corridor there were two screws and two convict orderlies. As they didn't speak to me, I didn't speak to them either. I merely followed them without a word. Two days later, the second symptom – noises in my ears.

'How are you, Papillon? Have you finished the magazine I sent you?'

'No, I've not read it. I spent all day and half the night trying to smother a mosquito or a little fly that's living in my ear. I shove in cotton wool, but it does no good. Their humming goes on and on – bzz-bzz-bzz. And it not only tickles, but it never stops buzzing. It gets you down in the end, Doctor. What do you think about it? Maybe, since I haven't managed to smother them we might try drowning them? What do you say?'

My mouth went on jerking all this time and I saw he took

412

notice of it. He took my hand and looked straight into my eyes. I could feel he was concerned and worried. 'Yes, Papillon, we'll drown them. Chatal, syringe his ears.'

We had these scenes every morning with variations, but it didn't look as though the doctor could make up his mind to send me to the asylum. When he was giving me a bromide injection Chatal said, 'It's all right for the moment. The doc's badly shaken, but it may still take him a long time before he sends you to the asylum. If you want him to make up his mind quick, show him you can be dangerous.'

'How are you, Papillon?' The doctor, accompanied by the medical warders and Chatal, greeted me kindly as he opened my cell door.

'Hold your horses, Doc.' My whole attitude was aggressive. 'You know damn well I'm sick. And I'm beginning to wonder whether you aren't in with the sod who's torturing me.'

'Who's torturing you? When? How?'

'Listen, Doc, in the first place do you know the work of Dr. d'Arsonval?'

'I should hope so.'

'Then you know he's invented a multiple-wave oscillator to ionize the air round a patient with duodenal ulcers. This oscillator sends electric currents. Right: well an enemy of mine knocked off one of these machines in the Cayenne hospital. Every time I'm really asleep, he presses on the button and the current gets me smack in the belly and thighs. I jerk out straight, and my whole body jumps six inches into the air. How do you expect me to resist that and go on sleeping? It went on all last night. I scarcely close my eyes and the current hits me. My whole body jerks like a spring being released. I can't bear it any more, Doc. Just you tell them all that if I find anyone helping that sod, I'll take him to pieces. I've no weapons, but I'm strong enough to strangle any man on earth. And if the cap fits, wear it. And you can stuff up your hypocritical good mornings and how are you Papillons. I tell you again, Doc, just you hold your horses.'

This scene paid off. Chatal told me the doctor warned the screws to be very careful. To never open my door unless there were two or three of them and to always speak to me nicely. 'He's got persecution,' said the doctor. 'We'll have to send him to the asylum as quick as possible.'

Chatal, meaning to spare me being put into a strait-jacket,

had said, 'I believe I could undertake to lead him to the asylum with just one warder.'

'Well, Papi, have you had a good dinner?'

'Yes, Chatal, it was fine.'

'Would you like to come with me and Monsieur Jeannus?'

'Where to?'

'We're just going up to the asylum to take them some medical stores: it would make a little walk for you.'

'OK. Let's go.' And we all three went out of the hospital and took the asylum road. Chatal kept on talking as we went along, and then, when we were almost there, he said, 'Aren't you sick of the camp, Papillon?'

'Oh, yes, I'm fed up with it, particularly since my friend Carbonieri's no longer there.'

'Then why don't you stay in the asylum for a few days? That way maybe the character with the electric machine won't be able to find you to send the current.'

'Well, that's an idea, mate. But do you think they'd take me in, me not being sick in the head?'

'You leave that to me: I'll put in a word for you,' said the screw, quite delighted at seeing me fall into Chatal's so-called trap.

So to cut it short, here I was in the asylum together with a hundred lunatics. It was no fun at all, living with madmen. We exercised in the yard in groups of thirty to forty while the orderlies cleaned the cells. Everyone was stark naked, night and day. Fortunately it was warm. As for me, I was allowed to keep my slippers.

An orderly had just given me a lit cigarette. Sitting there in the sun I reflected that I'd been inside five days now and yet I'd not been able to get into touch with Salvidia.

A lunatic came over to me. I knew about him: his name was Fouchet. His mother had sold her house to send him fifteen thousand francs through a warder so he could escape. The screw was supposed to keep five thousand and give him ten thousand. The screw swiped the lot and then left for Cayenne. When Fouchet heard his mother had sent him the money – heard it from another source – and that she had stripped herself all to no purpose, he went raving mad and that same day he attacked the warders. They got on top of him before he could do any damage. And from that day, three or four years back, he'd been in the asylum.

414

'Who are you?' I looked at this poor chap, a young fellow of about thirty, standing there questioning me. 'Who am I? Why, a man like you, mate; neither more nor less.' 'That's a stupid answer. I can see you're a man, since you've got a prick and balls: if you'd been a woman you'd have had a hole. I was asking who you were? I mean, what's your name?' 'Papillon.' 'Papillon? You're a butterfly? Poor fellow. Butterflies have wings – they fly. And where are yours?' 'I've lost them.' 'You must find them. That way you'd be able to escape. The screws have no wings. Give me your cigarette.' Before I had time to hold it out he'd snatched it from my fingers. Then he sat down opposite me and drew in the smoke with delight.

'And who are you?' I asked him.

'Me? I'm the one they call the fall-boy. Every time I ought to be given something that belongs to me I'm done right in the eye.' 'How come?' 'That's just the way it is. So that's why I kill as many screws as ever I can. I hanged a couple last night. But don't tell a soul.' 'What did you hang them for?' 'They stole my mother's house. My mother sent me her house, and as they liked the look of it they kept it and now they're living in it. I was right to hang them, wasn't I?' 'Quite right. Now they won't be able to profit by it.' 'Do you see that fat screw over there, behind the bars? He lives in the house too. Believe you me, I'll do him in.' And he stood up and walked off.

What a relief! It was no sort of picnic, being forced to live among all these lunatics; and it was dangerous. At night they roared and shrieked all round me, and when the moon was full they were more frantic than ever. How can the moon possibly affect the condition of mad people? I can't explain it; but often and often I've seen it happen.

The screws reported on the mental cases under observation. With me they made a whole lot of cross-checks. For example they'd purposely forget to let me out into the yard, to see whether I'd notice it and complain. Or else they'd leave out one of my meals. I had a stick with a piece of string and I went through the motions of fishing. 'Are they biting, Papillon?' asked the chief warder. 'Not likely. Because whenever I go fishing there's a little fish that follows me everywhere, and when it sees a big one just going to bite it says, "Watch out, don't bite – it's Papillon who's fishing." That's why I never catch any. But still, I go on. Maybe one day there'll be a fish that doesn't believe it.'

I heard the screw say to an orderly, 'Well, he's right round the bend.'

When I ate at the big table in the dining-hall, I never could manage to get my dish of lentils down. There was a gigantic creature well over six feet tall, with arms, legs and trunk as hairy as an ape, who had picked on me as his victim. He always sat down next to me. The lentils were served very hot, so you had to wait for them to cool before you could eat them. I'd take my wooden spoon, and by blowing on them I'd manage to swallow a few. As for Ivanhoe (he thought he was Ivanhoe), he'd take his bowl, make a funnel of his hands and gulp the whole lot down in one go. Then he'd take mine without so much as by your leave and do the same. When he'd licked it clean he'd bang it down in front of me and stare at me with his huge bloodshot eyes as though to say, 'There. You see how I eat lentils?' I was beginning to have had quite enough of Ivanhoe, and as I was not yet certified I made up my mind to use him as a pretext for something spectacular. It was lentil day again. Ivanhoe was right there. He sat down next to me. His mad face was beaming with delight – he already felt the ecstasy of scoffing down his own lentils and mine too. I pulled a big, full, heavy earthenware water-jug towards me. The giant had scarcely raised my bowl and begun to pour my lentils down his throat before I stood up and broke the jug over his head with all my strength. He went down with an animal cry. Instantly all the other lunatics set upon one another, armed with their dishes. There was an appalling uproar and throughout the whole scene every one of these characters kept roaring and howling.

I was back in my cell, carried like a lump by four burly orderlies, who moved fast and without tenderness. I bawled out like a maniac, saying Ivanhoe had stolen my wallet and identity-card. That did the trick. The doctor decided to certify me as irresponsible for my actions. All the screws agreed that I was a quiet looney, but with very dangerous moments. Ivanhoe had a splendid bandage on his head: it seems I'd given him a three-inch wound. Fortunately he did not exercise at the same time as me.

I was able to have a talk with Salvidia. He already had a copy of the key of the dispensary, where the barrels were kept.

He was trying to get hold of enough wire to fasten them together. I told him I was afraid wire might break with the straining of the barrels in the sea and that it would be better to use rope, as having more give. He was going to try to get it, so we'd have both rope and wire. He also had three keys to make – one for my cell, one for the passage leading to it, and one for the main gate of the asylum. There were very few patrols. Only one warder for every four-hour guard duty – from nine to one in the morning and from one to five. There were two screws who always slept right through their guard and never made any rounds – they relied on a convict orderly who went on duty with them. So everything was in train, and now it was only a matter of waiting. I had another month at the most to endure.

As I walked into the yard the head warder gave me a cigar – a very poor cigar – already lit. But poor or not, it seemed marvellous to me. I looked at this herd of mother-naked men, singing, weeping, mopping and mowing, talking to themselves. They were still all wet from the shower each one had to take before being allowed into the yard, and their poor bodies showed the marks of the blows they had received or that they had given themselves, and the marks of the too tightly laced strait-jackets. This was indeed the end of the way down the drain. How many of these lunatics had been judged responsible for their actions by psychiatrists in France?

Titin – that was his nickname – belonged to my 1933 convoy. He had killed a man in Marseilles, then he had taken a taxi, loaded his victim into it and had himself driven to the hospital: there he said, 'Here, see to this man: I believe he's ill.' He was arrested on the spot, and the jury had the nerve to say he hadn't the very least degree of irresponsibility. And yet he must already have been crazy to have done a thing like that. Ordinarily speaking, the very dimmest of minds would have known he was going to be grabbed right away. Titin was here, sitting next to me. He had chronic dysentery – a walking corpse. He said, 'There are little monkeys in my guts, you know, Papillon. Some of them are wicked and they bite when they're angry – that's why I shit blood. The others are the furry sort, covered with hair, and their hands are as soft as down. They stroke me gently and they stop the wicked ones biting. When the good monkeys stand up for me, why, then I don't shit blood.'

'Do you remember Marseilles, Titin?'

'I most certainly do. Indeed, I remember it very well. The Place de la Bourse with the ponces and the strong-arm gangs . . .'

'Do you remember any of their names? L'Ange le Lucre? Le Gravat? Clément?'

'No, I don't remember names: just a bastard of a cabby who took me to the hospital with my sick friend and then said it was because of me he was sick. That's all.'

'What about your friends?'

'Don't know.'

Poor Titin: I gave him the end of my cigar and got up. My heart was filled with an immense pity for this poor soul who would certainly die there like a dog. Yes, it was very dangerous living among all these lunatics, but what could I do about it? In any case, as far as I could see it was the only way of preparing a break without the risk of a death sentence.

Salvidia was almost ready. He had two of the keys and he only lacked the one for my cell. He had also got hold of a length of very good rope, and what's more he'd made another out of strips of hammock canvas – a five-way plait, he told me. Everything was going well as far as that was concerned.

I was in a hurry to get moving, for it was really tough, holding out in the asylum and keeping up this act. To have the right to stay in the part of the asylum where my cell was, I had to break out and be violent every now and then.

Once I had such a convincing fit that the medical warders put me into a very hot bath with two bromide injections. There was a very strong canvas cover over it, so I couldn't get out. All that could be seen was my head, poking up through a hole. I'd been in the bath, held down by this sort of strait-waistcoat, for a couple of hours when Ivanhoe walked in. I was terrified by the way the great brute looked at me. I had a horrible dread that he was going to strangle me. I couldn't defend myself in any way, because my arms were underneath the canvas.

He came up to me and his big eyes looked attentively into my face: he looked as though he were trying to make out where he'd seen this head before – this head that now emerged from the cloth as from a frame. He breathed all over me, and his breath stank of decay. I felt like shouting for help, but I was afraid that calling out might make him madder. I closed my eyes and waited, sure that he was just about to strangle

418

me with his enormous lumpish hands. I shan't forget those moments of terror in a hurry. At last he moved off, walked about the room and then went up to the little wheels that controlled the water. He turned off the cold and turned the hot, the boiling hot, full on. I howled and shrieked like a lost soul, for I was being literally boiled. Ivanhoe disappeared. The whole room was full of steam: I choked as I breathed and I made superhuman efforts to tear off the wretched canvas, but in vain. At last help arrived. The screws had seen the steam coming out of the windows. When they took me out of my cauldron I was horribly burnt and I was in the most hellish pain. It was particularly my thighs and my private parts, which had lost all their skin. They dressed my burns with picric acid and put me into the asylum's little infirmary. The burns were so bad they called the doctor. A few injections of morphia helped me through the first twenty-four hours. When the medico asked me what had happened, I told him a volcano had erupted in the bath. No one could make it out. The medical warder accused the character who'd run the bath of having misused the taps.

Salvidia came and treated my burns with picric acid ointment. He was ready, and he pointed out that it was lucky I was in the infirmary, because if the break were to fail we could get back into this part of the asylum without being seen. He was going to make a copy of the infirmary key right away – he'd already taken a print on a piece of soap and he would have the finished job tomorrow. It was up to me to let him know the day I felt well enough to take advantage of the sleeping screws being on guard.

It was for tonight, during the watch that lasted from one o'clock till five in the morning. Salvidia wasn't on duty. To gain time, he was going to empty the vinegar barrel about eleven o'clock. We'd roll the oil barrel down full, because the sea was very rough and perhaps the oil would help us calm it for the launch.

I had flour sack trousers cut off at the knee, a woollen sweater and a good knife in my belt. I also had a waterproof bag that I was going to hang round my neck – it held cigarettes and a tinder lighter. Salvidia had made a waterproof knapsack full of manioc flour that he had soaked in oil and sugar. About seven pounds, he told me. It was late. I sat there on my bed waiting for my friend. My heart was thumping hard. In a few minutes the break was going to begin. May good luck and almighty God be on my side, so that I may escape from the road down the drain and leave it for good and all!

It was strange, but my thoughts only touched on the past but faintly, glancing towards my father and my family. Not a single picture of the assizes, the jury or the prosecuting counsel. But just as the door opened, in spite of myself I once more had a vision of Matthieu standing there, carried along the surface of the sea by the sharks.

'Papi, let's go!' I followed him. Quickly he closed the door and hid the key in a corner of the passage. 'Quick, quick.' We reached the dispensary: the door was open. Getting the empty barrel out was child's play. He slung the ropes over his shoulder and I took the wire and the knapsack with flour in it. In the pitch dark night I started rolling my barrel down towards the sea. He came behind, with the oil barrel. Fortunately he was very strong and it was quite easy for him to keep it from plunging down the steep descent.

'Slowly, slowly, take care it doesn't run away with you.' I waited for him, in case he should lose his hold on the barrel – if he did, I could block its run with mine. I went down backwards, me in front and my barrel behind. We reached the bottom of the path without any sort of difficulty. There was a little path in the direction of the sea, but after that it was very hard going over the rocks.

'Empty the barrel: we'll never get across with it full.' There was a stiff wind blowing and the waves were crashing furiously against the rocks. Fine, the barrel was empty. 'Ram the bung in hard. Wait a minute: put this bit of tin over it.' The holes were already made. 'Drive the nails right home.' The hammering would never be heard over the roaring of the wind and sea.

We lashed the two barrels tight together; but carrying them over the rocks was very difficult. Each of them was made to hold fifty gallons: they took up a lot of space and they were very awkward to handle. The place my friend had chosen for the launching made things no easier, either. 'Shove, for God's sake! Up a bit. Look out for the wave!' Both of us and the two barrels were picked up and flung hard back on to the rock. 'Take care. They'll smash, to say nothing of us breaking an arm or a leg!'

'Take it easy, Salvidia. Either go in front, towards the sea, or stand here behind. That's right. Heave the moment I give a shout. I'll shove at the same second and then we'll certainly get free of the rocks. But to do it, we've just got to hold tight and stay where we are, even if the sea breaks right over us.'

I shouted these orders to my friend in the midst of the thunder of the wind and the waves, and I think he heard them: a big wave swept completely over us as we clung to the barrels. At this moment I shoved madly on the raft with all my strength. And he must certainly have done the same, because all at once there we were afloat, away from the rocks. He was up on the barrels before me, but just as I handed myself on, a huge breaker heaved up beneath us and tossed us like a feather on to a pointed rock farther out at sea. The impact was so shattering that the barrels smashed open, scattering in fragments. When the wave drew back it swept me more than twenty yards from the rock. I swam and let myself be carried in by the next wave that ran straight for the shore. I landed in a sitting position between two rocks. I just had time to cling on before being swept away. Bruised all over, I managed to scramble out; but when I reached dry land, I realized that I'd been carried more than a hundred yards from the place where we'd launched the raft.

Taking no sort of care I shouted, 'Salvidia! Romeo! Where are you?' There was no answer. Quite overwhelmed I lay down on the path: I took off my sweater and my trousers, and there I was again, naked, wearing just my slippers. Christ, where was my friend? And once again I shouted with all my strength, 'Where are you?' Only the wind, the sea and the waves replied. I stayed there I don't know how long, numbed, completely shattered, mentally and physically. Then, weeping with fury, I threw away the little bag I had round my neck for my tobacco and lighter – a mark of my friend's real affection, for he himself was no smoker.

Standing there facing the wind and the huge waves that had swept everything away, I raised my clenched fist and insulted God. 'You swine, You filthy bugger, aren't You ashamed of persecuting me like this? You're supposed to be a good God, aren't You? You're a disgusting brute, that's all. A sadist, a bloody sadist! A perverted sod! I'll never utter Your name again. You don't deserve it.'

The wind had dropped, and the seeming calm did me good – brought me back to a sense of reality. I'd go back to the asylum, and if I could I'd get back into the infirmary. With a little luck, it should be possible.

I climbed the hill with just one idea in my head – getting back and lying down in my bed. Neither seen nor heard. I got into the infirmary passage with no difficulty. I'd had to climb the asylum wall, because I didn't know where Salvidia had put the key of the main gate.

I didn't have to look long before I found the infirmary key. I went in and double-locked the door behind me. I went to the window and threw the key far out – it fell the other side of the wall. And I went to bed. The only thing that could give me away was the fact that my slippers were soaked. I got up and wrung them out in the lavatory. Gradually, with the sheet over my face, I began to get warm again. The wind and the salt water had chilled me through and through. Had my friend really been drowned? Perhaps he had been swept much farther out than me and had been able to get ashore at the far end of the island. Hadn't I gone away from the rocks too soon? I ought to have waited a little longer. I blamed myself for having given in too quickly – for having given up my friend for lost.

In the drawer of the bedside table there were two sleeping pills. I swallowed them without water. My saliva was enough to get them down.

I was still asleep when the warder shook me awake. The room was full of light and the window was open. Three patients were looking in from outside. 'What's the matter, Papillon? You're sleeping like one of the dead. Haven't you drunk your coffee? It's cold. Here, drink it up.'

I was scarcely awake, but even so I grasped that as far as I was concerned everything was normal. 'What have you woken me up for?'

'Because now your burns are better your bed is wanted. You're going back to your cell.'

'OK, Chief.' And I followed him. On the way he left me in the yard. I took advantage of this to dry my slippers in the sun.

It was three days now since the failure of the break. I had heard not the least reference to it. I went to and fro from my cell to the yard and then from the yard back to my cell. Salvidia did not turn up again: so the poor fellow was dead, no doubt smashed against the rocks. I myself had had a narrow escape, and the reason I came out alive was certainly because I was behind rather than in front. But who could tell? I'd have to get out of the asylum. It was going to be harder to get them to believe I was cured, or at least fit to go back to the camp, than it had been to get inside in the first place. I'd now have to persuade the doctor that I was better.

'Monsieur Rouviot (he was the chief attendant), I'm cold at night. If I promise not to dirty my clothes, would you please let me have trousers and a shirt?' The screw was amazed. He stared at me with wide open eyes for a while, and then he said, 'Sit down here by me, Papillon. Tell me what's going on.'

'I'm surprised to find myself here, Chief. It's the asylum, isn't it? And so I'm in with the loonies. Did I somehow come adrift from my senses? Why am I here? It would be kind of you to tell me, Chief.'

'Poor old Papillon, you've been ill: but now it looks to me as though you're getting better. Would you like to work?'

'Yes.'

'What would you like to do?'

'Anything.'

So I was given clothes and I helped clean out the cells. In the evening my door was left open until nine, and it was only when the night screw came on duty that they shut me in.

The other day a man from the Auvergne, a convict orderly, spoke to me for the first time. We were alone in the guardroom. The screw hadn't come yet. I didn't know this guy, but he said he knew me quite well. 'It's not worth going on with the act, mate,' he said.

'What do you mean?'

'What do I mean? You don't imagine it took me in, do you? I've been looking after lunatics for seven years and from the very first week I saw that you were swinging the lead.'

'So what?'

'I'll tell you what. I'm really sorry you didn't bring off your break with Salvidia. It cost him his life. I honestly regret him, because he was a good friend of mine, although he didn't let me in on it. But I don't hold that against him. If you need anything at all, just let me know – I'll be happy.'

There was such an open look in his eye that I was sure he was straight. And although I'd never heard anybody say any good of him, I'd never heard any bad either: so he was certainly a good guy.

Poor Salvidia! There must have been a hell of a turmoil when they discovered he was gone. Pieces of barrel were found along the shore. They were certain he'd been eaten by the sharks. The medico shrieked and howled about the wasted olive oil. He said that with the war on they weren't ever likely to see another drop.

'What do you advise me to do?'

'I'll put you on the fatigue that goes out of the asylum every day and fetches the stores from the hospital. That'll make a walk for you. Start behaving properly. Out of ten things you say, let eight of them be sensible. Because you mustn't get better too quickly, either.'

'Thanks. What's your name?'

'Dupont.'

'Thanks. I shan't forget your advice.'

It was nearly a month now since I'd mucked up that break. Six days after it they had found my friend's body floating. By some extraordinary chance the sharks had not eaten him. But it seems that other fishes had had all his entrails and part of one leg, or so Dupont told me. His skull had been bashed in. He was so far gone there was no post-mortem. I asked Dupont whether he could get a letter out by the post for me. It would have to be given to Galgani for him to slip it in just as the mail sack was being sealed. I wrote to Romeo Salvidia's mother in Italy.

'Madame, your son died without chains on his legs. He died bravely at sea, far from warders and from prison. He died free, struggling courageously to gain his liberty. We each promised the other to write to his family in case anything happened to either of us. I am doing this painful duty, and I kiss your hands as a son would do.

Papillon, your boy's friend.'

Once this duty was done, I determined never to think of that nightmare any more. That was what life was like. What I had to do now was to get out of the asylum, have myself sent to Devil's Island whatever the cost, and try another break. The screw gave me the job of looking after his garden. I'd been well for two months now and my work was so much appreciated that the bloody fool of a warder wouldn't let me go. The Auvergnat told me that after the last examination the doctor had wanted to let me out of the asylum and put me into the camp for a probationary period. The screw was dead against the idea, saying his garden had never been so carefully looked after.

So this morning I pulled up all the strawberry plants and tossed them on to the rubbish-heap. Where each had been, I stuck a little cross: one cross for each plant. Uproar and hullab-alloo! The great lump of a screw very nearly burst with indignation. He frothed, and it choked him as he tried to speak – the sounds wouldn't come out properly. In the end he sat down on the wheel-barrow and shed real tears. I had exaggerated a little: but then what else could I do?

The doctor didn't take such a serious view. 'This patient must be sent to the camp for a probationary period, so as to readapt himself to ordinary life,' he insisted. 'It was because he was all alone in the garden that this crazy notion came into his head. Tell me, Papillon, why did you pull up the straw-berries and put crosses in their places?'

'I can't explain, Doctor, and I beg the warder's pardon. He was so fond of those strawberries that I'm really very much upset. I'll ask God to send him some more.'

Here I was back in the camp with my friends again. Carbon-ieri's place was empty: I slung my hammock next to the empty space, just as though Matthieu were still there.

The doctor made me sew a label on my blouse saying 'under special treatment'. Nobody but the doctor was allowed to give me orders. He told me I was to sweep up the leaves in front of the hospital from eight until ten in the morning. I had coffee and cigarettes sitting with the doctor in front of his house. His wife was there too, and she helped him to get me to talk about my past. 'And what happened then, Papillon? What was it like after you left the pearl-diving Indians?' I spent the whole afternoon with those wonderful people. 'Come and see me every day, Papillon,' said the doctor's wife. 'In the first place I want to see you and then I also want to hear about your experiences.'

Every day I spent some hours with the doctor and his wife, and sometimes with his wife alone. They thought that if they made me talk about my past life, it would help to steady my mind for good and all. I decided to ask the doc to have me sent to Devil's Island.

It was done: I was to leave the next day. The doctor and

his wife knew why I was going to Devil's Island. They'd been so good to me I hadn't wanted to deceive them. 'Doc, I just can't stand penal any longer: have me sent to Devil's Island so I can either make a break or perish in the attempt. It's got to end somehow.'

'I know what you mean, Papillon. This system of repression makes me feel sick, and the service is rotten through and through. So good-bye and good luck!'

Dreyfus's Seat

This was the smallest of the three Iles du Salut. The most northerly, too, and the most directly in the path of the wind and the waves. First there was a narrow strip that ran right round the island at sea level, and then the ground rose steeply to a little plain with the warders' guard-house and a single block for the convicts – about ten of them. Convicts sentenced for common-law offences were not officially supposed to be sent to Devil's Island; it was reserved for political offenders, each of whom lived in his own little house with a corrugated-iron roof. On Mondays they were given their rations for the week, uncooked, and every day a loaf of bread. There were perhaps thirty of them. The medical attendant was Dr. Léger, who had poisoned his whole family in Lyons or thereabouts. The political prisoners would have nothing to do with the convicts and sometimes they would write to Cayenne, complaining about some transportee or other. When that happened he'd be taken away and sent back to Royale.

There was a cable, a wire rope, between Royale and Devil's Island, because quite often the sea was too rough for the boat from Royale to come over to the little concrete landing-stage.

The chief warder of the camp (there were three warders) was called Santori. He was a filthy great brute and he often had a week's beard on his face. 'Papillon, I hope you'll behave well on Devil's Island. If you don't get in my hair then I'll leave you in peace. Go on up to the camp. I'll see you again there.'

In the hall I found six convicts – two Chinese, two Negroes, a guy from Bordeaux and another from Lille. One of the Chinese knew me well: he'd been in Saint-Laurent with me, under investigation for a killing. He was an Indo-Chinese, one of the survivors of the mutiny at Pulo-Condor, a penal settlement in those parts. He was a pirate by trade, and he used to attack sampans, sometimes killing the whole crew and their families. He was exceedingly dangerous, but he was such a good member of our community that I liked and trusted him.

'OK, Papillon?'

'OK. And how are you, Chang?'

'Fine. It's good here. You eat along of me. You sleep there, along of me. Me cook twice a day. Papillon catch fish. Here plenty fish.'

Santori appeared. 'Oh, you've settled in already? Tomorrow morning you'll go with Chang and feed the pigs. He'll bring the coconuts and you'll chop them in two. You have to put the small, soft nuts on one side for the little pigs that have no teeth. At four in the afternoon, the same again. Apart from those two hours, one in the morning and one in the afternoon, you're free to do what you like on the island. Every man who goes fishing has to bring my cook two pounds of fish every day, or else some langoustines. Then everybody's pleased. Right?'

'Yes, Monsieur Santori.'

'I know you're a man who loves a break, but I shan't worry, because it's impossible from here. You're shut in at night, but I know very well there are some who get out. Take care of the political prisoners. They've all got jungle knives. If you go anywhere near their houses they think you're coming to steal chickens or eggs. So you may get yourself killed or wounded, because they can see you whereas you can't see them.'

When I'd fed more than two hundred pigs I wandered over the island all day long, together with Chang, who knew it inside out. On the road down by the sea we met an old man with a long white beard. He was a journalist from New Caledonia who'd written against France and in favour of the Germans during the 1914 war. I also saw the sod who'd had Edith Cavell shot, the English or Belgian nurse who'd saved the English airmen in 1915. This character was a big fat brute, and he was battering a huge moray-eel, five feet long and as thick as my thigh, with a stick.

The medical orderly also lived in one of those little houses that were supposed to be for political prisoners only. Dr. Léger was a tall, powerful, dirty man. His face, topped by long greying hair that hung down over his ears and neck, was the only clean part about him. His hands were covered with half-healed wounds that he must have got clinging to the sharp rocks in the sea.

'If you need anything, come and I'll give it you. Don't come unless you're ill. I don't like visitors and I like chat even less. I sell eggs and sometimes a hen or a chicken. If you ever secretly kill a young pig, bring me a ham and I'll give you a chicken and six eggs. Since you're here, take this bottle of a hundred and twenty quinine tablets. You've certainly come with the idea of escaping, and in the extraordinarily unlikely case of your bringing it off, you'll need them in the bush.'

Both morning and evening I caught wonderful quantities of red mullet. I sent the warders' mess eight or nine pounds every day. Santori was delighted: he'd never been given so many langoustines and different kinds of fish. Sometimes I got as many as three hundred langoustines, diving at low water.

Dr. Germain Guibert came to Devil's Island yesterday. As the sea was calm he came with the governor of Royale and Madame Guibert. That terrific person was the first woman to set foot on Devil's Island. According to the governor, no civilian had ever landed there at all, I was able to talk to her for more than an hour. I took her to the bench where Dreyfus used to sit, looking out to sea, towards the France that had rejected him.

'If this polished stone could tell us Dreyfus's thoughts . . .' she said, stroking its surface. 'Papillon, this is certainly the last time we shall ever see one another, since you tell me you're going to try a break quite soon. I'll pray for your success. And before you go, I ask you to come and sit on this bench I'm now touching – sit here for a moment and stroke it yourself to say good-bye.'

The governor gave me permission to send the doctor langoustines and fish by the wire rope whenever I wanted to. Santori agreed.

'Good-bye, Doc; good-bye, Madame.' I waved as naturally as possible before their boat drew away from the landing stage. Madame Guibert gazed steadily at me, as though to say, 'Remember us always: and we shall not forget you, either.'

Dreyfus's seat was on the northern tip of the island, a hundred and fifty feet above the sea.

I didn't go fishing today. In a natural reservoir I had more than two hundred pounds of mullet and more than five hundred langoustines in an iron drum fastened by a chain. So I could afford to neglect my fishing. I had enough for the doc, for Santori, and for the Chinese and myself.

This was 1941 and I'd been in prison eleven years. I was thirty-five. I'd spent the best years of my life either in a cell or in a black-hole. I'd only had seven months of total freedom with my Indian tribe. The children my Indian wives must have had by me would be eight years old now. How terrible! How quickly the time had flashed by! But a backward glance showed all these hours and minutes studding my calvary as terribly long, and each one of them hard to bear.

Thirty-five! Where was Montmartre, the Place Blanche, Pigalle, the Petit Jardin dance-hall, the Boulevard de Clichy? Where was Nénette, with her Madonna's face – a perfect cameo? Nénette at the assizes, her great despairing black eyes fixed on me, shouting, 'Don't worry, sweetheart. I'll come out there and find you!' Where was Raymond Hubert and his 'We shall be acquitted'? Where were the twelve bastards of the jury? And the cops? And the prosecuting counsel? What were my father and my sisters' families doing under the German yoke?

All those breaks! Let's see. Just how many of them were there?

The first, when I got away from the hospital, having knocked out the screws.

The second from Rio Hacha, in Colombia. That was the finest. That time I succeeded completely. Why did I ever leave my tribe? A thrill passed through me: it was as though I could still feel myself making love with those two Indian sisters.

Then the third, fourth, fifth and sixth at Baranquilla. What bad luck I had in all those breaks! The rising in the chapel, which failed so dismally. The dynamite that wasn't strong enough: and then Clousiot hooking up his trousers. And the sleeping-draught working so slowly.

The seventh on Royale, where that sod Bébert Celier informed on me. Without him that one would have succeeded for sure. If he'd kept his mouth shut, I'd now be free with my poor friend Carbonieri.

The eighth, the last, from the asylum. A mistake, a very bad mistake on my part. Letting the Italian choose the place for launching. Two hundred yards farther down towards the slaughter-house it would certainly have been easier to get the raft out to sea.

This bench, where the innocent and yet condemned Dreyfus had found the strength to go on living in spite of everything, must be an example to me. It must teach me not to give in. To try another break. Yes, this smooth, polished stone, high over the rocky chasm where the incessant waves came thundering in, must give me strength. Dreyfus never let himself be discouraged, and he fought for his rehabilitation right through to the very end. It's true he had Zola and his famous *J'accuse* to help him. Still, if he hadn't been a man of real courage so much injustice would certainly have made him throw himself over the precipice from this same bench. He stuck it out. I couldn't do less; and I must give up the idea of a fresh death-or-glory break. It was the word death I was to give up; I must think of nothing but how I was going to win and be free.

During the long hours I spent sitting on Dreyfus's seat my mind wandered, dreaming of the past and building up a rosy future. I was often dazzled by the powerful light and by the silvery gleam of the waves. I gazed at this sea so long without really seeing it that I came to know every possible turn and eddy of the wind-driven waves. The tireless, inexorable sea threw itself upon the outermost rocks of the island. It searched and stripped them, as though it were saying to Devil's Island, 'Get out. You've got to go. You're in my way as I run in towards the mainland – you bar my path. That's why I'm breaking off little bits of you every single day, never letting up.' When there was a storm the sea really let itself go, and not only did it rush in and sweep away everything it could destroy as it withdrew, but it also thrust water into every nook and cranny so as gradually to undermine those enormous rocks that seemed to say, 'No one gets past me.'

It was then that I made an important discovery. Immediately below Dreyfus's seat the waves came in, broke against some huge hump-backed rocks and rushed furiously back. The tons of water they brought in could not spread, because they were hemmed in by two rocks forming a horseshoe fifteen to twenty feet across. Beyond that rose the cliff, so the water could only get out by going back into the sea.

This was very important, for if I were to throw myself into

431

the sea with a sack of coconuts, plunging into the wave the moment it broke and flooded the horseshoe, it would, without a shadow of doubt, take me with it as it withdrew.

I knew where I could get several jute sacks, because you could have as many as you liked at the pig-house when you wanted to gather coconuts.

The first thing was to have a trial run. The tides were highest and the waves were strongest at the full moon. I should wait till then. I hid a well-sewn sack, filled with coconuts, in a kind of grotto you could only get into by diving. I had come across it one day when I was diving for langoustines. They clung to the ceiling of the cave – air got into it only at low tide. In another sack that I tied to the one with the coconuts, I put a rock weighing five or six stone. As I meant to go off with two sacks instead of one and as I weighed eleven stone, everything was in proportion.

I was very excited by this experiment. This side of the island was completely safe – no one would ever imagine a man would choose the most exposed and therefore the most dangerous place for getting away. Yet it was the only place from which – always providing I could get away from the shore – I would be swept out to the open sea, so that it would be impossible for me to be driven on to Royale. It was from that point therefore and no other that I must set off.

The sack with the nuts and the other with the rock were too heavy to carry easily. I could not manage to haul them over the slippery rocks, always wet from the breaking waves. I'd spoken to Chang and he was going to help me. He brought along a whole mass of fishing things – deep-sea tackle and so on – so that if anyone came upon us suddenly we could say we were laying out lines to catch sharks.

'Shove, Chang, A little more and it's there.' The full moon lit up the scene as though it were daylight. I was deafened by the roar of the breaking waves. 'Are you ready, Papillon?' asked Chang. 'Throw it into this one.' A curling fifteen-foot wave hurled itself furiously against the rock: it broke beneath us, but the impact was so violent that its crest passed over the rock, soaking us from head to foot. That didn't prevent us from flinging the sack in the very moment the water stood at its highest before the back-draught. The sack, swept away like a straw, was carried on to sea.

'We've done it, Chang! How terrific!'

'Wait: see if him come back.'

To my horror, scarcely five minutes later, I saw my sack driving in on the top of a huge roller, twenty-five or thirty feet high – a roller that carried the coconut sack and the stone as though they weighed nothing at all, bearing it along a little in front of the foam on the crest and flinging it with unbelievable force against the rock a little to the left of the place it had started from. The sack burst, the coconuts scattered, and the stone rolled down to the bottom of the chasm.

Soaked through and through (for the waves had broken over us and very nearly swept us off our feet – though fortunately in the landward direction), scraped and battered, Chang and I scrambled away from the accursed spot without a backward glance.

'Not good, Papillon. Not good, this idea of break from Devil. Royale, him better. From south side Royale you go better than from here.'

'Yes, but on Royale the escape would be discovered within two hours. As there's nothing but the push of the waves to get the sack along, the three boats on the island could hem me in. Whereas here to begin with there's no boat: and then I'm sure of having the whole night in front of me before they find out I've made a break: and lastly they may very well think I've been drowned fishing. There's no telephone on Devil's Island. If I set off in a heavy sea, there's no boat that can land here. So it's from Devil's Island that I must go. But how?'

The sun blazed down at noon. A tropical sun that made your brains feel they were boiling inside your skull. A sun that shrivelled every plant that hadn't had time to grow big enough to stand it. A sun that dried out the shallow pools of sea-water in a few hours, leaving a white film of salt. A sun that made the air dance and tremble. Yes, the air literally jigged about in front of my eyes; and the reflected blaze from the sea dazzled me. Yet there I was on Dreyfus's seat once more, and none of these things could prevent me from studying the sea. And it was then that I suddenly realized what a bloody fool I had been all this time. The great roller, twice as high as the other waves, that had flung my sack back against the rocks, shattering it – this roller only came once in every seven waves.

From noon until sunset I watched to see if this always

433

happened, to see if there was no sudden change and therefore an alteration in the rhythm and the shape of this huge seventh wave.

No. Not once did the great roller come before its turn or after. Six twenty-footers, and then, taking shape more than three hundred yards out, the big fellow. It drove absolutely straight in. The nearer it came, the bigger and taller it grew. Unlike the six others, it had almost no foam on its crest. Indeed very little. It had a sound all of its own, like thunder dying away in the distance. When it broke on the two rocks and rushed into the passage between them to reach the cliff, the quantity of water was so much greater than in the others that it was smothered – it swirled round and round the hollow and it took ten or fifteen seconds before these eddies, these whirlpools, could escape: and when they did so they carried boulders with them, great rocks that went round and round with such a rumbling noise that you would have said it was hundreds of cartloads of stone all being unloaded at once.

I put ten coconuts into the same sack, stuffed in a forty-pound stone, and tossed the whole lot into the great roller the moment it broke.

There was so much white spray I couldn't follow its movements, but I did catch a glimpse of the sack as the water was sucked furiously back into the sea. The sack did not return. The six following waves were not strong enough to throw it on to the shore, and when the seventh formed some three hundred yards out, the sack must already have been beyond that zone, for I never saw it again.

I walked back to the camp, filled with hope and joy. I'd done it! I'd found the perfect way of launching. No mere luck about this one. Still, I'd have a more serious try-out with exactly the same weights as for the real break – two well-joined sacks of coconuts with two or three stones amounting to a hundred and fifty pounds altogether on top of them. I told my mate Chang. This Pulo-Condor Chink listened to what I had to say with all his ears.

'Good, good, Papillon. I think you find him out. Me help with real trial. Wait for very high tide – twenty-five foot tide. Him come soon equinox.'

Chang and I took advantage of the twenty-five-foot equinoctial spring tide to throw two sacks of nuts and three stones weighing about a hundred and seventy-five pounds into this splendid seventh wave of mine.

'What you call 'um, little girl you swim for at Saint-Joseph?'

'Lisette.'

'We call 'um wave that carry you off one day Lisette. Right?'

'Right.'

Lisette came in with the noise of an express running into a station. She had formed two hundred and fifty yards out, and as upright as a cliff she rode in, growing bigger every moment. It was really most impressive. She broke with such force that Chang and I were washed off the rock and the weighted sacks fell into the chasm all by themselves. In the last tenth of a second we had realized there was no holding on to the rock and we had flung ourselves back: that had prevented us from being washed over the edge, but it had not saved us from being thoroughly soaked. It was ten in the morning when we made this experiment. There was no danger, because the three screws were busy stock-taking the other end of the island. The sack was swept out: we could see it clearly, far away from the shore. Had it been borne away beyond the place where the waves were formed? There was no fixed mark by which we could tell whether it was on the far side or not. The six waves that followed Lisette did not manage to get hold of it in their run. Once again Lisette reared up and drove in; and she did not bring the sacks with her either. So they must have gone beyond the zone where waves could have an effect upon them.

We hurried up to Dreyfus's bench to try to catch sight of the sacks again, and on four different occasions we had the delight of seeing them a great way off, bobbing on the top of waves that were not coming in towards Devil's Island but rather driving westward. The experiment was an undoubted success. I should set off on my great adventure riding on Lisette's back.

'Here she comes, look! One, two, three, four, five, six . . .' and here was Lisette.

The sea was always rough on the headland where Dreyfus had had his bench, but on that particular day it was in an uncommonly bad temper. Lisette came in with her usual roar. It seemed to me that she was bigger than usual, and that at the base of the wave even more water was rushing along. This vast mass struck the two rocks harder and straighter than ever; and when the wave broke in the space between them, the crash was even more deafening than before.

'And that's the place where you say we have to chuck ourselves in? Well, what a sweet choice you've made to be sure. I wouldn't touch it with a barge-pole. I'm quite willing to go off on a break, yes: but plain suicide, no thank you very much!' Sylvain was much impressed by the way I'd just described Lisette. He'd been on Devil's Island these last three days, and of course I'd suggested that we should go off together. Each on a raft. In that way, if he agreed, I should have a companion on the mainland to make another break with. All alone in the bush was no sort of fun.

'Don't let it get you down before you've thought it over. Certainly the first idea of it would startle anyone; but it's the only wave that can sweep you out so far that the others won't drive you on to the rocks again.'

'No worry,' said Chang. 'We've tried. Once you off, you never come back to Devil for sure, nor touch on Royale.'

It took me a week to persuade Sylvain. He was solid bone and muscle, five foot eleven, with a very well-proportioned athletic body.

'All right. I agree we'll be swept out far enough. But after that, how long do you think it would take for the tides to carry us to the mainland?'

'To be honest, Sylvain, I don't know. It might be longer or shorter: it would all depend on the weather. The wind wouldn't have much hold on us, because we'd be too low down in the water. But if the weather's bad, the waves will be higher and they'll drive us in towards the forest all the faster. In seven, eight, or ten tides at the most, we ought to be thrown up on the shore. So, counting slack water and all, it should be something like forty-eight or sixty hours.'

'How do you work that out?'

'From the islands to the coast in a straight line, it's not more than twenty-five miles. Drifting, you'd be following the hypotenuse of a right-angled triangle. Look at the direction of the waves. Roughly speaking, you'd have to travel between seventy-five or at the outside a hundred miles. The nearer we get to the coast, the more the waves carry us straight in. And then, isn't it obvious that at this distance from the shore a piece of driftwood must travel at least three miles an hour?'

He looked and listened very attentively: he was a bright boy, all right. 'No, I admit you're not talking balls, and if it weren't for the low tides losing us time by taking us out to sea, we'd certainly be on the coast in under thirty hours. But counting the ebbs, I think you're about right – we'll be there in forty-eight to sixty hours.'

'You're convinced, then? You'll come with me?'

'Almost convinced. Suppose we were in the bush on the mainland. What should we do then?'

'We'd have to get to the outskirts of Kourou. There's a fair-sized fishing village there and men who go out after wild rubber and gold. We'd have to take care when we get close, because there's also a convicts' logging-camp. There'll certainly be forest tracks leading to Cayenne or the Chinese camp called Inini. We'll have to hold up a convict or a black civilian and make him take us to Inini. If the character behaves well, we'll give him five hundred francs and then he can bugger off. If it's a convict, we'll make him join our break.'

'What do we want to go to Inini for? It's a special camp for Indo-Chinese.'

'Chang's brother is there.'

'Yes, my brother him there. Him go off on break with you: him find boat and food for sure. You meet Cuic-Cuic and you have everything for break. Chinese man never inform. So you find any Annamite in bush, you speak him, him tell Cuic-Cuic.'

'Why do they call your brother Cuic-Cuic?' asked Sylvain.

'Don't know. It was Frenchman call him Cuic-Cuic.' He went on, 'Take care. When you nearly reach mainland, you find mud. Never you walk on him: mud bad, mud suck you. Wait for next tide, float you into bush – catch creeper, tree-branch, pull. Otherwise you fucked.'

'That's right, Sylvain. Never walk on the mud even if you're very, very close in. You have to wait until you can grab hold of branches or creepers.'

'OK, Papillon, I've made up my mind to come.'

'We'll make the two rafts almost exactly the same, since we are both about the same weight – that will prevent us from drifting far apart. But there's no telling. In case we lose touch, how shall we find one another again? You can't see Kourou

437

from here, but when you were on Royale did you notice some white rocks about ten miles to the right of Kourou? You can see them clearly when the sun strikes them.'

'Yes.'

'Those are the only rocks anywhere along the coast. Stretching out for ever, right and left, it's just mud. The white on the rocks is birds' shit. There are thousands of them, and since nobody ever goes there, that will be a perfect place for us to recover before plunging into the bush. We'll eat eggs and the coconuts that we'll take with us. No fire. The first to get there will wait for the other.'

'How many days?'

'Five. It's impossible that the other shouldn't be at the meeting-place in five days.'

The two rafts were ready. We'd lined the sacks so they should be stronger. I asked Sylvain to wait ten days so that I could spend as many hours as possible, training myself to ride a sack. He did the same. I noticed that every time the sacks were just going to turn over it needed an extra effort to keep upright. Whenever we could, we'd have to lie down on them. And take care not to go to sleep, because falling into the sea might mean losing your sack and never being able to reach it again. Chang made me a little water-proof bag to hang round my neck with cigarettes and a tinder lighter. We were going to grate ten coconuts each and carry them with us – the meat would help us bear the hunger and it would quench our thirst. It seemed that Santori had a kind of leather wine-skin he never used, so Chang, who went to the screw's house from time to time, was going to try and knock it off.

The break was for ten o'clock on Sunday evening. With the full moon the tide would rise twenty-five feet. So Lisette would be coming in with all her strength. Chang was going to feed the pigs all by himself on Sunday morning. I was going to sleep all Saturday and all Sunday. We'd set off at ten, when the ebb would already have been running for two hours.

It was impossible for my two sacks to come apart: they were bound together by plaited hemp ropes and brass wire and sewn together with strong sail-thread. We had found bigger sacks than usual, and their mouths overlapped so the coconuts couldn't get out either.

Sylvain did exercises all the time and I let the little waves come breaking against my legs for hours on end. The continual

438

beating of the water against my thighs and the way I had to tense myself to withstand each wave made my legs and thighs as strong as steel.

There was a ten-foot chain in a disused well on the island. I wove it in and out of the ropes holding my sacks. I had a bolt that I passed through the links: in case I couldn't hold out any more, I would chain myself to the sacks. And perhaps like that I might be able to sleep without the risk of falling into the water, and losing my raft. If the sacks turned over, the water would wake me up and I would right them.

'Only three days to go, Papillon.' We were sitting on Dreyfus's bench, watching Lisette.

'Yes, only three days, Sylvain. I believe we're going to bring it off. What do you think, brother?'

'It's certain, Papillon. Tuesday night or Wednesday morning we'll be in the bush. And then hey-diddle-diddle, the cat and the fiddle for us.'

Chang was going to grate us ten coconuts apiece. And as well as knives, we'd take two machetes stolen from the tool store.

The camp lay to the east of Kourou. It was only by walking towards the sun in the morning that we could be sure of being in the right direction.

'Monday morning, Santori he'll be mad,' said Chang. 'Me no say you and Papillon vanish until three in the afternoon, when screw done siesta.'

'Why don't you rush in, saying a wave swept us away while we were fishing?'

'No. Me no want complication. Me say, "Chief, Papillon and Sylvain no come work today. Me feed pigs all alone." No more, no less.'

Sunday: seven o'clock in the evening. I'd just woken up. I'd been making myself sleep ever since Saturday morning. The moon didn't rise until nine. So outside the night was very dark. A few stars in the sky. Big rain-bearing clouds raced by over our heads. We'd just left the prison block. Though it was against the rules we often went fishing by night or just walked about the island, so the others thought this perfectly natural.

A boy went back in with his lover, a big fat Arab. They'd certainly been making love in some hiding-place or other. As I watched them lifting the plank to get into the block I reflected that the Arab, with his boy-friend at hand to stuff two or three times a day, must have reached his highest point of happiness. For him the possibility of fulfilling his erotic desires must change prison into paradise. It was no doubt much the same for the fairy. He might have been something between twenty-three and twenty-five. His body was no longer as youthful as all that – no languorous adolescent. He kept in the shade all the time to preserve his milk-white skin, but for all that he was beginning to lose the Adonis touch. Yet here in penal he had more lovers than he could ever have dreamt of having in the free world. Apart from his fancy-man, the Arab, he had customers at twenty-five francs a go, just like any tart on the Boulevard Rochechouart in Montmartre. He not only derived a good deal of pleasure from them, but he also made such a good thing of it that he and his 'husband' lived quite well. He and the men who frequented him wallowed in their vice and loved it; and ever since they had reached penal there had only been one idea in their heads – sex.

The prosecuting counsel, hoping to punish them by sending them down the drain, had mucked it up: for them, the drain was happiness itself. The plank closed behind the little pouffe, and Chang, Sylvain and I were alone. 'Let's go.' Quickly we made our way to the north end of the island.

We took the two rafts out of the cave. And straight away all three of us were soaked to the skin. The wind was blowing with the particular howl of a strong gale coming right in from the offing. Sylvain and Chang helped me shove my raft to the top of the rock. At the last moment I decided to chain my left wrist to the rope binding the sacks. All at once I was afraid of losing my hold and being swept away without them. Sylvain got up on to the opposite rock, helped by Chang. The moon was high now and we could see very well.

I had rolled a towel round my head. There were six waves to be waited for. Only a few minutes left now. Chang had come back to my side. He hugged me round the neck and then kissed me. He was going to lie there wedged in an angle of the rock and grip my legs to help me withstand the shock of Lisette's breaking.

'Only one more!' shouted Sylvain. 'Then we're away.' He was standing in front of his raft so as to protect it from the mass of water that was about to sweep over it. I was in the same position and in addition I had Chang's hands to hold me firm – in his excitement he had driven his nails into the flesh of my calf.

Lisette came for us, driving in as tall as a steeple. She broke on our two rocks with her usual enormous crash and rushed up the side of the cliff.

I flung myself in a fraction of a second before my friend: he was in immediately after, and it was with the two rafts tight against one another that Lisette swept us racing out to sea. In less than five minutes we were more than three hundred yards from the shore. Sylvain had not yet climbed up on to his raft. I'd got on to mine within two minutes. Chang had hurried up to Dreyfus's seat, and he was waving a scrap of white cloth – his last farewell. Now it was a good five minutes that we had been beyond the dangerous zone where the waves formed to drive right in for Devil's Island. Those that we were now riding were much longer; they had almost no foam, and they were so regular that we drifted along as though we were part of them; we were not tossed about and the rafts did not attempt to capsize. We rose and fell upon these great rollers, slowly moving out into the offing, for this was the ebb.

Once again, as I reached the top and turned my head right round, I caught a last glimpse of Chang's white handkerchief. Sylvain was not far from me – perhaps fifty yards farther out to sea. Several times he held up his arm and waved it by way of showing triumph and delight.

That night was fairly easy going, and we very clearly felt

the change in the sea's direction. The tide we left on had carried us out, but this one was now sweeping us in towards the mainland.

The sun rose on the horizon: so it was six o'clock. We were too low in the water to be able to see the coast. But I could tell we were very far away from the islands, because although the sun lit up their tops, we could scarcely make them out, let alone see that there were three of them. All I could see was a single mass. Since they could not be told apart, I judged they were at least fifteen miles away.

The feeling of triumph and success made me laugh. What if I were to try sitting up on my raft? The wind would then push me along, blowing on my back.

There, I was up. I undid the chain and took a turn round my belt. The bolt was well greased and it was easy to tighten the nut. I held my hands up for the wind to dry them. I was going to smoke a cigarette. There, I drew on it, inhaling deeply and letting the smoke out slowly. I was not frightened any more. There's no point in telling you about the stomach aches I had before, during the plunge and then just after. No, I wasn't afraid any more: so calm indeed that when I'd finished the cigarette I decided to eat a few mouthfuls of coconut meat. I got a pretty good handful down and then I lit another cigarette. Sylvain was a fair distance away. We caught fleeting glimpses of one another from time to time, when we both happened to be on top of a wave. The sun was blazing like hell on the top of my skull and my brains were coming to the boil. I wetted my towel and wrapped it round my head. I took off my woollen sweater – it was stifling me, in spite of the wind.

Christ! My raft had turned over and I'd very nearly drowned. Two big gulps of sea-water had gone down. In spite of all my efforts I could not manage to turn my sacks over again and get back on to them. The trouble was the chain – it did not leave me free enough in my movements. At last, having slipped the whole length over to the same side, I succeeded in treading water by the sacks and getting my breath back. I began trying to take the chain off altogether and I strained away at the nut. I got angrier and angrier, and perhaps because I was too nervous my fingers had not the strength to undo it.

God, what a relief! It had turned at last. A rough five minutes! It had almost sent me crazy, thinking I could never get free of that chain.

442

I didn't bother to turn the raft right side up; I was exhausted and I didn't feel I had the strength. I just worked myself up on to it the way it was. What did it matter that I was on its bottom? I'd never fasten myself on again, either with the chain or anything else. I'd already seen what a bloody-fool thing it was to do, chaining my wrist at the beginning. That ought to have been enough.

The pitiless sun burned my arms and legs. My face was on fire. It seemed to me that wetting it made it worse, because as soon as the water dried the burning was even fiercer.

The wind had almost entirely dropped, and although with the smaller waves it was more comfortable, I was not getting along so fast. A great deal of wind and a rough sea would really have been better.

I had such a violent cramp in my right leg that I called out, as though someone could hear me. I made the sign of the cross over the place, remembering that my grandmother had told me that would cure it. This homely remedy was a dismal failure. The sun was well down in the west. It was about four o'clock in the afternoon and this was the fourth tide since we had set out. It was a flood tide, and it seemed to me to be moving me in towards the coast with greater strength than the last.

Now I could see Sylvain all the time, and for his part he could see me very well, too. He hardly disappeared at all, because the waves were no height now. He'd taken off his shirt, and he was bare from the waist up. He waved: he was more than three hundred yards ahead of me, but farther out to sea. Judging from the white water round his raft, he was trying to row with his hands. It looked as though he were checking his raft's progress so that I could catch up. I lay down on my sacks, and thrusting my arms into the water I rowed too. If he braked and I hurried, perhaps we could lessen the distance between us. I'd chosen my companion in this escape very well. He could take it, one hundred per cent. I stopped rowing. I was tiring, and I must keep all my strength. I was going to try to turn the raft over, because the bag of food was underneath, together with the leather bottle of fresh water. I was hungry and thirsty. My lips were already cracked and burning. The best way of turning the sacks over was to cling to them on the side opposite the rising wave and then to kick just as they rose. After five attempts I was lucky enough to swing them over in one go. The effort exhausted me and I found it really hard to crawl up on to them again.

The sun was touching the horizon and presently it would disappear. So it was six o'clock, or nearly. Let's hope the night wouldn't be too rough, because as I saw it, it was the long soaking that was taking away my strength.

I had a good drink from Santori's leather bottle, but first I ate two handfuls of coconut meat. Quite happy, and with my hands dried in the wind, I got out a cigarette and smoked it – terrific. Before the darkness fell Sylvain waved his towel, and so did I; this was our way of saying good night. He was still the same distance from me. I sat with my legs stretched out: I dried my sweater as much as I could and put it on. Even wet, these sweaters kept you warm; and the moment the sun dipped I felt the cold.

The wind grew stronger. It was only the western clouds that were touched with pink low on the horizon. Now everything else was covered with a half-darkness that deepened every moment. The wind was blowing from the east, and over there I saw no clouds at all. So no danger of rain for the present.

Apart from holding on and not getting wetter than I had to, the only thing I thought about was whether it would be sensible to fasten myself to the sacks in case tiredness overcame me, or whether, seeing what I'd been through, it would be too dangerous. Then I discovered that the reason I'd been so hampered was that the chain was too short, one end being unnecessarily twisted in among the sacks' ropes and wires. It was easy to get at it. With that extra length I should be able to move about much more freely. I fixed the chain properly and attached it to my belt once more. The well greased nut worked properly this time – I'd turned it too hard at first. I felt easier in my mind now, because I'd been terrified of dropping off to sleep and losing my sacks.

Yes, the wind was getting stronger and so were the waves. The seas rose higher and the hollows were deeper; and in spite of these great differences in level the raft sailed wonderfully well.

It was wholly dark. The sky was studded with millions of stars, and the brightest of them all was the Southern Cross. I couldn't see my friend. The night now beginning was very important, because if we were lucky enough to have the wind blowing all the time at this strength, we'd go a long way before tomorrow morning.

As the night wore on, the wind blew harder and harder. Slowly the moon heaved up out of the sea: it was a reddish moon, and when at last it was quite risen I could clearly see those darkish patches that give it the look of a face.

So it was past ten. The darkness grew less and less. As the moon rose higher and higher, so the moonlight increased; the waves shone silvery, and their strange brilliance hurt my eyes. I could not prevent myself from looking at them, but they really stabbed and wounded, for my eyes were already stinging from the sun and the salt water. I told myself I was overdoing it, but nevertheless I smoked three cigarettes straight off, one after another.

The raft was behaving well; this heavy sea suited it and it rose and fell with an easy swing. I could no longer leave my legs stretched out on the sacks, for this sitting position gave me cramps that very soon became intolerably painful.

Of course I was continually wetted up to my middle. My chest was hardly wet at all, and once the wind had dried my sweater no later wave soaked me further up than my belt. My eyes stung more and more. I shut them, and from time to time I dozed 'You mustn't sleep, man!' Easy enough to say: but I couldn't hold out any longer. Hell! I struggled against this huge drowsiness: and every time I came back to full wakefulness it was with a stabbing pain in my head. I brought out my tinder lighter. Every now and then I burned myself, putting the glowing wick on to my right forearm or the side of my neck.

I was seized with dreadful anxiety, and I tried to thrust it aside with all my strength. Was I going to fall asleep? If I fell into the sea, would the cold water wake me up? It was sensible to have tied myself on with the chain. I mustn't lose those two sacks – they were my very life now. It would be so bloody silly to fall into the wet and then never wake up again.

For some minutes now I'd been absolutely soaked. A stray wave, one that ran across the path of the others, had struck me on the right-hand side. Not only did it soak me, but it set me askew on the sea, and the two next ordinary waves covered me from head to foot.

This second night was well on towards its end. What time could it be? Judging from the way the moon was beginning to dip towards the west it must be about two or three in the morning. We had been at sea for five tides now, that is to say thirty hours. This soaking I had just had was useful in a way – the cold woke me up completely. I was shivering, but it was no longer an effort to keep my eyes open. My legs were very stiff and I decided to sit on them: pulling each in turn with both hands I managed to fold them under me. Maybe my frozen toes would thaw in that position.

I sat there cross-legged for a long while. The change of attitude did me good. The moon lit up the sea wonderfully, and I tried to catch sight of Sylvain; but as it moved down the sky the moon was right in my face, and I found it hard to make anything out distinctly. No, I could see nothing. Sylvain had had nothing to tie himself on with: who could tell whether he was still there on his raft? I searched the sea desperately, but in vain. There was a strong wind, but it was steady – the important thing was that there were no sudden gusts. I'd grown used to its rhythm, and I sat on my sacks as though I were part of them.

I stared all round so hard and for so long that in the end I had only this one idea in my head – I must see my buddy. I dried my fingers in the wind and then I whistled through them as hard as ever I could. I listened. No reply. Did Sylvain know how to whistle with his fingers? I didn't know. I ought to have asked before we set off. After all, we could easily have made a couple of whistles. I blamed myself for not having thought of it. Then I put my hands each side of my mouth and called 'Hoo-hoo!' The only answer was the cry of the wind and the slap-slap of the waves.

I couldn't bear it any more, so I stood up and balanced there, holding my chain in my left hand, during the time five waves raised me one after the other. When I reached the crest I stood quite straight, and on the up and then again on the down I squatted. Nothing to the right, nothing to the left, nothing in front. Was he perhaps behind me? I didn't dare stand up and look back. The only thing I had been able to make out without the least possible doubt was a hard line away on my left, deep black in the moonlight. It was certainly the forest.

When it was daylight I should see the trees, and thinking of that did me good. 'At sunrise you'll see the forest, Papi! I hope to God you see your friend too!'

I rubbed my toes and stretched out my legs. Then I decided

to dry my hands and smoke a cigarette. I smoked two. What time was it? The moon was getting very low. I couldn't remember how long before sunrise the moon had set the night before. I tried to bring it back by closing my eyes and seeing the happenings of that first night. No good. Yes it was, though! All at once I had a clear vision of the sun rising in the east and at the same time the tip of the moon just visible on the western horizon. So it must now be about five o'clock. The moon took its time to sink. The Southern Cross had disappeared long before; so had the Great and Little Bears. There was only the North Star that shone brighter than the rest. Since the sinking of the Southern Cross the North Star had reigned supreme.

The wind seemed to be increasing. At least there was more body in it than during the night, as you might say. This meant the waves were both taller and deeper and there were more white horses on their crests than there had been when the night began.

Thirty hours now that I'd been at sea. There was no denying that up until now things had gone well rather than otherwise, and that the toughest day was the one that was now about to dawn.

Being exposed to the full sun yesterday from six in the morning until six at night had baked me quite horribly. It was going to be no sort of fun when the sun rose again today to have another go at me. My lips were already cracking, and yet this was still the cool of the night. My lips and eyes burned painfully. It was the same with my hands and forearms. If I could manage it I wouldn't expose my arms any more. I'd have to see whether I could bear my sweater. Another place that hurt badly was between my arms and my thighs: in that case it wasn't the sun but the salt water and the rubbing of the sacks.

Still and all, brother, cooked or not, you've made your break all right and it's worth putting up with all this and more to be where you are. You've got a ninety per cent chance of reaching the mainland alive and hell, that's something, isn't it? Even if I were to get there burnt bald and half flayed, that wouldn't be too high a price to pay for such a voyage and such a result. And then again I hadn't seen a single shark. Can you imagine that? Were they all on holiday? You can't deny that as lucky characters go, you're a lucky character all right. This is the true, the genuine break — you'll see. All the others were too carefully laid on, too perfectly organized: the one that really works will be the craziest of them all. Two sacks of coconuts and go wherever the wind and the sea carry you. To the mainland. You must admit you don't have to go to college to know that driftwood always ends up on the shore.

If the wind and the drive of the sea kept going during the day with the same strength as it had during this last night we'd reach land in the afternoon for sure.

The ogre of the tropics rose up behind me. It looked as though he was thoroughly determined to fry everything to a crisp today, for he came up in a blaze of glory. In the flash of an eye he had dispelled the moonlight, and he was not fully risen from the sea before he made it clear who was master — who was the unquestioned king of the tropics. In no time at all the wind grew warm. In an hour it was going to be really hot. A feeling of well-being filled my whole body: the first rays had hardly reached me before a gentle warmth flooded through me from my middle upwards. I took off my towel-turban and held my cheeks out to the sun, as I would have held them out to a log fire. Before scorching me, the ogre meant to show how he was the giver of life before being death itself. My blood flowed faster along my veins, and even my water-soaked thighs felt this new life racing through them.

I could see the bush quite clearly — I mean the very tops of the trees, of course. It seemed to me that it was no great way off. I'd wait a little longer for the sun to rise more and then I'd stand up on my sacks to see if I could catch sight of Sylvain.

In less than an hour's time the sun was well up: God above, it was going to be hot! My left eye had half gummed up. I scooped up water and rubbed my eye with it — how it stung! I took off my sweater. I'd keep it off for a while, until the sun began to burn too fiercely.

A higher wave than the rest heaved up beneath me, raising me right up into the air. In the split second that it was at its highest I saw my friend. He was sitting on his raft, stripped to the waist. He didn't see me. He was less than two hundred yards away, to my left and a little in front. The wind was still blowing strongly, so seeing he was ahead of me almost directly down-wind, I decided to put my arms into the sleeves of my sweater and hold them up, gripping the bottom of it with my teeth. This kind of sail would surely carry me along faster than he was going.

I sailed in this way for about half an hour. But the sweater hurt my teeth and the strength I had to exert, holding it up, was wearing me out too fast. Still, when I gave over I had the impression that I'd gone faster than if I'd just left it to the waves.

Hurrah! I'd just seen Sylvain. He wasn't a hundred yards away. But what was he up to? It didn't look as though he was worrying about whether I was there or not. When another wave heaved me well up I saw him again, once, twice, three times. I distinctly saw he was shading his eyes with his right hand: so he must be searching the sea. Look back, you bloody fool! He had certainly looked, that was for sure; but he hadn't seen me.

I stood up and whistled. When I rose up again from the hollow of the wave there I saw Sylvain standing up and facing me. He waved his sweater. We waved good morning at least twenty times before we sat down again. We signalled at the top of every rising wave, and it so happened we were both going up and down in the same rhythm. On the last two waves he stretched his arm out towards the bush, which could now be seen in detail – it was only about six miles away. I lost my balance and collapsed, sitting on my raft. The sight of my friend and the bush so close at hand filled my whole being with joy – I was so moved I wept like a child. The tears cleaned my gummed-up eyes, and through them I saw countless facets of every colour; stupidly I thought, 'Why, you would say it was stained glass windows in a church.' God is with you today, Papi. It is in the midst of the elements, of nature – the vastness of the ocean, the never-ending waves, the tremendous green roof of the forest – that one feels so infinitely small in comparison with everything around; and it is perhaps then that without looking for Him one finds God – lays one's very hand upon Him. Just as during the thousands of hours I had spent buried alive in those dismal black-holes without a ray of light I had felt Him in the darkness, so today by the light of this rising sun (rising to devour everything not strong enough to withstand Him) I truly touched God: I felt Him all about me and within me. He even whispered in my ear. 'You are suffering and you will suffer even more; but this time I have decided to be on your side. I promise you that you will win and that you will be free.'

I had never had any religious instruction; I didn't know the ABC of the Christian religion; I was so ignorant that I didn't know who was Jesus's father nor whether His mother was really the Virgin Mary; nor whether His father was a carpenter or a camel driver – but all that gross ignorance does not prevent one from meeting God when one really looks for Him: He is to be found in the wind, the sea, the sun, the jungle, the stars, and even in the fishes that He must have scattered with so free a hand so that man might be fed.

The sun rose fast. It must be ten in the morning. I was completely dry from the waist upwards. I soaked my towel again and wrapped it round my head. I put on my sweater, because my shoulders, back and arms were burning horribly. And although my legs were very often in the water, they too were as red as lobsters.

Now that the coast was nearer, the indraught was greater and the waves ran almost straight towards the shore. I could see the details of the forest, and that made me think that merely in these four or five morning hours we had moved in a great deal. My first break had taught me how to calculate distances. When you can see details clearly, you're less than three miles away: now at present I could tell the difference between the thickness of one trunk and another; and once, from the crest of a particularly high wave, I very clearly saw a huge monster of a tree lying over sideways, with its leaves dipping into the sea.

Dolphins and birds! God send that the dolphins don't play with my raft, pushing it around. I'd heard that they have a way of shoving driftwood and men in towards the shore and of drowning them by pushing with their noses, all with the best intentions in the world, since they only mean to help. No: although there were three or four of them and they circled round and round, it was only to see what it was all about, and they went away without even touching my raft. Thank God for that!

Noon, and the sun was right over my head. The bastard must certainly mean to boil me alive. My eyes were oozing continuously and the skin had quite gone from my lips and nose. The waves were choppier and now they were running in towards the shore with a deafening noise.

I could see Sylvain nearly all the time. He scarcely ever disappeared – the waves weren't deep enough. There was a kind of bar where they broke with a shocking din; and then, once they were over this foaming barrier, they drove right in to attack the forest.

We were about half a mile from the shore and I could make out the pink and white birds with aristocratic plumes, walking about and thrusting their beaks into the mud. There were thousands and thousands of birds. Scarcely any of them flew higher than about six feet, and these short, low flights were merely to avoid being wetted by the spray. There was spray everywhere and the sea was a filthy yellow muddy colour. We were so close in that I could see the dirty high-water mark on the trunks of the trees.

The crash of the rollers did not drown the shrill cry of these myriads of many-coloured waders. Thump. Thump. Then two or three yards further. Thump. I had grounded – I was aground on the mud. There was not enough water to float me. By the sun, it was two in the afternoon. So it was forty hours since I had left. That had been two days back, at ten at night, when the ebb had been running for two hours. So this was the seventh tide, and it was natural that I should be stranded, for this was the ebb once more. The flood would start to run at about three. By nightfall I should be in the bush. I'd keep the chain so as not to be swept off the sacks at the most dangerous moment – the time when the rollers began breaking over me without floating the raft, the sea not being deep enough. I shouldn't be afloat before the tide had been flowing for at least two or three hours.

Sylvain was more than a hundred yards over on my right, and somewhat ahead. He looked at me and waved his arms about. It seemed to me he was trying to shout something but his throat couldn't produce any sound; otherwise I should have heard him. Now that the noise of the rollers had died away behind us there we were on the mud with no sound apart from the cry of the waders. As for me, I was about five hundred yards from the forest: Sylvain was a hundred or a hundred and fifty yards away from me and farther in. But what was the bloody great fool doing now? He was standing up, and he had left his raft. Surely he hadn't gone out of his mind? He mustn't start walking or he'd sink in a little more with every step and maybe he wouldn't be able to get back to his raft. I tried to whistle: I couldn't. There was a little water left so I emptied the bottle: then I tried to shout to stop him. I couldn't utter a sound. Bubbles of gas were coming up out of the mud. So it was only a thin crust with ooze beneath, and any guy that let himself be caught in it – his number would be up for sure.

Sylvain turned round; he looked at me and made signs I couldn't understand. I waved furiously, meaning 'No, no! Don't stir from your raft! You'll never get to the forest!' As he was the far side of his sacks of coconuts, I couldn't make out whether he was near the raft or far from it. At first I thought he must be very close, and so if he bogged down he'd be able to catch hold of it.

All at once I realized that he'd gone quite a distance – that he'd sunk in and couldn't get himself out and so back to his raft. I heard a shout. I lay flat on my sacks, dug my hands into the mud and heaved with all my strength. My sacks moved forward beneath me and I managed to slide along for twenty yards. I'd moved over to the left and it was then, standing, with the sacks no longer blocking my view, that I saw my friend, my buddy, buried to the waist. He was more than ten yards from his raft. Terror gave me back my voice and I shouted 'Sylvain! Sylvain! Don't move! Lie flat in the mud. Get your legs out if you can.' The wind carried my words along and he heard them. He nodded his head to say yes. I flung myself down again and I heaved at the mud, sliding my raft along. My frantic anxiety gave me superhuman strength and I covered another thirty yards and more. It's true I'd taken over an hour to do it, but I was very close to him now – perhaps fifty or sixty yards. I couldn't see very well.

Sitting up, with my hands, arms and face all covered with ooze, I tried to wipe my left eye – salt mud had got into it and it was burning. It not only stopped me seeing out of that one, but it also spoilt the sight of the other, which had now begun to run, just to make things easier. At last I saw him: he was no longer lying down; he was upright, with only his chest rising from the mud.

The first wave arrived. It passed over me without knocking me off my seat and broke farther up, covering the mud with its foam. It also swept over Sylvain: his chest was still out of the mud. At once the thought came to me – 'The more the breakers come in, the softer the mud will be. I must reach him whatever happens.'

I was seized with the furious energy of a wild animal whose cubs are in danger, and I thrust, thrust, thrust at this mud to reach him, like a mother trying to save her child. He gazed at me without a word or a movement, his eyes fixed on me and mine on him. It was essential not to lose his gaze, and I no longer looked to see where I was to drive in my hands. I dragged myself on a little, but now two rollers had passed over me, quite covering me, and the mud had become thinner: I was moving much slower than an hour ago. A big roller came in, almost smothering me and pulling me off my raft. I sat up to see better. The mud was up to Sylvain's armpits. I was less than forty yards from him. He was gazing intently at me, I saw he knew he was going to die there – the poor unfortunate bastard, bogged down three hundred yards from the Promised Land.

I flattened myself again and dug into the mud – it was almost liquid now. My eyes and his were inseparably joined. He shook his head to say no, don't struggle any more. I went on nevertheless and I was less than thirty yards away when a great roller smothered me under its mass of water and very nearly tore me off my sacks – they floated and moved me five or six yards forward.

When the roller had gone I looked round. Sylvain had vanished. The mud, with its thin layer of foaming water, was perfectly smooth. There was not even my friend's hand showing to say a last farewell. I had an utterly disgusting, brutish reaction, the instinct for self-preservation overcoming all decent feeling. 'You're alive, Papi. You're alone, and when you're in the jungle alone with no friend, it won't be so bloody easy to make a success of this break.'

A roller crashed over my back (for I was sitting up) and brought me back to my senses. It bent me right over and knocked all the wind out of my body – it was minutes before I could draw breath. The raft was driven up a few yards, and it was only then, as I watched the wave dying away far up near the trees, that I mourned for Sylvain. 'We were so close: if only you hadn't moved, brother! Less than three hundred yards from the trees. Why? Just tell me why you did such a bloody fool thing. What made you think that crust was firm enough for you to walk on? The sun? The glare? Who knows?

Couldn't you stand the hellish discomfort any longer? How come a man like you couldn't bear a few more hours on the gridiron?'

The breakers came in one after another with a thunderous roar. They were coming in faster, and the waves were bigger. Each one washed right over me, and each one heaved me up a few yards, still leaving me on the mud. At about five o'clock the breakers suddenly changed into flowing sea and I was water-borne, right off the bottom. Now that the waves had some depth beneath them they made almost no noise. The thunder of the breakers died away. Sylvain's raft had already been washed up among the trees. I was set down not too violently, carried up to some twenty yards from the virgin forest. When the wave drew back there I was stranded on the mud again, firmly determined not to stir from my raft until I had hold of a branch or a creeper. Only twenty yards to go. It took more than an hour before there was depth enough for me to be lifted up again and carried into the forest. The roaring wave that carried me up literally flung me in among the trees. I undid the bolt and freed myself from the chain. I did not throw it away: it might come in useful.

In the Bush

I hurried into the forest as fast as I could, before the sun should go down; I made my way half walking, half swimming, for here too there was mud that sucked you down. The water ran far in among the trees and night had fallen before I reached dry land. My nose was filled with the smell of rotting vegetation and there was so much gas that it stung my eyes. My legs were wrapped round and round with stalks and leaves. I still pushed my raft in front of me. At every stop I tried the ground beneath the water, and it was only when it did not give that I went on.

I spent my first night on a great fallen tree. Hundreds of

creatures of every kind walked about on me. My body burnt and stung. I put on my sweater, having hauled up my sack and made it fast at both ends to the tree-trunk. I had life inside the sacks, for once I'd opened the coconuts they would provide me with food so that I could hold out. I had my jungle-knife looped to my right wrist. I stretched out exhausted in the crotch of the tree – it made a kind of large hollow or nest – and went to sleep without having time to form a single thought. No: perhaps I did just mutter 'Poor Sylvain' once or twice before I sank right down.

It was the noise of the birds that woke me. The rays of the sun were coming horizontally, shining far in among the trees; so it would be seven or eight in the morning. There was a great deal of sea all round me, so it must be high water. Maybe this was the end of the tenth tide.

That made sixty hours since I'd left Devil's Island. I couldn't make out whether I was far from the sea or not; in any case I was going to wait for the water to go down before I went to the shore to dry myself and take a little sun. I had no fresh water left. There were still three handfuls of coconut meat, and I ate it with very great pleasure. I also rubbed some on my burns – the oil it contained soothed them. Then I smoked two cigarettes. I thought about Sylvain, and this time I did so with no selfishness. Shouldn't I, in the first place, have escaped without any friend? After all, I claimed I could manage all alone – could shift for myself. So in that case it was all one: but my heart was filled with a great sadness and I closed my eyes, as though that would prevent me from seeing my friend going down into the mud. As far as he was concerned it was all over.

I wedged my sack carefully into the crotch of the tree and brought out a coconut. I managed to open two by hitting them as hard as I could on the wood between my legs, bringing them point down so that the shell split open. That was better than using the jungle-knife. I ate a whole one and drank the little over-sweet milk it had. The tide ebbed quickly, and when the water had gone the mud bore me perfectly well as I walked down to the shore.

There was a brilliant sun and the sea was incomparably beautiful. I gazed for a long while towards the place where I thought Sylvain must have disappeared. I washed in a pool of sea-water, and my clothes and body were soon dry. I smoked a cigarette. One last look towards my friend's grave and I went back into the forest, making my way quite easily. With my sack on my shoulder I pushed in slowly among the undergrowth. In about two hours I came to dry land at last, where the trees showed no sign of flooding or of the tide. Here I would camp and rest completely for twenty-four hours. I'd open the nuts one by one, take out the meat and put it all in the sack, ready to be eaten when it was needed. I could have lit a fire, but I thought it wouldn't be wise.

The rest of that day and then the night passed off quietly. The din of the birds woke me at sunrise. I finished taking out the coconut meat, and then, with a very small bundle on my shoulder, I set off towards the east.

Towards three in the afternoon I came across a path. It was a track used either by the men who went out looking for balata – natural rubber – or for timber, or by those who carried supplies to the gold-diggers. It was a narrow path, but it was clean – no branches lying across it – so it must be well used. Here and there I saw the tracks of an ass or an unshod mule. In the dried mud, men's footprints, the big toe clearly marked. I walked until nightfall. I chewed coconut, which both nourished me and quenched my thirst. Sometimes I rubbed my nose, lips and cheeks with well-chewed pulp, mixed with spit. My eyes ran a great deal, and they often gummed up. As soon as I could, I'd wash them with fresh water. As well as the coconuts, my sack held a water-proof box with a piece of common soap, a Gillette razor, twelve blades and a shaving-brush. It had survived the voyage perfectly.

I walked with my machete in my hand, but I did not need to use it, since the path was quite free and open. Indeed, at the sides I noticed places where branches had been trimmed off not long before. A good many people must pass along, so I should have to take great care.

Here the bush was not the same as what I'd experienced during my first break, at Saint-Laurent-du-Maroni. Here the forest was at two levels, and it was not as thick as it was on the Maroni. The first level was vegetation rising fifteen or twenty feet, and then over that there was the forest roof, more than sixty feet above the ground. There was daylight only to the right of the path; on the other side it was almost entirely dark.

I moved along fast, sometimes crossing a clearing where

the trees had been burnt either by men or by lightning. I kept an eye on the sun's rays: their slope showed that it was not far from setting. My back was turned towards it, for I was going eastwards – that is to say, in the direction of the Negro village of Kourou or the prison camp of the same name.

Night would fall suddenly: I mustn't walk in the darkness. I'd push into the forest and find a place where I could lie down. Thirty yards and more from the path I made myself a bed, cutting smooth leaves from a tree like a banana-palm and sheltering myself with others. I and my bed were perfectly dry, and as luck would have it, no rain fell. I smoked two cigarettes

I was not too tired that evening. The coconut meat satisfied my hunger and kept me going. But my mouth was parched with thirst and my saliva would hardly flow at all.

The second part of the break had begun; and this was the third night without a hitch that I had spent on the mainland. Ah, if only Sylvain were with me! He's not here, brother, and what is there you can do about it? Have you ever needed anyone's advice or support at any time in your life? Are you a leader or a follower? Don't you be a bloody fool, Papillon: apart from natural grief at having lost a friend you're no worse off just because you're alone in the bush. Royale, Saint-Joseph and Devil's Island are far away now; it's six days since you left them. Kourou must have been warned. First the screws in the logging camp and then the darkies in the village. There must be a police post there, too. Was it really sensible to walk towards the village? I knew nothing about its surroundings. The camp lay between the village and the river. That was all I knew about Kourou.

When I was on Royale I thought I'd hold up the first person I came across and force him to take me to the neighbourhood of Inini, the camp for the Chinese with Cuic-Cuic, Chang's brother, among them. Why should I alter my plan? If the people on Devil's Island had made up their minds we'd been drowned, then there'd be no trouble. But if they thought we'd escaped then Kourou would be dangerous Since it was a logging camp, there'd be a great many Arabs – that is to say, plenty of trackers. Watch out for the manhunt, Papi! Don't slip up. Don't get yourself caught between two fires. You've got to see these characters, whoever they may be, before they see you. Moral: I mustn't walk on the path but through the forest, alongside the track. All today you've been behaving like a bleeding half-wit, rushing about on this path with nothing but a jungle-knife as a weapon. It wasn't so much ignorance as raving madness. So tomorrow I'd walk through the forest.

I got up early, woken by the birds and the animals greeting the sunrise – indeed, I got up at the same time as the rest of the jungle. Another day was beginning for me too. I swallowed a well-chewed handful of coconut. I rubbed some over my face and started on my way.

Although I was very close to the path I could not be seen: the going was hard, because though the creepers and branches were not very thick I still had to push them aside to get along. Still, it had been very wise to leave the track, because I heard someone whistling. Ahead of me the path ran straight for a good fifty yards: I could not see the whistler. Ha, here he was! A coal-black Negro. He had a pack on his back and a gun in his right hand. He was wearing a khaki shirt and a pair of shorts: legs and feet bare. He walked with his head down, his back bowed under his bulky load, and his eyes on the ground.

I hid behind a big tree on the very edge of the path and waited with my knife open in my hand until he reached me. The second he passed the tree I flung myself upon him. My right hand caught his gun arm and twisted it: the gun dropped. 'Don't kill me! Oh God, have mercy!' He stood there with my knife-point against the lower left side of his throat. I bent and picked up the gun, an old single-barrelled job, but one that was certainly crammed with powder and shot to the muzzle. I cocked it, stood back a couple of paces and said, 'Undo your pack: drop it. Don't you try and run or I'll kill you like a dog.'

The poor petrified black obeyed. Then he looked at me. 'You're an escaped convict?'

'Yes.'

'What do you want? Take everything I have. But I beg you not to kill me – I've got five children. Leave me my life, for pity's sake.'

'Shut up. What's your name?'

'Jean.'

'Where are you going?'

'I'm carrying stores and medicines to my two brothers: they're cutting wood in the bush.'

'Where do you come from?'

'Kourou.'

'Do you belong there?'

'That's where I was born.'

'Do you know Inini?'

'Yes. Sometimes I do a deal with the Chinese in the prison camp.'

'Do you see this?'

'What is it?'

'A five hundred franc note. Take your choice, brother: either you do what I say and I give you these five hundred francs and hand you back your gun, or you refuse or try to deceive me. And in that case I kill you. Make your choice.'

'What have I got to do? I'll do anything you say, even for nothing.'

'You must take me to somewhere near Inini camp without my running any danger. When I've got into touch with a Chinese you can go. OK?'

'OK.'

'Don't you try to pull a fast one on me or you're a dead man.'

'No, I swear I'll help. I'll be straight with you.'

He had some condensed milk with him. He brought out six tins and gave them to me, together with a two-pound loaf and some bacon.

'Hide your pack in the bush: you can pick it up later. Look, I'll mark this tree with my machete.'

I drank a tin of milk. He also gave me a new pair of trousers – workingman's blue trousers. I put them on, never leaving hold of the gun.

'On your way, Jean. Take care no one sees us, because if they do it'll be your fault. And in that case, you've had it.'

Jean was better at going through the bush than me and I found it hard to keep up, so clever he was at avoiding branches and creepers. The nimble bastard went through the jungle with the greatest of ease.

'You know, they've been told at Kourou that two convicts have escaped from the islands. So I must tell you straight – it'll be very dangerous for you when we go by near the Kourou prison camp.'

'You seem a straightforward type, Jean. I hope you won't let me down. What do you think is the best way of getting to Inini? Remember that my safety means your life, because if the screws or the trackers come on me suddenly, I'll be forced to kill you.'

'What should I call you?'

'Papillon.'

'Right, Monsieur Papillon. We ought to go deep into the bush and get round a long way from Kourou. I'll guarantee to take you to Inini through the forest.'

'I'll trust you. Take whatever path you think the safest.'

Right inside the forest we went slower, but ever since we had left the neighbourhood of the path I felt that the Negro was more relaxed. He didn't sweat so heavily and his face was less tense: he seemed much calmer.

'It looks to me you're not so frightened now, Jean?'

'That's right, Monsieur Papillon. Being on the edge of the track was very dangerous for you, and so for me too.'

We were getting along fast. He was bright, this darkie: he never moved more than three or four paces from me. 'Stop. I want to roll a cigarette.'

'Here's a packet of Gauloises.'

'Thanks, Jean, you're a good fellow.'

'That's true: I am very good. I'm a Catholic, you understand, and it grieves me to see the way the white warders treat the convicts.'

'Have you seen many? Where?'

'In the Kourou logging camp. It wounds your heart to see them dying slowly, eaten away by the labour of wood cutting and by the fever and dysentery. You're better off on the islands. This is the first time I've ever seen a prisoner in perfect health, like you.'

'Yes: it's better on the islands.'

We'd sat down for a while on a big branch. I offered him one of his tins of milk. He said he'd rather have some coconut.

'Is your wife young?'

'Yes, she's thirty-two. I'm forty. We have five children, three girls and two boys.'

'Do you earn a decent living?'

'I get along fairly well with the rosewood, and my wife washes and irons for the warders. That helps a little. We're very poor, but we all have enough to eat and the children all go to school. They've always got shoes to put on.'

Poor Negro, he thought everything was fine just because his children had shoes to their feet. He was almost my size and there was nothing at all unpleasant in his black face. Far from it: you could see in his eye that he had feelings that did him honour – he was hard-working, healthy, a good father, a good husband, a good Christian.

'And what about you, Papillon?'

'I'm trying to make myself a new life. These last ten years I've been buried alive, and yet I've escaped again and again so as to be like you one day – free, with a wife and kids, without doing anyone any harm, even in thought. As you said yourself, the penal settlement is rotten through and through, and a man with any self-respect must get out of that filth.'

'I'll help you to succeed – I'll not let you down. Let's go.'

Jean had a wonderful sense of direction, and without any hesitation he led me straight to the neighbourhood of the Chinese camp: we got there about two hours after nightfall. We heard far-off noises: we saw no lights. Jean said that to get really close to the camp we should have to avoid one or two outposts. We decided to stop for the night.

I was dead with tiredness; yet I was afraid to sleep. What if I was wrong about the Negro? Suppose he'd been playing a part? Suppose he took the gun while I was asleep and killed me? He'd gain double by doing so: in the first place he'd get rid of the danger I represented, and in the second he'd get a reward for having killed an escaped convict.

Yes, he was very intelligent. Without a word, without waiting about, he lay down to go to sleep. I still had the chain and the bolt. I felt like putting it on him, but then I reflected that he could undo the nut as easily as I could and that if he were to move carefully while I slept flat out, I'd feel nothing. I'd try not to go to sleep. I had a whole packet of Gauloises. I'd do anything to keep awake. I couldn't put myself into this man's hands – after all, he was honest and he would certainly have put me down as a crook.

The night was completely dark. He was lying a couple of yards from me and all I could see was the paleness of the soles of his feet. The forest has its own particular night noises

461

– one is the hoarse, powerful cry of the howler monkey, which can be heard for miles. It's very important, because if the howl is regular it means the rest of the band can eat and sleep in peace. It's not an alarm or a danger call; it says that there are neither wild animals nor men around.

I was all tensed up, and with the help of some cigarette burns and above all the thousands of mosquitoes that were determined to extract every last drop of my blood, I held out against sleep without too much difficulty. I might have kept the mosquitoes off by rubbing myself with a mixture of spit and nicotine, but I knew I'd drop off without them to keep me awake. I just hoped there were no carriers of malaria or yellow fever among them.

So here I was, no longer on the way down the drain – perhaps only for the moment, but at all events away from it. In 1931, when I'd been arrested, I was twenty-five. Now it was 1941. Ten years. It was in 1932 that that prosecutor Pradel had uttered an inhuman and pitiless indictment to throw me, young and strong as I was, into that pit they call the prison system, a pit full of a sticky liquid that was to dissolve me slowly and cause me to disappear. Now I'd brought off the first part of this break. I'd climbed from the bottom of the pit to its edge. I must concentrate all my intelligence and all my strength so as to bring off the second part.

The night passed slowly, but pass it did; and I did not go to sleep. I never even put down the gun. With the burns and the stinging of the mosquitoes I stayed so thoroughly awake that it never once dropped from my hands. I had the right to feel pleased with myself: I'd not risked my freedom by giving way to fatigue. Mind had triumphed over matter and I congratulated myself upon that fact when I heard the first bird-calls that announced the coming of the day. These early risers were soon joined by hundreds of others.

The Negro stretched his whole length and then sat up. 'Good morning,' he said, rubbing his feet, 'didn't you go to sleep?'

'No.'

'That was stupid, because I promise you you had nothing to fear from me. I've really made up my mind to help you to succeed.'

'Thanks, Jean. Does it take long for the daylight to get into the forest?'

462

'It won't be here for more than an hour yet. It's only the animals that can tell the dawn's coming so far ahead. Down here we'll be able to see pretty well in an hour's time. Lend me your knife, Papillon.'

I held it out to him without hesitation. He took two or three paces and cut off the branch of a cactus. He gave me one piece and kept the other for himself.

'Drink the water it has in it and rub some on your face.'

Using this strange sort of a basin I drank and washed. Daylight was coming. Jean gave me back the knife. I lit a cigarette and Jean had one too. We set off. We had to wade through a good many very difficult patches of marsh, and then, without having met anyone, friend or enemy, we reached the outskirts of the Inini camp at about midday.

It was a regular highway that we came to. On one side of the broad clearing there ran a narrow-gauge railway. 'It's a line with nothing but trucks pushed by the Chinese,' he told me. 'The wheels make a terrible noise and you can hear them a great way off.' We were there when one went by: it had a bench with two screws sitting on it. Behind there were two Chinese with long poles to act as brakes. Sparks flew from the wheels. Jean told me the poles were tipped with steel and they were used either for pushing with or braking.

There were a great many people on the road. Chinese went by, some carrying coils of creeper on their shoulders, some a wild pig, and others bundles of palm fronds. They all looked as though they were going to the camp. Jean told me there were many reasons for them to go out into the forest – hunting game, looking for creepers to make furniture with, or palm fronds for the mats that shaded the vegetable gardens from the burning sun, catching butterflies, insects, snakes, etc. Some Chinese were allowed to go into the forest for a few hours once they had finished the work they were set. They all had to be back before five o'clock in the afternoon.

'Here, Jean. Here's the five hundred francs and your gun [I'd already unloaded it]. I've got my knife and my machete. You can go now: and thanks. I hope God will reward you better than I can for having helped an unfortunate bastard to try and make a new life. You've been dead straight, so thanks again. I hope when you tell your children all about this you'll say, "The convict looked a decent type; I'm not sorry I helped him."'

'Monsieur Papillon, it's late. I couldn't get far before night-fall. Keep the gun: I'll stay with you until tomorrow morning. If you don't mind, I'd rather it was me that stopped the Chinese to go and tell Cuic-Cuic – you pick him out. He won't be so frightened as if he saw a white man on the run. You let me go out on the road. Even if a screw turns up, he won't think it strange to see me here. I'll say I'm looking for rosewood for the Symphorien Company in Cayenne. Rely on me.'

'Well, in that case take your gun – an unarmed man in the forest would look queer.'

'That's true.'

Jean stood there on the road. I was going to give a low whistle when a Chinese I liked the look of came along.

'Good day, Mouché,' said a little old Chinaman in pidgin-French: he was carrying what must certainly be a length of cabbage-palm on his shoulder – delicious eating. I whistled, because this polite old man who greeted Jean first seemed to me the right sort.

'Good day, Chink. Stop: me want talk to you.'

'What you want, Mouché?' he asked, stopping.

They talked together for close on five minutes. I couldn't hear what they said. Two Chinese went by, carrying a big deer on a pole: it hung from its feet, and its head dragged along the ground. They went by without greeting the Negro, but they said a few words in Chinese to their countryman, who made a short reply.

Jean brought the old man into the trees. He came towards me, holding out his hand. 'You makee break?'

'Yes'

'Where from?'

'Devil.'

'Good, good.' He laughed, staring at me with his slit eyes. 'Good, good. What your name?'

'Papillon.'

'Me not know.'

'Me, friend of Chang. Chang Vauquien, Cuic-Cuic's brother.'

'Oh? Good, good.' He shook my hand again. 'What you want?'

'Tell Cuic-Cuic me waiting here.'

'No can do.'

'How come?'

'Cuic-Cuic him steal sixty ducks belong head of camp. Head go to kill Cuic-Cuic, Cuic-Cuic him run'

'How long ago?'

'Two month.'

'Gone by sea?'

'No can tell. Me go to camp, talk other Chinaman, great friend of Cuic-Cuic. Him say what to do. You no go away from here. Me come back tonight.'

'What time?'

'Don't know. But me come, bring food, cigarettes: you no lightee fire here. Me whistle La Madelon. When you hear, you come out on road. Savvy?'

'Me savvy.' He disappeared. 'What do you think about it, Jean?'

'There's no harm, because if you like we'll go straight back the way we came to Kourou and I'll find you a canoe, some food and a sail so that you can get away by sea.'

'I'm going very far, Jean: it wouldn't be possible to set off alone. But thanks for your offer. If the worst comes to the worst I'll accept it.'

The Chinese had given us a big piece of cabbage-palm, and we ate it. It was fresh and very good indeed – a strong nutty flavour. Jean was going to keep watch: I felt quite sure of him. I daubed my face and hands with tobacco-juice, for the mosquitoes were beginning their attack.

Jean shook me awake. 'Papillon, someone's whistling La Madelon.'

'What's the time?'

'Not late: maybe nine o'clock.'

We went out on to the road. The night was very dark. The whistler came nearer and I answered. He came closer still: we were very near, but I couldn't see him. We each whistled in turn, and presently we came together. There were three of them. Each shook me by the hand. The moon would be rising soon.

'Let's sit here by the side of the road,' said one of them in perfect French. 'No one can see us in the darkness.' Jean came with us. 'Eat first; we'll talk afterwards,' said the educated Chinese. Jean and I ate some piping hot vegetable soup. It warmed us through and through and we decided to keep the rest of the food for later. We drank hot sweet tea that tasted of mint – it was delicious.

'So you're a close friend of Chang's?'

'Yes. He told me to come and look for Cuic-Cuic so we could escape together. I've already made a break that took me a very long way – as far as Colombia. I'm a good sailor, and that's why Chang wanted me to take his brother. He trusts me.'

'I see. What are Chang's tatoo marks?'

'A dragon on his chest and three spots on his left hand. He told me those three spots meant he was one of the leaders of the rising at Pulo-Condor. His best friend was another leader of the rising called Van Hue. He's lost an arm.'

'That's me,' said the educated one. 'You're certainly a friend of Chang's, and that means you're our friend. Listen: Cuic-Cuic has not been able to get out to sea yet because he doesn't know how to sail a boat. He's alone: he's in the bush, about five miles from here. He makes charcoal. Friends sell it for him and give him the money. When he's saved enough he'll buy a boat and look for somebody who'll escape with him by sea. He's in no danger where he is. He's on a kind of island surrounded by treacherous mud and no one can get on to it. Anyone who doesn't know the way through the marsh would be sucked down. I'll fetch you at dawn and take you to Cuic-Cuic. Come with us.'

We went along the edge of the road, because the moon had risen and it was light enough to see anyone at fifty yards. When we reached a wooden bridge he said, 'Shelter under this bridge. Sleep here and I'll come and fetch you tomorrow morning.'

We shook hands and they went off. They walked along quite openly: if they were found they were going to say they had been out to look at traps they had set in the bush during the day. Jean said to me, 'Papillon, don't you sleep here. You sleep in the bush and I'll stay. When he comes I'll call you.'

'Fine.' I went back into the bush and with my belly full of good soup I dropped off happily after I'd smoked a few cigarettes.

Van Hue was at the meeting place before sunrise. To gain time we were going to walk on the road until daylight. We went along fast for about forty minutes. Then suddenly there was the sun and far off we could hear the noise of a truck coming towards us down the line. We got under cover.

'Good-bye, Jean, and good luck. God bless you and your

family.' I made him take the five hundred francs. In case things went wrong with regard to Cuic-Cuic, he told me how to reach his village, and how to get round it and post myself on the path where we'd met in the first place. He had to go along it twice a week. I shook hands with that great-hearted Guiana Negro and he leapt on to the path.

'Let's go,' said Van Hue, thrusting his way into the forest. He steered without hesitation and we moved along fairly quickly, for the bush was not very thick. When branches and creepers got in his way he did not cut them with his machete. He pushed them aside.

Cuic-Cuic

In something under three hours there we were in front of a great pool of mud. Floating on the ooze, water-lilies and plants with great flat green leaves. We walked along the bank.

Van Hue saw me trip and said, 'Take care you don't fall, because if you do you sink for good – no hope whatsoever.'

'Go ahead. I'll follow you and take more care.'

There was a little island ahead of us, perhaps a hundred and fifty yards away. Smoke was rising from the middle. Those must be the charcoal mounds. I detected a crocodile in the mud, with only its eyes showing. What could it possibly live on, there in that marsh?

We walked another half mile along the bank of this sort of mud-lake. Van Hue stopped and began singing very loudly in Chinese. A man came towards the edge of the little island. A small man, wearing nothing but a pair of shorts. The two Chinese began talking. It went on and on and I was getting impatient when at last they stopped.

'Come this way,' said Van Hue. I followed him, and we went back the way we had come. 'It's all right: that was a friend of Cuic-Cuic's. Cuic-Cuic has gone hunting, but he'll be back soon. We have to wait for him here.'

We sat down. In less than an hour's time Cuic-Cuic appeared. He was a little dried-up bastard, Annamite yellow, with heavily lacquered teeth – almost shining black: he had an open, intelligent look.

'You're my brother Chang's friend?'

'Yes.'

'That's fine. You can go, Van Hue.'

'Thanks,' said Van Hue.

'Here, take this bird with you.'

'No thanks.' He shook my hand and left.

Cuic-Cuic led me along: there was a pig that walked in front of him. He followed this pig very carefully. 'Take great care, Papillon. Put a foot wrong, make the slightest mistake, and you're in the mud. If there's an accident, one can't help the other, because that would only mean two instead of one being sucked down. The way across is never the same, because the mud shifts; but the pig always finds a path. Only once did I ever have to wait two days before I could get over.'

And indeed the black pig sniffed the mud and paced swiftly out on to it. The Chinese spoke to the pig in his own language. I followed, quite taken aback at the sight of this little creature obeying him like a dog. Cuic-Cuic watched closely, and I stared, fascinated. The pig crossed to the other side without ever sinking in more than a few inches. My new friend hurried after the pig, saying 'Tread in my footsteps. We've got to move quick, because the pig's tracks will fade at once.' We crossed without any difficulty. The mud never came up higher than my calves; and that was only towards the end.

The pig had made two long detours, and this forced us to walk over the crusted mud for more than two hundred yards. Sweat poured off me. I can't say I was just frightened: I was absolutely terrified. During the first part of the crossing I wondered whether it was my fate to die as Sylvain had died. I could see him again, poor chap, in his last moments: and although I was as wide awake as possible and although I could see his body all right, his face seemed to have my features. How that crossing put me through the mangle! I won't forget it in a hurry.

'Give me your hand.' And the little skin-and-bone Cuic-Cuic helped me climb up on to the bank.

'Well, mate, the trackers aren't likely to come for us here!'

'Oh, as far as that's concerned you can rest easy.'

468

We made our way into the little island. The smell of charcoal gas caught my throat. I coughed. It was the two smoking mounds. There was no danger of my being eaten alive by mosquitoes here. Down-wind, with the smoke all round it, there was a hut, its roof and walls made of plaited fronds – a carbet. It had a door, and in front of this door stood the little Indo-Chinese I'd seen before we met Cuic-Cuic.

'Good afternoon, Mouché.'

'Talk to him in French, not pidgin,' said Cuic-Cuic. 'He's a friend of my brother's.'

The Chink, a half-portion of a man, inspected me from head to foot. Satisfied with his examination, he held out his hand, his gap-toothed mouth spread in a smile. 'Come in and sit down.'

This single room, this kitchen, was clean. There was something cooking over the fire in a big pot. Only one bed: it was made of branches, and it stood at least three feet from the ground.

'Help me to make a place for him to sleep tonight.'

'Yes, Cuic-Cuic.'

In less than half an hour there was my bunk. The two Chinese laid the table and we ate some splendid soup, then white rice and meat cooked with onions.

This chap, Cuic-Cuic's friend, was the one who sold the charcoal. He didn't live on the island and so at nightfall Cuic-Cuic and I were alone together.

'Yes, I stole all the commanding officer's ducks, and that's why I'm on the run.'

We were sitting one on each side of the little fire, and from time to time the flames lit up our faces. We looked hard at one another; and each, talking about himself, tried to find out what the other was like.

There was almost no yellow in Cuic-Cuic's face: the sun had turned it nearly copper coloured. His very slanting bright black eyes looked me straight in the face when he spoke. He smoked long cigars he rolled himself, using black leaf. I went on smoking cigarettes, making them with the rice-paper the one-armed man had given me.

'So I made a break, seeing the chief, the ducks' owner, meant to kill me. That was three months ago. The worst of it is, I've gambled away not only the money for the ducks but everything from the two charcoal kilns.'

469

'Where do you play?'

'In the bush. The Chinese from the Inini camp and the discharged prisoners from Cascade get together every night.'

'You've made up your mind to get away by sea?'

'That's the one thing I aim at; and by selling charcoal I thought I'd be able to buy a boat and then find a man who knew how to sail it and who'd like to go off with me. But in three weeks' time there'll be more charcoal to sell and then we'll buy a boat and set off in it, since you understand the sea.'

'I've got money, Cuic-Cuic. We don't have to wait for the charcoal to buy a boat.'

'That's fine, then. There's a good boat for sale at one thousand five hundred francs. It's a Negro, a wood-cutter, who's selling it.'

'You've seen it, then?'

'Yes.'

'Well, I'd like to see it too.'

'Tomorrow I'll go and see Chocolate, as I call him. Tell me about your break, Papillon, will you? I thought it was impossible to escape from Devil's Island. Why didn't my brother Chang come with you?' I told him all about the break, the wave called Lisette, and Sylvain's death. 'I can see Chang didn't want to go with you. It was terribly risky. You have luck on your side, that's the only reason you've reached here alive. I'm glad of it.'

Cuic-Cuic and I talked for more than three hours. We turned in early, because he wanted to go and see Chocolate at daybreak. We put a big log on the fire to keep it in all night and went to bed. The smoke caught my throat and made me cough, but there was the advantage that not a single mosquito came in.

Lying there on my pallet with a good warm blanket over me, I closed my eyes. But I could not go to sleep. I was too excited. Yes, the break was going well. If the boat was good, I'd be at sea in under a week. Cuic-Cuic was a small, lean type, but he must have uncommon strength and great powers of resistance. He was certainly dead straight with his friends, but he would be very cruel to his enemies, for sure. It is difficult to make out an Asiatic face – it gives nothing away: but his eyes spoke in his favour.

I dropped off and I dreamt of a sunlit sea with my boat tearing happily through the waves on its way to freedom.

'Would you like coffee or tea?'

'What do you drink?'

'Tea.'

'Give me tea, then.'

Dawn was just beginning to break: the fire had kept in overnight and water was boiling in a pot. There was the cheerful sound of a cock crowing. No other bird-cries anywhere near us: no doubt the smoke of the charcoal heaps kept them away. The black pig was lying on Cuic-Cuic's bed. It went on sleeping, which seemed to me to show idleness. Dampers made of rice flour were cooking in the ashes. When he'd given me some sugared tea, my mate cut a damper in two, spread it with margarine and gave it to me. We made a huge breakfast. I ate three well-cooked dampers.

'I'm off: come a little way with me. If anyone calls or whistles, don't you answer. You're in no danger – it's impossible for anyone to reach this place. But if you show yourself on the bank you might get shot.'

His master called him and the pig got out of bed. It ate and drank. Then it walked out, with us following. It went straight towards the mud. Some way from the place we landed the day before, it went down. It paced out for about ten yards and then turned back. It didn't like the mud there. It tried three times and then it found the right crossing. At once Cuic-Cuic hurried without any hesitation over to the mainland.

He didn't intend to come back until the evening. He'd put the soup on the fire and I ate it by myself. Then I found eight eggs in the hen-run and made a little omelette with three of them, using margarine. The wind had changed and the smoke from the heap opposite the hut drove away to one side. In the afternoon I lay there, sheltering comfortably from the rain on my bed of branches, and the charcoal gas did not worry me at all.

During the morning I walked about all over the island. There was quite a big clearing near the middle. The fallen trees and the piles of logs showed that this was where Cuic-Cuic got the wood for his mounds. I also found a pit of white clay where he must certainly take the earth he needed to cover the heaps and prevent them from burning away. The hens pecked about in the clearing. A huge rat darted away from under my feet, and a few yards farther on I found a dead snake nearly six feet long. The rat must just have killed it.

I made a whole series of discoveries during this day alone on the island. For instance, I found a family of ant-eaters. The mother and three little ones. They were in the middle of a huge ant-hill, with ants milling about in every direction. And then there were a dozen very small monkeys, leaping from tree to tree in the clearing. They were marmosets, and when I appeared they uttered heart-breaking cries.

Cuic-Cuic came back that evening. 'I didn't see Chocolate or his boat, either. He must have gone to get stores at Cascade, the little village where his house is. Did you have enough to eat?'

'Yes.'

'Would you like some more?'

'No.'

'I've brought you two packets of ration tobacco. That's all there was.'

'Thanks. It doesn't matter. When Chocolate goes to the village, how long does he stay?'

'Two or three days: but still I'll go tomorrow and every day after that, because I don't know when he left.'

The next day the rain came pouring down in torrents. That did not prevent Cuic-Cuic from setting off completely naked, with his clothes under his arm wrapped in a piece of oilskin. I didn't go with him. 'It's not worth your getting wet too,' he said.

The rain stopped. From the sun I could see it was between ten and eleven o'clock. One of the two heaps, the farther one, had caved in under the enormous downpour. I went over to have a look at it. The rain had not put the fire out altogether. Smoke was still rising from the shapeless mound. All at once I rubbed my eyes and stared again – I could hardly believe what I had just seen. Five shoes protruding from the charcoal. I realized at once that these shoes, upright on their heels, each had a foot and a leg in it. So there were three men cooking away in the heap. I don't have to spell out my first reaction. Chancing on a thing like that sends a shiver right down your back. I bent over, and kicking the half charred wood aside I found the sixth shoe.

That Cuic-Cuic is a fast worker: as soon as he does any characters in, he reduces them to ashes by wholesale. It was so striking that to begin with I walked away from the heap and into the clearing. I needed the warmth of the sun. Yes, suddenly, in that stifling temperature, I felt cold through and through and I had to have the tropical sun to warm me.

Reading this, you may think it unnatural; you may think I ought to have been in a muck-sweat after making a discovery like that. Well, no: I was utterly chilled, frozen spiritually and physically. It was not until long after, almost an hour, that the sweat started pouring down my face, because the more I thought about it the more it seemed a miracle to me that I was still alive, seeing I'd told him I had a lot of money in my charger. Or was he maybe reserving me for the bottom of a third mound?

I remembered how his brother Chang had told me Cuic-Cuic had been convicted of piracy and murder aboard a junk. When they attacked a vessel with the idea of robbing it they wiped out the whole family – always on so-called political grounds, of course. So these were characters who were already quite used to wholesale killings. And then again, I was a prisoner here. I was in a queer sort of a position, all right.

Let's get things straight. If I kill Cuic-Cuic here on the island and stuff him into the heap in his turn, nobody's any the wiser. But the pig won't obey me: not so much as a word of French does this fool of a tame pig understand. So there's no way of getting off the island. If I turn a gun on him, the Chink will obey me: but then, having got off the island, I'll be forced to kill him on the other side. If I throw him into the mud, he'll vanish: but there must be some reason why he burns these types rather than tosses them over the bank, which would be so much easier. As far as the screws are concerned, I don't give a hoot in hell, but if his Chinese friends find out I've killed him, they'll turn man-hunters, and with their knowledge of the bush it wouldn't be any sort of fun having them after me. Cuic-Cuic's only got a single-barrelled muzzle-loader. He never lets go of it, not even when he's cooking. He sleeps with it and he even carries it with him when he leaves the hut to relieve himself. I must keep my knife open all the time of course: but even so, I have to sleep sometimes. Well, I did make a splendid choice of a companion to escape with, didn't I?

I couldn't eat all day. And I'd still not made up my mind when I heard somebody singing. It was Cuic-Cuic coming back. Hidden behind the leaves I watched him. He had a bundle balanced on his head, and when he was very close to the bank I showed myself. With a smile he handed me a parcel wrapped up in a flour sack, climbed up beside me and hurried towards the hut. I followed him.

'Good news, Papillon: Chocolate's back. He still has the boat. He says it'll carry more than half a ton without sinking. The things you're carrying are flour sacks to make a mainsail and a jib. This is the first bundle. Tomorrow we'll bring the rest, because you'll come with me and see whether you like the boat.' Cuic-Cuic said all this without turning round. We were walking in a line. The pig first, then him and then me. It occurred to me that it didn't look as though he was planning to stuff me into the charcoal, seeing that he was going to take me to see the boat tomorrow and since he was already beginning to spend money on the escape – he'd bought these flour sacks. 'Why, a heap has caved in. The rain, I dare say. It doesn't surprise me, all this bleeding wet.'

He didn't even turn aside to go and look at the heap but went straight into the hut. I couldn't tell what to say, or what decision to make. Pretending not to have seen anything wouldn't wash. It would seem unnatural never to have stepped over to the charcoal mound, a mere twenty-five yards from the hut, all day long.

'You let the fire go out?'

'Yes. I didn't notice.'

'But you haven't had anything to eat?'

'No. I wasn't hungry.'

'Are you sick?'

'No.'

'Then why didn't you eat the soup?'

'Cuic-Cuic, sit down. I've got to talk to you.'

'Let me just light the fire first.'

'No. I want to talk to you right away, while it's still daylight.'

'What's the matter?'

'Those three men in the charcoal heap – now it's fallen in they show. Tell me about it, will you?'

'Oh, that's why you were so upset!' And quite unmoved he looked me straight in the eye. 'After you'd seen that, you were uneasy in your mind. I understand you perfectly well; it's natural enough. Indeed, it was lucky for me you didn't knife me from behind. Listen, Papillon, those three men were trackers. Now a week ago, or rather ten days to be exact, I sold Chocolate a fair amount of charcoal. The Chinese you saw helped me get the sacks off the island. It's a tricky business: we have two hundred yards of rope or more and we slide a little train of sacks over the mud. I'll keep it short. Between here and the little channel where Chocolate's canoe was lying, we left a good many traces. Some worn old sacks had leaked charcoal. That was when the first tracker started hanging about. I could tell from the noises the animals made that there was someone in the bush. I saw the character without him seeing me. It wasn't difficult to cross over, make a half circle and come up behind him unawares. He died without ever seeing who killed him. As I'd noticed that some days after a body has sunk into the mud it comes up again, I carried him here and put him into the charcoal.'

'And what about the other two?'

'That was three days before you came. The night was very dark and silent, which is uncommon here in the bush. These two had been moving round the marsh since nightfall. When the smoke drifted towards him, one of them coughed from time to time. That was how I knew they were there. Before dawn I risked a crossing on the far side from where I had pinpointed the cough. As for the first tracker, to keep things short, I just cut his throat. He didn't even have time to scream. The other one, who had a gun, was stupid enough to let me see him – he was too taken up with staring into the bush on the island, trying to see what was happening over there. I shot him, and then seeing he wasn't dead I slid my knife into his heart. There, Papillon, that's the story of the three stiffs you found in the charcoal. Two were Arabs and one was French. It was very tricky getting over the mud with a corpse on my shoulder. They were heavy, and I had to make two journeys. In the end I managed to get them all into the mound.'

'And that's really how it happened?'

'Yes, Papillon, I swear that's exactly how it was.'

'Why didn't you chuck them into the mud?'

'As I just told you, the mud throws up corpses. Sometimes big deer fall in and then a week later they come to the surface again. They stink until the vultures have eaten them. It takes quite a while, and the vultures flying about and making a noise brings people to look. I swear to you, Papillon, you've nothing to be afraid of with me. Listen, take the gun, if that would make you any happier.'

I had a wild desire to accept but I fought it down, and as naturally as I could I said, 'No, Cuic-Cuic. I'm here because I feel I'm with a friend – perfectly safe. But you'll have to burn the trackers again tomorrow, because who can tell what'll happen when we leave this place? I don't want anyone to accuse me of three murders, even if I'm not here.'

'OK, I'll burn them again tomorrow. But don't you worry, no one will ever set foot on this island. It's impossible to get over without sinking in the mud.'

'And what if they use a rubber dinghy?'

'I hadn't thought of that.'

'If someone brought the gendarmes here and they took it into their heads to cross to the island, believe me they'd cross with a rubber dinghy all right. And that's why we must get out as soon as we possibly can.'

'Right. Tomorrow we'll light the mound again – in any case it's not gone right out. All we have to do is to make two holes for the air.'

'Good-night, Cuic-Cuic.'

'Good-night, Papillon. And I say again, sleep well – you can trust me.'

With the blanket pulled up to my chin, I luxuriated in its warmth. I lit a cigarette. Not ten minutes later, Cuic-Cuic was snoring. And there was the heavy breathing of his pig, lying there next to him. There were no more flames, but the tree-trunk on the hearth glowed red every time the breeze wafted into the hut, and this glow gave me a feeling of peace and calmness. I delighted in this comfort and I dropped off thinking. 'Either I wake up tomorrow, and in that case everything will be fine between Cuic-Cuic and me; or else the Chinese is a better actor than Sacha Guitry, a marvel at hiding what he means to do and at telling tales, and in that case I shall never see the sun again, because I know too much – I might be dangerous to him.'

The specialist in mass-murder woke me, a mug of coffee in his hand; and as though nothing had happened he wished me good morning with a wonderfully cordial smile. Dawn had broken. 'Here, drink your coffee and have a damper – it's already spread.'

When I'd eaten and drunk I washed outside, taking water from a barrel that was always full.

'Will you give me a hand, Papillon?'

'Yes,' I said, without asking what he wanted me to do.

We pulled the half burnt corpses out by their feet. I didn't say anything, but I noticed that all three of them had had their bellies opened: the kindly Chinese must have rummaged through their guts to see whether they had chargers. Were they in fact trackers? Man hunters? Why might not they have been after butterflies or game? Had he killed them to protect himself or to rob them? Enough of that. They were back in a hole in the mound, well covered with wood and clay. We opened two passages for the air and the heap went back to its two jobs – making charcoal and turning the three stiffs into cinders.

'Let's go, Papillon.'

The little pig quickly found a crossing. Hurrying along one after the other we passed over the mud. I could not overcome my dread at the moment of setting out upon it. Sylvain's end had made such an appalling impression on me that I could not set foot on the marsh with an easy mind. At last, the cold sweat running off me, I darted after Cuic-Cuic. I walked carefully in his footsteps. There was no reason why I should sink: if he got over, I could get over.

Rather more than two hours of walking brought us to the place where Chocolate was cutting wood. We'd met nobody in the bush and so we'd never had to hide.

'Good-day, Mouché.'

'Good-day, Cuic-Cuic.'

'OK?'

'Fine. How are you?'

'Show my friend the boat.'

It was a very strong-built boat, something like a lighter. It was very heavy, but it was solid. I dug my knife in all over it: nowhere did the point go in more than a quarter of an inch. The planking was sound, too. It had been made of the very best quality wood.

'What are you asking for it?'

'Two thousand five hundred francs.'

'I'll give you two thousand.' It was a deal. 'This boat has no keel. I'll give you an extra five hundred francs, but you've got to fix a keel, a rudder and a mast. Hardwood keel and rudder. The mast, ten foot of light whippy wood. When will it be ready?'

'In a week.'

'Here are two thousand franc notes and one five hundred. I'm going to cut them in two and I'll give you the other half on delivery. You keep these three halves. Right?'

'Yes.'

'I want some permanganate, a keg of water, cigarettes and matches, stores for four men for a month – flour, oil, coffee and sugar – I'll pay for them separately. You must hand everything over to me on the river, on the Kourou.'

'Mouché, I can't take you down to the mouth of the river.'

'I never asked you to. All I said was to deliver the boat on the river and not in this creek.'

'Here are the flour sacks, some rope, needles and sail thread.'

Cuic-Cuic and I went back to our hide-out. We got there without any trouble before nightfall. On the way back he carried the pig on his shoulders, because it was tired.

The next day I was alone, busy sewing the sail, when I heard shouts. I went towards the mud, hiding behind the trees, and looked over to the opposite bank: Cuic-Cuic and the Chinese intellectual were arguing and waving their arms. It seemed to me that the intellectual wanted to cross to the island and Cuic-Cuic was against it. Each had a machete in his hand. The one-armed man was the more excited of the two. Christ, he mustn't kill Cuic-Cuic on me! I decided to show myself. I whistled. They turned towards me.

'What's up, Cuic-Cuic?'

'I want to talk to you, Papillon,' shouted the other. 'Cuic-Cuic won't let me across.'

After another ten minutes of argument in Chinese the pig walked in front of them and they both came over to the island. We sat in the hut with mugs of tea in our hands, and I waited until they should make up their minds to speak.

'Well,' said Cuic-Cuic, 'this is what it's all about: he wants to come on the break with us, cost what it may. I keep telling him it's not for me to make any decision – you're the one who pays and who gives all the orders. He won't believe me.'

'Papillon,' said the other, 'Cuic-Cuic just has to take me with him.'

'How come?'

'Because two years ago he cut off my arm in a fight over

478

a card-game. He made me swear not to kill him. I swore on one condition – he'd got to feed me all my life long, or at least whenever I insisted upon it. Now if he goes off, I'll never see him again as long as I live. That's why he's either got to let you go alone or he's got to take me with him.'

'Well, for God's sake! Now I really have seen everything. Listen, I'm quite willing to take you. It's a big, solid boat, and we could take more if we wanted. If Cuic-Cuic agrees, you can come.'

'Thanks,' said the one-armed man.

'What do you say, Cuic-Cuic?'

'Fine, if you want it that way.'

'There's one important thing. Can you get out of the camp without being reported missing and reach the river before night? Will they think you've escaped and send out a search-party?'

'No difficulty there at all. I'm allowed out at three in the afternoon, and I can get to the river bank in under two hours.'

'Cuic-Cuic, would you be able to find the place in the dark, for us to take your friend aboard, losing no time?'

'Oh, no sort of doubt about it at all.'

'Come here in a week's time and I'll tell you what day we leave.'

Delighted, the one-armed man shook my hand and went away. I watched them as they said good-bye to one another on the far bank – they shook hands before separating. So that was all right. When Cuic-Cuic was back in the hut I said, 'That was a quaint sort of agreement you made with your enemy, feeding him for the rest of his life. I've never heard of such a thing. What did you cut his arm off for?'

'It was in a fight about cards.'

'It would have been better to have killed him.'

'No, because he's a very good friend of mine. When I was brought up in front of the court-martial because of the squabble, he stood up for me right through – he said he'd attacked me and I'd only acted in self-defence. I accepted the agreement of my own free will and I must never let him down in any way. The only thing is I didn't like to mention it to you because you're the one that's paying for this whole break.'

'OK, Cuic-Cuic, let's not talk about that any more. Once we're free, God willing, it'll be up to you to do what you think's right.'

'I'll keep my word.'

'What do you reckon you'll do, supposing we do get free one of these days?'

'A restaurant. I'm a very good cook and he's a specialist in chow mein.'

This whole business put me in a good temper. It was so funny from beginning to end that I couldn't help teasing Cuic-Cuic about it from time to time.

Chocolate kept his promise: in five days everything was ready. We went through a driving rain storm to look at the boat. All in order. The mast, rudder and keel had been fitted extremely well, and they were made of the finest wood. The boat was waiting for us with its water-barrel and the stores in a backwater. All that was needed now was to let Van Hue know. Chocolate said he would go to the camp and tell him. So that we shouldn't have to run the risk of coming in to the side to pick him up, Chocolate would take him directly to the hide-out.

The mouth of the Kourou river was marked by two lights. If it was raining we could run out right in the middle of the stream without any risk – the sails furled, of course, so as not to be picked up. Chocolate gave us some black paint and a brush. We were to paint a big K on the mainsail and the number 21. K21 was the registration number of a fishing-boat that sometimes went out at night. If we were seen hoisting the sail as we put out to sea, they would take us for the other boat.

It was for tomorrow evening at seven, an hour after nightfall. Cuic-Cuic assured me he had found a path that would take us to the hiding-place for sure. We'd leave the island at five so as to have an hour's daylight to walk in.

We were in very high spirits as we went back to the hut. Cuic-Cuic walked along in front of me, carrying the pig on his shoulder, and he never stopped talking. 'At last I'm going to get clear of prison,' he said, without turning round. 'It's thanks to you and my brother Chang. Maybe one day, when the French have left Indo-China, I'll be able to get back to my own country.'

In short, he believed in me; and the knowledge that I liked the boat made him as happy as a sandboy. I slept on the island for the last time – my last night, I hoped, on the soil of Guiana.

If I could get away from the river and out into the open

sea, it was certain freedom. Shipwreck was the only danger; for now that the war was on no country handed back escaping fugitives. In that respect at least, the war had been of some use to us. If the French caught us, we were condemned to death, true enough: but they had to catch us first. I thought of Sylvain: if he hadn't made that mistake he'd have been here by my side now. I dropped off, composing this cable: 'Monsieur Pradel, public prosecutor: at last I have conquered. I have left the sewer you flung me into, left it for ever. It has taken me nine years.'

The sun was quite high by the time Cuic-Cuic woke me up. Tea and dampers. There were boxes all over the place. I caught sight of two wickerwork cages. 'What are you going to do with them?'

'They're for the hens, so we can eat them on the voyage.'

'You're crazy, Cuic-Cuic! We can't take the hens.'

'But I'm going to take them, though.'

'Are you out of your mind? What if the ebb only takes us out round about daybreak and the cocks and hens start cackling out there on the river – don't you see the danger?'

'Me no leave hens.'

'Cook them then, and put them up in their own fat and some oil. They'll keep, and we'll eat them during the first three days.'

Persuaded at last, Cuic-Cuic went out to fetch the hens; but the noise of the first four made the others smell a rat, because he was never able to catch the rest – they all vanished into the bush and hid. I can't tell how they had foreseen the danger, but they had – mystery of nature!

Loaded like pack-horses we crossed the mud behind the pig. Cuic-Cuic had begged me to take it with us.

'Can you give me your word the creature won't make a noise?'

'I promise you he won't. When I give the word he is quite silent. Two or three times we've been hunted by a jaguar – the jaguar circling round to take us unawares – and he's not made a sound. And yet every bristle on his body was on end.'

I was sure that Cuic-Cuic was telling the truth, so I agreed to take his beloved swine aboard. It was dark, by the time we reached the hiding-place. Chocolate was there with Van Hue. I checked everything with a couple of electric torches. There was nothing missing: the parrels of the sail were already shipped and the jib was in its place, ready to be set. I showed Cuic-Cuic how to hoist it and he went through the motions two or three times. He quickly grasped what I wanted of him. The Negro had behaved wonderfully; I paid him: he was such a simple-minded creature that he had brought gummed paper and the other halves of the notes – he asked me to stick them together for him. Never for a moment had it occurred to him that I might take the money back. When people don't think evil of others, it means they're decent and straightforward themselves. Chocolate was a fine man, honest and direct. He'd seen how the convicts were treated, and he had no sort of hesitation in helping three of them escape from that hell.

'Good-bye, Chocolate. Good luck to you and your family.'

'Thank you very much.'

Eleventh Exercise-Book
Farewell to Penal

The Break with the Chinese

I got in last: Chocolate shoved us off and the boat moved out into the stream. No paddles, but two good oars: Cuic worked one in the bows and I worked the other. In less than two hours we reached the main river.

It had been raining for the last hour and more. A painted flour sack was my oilskin, and Cuic-Cuic and Van Hue each had one too. The Kourou was running fast, and it was full of eddies, but in spite of the current we were in the middle of the stream within an hour. Three hours later, with the ebb-tide carrying us, we passed between the two lights. I knew the sea was near at hand, because they stood on the farthest points of the estuary. With our jib and mainsail set, we ran out of the Kourou without the slightest hitch. The wind took us on the beam with such force that I was obliged to pay the sheet right out. We ran abruptly into the sea, racing through the narrow strait: rapidly the shore dropped away behind us. Twenty-five miles ahead, the lighthouse on Royale gave us our position. Thirteen days ago I was behind that light, on Devil's Island. My two Chinese companions did not burst out into cries of delight at this clean break with the mainland, at getting out to sea in the darkness. The Orientals do not express their feelings in the same way that we do. Speaking in an ordinary voice, once we were well out, Cuic-Cuic merely observed, 'We managed that very well,' and that was all.

Van Hue added, 'Yes: we got out to sea without anything going wrong.'

'Cuic-Cuic, I want a drink. Pass me a little tafia.' They poured some out for me and then they knocked back a stiff tot themselves.

I'd set off without a compass, but my first break had taught me how to navigate by the sun, the moon, the stars and the wind, so without hesitation I brought the mast to bear on the North Star and headed straight out to sea. The boat handled well: it rose easily to the swell and scarcely rolled at all. The wind was very strong, and by the morning we were a great distance from the coast and from the Iles du Salut. If it hadn't been too dangerous I should have run in towards Devil's Island to have a good stare at it as I sailed by, sitting there at my ease.

Now for six days we had had a heavy swell, but no rain and no violent wind. The stiff breeze had carried us westward at a fair speed. Cuic-Cuic and Hue were excellent shipmates. They never complained either of the rough sea, or of the sun, or of the cold at night. There was only one thing – neither would lay a finger on the tiller or take over the boat for a few hours so that I could sleep. They produced something to eat three or four times a day. All the hens and the cocks made their way into the pot. Yesterday, by way of a joke, I said to Cuic-Cuic, 'When are we going to eat the pig?'

He took it terribly to heart. 'That creature is my friend, and before anyone kills him he'll have to kill me first.'

My companions took great care of me. They gave up smoking so that I should have as much tobacco as I wanted. There was hot tea ready all the time. They did everything without having to be told.

We had been gone a week. I was at the end of my tether. The sun was beating down with such strength that even my Chinks were done an elegant brown. I just had to sleep. I lashed the tiller and left the boat with the merest scrap of sail – it could go wherever the wind took it. I slept like one of the dead for four hours.

A harder thump than usual started me violently out of my sleep. When I dipped my face into the water I had the pleasant surprise of finding that Cuic-Cuic had shaved me while I was asleep – I'd felt nothing. He'd also put oil on my face.

Since yesterday evening I'd been steering west by south, because it seemed to me I'd made too much northing. This heavy boat not only held the sea well, but it also made little leeway. That was why I thought I'd got too far to the north, seeing that I'd reckoned on a good deal of drift when maybe there had been almost none. God above, an airship! This was the first time in my life I'd ever seen one. It didn't look as though it was coming towards us and it was too far off to be able to tell how big it was. Its aluminium-coloured sides sent back the sun with such a silvery brilliance that you couldn't look at it for long. Now it had changed direction and it looked as though it was steering for us. Yes: it grew larger and larger and in less than twenty minutes it was over our heads. Cuic-Cuic and Hue were so astonished at the spectacle that they never stopped jabbering in Chinese.

'For Christ's sake, talk French, so I can understand you.'

'English sausage,' said Cuic-Cuic.

'No, it's not exactly a sausage: it's an airship.'

The huge contraption was so low now that we could see every detail: it kept turning above us in narrow circles. Flags came out and made signals. We couldn't understand, so we couldn't reply. The airship went on signalling, coming even closer – so close we could see the people in the cabin. Then it went straight off in the direction of the land. Less than an hour later an aeroplane appeared and passed over us several times.

The swell had increased and quite suddenly the wind had strengthened. The horizon was clear all round, so there was no danger of rain.

'Look,' said the one-armed man.

'Where?'

'That black speck over there where the land should be. That speck is a ship.'

'How do you know?'

'I'm sure of it: and I'll go so far as to say it's a fast destroyer.'

'Why?'

'Because it's making no smoke.'

And indeed after a long hour we could very clearly see a grey man-of-war apparently coming straight for us. It grew bigger and bigger, which meant it was coming at an enormous speed, and its bows were pointing directly at us – so much so that I was afraid it would shave us too close. That would be dangerous, because with the heavy seas running across its wake it might sink us.

It began a turn, showing us its side, and we saw its name, the *Tarpon*. The destroyer, with the English flag at its bows, finished its turn and came gently towards us, stern first. It moved alongside, keeping to the same speed as us. Most of the crew were on deck, dressed in the blue of the Royal Navy. On the bridge an officer in white with a loudspeaker hailed us in English, 'Heave to. Heave to at once.'

'Lower the sails, Cuic-Cuic.'

In under two minutes mainsail, foresail and jib were down. With the sails furled we hardly moved at all, except that the waves kept heaving us sideways. I could not stay long in this position without danger: a boat with no motion of its own, either from sails or motor, doesn't obey the helm. It's very dangerous when the sea is high. Putting my hand up to my mouth I shouted. 'Do you speak French, Captain?' Another officer took the loud-hailer. 'Yes, Captain, I understand French.'

'What do you want with us?'

'We want to hoist your boat aboard.'

'No, it's too risky: I don't want my boat smashed up.'

'We are a man-of-war on patrol. You just have to obey.'

'I don't give a damn: the war's nothing to do with us.'

'Aren't you survivors from a torpedoed ship?'

'No, we've escaped from the French *bagne*.'

'What's a *bagne*? What do you mean, with your *bagne*?'

'Prison, gaol. In English *convict*. Hard labour.'

'Oh, yes. I understand. Cayenne?'

'Yes, Cayenne.'

'Where are you going?'

'British Honduras.'

'That's impossible. You must steer by west and go to Georgetown. That's an order.'

'OK.' I told Cuic-Cuic to haul up the sails and we set off in the direction given by the destroyer.

We heard the noise of a motor behind us: it was a boat from the man-of-war and it very soon overtook us. There was a sailor with a rifle slung over his shoulder standing in the bows. The boat came up on our starboard side, just shaving us, neither stopping nor asking us to stop. With one step the sailor came aboard: the boat went on and turned to rejoin the destroyer.

'Good afternoon,' said the sailor. He came and sat down at my side. Then he took the tiller and steered rather more south than I had been going. I gave the steering over to him, watching how he did it. He knew how to handle a boat, there was no sort of doubt about that. In spite of it all I stayed where I was. You never know.

'Cigarettes?' He took out three packets of English cigarettes and gave us one each.

'God above,' said Cuic-Cuic, 'they must have given him

these the moment he got into the boat: he certainly wouldn't have been walking about with three packets on him.'

I laughed at Cuic-Cuic's remark and then went back to watching the English sailor, who was better at managing a boat than I was. I had plenty of time for reflection. This time the break had succeeded for good and all. I was free, free. A warmth flooded up from my heart and indeed I believe my eyes filled with tears. It was true: here I was, free for ever, because now the war was on no country ever handed fugitives back.

Before the war was over, I'd have time to make myself known and liked in any country where I happened to have settled. The only difficulty was that maybe the war would prevent me from choosing the country where I'd like to live. That didn't matter at all: wherever I lived my conduct would soon win the authorities' and the people's trust and esteem. My behaviour must be and would be irreproachable. Even more: it would be exemplary.

This feeling of security, of having at last overcome the way down the drain, was so great that I thought of nothing else. You've won at last, Papillon! After nine years you've come out on top. Thank you, Lord: You might have done it sooner, but Your ways are mysterious and I have no complaints, because thanks to Your help I'm still young and healthy, and I'm free.

I was still reflecting upon the distance I'd come during these nine years of penal, plus the two served in France before – a total of eleven – when I looked where the sailor was pointing as he cried, 'Land!'

At four in the afternoon, having passed an unlit lighthouse, we ran up an enormous river, the Demerara. The ship's boat reappeared: the sailor handed back the tiller and went into the bows. He caught the tow-line they threw and made it fast to the thwart. He lowered the sails himself, and gently towed by the boat we went about ten miles up the yellow river, with the destroyer following two hundred yards behind. A bend in the stream, and then a big town appeared. 'Georgetown,' said the English sailor.

This was the capital of British Guiana, and the boat towed us slowly in. A great many merchant ships, launches and men-of-war. Guns in turrets, standing on the banks of the river. What with these and all the others aboard the naval vessels, it was a positive arsenal.

It was war time. The war had been going on for two years, but I had not really been conscious of it. Georgetown, the capital of British Guiana, was an important port on the Demerara river, and it was in the war up to its neck – involved a hundred per cent. I found it very queer indeed, this feeling of a town under arms. We had scarcely touched the naval landing-stage before our accompanying destroyer came smoothly in and moored beside us. We climbed up on to the wharf, Cuic-Cuic and his pig, Hue with a little bundle in his hand, and me without anything at all. No civilians at all at this Royal Navy landing-place: only soldiers and sailors. An officer I recognized came up. He was the one who'd talked to me in French from the bridge of the destroyer. Kindly he held out his hand and said, 'Are you pretty fit?'

'Yes, Captain.'

'Fine. Still, you'll have to go to the infirmary and have some injections. And your two friends as well.'

Life in Georgetown

In the afternoon, after they had given us several shots, we were transferred to the central police-station, a kind of headquarters with hundreds of policemen continually going in and out. The chief of the Georgetown police, the authority directly responsible for public order in this considerable port, received us in his office right away. Around him there were English officers in khaki, impeccable in their shorts and white stockings. The colonel motioned us to sit down in front of him, and speaking excellent French he said, 'Where were you coming from when you were picked up at sea?'

'From the penal settlement in French Guiana.'

'Please tell me exactly where you escaped from.'

'I escaped from Devil's Island. The others from the semi-political camp at Inini, near Kourou in French Guiana.'

'What was your sentence?'

'Life: for manslaughter.'

'And the Chinese?'

'Manslaughter too.'

'Their sentence?'

'Life.'

'Your trade?'

'Electrician.'

'And theirs?'

'Cooks.'

'Are you for de Gaulle or Pétain?'

'We know nothing about that at all. We're just men from prison trying to make ourselves a new life – to go straight and live free.'

'We'll give you a cell that will be open day and night. We'll let you out when we've looked into your statements. You've nothing to fear if you've told the truth. You must understand that we're at war and that we have to take even more care than usual.'

To cut it short, in a week's time they set us free. We'd taken advantage of this spell in the police-station to get some decent clothes. At nine one morning there we were in the street, my two Chinamen and me, properly dressed and carrying identity-cards with our photographs on them.

This was a town of two hundred and fifty thousand inhabitants, and it was almost entirely built of wood in the English way – ground floor masonry and the rest wood. The streets and avenues were stiff with people of every race, white, brown and black men, Indian, coolies, English and American sailors, Scandinavians. Our heads swam as we walked about in this multi-coloured crowd. We were filled with an overflowing happiness – our hearts were so full of it that it must have showed in our faces, even in Cuic-Cuic's and Hue's Chinese faces, because several people looked at us and smiled kindly.

'Where are we going?' asked Cuic-Cuic.

'I've got a sort of address. A black policeman told me where two Frenchmen live, at Penitence Rivers.'

As I understood it, it was a district in which only Indians lived. I went up to a policeman in spotless white and showed him the address. Before answering he asked for our identity-cards. Proudly I showed them. 'Thank you; that's fine.' Then he took the trouble to put us on to a tram, having spoken to the conductor. We left the middle of the town and after twenty minutes the conductor told us to get out. This must be the place. We questioned people in the street, saying 'Frenchmen?' A young fellow made signs for us to follow him and he led us straight to a little one-storeyed house. As soon as I went towards it three men came out with welcoming gestures.

'Can it be you, Papi? How in God's name did you get here?'

'It's just not true!' cried the oldest, the one with snow-white hair. 'Come on in. This is my place. Are the Chinese with you?'

'Yes.'

'Come in, all of you. You're very welcome.'

The old convict was called Auguste Guittou: he was born and bred in Marseilles and he'd crossed in the 1933 convoy with me, aboard the *Martinière* nine years before. After a break that ended badly his main sentence had been commuted, and he told me that it was as a ticket-of-leave man that he had escaped some three years back. Of the others, one was a character from Arles called Petit-Louis; and the third came from

490

Toulon – his name was Julot. They too had gone off after they had served their time; but by law they should have stayed there in French Guiana for the same number of years as they had been sentenced to – ten and fifteen years. That second period was called the *doublage*.

The house had four rooms, two for sleeping, one for cooking and eating in, and one that served as a workshop. They made shoes out of balata, a kind of natural rubber collected in the bush that could easily be worked and shaped with the help of hot water. The only drawback was that if it was exposed to the sun too long it melted, because the rubber was not vulcanized. They coped with that by putting strips of strong cloth between the layers of balata.

We were welcomed nobly, for they too had suffered, and suffering makes men great-hearted: without a second thought Guittou took us into his house, fixing a bedroom for the three of us. The only point of doubt was Cuic-Cuic's pig, but Cuic-Cuic said he was certain it would never make a mess in the house: it would go out all by itself whenever it needed to.

Guittou said, 'All right. We'll see. Keep it with you for the time being.'

And for the time being we settled in with old army blankets on the floor by way of beds. We sat there in front of the door, the six of us, smoking, and I told Guittou all my adventures of the last nine years. He and his two friends listened with all their ears, vividly experiencing everything I had been through, for they had known the same kind of thing, and they knew what it was like. Two of them had been acquainted with Sylvain and they were deeply grieved at his horrible death. Many people of every colour and nationality went up and down in front of us: from time to time one of them would buy shoes or a broom, for Guittou and his friends also made brooms to earn their living. They told me that here in Georgetown, counting both convicts and relégués, there were about thirty men who had escaped from penal. At night they met in a bar in the middle of town and drank beer or rum together. Julot said that they all worked to keep themselves and that most of them behaved well.

While we were sitting there in the shade in front of the house door a Chinese passed by, and Cuic-Cuic called out to him. Without saying anything to me Cuic-Cuic and Hue went off with this stranger: it was clear they were not going far, because the pig followed behind. Two hours later Cuic-Cuic came back with an ass pulling a little cart. As proud as a peacock he reined in and spoke to the donkey in Chinese. The creature gave every appearance of understanding this language. There were three camp beds in the cart, three mattresses, pillows and three suitcases. The one he gave me was full of shirts, drawers and vests, as well as ties, two pairs of shoes, etc.

'Where did you find all this, Cuic-Cuic?'

'It's my countrymen who've given them to me. We'll go and see them tomorrow if you like.'

'Fine.'

We expected Cuic-Cuic to go off again with the donkey and cart, but not at all – he unharnessed the donkey and hitched it to a ring in the courtyard.

'They gave me the ass and the cart too. I'd easily be able to earn my living with them, they said. Tomorrow morning another Chinese is coming to show me how.'

'They're quick movers, your countrymen.'

Guittou said that the donkey and cart could stay in the courtyard for the present. Everything went well, this first day of our freedom. That evening we all six sat round the work-bench: we ate a good vegetable soup made by Julot and an excellent dish of spaghetti.

'Everyone will do the washing up and the housework in turn,' said Guittou.

This meal together was the symbol of the beginning of a little warm-hearted community. The knowledge that we were going to be helped in our first attempts at living free was wonderfully comforting. Cuic-Cuic, Hue and I were truly happy, through and through. We had a roof, a bed, and open-handed friends who in their poverty were great-hearted enough to help us. What more could we ask?

'What would you like to do tonight, Papillon?' asked Guittou. 'Would you like to go down-town to the bar where all the other lags go?'

'I'd rather stay here tonight. You go, if you like – don't let me stop you.'

'Yes, I'll go, because I've got to see someone.'

'I'll stay with Cuic-Cuic and the one-armed guy.'

Petit-Louis and Guittou dressed and put on ties and went into the town. Only Julot stayed, to finish off a few pairs of shoes. My companions and I wandered about the nearby streets to get to know the district. Here everything was Indian. Very few blacks, almost no whites, just two or three Chinese restaurants.

Penitence Rivers was its name, and it might have been a little piece of India or Java. The young women were really lovely, and the old men wore long white robes. Many of the people went barefoot. It was a poor district, but everybody was cleanly dressed. The streets were ill-lit; the bars were full of people eating and drinking; and there was Indian music everywhere.

A shining black Negro dressed in white and wearing a tie stopped me. 'You're French, Monsieur?'

'Yes.'

'What a pleasure to meet a fellow-countryman. Will you come and have a drink?'

'All right: but I've two friends with me.'

'That doesn't matter. Do they speak French?'

'Yes.'

There we were all four of us, sitting at a table looking out on to the pavement. This black man from Martinique spoke purer French than we did. He told us to beware of the English Negroes, for, said he, they were all liars. 'They're not like us French: we can be trusted – they can't.'

I smiled inwardly at hearing this coal-black Negro say 'us Frenchmen'. But then immediately afterwards it worried me badly. For indeed this gentleman was French, and it seemed to me he was more French than me, since he laid claim to his country, believing in it wholeheartedly. He was capable of giving his life for France: I wasn't. So he was a more genuine Frenchman than I was. However, I went along with the current. 'Yes. I'm happy to meet a fellow-countryman too, and to talk my own language – I'm very bad at English.'

'I speak it fluently and correctly. If I can be of any use to you, here I am. Have you been in Georgetown long?'

'Only a week.'

'Where do you come from?'

'French Guiana.'

'Really? Are you an escaped prisoner or a warder who wants to join de Gaulle?'

'No, I'm an escaped prisoner.'

'And your friends?'

'The same.'

'Monsieur Henri, I don't want to know anything about your past, but now's the moment to come to the help of France and to redeem yourself. I'm for de Gaulle and I'm waiting for a ship for England. Come and see me tomorrow at the Mariners' Club – here's the address. I'd be glad to have you join us.'

'What's your name?'

'Homère.'

'Monsieur Homère, I can't make up my mind right away. In the first place I've got to find out about my family; and then before taking such an important decision I've got to analyse it. Objectively. You must understand, Monsieur Homère, that France has knocked me about cruelly – treated me in the most inhuman sort of way.'

With splendid zeal and ardour the Martiniquais did all he could to persuade me. It was really moving to hear him produce all these arguments in favour of our poor suffering France.

We went home very late, and as I lay in bed I thought over all this French patriot had said. I had to consider his suggestion very seriously. After all, the cops, the lawyers and the prison service weren't France. I knew in my heart that I hadn't stopped loving my country. And to think there were Huns all over it! Christ, how my people must suffer: how it must humiliate the whole nation.

When I woke up, the donkey, the cart, the pig, Cuic-Cuic and Van Hue had disappeared.

'Well brother, did you sleep well?' asked Guittou and his friends.

'Yes, thanks.'

'Listen, would you like black coffee or café au lait or tea? Coffee and bread and butter?'

'Yes please.' I ate the lot, watching them at their work. Julot prepared the lump of balata as it was called for: he took hard bits out of the hot water and kneaded them into the soft mass. Petit-Louis cut out the pieces of cloth and Guittou made the shoes. 'Do you turn out many?'

'No. We aim at making twenty dollars a day. Five dollars looks after the rent and the food. That leaves five over for each man's pocket-money, clothes and laundry.'

'Do you sell them all?'

'No. Sometimes one of us has to go out and peddle shoes and brooms in the streets of Georgetown. On foot and in the blazing sun, it's tough.'

'I'd be happy to do it, when it has to be done. I don't want to be a parasite here. I must do something to chip in for the food too.'

'OK, Papi.'

All day long I wandered about Georgetown's Indian quarter. I noticed a big cinema poster and I was seized with a violent longing to see a talking film in colour for the first time in my life. I'd ask Guittou to take me that evening. I walked round and round the streets of Penitence Rivers for hours and hours. I was delighted with the politeness of the people. There were two outstanding things about them – they were clean and they were very polite. I found this day strolling alone through the Hindu district of Georgetown even more exalting than my arrival in Trinidad nine years before.

In Trinidad, in the midst of all the wonderful feelings that arose from mingling with the crowd, there was always this question hanging over my head – 'One day, in two weeks' time or at the very most three, I'll have to go out to sea again: what country will take me in? Will there be any nation that will accept me? What will the future bring?' Here it was quite different. I was free for good and all; if I wished, I could even go to England and enlist in the Free French forces. What should I do? If I made up my mind to join de Gaulle wouldn't they say I'd just come because I didn't know what else to do? Among all those people who'd always gone straight, wouldn't I be treated like a criminal who was on their side because he had no other refuge? They said France was divided in two – divided between Pétain and de Gaulle. How could a Marshal of France possibly not know where honour lay and what was the best for the country? If I joined the Free French, wouldn't I be forced to fight against my own countrymen later on?

It was going to be very hard, very hard, to make a decent living here. Guittou, Petit-Louis and Julot were no sort of fools and yet they were working for five dollars a day. To begin with, I would have to learn to live as a free man. I had been a prisoner since 1931; and this was 1942. I couldn't solve all these problems the very first day of my freedom. I didn't even know the ABC of making a place for myself in life. I'd never worked with my hands. Just a smattering of electricity – absolutely any workman in the trade knew more than me. There was only one thing I had to promise myself, and that

495

was to go straight, at least according to my own code. It was four o'clock when I got back to the house.

'Well, Papi, and how did you like the air of freedom? Pretty good, eh? Did you enjoy your walk?'

'Yes, Guittou, I've been wandering all over the place – all over this whole quarter.'

'Did you see your Chinamen?'

'No.'

'They're in the yard. They know how to take care of themselves, those friends of yours. They've made forty dollars already and they tried to make me take twenty. I wouldn't, of course. Go and see them.'

Cuic-Cuic was cutting up a cabbage for his pig. Van Hue was washing the donkey, which stood there quiet, delighting in it.

'OK, Papillon?'

'Fine. And what about you two?'

'We're very pleased with ourselves: we've made forty dollars.'

'What did you do?'

'We went out into the country at three in the morning, with another Chinese to show us. He had two hundred dollars with him and we used it to buy tomatoes, lettuces, aubergines – fresh vegetables of every kind. And a few chickens, eggs and some goat's milk. Then we went to the market down by the harbour. At first we sold just a little to the locals and then all the rest to some American sailors. They were so pleased with our prices that I don't have to go into the market tomorrow: they told us to wait for them outside the harbour gates. They'll buy the lot. Here's the money. You're the leader, so you still have to look after it.'

'You know I've got money, Cuic: I don't need this.'

'Keep the money or we shan't work any more.'

'Listen, these Frenchmen live on about five dollars a day each. We'll take five apiece and give five to the house for food. The rest we'll put aside to give your Chinese friends back the two hundred they lent you.'

'OK.'

'Tomorrow I'll come with you.'

'No. You stay bed. If you like, meet us at seven o'clock in front of the main harbour gates.'

'OK.'

Everybody was happy. Us to begin with, because we knew

we could earn our living and not be a burden on our friends. And then Guittou and the two others, who in spite of their kindness must have been wondering how soon we should be able to stand on our own feet.

'Your friends are terrific, Papillon. We'll make a couple of bottles of pastis and celebrate.' Julot went out and came back with sugar-cane, alcohol and various essences. An hour later we were drinking a pastis worthy of Marseilles. Helped on by the alcohol our voices grew louder and our happy laughter was more cheerful and stronger than usual. Some Indian neighbours gathered that there was a party in the Frenchmen's house, and five of them, three men and two girls, came without any sort of ceremony and joined us. They brought skewers of chicken and pork, all very highly seasoned and peppered. The two girls were most remarkably beautiful. They were dressed all in white; their feet were bare; and each wore a silver anklet on her left leg. Guittou said to me, 'Take care. These are good girls. Don't you go and make a pass just because you can see their bare breasts under that veil. It's natural for them. As for me, I'm too old. But Julot and Petit-Louis had a go when we first arrived and they came to grief. The girls wouldn't come to see us again for a long while.'

These two Indians were really lovely. They had a little round tattooed mark in the middle of their foreheads, and that gave them a strange, exotic look. They talked to us kindly, and from what little English I knew I gathered they were bidding us welcome to Georgetown.

That night Guittou and I went down to the middle of the city. You would have said it was another civilization, utterly different from the one we lived in. The town was crammed with people. Whites, blacks, Indians, Chinese, soldiers and sailors in uniform, and a great many merchant marine-sailors. Great numbers of bars, restaurants, pubs and night-clubs: and their glare lit up the streets as though it was midday.

That evening I'd been to the first talking film in colour I'd ever seen in my life, and still astonished by this new experience, I followed Guittou into a huge bar. One corner was filled with Frenchmen, at least a score of them. Their drink was Free Cubas – Coca-Cola and spirits. All these men were convicts, escaped convicts. Some had got away after they had been let out: they'd served their sentence and they were supposed to serve their *doublage* in Guiana. But they starved, they couldn't find jobs, and both the locals and the officials looked upon them with disfavour: they preferred running for it and trying to reach a country where they hoped they'd be able to lead a better life. But it was tough, they told me.

'Take me, for example. I cut timber in the forest for John Fernandes at two dollars fifty a day. I come down to Georgetown for a week every month. I'm desperate.'

'And what about you?'

'I make butterfly collections. I go out after them into the bush and when I've caught a good many of different sorts I arrange them in glass-topped boxes and sell them as a collection.'

Others were stevedores in the port. They all worked, but they only just made enough to live on. 'It's tough, but we're free,' they said. 'And freedom, Christ, it's good.'

That evening a relégué called Faussard came to see us. He stood drinks all round. He'd been on board a Canadian ship carrying bauxite that had been torpedoed in the mouth of the Demerara river. As a survivor he'd been given a sum of money on account of the sinking. Almost the whole of the crew had been drowned. He'd been lucky enough to be able to get into a lifeboat. He told us the German submarine surfaced and spoke to them. It had asked them how many ships were still in the port, waiting to sail with cargoes of bauxite. When they said they didn't know, the man who had been questioning them laughed. 'Yesterday I was in such-and-such a cinema in Georgetown,' he said. 'Look at this half of the ticket.' And it seems he opened his coat and said, 'This suit comes from Georgetown.' Unbelievers said it was just bluff, but Faussard would have it that it was so, and I've no doubt he was telling the truth. He said the submarine even told them what ship was going to come and pick them up: and indeed that very ship did save their lives.

Every man had a tale to tell. Guittou and I were sitting next to an old Parisian from the Halles called Petit-Louis de la rue des Lombards: he said, 'Papillon, I'll tell you what, my old mate, I found a little racket that meant I could live without doing a hand's turn. In the paper there's a heading *Died for his King* or *for the Queen* or something like that; and whenever a Frenchman's name appeared I'd go to a mason's yard and take a photo of a tombstone with the name of the ship, the date it was torpedoed and the name of the Frenchman – I painted them on. Then I'd go round to the rich English houses and say they ought to give something for a monument to this Frenchman who'd died for England, so there'd be something in the graveyard to remember him by. It worked perfectly up until last week, when a bloody fool of a Breton, who'd been reported lost, turned up, not only alive but in terrific health. He went to see some of the very women who'd given me five dollars for his memorial – a stiff who went about saying he was alive and that I'd never bought a stone from any mason's yard in my life. I'll have to find something else to live on, because at my age I can't work any more.'

Stimulated by the Free Cubas everyone roared away at full blast, telling the most extraordinary tales: we were all certain we were the only ones who understood French.

'Look at me,' said one guy, 'I make balata dolls and bicycle handles. The only thing is, when the little girls leave their dolls out in the sun in their gardens they melt or go out of shape. Oh, it's a bloody wasps' nest when I forget what street I've already worked. This last month I haven't dared go along half the streets in Georgetown by daylight. The same thing with the bicycles. You leave them in the sun and when you come back your hands stick to the grips I've sold.'

'Or take me,' said another man. 'I use balata too – I make sticks with black girls' heads as decorations. I tell the sailors I'm a survivor from Mers-el-Kébir and that they just have to buy one, because it's not their fault I'm still alive. Eight out of ten fall for it.'

This modern Alsatia made me laugh, but it also made me realize that in fact earning a living was by no means easy. Someone turned on the radio at the bar: it was de Gaulle making a speech. A French voice from London, encouraging the French overseas and in the colonies: everyone listened. It was a moving appeal and nobody uttered a sound. All at once one of the lags who'd had too many Free Cubas sprang up and said, 'Brothers, this is terrific! All of a sudden I understand English! I followed every word Churchill said!' Everyone burst out laughing: not a man there tried to make him see he'd got it wrong.

Yes, I'd have to take my first steps towards earning my own living; and as I could see from the others, it wasn't going to be easy. This didn't weigh on my mind. Between 1930 and 1942 I'd totally lost all sense of responsibility and all knowledge of how to make a living. A man who's been a prisoner as long as that, without having to worry about food, rent or clothing, a man who's been put on a lead, managed, shoved around, and who's grown used to doing nothing off his own bat and to obeying every kind of order without thinking about it, a man who's grown used to being given food and drink at set hours – this man has to re-learn how to live when all of a sudden he finds himself in the middle of a big town, no longer knowing how to walk on a pavement without bumping into people or crossing a road without getting himself run over. And then again there are some reactions you'd never expect: for example, among all those different kinds of lags, all talking French sprinkled with English or Spanish words, I was listening as hard as ever I could when suddenly I wanted to go to the lavatory there in that English pub. Well, you'll scarcely believe it, but for a fleeting second I looked round for the warder whose permission I ought to ask. It was very short: but it was also very funny when I understood what was the matter and said to myself, 'Papillon, when you want to have a piss or do anything else, from now onwards there's no one whose permission you have to ask.'

And at the cinema too, when the girl was looking for a place for us, for a moment I felt like saying, 'Please don't you trouble about me. I'm only a mere convict – I'm not worth bothering with.' And going along the street between the cinema and the pub I turned round several times. Guittou knew all about this, and he said to me, 'Why do you keep turning round all the time? Are you looking to see if the screw's following you? No screws here, old Papi: you left them all behind in penal.'

In the lags' language they say you have to get rid of your convict's shirt. But it's more than that, because prison clothes are only a symbol. It's not only your shirt you have to get rid of, but the brand made with a red-hot iron on your heart and spirit.

A police patrol came into the bar – impeccably-dressed English Negroes. They went round, table by table, asking for identity cards. When they reached our corner the sergeant carefully scanned all the faces. He saw one he didn't know – mine. 'Identity card, sir, if you please.' I passed it: he looked at me and gave it back, saying, 'Excuse me, I didn't know you. Welcome to Georgetown.' And with that he went away.

When he'd gone, Paul le Savoyard observed, 'These rosbifs are wonderful. The only foreigners they trust a hundred per cent are the escaped lags. If you can prove that you made a break from penal, the English authorities will set you free straight away.'

Although we got home late, I was at the main harbour gate at seven the next morning. Less than half an hour later Cuic-Cuic and Hue appeared with the little cart full of vegetables gathered that morning, together with eggs and a few chickens. They were by themselves. I asked where their friend was – the Chinese who was to show them how to manage. Cuic said, 'He showed us yesterday. That was enough. Now we don't need anyone.'

'Did you have to go far to find all that?'

'Yes. Two and a half hour's journey and more. We set off at three this morning and we're only just back.'

As if he'd been living there for twenty years, Cuic-Cuic produced hot tea and then dampers. Sitting on the pavement close to the cart, we ate and drank, waiting for customers.

'Do you think they'll come, your Americans of yesterday?'

'I hope so; but if they don't, we'll sell to other people.'

'What about the prices? How do you fix them?'

'I don't say this costs so-and-so: I say, what'll you give me?'

'But you can't speak English.'

'That's so. But I do know how to use my hands and fingers. Then it's easy enough.'

'Anyhow, you can talk well enough to buy and sell,' said Cuic-Cuic to me.

'Yes, but first I'd like to see you do it by yourself.'

I didn't have long to wait, because soon there appeared a huge kind of jeep called a command car. The driver, a petty officer and two sailors got out of it. The petty officer climbed into the cart and looked at all the lettuces, aubergines and so on. He inspected every crate and he prodded the chickens.

'How much the lot?' And the bargaining began.

The American sailor talked through his nose. I couldn't understand a word he said. Cuic-Cuic jabbered away in Chinese and French. Seeing that they'd never come to an agreement I called Cuic-Cuic aside. 'What did you lay out altogether?' He looked through his pockets and found seventeen dollars. 'A hundred and eighty-three dollars,' he said.

'What's he offering you?'

'Two hundred and ten, I think. It's not enough.'

I went over to the petty officer. He asked if I spoke English. A very little. 'Talk slowly,' I said.

'OK.'

'What do you offer? No, two hundred and ten dollars is impossible. Two hundred and forty.'

He wasn't having any.

He pretended to go and then came back: went off again and got into his jeep. But I had the feeling it was all an act. Just as he was getting out of it again our two pretty neighbours arrived, the Indian girls, half-veiled. They had certainly been watching the scene, because they pretended not to know us. One of them got into the cart, looked at our wares and said, 'How much the lot?'

'Two hundred and forty dollars,' I replied.

'It's a deal,' she said.

But the American brought out two hundred and forty dollars and gave them to Cuic-Cuic, telling the Indian girls he'd already bought the stuff. Our neighbours did not go away but stood watching the Americans unload the cart and pile the things into the command car. At the last moment a sailor laid hold of the pig, thinking it was part of the bargain. Naturally Cuic-Cuic wouldn't have that. An argument began and we couldn't manage to make them understand that the pig was not included in the deal.

I tried to explain to the Hindus, but it was very hard. They couldn't get it either. The American sailors wouldn't let go of the pig: Cuic-Cuic wouldn't give back the money. The whole thing threatened to degenerate into a brawl. Van Hue had already picked up a shaft when an American military police jeep went by. The petty officer whistled. The military police came over. I told Cuic-Cuic to give back the money: he wouldn't listen to me for a moment. The sailors still had hold of the pig, and they wouldn't give it back either, Cuic-Cuic was standing there in front of their jeep, so that they couldn't drive away. Quite a crowd had gathered round this noisy little scene. The military police said the Americans were in the right; and in any case, they couldn't understand a word of our gibberish either. They really believed we had been trying to swindle the sailors.

I was at my wits' end when I suddenly remembered that I

502

had the name of the Negro from Martinique with the telephone number of the Mariners' Club. I showed it to the policeman, saying, 'Interpreter'. He took me to a phone. I put the call through and I was lucky enough to find my Gaullist friend. I asked him to tell the policeman that the pig was not part of the deal, that it was a tame pig, that Cuic-Cuic looked upon it in the same light as a dog, and that we'd forgotten to tell the sailors it wasn't included. Then I handed the telephone to the policeman. In three minutes he had understood everything. With his own hands he took the pig and gave it back to the delighted Cuic-Cuic, who caught it in his arms and hurried it into the cart. The whole thing ended well and the Yanks laughed like a pack of children. The crowd dispersed: everybody was happy. Back at the house that night we thanked the Hindu girls, and when they understood what it was all about they too laughed as much as anybody else.

We had been in Georgetown three months now. Today we moved into one half of our Indian friend's house. Two big, airy bedrooms, a dining-room, a little kitchen with a charcoal stove and a huge yard with a corner roofed over with corrugated iron for a stable. The donkey and cart were under cover. I was going to sleep alone in a big second-hand bed with a good mattress. In the next room, each in his own bed, my two Chinese friends. We also had a table and six chairs, as well as four stools. In the kitchen, everything necessary for cooking. We thanked Guitton and his friends for their hospitality and then, as Cuic-Cuic said, we took possession of our own house.

In front of the dining-room window and looking out on to the street there stood a wickerwork armchair in all its glory – a present from the Indian girls. On the table, some fresh flowers in a glass pot, produced by Cuic-Cuic.

This feeling of being here, in the first home of my own, gave me confidence in myself and in the future. It was a very modest house, but it was clean, light and airy; and it was the first fruit of three months of team-work.

Tomorrow was Sunday, and there would be no market, so we'd be free all day long. What's more, we'd all three made up our minds to invite Guitton and his friends as well as the Indian girls and their brothers to dinner. The guest of honour was to be the Chinese who'd helped Cuic-Cuic and Van Hue – the one who'd given the donkey and cart and who'd lent us the two hundred dollars to get going. In his plate he'd find an envelope with the two hundred dollars and a note of thanks from us in Chinese.

After his beloved pig, I was the one who had all Cuic-Cuic's affection. He was always doing kind things for me – I was the best dressed of the three, and he'd often come home with a present, a shirt, a tie, or a pair of trousers. He bought all these things with his own money. Cuic-Cuic didn't smoke and he hardly drank at all; his only vice was gambling. He had but one dream – saving up enough to go to the Chinese club to gamble.

We had no real difficulty at all in selling our morning's purchases. I could already speak enough English to buy and sell. Between the three of us, we made twenty-five to thirty-five dollars. It wasn't much, but we were very pleased at having found a way of earning our livings so quickly. I didn't always go out buying, although I made better bargains than they did, but now I was always the one that did the selling. There were plenty of English and American sailors, posted ashore to do the buying for their ships, who knew me. We'd talk over the prices pleasantly, not getting too worked up about it. There was one big Italian-American who looked after the supplies for an officers' mess, and he always talked to me in Italian – he was delighted when I answered in his own language and he only bargained for the hell of it. He always ended up by paying the price I'd asked in the first place.

By about half past eight or nine we were back at the house. Van Hue and Cuic-Cuic would go to bed after we'd all three had something to eat. As for me, I'd go and see Guittou and his friends or else the Indian girls would call on me. No real housework to do: the sweeping, making of beds, laundry, dusting, was all done for us by the two sisters, and they did it very well for almost nothing – two dollars a day. I fully appreciated what it was to be free, without any anxiety for the future.

In this town the usual way of getting about was by bicycle. So I bought one in order to go wherever I wanted without difficulty; and since both the town and the surrounding countryside were quite flat, one could cover long distances without effort. The machine had two strong carriers, one in front and the other behind: so like many of the locals I could easily take two people with me.

At least twice a week I went out for an hour or two with my friends the Indian girls. They were absolutely delighted, and I began to see that one of them, the younger girl, was beginning to fall in love with me.

I'd never seen her father, but the other day he appeared. He lived not far from our place, but he'd never come to see us and I only knew her brothers. He was a tall old man with a very long snow-white beard. His hair was silvery, too, and it parted to show a noble and intelligent forehead. He only spoke his Hindu language, and his daughter translated. He invited me to come and see him at his house. Through the little princess (that was my name for his daughter) he said it was no distance by bicycle. I promised to return his call before long.

When he'd eaten a few cakes and drunk some tea he went away, but I noticed that first he inspected the house in all its details. The little princess was delighted to see that her father was pleased with his visit and with us.

I was thirty-six and I was in perfect health: I still felt young and fortunately everybody looked upon me as young too – all my friends said I didn't look more than thirty. Now this girl was nineteen, and she had all the calm, placid beauty of her race as well as all its fatalism in her attitude to life. To love and to be loved by such a wonderful girl would be a gift from heaven.

When the three of us went out she always got on to the carrier in front, and she knew very well that when she sat up quite straight and I leant forward to pedal harder, my face was very close to hers. If she held her head back I could see all the beauty of her bare bosom under her veil, better than if she'd worn nothing at all. Her great black eyes blazed as we almost touched, and her mouth – dark red against her tea-coloured skin – opened just a little in her longing to be kissed. A mouth adorned with beautiful, perfect teeth. She had a way of saying certain words and of showing the tip of her pink tongue in her half-opened mouth that would have inflamed the holiest of the holy saints who have bequeathed the Catholic religion to us.

We were to go to the cinema one evening, just the two of us, because it seemed her sister had a headache – one of those headaches invented to leave us to ourselves, in my opinion. She appeared in a white muslin dress that came down to her ankles; there were three silver rings round them which showed as she walked. She was wearing sandals whose thongs went round her big toe: this made her feet seem very elegant. There was a very small gold shell in her right nostril. On her head, held by a golden ribbon, a short muslin veil came a little lower than her shoulders. Hanging from this ribbon there were three strings of many-coloured stones, reaching to the middle of her forehead. It was a charming piece of nonsense, of course: and when her head swayed it showed the striking blue spot tattooed on her forehead.

The whole Indian household and mine, in the persons of Cuic-Cuic and Van Hue, watched us leave: they looked charmed at seeing our open happiness. They all looked as though they knew we'd come back from the cinema engaged.

We rode along towards the middle of the town, with her well settled on the cushion of my carrier. It was during a long stretch of free-wheeling down an ill-lit avenue that this magnificent girl, of her own accord, brushed my mouth with a light and fleeting kiss. I had had so little idea that she would take the first step that I nearly fell off the bicycle.

We sat at the back of the cinema, holding hands: I spoke to her with my fingers and she replied. We didn't watch the film; and our first loving exchanges, sitting there in that cinema, were completely silent. There was a singing in her fingers, her long, carefully trimmed and varnished nails, and in the pressure of her palm; they told me much better than words about her love for me and her desire to be mine. She laid her head on my shoulder, and this allowed me to kiss her pure and lovely face.

This shy, timid love, so long in coming to flower, quickly developed into a whole-hearted passion. I'd told her, before she was mine, that I couldn't marry her, since I already had a wife in France. That hardly worried her for so long as a day. One night she stayed with me. She said that because of her brothers and certain Indian neighbours she would rather I went and lived with her at her father's place. I agreed and moved over to his house: he lived there alone with a young Indian woman, a distant relation, who looked after him and did all the housework. It was only about a quarter of a mile from the house where Cuic-Cuic went on living. So my two friends came to see me every evening and spent an hour or so with us. Quite often they stayed to supper.

We still went on selling vegetables down by the harbour. I'd leave at half past six and my Indian girl nearly always came with me. We took a big thermos full of tea and a bag with toast and a pot of jam; we waited for Cuic-Cuic and Hue so that we could all eat together. She was the one who produced breakfast and she was very particular about this rite of the first meal of the day, all four of us together. She brought everything that was needed in her bag – a very small lace-trimmed mat that she ceremoniously laid on the pavement, having swept the stones first with a little brush, and four china cups and saucers. And sitting there on the ground, we solemnly had our breakfast.

It amused me to drink tea sitting on the pavement as though we were in a room; but both she and Cuic-Cuic thought it perfectly natural. They took no sort of notice of the passers-by, for in their opinion they were behaving quite ordinarily. It gave her so much pleasure to pour out the tea for us and spread marmalade on the toast that it would have wounded her if I hadn't gone along with it.

Last Saturday something happened that gave me the key to a mystery. We'd been together for two months now and she'd often given me small quantities of gold. It was always pieces of broken-up jewellery – half of a ring, a bit of chain, the quarter or the half of a medal or gold coin, a single earring. I didn't need money for living, so although she told me to sell the gold I always kept it in a box. I had close on fourteen ounces. When I asked her where it came from she hugged me, kissed me, and laughed; but gave me no explanation.

But at about ten o'clock on Saturday morning my Indian girl asked me to take her father on my bicycle – to take him somewhere: I forget the name of the place. 'My father will show you the way,' she said. 'I must stay at home and do the

507

ironing.' I was puzzled, but I thought the old man wanted to see a friend some way off, so I agreed quite cheerfully.

He sat there on the front carrier and he pointed out the way without a word, because he only spoke his own language. It was a long way, and I had to ride for the best part of an hour. We came to a wealthy district by the sea – splendid villas everywhere. My 'father-in-law' made a sign: I stopped and watched him. He took a round white stone from under his robe and knelt at the bottom of the steps leading up to a house. He rolled the stone on the step and at the same time he chanted. A few minutes went by and then a woman dressed in Indian clothes came out of the house and gave him something without saying a word.

He went on from house to house, doing the same thing until four o'clock in the afternoon. It was a long business, and I could not make it out. At the last house it was a man dressed in white who came out. He made the old boy stand up and taking his arm he led him into the house. He stayed there more than a quarter of an hour and then came out again, still with the man in white, who kissed his forehead or rather his white hair before taking leave of him. We went home, and I pedalled as hard as I could to get there quickly, because by now it was half past four.

Fortunately we reached the house before nightfall. First my pretty Indara took her father to his room; then she hung round my neck, kissing me and pulling me along towards the bath-room so I could have a shower. There was cool, fresh linen waiting for me, and I sat down at the table, washed, shaved and changed. I was on fire with curiosity. Only I knew you must never try to force an Indian or a Chinese to tell you anything – there always has to be a certain waiting period. Then they'll tell you of their own accord, because they can sense you're asking for their trust; and if they think you worthy of it, they'll give it you. And that's what happened with Indara.

After we'd made love for a long while and she was lying, quite relaxed, with her still-hot cheek on my bare arm, she said, without looking at me, 'You know, sweetheart, when my father goes out to look for gold, he doesn't do any harm: far from it. He calls up spirits to protect the houses where he rolls his stone. They give him a piece of gold to say thank you. It's a very old custom in Java, where we come from.'

That was what my princess told me. But one day a friend of hers had a talk with me in the market. It so happened that neither Indara nor the Chinese had arrived yet. This pretty girl – she was from Java too – told me something quite different. 'Why on earth do you go on working, now you live with the sorcerer's daughter? Isn't she ashamed of making you get up so early, even when it rains? You could live without doing anything, what with all that gold her father earns. She can't love you, or she would never let you get up so early.'

'And what does her father do? Tell me about it – I don't know a thing.'

'Well, her father's a sorcerer from Java. If he likes, he can bring death on you or your family. The only way of escaping the spell he casts with his magic stone is to give him so much gold that he'll roll it the way opposite to the way he rolls it to bring death. When he does that he undoes all the curses – he brings health and life for you and everybody in your household.'

'That's not at all the way Indara told it.'

I decided to make a check to see which of them was right. Some days later I was with my white-bearded 'father-in-law' on the bank of a stream that ran through Penitence Rivers and joined the Demerara. The look on the Indian fishermen's faces told me all I wanted to know. Every one of them gave him a fish and hurried away from the water's edge as quickly as possible. It was quite clear. I no longer needed to ask anybody anything.

As far as I was concerned, my Indian father-in-law didn't worry me in the very least. He never spoke to me in anything but his own language, and he imagined I understood a little. I never could manage to make out what he meant. That had its good side – it was impossible for us to disagree. And then in spite of everything he did find me work to do: I tattooed their foreheads for the girls of between thirteen and fifteen. Sometimes he bared their bosoms and I tattooed their breasts with leaves or coloured petals – green, pink and blue – letting the tip rise like the pistil of a flower. The brave ones (it hurt a great deal) had the dark circle round their nipples tattooed bright yellow; and a few even had the tip itself yellowed too.

He put up a notice in front of the house, written in Hindu, and they told me it said 'Tattoo artist – moderate prices – all work guaranteed'. The tattooing was well paid, and so I had a double pleasure – that of admiring the Javanese girls' lovely bosoms and that of making money.

Cuic-Cuic found a restaurant for sale down by the harbour. He proudly brought me the news and suggested we should buy the place. The price was right: eight hundred dollars. By selling the sorcerer's gold and adding our savings, we could buy the restaurant. I went to have a look at it. It was in a little street, but it was very close to the harbour, and the district was crowded at all hours of the day and night. There was one fairly big black-and-white tiled room, eight tables on the left, eight on the right, and in the middle a round table where you could show the hors d'oeuvres and the fruit. A big, airy, well lit kitchen: two large ovens and two huge ranges.

Restaurant and Butterflies

We bought the place. Indara herself sold all our gold. Her father was surprised I'd never touched the scraps he'd given his daughter for us both. He said, 'I gave them to you so you could make use of them. They belong to you two – you don't have to ask me if you want to sell them. Do whatever you please.'

My sorcerer father-in-law wasn't such a bad old stick. As for Indara, she was in a class apart as a mistress, as a wife and as a friend. There was no danger of our quarrelling, because she always answered yes to everything I said. The only time she looked a trifle sour was when I tattooed the other girls' tits.

So here I was, the owner of the Victory Restaurant in Water Street, in the heart of Georgetown's harbour district. Cuic-Cuic was to do the cooking: he liked it and it was his trade. Hue was to look after the buying and to make the chow mein. This was how it was made: best wheat flour was mixed with a great many yolks of eggs and then beaten. The dough was worked long and hard without any water being added. The work of

510

kneading was very hard – so much so that he had to do it with his feet, riding a well-polished pole fixed to the middle of the table. He had one leg round the pole and he held it with his only hand while at the same time he hopped round and round on the table, thus kneading the dough: worked as powerfully as this, the mixture became light and delicious. A little butter at the last moment gave it a wonderful taste.

The restaurant had gone broke, but now it became very well known. Indara and another young and very pretty Indian girl called Daya served the many customers who came hurrying to try our Chinese food. All the escaped lags appeared. The ones who had money paid and the others ate for free. 'It brings luck to give food to a hungry man,' said Cuic-Cuic.

There was only one snag – the glamour of Indara and the other waitress. Both of them showed their naked tits under their transparent veils. What's more, they'd slit their dresses from the ankle to the hip. In certain positions they showed their whole leg, right up their thighs. The American, English, Swedish, Canadian and Norwegian sailors sometimes came in and ate twice a day to enjoy the spectacle. My friends called the restaurant the voyeurs' paradise. As for me, I was the owner. I was the boss, and that went for everybody. There was no till: the waitress brought me the money and I put it in my pocket, giving change when necessary.

The restaurant opened at eight in the evening and stayed open until five or six the next morning. I hardly need say that about three all the tarts in the parish who'd had a profitable night came and ate curried chicken or bean-sprout salad with their ponce or with a customer. They also drank beer, particularly English beer, whiskey, and the very good local rum with soda or Coca-Cola. Since the place became the meeting-point for all the French who had made a break, I was the refuge, the adviser, the judge and the confidential friend of the whole colony of lags and relégués.

This sometimes caused difficulties. A butterfly-collector told me about the way he went out into the bush to look for them. He'd cut out a piece of cardboard the shape of a butterfly and then stick on the wings of the kind he wanted to catch. The cardboard was fixed to the end of a stick about a yard long. When he was hunting he held the stick in his right hand and twirled it about so the fake butterfly looked as though it was flying. He always hunted in sun-filled clearings. He knew the

511

times when each kind of butterfly came out of its chrysalis: there were some that only lived forty-eight hours. So when the sun came into the clearing, the butterflies that had just hatched hurried into the light to find love as soon as ever they could. When they caught sight of the bait they would rush at it from a great way off. If the phony butterfly was a male, then it would be a male coming to fight it. My friend had a little net in his left hand and he'd catch the butterfly straight away. It had a closable neck, so the hunter could go on catching butterflies without being afraid the others would escape. And if the bait was a female, then the males would come so as to make love, and the result would be the same.

The most beautiful of these insects were the moths, but as they often flew into things, it was very hard to find one whose wings were perfect – they were nearly always ragged. To catch moths, he would climb to the top of a high tree, spread a white sheet over a frame and light it from behind with a carbide lamp. The big moths, four to six inches across, would come and cling to the sheet. Then all he had to do was to kill them by squeezing their thoraxes with a strong, sudden pinch that did not crush them. They must not be allowed to struggle or else they would spoil their wings and their value would be lost.

In a show-case I always had little collections of butterflies, insects, small snakes and vampires. There were more buyers than goods. So the prices were high.

An American pointed out one butterfly whose back wings were steel-blue and whose front wings were light blue. He offered me five hundred dollars if I could find one like that, only a hermaphrodite.

I talked about this to my friend, and he said that he had once caught a very pretty specimen of that sort, and he'd got fifty dollars for it: later a serious collector had told him it was worth close on two thousand.

'That Yank's playing you for a sucker, Papillon,' he said. 'He takes you for a lemon. Even if the rare specimen was only worth fifteen hundred dollars he'd still be making a hell of a packet out of your ignorance.'

'You're dead right: he's a sod. What about making a sucker out of him?'

'How?'

'We'd have to stick two male wings on to a female, or the

other way about. The snag is sticking them on without its showing.'

After a good many attempts that didn't work, we managed to fix two male wings to a splendid female without its showing: we did this by making a tiny cut in her thorax and glueing the ends of the wings with diluted balata. It held so well you could pick the butterfly up by the phony wings. I put it into a glass case with others belonging to an ordinary twenty-dollar collection, as if I'd not noticed it. The bait took. The American had hardly caught sight of it before he had the nerve to walk in with a twenty-dollar bill in his hand, wanting to buy the collection. I told him it was reserved – a Swede had asked me for a case and this one was for him. During the next couple of days the American had the box in his hands at least a score of times. At last he couldn't bear it any longer and he said to me, 'I'll buy the butterfly in the middle for twenty dollars and you can keep the rest.'

'What's so unusual about the middle one?' I asked, and looked at it closely. Then I exclaimed, 'My God, it's a hermaphrodite!'

'Eh? Why, yes: so it is. I hadn't been quite sure,' said the Yank. 'With the glass you can't see very well. Do you mind if I take it off?' He stared at the butterfly from every angle. 'What do you want for it?'

'Didn't you tell me one day that a specimen like that was worth five hundred dollars?'

'I've told several butterfly-hunters the same thing: I don't want to profit by the ignorance of the man who caught this one.'

'Then it's five hundred dollars or nothing.'

'It's a deal. Keep it for me. Look, here's all I have on me to show it's a sale – sixty dollars. Give me a receipt and tomorrow I'll bring the rest. And whatever you do, take it out of this box.'

'OK. I'll keep it somewhere else. Here's your receipt.'

As we opened the descendant of Lincoln appeared. He examined the butterfly again, this time with a little magnifying-glass. My heart was in my mouth when he turned it upside down. He was satisfied: he paid me, put the butterfly in a box he'd brought himself, asked me for another receipt and went away.

Two months later the cops picked me up. When we got to

the station the superintendent told me in French that I'd been arrested because an American accused me of swindling him. 'It's to do with a butterfly whose wings you stuck on,' said the policeman. 'It seems that the hoax brought you in five hundred dollars.'

Within two hours Cuic-Cuic and Indara were there with a lawyer. He spoke French very well. I told him I knew nothing whatsoever about butterflies – I was neither a catcher nor a collector. I just sold boxes of them to oblige butterfly-hunters who were customers of mine. It was the Yank who'd offered me the five hundred dollars, not me who'd asked for it: and anyhow if the butterfly had been the genuine article, as he believed, it was the American who was the thief, because in that case it would have been worth about two thousand dollars.

Two days later I came up before the court. The lawyer acted as interpreter. I told my story over again. To back it up my lawyer had a price-list of butterflies in which the specimen we were talking about was shown at something over one thousand five hundred dollars. The American lost the case: he had to pay the costs of the proceedings, my lawyer's fees and two hundred dollars on top of it all.

All of us – Indians and convicts – celebrated my acquittal with home-made pastis. Every member of Indara's family had come to the hearing, and now that I had been found not guilty they were all wonderfully proud of being related to a superman. For they weren't taken in: they knew damn well it was me that had stuck on the wings.

There: it was bound to happen – we were forced to sell the restaurant. Indara and Daya were too lovely, and their kind of strip-tease, always beginning but going no distance, made more effect on the full-blooded sailors than if they'd been stark naked. They'd noticed that the nearer they put their barely-covered tits to the sailor's noses the bigger tips they got: they'd bend right over the table, slowly working out the bill or the change. After a carefully calculated period of exposure, when the sailor's eyes were starting out of his head so as to see better, they'd straighten up and say, 'And what about my tip?' 'Ah!' The poor bastards were open-handed: they were set ablaze and the fire was never put out – they hardly knew what to do with themselves.

One day what I'd always been afraid of happened. A great

freckled lump of a red-head wasn't satisfied with just the sight of a naked thigh. When the panties put in their fleeting appearance his hand darted out and his brutish fingers gripped my Javanese like a vice. As she happened to have a full water jug in her hand it didn't take her a second to smash it on his head. The sailor went down under the blow, tearing off her panties as he fell. I rushed to pick him up, but his friends thought I was going to hit him, and before I could utter one of them had hit me right in the eye. Did the sea-going boxer really mean to stand up for his shipmate, or did he just want to give the husband a black eye – the husband who prevented him from getting at the pretty Indian girl? Who knows? At all events, my eye copped it good and hard. But he was altogether too sure of winning, for he stood there in front of me with his fists up calling out, 'Box, man, box!' A kick in the balls followed by my own particular kind of butt laid the boxer flat.

Now the fight spread. Van Hue came to my help from the kitchen and laid about him with his chow mein stick. Cuic-Cuic darted in with a long two-pronged fork and jabbed right and left. A Parisian tough, a former pillar of the rue de Lappe dance halls, used a chair by way of a club. No doubt feeling handicapped by the loss of her panties, Indara withdrew from the battle.

The final count was five Yanks with bad head wounds and others with double holes in various parts of their bodies, made by Cuic-Cuic's fork. Blood everywhere. A gleaming black Negro policeman had posted himself at the door so that no one could get out. And it was lucky that he had, because an American military police jeep turned up. With their clubs raised, the white gaiters tried to force their way in: and since they'd seen their own sailors all covered with blood it was certainly their intention to revenge them. The black policeman shoved them back and put his arm and his truncheon across the door, saying, 'His Majesty's police.'

It was only when the English police arrived that we were brought out and put into the black maria. We were taken to the police station. Apart from my black eye, none of us was hurt, which meant that they did not have much faith in our plea of self-defence. At the trial, a week later, the judge accepted our statement and let us all go except for Cuic-Cuic, who got three months for assault and battery. He had handed

515

out a very great many of his two-pronged stabs, and it was difficult to explain them away.

After that there were six more fights in under a fortnight, and we felt we couldn't go on. The sailors had determined not to call it a day, and as the newcomers always had different faces, how could we tell who were our friends and who were our enemies?

So we sold the restaurant, not even getting the price we'd paid for it. It was true that with the reputation it had acquired, the buyers didn't stand in line for it.

'What are we going to do, Hue?'

'Until Cuic-Cuic comes out, let's rest. We can't take to the donkey and cart again, because they were sold together with the stock and the goodwill. The best thing is to do nothing – just rest. Then later we'll see.'

Cuic-Cuic came out. He told us he'd been well treated. 'The only thing,' he said, 'is that I was near two men who'd been condemned to death.' The English have a disgusting way of giving a man with a death sentence forty-five days' notice that he's going to be hanged high and dry on such-and-such a day and at such-and-such an hour and that the King's reprieve has been refused. 'So,' said Cuic, 'every morning the two men who were to be topped called out to one another, "One day less, Johnny: only so many days now!" And then the other would go on shouting insults at his accomplice for hours on end.' Apart from that Cuic-Cuic had had an easy time, and they had thought highly of him.

The Bamboo Hut

Pascal Fosco came down from the bauxite mines. He was one of the men who'd tried to hold up the Marseilles post-office. His accomplice had been guillotined. Pascal was the toughest of us all. He was a clever mechanic, but he only made four dollars a day: even so, he always managed to keep one or two of the other convicts who were having a bad time.

This bauxite mine was deep in the bush. A little village had grown up round the camp, and the miners and engineers lived there. There was a continual stream of aluminium-ore coming down to the port to be loaded into the many ships. An idea came into my head: why shouldn't we start a joint in that village at the back of beyond? At night the men must be bored black – bored through the ground.

'That's quite true,' said Fosco. 'It's not a bleeding fun-fair. There's absolutely nothing.'

A little later Indara, Cuic-Cuic, Van Hue and I were aboard a tub steaming up the river: in two days' time we reached the Mackenzie mine. The engineers, overseers and skilled crafts-men had a camp made up of comfortable little houses, all provided with metal screens against the mosquitoes. But the village was revolting. Nothing built of brick, stone or concrete. Nothing but mud-and-bamboo huts with palm-frond roofs or, on the more modern ones, sheets of corrugated iron. There were four horrible overcrowded restaurants with bars. The miners had to fight to get a glass of warm beer. Not a single place had a refrigerator.

Pascal was right: there was business to be done in this remote backwater. After all, I was making a break, I was on the run – this was adventure – I couldn't live ordinarily, like my friends. Working just to make enough to live on didn't interest me at all.

As the streets were ankle-deep in mud every time it rained I picked on a higher place a little back from the middle of the village. That way I was sure that when it rained neither the inside nor the surroundings of the building I had in mind would be flooded.

In ten days, helped by the Negro carpenters who worked in the mine, we ran up a rectangular hall twenty yards long and eight wide. Thirty tables for four would mean that we could get a hundred and twenty customers in easily. A raised stage for the performance, a bar the width of the room and a dozen high stools. Next to this hall another building with eight bed-rooms that would easily house sixteen people.

When I went down to Georgetown to buy the equipment, chairs, tables, etc., I took on four splendid black girls to wait on the customers. Daya, who used to work in the restaurant,

517

decided to come with us. An Indian girl would thump the old piano I'd hired. All that remained for me to do was to fix the show.

After a great deal of trouble and soft soap I managed to persuade six girls, two of them Javanese, one Portuguese, one Chinese and two just brown, to give up whoring and become strip-tease artistes. I bought an old red curtain in a junk shop for the start and the finish of the show.

I went upstream with all my people, hiring a Chinese fisherman's bongo specially for the purpose. A spirit merchant had provided me with every conceivable kind of drink on credit. He trusted me, and every month I'd pay for what I'd sold, checking the inventory, while he would send up new supplies as they were needed. An old gramophone and some secondhand records would provide music when the pianist stopped tormenting the piano. I found an Indian who'd bought a theatrical touring company's wardrobe and I picked out all kinds of dresses, petticoats, black and coloured stockings, suspender belts and bra's: they were all still in very good condition, and I chose them for their violent colours.

Cuic-Cuic bought the chairs, tables and bedding; Indara looked after the glasses and everything else needed for the bar; I bought the drinks and made all the arrangements for the show. We had to go at things very hard to get it all ready in a week. Still, we managed it, and the girls and the equipment filled the entire boat.

Two days later we reached the village. The appearance of ten girls in this dismal hole, deep in the bush, caused an uproar. Each carrying a bundle, we made our way up to the Bamboo Hut, which was the name we'd given our joint. The rehearsals began. Teaching my artistes to strip was not at all an easy job. In the first place because I spoke English very badly, so that no one understood what I said; and in the second all their lives they'd whipped off their clothes so as to have a quicker turn-over of customers. Whereas now it was quite the opposite – the slower, the sexier. There were different tactics for each girl. And her way of doing it also had to harmonize with her clothes.

There was the Marquise, in a pink corset and a crinoline, with long white lace drawers: she undressed slowly behind a screen but in front of a large mirror that allowed the audience to see every morsel of flesh as she gradually uncovered it.

518

Then there was the Express, a very light café-au-lait girl with a smooth belly, a splendid example of cross breeding – a white man with an already very light Negress, no doubt. She had a lovely, very well proportioned shape, and her colour brought it out to perfection. Her long, naturally curling hair fell on to her exquisitely rounded shoulders. Full, high breasts, proud in spite of their size, with tips hardly any darker than her flesh. And we called her the Express. All the parts of her costume opened with zips. She appeared in cowboy's trousers, a wide brimmed hat and a white shirt with leather fringes at the wrists. She came on to the sound of a military march and kicked off her shoes, sending them flying. Her trousers zipped on each side and fell straight off in one go. The shirt came off in two pieces, with zips on either arm. For the audience the shock was terrific, because her naked breasts burst out as though they were angry at having been shut in so long. She stood there astraddle, with her hands on her hips, her legs and top bare, looked the audience straight in the eye and took off her hat, tossing it on to a table near the stage. The Express had no prudery about taking off her panties, either. She unbuttoned them each side and ripped the little object off rather than step out of it. She stood there, dressed like Eve, her woolly sex showing; and at the same moment another girl passed her a huge fan made of white feathers. She opened it wide and hid behind it.

On the opening night the Bamboo Hut was crammed. The management of the bauxite mine was there to the last man. The show ended with a dance and it was dawn by the time the last customers left. It was a great success: we couldn't have asked for better. There were overheads, but the prices were high and that made up for it; and I firmly believed that on a great many nights this cabaret in the heart of the bush would have more customers than it had room for.

My four black waitresses couldn't keep pace with the orders. Their skirts were very short, their necklines were very low and they had red handkerchiefs on their heads: they made a great impression upon the customers. Indara and Daya each looked after one part of the room. Van Hue and Cuic-Cuic were behind the bar to hand out the orders. And I was everywhere, putting things right when they went wrong and helping out in moments of stress.

'It's a hit for sure,' said Cuic-Cuic, when the waitresses,

artistes and boss were alone once more in the big hall. We all ate together as one big family, boss and employees, quite worn out but delighted with the result. Everyone went off to bed.

'Well, Papillon, aren't you going to get up?'

'What's the time?'

'Six o'clock in the afternoon,' said Cuic-Cuic. 'Your princess has been helping us. She's been up since two. Everything's in order and we're ready to begin again tonight.'

Indara appeared with a jug of hot water. Shaved, washed and full of life I put my arm round her waist and we walked into the Bamboo Hut. There I was met with innumerable questions.

'How was it, boss?'

'Did I strip well? Did you think there was any place where it was dull?'

'Did I sing more or less in tune? Luckily they aren't hard to please.'

I really liked my new team. These tarts turned strip-tease artistes took their job seriously and they seemed happy to have left their earlier calling.

We did a roaring trade. The only difficulty was this – all these single men and too few girls. Every customer wanted to have one with him, if not all night long, then at least a good deal longer than she would stay – the artistes were particularly in demand. This created jealousies. Now and then, when there happened to be two girls at the same table, the customers would burst out in protest.

The black girls were much sought-after too, in the first place because they were lovely and in the second because there were no women at all in the bush. Daya would sometimes go behind the bar to serve drinks and then she'd talk to everybody. There would be as many as twenty men standing there, enjoying the Indian girl's company – and indeed she was a most uncommon beauty.

So as to do away with jealousy and discontent among the customers who wanted an artiste at their table, I set up a lottery. There was a big wheel with numbers from one to thirty-two – one for each table and two for the bar – that decided where the girl should go after each strip-tease turn or song. To be in on it, you had to buy a ticket, which was the price of a bottle of whiskey or champagne.

As I saw it this system should have two advantages. In the first place it did away with all arguments. The winner had the pleasure of the chick at his table for an hour, all at the cost of his bottle. It was brought to him like this: when the artiste was mother-naked behind her fan, we span the wheel, and when the number came up she got on to a big silver-painted wooden tray. Four men took hold of it and carried her to the winning table. She uncorked the champagne herself and had a drink, still stark naked; then she'd excuse herself and come back five minutes later and sit at the table, dressed again.

For six months everything went fine; but when the rainy season was over a new set of customers appeared. These were the gold and diamond prospectors, who wandered about all over the bush, searching its many alluvial deposits. It was a very, very tough life, this looking for gold and diamonds with rudimentary equipment. The diggers often killed or robbed one another, so everybody carried weapons. And when they had a little poke of gold-dust or a handful of diamonds they just couldn't withstand the temptation of flinging it about. The girls were given a high commission on each bottle. So obviously when they were entwined with the customers they would pour their champagne or whiskey into the ice-bucket so as to finish the bottle sooner. In spite of all they drank, some customers realized what was going on, and then their reactions were so violent that I was forced to have the chairs and tables screwed to the floor.

With these new customers, what was bound to happen did happen. We called this particular girl Cinnamon-Flower, on account of her skin which was just the colour of cinnamon. I'd brought back this new chick from the gutters of Georgetown, and her way of stripping drove the audience right out of their minds.

When it was time for her act, we brought on a white satin sofa, and then not only did she strip with some wonderful fancy touches, but once she was absolutely naked she'd stretch out on the sofa and fondle herself. Her long, tapering fingers wandered all over her bare body from top to toe, playing with every single part of it. I don't have to describe the reactions of these rough bush characters, already full of drink.

She was very keen on the main-chance, and to take part in the lottery she'd insisted that the players should have to pay for two bottles of champagne and not just one, as they did for the other girls. There was a big, powerful digger with a bushy black beard who'd taken a good many tickets in the hope of winning Cinnamon-Flower, but in vain: and when Indara went round selling the numbers for the Flower's last turn he bought the tickets for all thirty tables. The only ones left were the two for the bar.

Our bearded customer was sure of winning now he'd bought sixty bottles of champagne, and he confidently waited for Cinnamon-Flower's act and the drawing of the lottery. Cinnamon-Flower had drunk a great deal that night, and it had gone to her head. It was four in the morning when she began her last turn. With drink on top of everything else, she was sexier than usual, and the things she did were even more suggestive. Whirr! We span the wheel, and its little horn pointer was going to show who was the winner.

Having seen the chick's performance, the bearded type was drooling with excitement. He waited, certain they were just about to bring her to him naked on the silver plate, with the fan over her and two bottles of champagne between her splendid legs. Disaster! The guy with the thirty tickets lost. It was number thirty-one that came up – the bar. At first he couldn't really understand: he only fully grasped what had happened when he saw the artiste picked up and put down on the bar. At that the bloody great fool went right off his head: he knocked over the table and reached the bar in three strides. It didn't take him three seconds to bring out his gun and pump three shots into the girl.

Cinnamon-Flower died in my arms. I picked her up after having knocked out the brute with an American police blackjack I always carried. If I hadn't been delayed by tripping over a waitress and her tray the maniac would never have had time to do what he did. Result: the police closed the Bamboo Hut and we all went back to Georgetown.

So here we were at home again. Indara, a genuine Hindu fatalist, never changed in her attitude. As far as she was concerned this disaster was of no importance. We'd do something else, that was all. The Chinese were the same and our team was as united as ever. Never a word of blame for my crazy idea of having the girls drawn by number, although that was the idea that had brought us to grief. We scrupulously paid all our debts with what we'd been able to save, and we gave Cinnamon-Flower's mother a sum of money. We didn't worry. Every evening we went to the bar where the lags all met. We spent some very happy evenings there, but what with all the war-time restrictions, I began to grow tired of Georgetown. What's more, up till now my princess had never been jealous and I had been as free as a bird: but now she never let me move an inch without her, and she'd sit close to me for hours and hours, no matter where we were.

The possibilities of doing business in Georgetown grew fainter. So one fine day I was seized with a longing to leave British Guiana for some other country. There was no danger about it, because this was war-time. No country would hand us back; or at least that was what I thought.

Break from Georgetown

Guittou was of the same opinion. He too thought there must be countries where it would be easier to make a living than British Guiana. We began to prepare for a break. For indeed, leaving British Guiana was a very serious crime. There was a war on and we none of us had a passport.

Three months before this Chapar had escaped from Cayenne, having been un-interned. He was now making ices in a Chinese cake-shop for one dollar fifty a day. He wanted to quit Georgetown too. And there were two others who wanted to come – a lag from Dijon called Deplanque and another guy from Bordeaux. Cuic-Cuic and Van Hue preferred to stay. They were quite happy here.

The mouth of the Demerara river was very carefully watched and guarded by nests of machine-guns, torpedo-tubes and heavy artillery, so we decided to make an exact copy of a fishing-boat registered at Georgetown and sail out, passing ourselves off as the same vessel. I blamed myself for being ungrateful to Indara and for not returning her total devotion as I ought. But there was nothing I could do about it: she clung to me so these days that it got on my nerves – she angered me. There are plain, uncomplicated beings who don't hold back their desires in any way and they don't wait for their lovers to take the first step. This Indian girl behaved exactly like the two Goajira sisters. As soon as their senses felt like coming into flower they offered themselves, and if you didn't take them, then there was all hell to pay. Deep inside them there grew up a gnawing, lasting unhappiness, and this distressed me all the more since I hadn't the least wish to hurt Indara, any more than I had wanted to hurt Lali and Zoraïma. I was obliged to force myself so that she should enjoy herself as much as possible in my arms.

The other day I watched the prettiest miming to express emotion that can possibly be imagined. There exists a sort of modern slavery in British Guiana. Javanese come to work in the cotton, sugar or cocoa plantations with five or ten year contracts. Husband and wife are both obliged to go out and work every day except when they are sick. But if the doctor doesn't agree that they are, they have to do an extra month's work at the end of their contract by way of punishment. And there are other months for other minor faults. They are all great gamblers and so they run into debt with the plantation; and they sign on for an additional period of one or more years so as to pay their creditors with the bonus they get for signing.

Generally speaking they never get free at all. They would stake their wives and keep their words exactly if they lost, but there was one thing they held sacred – their children. They do all they possibly can to keep them free. They put up with very great difficulties and privations, but they overcome them, and it is extremely rare for any of their children to sign a contract with a plantation.

So on this particular day it was the marriage of an Indian girl. Everybody was dressed in long gowns, the women in white veils and the men in white robes that came down to their feet. Quantities of orange blossom. After a good many religious ceremonies things had reached the point where the husband was to carry off his wife. The guests were standing there at the door of the house, the women on the right and the men on the left. The door was open, and there on the threshold sat the mother and father. The newly-married couple kissed the members of their family and walked between the two lines of people – lines that were some yards long. Suddenly the bride broke away from her husband's arm and ran to her mother. The mother hid her eyes with one hand and with the other she waved the girl back to the husband.

The young man held out his arms and called her: her movements showed that she couldn't tell what to do. Her mother had borne her: her gestures made one see the birth. Then her mother had suckled her. Could she forget all that to follow the man she loved? Maybe: but don't be in such a hurry, said her hands; just wait a moment and let me gaze a little longer at these dear parents of mine who, until I met you, were all I had to live for.

Then his gestures showed that life required that she too should be a wife and a mother. And all this went on to the sound of the girls' chanting and the answering song of the boys. Finally, having once more escaped from her husband's embrace and having kissed her parents, she ran a few steps and leapt into his arms. He hurried her off and took her away in the little flower-covered cart that was waiting for them.

We prepared the break with scrupulous care. We got a long, broad boat ready, with a good mainsail and jib and a first-class rudder, taking care the police shouldn't see what we were doing. We hid it downstream from our district in Penitence River, a tributary of the Demerara. It had exactly the same paintwork and number as a Chinese fishing boat registered in Georgetown. If a searchlight picked it out, only the crew would look different. To make the deception perfect we'd have to squat, because the Chinese in the boat we were copying were wizened little characters, whereas we were all big men.

It all went without a hitch and we ran out of the Demerara river in triumph, getting right out to sea. But in spite of the pleasure of having got away and of having avoided the danger of being discovered, I couldn't savour it to the full: there was just one thing that rather spoilt it for me, and that was having stolen off without a word to my Indian princess. I was not pleased with myself. She, her father and all her people had done me nothing but good and I was making a poor return. I didn't try and find reasons to justify my behaviour. It seemed to me that what I was doing wasn't at all pretty, and I wasn't in the least proud of myself. I'd left six hundred dollars just lying there on the table; but money doesn't pay for the kind of things I'd been given.

We were to steer due north for forty-eight hours. I'd returned to my old idea and I wanted to reach British Honduras: that would mean two days and more on the open sea.

The party was made up of five men, Guittou, Chapar,

Barrière from Bordeaux, Deplanque from Dijon, and me, Papillon, captain in charge of navigation. We'd hardly been thirty hours at sea before we ran into an appalling storm, followed by a kind of typhoon – a cyclone. Thunder, lightning, rain, huge irregular waves, hurricane-force whirlwinds, and we were carried along, quite unable to resist, in a wild ride over such a sea as I had never seen or even imagined. For the first time in my experience the trade-winds were completely done away with by these furious blasts, and the storm took us racing down in the opposite direction. If it had lasted a week we should have been right back in penal.

It was a memorable cyclone, as Monsieur Agostini, the French consul, told me later in Trinidad. He'd had more than six thousand coconut palms destroyed in his plantation – the cyclone had snapped them off at head height. Houses were picked up and carried a great way, falling back on to the land or out at sea. We lost everything – stores, baggage and even our water barrels. The mast broke about six feet up; the sails carried away; and worst of all, the rudder broke. By some miracle Chapar managed to save a small paddle, and it was with that little spade-like object that I tried to steer the boat. We all stripped to the skin to make some sort of a sail: everything went into it – jackets, trousers, shirts. We were all five of us down to our drawers. Our stump of a mast and this sail, made up of our clothes and held together with a coil of wire that happened to be aboard, meant that we could make something like progress.

The trade-winds came back, blowing in their natural direction, and I took advantage of this to head due south to reach land – any land, even British Guiana. The sentence waiting for us there would have been a welcome relief. During and after this – I won't call it a storm because that's not strong enough – this upheaval, this prodigious turmoil, or rather this cyclone, my companions behaved splendidly.

It was not until six days later – two of them dead calm – that we saw land. Our scrap of sail drew in spite of its holes, but even so we couldn't take the wind as I should have liked; and the little paddle was not up to steering the boat accurately or steadily. Since we were all naked we were horribly sunburnt all over our bodies, and that diminished our resistance. We none of us had any skin left on our noses – every nose aboard was flayed. Lips, feet, thighs and the flesh between our thighs were all in the same state: completely raw. We were so tortured by thirst that Deplanque and Chapar went so far as to drink salt water. After that they suffered even worse. In spite of our thirst and our gnawing hunger, there was one good thing – no one, absolutely no one, complained. No one handed out any advice, either. If anyone chose to drink salt water or throw it over himself, saying it cooled him, he could do so and find out all by himself that it bit into his wounds and made him even hotter when it evaporated.

I was the only one to have a completely open, healthy eye; all the others were suppurating and constantly gumming up. This meant they had to bathe their eyes however much it hurt, because they had to be able to open their eyes and see properly. The furious sun beat down on our sores with such force that we could hardly bear it. Deplanque was half out of his mind, and he kept on talking about throwing himself into the sea.

For the last hour it had seemed to me that I could make out land on the horizon. Of course I steered for it straight away, but without saying anything, because I was not sure. Birds appeared and flew around us: so I hadn't been mistaken. Their cries roused my companions, who were lying in the bottom of the boat, stupefied by the sun and their weariness – they lay there shielding their faces with their arms.

Guittou rinsed his mouth so as to be able to speak and said, 'Do you see the land, Papi?'

'Yes.'

'How long do you think it'll take us to get there?'

'Between five and seven hours. Listen, brothers: I'm all in. I've got the same sunburn as you, and on top of that my buttocks are raw with the rubbing of the wood and the salt water. There's not much wind, and we're only going along slowly: the muscles of my arms are cramping all the time and so are my hands, worn out with gripping this paddle I use as a rudder. Will you agree to what I say, now? Let's lower the sail and spread it over the boat like an awning to shelter us from this bloody sun until night falls. The boat'll drift towards the land all by itself. That's what we must do unless one of you will take my place steering.'

'No, no, Papi. Let's do what you say, and all of us except one sleep in the shadow of the sail.'

The sun was just beyond its height when I put this decision

527

to them. With an animal pleasure and relief I stretched out in the bottom of the boat, in the shade at last. My friends gave me the best place, so that I could get the outside air, coming in over the bows. The one keeping watch sat up, but he too was in the shadow. Everybody, including him, soon dropped off. We were shattered with tiredness, and were so delighted in this awning, sheltering us at last from the pitiless sun, that we sank into a profound sleep.

All at once every man aboard was woken by the howl of a siren. I pushed back the sail: outside it was dark. What time could it be? When I sat there in my place at the rudder a cool breeze whispered over my poor flayed body and straight away I was cold. But what a delightful feeling not to be on fire any more! We hoisted the sail. When I'd bathed my face in sea-water – fortunately there was only one suppurating eye that hurt – I could see land very clearly both to my right and my left. Where were we? Which of the two should I make for? Again we heard the howling of the siren. I located it: it was coming from the land on my right. What the hell was it trying to tell me?

'Where do you think we are, Papi?' asked Chapar.

'Frankly, I don't know. If that land isn't an island and all this is a gulf, then maybe we're at the tip of British Guiana, the part that runs out as far as the Orinoco [the great Venezuelan river that makes the frontier]. But if there's a pretty considerable distance between the land on the right and the land on the left, then that point is an island, and it's Trinidad. And in that case the one on the left would be Venezuela, which would mean we're in the Gulf of Paria.'

The charts I'd happened to study showed me that this was the choice. If it was Trinidad to the right and Venezuela to the left, which should we choose? Our fate would depend upon the decision. This fine fresh breeze would make it quite easy to run for either shore. For the moment we were moving neither towards the one nor the other. There were rosbifs on Trinidad – the same government as British Guiana.

'We're sure of being well treated,' said Guittou.

'Yes, but what are they going to say about our having left their territory illegally in war-time?'

'What do you know about Venezuela?'

'There's no telling what it's like now,' said Deplanque. 'In President Gomez' time escaped convicts were made to work on the roads in wicked conditions and then they were handed back to France.'

'Yes, but it's not the same now. There's a war on.'

'According to what I heard in Georgetown, they're not at war. They're neutral.'

'Are you sure of that?'

'Dead sure.'

'Well, in that case it would be dangerous for us.'

We could see the lights on land both to the right and to the left. The siren again, and this time it gave three quick howls. Lights flashed at us from the right-hand shore. The moon had just risen, far ahead of us, but on our path. Right in front of us two huge pointed black rocks soared up from the water. So that must be what the siren was for – it was warning us that the place was dangerous.

'Why, look! Buoys. A whole string of them. Why don't we tie up and wait for daylight? Chapar, lower the sail.'

Straight away he let go the collection of trousers and shirts that I so pompously called the sail. I braked with my paddle and brought the boat's bows to one of these 'buoys'. Fortunately there was a fair length of rope so well tied to the mooring ring that the cyclone had not been able to rip it off. There we were, made fast. Not moored directly to this strange looking buoy, because there was nothing on its surface to get a hold on, but to the cable that linked it to another a little farther on. They were no doubt there to mark a channel, and so there we rode, firmly moored to the cable. Without bothering about the howling that still kept on coming from the shore to our right we all lay down in the bottom of the boat, sheltering ourselves from the wind with the sail. I had been chilled through and through by the breeze and the night air, but now a gentle warmth flooded over me and I was certainly one of the first to go fast asleep.

The day was clear and bright when I woke up. The sun was rising: there was quite a sea running, and the blue-green of the water showed that the bottom was coral.

'What are we going to do? Shall we make up our minds to go ashore? This hunger and thirst are killing me.'

This was the first time anyone had complained since the beginning of these days with nothing to eat – just seven of them now.

'We're so close in it'd be no great crime,' said Chapar.

Sitting there in the stern and looking right ahead beyond the huge rocks that rose from the sea, I could plainly see the great cleft in the land. So it was Trinidad to our right and Venezuela to our left. There was no sort of doubt that we were in the Gulf of Paria; and the reason why the water was blue and not yellow from the current of the Orinoco was that we were lying in the channel of the current that passes between the two countries and then runs far out to sea.

'What are we going to do? That's for all of you guys to say: it's too serious for just one man to take the decision. To the right, that's the English island of Trinidad. To the left, Venezuela. Which do you want to go to? We ought to get ashore as quickly as possible, our boat and ourselves in the state we are. There are two time-expired men here, Guitton and Barrière. The other three, Chapar, Deplanque and me, run a greater risk. It's for us to decide. What do you people say?'

'The wisest thing is to go to Trinidad. Venezuela – we know nothing about it.'

'There's no need to make any decision,' said Deplanque. 'This launch that's coming will make it for us.'

And there it was in fact was a launch, coming fast in our direction. Here it was: it stopped fifty yards away. A man was picking up a loud-hailer. I caught sight of a flag – not an English flag. It was a flag I'd never seen before, a very beautiful flag all covered with stars. It must be Venezuelan. Later it was to be 'my flag', the standard of my new country and the most moving of all symbols for me – a symbol that meant that I, like every other ordinary man, had concentrated all the noblest qualities of a great nation, of my nation, into a scrap of cloth.

'*Quien son vosotros*? (Who are you?)'

'We're French.'

'*Estan locos*? (Are you mad?)'

'Why?'

'*Porque son encarados a mines* (Because you are tied up to a mine).'

'Is that why you don't come any closer?'

'Yes. Cast off right away.'

'OK.'

Chapar had undone the rope in three seconds. We'd been moored to a string of floating mines. We went alongside the launch, and its captain told us that it was a miracle we had not been blown up. They didn't come aboard, but handed us coffee, hot milk with plenty of sugar in it, and some cigarettes.

'Go to Venezuela. You'll be well treated, I promise you. We can't tow you in because we're on our way to pick up a badly wounded man on the Barimas lighthouse – it's urgent. Whatever you do don't try to run for Trinidad, because it's ten to one you'll hit a mine. And then . . .'

Calling out '*Adios, buena suerte* (Good-bye, good luck)' the launch went off. They left us two bottles of milk. We hoisted the sail. It was ten in the morning, my stomach was beginning to return to normal, thanks to the coffee and hot milk, and I had a cigarette in my mouth when I ran ashore, taking no sort of precautions and landing on the soft sand of a beach with some fifty people on it – they had all come down to watch the arrival of this strange craft with its stump of a mast and a sail made of jackets, trousers and shirts.

The Fishermen of Irapa

I discovered a world, a people, and a civilization that were entirely unknown to me. Those first moments on Venezuelan soil were so moving that it would need more than my small amount of talent to explain, express and describe the atmosphere – the welcome these warm, open-handed people gave us. Some of the men were black, others white; but the great majority were a very light colour – that of a European after several days in the sun: and they almost all had their trousers rolled up to the knees.

'Poor fellows, what a state you're in!' they said.

The fishing village where we'd landed was called Irapa, and administratively it belonged to the state of Sucre. All the women without exception turned themselves into nurses, nuns and guardian angels. The young ones (every one of them pretty – rather small, but Lord, how graceful), the middle-aged and the really old. They took us all to a house where they had hung five woollen hammocks and set out a table and chairs in the lean-to, and there they rubbed us from head to foot with cocoa butter. Not an inch of raw flesh was overlooked. We were dying of hunger and exhaustion and our long fast had brought on a fair degree of dehydration: these fishing people knew very well that we should sleep but that we should also eat small quantities at a time.

We each of us lay at our ease in a hammock, and even while we were sleeping, we were given little spoonfuls of food by our amateur nurses. My strength completely deserted me the moment they laid me in my hammock with my naked sores covered with the cocoa butter, and I collapsed entirely, sleeping, eating and drinking without really knowing what was going on around me.

My empty stomach would not hold the first spoonfuls of their kind of tapioca. I wasn't the only one, either. We all of us threw up at least some of the food these kind women put into our mouths, and we did so several times.

The people of this village were exceedingly poor, but there was not a single one of them that did not help us. In three days' time, thanks to the care they took and to our youth we were almost on our feet again. We got up for hours on end, and sitting there under the cool shade of the palm fronds of the lean-to my friends and I talked to the people of Irapa. They were not wealthy enough to dress us all in one go, so they formed little groups, one looking after Guittou, another after Deplanque, etc. There were nearly a dozen who took care of me. The first days they dressed us in any old clothes that came to hand – old, but scrupulously clean. Now every time they could they bought us a new shirt, a pair of trousers, a belt, a pair of shoes. Among the women who looked after me there were two very young girls: they looked mostly Indian, but there must already have been a mixture of Spanish or Portuguese blood. One was called Tibisay and the other Nenita. They bought me a shirt, a pair of trousers and a pair of the shoes they called aspargatas. They had heel-less leather soles and their uppers were made of plaited cloth. The cloth only covered the instep and heel – it left the toes free.

'There's no need to ask where you come from. We can see from your tattooings that you escaped from the French penal settlement.'

That moved me even more deeply. What! Knowing that we were men condemned for serious crimes, men who had escaped from a prison whose harshness they knew from magazines and newspapers, these humble people thought it quite natural to take us in and help us? It is already a striking proof of goodness when a fairly well-to-do or wealthy man gives another clothes, or when, from his copious store, he gives food to hungry strangers. But there is something truly wonderful about cutting a home-baked cassava or maize loaf in two when it's insufficient for you and your own family; sharing a meal – that was not enough in the first place – with a stranger, a fugitive from justice into the bargain.

This morning everybody was very quiet, both men and women too. They seemed concerned and worried. What was up? Tibisay and Nenita were with me. I'd managed to shave for the first time for a fortnight, for now it was a week since

533

we'd been with these great-hearted people. A thin film of skin had formed over my burns, so I was able to use a razor. Because of my beard, these girls had only had a vague notion of my age. They were absolutely delighted to find that I was young, and they naively told me so. Yet I was thirty-five, although I only looked twenty-eight or thirty. Yes, I could certainly feel that all these hospitable men and women were worried for us.

'What can be happening? Tell me, Tibisay, what's the matter?'

'We're expecting the authorities from Guiria, a village near Irapa. There's no administrator here, and the police know about your being with us, though we can't tell how. Anyway they're going to come.'

A tall and lovely black girl came to see me, bringing with her a splendidly-proportioned young man, bare to the waist and with his trousers rolled up to his knees. In Venezuela they often call coloured women La Negrita as a pet name – there is no kind of religious or racial discrimination about it whatsoever. So La Negrita said to me, 'Señor Enrique [Monsieur Henri], the police are coming. I don't know whether they're going to do you harm or not. Would you like us to hide you in the mountains for a while? My brother could take you to a hut where no one would ever find you. Tibisay, Nenita and me, between us we would bring you food every day and tell you what was going on.'

I was very deeply touched and I tried to kiss the noble girl's hand, but she pulled it away, and very sweetly and chastely kissed me on the cheek.

A party of horsemen arrived at a gallop. They all had machetes, the long knives used for cutting sugar cane, hanging like swords at their left sides; and they all had a broad, full cartridge-belt with a huge revolver in a holster. They dismounted. A tall, lean man with a Mongolian-looking face, the slit eyes of an Indian and a copper-coloured skin – a man of about forty – came towards us. He was wearing an enormous rice-straw hat.

'Good morning. I am the administrator.'

'Good morning, señor.'

'You people, why didn't you tell us you had five escaped French prisoners here? I'm told they've been in Irapa a week. Answer me.'

534

'We were waiting for them to be able to walk and for their burns to heal.'

'We've come to fetch them and take them to Guiria. A lorry is on its way.'

'Coffee?'

'Yes, please.'

We sat there in a circle and everybody had some coffee. I considered the administrator and his men. They did not seem wicked. I had the impression that they were obeying orders from above without necessarily agreeing with them.

'Have you escaped from Devil's Island?'

'No, we come from Georgetown, in British Guiana.'

'Why didn't you stay there?'

'It's hard to earn a living in those parts.'

He smiled and said, 'You think you'll be better off here than with the English?'

'Yes, because we're Latins, like you.'

A group of seven or eight men came towards our circle. They were led by a white-haired man of about fifty with very light chocolate-coloured skin. He was five foot eight, and his huge black eyes showed remarkable intelligence and strength of mind. His right hand rested on the hilt of a machete hanging at his side.

'Chief, what are you going to do with these men?'

'I'm going to take them to the prison at Guiria.'

'Why don't you let them stay with us, living with our families? Each will take one.'

'It's impossible – I have orders from the governor.'

'But they've committed no crime on Venezuelan soil.'

'I agree. But still, these are very dangerous men; because to be sent to the French penal settlements they must have been guilty of really serious crimes. What's more, they've escaped without any papers, and their country will certainly ask for them back when it's known they're in Venezuela.'

'We want to keep them with us.'

'Impossible – governor's orders.'

'Everything's possible. What does the governor know about truly unfortunate people? A man is never lost. Whatever he may have done, there's always some moment in his life when he has a chance of retrieving himself and becoming a good and useful member of the community. Isn't that right, all of you?'

535

'Yes,' said all the men and women with one voice. 'Leave them with us and we'll help them make a new life for themselves. In a week we've come to know them quite well enough to be sure they're decent people.'

'People more civilized than we are have shut them up in cells so they should do no more harm,' said the administrator.

'What do you mean by civilization, Chief?' I asked. 'Do you think that because we have lifts, aeroplanes and a train that runs under the ground it proves the French are more civilized than these people who have taken us in and looked after us? Let me tell you that in my humble opinion the greater human civilization and the greater understanding is to be found in each member of this community, living simply and naturally; even if it is a community that lacks all the advantages of an industrial civilization. But though they may not have the benefits of progress, they have a much higher notion of Christian charity than all the other so-called civilized nations in the world. I'd rather have a man belonging to this village, unable to read or write, than a Sorbonne graduate, if that meant he would come to have the heart of the lawyer who got me sent down. The first is always a man; the other has forgotten how to be one.'

'I know what you mean. Still, I'm just obeying orders. Here's the lorry coming. Please make it easier for me and behave so that everything passes off without a scene.'

Each group of women embraced the man they'd looked after. Tibisay, Nenita and La Negrita wept bitterly as they kissed me. All the men shook us by the hand, thus showing how it grieved them to see us going off to prison.

Farewell, people of Irapa, who had the nobility and courage to stand up to the authorities of your own country, and to criticize them so as to protect a band of poor devils unknown to you only a few days before. For me the bread that I ate among you, the bread you had strength enough to take from your own mouths to give to me, the bread that symbolizes the brotherhood of man, was the sublime example of the ancient wisdom – *Thou shalt not kill: thou shalt do good unto those that suffer even if thou thyself must go hungry: always help those more unfortunate than thou.* 'And if one day I am free,' I went on to myself, 'I'll help others whenever I can, as I've been taught to do by these first Venezuelans I've ever come across.' And later I was to meet a great many more.

536

Two hours later we reached a big village, a seaport that aspired to be a town: its name was Guiria. The administrator handed us over to the district chief of police himself. They treated us fairly well in the police station, but we were closely questioned, and the stupid official in charge of the interrogation absolutely refused to believe that we had come from British Guiana, where we had been free. And on top of that, when he asked us to explain how we came to reach Venezuela so exhausted and in such a state of destitution after so short a voyage as that from Georgetown to the Gulf of Paria, and I told him about the cyclone, he said we were making game of him.

'Two big banana-boats sunk in that storm, crew and all,' he said, 'and so did a ship loaded with bauxite. And you tell me you lived through it in a sixteen foot boat, open to the four winds? Who can believe such stuff? Even the old fool who begs in the market-place couldn't swallow that one. You're lying: there's something very dubious about your whole story.'

'Check what I say at Georgetown.'

'I don't want to make myself a laughing-stock for the English.'

I don't know what kind of a report this stupid, obstinate, unbelieving pompous fool of a secretary wrote or who he sent it to, but in any case we were woken up at five o'clock one morning, chained together and put aboard a lorry for an unknown destination.'

As I've said, the port of Guiria is on the Gulf of Paria, over against Trinidad. It also has the advantage of being on the mouth of a huge river, the Orinoco, which is almost as big as the Amazon.

There we were, the five of us chained and ten policemen to look after us, and we travelled in the direction of Ciudad Bolivar, a big town that was the capital of the state of Bolivar. On these earth roads the journey was very tiring; we were all of us, prisoners and police, jerked and flung about like so many sacks of potatoes in the back of the lurching, bounding lorry; and it lasted for five days on end. Every night we slept in the lorry and the next morning we set off again on this mad rush towards God knows where.

At last, five or six hundred miles from the sea, we reached our journey's end: it was where the earth road through the virgin forest from Ciudad Bolivar to El Dorado came to a halt. Both guards and prisoners, we were utterly exhausted by the time we reached the village.

Let me tell you about this El Dorado. To begin with it was the great hope of the Spanish conquistadores who saw that the Indians from those parts possessed gold and who firmly believed that there was a mountain of gold there: or if not entirely of gold then at least half gold and half earth. Now El Dorado is a village on the bank of a river full of caribes, of piranhas, those carnivorous fish that can entirely devour a man or an animal in a few minutes, and of trembladores – electric eels that instantly knock out their victim with an electric shock and then later suck his rotting carcass. In the middle of the river there is an island, and on the island there was a real genuine concentration camp. This was the Venezuelan penal settlement.

This hard-labour colony was the roughest thing I'd ever seen in my life: and it was the most savagely inhuman, too, because of the way the men were knocked about. It formed a square, each side being a hundred and fifty yards long, and it was surrounded by barbed wire. There were close on four hundred men who slept there in the open air, because there were only a few zinc-roofed shelters scattered here and there about the camp.

We were not asked for any explanation and we were given none: we were clapped into this prison of El Dorado the moment we arrived in the lorry at three in the afternoon, exhausted and in chains. They didn't trouble to write down our names or even ask them; but at half past three we were called out – two of us were given shovels and the other three picks. Five soldiers surrounded us: they carried rifles and bull's pizzles and they were commanded by a corporal. Under the threat of being beaten we were forced to march to a place where men were working. We grasped straight away that the prison guards were putting on a demonstration of strength and that it would be extremely dangerous to disobey for the moment. We'd see about it later.

When we got to the place where the men were working

they made us dig a trench along the side of a road they were driving through the virgin forest. We set to without a word and each one of us worked steadily, as far as his strength would allow. This didn't prevent us from hearing the insults and the savage blows that rained down on the prisoners without a pause. Not one of us was beaten. The object of putting us to work like this the moment we arrived was above all to let us see how prisoners were treated here.

It was a Saturday. Sweating and dusty, we were taken into the camp when our work was over, but still without any formalities of any kind.

'The five Frenchmen, over here!' It was the *presso* corporal speaking – the provost. He was a six-foot half-caste and he carried a bull's pizzle in his hand. This foul brute was in charge of discipline, but only inside the camp. We were shown where to sling our hammocks: it was in the open air, near the gate. But at least there were some sheets of corrugated iron, which meant that we would be sheltered from the sun and the rain.

The great majority of the prisoners were Colombians: the rest Venezuelans. None of the punishment camps in our penal settlement could compare with this labour-colony for brutality. The treatment these men underwent would have killed a mule. Yet nearly all of them were remarkably well, because there was one thing about the place – there was an extraordinary amount of food and it was very good.

We held a little council of war. If any one of us was hit by a soldier, the best thing for us was to lie flat on the ground and not get up whatever they did to us. It would certainly reach the ears of an officer and then we could ask him how we came to be in this hard-labour prison without having committed any crime. The two time-expired men, Guittou and Barrière, spoke about asking to be handed back to France. Then we decided to call the *presso* corporal. I was the one who was to speak to him. They called him Negro Blanco [the White Negro]. Guittou went and fetched him. The brute appeared, still carrying his bull's pizzle. The five of us surrounded him.

'What do you want with me?'

I spoke. 'We want to tell you just one thing. We'll never disobey any of the rules here, so there'll be no reason for you to hit us. But we've noticed that you lash out quite unprovoked, hitting whoever happens to be within your reach. That's why we asked you to come here for us to tell you that the day you hit any one of us, you're a dead man. Do you get my meaning?'

'Yes,' said Negro Blanco.

'One last piece of advice.'

'What?' he said in a toneless voice.

'If what I've just said has to be repeated, let it be to an officer, not to a soldier.'

'OK.' And he went off.

All this happened on a Sunday, the day the prisoners didn't go to work. An officer appeared. 'What's your name?'

'Papillon.'

'You're the leader of the Frenchmen?'

'There are five of us and we're all leaders.'

'Why was it you that acted as spokesman with the provost?'

'Because I speak Spanish best.'

The man who was talking to me was a captain in the National Guard. He told me that he was not the commanding officer – there were two others above him, but they weren't there. He'd been in command since our arrival. The other two would come back on Tuesday. 'Speaking in your own name and in the name of your friends you have threatened to kill the provost if he hits any one of you. Is that true?'

'Yes, and it is a very serious threat. But I also said we'd do nothing that would in any way justify corporal punishment. As you know, Captain, no court has sentenced us, because we've committed no crime in Venezuela.'

'I know nothing about it. You reached the camp with no papers at all, only a note from the chief who's in the village, saying ''Put these men to work as soon as they arrive.'' '

'Well, Captain, since you're a soldier, be fair enough to have your men told not to treat us like other prisoners, until your chiefs get here. Once again I assure you we've not been condemned and it's impossible that we should be, because we've committed no crime of any sort in Venezuela.'

'All right: I'll give orders accordingly. I hope you haven't lied to me.'

I had plenty of time that Sunday afternoon to study the other prisoners. The first thing that struck me was that physically they were all in good shape. Secondly, that blows were such an everyday matter, were handed out so freely, that they'd grown used to them – so much so that even on Sunday, the

540

day of rest, when they could easily have avoided them by behaving properly, they seemed to take a masochistic pleasure in playing with fire. They never stopped doing things that were forbidden – playing craps, stuffing a boy in the latrines, stealing from other prisoners, calling out obscene words to the women who came from the village bringing sweets or cigarettes for the prisoners. They also traded things – a plaited basket or a carving for a few coins or packets of cigarettes. Well, there were some prisoners who managed to grab what the woman was offering through the barbed wire, run off without giving anything in exchange and hide among the other men. It all amounted to this: corporal punishment was dealt out so unjustly and so capriciously that the prisoners were thoroughly hardened to it; the reign of terror in the camp neither benefited society nor kept order – it had no sort of good effect whatsoever upon the unfortunate prisoners.

With its silence, the solitary confinement prison of Saint-Joseph was far more dreadful than this. Here the fear only lasted a matter of moments, and what with being able to talk at night, on Sundays and at times when there was no work, and with the great quantities of good food, a man could very well manage his sentence, which never exceeded five years in any case.

We spent Sunday smoking and drinking coffee, talking among ourselves. A few Colombians came over to us; we kindly but firmly sent them about their business. We had to be looked upon as prisoners of a different kind: otherwise we should be done for.

At six o'clock on Monday morning, after a hearty breakfast, we marched out to work with the others. This was how the job was set in hand: two lines of men opposite one another – fifty prisoners, fifty soldiers. One soldier to each prisoner. Between the two ranks, fifty tools: picks, shovels or axes. The two lines watched one another. The line of prisoners all on edge; the line of soldiers eager and sadistic.

A sergeant bawled out, 'So-and-So, pick!'

The poor bastard rushed forward and the moment he caught it up, put it on his shoulder and raced off towards his work, the sergeant shouted, 'Private number so-and-so!' The soldier tore along after the wretched prisoner, flogging him with his bull's pizzle. This horrible spectacle was repeated twice a day. Anyone would have thought that the place between the camp and the working site was filled with donkey drivers beating their animals along at full speed. As we waited for our turn we were rigid with apprehension. Fortunately it was different for us. 'You five Frenchmen, come here! The young ones take these pick-axes and the older ones these two shovels.'

We did not run to the working site, but we walked there very briskly, escorted by four soldiers and a corporal. This day was longer and more sickening than the first. There were some men who were specially picked upon, and when they were completely exhausted they flung themselves down on their knees howling like madmen and begging not to be hit any more. In the afternoon the men had to make one big pile from several heaps of logs that had not burnt away properly. Others had to clean up behind them. And then again, there were between eighty and a hundred half burnt faggots that had to be converted into one huge blaze in the middle of the camp. Each soldier flogged his prisoner as he picked up the wood and ran to the camp with it. During this hellish race some of them went absolutely out of their senses, and in their hurry they took hold of branches by the glowing end. This hideous scene lasted three hours, as they went barefoot over the embers, burning their hands and suffering under the rain of blows. None of us was asked to join in the cleaning up of this fresh clearing. It was just as well, because as we worked we had agreed – keeping our heads well down and using few words – each to tackle a soldier, including the corporal, take their rifles and fire right into the middle of all these brutes.

On Tuesday we didn't go to work. We were summoned to the office of the two National Guard majors. They were perfectly amazed at the fact of our being in El Dorado without any papers to show that some court had sent us there. They promised that at all events they would ask the governor of the settlement for an explanation.

It didn't take long. These two majors in command of the prison guard were certainly very strict – indeed they might be said to carry repression much too far – but they behaved correctly and they made the governor himself come to make things clear to us.

Here he was before us, with his brother-in-law, a Russian, and the two National Guard officers.

'Frenchmen, I am the governor of the settlement of El Dorado. You have asked to speak to me. What is it that you want?'

'In the first place, what court has condemned us to serve a sentence in this hard-labour colony – condemned us unheard? How long and for what crime? We came to Venezuela, to Irapa, by sea. We haven't committed the slightest crime. So what are we doing here? And how can you say it's right that they should force us to work?'

'To begin with, we're at war. So we have to know exactly who you are.'

'Certainly; but that doesn't mean that we should be thrown into your penal settlement.'

'You are men who have escaped from French justice, so we have to find out whether they want you.'

'I accept that; but again I say, why treat us as though we had a sentence to serve?'

'For the moment you're being held under the *vagos y male-antes* [rogues and vagabonds] act while inquiries are made about you.'

This argument would have gone on and on if one of the officers hadn't cut it short by giving his opinion. 'Governor, we can't decently treat these men like the other prisoners. I suggest that until Caracas has decided how to deal with this particular state of affairs, we should find some other way of keeping them busy apart from road work.'

'They are dangerous characters: they've threatened to kill the *presso* corporal if he strikes them. Isn't that true?'

'Not only him, Governor; we'll kill *anyone else whatsoever* who hits a single one of us.'

'And what if it's a soldier?'

'The same thing. We've done nothing to deserve treatment like this. Our law and our prison system may be more hideous and inhuman than yours, but we won't put up with being flogged like animals.'

The governor turned triumphantly towards the officers. 'You see what very dangerous men they are!'

The older major paused for a moment or two and then to everybody's amazement he said, 'These escaped Frenchmen are right. They've done nothing in Venezuela to justify their being made to undergo a sentence or submit to the rules of this settlement. I think they're right. So there are two solutions, Governor: either you find them some work apart from the other prisoners or you don't send them out to work at all. If they are with all the rest, they'll certainly get hit by a soldier one of these days.'

'We'll see. Leave them in the camp for the moment. I'll tell you what must be done tomorrow.' And the Governor withdrew, together with his brother-in-law.

I thanked the officers. They gave us some cigarettes and promised to add a piece in the evening orders that would tell the officers and soldiers that on no account were we to be struck.

We'd been here a week now. We no longer went out to work. Yesterday – that is to say Sunday – something terrible happened. The Colombians drew lots to find who would kill the provost Negro Blanco. It was a man of about thirty who lost. They gave him an iron spoon whose handle had been sharpened on the cement and turned into a very pointed double-edged spearhead. The man kept his word bravely: he stabbed Negro Blanco three times near the heart. The provost was hurried off to the hospital and the killer was tied to a stake in the middle of the camp. The soldiers ran about like madmen, searching for other weapons. They were in a furious rage, and as I didn't take my trousers off quickly enough, one of them fetched me a blow with his bull's pizzle on my thigh. Barrière caught up a bench and swung it over the soldier's head. Another soldier stabbed him through the arm with his bayonet just as I flattened my soldier with a kick in the guts. I'd already got his rifle when we heard a shouted order. 'Hold it, all of you! Don't touch the Frenchmen! Frenchie, drop that rifle!' It was Captain Flores, the one who had received us the first day.

He stepped in at the very moment I was about to fire into the general mass. If it hadn't been for him we might perhaps have killed one or two, but we should certainly have lost our lives, dying there stupidly in the Venezuelan forest at the back of beyond, in that penal settlement that had nothing to do with us nor we with it.

Thanks to the captain's forceful interference the soldiers left our group and went off to satisfy their appetite for butchery elsewhere. It was then that we witnessed the ugliest, basest sight a man can well imagine.

Tied to a stake in the middle of the camp, the Colombian was flogged and beaten continuously by three men at a time, soldiers and *presso* corporal included. This went on from five in the afternoon until the sun rose at six the next morning.

544

How a man can last when it is only his body that is hit! There were very short pauses in the butchery during which he was asked who were his accomplices, who had given him the spoon and who had sharpened it. He betrayed no one, even when they promised they would stop the torture if he spoke. He lost consciousness several times. They brought him round by throwing buckets of water over him. It reached its climax at four in the morning. They saw that his skin was no longer reacting to the blows, not even by twitching, and they left off.

'Is he dead?' asked an officer.

'We don't know.'

'Untie him and set him on all fours.'

Four men propped him up, more or less on hands and knees. Then one of the torturers hit him with his whip so that the lash struck the division between his buttocks: the tip certainly went beyond his sexual organs. The master-stroke of torture at last forced out a shriek of agony.

'Go on,' said the officer. 'He's not dead.'

They went on beating him until daybreak. This mediaeval flogging would have killed a horse, but it did not finish off the Colombian. They left him alone for an hour and threw several buckets of water over him; at the end of this time he had the strength to get to his feet, helped by the soldiers. He even managed to stand upright by himself for a moment. The medical orderly appeared carrying a glass.

'Drink this purge,' ordered the officer. 'It'll pull you together.'

The Colombian hesitated, then drained the glass in one gulp. A moment later he fell to the ground, and this time for good. In this death agony he gasped out the words 'Fool. They've poisoned you.'

I need hardly say that none of the prisoners, nor any one of us, had the least intention of lifting a finger to help him. Every single man there was terrorized. This was the second time in my life I longed for death. A soldier a little way from me was holding his rifle carelessly, and for some minutes I was on the edge of grabbing it: the only thing that held me back was the idea that I might perhaps be killed before I had time to work the breech and fire into them.

A month later Negro Blanco was once more the terror of the camp – even more so this time. Yet it was written that he was fated to die at El Dorado. One night a soldier belonging to the guard pointed his rifle at him as the *presso* passed close by.

'Get down on your knees,' said the soldier.

Negro Blanco obeyed.

'Say your prayers. You're going to die.'

He let him say a short prayer and then shot him three times, killing him. The prisoners said he had done it because he was sickened at the way the brute flogged the unfortunate men under him. Others said that Negro Blanco had denounced the soldier to his officers, saying he'd known him in Caracas and that before he went into the army he'd been a thief. He was buried not far from the Colombian, who was a thief without any doubt, but also a man of most unusual worth and courage.

All these happenings prevented the authorities from coming to a decision about us. What's more, the other prisoners stayed in the camp for a fortnight without ever going out to work. Barrière was very carefully treated for his bayonet wound by a doctor from the village.

For the time being we were properly treated. Chapar left the other day for the village, where he was going to cook for the governor. Guittou and Barrière were set free, because France had provided information about us all and it was clear that they had served their time. As for me, I had given an Italian name. My real name came in this report, together with my finger-prints and the news of my life sentence: it also said that both Chapar and Deplanque had been given twenty years apiece. The governor was very pleased with himself as he told us about what he had heard from France. 'Still,' he said, 'since you have done nothing wrong in Venezuela we'll just keep you here for a while and then let you go. But you'll have to behave yourselves and work properly: we are holding you for observation.'

Quite often, when they were talking to me, the officers had complained of the difficulty of getting fresh vegetables in the village. The settlement had a farming camp, but no vegetables at all. They grew rice, maize, black beans and that was the lot. I said I would make them a kitchen garden if they would provide me with the seeds. Done.

The first advantage was that it got Deplanque and me out of the camp; and as two relégués had arrived, having been arrested in Ciudad Bolivar, they joined us. One of them was called Toto, and he came from Paris; the other was a Corsican. We four built a couple of solid little wooden houses, roofed over with palm-fronds – one for Deplanque and me and the other for our two companions.

Toto and I made high stands with their feet in tins full of paraffin so that the ants should not eat the seeds, and very soon we had strong tomato plants, as well as aubergines, melons and haricot beans. We began planting them out in their beds, for now they were strong enough to withstand the ants. The little tomatoes had a kind of ditch or hollow round them that we often filled with water, to keep them moist all the time and to prevent the many parasites of this untouched ground from getting at them.

'Here, what's this?' said Toto. 'Look how this pebble sparkles.'

'Wash it, man.'

He passed it to me. It was a little crystal the size of a chickpea. Once it was washed it shone even more on the side where it was broken from the mother-rock – it had been embedded in a sort of very hard stone.

'Could it be a diamond?'

'Shut up for Christ's sake, Toto. If it is one, this isn't the moment to bellow about it. Suppose we've been lucky enough to hit on a diamond mine? Hide it and let's wait until this evening.'

That evening I was giving a lesson in mathematics: my pupil was a corporal (now a colonel) who was then getting ready for his officer's examination. This man, unshakeably straight and great-hearted (he has proved it over a friendship of twenty-five years) is now called Colonel Francisco Bolagno Utrera.

'Francisco, what's this? Is it a piece of quartz?'

'No,' he said, having inspected it very thoroughly. 'It's a diamond. Hide it carefully and don't show it to anybody. Where did you find it?'

'Under my tomato seedlings.'

'That's odd. Maybe you carried it there when you brought water up from the river. Do you scrape the bottom with your bucket and so scoop up sand too?'

'Yes, sometimes.'

'Then that's the answer for sure. You carried your diamond up from the river, from the Caroni. Look very carefully to see whether you didn't bring up any others, because you never find just one gem stone. Where you find one, there have to be others.'

Toto set to work; he'd never worked like this in his life; he went at it so hard that our two companions, whom we hadn't told, said, 'Don't bash away like that, Toto. You'll kill yourself, carrying all this water up from the river. And you keep carrying up sand with it too.'

'That's just to make the earth lighter, mate,' said Toto. 'If you mix sand in, it drains better.'

We all made fun of him, but for all that Toto went on bringing up his buckets without a pause. At noon one day as the rest of us were sitting in the shade, he tripped and fell as he passed us. And out of the sand there rolled a diamond the size of two chick-peas. Once again the mother-rock was broken, or else the stone would never have been seen. He made the mistake of grabbing it too fast.

'Why,' said Deplanque, 'isn't that a diamond? The soldiers say the river has diamonds in it, and gold, too.'

'That's why I carry all this water. Now you see that I'm not such a bloody fool after all,' said Toto. He was relieved that now at last he could say why he had been working so hard.

To cut the story of the diamonds short, in six months Toto had found between seven and eight carats; and I had about twelve, in addition to over thirty stones so small that they came into what the miners call the industrial category. But one day I found a single stone weighing more than six carats. When I had cut it at Caracas in later days it produced a diamond of very nearly four carats: I still have it, and I wear it on my finger day and night. Deplanque and Antartaglia also collected a certain number of stones. I still had my charger from prison and I kept mine in it. They made themselves something of the same kind out of the tips of horns, and that was where they kept their treasure.

No one knew a thing, apart from the future colonel, Corporal Francisco Bolagno. The tomatoes and the other plants grew: the officers scrupulously paid us for the vegetables that we took to their mess every day.

We had a fair amount of freedom. We worked without any guard and we slept in our two huts. We never went to the camp. We were left alone and quite well treated. Of course every time we could we urged the governor to let us out. And every time he replied, 'Presently'. But now we'd been here eight months and nothing had happened. So I began to talk about making a break. Toto wouldn't have anything whatsoever to do with it. Nor would the others. I bought a hook and line so that I could study the river. I also took to selling fish, especially the well-known caribes, those carnivorous fish that weigh up to a couple of pounds and that have teeth arranged like a shark's – quite as dangerous, too.

There was a tremendous scene today. Gaston Duranton, known to his friends as Tordu, or Bent Gaston, had gone off on a break, carrying with him seventy thousand bolivars from the governor's safe.

This lag had a curious story of his own. When he was a child he was in the reformatory school on the Ile d'Oléron and he worked there in the bootmakers' shop. One day the leather band that held the shoe on his knee, going under his foot, broke and the jerk dislocated his hip. It was not looked after properly and it only went half way back into its socket; so all the rest of his life as a boy and part of his life as a man he was bent – lopsided. It was painful to see him walk – a thin, crooked boy who could only get along by dragging the leg that would not obey him. He came over to the penal settlement when he was twenty-five. After those long spells of reformatory school there was nothing surprising about his emerging as a thief.

Everyone called him Tordu. Almost nobody knew his real name of Gaston Duranton. Bent he was, Bent they called him. But although he was so lopsided he escaped from penal and got as far as Venezuela. Those were the days when Gomez was dictator. Not many men from penal survived his régime. There were a few exceptions, the most notable being Dr. Bougrat, because he saved the whole population of the pearl fishing island of Margarita, where there was an epidemic of yellow fever.

Tordu was picked up by Gomez' special police, and sent to work on the Venezuelan roads. The French and Venezuelan prisoners were chained to iron balls that had the Toulon fleur de lys stamped on them. When the Frenchmen complained they were told, 'But all these chains, shackles and balls come from your own country! Just you have a look at the fleur de lys.' Well, Tordu escaped from the mobile camp when he was working on the road. They caught him a few days later and brought him back to this perambulating gaol. He was stretched out naked, flat on his belly, in front of all the prisoners, and he was sentenced to a hundred lashes.

It was exceedingly uncommon for a man to survive more than eighty. As luck would have it Tordu was thin, and as he lay there flat the blows could not reach his liver, which may burst if it is hit. It was the custom, after a beating of this kind, which left a man's buttocks cut to pieces, to sprinkle salt on the wounds and to leave the man in the sun. Yet his head was always covered with a big fleshy leaf, because although it was all right for him to die from the flogging, it was wrong for him to die of sunstroke.

Tordu survived this mediaeval torture and when he got to his feet he found to his astonishment that he was no longer bent. The blows had broken the imperfect joint and had put his hip right back where it ought to have been. No one could understand it and everybody, soldiers and prisoners too, said it was a miracle. In that superstitious country they believed it was God's reward for having withstood his terrible punishment so bravely. They took off his shackles and his iron ball at once. He was given special treatment and the job of carrying water for the convicts at work. He grew and filled out, and as he ate a great deal he became a powerful, athletic character.

France found out that men from the penal settlement were building the Venezuelan roads and came to the opinion that their energies would be better employed in French Guiana. Marshal Franchet d'Esperey was sent on a mission to the dictator, who was very pleased at having all this free labour; the marshal was to ask him to be so kind as to hand the men back to France. Gomez agreed and a boat came to Puerto Cabello to fetch them. At this point there were some splendid scenes of confusion, because there were men from other road-building sites who knew nothing about what had happened to Tordu.

'Hi, Marcel! How are you, brother?'

'Who are you?'

'Tordu.'

'Don't talk such balls,' they all replied, seeing this fine, well-built type standing there on his two straight legs. Tordu was young and he loved his joke: and during the time the French convicts were being loaded on to the ship he never stopped calling out to all the men he knew. And of course not a single one of them could believe that Tordu had been straightened out. When I was taken back to penal myself I heard the story from his own mouth on Royale; and from others, too.

He escaped again in 1943 and landed up in El Dorado. He told them he'd lived in Venezuela before, though he certainly didn't add that he'd done so as a prisoner, and straight away they gave him Chapar's job as a cook: for Chapar had turned gardener. So Tordu was over at the village, in the governor's house – that is to say, on the other side of the river.

In the governor's office there stood the colony's safe, with all the money in it. On this particular day, then, Tordu took these seventy thousand bolivars, which at that time were worth about twenty thousand dollars. Hence the turmoil in our garden – governor, governor's brother-in-law and the two guard majors milling frantically about. The governor wanted to put us back in the camp. The officers wouldn't have it. They stood up for us and at the same time for their supplies of vegetables. At last they managed to persuade the governor that we had no information to give him; that if we'd known anything, we'd have gone off with Tordu; and that our object was to be set free in Venezuela, not in British Guiana, which was the only place he could possibly go to.

Tordu was found dead nearly fifty miles away, in the bush very near the British Guiana frontier; and it was the vultures circling over him that gave him away. The first, most convenient, version of his death was that he had been murdered by the Indians. Much later a man was arrested in Ciudad Bolivar, changing brand-new five-hundred-bolivar notes. The bank that had sent the governor of El Dorado the notes had kept the numbers and they saw that these were the same – that these notes had been stolen. The man confessed and informed on two others, who were never arrested. That, then, was the life and death of my good friend Gaston Duranton, known by the name of Tordu.

Some of the officers secretly and illegally set prisoners to work, looking for gold and diamonds in the river Caroni. They found some – not in extraordinary quantities, but enough to make them very keen. Below my garden there were two men working all day long with a wash-trough, a cone with its point down; they filled it with earth and swilled it about – diamonds, being heavier than anything else, would sink down to the bottom. Very soon someone was killed: he had been robbing his boss. This little scandal put an end to the illicit mine.

In the camp there was a man whose body was covered with tattooing. The one on his neck read *Barber: shit to you*. His right arm was paralysed. His mouth was twisted and sometimes his big tongue hung out, drooling; so it was obvious he had had a stroke. Where? No one knew. He had been brought here before the rest of us. Where had he come from? The one thing that was certain was that he was an escaped lag or relégué. *Bat d'Af* – the French army's penal battalion – was tattooed on his chest, and that together with the shit to the barber on his neck made it dead certain he was a convict.

The screws and the prisoners called him Picolino. He was well treated and they conscientiously gave him his food three times a day, and cigarettes. His blue eyes were intensely alive and they were by no means always sad. When he was looking at someone he liked they sparkled with pleasure. He understood everything that was said to him, but he could neither speak nor write – his paralysed right arm was incapable of holding a pen and his left hand lacked the thumb and two fingers. This wreck of a man leant up against the barbed wire for hours on end waiting for me to go by with the vegetables, because this was the path I took to go to the officers' mess. So every morning, as I carried up my stuff, I stopped to have a talk with Picolino. Leaning there on the barbed wire he would gaze at me with his fine blue eyes, so full of life in that almost dead body. I passed the time of day and then by nodding or winking he made me understand that he followed what I said. His poor paralysed face would light up for a moment and his eyes gleam as he tried to tell me God knows how many things. I always took him some little treat – tomatoes, lettuces or cucumbers made into a salad with a vinaigrette sauce, a little melon, or a fish cooked over the embers. He was never hungry, because the Venezuelan prison provided plenty of food; but it made a change from the official rations. And I always added a few cigarettes. This chat with Picolino became a settled habit, so much so that the soldiers and prisoners called him Picolino, son of Papillon.

The Venezuelans were so pleasant, kindly and charming, that an extraordinary thing happened: I made up my mind to put my faith in them. I would not make a break. I'd accept this wrongful situation of being a prisoner in the hope that some day I might belong to their nation. This may seem absurd. Their brutal way of treating the convicts was not calculated to make me feel like living among them; but on the other hand I came to realize that both prisoners and soldiers looked upon corporal punishment as something that was perfectly natural. If a soldier did something wrong, he too was given several lashes. And a few days later this same soldier would talk to the corporal, sergeant or officer who had knocked him about as though nothing had happened. The dictator Gomez had ruled them in this way for years and years, and it was from him that they had inherited the barbarous system. It had become customary – so much so that a civil administrator would punish the people under his authority with a whip.

I was on the eve of being set free; and the reason for this was that there had been a revolution. The president of the republic, General Angarita Medina, had been overthrown by a half military and half civilian *coup d'état*; he was one of the greatest liberals in the history of Venezuela, and he was so good, so democratic, that he had been both unable and unwilling to withstand this rising. It seems he had flatly refused to allow Venezuelans to shed one another's blood to keep him in office. This great democratic soldier certainly knew nothing about what went on in El Dorado.

At all events, a month after the revolution all the officers were changed. The authorities began an inquiry into the so-called purge and into the death of the Colombian. The governor and his brother-in-law vanished, and they were replaced by a lawyer who had also been a diplomat.

'Yes, Papillon, I'm going to set you free tomorrow; but I'd like you to take that poor Picolino with you. I know you take an interest in him. He has no official identity, so I'll give him one. As for you, here's a *cédule*, an identity-card; it's all in order, and it's made out in your real name. The conditions are

these: you must live somewhere in a small village for a year
before you're allowed to settle in a big town. This is a kind
of probationary period, not so that the police can supervise
you, but so that we can see what progress you make and how
you can manage in life. If the administrator of the district
gives you a certificate of good behaviour at the end of that
time, as I'm sure he will, then that will put an end to your
confinamiente, your obligatory residence. I think Caracas
would be a perfect town for you. At all events, you're legally
authorized to live in this country. Your past doesn't mean
anything to us. It's up to you to show that you're worthy of
being given this chance of once more becoming a respectable
member of society. I hope that before five years have gone by
you will be my compatriot – that naturalization will give you
a new country of your own. May God be with you. Thank
you for being willing to take care of that poor helpless Picolino.
I can only let him out if someone gives a signed undertaking
that he will look after him. Let's hope that some hospital will
be able to cure him.'

It was at seven the next morning that I was to go out into
real freedom, together with Picolino. My heart was flooded
with warmth: at last I had escaped from the road down the
drain, and now it was for good. I had been waiting for this
for thirteen years: for now it was 18 October 1945.

I went down to my shed in the garden. I asked my friends
to forgive me, but I just had to be alone. My feelings were
too powerful for me to be able to express them with anyone
there. I examined the identity-card the governor had given me:
my photograph in the left-hand corner: on top, the number
1728629: valid from 3 July 1944. Plumb in the middle, my
name: beneath it, my Christian name. On the back, date of
birth: 16 November 1906. The identity-card was perfectly in
order, and it was even signed and stamped by the Director of
the Identity Bureau. Status in Venezuela: resident. This word
resident was terrific: it meant I was domiciled in Venezuela.
My heart beat wildly. I felt like going down on my knees and
thanking God. You don't know how to pray, Papillon; and
you've never been baptized. What God are you going to speak
to, when you don't belong to any specific religion? The God of
the Catholics? The Protestants? The Jews? The Mahometans?
Which was I going to choose to address my prayer to – a
prayer that I'd have to invent, since I knew none right through.

But why should I worry about which God to pray to on this particular day? When I had called upon Him during the course of my life, or even when I cursed Him, hadn't I always thought of the God of the Infant Jesus in His basket with the ass and the ox around Him? Did my subconscious mind still bear a grudge against those Colombian nuns? In that case, why not think just of the splendid, noble-hearted bishop of Curaçao, Mgr Irénée de Bruyne; or farther back still, of the good chaplain of the Conciergerie?

Tomorrow I would be free, completely free. In five years I would be a naturalized Venezuelan, for I was certain I should commit no wrong-doing upon this soil that had given me asylum and that had trusted me. In the life before me I must be twice as honest as anybody else.

For indeed, although I was innocent of the killing for which a public prosecutor, some cops and the twelve bastards of the jury had sent me to penal, they could only have done so because I was already something of a bad hat. It was because I was in fact outside the law that it was so easy for them to spin a web of falsehoods around my character. Opening other people's safes is not a really praiseworthy occupation and society has both the right and the duty to defend itself. I must honestly confess that the reason I was tossed down the drain was that I was a standing candidate for it. The fact that such a punishment was unworthy of a nation like France; the fact that although society has the duty of defending itself it does not have that of taking such ignoble revenge – all that is something else again. I could not wipe out my past just like that; I had to rehabilitate myself by my own efforts: first in my own eyes and then in those of others. So thank the God of the Catholics, Papi: promise Him something very important.

'Lord, forgive me if I do not know how to pray; look into me and You will see I don't possess words enough to express my gratitude to You for having brought me as far as this. It has been a hard struggle; making my way along the calvary inflicted upon me by other men has not been always very easy; and the reason I have been able to overcome all these obstacles and go on living in good health up until this blessed day is certainly because of Your helping hand. What can I do to show You that I am sincerely grateful for Your care of me?'

'Renounce thy vengeance.'

Did I really hear these words or did I only think I heard

them? I don't know: but they came so suddenly, like a smack in the face, that I'd almost swear I really did hear them.

'Oh no! Not that! Don't ask me that. These people have made me suffer too much. How can You expect me to forgive those bent cops, or Polein, that perjured witness? How can I give up the idea of ripping out that inhuman lawyer's tongue? I can't do it. You're asking me too much. No, no, no. I'm sorry to offend You, but at no price whatsoever will I give up carrying out my revenge.'

I went outside: I was afraid of weakening and I didn't want to yield. I walked up and down my garden. Toto was curling the tips of the climbing beans round their stakes so that they should get a hold. They were all three there, Toto, the optimistic Parisian from the gutters of the rue de Lappe, Antartaglia, the Corsican-born pickpocket who had spent years relieving Parisians of their purses, and Deplanque, the guy from Dijon who'd killed a fellow-ponce, and they all came towards me. They were looking at me, and their faces were full of happiness because I was to be free at last. It would be their turn soon, no doubt.

'Didn't you bring a bottle of wine or rum from the village to celebrate being let out?'

'Forgive me. I was knocked all of a heap and I never even thought about it. Don't hold it against me. I'm very sorry I forgot.'

'No, no, there's nothing to be sorry about. I'll make us all a pot of coffee.'

'Brother, you're happy, because you're going to be free for good and all at last, after all these years of struggle. We're happy for you.'

'I hope your turn will come soon.'

'That's for sure,' said Toto. 'The captain told me that he was going to let one of us out each fortnight. What are you going to do once you're free?'

I hesitated for a second or two, but then, in spite of my dread of looking ridiculous in front of the relégué and these two lags, I bravely said, 'What am I going to do? Well, it's simple enough. I'll get a job and I'll go straight: for good. I'd be ashamed of committing a crime in this country that has put its trust in me.'

I was astonished when, instead of an ironic crack, I heard them all three say, 'I've made up my mind to go straight too.

You're dead right, Papillon: it'll be tough, but it's worth it; and these Venezuelans deserve we should treat them right.'

I couldn't believe my ears. Toto, the tough from the Bastille gutters, with notions of this kind? It was staggering. Antartaglia, who'd spent his long life rifling other people's pockets, reacting like this? It was wonderful. And it was even more amazing that Deplanque, a professional ponce, should have no plans for finding a woman and putting her to work. We all burst out laughing.

'Well, what do you know! If you were to go back to Montmartre tomorrow and tell them in the Place Blanche, nobody would believe you.'

'The men of our world would. They'd understand, brother. It's only the squares who wouldn't agree. The great majority of Frenchmen won't have it that guys like us, with the kind of past we have behind us, can become decent citizens from every point of view. That's the difference between the Venezuelan nation and ours.'

I've already told you what the poor fisherman of Irapa had to say, when he was telling the administrator that a man was never wholly lost and that he must be given a chance so that with help he might go straight. These almost illiterate fishermen of the Gulf of Paria, away at the far end of the world, lost in the huge estuary of the Orinoco, have a humane philosophy that is lacking in a good many of our fellow-countrymen. Too much material progress, a rat-race of a life, a society with only one ideal – more mechanical inventions, a life that grows easier and easier all the time, a higher standard of living. Lapping up scientific discoveries in much the same way that one laps up an ice-cream brings about a longing for greater comfort and a perpetual struggle to attain it. This dries up people's hearts: it does away with pity, understanding and nobility. They no longer have the time to care for others, least of all habitual criminals. And even the authorities here at the back of beyond are unlike ours; for although they are responsible for public order they will nevertheless run the risk of getting into serious trouble in order to save a fellow man. And I think that is splendid.

I had a fine navy-blue suit given me by my pupil, the one who is now a colonel. A month back he had gone off to the officers' school, having passed the examination, one of the top three,

I was happy to have done a little something towards his success by the lessons I'd given him. Before he left he'd given me some almost new clothes that fitted me very well. I'd leave prison decently dressed thanks to Francisco Bolagno, a corporal in the National Guard, a married man and the father of a family.

This field officer, at present a colonel in the National Guard, has honoured me with his great-hearted, unshakeable friendship for twenty-six years now. He is the embodiment of integrity, nobility and the most elevated feelings a man can possess. In spite of his high position in the army, his faithful friendship has never faltered, and he has never failed to help me on every possible occasion. I owe a great deal to Colonel Francisco Bolagno Utrera.

Yes, I'd do everything I possibly could to go straight and to stay straight. The only difficulty was that I'd never done any work – I had no trade. I'd have to take any sort of job at all to earn my living. It wouldn't be easy, but I'd get there: that was for sure. Tomorrow I'd be a man like other men. Prosecutor, you've lost the game: *I have left the road down the drain for good.*

In the nervous excitement of this last night of my odyssey as a prisoner I tossed and turned in my hammock. I got up and walked through the garden that I had looked after so carefully all these last months. The moonlight was almost as bright as day: silently the water of the river flowed down towards its mouth. No birdsong: they were all asleep. The sky was full of stars, but the moon was so bright you had to turn your back to it to see them. Opposite me the mass of the forest, with just one clearing, the space where the village of El Dorado stood. Nature's deep tranquillity soothed me. Gradually my painful excitement died away, and the calmness of the night gave me the peace of mind I needed.

I could clearly picture the place where I should land from the boat tomorrow – in the country of Simon Bolivar, the man who freed Venezuela from the Spanish yoke and who bequeathed to his sons those feelings of humanity and understanding that made it possible for me to make a new life for myself.

I was thirty-seven: still young. I was absolutely fit. I'd never had any serious illness, and it seemed to me that I could say that I was perfectly well balanced mentally. The way down the drain had left no degrading marks upon me; and I think the real reason for that was that I had never truly belonged there.

During these first weeks of freedom I would not only have to find some way of earning my living but also look after poor Picolino and keep him too. It was a serious responsibility that I had taken upon myself. Yet although he would be a heavy burden I'd keep my promise to the governor and I'd never leave the poor fellow until I'd managed to get him into a hospital, where he would be cared for by people who knew what they were about.

Should I tell my father that I was free? He'd not heard from me for years. In any case where was he? The only news of me he'd had was the visits of the gendarmes whenever I made a break. No, I mustn't be in too much of a hurry. I had no right to open a wound that had perhaps been almost healed by the passing of the years. I'd write when I was really on my feet, when I had a solid and straightforward, though perhaps modest job, so that I'd be able to say, 'Dear Papa, your little boy is free and he has become an honest man – he has gone straight. He lives in such-and-such a way and he has such-and-such a position. You no longer have to hang your head when he is mentioned, and that is why I am writing to tell you that I always have loved and honoured you and always will.'

This was war-time: who could tell whether the Germans were there in my little village? The Ardèche was not a very important part of France. It wouldn't be completely occupied. What could they find there, apart from the chestnuts? Yes, it was only when I was properly established and worthy of it that I'd write home, or rather try to write.

Where should I go now? I'd settle in a village called La Callao, by the goldmines. There I'd live the year I was required to spend in the country. What should I do? God knows. Cross those bridges when you come to them. If you have to dig to earn your bread, why then you'll just dig and that's all there is to it. To begin with I've got to learn how to live as a free man. It won't be easy. Apart from these few months in Georgetown. I'd not had to worry about earning my daily bread for the last thirteen years. Still, at Georgetown I'd not done so badly. The adventure would go on, and it was up to me to find ways of earning my living – without doing anyone any harm, of course. I'd see. So tomorrow it would be La Callao.

Seven o'clock in the morning. A splendid tropical sun, a cloudless blue sky, birds singing their delight in life, my friends gathered at the garden gate. Picolino, newly shaved and cleanly dressed in civilian clothes. There was an officer there waiting with my friends, and he was going with us as far as the village of El Dorado.

'Embrace us,' said Toto, 'and then just go. That'll be best for everyone.'

'Good-bye, brothers. If ever you pass by La Callao, look me up. If I have a place of my own, it'll be yours.'

'Good-bye, Papi. Good luck!'

Quickly we went down to the landing stage and got into the boat. Picolino walked very well: it was only above the waist that he was paralysed – his legs were quite all right. In under a quarter of an hour we were on the other side of the river.

'Right: here are Picolino's papers. Good luck, you two. From this moment on you're free. Adios!'

It's as easy as that to drop the chains you've been dragging for thirteen years. 'From this moment on you're free.' They turn their backs, which means that nobody is keeping watch on you any more. And that's all. In a few minutes we had climbed the cobbled path from the river. All we had was a little bundle with three shirts in it and a spare pair of trousers. I was wearing my navy-blue suit, a white shirt and a blue tie to match.

But as you may imagine, making a new life for oneself is not quite as easy as sewing on a button. And although today, twenty-five years later, I am a married man with a daughter of my own, a Venezuelan citizen living happily in Caracas, I only got there after a great many other adventures, some of them successful and others disastrous, but all of them the adventures of a free man and an upright citizen. Maybe one day I'll tell them, together with a good many other remarkable stories that I didn't have room for here.

BANCO

The Further Adventures of Papillon

Translated from the French by
Patrick O'Brian

To the memory of Dr Alex Guibert-Germain,
to Madame Alex Guibert-Germain,
to my countrymen, the Venezuelans,
to my French, Spanish, Swiss, Belgian, Italian, Yugoslav,
German, English, Greek, American, Turkish, Finnish,
Japanese, Israeli, Swedish, Czechoslovak, Danish, Argentine,
Colombian, and Brazilian friends and all those friends who
are faceless but who have done me the honour of writing to me.

'What you think of yourself matters more than what others
think of you.'

(*author unknown to Papillon*)

Contents

Translator's Introduction

MIDDLE-AGED, impoverished by an earthquake and worried about his future, Henri Charrière sat down to write a book to restore his fortunes: it was his first, and he called it *Papillon*, the name by which he had been known in the underworld of Paris and in the French penal settlements. He had no great opinion of himself as an author and he was quite willing to have it improved, cut about and put into 'good French'; but the first publisher he sent it to happened to employ a brilliant editor who at once realized the exceptional quality of the manuscript and who delivered it to an astonished public in its original state, merely tidying up the punctuation, the spelling and a very few points of style.

That was in 1970, the year of the *phénomène Papillon*, a phenomenon almost unparalleled in the annals of publishing: it was not only that an extraordinary number of people read the book (850,000 copies were sold in the first few months), but that the readers embraced the whole spectrum of literary opinion, from the Académie Française to those whose lips moved slowly as they made their fascinated way through the strange adventures of an indomitable man struggling against the society that had sent him to rot in the infamous tropical prisons of Guiana with a life-sentence for a murder that he had never committed.

They were all deeply moved by the burning sense of injustice that runs right through the book and that gives it its coherence and validity, but even more by Papillon's sheer narrative power, his innate genius for telling a story. 'This is a literary prodigy,' said François Mauriac. 'It is utterly fascinating reading . . . This new colleague of ours is a master!' And he pointed out that it was not enough to have been a transported convict and to have escaped again and again; extraordinary talent was required to give the book its ring of truth and to make its value 'exactly proportional to its immense success'.

9

The soundness of Mauriac's words can be seen not only from the immense quantities of hopeless manuscripts by other ex-prisoners (purple characters, but untouched by genius) that flow into publishers' offices every week, but also by the baldness of the following summary that is intended to put the reader of this second volume into the picture: the main facts are here, but I am the first to admit that the heart of the matter is lacking.

The facts, then: in 1931 Henri Charrière, alias Papillon, was sentenced to transportation for life and he was taken away with some hundreds of others in a prison-ship bound for South America, for French Guiana. Here he found himself in an appallingly tough and savage world where corruption, terrorism, sodomy and murder were commonplace; he was well equipped for survival in this world, being as tough as any man there, perfectly loyal to his friends and perfectly uncompromising in his hatred of the official establishment, and in time he could have carved out a respectable place for himself. But he had no intention of staying; he had sworn not to serve his unjust sentence, and forty-two days after his arrival he made a break. With two companions (one broke his leg in escaping) he made his way down the Maroni river in a crazy boat; at a remote lepers' island they changed boats and so rode out to sea, sailing under the broiling sun day after day until at last they reached Trinidad. On and on to Curaçao, where the boat was wrecked; on to Rio Hacha in Colombia, where the wind failed them and they were taken prisoner. Another break, this time with a Colombian friend, and eventually Papillon reached hostile Indian territory, alone and on foot. They took him in, gave him two wives, and then, when at last he would stay no longer, a bag of pearls. Back to Colombia, only to be arrested and imprisoned once more, and, after several abortive breaks, handed over to the French authorities. Then solitary confinement on the Île Saint-Joseph—a deeply moving account of the silence, the heat and the utter loneliness of that dim, timeless, underground cage—two years of it. When at last it was over and he was out in the light again, he began to make a raft for another break; but a fellow convict informed upon him, and having killed the informer he went back to solitary—an eight years' sentence cut to nineteen months for rescuing a little girl from the sharks. Another attempt to escape; transfer to Devil's Island and then the final break at last, riding two sacks of coconuts through the shark-infested sea to the mainland. A new boat and a new series of adventures brought him, by way of British Guiana (and a new wife), to Venezuela and to the Venezuelan penal settlement at El Dorado, where he was held on the charge of being a rogue and a vagabond. But a *coup d'état* in Caracas brought the promise of release, and the last pages of the book show Papillon, equipped with genuine papers at last, and dressed in good civilian clothes, ready to walk out into freedom after thirteen years of being in prison or on the run. That is where the present volume starts, and from now on his story is told in his own infinitely more living words.

But, before I leave Henri Charrière to tell his own story, perhaps I may be permitted to say a word about the translation. I had followed *Papillon*'s wild success; I had watched the splendid time the author was having (Papillon in a sledge with Brigitte Bardot, Papillon with an immense cigar and a diamond ring, Papillon in a dinner-jacket, painting Paris red) with delight and with admiration for his iron resistance; but I had been afraid that fame and wealth might alter his style and complicate my task. Not at all: as soon as I looked into *Banco* I recognized exactly the same voice: here and there a slightly more literary turn of phrase, here and there a literary allusion, but not the least change in the essential Papillon. So I made no alteration in the techniques I had adopted for translating his earlier book: of these the only one that seems to call for any explanation is my use of a somewhat archaic Americanized slang, particularly in the dialogue. This seemed to me the only way of rendering Papillon's equally archaic argot; and in the few cases where even American would not quite yield the liveliness of the French, I comforted myself with the proverb from Papillon's own country: 'If you cannot have thrushes to eat, then you must make do with blackbirds.'

PATRICK O'BRIAN

11

'GOOD luck, Frenchman! From this moment, you're free. *Adios!*'

The officer of the El Dorado penal settlement waved and turned his back.

And it was no harder than that to get rid of the chains I had been dragging behind me these thirteen years. I held Picolino by the arm and we took a few steps up the steep path from the river-bank, where the officer had left us, to the village of El Dorado. And now, sitting here in my old Spanish house on the night of 18-August 1971, to be exact, I can see myself with unbelievable clarity on that pebbly track; and not only does the officer's voice ring in my ears in just the same way, deep and clear, but I make the same movement that I made twenty-seven years ago—I turn my head.

It is midnight: outside, the night is dark. And yet it's not. For me, for me alone, the sun is shining: it's ten o'clock in the morning and I stare at the loveliest shoulders, the loveliest back I have ever seen in my life—my gaoler's back moving farther and farther away, symbolizing the end of the watching, the spying, the surveillance that had gone on every day, night, minute and second, never stopping for thirteen years.

A last look at the river, a last look beyond the warder at the island in the middle with the Venezuelan penal settlement on it, a last look at a hideous past that lasted thirteen years and in which I was trampled upon, degraded and ground down.

All at once pictures seemed to be forming against the mists raised from the water by the blazing tropical sun, to show me the road I had travelled these thirteen years, as though it were on a screen. I refused to watch the film; I caught Picolino by the arm, turned my back on the weird picture and led him quickly up the path, first giving myself a shake to get rid of the filth of the past for good and all.

Freedom? Yes, but where? At the far end of the world, way back in the plateaux of Venezuelan Guiana, in a little village deep in the most luxuriant virgin forest you can imagine. This was the south-east tip of Venezuela, close to the Brazilian frontier: an enormous sea of green broken only here and there by the waterfalls of the rivers and streams that ran through it—a green ocean with widely-scattered little communities with ways and customs worthy of biblical times, gathered round a chapel, where no priest even had to talk about love for all men and simplicity because that was the way they lived naturally, all the year round. Often these *pueblitos* are only linked to others, as remote as themselves, by a truck or two: and looking at the trucks, you wondered how they ever got so far. And in their way of life these simple, poetic people live just as people did hundreds and hundreds of years ago, free from all the taints of civilization.

When we had climbed up to the edge of the plateau where the village of El Dorado begins, we almost stopped; and then slowly, very slowly, we went on. I heard Picolino draw his breath, and like him I breathed in very deeply, drawing the air right down into the bottom of my lungs and letting it out gently, as though I were afraid of living these wonderful minutes too fast—these *first minutes of freedom*.

The broad plateau opened in front of us: to the right and the left, little houses, all bright and clean and surrounded by flowers. Some children had caught sight of us: they knew where we came from. They came up to us, not unfriendly at all; no, they were kind, and they walked beside us without a word. They seemed to understand how grave this moment was, and they respected it.

There was a little wooden table in front of the first house with a fat black woman selling coffee and *arepas*, maize cakes.

'Good morning, lady.'

'*Buenas dias, hombres!*'

'Two coffees, please.'

'*Si, señores.*' And the good fat creature poured us out two cups of delicious coffee: we drank them standing, there being no chairs.

'What do I owe you?'

'Nothing.'

'How come?'

'It's a pleasure for me to give you the first coffee of your freedom.'

14

'Thank you. When's there a bus?'

'Today's a holiday, so there's no bus; but there's a truck at eleven.'

'Is that right? Thanks.'

A black-eyed, light-skinned girl came out of a house. 'Come in and sit down,' she said with a lovely smile.

We walked in and sat down with a dozen people who were drinking rum.

'Why does your friend loll out his tongue?'

'He's sick.'

'Can we do anything for him?'

'No, nothing: he's paralysed. He's got to go to hospital.'

'Who's going to feed him?'

'Me.'

'Is he your brother?'

'No; my friend.'

'You got money, Frenchman?'

'Very little. How did you know I was French?'

'Everything gets known here in no time. We knew you were going to be let out yesterday: and that you escaped from Devil's Island and that the French police are trying to catch you to put you back there again. But they won't come and look for you here: they don't give orders in this country. We are the ones who are going to look after you.'

'Why?'

'Because . . .'

'What do you mean?'

'Here, drink a shot of rum and give one to your friend.'

Now it was a woman of about thirty who took over. She was almost black. She asked me whether I was married. Yes, in France. If my parents were still alive. Only my father.

'He'll be glad to hear you are in Venezuela.'

'That's right.'

A tall dried-up white man then spoke—he had big, staring eyes, but they were kind—'My relation didn't know how to tell you why we are going to look after you. Well, I'll tell you. Because unless he's mad—and in that case there's nothing to be done about it—a man can be sorry for what he's done and he can turn into a good man if he's helped. That's why you'll be looked after in Venezuela. Because we love other men, and with God's help, we believe in them.'

'What do you think I was a prisoner on Devil's Island for?'

'Something very serious, for sure. Maybe for having killed someone, or for a really big theft. What did you get?'

'Penal servitude for life.'

'The top sentence here is thirty years. How many did you do?'

'Thirteen. But now I am free.'

'Forget all that, *hombre*. As quick as you can forget everything you suffered in the French prisons and here in El Dorado. Forget it, because if you think about it too much you'll be forced to feel ill-will towards other men and maybe even hate them. Only forgetting will let you love them again and live among them. Marry as soon as ever you can. The women in this country are hot-blooded, and the love of the woman you choose will give you happiness and children, and help you forget whatever you have suffered in the past.'

The truck arrived. I thanked these kind, good people and went out, holding Picolino by the arm. There were about ten passengers sitting on benches in the back of the truck. In their kindness these humble people left us the best seats, next to the driver.

As we lurched wildly along the bumpy, pot-holed track, I thought about this strange Venezuelan nation. Neither the fishermen of the Gulf of Paria, nor the ordinary soldiers of El Dorado, nor the humble working-man who talked to me in that thatched mud hut had had any education. They could hardly read and write. So how did they come to have that sense of Christian charity and nobility of heart that forgives men who have done wrong? How did they manage to find just the right encouraging words, helping the ex-convict with their advice and what little they possessed? How did it come about that the heads of the penal settlement of El Dorado, both the officers and the governor—educated men, those—had the same ideas as the simple people, the idea of giving the man who is down his chance, whoever he is and however bad the thing he's done? Those were not qualities that could ever come from Europeans: so the Venezuelans must have got them from the Indians.

*

16

Here we are in El Callao. A big square: music. Of course: it is 5 July, the national holiday. People dressed in their best clothes, the motley crowd of tropical countries where all sorts of colours are mixed—black, yellow, white, and the copper of the Indians, whose race always comes out in the slightly slanting eyes and the lighter skin. Picolino and I got out, as well as some passengers from the back of the truck. One of them, a girl, came up to me and said, 'Don't pay: that has been looked after.' The driver wished us good luck and the truck set off again. With my little bundle in one hand and Picolino holding the other with the three fingers he had left, I stood there wondering what to do. I had some English pounds from the West Indies and a few hundred bolivars (one bolivar is worth about ten new pence) given me by my mathematical pupils at the penal settlement. And a few raw diamonds found among the tomatoes in the kitchen-garden I had made.

The girl who had told us not to pay asked me where we were going and I told her my idea was to find a little boarding-house.

'Come to my place first: then you can look around.'

We crossed the square with her and in a couple of hundred yards we reached an unpaved street lined with low houses; they were all made of baked clay, and their roofs were thatch or corrugated iron. At one of them we stopped.

'Walk in. This house is yours,' said the girl. She must have been about eighteen.

She made us go in first. A clean room with a floor of pounded earth; a round table; a few chairs; a man of about forty, medium height, smooth black hair, the same colour as his daughter's; Indian eyes. And three girls of about fourteen, fifteen and sixteen.

'My father and my sisters,' she said, 'here are some strangers I have brought home. They've come from the El Dorado prison and they don't know where to go. I ask you to take them in.'

'You're welcome,' said the father. And he repeated the ritual words, 'This house is yours. Sit down here, round the table. Are you hungry? Would you like coffee or rum?'

I didn't want to offend him by refusing so I said I'd like some coffee. The house was clean, but I could see from the simple furniture that they were poor.

'My daughter Maria, who brought you here, is the eldest. She takes the place of her mother, who left us five years ago with a gold-prospector. I'd sooner tell you that myself, before you hear it from someone else.'

Maria poured coffee for us. Now I could look at her more closely, seeing she had come to sit down next to her father, right opposite me. The three sisters stood behind her. They looked closely at me, too. Maria was a girl of the tropics, with big black almond-shaped eyes. Her jet-black curling hair, parted in the middle, came down to her shoulders. She had fine features, and although you could make out the drop of Indian blood from the colour of her skin, there was nothing Mongolian about her face. She had a sensuous mouth: splendid teeth. Every now and then she showed the tip of a very pink tongue. She was wearing a white, flowered, wide-open blouse that showed her shoulders and the beginning of her breasts, hidden by a brassière that could be seen under the blouse. This blouse, a little black skirt and flat-heeled shoes were what she had put on for the holiday—her best. Her lips were bright red, and two pencilled lines at the corners of her huge eyes made them seem even larger.

'This is Esmeralda [Emerald],' she said, introducing her youngest sister. 'We call her that because of her green eyes. This is Conchita; and the other is Rosita, because she looks like a rose. She is much lighter coloured than the rest of us and she blushes at the least thing. Now you know the whole family. My father's name is José. The five of us are the same as one, because our hearts beat all together. And what's your name?'

'Enrique.' [Henri: in Spanish they say Enrique.]

'Were you in prison long?'

'Thirteen years.'

'Poor thing. How you must have suffered.'

'Yes: a great deal.'

'Papa, what do you think Enrique can do here?'

'I don't know. Do you have a trade?'

'No.'

'Well then, go to the gold-mine. They'll give you a job.'

'And what about you, José? What do you do?'

'Me? Nothing. I don't work—they pay you very little.'

18

Well, well, well. They were poor, sure enough; yet they were quite well dressed. Still, I couldn't very well ask him what he used for money—whether he stole instead of working. Wait and see, I said to myself.

'Enrique, you'll sleep here tonight,' said Maria. 'There's a room where my father's brother used to sleep. He's gone, so you can have his place. We'll look after the sick man while you go to work. Don't thank us; we're giving you nothing—the room's empty in any case.'

I didn't know what to say. I let them take my little bundle. Maria got up and the other girls followed her. She had been lying: the room was in use, because they brought out women's things and put them somewhere else. I pretended not to notice anything. No bed, but something better, something you see most of the time in the tropics—two fine wool hammocks. A big window with just shutters—no glass—opening on to a garden full of banana palms.

As I swung there in the hammock I could hardly believe what had happened to me. How easy this first day of freedom had been! Too easy. I had a free room and four sweet girls to look after Picolino. Why was I letting myself be led by the hand like a child? I was at the world's end, to be sure; but I think the real reason why I let myself be managed was because I had been a prisoner so long that obeying was the only thing I understood. Yet now I was free and I ought to make my own decisions; but still I was letting myself be led. Just like a bird when you open the door of its cage and it doesn't know how to fly any more. It has to learn all over again.

I went to sleep without thinking about the past, exactly as the humble man of El Dorado had advised me. Just one thought before I dropped off: these people's hospitality was something staggering and wonderful.

I had just breakfasted off two fried eggs, two fried bananas covered with margarine and black bread. Maria was in the bedroom, washing Picolino. A man appeared in the doorway: a machête in his belt.

'Gentes de paz,' said he. Men of peace, which is their way of saying I'm a friend.

'What do you want?' asked José, who had had breakfast

with me.

'The chief of police wants to see the men from Cayenne.'

'You don't want to call them that. Call them by their names.'

'OK, José. What are their names?'

'Enrique and Picolino.'

'Señor Enrique, come with me. I am a policeman, sent by the chief.'

'What do they want with him?' asked Maria, coming out of the bedroom. 'I'll come too. Wait while I dress.'

In a few minutes she was ready. As soon as we were in the street she took my arm. I looked at her, surprised, and she smiled at me. We soon reached the little administrative building. More police, all in plain clothes apart from two in uniform with machêtes hanging from their belts. In a room full of rifles, a black man with a gold-braided cap. He said to me, 'You're the Frenchman?'

'Yes.'

'Where's the other?'

'He's sick,' said Maria.

'I command the police. I'm here to be useful and to help you if you need it. My name's Alfonso.' And he held out his hand.

'Thanks. Mine's Enrique.'

'Enrique, the chief administrator wants to see you. You can't go in, Maria,' he added, seeing she was about to follow me. I went into the next room.

'Good morning, Frenchman. I am the chief administrator. Sit down. Since you're in compulsory residence here in El Callao I sent for you so that I could get to know you: because I'm responsible for you.' He asked me what I was going to do—where I wanted to work. We talked a while and then he said to me, 'If there's anything at all, come and see me. I'll help you work out as good a life as we can manage.'

'Thank you very much.'

'Oh, there's one thing. I must warn you that you're living with very good, honest girls; but their father, José—he's a pirate. Be seeing you.'

Maria was outside, at the station door, settled into that attitude of Indians when they are waiting, neither moving nor talking to anyone at all. She was not an Indian: yet in spite of everything, because of that little drop of Indian blood she had, the race came out. We took another way back to the house and walked through the whole village, her arm in mine.

'What did the chief want with you?' asked Maria, calling me *tu* for the first time.

'Nothing. He told me I could count on him to help me find a job or in case I was in a hole.'

'Enrique, you don't need anyone now. Nor does your friend.'

'Thanks, Maria.'

We passed by a pedlar's stall, full of women's trinkets—necklaces, bracelets, earrings, brooches, etc.

'Hey, look at this.'

'Oh, how pretty!'

I took her over to the stall and picked out the best necklace together with matching earrings, and three other smaller ones for her sisters. I gave thirty bolivars for these tinselly little things, paying with a hundred note. She put on the necklace and the earrings straight away. Her big black eyes sparkled with joy and she thanked me as though they were really valuable jewels.

We went back to the house, and the three girls shrieked with delight over their presents. I went to my room, leaving them. I had to be alone to think. This family had offered me their hospitality with a splendid generosity; but should I accept it? I had a little Venezuelan money and some English pounds, not to mention the diamonds. Reckoning it all together, I could live four months and more without worrying and I could have Picolino looked after.

All these girls were lovely, and like tropical flowers they were surely all warm, sexy, ready to give themselves only too easily, almost without thinking. I had seen Maria looking at me today almost as if she were in love. Could I resist so much temptation? It would be better for me to leave this too welcoming house, because I did not want my own weakness to bring trouble and suffering. On the other hand, I was thirty-seven and although I looked younger, that did not change my real age. Maria was not quite eighteen and her sisters were younger still. I ought to go, I thought. The best thing would be to leave Picolino in their care: paying for his board, of course.

'Señor José, I'd like to talk to you alone. Shall we go and have a rum at the café in the square?'

'All right. But don't call me señor. You call me José and I'll call you Enrique. Let's go. Maria, we're going out to the square for a minute.'

'Enrique, change your shirt,' said Maria. 'The one you've got on is dirty.'

I went and changed in the bedroom. Before we left, Maria said to me, 'Don't stay long, Enrique; and above all, don't you drink too much!' And before I had time to step back she kissed me on the cheek. Her father burst out laughing, and he said, 'That Maria—she's in love with you already.'

As we walked towards the bar I began, 'José, you and your family took me in the first day of my freedom, and I thank you more than I can say. I'm about your age; and I don't want to make you a bad return for your hospitality. You're a man, so you will understand that if I lived among your daughters it would be hard for me not to fall in love with one of them. But I'm twice as old as the eldest and I'm legally married in France. So let's go and have a drink or two together, and then you take me to some cheap little boarding-house. I can pay.'

'Frenchie, you're a real man,' said José, looking me straight in the eye. 'Let me shake your hand good and hearty, like a brother, for what you've just said to a poor guy like me. In this country, do you see, it's not like it is where you come from, maybe. Here almost nobody's married legally. You like one another, you make love, and if there's a child you set up house together. You join up as easily as you leave one another. It's very hot here, and on account of the heat the women are very full-blooded. They thirst for love and the pleasures of the flesh. They mature early. Maria's an exception; she's never had an affair although she's nearly eighteen. I think your country's morality is better than ours, because here there are any number of women who have children without a father, and that's a very serious problem. But what can you do about it? The good Lord says you must love one another and have children. In this country the women don't calculate when they give themselves to a man—they aren't after a social position.

They want to love and be loved, just like that, quite naturally: nothing more. They are faithful so long as they like you sexually. When that's over, it's another story. Yet they are wonderful mothers, willing to make any sacrifice at all for their children, even keeping them when they could work for themselves. So although I quite see you are surrounded by temptation all the time, I ask you again to stay with us. I'm glad to have a man like you in the house.'

We were in the bar before I answered. It was a bar and at the same time a grocer's shop. A dozen men were sitting about. We drank a few *Cuba Libres*, a mixture of rum and Coca-Cola. Several people came up to shake my hand and bid me welcome to their village. Each time José introduced me as a friend who was living at his house. We had a good many drinks. When I asked what they came to, José became almost annoyed. He wanted to pay for everything. Still, I did manage to persuade the barman to refuse his money and take mine.

Someone touched me on the shoulder: it was Maria. 'Come home. It's lunch-time. Don't drink any more: you promised me not to drink too much.' She was saying 'thee' to me now.

José was arguing with another man; she said nothing to him but took me by the arm and led me out.

'What about your father?'

'Let him be. I can never say anything to him when he's drinking and I never come to fetch him from the café. He wouldn't have it, anyway.'

'Why did you come and fetch me, then?'

'You're different. Be good, Enrique, and come along.' Her eyes were so brilliant and she said it so simply that I went back to the house with her.

'You deserve a kiss,' she said when we got there. And she put her lips to my cheek, too near my mouth.

José came back after we had had lunch together at the round table. The youngest sister helped Picolino eat, giving him his food little by little.

José sat down by himself. He was tolerably high, so he spoke without thinking. 'Enrique is frightened of you, my girls,' he said. 'So frightened he wants to go away. I told him that in my opinion he could stay, and that my girls were old enough to know what they were doing.'

Maria gazed at me. She looked astonished, perhaps disappointed. 'If he wants to go, Papa, let him. But I don't think he'd be better off anywhere else than he is here, where everyone likes him.' And turning to me she added, 'Enrique, don't be a coward. If you like one of us and she likes you, why should you run away?'

'On account of he's married in France,' said her father.

'How long since you saw your wife?'

'Thirteen years.'

'The way we see it, if you love a man you don't necessarily marry him. If you give yourself to a man, it's to love him, nothing more. But it was quite right of you to tell our father you were married, because like that you can't promise any of us anything at all, apart from love.' And she asked me to stay with them without committing myself. They would look after Picolino and I would be free to work. She even said I could pay a little, as if I were a lodger, to make me feel easier in my mind. Did I agree?

I had no time to think properly. It was all so new and so quick after thirteen years of life as a convict. I said, 'OK, Maria. That's fine.'

'Would you like me to go with you to the gold-mine this afternoon to ask for a job? We could go at five, when the sun is lower. It's a mile and a half from the village.'

'Fine.'

Picolino's movements and his expression showed how pleased he was that we were going to stay. The girls' kindness and their care had won his heart. My staying was chiefly on account of him. Because here I was pretty sure of having an affair before long: and maybe it would not suit me.

With all that had been going on inside my head these last thirteen years, with all that had stopped me sleeping these thirteen years on end, I was not going to come to a halt as quickly as all this and settle down in a village at the far end of the world just because of a girl's pretty face. I had a long road in front of me, and my stops must be short. Just long enough to get my wind and then full speed ahead. Because there was a reason why I had been fighting for my liberty these thirteen years and there was a reason why I had won the fight: and that reason was *revenge*. The prosecuting counsel, the false witness, the cop: I had a score to settle with them. And that was something I was never to forget. Never.

I wandered out to the village square. I noticed a shop with the name Prospéri over it. He must be a Corsican or an Italian, and indeed the little shop did belong to the descendant of a Corsican. Monsieur Prospéri spoke very good French. He kindly suggested writing a letter for me to the manager of La Mocupia, the French company that worked the Caratal gold-mine. This splendid man even offered to help me with money. I thanked him for everything and went out.

'What are you doing here, Papillon? Where the hell have you come from, man? From the moon? Dropped by parachute? Come and let me kiss you!' A big guy, deeply sunburnt, with a huge straw hat on his head, jumped to his feet. 'You don't recognize me?' And he took off his hat.

'Big Charlot! Stone the crows!' Big Charlot, the man who knocked off the safe at the Place Clichy Gaumont in Paris, and the one in the Batignolles station! We embraced like two brothers. Tears came into our eyes, we were so moved. We gazed at one another.

· 'A far cry from the Place Blanche and the penal, mate, eh? But where the hell have you come from? You're dressed like an English lord: and you've aged much less than me.'

'I'm just out of El Dorado.'

'How long were you there?'

'A year and more.'

'Why didn't you let me know? I'd have got you out straight away, signed a paper saying I was responsible for you. Christ above! I knew there were some hard cases in El Dorado, but I never for a moment imagined you were there, you, a buddy!'

'It's a bloody miracle we should have met.'

'Don't you believe it, Papi. The whole of Venezuelan Guiana from Ciudad Bolivar to El Callao is stuffed with right hard guys or detainees making a break. And as this is the first bit of Venezuelan territory you come across when you escape, there's no miracle in meeting anyone at all between the Gulf of Paria and here—every last son of a bitch comes this way. All those who don't come apart on the road, I mean. Where are you staying?'

'With a decent type called José. He has four daughters.'

'Yes, I know him. He's a good chap, a pirate. Let's go and get your things: you're staying with me, of course.'

'I'm not alone. I've got a paralysed friend and I have to look after him.'

'That doesn't matter. I'll fetch an ass for him. It's a big house and there's a negrita [a black girl], who'll look after him like a mother.'

When we had found the second donkey we went to the girls' house. Leaving these kind people was very painful. It was only when we promised we should come and see them and said they could come and see us at Caratal that they calmed down a little. I can never say too often how extraordinary it is, the Venezuelan Guianans' hospitality. I was almost ashamed of myself when I left them.

Two hours later we were at Charlot's 'château', as he called it. A big, light, roomy house on a headland looking out over the whole of the valley running down from the hamlet of Caratal almost to El Callao. On the right of this terrific virgin forest landscape was the Mocupia gold-mine. Charlot's house was entirely built of hardwood logs from the bush: three bedrooms, a fine dining-room and a kitchen; two showers inside and one outside, in a perfectly kept kitchen-garden. All the vegetables we had at home were growing there, and growing well. A chicken-run with more than five hundred hens; rabbits, guinea-pigs, two goats and a pig. All this was the fortune and the present happiness of Charlot, the former hard guy and specialist in safes and very delicate operations worked out to the second.

'Well, Papi, how do you like my shack? I've been here seven years. As I was saying in El Callao, it's a far cry from Montmartre and penal! Who'd ever have believed that one day I'd be happy with such a quiet, peaceful life? What do you say, buddy?'

'I don't know, Charlot. I'm too lately out of stir to have a clear idea. For there's no doubt about it, we've always been on the loose and our young days were uncommonly active! And then ... it sets me back a little, seeing you quiet and happy here at the back of beyond. Yet you've certainly done it all yourself and I can see it must have meant a solid dose of hard labour, sacrifices of every kind. And as far as I am concerned, you see, I don't feel myself up to it yet.'

When we were sitting round the table in the dining-room and drinking Martinique punch, Big Charlot went on, 'Yes, Papillon, I can see you're amazed. You caught on right away that I live by my own work. Eighteen bolivars a day means a small-time life, but it's not without its pleasures. A hen that hatches me a good brood of chicks, a rabbit that brings off a big litter, a kid being born, tomatoes doing well ... All these little things we despised for so long add up to something that gives me a lot. Hey, here's my black girl. Conchita! Here are some friends of mine. He's sick; you'll have to look after him. This one's called Enrique, or Papillon. He's a friend from France, an old-time friend.'

'Welcome to this house,' said the black girl. 'Don't you worry, Charlot, your friends will be properly looked after. I'll go and see to their room.'

Charlot told me about his break—an easy one. When he reached penal in the first place he was kept at Saint-Laurent-du-Maroni, and after six months he escaped from there with another Corsican called Simon and a detainee. 'We were lucky enough to reach Venezuela a few months after the dictator Gomez died. These open-handed people helped us make a new life for ourselves. I had two years of compulsory residence at El Callao, and I stayed on. Little by little, I took to liking this simple life, you get it? I lost one wife when she was having a baby, and the daughter too. Then this black girl you've just seen, Conchita, she managed to comfort me with her real love and understanding, and she's made me happy. But what about you, Papi? You must have had a cruelly hard time of it: thirteen years is a hell of a stretch. Tell me about it.'

I talked to this old friend for more than two hours, spilling out everything these last years had left rankling in me. It was a wonderful evening—wonderful for us both to be able to talk about our memories. It was odd, but there was not a single word about Montmartre, not a word about the underworld, no reminders of jobs that were pulled off or that misfired, nothing about crooks still at large. It was as though for us life had begun when we stepped aboard *La Martinière*, me in 1933, Charlot in 1935.

Excellent salad, a grilled chicken, goat cheese and a delicious mango, washed down with good Chianti and all put on the table by the cheerful Conchita, meant that Charlot could welcome me properly in his house and that pleased him. He suggested going down to the village for a drink. I said it was so pleasant here I didn't want to go out.

'Thanks, my friend,' said my Corsican—he often put on a Paris accent. 'You're dead right: we are comfortable here. Conchita, you'll have to find a girl-friend for Enrique.'

'All right: Enrique, I'll introduce you to friends prettier than me.'

'You're the prettiest of them all,' said Charlot.

'Yes, but I'm black.'

'That's the very reason why you're so pretty, poppet. Because you're a thoroughbred.'

Conchita's big eyes sparkled with love and pleasure: it was easy to see she worshipped Charlot.

Lying quietly in a fine big bed I listened to the BBC news from London on Charlot's radio: but being plunged back into the life of the outside world worried me a little—I was not used to it any more. I turned the knob. Now it was Caribbean music that came through: Caracas in song. I did not want to hear the great cities urging me to live their life. Not this evening, anyway. I switched off quickly and began to think over the last few hours.

Was it on purpose we had not talked about the years when we both lived in Paris? No. Was it on purpose we had not mentioned the men of our world who had been lucky enough not to be picked up? No again. So did it mean that for tough guys like us what had happened before the trial no longer mattered?

I tossed and turned in the big bed. It was hot: I couldn't bear it any more and I walked out into the garden. I sat down on a big stone, from where I was I looked out over the valley and the gold-mine. Everything was lit up down there. I could see trucks, empty or loaded, coming and going.

Gold: the gold that came out of the depths of that mine. If you had a lot of it, in bars or turned into notes, it would give you anything on earth. This prime mover of the world, that cost so little to mine, since the workers had such miserable wages, was the one thing you had to have to live well. And there was Charlot who had lost his freedom because he had wanted a lot of it: yet now he hadn't even mentioned the stuff. He never told me whether the mine had plenty of gold in it or not. These days his happiness was his black girl, his house, his animals and his kitchen-garden. He had never even referred to money. He had become a philosopher. I was puzzled.

I remembered how they caught him—a guy by the name of Little Louis had tipped off the police; and during our short meetings in the Santé he never stopped swearing he would get him the first chance he had. Yet this evening he had not so much as breathed his name. And as for me—Christ, how strange!—I had not said a word about my cops, nor Goldstein, nor the prosecuting counsel, either. I ought to have talked about them! I hadn't escaped just to end up as a cross between a gardener and a working-man.

I had promised to go straight in this country and I'd keep my word. But that didn't mean I had given up my plans for revenge. Because you mustn't forget, Papi, that the reason why you're here today is not only that the idea of revenge kept you going for thirteen years in the cells but because it was your one religion too; and that religion is something you must never give up.

His little black girl was very pretty, all right; but still I wondered whether Big Charlot wouldn't be better off in a city than in this hole at the far end of creation. Or maybe it was me who was the square, not seeing that my friend's life had its charm. Or then again was it Charlot who was afraid of the responsibilities that modern big-town life would put upon him? That was something to chew over and reflect upon.

Charlot was forty-five, not an old man. Very tall, very strong, built like a Corsican peasant fed on plenty of good healthy food all his young days. He was deeply burnt by the sun of this country, and with his huge straw hat on his head, its brim turned up at the sides, he really looked terrific. He was a perfect example of the pioneer in these virgin lands, and he was so much one of the people and the country he did not stand out at all. Far from it: he really belonged.

Seven years he'd been here, this still-young Montmartre safe-breaker! He must certainly have worked more than two years to clear this stretch of plateau and build his house. He had to go out into the bush, choose the trees, cut them down, bring them back, fit them together. Every beam in his house was made of the hardest and heaviest timber in the world, the kind they call ironwood. I was sure all he earned at the mine had gone into it, because he must have had help and have paid for the labour, the cement (the house was concreted), the well and the windmill for pumping the water up to the tank.

That well-rounded young negrita with her big loving eyes: she must be a perfect companion for this old sea-dog on shore. I'd seen a sewing-machine in the big room. She must make those little dresses that suited her so well. Not many dressmaker's bills for Charlot, no sir.

Maybe the reason why he hadn't gone to the city was that he was not sure of himself, whereas here he enjoyed a life with no problems at all. You're a great guy, Charlot! You're the very picture of what a crook can be turned into. I congratulate you. But I also congratulate the people who helped you to change not only your life but even your way of seeing what a life can be or ought to be.

But still these Venezuelans are dangerous, with their generous hospitality. Being surrounded with human kindness and good will all the time soon turns you into a prisoner if you let yourself be caught. I'm free, free, free, and I mean to stay that way for ever.

Watch it, Papi! Above all, no setting up house with a girl. You need love when you've been cut off from it for so long. But fortunately I'd already had a girl in Georgetown two years ago, my Hindu, Indara. So from that point of view I was not so vulnerable as if I'd come straight from penal, which was the case with Charlot. Yet Indara was lovely and I was happy; but it wasn't for that I had settled in Georgetown, living there in clover. Then again if the quiet life is too quiet though it's happy, it's not for me: that I know very well.

Adventure! Adventure so you feel alive, alive all through! Besides, that was why I left Georgetown and why I landed up at El Dorado. But that's the reason too why I'm here today, in this very spot.

OK. Here the girls are pretty, full-blooded and charming and I certainly cannot live without love. It's up to me to avoid complications. I must promise myself to stay here a year, since I'm forced to do so anyway. The less I own, the easier I'll be able to leave this country and its enchanting people. I'm an adventurer, but an adventurer with a shift of gear—I must get my money honestly, or at least without hurting anyone. Paris, that is my aim: Paris one day, to present my bill to the people who put me through so much suffering.

I was calmer now, and my eyes took in the setting moon as it dipped towards the virgin forest, a sea of black tree-tops with waves of different heights—but waves that never stirred. I went back to my room and stretched out on the bed.

Paris, Paris, you're still a great way off yet; but not so far that I shan't be there again one day, walking the asphalt of your streets.

2: The Mine

A WEEK later, thanks to the letter that Prospéri, the Corsican grocer, wrote for me, I was taken on at the Mocupia mine. Here I was, looking after the working of the pumps that sucked up the water from the shafts.

The mine looked like a coal-pit: the same underground galleries. There were no veins of gold and very few nuggets. The gold was found in very hard rock: they blasted this rock with dynamite and then broke the oversized lumps with a sledge-hammer. The pieces were put into trucks, and the trucks came to the surface in lifts; then crushers reduced the rock to a powder finer than sand. This was mixed with water, making a liquid mud that was pumped up into huge tanks as big as the reservoirs in an oil-refinery: these tanks had cyanide in them. The gold dissolved into a liquid heavier than the rest and sank to the bottom. Under heat, the cyanide evaporated, carrying off the particles of gold; they solidified and were caught by filters very like combs as they went past. Then the gold was collected, melted into bars, carefully checked for 24-carat purity and put into a strictly guarded store. But who did the guarding? I still can't get over it. Simon, no less, the hard guy who had made his break from penal with Big Charlot.

When my work was over, I went to gaze at the sight: I went to the store and stared at the huge pile of gold ingots neatly lined up by Simon, the ex-convict. Not even a strong-room: just a concrete store-house with walls no thicker than usual and a wooden door.

'OK, Simon?'

'OK. And what about you, Papi? Happy at Charlot's?'

'Yes, I'm fine.'

'I never knew you were in El Dorado. Otherwise I'd have come to get you out.'

'That's civil. Are you happy here?'

'Well, you know, I have a house: it's not as big as Charlot's, but it's made of bricks and mortar. I built it myself. And I've got a young wife, very sweet. And two little girls. Come and see me whenever you like—my house is yours. Charlot tells me your friend is sick: now my wife knows how to give injections, so if you need her don't hesitate.'

We talked. He too was thoroughly happy. He too never spoke of France or Montmartre, though he had lived there. Just like Charlot. The past no longer existed; the only thing that mattered was the present—wife, children, the house. He told me he earned twenty bolivars a day. Fortunately their hens gave them eggs for their omelettes and the chickens were on the house; otherwise they wouldn't have gone far on twenty bolivars, Simon and his brood.

I gazed at that mass of gold lying there, so carelessly stored behind a wooden door and these four walls only a foot thick. A door that two heaves on a jemmy would open without a sound. This heap of gold, at three bolivars fifty the gramme or thirty-five dollars the ounce, would easily tot up to three million five hundred thousand bolivars or a million dollars. And this unbelievable great fortune was within hand's reach! Knocking it off would be almost child's play.

'Elegant, my neat pile of ingots? Eh, Papillon?'

'It'd be more elegant still well salted away. Christ, what a fortune!'

'Maybe: but it's not ours. It's holy, on account of they've entrusted it to me.'

'Entrusted it to you, sure; but not to me. You must admit it's tempting to see something like that just lying about.'

'It's not just lying about, because I'm looking after it.'

'Maybe. But you aren't here twenty-four hours out of the twenty-four.'

'No. Only from six at night to six in the morning. But during the day there's another guard: maybe you know him— Alexandre, of the forged postal orders.'

'Oh yes, I know him. Well, be seeing you, Simon. Say hello to your family for me.'

'You'll come and see us?'

'Sure. I'd like to. Ciao.'

I left quickly, as quickly as I could to get away from this scene of temptation. It was unbelievable! Anyone would say they were yearning to be robbed, the guys in charge of this mine. A store that could hardly hold itself upright and two one-time high-ranking crooks taking care of all that treasure!

In all my life on the loose I'd never seen anything like it!

Slowly I walked up the winding path to the village. I had to go right through it to reach the headland with Charlot's château on it. I dawdled; the eight-hour day had been tough. In the second gallery down there was precious little air, and even that was hot and wet, in spite of the ventilators. My pumps had stopped sucking three or four times and I had had to set them right away. It was half past eight now and I had gone down the mine at noon. I'd earned eighteen bolivars. If I had had a working-man's mind, that wouldn't have been so bad. Meat was 2·50 bolivars the kilo; sugar 0·70; coffee 2. Vegetables were not dear either : 0·50 for a kilo of rice and the same for dried beans. You could live cheaply, that was true. But did I have the sense to put up with that kind of life?

In spite of myself, as I climbed up the stony path, walking easily in the heavy nailed boots they had given me at the mine—in spite of myself, and although I did my best not to think about it, I kept seeing that million dollars in gold bars just calling out for some enterprising hand to grab it. At night, there wouldn't be any difficulty in jumping on Simon and chloroforming him without being recognized. And then the whole thing was in the bag, because they carried their feckless-ness to the point of leaving him the key of the store so he could take shelter if it rained. Criminal irresponsibility! All that would be left to do then was carry the two hundred ingots out of the mine and load them into something—a truck or a cart. I'd have to prepare several caches in the forest, all along the road, to salt the ingots away in little packets of a hundred kilos each. If it was a truck, then once it was unloaded I'd have to carry right on as far as possible, pick the deepest place in the river and toss it in. A cart? There were plenty in the village square. The horse? That would be harder to find, but not impossible. A night of very heavy rain between eight and six in the morning would give me all the time I needed for the job and it might even let me get back to the house and go to bed meek as a monk.

By the time I reached the lights of the village square, in my mind I had already brought it off, and was slipping into the sheets of Big Charlot's bed.

'*Buenos noches*, Francès,' called a group of men sitting at the village bar.

'Hello there, one and all. Good night, *hombres*.'

'Come and join us for a while. Have an iced beer: we'd like you to.'

It would have been rude to refuse so I accepted. And here I was sitting among these good souls, most of them miners. They wanted to know whether I was all right, whether I'd found a woman, whether Conchita was looking after Picolino properly, and whether I needed money for medicine or anything else. These generous, spontaneous offers brought me back to earth. A gold-prospector said that if I didn't care for the mine and if I only wanted to work when I felt like it I could go off with him. 'It's tough going, but you make more. And then there's always the possibility you'll be rich in a single day.' I thanked them all and offered to stand a round.

'No, Frenchman, you're our guest. Another time, when you're rich. God be with you.'

I went on towards the château. Yes, it would be easy enough to turn into a humble, honest man among all these people who lived on so little, who were happy with almost nothing, and who adopted a man without worrying where he came from or what he had been.

Conchita welcomed me back. She was alone. Charlot was at the mine—when I left for work so he came back. Conchita was full of fun and kindness: she gave me a pair of slippers to rest my feet after the heavy boots.

'Your friend's asleep. He ate well and I have sent off a letter asking for him to be taken into the hospital at Tumereno, a little town not far off, bigger than this.'

I thanked her and ate the hot meal that was waiting for me. This welcome, so homely, simple and happy, made me relax; it gave me the peace of mind I needed after the temptation of that ton of gold. The door opened.

'Good evening, everybody.' Two girls came into the room, just as if they were at home.

'Good evening,' said Conchita. 'Here are two friends of mine, Papillon.'

One was dark, tall and slim; she was called Graciela, and was very much the gypsy type, her father being a Spaniard. The other girl's name was Mercedes. Her grandfather was a

35

German, which explained her fair skin and very fine blonde hair. Graciela had black Andalusian eyes with a touch of tropical fire; Mercedes' were green and all at once I remembered Lali, the Goajira Indian. Lali ... Lali and her sister Zoraïma: what had become of them? Might I not try to find them again, now I was back in Venezuela? It was 1945 now, and twelve years had gone by. That was a long, long time, but in spite of all those years I felt a pain in my heart when I remembered those two lovely creatures. Since those days they must have made themselves a fresh life with a man of their own race. No, honestly I had no right to disturb their new existence.

'Your friends are terrific, Conchita! Thank you very much for introducing me to them.'

I gathered they were both free and neither had a fiancé. In such good company the evening went by in a flash. Conchita and I walked them back to the edge of the village, and it seemed to me they leant very heavily on my arms. On the way back Conchita told me both the girls liked me, the one as much as the other. 'Which do you like best?' she asked.

'They are both charming, Conchita; but I don't want any complications.'

'You call making love "complications"? Love, it's the same as eating and drinking. You think you can live without eating and drinking? When I don't make love I feel really ill, although I'm already twenty-two. They are only sixteen and seventeen, so just think what it must be for them. If they don't take pleasure in their bodies, they'll die.'

'And what about their parents?'

She told me, just as José had done, that here the girls of the ordinary people loved just to be loved. They gave themselves to the man they liked spontaneously, wholly, without asking anything in exchange apart from the thrill.

'I understand you, poppet. I'm as willing as the next man to make love for love's sake. Only you tell your friends that an affair with me doesn't bind me in any way at all. Once warned, it's another matter.'

Dear Lord above! It wasn't going to be easy to get away from an atmosphere like this. Charlot, Simon, Alexandre and no doubt a good many others had been positively bewitched. I saw why they were so thoroughly happy among these cheerful people, so different from ours. I went to bed.

'Get up, Papi! It's ten o'clock. And there's someone to see you.'

'Good morning, Monsieur.' A greying man of about fifty; no hat; candid eyes; bushy eyebrows. He held out his hand. 'I'm Dr Bougrat.* I came because they told me one of you is sick. I've had a look at your friend. Nothing to be done unless he goes into hospital at Caracas. And it'll be a tough job to cure him.'

'You'll take pot-luck with us, Doctor?' said Charlot.

'I'd like to. Thanks.'

Pastis was poured out, and as he drank Bougrat said to me, 'Well, Papillon, and how are you getting along?'

'Why, Doctor, I'm taking my first steps in life. I feel as if I'd just been born. Or rather as if I'd lost my way like a boy. I can't make out the road I ought to follow.'

'The road's clear enough. Look around and you'll see. Apart from one or two exceptions all our old companions have gone straight. I've been in Venezuela since 1928. Not one of the convicts I've known has committed a crime since being in this country. They are almost all married, with children, and they live honestly, accepted by the community. They've forgotten the past so completely that some of them couldn't tell you the details of the job that sent them down. It's all very vague, far away, buried in a misty past that doesn't matter.'

'Maybe it's different for me, Doctor. I have a pretty long bill to present to the people who sent me down against all justice—thirteen years of struggle and suffering. To see the bill is paid, I have to go back to France; and for that I need a lot of money. It's not by working as a labourer that I'm going to save up enough for the voyage out and back—if there is any return—quite apart from what my plan will cost. And then the thought of ending my days in one of these God-forsaken holes ... I like the idea of Caracas.'

* The hero of a well-known criminal affair in Marseilles during the twenties. A dead man was found in a cupboard in his consulting-room. Bougrat pleaded professional error in the amount of an injection. The court said it was murder. They gave him a life-sentence, but he soon escaped from Cayenne and made himself a new life in Venezuela.

'And do you think you're the only one of us with an account to settle? Just you listen to the story of a boy I know. Georges Dubois is his name. A kid from the slums of La Villette—alcoholic father, often inside with delirium tremens, the mother with six children: she was so poor she went around the North African bars looking for customers. Jojo, they called him; and he'd been going from one reformatory to the next since he was eight. He started with the crime of knocking off fruit outside shops—did it several times. First a few terms in the Abbé Rollet's homes, then, when he was twelve, a tough stretch in a really hard reformatory. I don't have to tell you that the four-teen-year-old Jojo, surrounded by young fellows of eighteen, had to look out for his arse. He was a weakly kid, so there was only one way of defending himself—a knife. One of these per-verted little thugs got a stab in the belly, and the authorities sent Jojo to Esse—the toughest reformatory of the lot, the one for hopeless cases—until the age of twenty-one. Then they gave him his marching orders for the African disciplinary bat-talions, because with a past like his, he was not allowed into the ordinary army. They handed him the few francs he had earned and farewell, adieu! The trouble was that this boy had a heart. Maybe it hardened, but it still had some sensitive corners. At the station he saw a train destined for Paris. It was as if a spring had been triggered off inside him. He jumped in double quick, and there he was in Paris. It was raining when he walked out of the station. He stood under a shelter, working out how he would get to La Villette. Under this same shelter there was a girl; she too was keeping out of the rain. She gave him a pleasant sort of a look. All he knew about women was the chief warder's fat wife at Esse and what the bigger boys at the reformatory had told him—more or less true. No one had ever looked at him like this girl: they began to talk.

'"Where do you come from?"'

'"The country."'

'"I like you, boy. Why don't we go to a hotel? I'll be nice to you and we'll be in the warm."'

'Jojo was all stirred up. To him this chick seemed some-thing wonderful—and what's more her gentle hand touched his. Discovering love was a fantastic, shattering experience for him. The girl was young and very amorous. When they had made love until they could no more, they sat on the bed to smoke, and the chick said to him, "Is this the first time you've been to bed with a girl?"

' "Yes," he confessed.

' "Why did you wait so long?"

' "I was in a reformatory."

' "A long time?"

' "Very long."

' "I was in one too. I escaped."

' "How old are you?" asked Jojo.

' "Sixteen."

' "Where are you from?"

' "La Villette."

' "What street?"

' "Rue de Rouen."

'So was Jojo. He was afraid to understand. "What's your name?" he cried.

' "Ginette Dubois."

'It was his sister. They were completely overwhelmed and they both began to cry with shame and wretchedness. Then each told the road they had travelled. Ginette and her other sisters had had the same kind of life as Jojo—homes and re-formatories. Their mother had just come out of a sanatorium. The eldest sister was working in a brothel for North Africans in La Villette—sweated labour. They decided to go and see her.

'They had scarcely left the hotel before a pig in uniform called out to the chick. "Now you little tart, didn't I tell you not to come soliciting on my beat?" And he came towards them. "This time I'll run you in, you dirty little whore."

'It was too much for Jojo. After everything that had just happened, he no longer really knew what he was doing. He brought out a many-bladed pocket-knife he had bought for the army and shoved it into the pig's chest. He was arrested and twelve "qualified" jurymen condemned him to death: he was reprieved by the President of the Republic and sent to the penal settlement.

'Well now, Papillon, he escaped and at present he's living at Cumana, a fair-sized port. He's a shoemaker, he's married, and he has nine children, all well cared for and all going to school. Indeed, one of the elder children has been at the university this last year. Every time I'm in Cumana I go and see them. That's a pretty good example, eh? Yet believe you me, he too had a long bill to present to society. You're no exception, Papillon, you see. Plenty of us have reasons for revenge. But as far as I know, not one of us has left this country to take it. I trust you, Papillon. Since you like the idea of Caracas, go there: but I hope you'll have the sense to live the city life without falling into any of its traps.'

Bougrat left very late that afternoon. My ideas were in a turmoil by having seen him. Why had he made such an impression on me? Easy to see why. During these first days of freedom I had met convicts who were happy and readjusted; but even so, there was nothing extraordinary about the lives they led. It was more a prudent, very small-time kind of living. Their position was way down—workmen or peasants. Bougrat was different. For the first time I had seen an ex-con who was now a monsieur, a gentleman. That was what had made my heart thump. Would I be a monsieur too? Could I become one? For him, as a doctor, it had been comparatively easy. It would be harder for me, maybe; but even if I didn't yet know how to set about it, I was sure that one day I was going to be a monsieur too.

Sitting on my bench at the bottom of the second gallery I watched my pumps: today they had run without a hitch. Keeping time with the engine I repeated Bougrat's words, 'I trust you, Papillon! Watch out for the pitfalls of the city.' There must be some, for sure; and it wouldn't be so easy to change my outlook either. I had had proof of that: only yesterday the sight of the gold store-house had knocked me absolutely flat. I had been out only a fortnight, and already, as I climbed up the path, dazzled by that fortune within hand's reach, I was working out the details of how to get hold of it. And I'd certainly not yet completely made up my mind to leave those ingots lying there in peace.

The thoughts ran pell-mell through my head. 'Papillon, I trust you.' But could I put up with living like my companions? I didn't think so. After all, there were plenty of other ways of getting enough money honestly. I was not forced to accept a life that was too small for me. I could carry on as an adventurer—I could prospect for gold or diamonds, vanish into the bush and come out some day with enough to set me up in the kind of position I was after.

It wouldn't be easy to give up running risks and taking chances. But I thought, in spite of the temptation of that heap of gold, you mustn't do it; you can't do it; you haven't the right to do it. A million dollars ... You get that, Papi? Especially, since the job's already in the bag. You don't even have to work it out—it can't miss. Tempting, by God, tempting. Lord above, they had no right to shove a mountain of gold right under a crook's nose and then say to him 'You mustn't touch.' The tenth part of that gold would be enough for me to carry out everything, revenge included—to carry out everything I'd dreamt of during those thousands of hours when I was buried alive.

At eight o'clock the hoist brought me up to the surface. I took the long way round so as not to go by the store-house. The less I saw of it, the better. I passed quickly through the village, greeting people and saying sorry to the ones who wanted me to stop—I was in a hurry; and I climbed fast to the house. Conchita was waiting for me, as black and cheerful as ever.

'Well, Papillon, and how are you doing? Charlot told me to pour you out a stiff pastis before dinner. He said you looked as though you had problems. What's wrong, Papi? You can tell me, your friend's wife. Would you like me to fetch Graciela for you, or maybe Mercedes if you like her better? Don't you think that would be a good idea?'

'Conchita, you're my little black pearl of El Callao, you're wonderful, and I see why Charlot worships you. Maybe you're right: maybe to set me up I need a girl beside me.'

'That's for sure. Unless it's Charlot who was right.'

'How do you mean?'

'Well, there was me saying that what you needed was to love and be loved. And he told me to hold on before I put a girl in your bed—perhaps it was something else.'

'How do you mean, something else?'

She hesitated for a moment and then all at once she said, 'I don't care if you do tell Charlot; but he'll box my ears.'

'I shan't tell him anything. I promise.'

'Well, Charlot says you aren't built for the same kind of life as he and the other Frenchmen here.'

'What else? Come on, Conchita; tell me the lot.'

'And he said you must be thinking that there's too much useless gold lying about at the mine and that you'd find something better to do with it. There! And he went on that you aren't a type that can live without spending a lot; and that you had a revenge you couldn't give up and for that you wanted a great deal of money.'

I looked her straight in the eye. 'Well, Conchita, your Charlot got it wrong, wrong, wrong. You're the one who was right. As for my future—no problem at all. You guessed it: what I want is a woman to love. I didn't like to say so, on account of I'm rather shy.'

'That I don't believe, Papillon.'

'OK. Go and fetch the blonde, and just you see if I'm not happy when I have a girl of my own.'

'I'm on my way,' she said, going into the bedroom to change her dress. 'Oh that Mercedes, how happy she will be!' she called. Before she had time to come back there was a knock at the door. 'Come in,' said Conchita. The door opened and there was Maria, looking a trifle confused.

'You, Maria, at this time of night? What a marvellous surprise! Conchita, this is Maria, the girl who took me in when Picolino and I first landed up in El Callao.'

'Let me kiss you,' said Conchita. 'You're as pretty as Papillon said you were.'

'Who's Papillon?'

'That's me. Enrique or Papillon, it's all one. Sit down by me on the divan and tell me everything.'

Conchita gave a knowing laugh. 'I don't think it's worth my while going out now,' she said.

Maria stayed all night. As a lover she was shy, but she reacted to the slightest caress. I was her first man. Now she was sleeping. The two candles I had lit instead of the raw electric light were guttering. Their faint glow showed the beauty of her young body even better, and her breasts still marked by our embrace. Gently I got up to make myself some coffee and to see what time it was. Four o'clock. I knocked over a saucepan and woke Conchita. She came out of her room wearing a dressing-gown.

'You want some coffee?'

'Yes.'

'Only for you, I'm sure. Because she must be sleeping with those angels you've introduced her to.'

'You know all about it, Conchita.'

'My people have fire in their veins. You must have noticed it tonight. Maria has one touch of Negro, two touches of Indian and the rest Spanish. If you're not happy with a mixture like that, go and hang yourself,' she said, laughing.

The splendid sun was high in the sky when it saw Maria wake up. I brought her coffee in bed. There was a question already on my lips. 'Aren't they going to worry, not finding you at home?'

'My sisters knew I was coming here, so my father must have known an hour later. You aren't going to send me away to-day?'

'No, sweetie. I told you I didn't want to set up house, but between that and sending you away is a long chalk, if you can stay without any trouble. Stay as long as you like.'

It was close on twelve and I had to leave for the mine. Maria decided to go home, hitching a lift in a truck, and to come back in the evening.

'Hey there,' said Charlot. He was standing in the door of his room, wearing pyjamas; and he spoke to me in French. 'So you've found the chick you needed all by yourself. A luscious piece, too: I congratulate you, cock.' He added that as it was Sunday tomorrow we might drink to the marriage.

'Maria, tell your father and sisters to come and spend Sunday with us to celebrate this. And you come back whenever you like—the house is yours. Have a good day, Papi; watch out for the number three pump. And when you quit work, you don't have to drop in on Simon. If you don't see the stuff he is looking after so badly, you'll feel it less.'

'You dirty old crook. No, I shan't go and see Simon. Don't you worry, mate. *Ciao*.'

Maria and I walked through the village arm in arm, tight together, to show the girls she was my woman.

The pumps ran sweetly, even number three. But neither the hot, wet air nor the beat of the motor stopped me thinking about Charlot. He had grasped why I was so thoughtful, all right. It hadn't taken long for him, an old crook, to see that the heap of gold was at the bottom of it all. Nor for Simon either: and Simon must certainly have told him about our conversation. Those were the sort of friends a man should have—real friends, aglow with joy because I'd got myself a woman. They were hoping that this black-haired godsend would make me forget the blazing heap of loot.

I turned all this over and over in my head, and in time I began to see the position more clearly. These good guys were now as straight as so many rulers; they were leading blameless lives. But in spite of living like squares they had not lost the underworld outlook and they were utterly incapable of tipping off the police about anyone whatsoever, even if they guessed what he was up to and they knew for sure it would mean bad trouble for them. The two who would be taken in straight away if the thing came off were Simon and Alexandre, the men who guarded the treasure. Charlot would come in for his share of the wasps' nest too, because every single one of the ex-convicts would be trundled off to jail. And then farewell peace and quiet, farewell house, kitchen-garden, wife, kids, hens, goats and pigs. So I began to see how these former crooks must have quaked not for themselves but for their homes, when they thought how my caper was going to ruin everything. 'How I hope he doesn't go and bugger it all,' they must have said. I could see them holding a council of war.

I had made up my mind. I'd go and see Simon that evening and ask him and his family to the party tomorrow, and I'd tell him to invite Alexandre too if he could come. I must make them all think that for me having a girl like Maria was the finest thing in the world.

The hoist brought me up to the open air. I met Charlot on his way down and I said to him, 'The party's still on, mate?'

'Of course it is, Papillon. More than ever.'

'I'm going to ask Simon and his family. And Alexandre too, if he can come.'

Old Charlot was a deep one. He looked me straight in the eye and then in a rather flip tone he said, 'Why, that's a sweet idea, my friend.' Without another word he stepped into the hoist, and it took him down to where I had just come from. I went round by the store and found Simon.

'OK, Simon?'

'Fine.'

'I've dropped in to say hello, in the first place, and then to ask you to lunch with us on Sunday. Bring your family, of course.'

'That'll be great. What's the party for? Your being let out?'

'No, my marriage. I've found a girl. Maria from El Callao, José's daughter.'

'Congratulations, with all my heart. I truly hope you'll be happy, mate, upon my oath I do.' He shook my hand good and hard and I left him. Half way down the path I found Maria coming to meet me, and arms round each other's waists we went up to the château. Her father and sisters would be there around ten tomorrow morning to help get the food ready.

'So much the better, because there are going to be more of us than we had reckoned on. And what did your father say?'

'He said, "Be happy, daughter, but don't you kid yourself about the future. I only have to look at a man to know what he's like. The man you've chosen is a good one, but he won't stay here. He's not the sort to put up with a simple life like ours."'

'What did you say to that?'

'I said I'd do everything to keep you as long as ever I could.'

'Come and let me kiss you: you've got a lovely heart, Maria. Let's live in the present: the future can look after itself.'

Having eaten something we went to bed; we should have to be up early the next day to help Conchita kill the rabbits, make the big cake, fetch the wine, etc. This night was even more splendid and passionate and enchanting than the first. Maria really had fire in her veins. Straight away she learnt to call up and increase the pleasure she had been taught. We made love long and hard until we fell fast asleep wrapped tight together.

The next day was Sunday, and the party was a marvellous success. José congratulated us on loving one another and Maria's sisters whispered questions in her ear—full of curiosity. Simon and his fine family were there. And Alexandre too, since he had been able to find someone to fill in for him guarding the treasure. He had a charming wife, and a well-dressed little boy and girl came with them. The rabbits were delicious, and the huge cake, shaped like a heart, lasted no time at all. We even danced to the radio and the gramophone, and an old convict played the accordion.

After a good many liqueurs I set about my old crooks in French. 'Well, and what have you guys been thinking? Did you really believe I was going to pull something off?'

'Yes, mate,' said Charlot. 'We shouldn't have said a word if you hadn't brought it up yourself. But it's dead certain you had the notion of knocking off that ton of gold, right? Give the straight answer, Papillon.'

'You know I've been chewing over my revenge these thirteen years. Multiply thirteen years by three hundred and sixty-five days and then by twenty-four hours and each hour by sixty minutes and you still won't have the number of times I've sworn to make them pay for what I went through. So when I saw that heap of gold in such a place, why true enough, I did think of working out a job.'

'What then?' said Simon.

'Then I looked at the position from every side and I was ashamed. I was running the risk of destroying the happiness of you all. I came to see that this happiness of yours—a happiness I hope to have myself one day—was worth much more than being rich. So the temptation of knocking off the gold quite disappeared. You can take it for a certainty, and I give you my word: I shan't do anything here.'

'There you are, then,' said Charlot, grinning all over his face. 'So now we can sleep easy. It's not one of our crooks that would ever give way to temptation. Long live Papillon! Long live María! Long live love and freedom! And long live decency! Hard guys we were, hard guys we are still, but only towards the pigs. Now we're all of the same mind, including Papillon.'

Six months I'd been here. Charlot was right. On the day of the party I had won the first battle against my longing to pull something off. I had been drifting away from the 'road down the drain' ever since I had escaped. Now thanks to my friends' example I had gained an important victory over myself: I had given up the idea of grabbing that million dollars. One thing was sure: for the future it would not be easy for any job to tempt me. Once I'd given up a fortune like that, it would be very hard for anything else to make me change my ideas. Yet I wasn't entirely at peace with myself. I had to make my money some other way than stealing it, fair enough; but still I had to get enough together to be able to go to Paris and hand in my bill. And that was going to cost me a packet.

Boom-bom, boom-bom, boom-bom: all the time my pumps sucked up the water that flowed into the galleries. It was hotter than ever. Every day I spent eight hours down there in the bowels of the mine. At this time I was on duty from four in the morning until noon. When I knocked off I'd have to go to Maria's house in El Callao. Picolino had been there this last month, because in El Callao the doctor could see him every day. He was being given a course of treatment and Maria and her sisters looked after him wonderfully. So I was going to see him and to make love to Maria: it was a week since I'd seen her, and I wanted her, physically and mentally.

I found a lorry that gave me a lift. The rain was pouring down when I opened the door at about one o'clock. They were all sitting round the table, apart from Maria, who seemed to be waiting near the door. 'Why didn't you come before? A week's a long, long time. You're all wet. Come and change right away.'

She pulled me into the bedroom, took my clothes off and dried me with a big towel. 'Lie down on the bed,' she said. And there we made love, not minding about the others who were waiting for us the other side of the door, nor about their impatience. We dropped off to sleep, and it was Esmeralda, the green-eyed sister, who gently woke us up late that afternoon, when night was already coming on.

When we had all had dinner together, José the Pirate suggested going for a stroll.

'Enrique, you wrote to the chief administrator asking him to get Caracas to put an end to your *confinamiento* [compulsory residence]: is that right?'

'Yes, José.'

'He's had the reply from Caracas.'

47

'Good or bad?'

'Good. Your *confinamiento* is over.'

'Does Maria know?'

'Yes.'

'What did she say?'

'That you'd always said you wouldn't stay in El Callao.' After a short pause he asked me, 'When do you think you'll leave?'

Although I was bowled over by this news, I thought and then answered straight away, 'Tomorrow. The truck-driver who brought me said he was going on to Ciudad Bolivar tomorrow.' José bowed his head. '*Amigo mio*, are you sore at me?'

'No, Enrique. You've always said you'd never stay. But it's sad for Maria—and for me, too.'

'I'll go and talk to the driver if I can find him.'

I did find him: we were to leave tomorrow at nine. As he already had one passenger, Picolino would travel in the cab and myself on the empty iron barrels behind. I hurried to the chief administrator; he handed over my papers and, like the good man he was, he gave me some advice: and he wished me good luck. Then I went round seeing everybody who had given me their friendship and their help.

First to Caratal, where I picked up the few things I possessed. Charlot and I embraced one another, deeply moved. His black girl wept. I thanked them both for their wonderful hospitality.

'It's nothing, mate. You would have done the same for me. Good luck. And if you go to Paris, say hello to Montmartre from me.'

'I'll write.'

Then the ex-cons, Simon, Alexandre, Marcel, André. I hurried back to El Callao and there I said good-bye to all the miners and the gold- and diamond-prospectors and my workmates. All of them, men and women, said something from the heart to wish me good luck. It touched me a great deal and I saw even more clearly that if I had set up with Maria I should have been like Charlot and the others—I should never have been able to tear myself away from this paradise.

The hardest of all my farewells was to Maria. Our last

night, a mixture of love and tears, was more violent than anything we had ever known. Even our caresses broke our hearts. The horrible thing was that I had to make her understand there would be no hope of my coming back. Who could tell what my fate would be when I carried out my plans?

A shaft of sunlight woke me. My watch said eight o'clock already. I hadn't the heart to stay in the big room, not even the few moments for a cup of coffee. Picolino was sitting in a chair, tears running down his face. Esmeralda had washed and dressed him. I looked for Maria's sisters, but I couldn't find them. They'd hidden so as not to see me go. There was only José standing there in the doorway. He grasped me in the Venezuelan *abrazo* (one hand holds yours and the other is round your shoulders), as moved as I was myself. I couldn't speak, and he said only this one thing: 'Don't forget us; we'll never, never forget you. Good-bye: God go with you.'

With all his clean things carefully made up into a bundle, Picolino wept bitterly, and his movements and the hoarse sounds he uttered conveyed his wretchedness at not being able to bring out the millions of thanks he had in his heart. I led him away.

Carrying our baggage, we reached the driver's place. A splendid exit from the town, all right: his truck had broken down; no leaving today. We had to wait for a new carburettor. There was no way out of it—I returned to Maria's with Picolino. You can imagine the shrieks when they saw us coming back.

'God was kind to have broken the truck, Enrique! Leave Picolino here and walk around the village while I get the meal ready. It's an odd thing,' Maria added, 'but it could be you're not fated to go to Caracas.'

While I was strolling about I thought over this remark of Maria's. It worried me. I did not know Caracas, a big city, but people had talked about it and I could imagine what it was like. The idea certainly attracted me; but once I was there, what should I do, and how could I do it?

I walked slowly across the square of El Callao with my hands behind my back. The sun was blazing down. I went over to an almendron, a huge, very leafy tree, to shelter from the furious heat. Under the shade there stood two mules, and a

49

little old man was loading them. I noticed the diamond-prospector's sieve and the gold-prospector's trough, a kind of Chinese hat they use to wash the gold-bearing mud in. As I gazed at these things—they were still new to me—I went on pondering. In front of me there was this biblical picture of a quiet, peaceful life with no sounds apart from those of nature and the patriarchal way of living; and I thought of what it must be like at that very moment in Caracas, the busy, teeming capital that drew me on. All the descriptions I had heard turned into exact images. After all, it was fourteen years since I had seen a big town! Since I could now do as I liked, there was no doubt about it—I was going to get there, and as quick as I could.

3 : Jojo La Passe

JESUS, the song was in French! And it was the little old prospector singing. I listened.

> The old sharks are there already
> They've smelt the body of a man.
> One of them chews an arm like an apple
> Another eats his trunk and tra-la-la
> The quickest gets it, the rest have none
> Convict farewell; long live the law!

I was thunderstruck. He sang it slowly, like a requiem. The 'tra-la-la' had an ironic merriment, and the 'long live the law' was full of the mockery of the Paris underworld: it sounded like an unanswerable truth. But to feel the full irony of it you had to have been there.

I looked closely at the man. The size of three apples one on top of the other: just five foot one, I learnt afterwards. One of the most picturesque ex-convicts I had ever come across. Snowy white hair with long, grey side-whiskers cut on the slant. Blue jeans; a big, broad leather belt; on the right, a long sheath with a curved handle coming out of it at the height of his groin. I walked over to him. He had no hat on—it was lying on the ground—so I could see his broad forehead, speckled with a red even darker than his old sun-baked pirate's tan. His eyebrows were so long and thick he surely had to comb them. Beneath them, steely grey-green eyes, gimlets that bored through me. I hadn't taken four steps before he said to me, 'You come from penal, as sure as my name's La Passe.'

'Right. My name's Papillon.'

'I'm Jojo La Passe.' He held out his hand and took mine frankly, just as it should be between men, not so hard it crushes your fingers the way the show-offs do, nor too flabby, like hypocrites and fairies. I said, 'Let's go to the bar and have a drink. It's on me.'

'No. Come to my place over the way, the white house. It's called Belleville, after where I lived when I was a kid. We can talk there in peace.'

Indoors it was swept and clean—his wife's field of action. She was young, very young; perhaps twenty-five. He—God knows: sixty at least. She was called Lola, a dusky Venezuelan.

'You're welcome,' she said to me, with a pleasant smile.

'Thanks.'

'Two pastis,' said Jojo. 'A Corsican brought me two hundred bottles from France. You'll see whether it's good or not.'

Lola poured it out and Jojo tossed back three-quarters of his glass in one gulp. 'Well?' said he, fixing me with his eye.

'Well what? You don't think I'm going to tell you the story of my life, do you?'

'OK, mate. But Jojo La Passe, doesn't that ring any bells?'

'No.'

'How quickly they forget you! Yet I was a big shot in penal. There was no one that came within miles of me for throwing the seven and eleven with dice just touched with a file—not loaded, of course. That wasn't yesterday, to be sure; but after all, men like us, we leave traces—we leave legends. And now according to what you tell me, in a few years it's all forgotten. Did not one single bastard ever tell you about me?' He seemed deeply outraged.

'Frankly, no.'

Once again the gimlets bored right into my guts. 'You stayed no great time in penal: you've scarcely got the face at all.'

'Thirteen years altogether, counting El Dorado. You think that's nothing?'

'It's not possible. You're scarcely marked, and only another con could tell that's where you come from. And even then, a con who was not a diabolically clever face-reader might get it wrong. You had it easy in penal, right?'

'It wasn't as easy as all that: the islands; solitary.'

'Balls, man, balls! The islands—they're a holiday camp! All they lack is a casino. For you, penal meant the sea-breeze, crayfish, no mosquitoes, fishing, and now and then a real treat— the pussy or the arse of some screw's wife kept too short of it by her bastard of a husband.'

'Still, you know . . .'

52

'Blah-blah-blah: don't you try to fool me. I know all about it. I wasn't on the islands, but I've been told about them.' This man, maybe he was picturesque, but things were likely to turn nasty for him: I felt my temper rising fast. He went on, 'Penal, the real penal, was Kilometre 24. That doesn't mean anything to you? No, it doesn't, and that's for sure. With your mug, you've certainly never pissed in those parts. Well, mate, I have. A hundred men, every one of them with diseased guts. Some standing, some lying down, some groaning like dogs. There's the bush in front of them, like a wall. But it's not them that are going to cut the bush down: it's the bush that's going to do the cutting. It's not a working camp. As the prison administration puts it, Kilometre 24 is a conveniently hidden little dell in the Guiana forest—you toss men into it and they never bother you again. Come, Papillon; don't try and stuff me up with your islands and your solitary. It won't wash with me. You've got nothing of the look of a dog with all the spirit beaten out of it, nor the hollow face of a skin-and-bones lag with a life-sentence, nor the dial you see on all those poor buggers who escaped from that hell by some miracle—unfortunate sods who look as if they'd been worked over with a chisel to give them an old man's face on a young man's head. There's nothing like that about you at all. So there's no possible mistake about my diagnosis: for you, penal meant a holiday in the sun.'

How he did nag on and on, this little old bastard. I wondered how our meeting was going to end.

'For me, as I've been telling you, it meant the hollow nobody ever comes out of alive—amoebic dysentery, a place where you gradually shit your guts out. Poor old Papillon: you didn't even know what penal was all about.'

I looked closely at this terribly energetic little man, working out just where to plant my fist on his face, and then all at once I shifted into reverse and decided to make friends. No point in getting worked up: I might need him. 'You're right, Jojo. My penal didn't amount to much, since I'm so fit it takes a really knowing type like you to tell where I come from.'

'OK, we're in agreement, then. What are you doing now?'

'I'm working at the Mocupia gold-mine. Eighteen bolivars a day. But I've got a permit to go wherever I like; my *confina-*

53

miento is over.'

'I bet you want to light off for Caracas and go on the loose again.'

'You're right: that's just what I want to do.'

'But Caracas, it's the big city; so trying to pull off anything there means a hell of a risk. You're scarcely out, and you want to go back inside again?'

'I've got a long bill for the sods who sent me down—the pigs, the witnesses, the prosecutor. A thirteen-year stretch for a crime I never committed: the islands, whatever you may think of them, and solitary at Saint-Joseph, where I went through the most horrible tortures the system could think up. And don't forget I was only twenty-four when they framed me.'

'Hell: so they stole the whole of your youth. Innocent, really innocent, cross your heart, or are you still pleading in the dock?'

'Innocent, Jojo. I swear by my dead mother.'

'Christ. Well, I see that must lay heavy on your chest. But you don't have to go to Caracas if you want dough to straighten out your accounts—come with me.'

'What for?'

'Diamonds, man, diamonds! Here the government is generous: this is the only country in the world where you can burrow wherever you like for gold or diamonds. There's only one thing: no machinery allowed. All they let you use is shovel, pickaxe and sieve.'

'And where's this genuine El Dorado? Not the one I've just come out of, I hope?'

'A good way off. A good way off in the bush. A good many days on a mule and then in a canoe and then on foot, carrying your gear.'

'It's not what you'd call in the bag; hardly child's play.'

'Well, Papillon, it's the only way of getting hold of a fa sack of dough. You find just one bomb and there you are, a wealthy man—a man who has women that smoke and fart in silk. Or, if you like it that way, a man who can afford to g and present his bill.'

Now he was in full flow; his eyes blazed; he was all worke up and full of fire. A bomb, he told me—and I'd already hear it at the mine—was a little mound no bigger than a peasant's handkerchief, a mound where by some mystery of nature a hundred, two hundred, five hundred, even a thousand carats' of diamonds were clustered together. If a prospector found a bomb in some far-off hole, it didn't take long—presently men started coming in from north, south, east and west, as if they'd been told by some grapevine. A dozen, then a hundred, then a thousand. They smelt the gold or the diamonds like a starving dog smells a bone or an old bit of meat. They came flooding in from every point of the compass. Rough types with no trade who'd had enough of battering away with a pick at twelve bolivars a day for some employer. They got sick of it, and then they heard the call of the jungle. They didn't want their family to go on living in a rabbit-hutch, so they went off, knowing very well what they were in for—they were going to work from one sun to the next in a wicked climate and a wicked atmosphere, condemning themselves to several years of hell. But with what they sent home, their wife would have a light, roomy little house; the children would be properly fed and clothed and they'd go to school—even go on with their own schooling, perhaps.

'So that's what a bomb gives?'

'Don't talk balls, Papillon. The guy that finds a bomb never goes back to mining. He's rich for the rest of his life, unless he goes so crazy with joy that he feeds his mule with hundred-bolivar notes soaked in kummel or anis. No, the man I'm talking about, the ordinary guy, he finds a few little diamonds every day, even though they may be very, very small. But even that means ten or fifteen times what he gets in the town. Then again, he lives as hard as possible, right down to bed-rock; because out there you pay for everything in gold or diamonds. But if he lives hard, he can still keep his family better than before.'

'What about the others?'

'They come in every shape and size. Brazilians, types from British Guiana and Trinidad: they all of them escape from exploitation in the factories or cotton-plantations or whatever. And then there are the real adventurers, the ones who can only breathe when they're not hemmed in by the horizon, the ones who will always stake everything for the jackpot—Italians,

Englishmen, Spaniards, Frenchmen, Portuguese—men from all over. Christ, you can't imagine the types that come rushing into this promised land! The Lord above may have filled it with piranhas and anacondas and mosquitoes and malaria and yellow fever, but He's also scattered gold, diamonds, topazes and emeralds and such all over its surface. There's a swarm of adventurers from everywhere in the world, and they stand there in holes up to their bellies in the water, working so hard they never feel the sun nor the mosquitoes nor hunger nor thirst, digging, tossing out the slimy earth and washing it over and over again, straining it through the sieve to find the diamonds. Then again, Venezuela has enormous frontiers and there you won't meet anyone who asks you for your papers. So there's not only the charm of the diamonds, but you can be sure of the pigs leaving you in peace. A perfect place to lie up and get your breath if you're on the run.'

Jojo stopped. There was nothing he had forgotten: I now knew the lot. A quick moment of thought and then I said, 'You go off alone, Jojo. I can't see myself working like a Trojan. You'd have to be possessed—you'd have to believe in your bomb like you believe in God Almighty to stand it in that kind of a hell. Yes, you go off by yourself. I'll look for my bomb in Caracas.'

Once again his hard eyes pierced me through and through. 'I get it: you haven't changed. Do you want to know what I really think?'

'Go ahead.'

'You're quitting El Callao because it makes you sick, knowing there's an unprotected heap of gold at La Mocupia. Right or wrong?'

'Right.'

'You're leaving it alone because you don't want to muck things up for the old lags who are living here in retirement. Right or wrong?'

'Right.'

'And you think that when it comes to finding the bomb there where I said, it's a matter of many are called and few are chosen? Right or wrong?'

'Right.'

'And you'd rather find the bomb in Caracas, wrapped up

and prepared, the diamonds already cut—find it in a jeweller's shop or a gem wholesaler's?'

'Maybe: but that's not certain. Remains to be seen.'

'On my oath, you're a right adventurer; nothing will cure you.'

'That's as it may be. But don't you forget this thing that keeps eating me all the time—this revenge. For that I really think I'd do anything at all.'

'Adventure or revenge, you still need dough. So come along into the bush with me. It's terrific, you'll see.'

'With a pickaxe and a shovel? Not for me.'

'You got a fever, Papillon? Or has it turned you into a lemon, knowing that you can go where you like since yesterday?'

'I don't feel that way.'

'You've forgotten the main thing—my name. Jojo *La Passe*: Jojo the Craps.'

'OK, so you're a professional gambler: but I don't see what that's got to do with this notion of labouring away like brutes.'

'Nor do I,' said he, doubling up with laughter.

'How come? We aren't going to the mines to dig up diamonds? Where do we get them from, then?'

'Out of the miners' pockets.'

'How?'

'By shooting craps every night, and by sometimes losing.'

'I get you, mate. When do we leave?'

'Wait a minute.' He was very pleased with the effect of his words: slowly he stood up, pulled a table out into the middle of the room, spread a blanket over it and brought out six pairs of dice. 'Have a good look.' Very carefully I examined them. They were not loaded.

'No one could say those dice were cogged, could they?'

'Nobody.'

He brought a gauge out of a felt case, gave it to me and said, 'Measure.' One of the sides had been carefully filed and polished, reducing it less than a tenth of a millimetre. All you could see was shine. 'Try and throw seven or eleven.' I rolled the dice. Neither seven nor eleven. 'My turn now.' Jojo deliberately made a little ruck in the blanket. He held the dice with the tips of his fingers. 'That's what we call the nippers,' he observed. 'Here we go! And there's seven! And there's eleven! And eleven! And seven! You want six! Boom, there's six! Six with four and two or five and one? There you are. Is the gentleman satisfied?'

I was fascinated, utterly fascinated. I'd never seen such a thing: it was extraordinary. You couldn't make out the slightest false move.

'Listen, mate, I've been shooting craps for ever. I started on the Butte when I was eight. I've risked shooting them, mate, I've risked shooting them with dice like that, and do you know where? On the crap-table at the Gare de l'Est, in the days of Roger Sole and Co.'

'I remember. There were some very quaint specimens there.'

'You don't have to tell me. And among the regulars, as well as the wide boys and the pimps and the odds and sods, there were cops as famous as Jojo-le-Beau, the pimp-cop from La Madeleine, and specialists from the gambling squad. And they were done as brown as the rest. So you see there's no coming unstuck if you shoot these craps in a miners' camp.'

'True enough.'

'But get this: the one place is as dangerous as the other. At the Gare de l'Est the crooks were as quick on the draw as the miners. Just one difference: in Paris you shoot and you light out as quick as you can. At the mine, you shoot and stay put. There are no pigs: the miners make their own laws.' He paused, slowly emptied his glass, and went on, 'Well now, Papillon, are you coming with me?'

I reflected for a moment; but not for long. The adventure tempted me. It was risky, without doubt; those miners would not be choir-boys—far from it; but there might be big money to be picked up. Come on, Papillon, banco on Jojo! And again I said to him, 'When do we leave?'

'Tomorrow afternoon, if you like: at five, after the heat of the day. That'll give us time to get things together. We'll travel by night at first. You got a gun?'

'No.'

'A good knife?'

'No knife.'

'Never mind. I'll look after that. *Ciao*.'

I went back to the house, thinking about Maria. She'd certainly rather I went into the bush than to Caracas. I'd leave Picolino with her. And then tomorrow, on my way for the diamonds! And seven! And eleven! *Once, siete! Et sept, et onze!* I was there already: all I had left to do was to learn all the numbers in Spanish, English, Brazilian and Italian.

I found José at home. I told him I'd changed my mind. Caracas would be for another time; at present I was going off with an old white-haired Frenchman called Jojo to the diamond-mines.

'What are you going with him as?'

'As his partner, of course.'

'He always gives his partners half his winnings.'

'That's the rule. Do you know men who've worked with him?'

'Three.'

'Did they make plenty of money?'

'I don't know. I dare say they did. Each one of them made three or four trips.'

'And what about after those three or four trips?'

'After? They never came back.'

'Why not? Did they settle down there at the mines?'

'No. They were dead.'

'Is that right? Fever?'

'No. Killed by the miners.'

'Oh. Jojo must be a lucky guy, if he always got out of it.'

'Yes. But Jojo, he's very knowing. He never wins much himself: *he works it so that his partner wins.*'

'I see. So it's the other man who's in danger; not him. It's as well to know. Thanks, José.'

'You're not going, now that I've told you that?'

'One last question, and give me the straight answer: is there a chance of coming back with a lot of dough after two or three trips?'

'Sure.'

'So Jojo is rich. Why does he go back there, then? I saw him loading the mules.'

'To begin with Jojo doesn't risk anything, as I said. Secondly, he was certainly not going off. Those mules belong to his father-in-law. He made up his mind to go because he met you.'

'But what about the stuff he was loading, or getting ready to load?'

'How do you know it was for him?'

'Oh-ho. What other advice have you got?'

'Don't go.'

'Not that. I've made up my mind to go. What else?'

José bent his head as if to think. A long pause. When he looked up again his face was bright. His eyes shone with intelligence, and slowly, drawing out his words, he said, 'Listen to the advice of a man who knows that world through and through. Every time there's a big game, a real big game—when there's a heap of diamonds in front of you and everything is at the boiling-point, get up unexpectedly and don't sit there with your winnings. Say you've got a belly-ache and go straight to the john. You don't come back, of course; and that night you sleep somewhere else, not in your own place.'

'Pretty good, José. And what else?'

'Although the buyers at the mine pay a good deal less than the ones in El Callao or Ciudad Bolivar, you want to sell them all the diamonds you win—sell them every day. And *don't ever take the cash*. Make them give you receipts in your name so as to cash them at El Callao or Ciudad Bolivar. Do the same with foreign banknotes. You say you're afraid of losing everything you've won in a single day and so you avoid the risk by never having much on you. And you tell everybody just what you're doing, so it becomes well known.'

'So that way I'll have a chance of coming back?'

'Yes. You'll have a chance of coming back alive, if God wills.'

'Thanks, José. *Buenas noches*.'

Lying in Maria's arms, exhausted with love, my head in the hollow of her shoulder, I felt her breath on my cheek. In the darkness, before I closed my eyes, I saw a heap of diamonds in front of me. Gently I picked them up, as though I were playing with them, and put them into the little canvas bag that all miners carry; then I got up right away and having looked round I said to Jojo, 'Keep my place. I'm going to the john. I'll be back in a minute.' And as I dropped off, there were José's knowing eyes, shining full of light—only people who live very close to nature have eyes like that.

The morning passed quickly. Everything was settled. Pico-lino was to stay there: he would be well cared for. I kissed everybody. Maria shone with delight. She knew that if I went to the mines I should have to come back this way, whereas Caracas never gave back the men who went to live there. She went with me as far as the meeting-place. Five o'clock; Jojo was there, and in great form. 'Hello there, mate! OK? You're prompt—fine, fine! The sun will be down in an hour. It's better that way. There's no one who can follow you at night.'

A dozen kisses for my true love and I climbed into the saddle. Jojo fixed the stirrups for me and just as we were setting off Maria said to me, 'And above all, *mi amor*, don't forget to go to the lavatory at the right moment.'

I burst out laughing as I dug my heels into the mule. 'You were listening behind the door, you Judas!'

'When you love, it's natural.'

Now we were away, Jojo on a horse and me on a mule. The virgin forest has its roads, and they are called *piques*. A *pique* is a passage about two yards wide that has gradually been cut out through the trees; and the men who pass along keep it clear with their machêtes. On either side, a wall of green: above, a roof of millions of plants, but too high to be reached with a machête even if you stand in your stirrups. This is the *selva*, the tropical forest. It is made up of an impenetrable tangle of two kinds of vegetation: first comes a mixture of creepers, trees and plants that does not rise much above twenty feet, then over that, mounting to seventy-five or a hundred feet, there are the splendid great tops of the huge trees that climb higher and higher to reach the sun. But although their tops are in the sunlight, the foliage of their wide, leafy branches makes a thick screen, keeping off all but a dim, filtered day. In a tropical forest you are in a wonderful landscape that bursts into growth all over, so as you ride along a *pique* you have to hold the reins in one hand and keep slashing at everything that gets in your way. A *pique* where a certain number of people keep coming and going always looks like a well-kept corridor.

There's nothing that gives a man such a sense of freedom as

being in the bush and well armed. He has the feeling of being as much part of the landscape as the wild animals. He moves cautiously, but with unbounded self-confidence. He seems to be in the most natural of all possible elements, and all his senses are on the alert—hearing, sight and smell. His eyes dart perpetually from point to point, sizing up everything that moves. In the bush there is only one enemy that matters, the beast of beasts, the most intelligent, the cruellest, the wickedest, the greediest, the vilest and also the most wonderful—man.

We travelled all that night, going fairly well. But in the morning, after we had drunk a little coffee from the Thermos flask, my whore of a mule started dragging its feet, dawdling along sometimes as much as a hundred yards behind Jojo. I stabbed its arse with all kinds of thorns, but nothing did any good. And to aggravate matters, Jojo started bawling out, 'Why, you know nothing about riding, man. It's easy enough. Watch me.' And he would just touch his creature with his heel and set off at a gallop. And he'd stand in his stirrups and bellow, 'I'm Captain Cook' or 'Hey there, Sancho! Are you coming? Can't you keep up with your master, Don Quixote?'

This riled me and I tried everything I could think of to make the mule get along. At last I hit on a terrific idea and straight away it broke into a gallop. I dropped a lighted cigar-end into its ear. It tore along like a thoroughbred; I rejoiced, full of glee; I even passed the Captain, waving as I went flashing by. But a mule being a vicious brute this only lasted the length of the gallop. It rammed me up against a tree, nearly crushing my leg, and there I was on the ground, my arse filled with the prickles of some plant. And there was old Jojo, screeching with laughter like a child.

I won't tell the whole story of chasing the mule (two hours!) nor its kicking and farting and all the rest. But at last, out of breath, full of thorns, perishing with heat and weariness, I did manage to hoist myself on to the back of that cross-grained, obstinate bastard. This time it could go just as it chose: I was not going to be the one to cross it. The first mile I rode not sitting but lying on its back, with my arse in the air, trying to get the fiery thorns out of it.

The next day we left the pig-headed brute at a *posada*, an

inn: then two days in a canoe, and then a long day's walk with packs on our back brought us to the diamond-mine.

I dumped my load on the log table of an open-air eating-house. I was at the end of my tether, and I could have strangled old Jojo—he stood there with no more than a few drops of sweat on his forehead, looking at me with a knowing grin. 'Well, mate, and how are you feeling? OK?'

'Fine, fine! Is there any reason why I shouldn't be feeling fine? But just you tell me this: why have you made me carry a shovel, a pickaxe and a sieve all day long when we aren't going to do any digging at all?'

Jojo put on a sorrowful air. 'Papillon, you disappoint me. Think a little: use your loaf. If a guy turned up here, not carrying these tools, what would he have come for? That's the question everybody would ask—all these eyes that watched you coming into the village through the holes in the walls and the tin roofs. With you loaded as you were, no questions. You get it?'

'I get it, man.'

'It's the same for me, since I'm carrying nothing. Suppose I turn up with my hands in my pockets and I set up my table without doing anything else: what are the miners and their girls going to say, eh, Papi? This old French type is a professional gambler, that's what they are going to say. Well now, you'll see what I'm going to do. If I can, I'll try and find a secondhand motor-pump here in the village: otherwise I'll send for one. And twenty yards of big piping and two or three sluices. A sluice is a long wooden box with divisions, and these divisions have holes in them. You pump the mud into it, and that means a team of seven men can wash fifty times more earth than a dozen working the old-fashioned way. And it's still not looked upon as machinery. Then as the owner of the pump I get twenty-five per cent of the diamonds; and what's more, I have a reason for being here. No one can say I live off gambling, because I live off my pump. But since I'm a gambler *as well*, I don't stop gambling at night. That's natural, because I don't take part in the actual work. You get it?'

'It's as clear as gin.'

'There's a bright boy. Two *frescos*, Señora.'

A fat, friendly old light-skinned woman brought us glasses full of a chocolate-coloured liquid with an ice-cube and a bit of lemon swimming in it.

'That'll be eight bolivars, *hombres*.'

'More than two dollars! Hell, life is not cheap here.'

Jojo paid. 'How are things going?' he asked.

'So-so.'

'Are there any or are there not?'

'Men in plenty. But very, very few diamonds. They found this place three months ago, and since then four thousand men have come rushing in. Too many men for so few diamonds. And what about him?' she said, jerking her chin towards me. 'German or French?'

'French. He's with me.'

'Poor soul.'

'How come, poor soul?' I asked.

'Because you're too young and too good-looking to die. The men who come with Jojo never have any luck.'

'You shut your trap, you old fool. Come on, Papi, let's go.'

As we stood up, the fat woman said to me by way of good-bye, 'Look out for yourself.'

Of course, I'd said nothing about what José had told me, and Jojo was amazed that I did not try to find out what there was behind her words. I could feel him waiting for the questions that didn't come. He seemed upset and he kept glancing at me sideways.

Pretty soon, after he had talked to various people, Jojo found a shack. Three small rooms; rings to hang our hammocks; and some cartons. On one of them, empty beer and rum bottles; on another, a battered enamel bowl and a full watering-can. Strings stretched across to hang up our clothes. The floor was pounded earth, very clean. The walls of this hutch were made of planks from packing-cases—you could still read Savon Camay, Aceite Branca, Nestlé's Milk. Each room was about ten foot by ten. No windows. I felt stifled and took off my shirt.

Jojo turned, deeply shocked. 'Are you crazy? Suppose somebody came in? You've got a wicked mug already, and now if you go and show your tattooed hide, man it's as if you were advertising the fact that you're a crook. Behave yourself.'

'But I'm stifling, Jojo.'

'You'll get used to it—it's all a matter of habit. But behave yourself, almighty God: above all, behave yourself.'

I managed to keep myself from laughing: he was a priceless old party, that Jojo.

We knocked two rooms into one. 'This will be the casino,' said Jojo, with a grin. It made a room twenty foot by ten. We swept the floor, went out to buy three big wooden crates, some rum and paper cups to drink out of. I was eager to see what the game would be like.

I didn't have to wait long. Once we had been round a number of wretched little drinking-joints, to 'make contact' as Jojo put it, everyone knew that there would be a game of craps in our place at eight that evening. The last joint we went to was a shed with a couple of tables outside, four benches and a carbide lamp hanging from a covering of branches. The boss, a huge, ageless redhead, served the punch without a word. As we were leaving he came over to me and, speaking French, he said, 'I don't know who you are and I don't want to know. But I'll just give you this tip. The day you feel like sleeping here, come along. I'll look after you.'

He spoke an odd sort of French, but from his accent I realized he was a Corsican. 'You a Corsican?'

'Yes. And you know a Corsican never betrays. Not like some guys from the north,' he added, with a knowing smile.

'Thanks. It's good to know.'

Towards seven o'clock, Jojo lit the carbide lamp. The two blankets were laid out on the ground. No chairs. The gamblers would either stand or squat. We decided I shouldn't play that night. Just watch, that's all.

They started to arrive. Extraordinary mugs. Few short men: most were huge, bearded, moustachio'd types. Hands and faces were clean; they didn't smell; yet their clothes were all stained and very nearly worn out. But every single one of the shirts—mostly short-sleeved—was spotlessly clean.

In the middle of the cloth, eight pairs of dice were neatly arranged, each in a little box. Jojo asked me to give each player a paper cup. There were about twenty of them. I poured out the rum. Not a single guy there jerked up the neck of the bottle to say enough. After just one round, three bottles vanished.

Each man deliberately took a sip, then put his cup down in front of him and laid an aspirin tube beside it. I knew that there were diamonds in those tubes. A shaky old Chinese set up a little jeweller's scales in front of him. Nobody said much. These men were shagged out: they'd been labouring under the blazing sun, some of them standing in water up to their middles from six in the morning till the sun went down.

Ha, things were beginning to move! First one, then two, then three players took up a pair of dice and examined them carefully, pressing them tight together and passing them on to their neighbour. Everything must have seemed to be in order, because the dice were tossed back on to the blanket without anything being said. Each time, Jojo picked up the pair and put them back in their box, all except for the last, which stayed there on the blanket.

Some men who had taken off their shirts complained of the mosquitoes. Jojo asked me to burn a few handfuls of damp grass, so that the smoke would help to drive them out.

'Who kicks off?' asked a huge copper-coloured guy with a thick black curly beard and a lopsided flower tattooed on his right arm.

'You, if you like,' said Jojo.

Out of his silver-mounted belt, the gorilla—for he looked very like a gorilla—brought an enormous wad of bolivar-notes held in an elastic band.

'What are you kicking off with, Chino?' asked another man.

'Five hundred bolos.' Bolos is short for bolivars.

'OK for five hundred.'

And the craps rolled. The eight came up. Jojo tried to shoot the eight.

'A thousand bolos you don't shoot the eight with double fours,' said another player.

'I take that,' said Jojo.

Chino managed to roll the eight, by five and three. Jojo had lost. For five hours on end the game continued without an exclamation, without the least dispute. These men were uncommon gamblers. That night Jojo lost seven thousand bolos and a guy with a game leg more than ten thousand.

It had been decided to stop the game at midnight, but

everyone agreed to carry on for another hour. At one o'clock Jojo said this was the last crack.

'It was me that kicked off,' said Chino, taking the dice. 'I'll close it. I lay all my winnings, nine thousand bolivars.'

He had a mass of notes and diamonds in front of him. He covered a whole lot of other stakes and rolled the seven first go.

At this terrific stroke of luck, for the first time a murmur went round. The men stood up. 'Let's get some sleep.'

'Well, you saw that, mate?' said Jojo when we were alone.

'Yes: and what I noticed most were those right hard mugs. They all carry a gun and a knife. There were even some who sat on their machêtes, so sharp they could take your head off in one swipe.'

'That's a fact: but you've seen others like them.'

'Even so ... I ran the table on the islands, but I tell you I never had such a feeling of danger as tonight.'

'It's all a matter of habit, mate. Tomorrow you'll play and we'll win: it's in the bag. As you see it,' he added, 'which are the guys to watch closest?'

'The Brazilians.'

'Well done! That's how you can tell a man—the way he spots the ones who may turn lethal from one second to another.'

When we had locked the door (three huge bolts) we threw ourselves into our hammocks, and I dropped off right away, before Jojo could start his snoring.

The next day, a splendid sun arose fit to roast you—not a cloud nor the least hint of a breeze. I wandered about this curious village. Everyone was welcoming. Disturbing faces on the men, sure enough, but they had a way of saying things (in whatever language they spoke) so there was a warm human contact right away. I found the enormous Corsican redhead again. His name was Miguel. He spoke fluent Venezuelan with English or Brazilian words dropping into it every now and then, as if they'd come down by parachute. It was only when he spoke French, which he did with difficulty, that his Corsican accent came out. We drank coffee that a young brown girl had strained through a sock. As we were talking he said to me, 'Where do you come from, brother?'

'After what you said yesterday, I can't lie to you. I come from penal.'

'Ah? You escaped? I'm glad you told me.'

'And what about you?'

He drew himself up, six foot and more, and his redhead's face took on an extremely noble expression. 'I escaped too, but not from Guiana. I left Corsica before they could arrest me. I'm a bandit of honour—an *honourable* bandit.'

His face, all lit up with the pride of being an honest man, impressed me. He was really magnificent to see, this honourable bandit. He went on, 'Corsica is the paradise of the world, the only country where men will give their lives for honour. You don't believe it?'

'I don't know whether it's the only country, but I do believe you'll find more men in the maquis who are there on account of their honour than just plain bandits.'

'I don't care for town-bandits,' he said thoughtfully.

In a couple of words I told him how things were with me; and I said I meant to go back to Paris to present my bill.

'You're right; but revenge is a dish you want to eat cold. Go about it as carefully as ever you can; it would be terrible if they picked you up before you had had your satisfaction. You're with old Jojo?'

'Yes.'

'He's straight. Some people say he's too clever with the dice, but I don't believe he's a wrong 'un. You've known him long?'

'Not very; but that doesn't matter.'

'Why, Papi, the more you gamble the more you know about other men—that's nature; but there's one thing that worries me for you.'

'What's that?'

'Two or three times his partner's been murdered. That's why I said what I did yesterday evening. Take care: and when you don't feel safe, you come here. You can trust me.'

'Thanks, Miguel.'

Yes, a curious village all right, a curious mixture of men lost in the bush, living a rough life in the middle of an explosive landscape. Each one had his story. It was wonderful to see them, wonderful to listen to them. Their shacks were sometimes no more than a roof of palm-fronds or bits of corrugated iron, and God knows how they got there. The walls were strips of cardboard or wood or sometimes even cloth. No beds; only hammocks. They slept, ate, washed and made love almost in the street. And yet nobody would lift a corner of the canvas or peer between the planks to see what was going on inside. Everybody had the utmost respect for others' privacy. If you wanted to go and see anyone, you never went nearer than a couple of yards before calling out, by way of ringing the bell, 'Is there anyone at home?' If there was and he didn't know you, you said, '*Gentes de paz*,' the same as saying I'm a friend. Then someone would appear and say politely, '*Adelante. Esta casa es suya.*' Come in; this house is yours.

A table in front of a solid hut made of well-fitting logs. On the table, necklaces of real pearls from Margarita Island, some nuggets of virgin gold, a few watches, leather or expanding metal watch-straps, and a good many alarm-clocks. Mustafa's jewellery shop.

Behind the table, there was an old Arab with a pleasant face. We talked a while: he was a Moroccan and he'd seen I was French. It was five in the afternoon, and he said to me, 'Have you eaten?'

'Not yet.'

'Nor have I. I was just going to. If you'd like to share my meal...?'

'That would be fine.'

Mustafa was a kind, cheerful guy. I spent a very pleasant hour with him. He was not inquisitive and he didn't ask me where I came from.

'It's odd,' he said, 'in my own country I hated the French, and here I like them. Have you known any Arabs?'

'Plenty. Some were very good and others were very bad.'

'It's the same with all nations. I class myself among the good ones. I'm sixty, and I might be your father. I had a son of thirty: he was killed two years ago—shot. He was good-looking; he was kind.' His eyes brimmed with tears.

I put my hand on his shoulder: this unhappy father so moved by the memory of his son reminded me of my own—he too, retired in his little house in the Ardèche must have his eyes filled with tears when he thought of me. Poor old Papa.

Who could tell where he was, or what he was doing? I was sure he was still alive—I could feel it. Let's hope the war had not knocked him about too much.

Mustafa told me to come to his place whenever I felt like it—for a meal or if ever I needed anything: I'd be doing a kindness if I asked him a favour.

Evening was coming on: I said thank you for everything and set off for our shack. The game would soon be beginning.

I was not at all on edge about my first game. 'Nothing ventured, nothing gained,' Jojo had said, and he was quite right. If I wanted to deliver my trunk filled with dynamite at 36, quai des Orfèvres and to deal with the others I needed dough, plenty of dough. I'd be getting my hands on it precious soon: and that was a certainty.

As it was a Saturday, and as the miners religiously took their Sundays off, the game was not to begin before nine, because it would last until sunrise. The men came crowding to the shack, too many of them to get inside. It was impossible to find room for them all, so Jojo sorted out the ones who could play high. There were twenty-four of them: the rest would play outside. I went to Mustafa's, and he very kindly lent me a big carpet and a carbide lamp. As the big-time gamblers dropped out, so they could be replaced from outside.

Banco, and banco again! On and on: every time Jojo rolled the dice so I kept covering the stakes. 'Two to one he won't shoot six with double threes ... ten with double fives ...' The men's eyes were ablaze. Every time one of them lifted his cup an eleven-year-old boy filled it with rum. I'd asked Jojo to let Miguel supply the rum and the cigars.

Very soon the game heated up to boiling-point. Without asking his permission, I changed Jojo's tactics. I laid not only on him but also on the others, and that made him look sour. Lighting a cigar, he muttered angrily, 'Stuff it, man. Don't scatter the gumbo.' By about four in the morning I had a pile of bolivars, cruzeiros, American and West Indian dollars, diamonds and even some little gold nuggets in front of me.

Jojo took the dice. He staked five hundred bolivars. I went in with a thousand.

And he threw the seven!

I left the lot, making two thousand bolivars. Jojo took out

the five hundred he had won. And threw the seven again!
Once more he pulled out his stake. And seven again!

'What are you going to do, Enrique?' asked Chino.

'I leave the four thousand.'

'Banco alone!' I looked at the guy who had just spoken. A
little thickset man, as black as boot-polish, his eyes bloodshot
with drink. A Brazilian for sure.

'Put down your four thousand bolos.'

'This stone's worth more.' And he dropped a diamond on
the blanket, just in front of him. He squatted there in his pink
shorts, bare to the waist. The Chinese picked up the diamond,
put it on his scales and said, 'It's only worth three and a
half.'

'OK for three and a half,' said the Brazilian.

'Shoot, Jojo.'

Jojo shot the dice, but the Brazilian grabbed them as they
rolled. I wondered what was going to happen: he scarcely
looked at the dice but spat on them and tossed them back to
Jojo. 'Shoot them like that, all wet,' he said.

'OK, Enrique?' asked Jojo, looking at me.

'If that's the way you want it, *hombre*.'

Jojo hitched the fold in the blanket deeper with his left
hand, and without wiping the dice he shot them—a long, long
roll. And up came the seven again.

As if he was jerked by a spring, the Brazilian leapt to his
feet, his hand on his gun. Then quietly he said, 'It's not my
night yet.' And he went out.

The moment he shot up like a jack-in-the-box my hand
darted to my gun—it had a round in the breech. Jojo never
stirred nor made a move to defend himself. And yet it was him
the black man was aiming at. I saw I still had a lot to learn
before I knew the exact moment when to draw and fire.

At sunrise we stopped. What with the smoke of the damp
grass and the cigars and cigarettes, my eyes stung so much
they ran. My legs were completely numb from having squatted
like a tailor more than nine hours on end. But there was one
thing that pleased me: I hadn't had to get up and piss, not
once, and that meant I was entirely in control of my nerves
and of my life.

We slept until two in the afternoon. When I woke up, Jojo

wasn't there. I put on my trousers—nothing in the pockets! Shit! Jojo must have swiped the lot. But we hadn't settled our accounts yet: he shouldn't have done that. He was taking too much upon himself—coming it the boss, and coming it a trifle high. I wasn't and never had been a boss; but I couldn't bear people who thought themselves superior—who thought they could get away with anything. I went out and I found Jojo at Miguel's, eating a dish of macaroni and mince. 'OK, buddy?' he said to me.

'Yes and no.'

'How come, no?'

'Because you never ought to have emptied my pockets when I wasn't there.'

'Don't talk balls, boy. I know how to behave and the reason why I did that is on account of everything depends on mutual trust. Don't you see, during a game you might very well stuff the diamonds or the liquid some place else besides your pockets, for example? Then again, you don't know what I won either. So whether we empty our pockets together or not, it's all one. A matter of confidence.'

He was right: let's say no more. Jojo paid Miguel for the rum and the tobacco of last night. I asked whether the guys wouldn't think it odd that he paid for them to drink and smoke.

'But I'm not the one who pays! Each man who wins a packet leaves something on the table. Everyone knows that.'

And night after night this life went on. We'd been here two weeks, two weeks in which every night we played high and wild, gambling with the dice and gambling with our lives too.

Last night an appalling rain came hurtling down. Black as ink. A gambler got up after winning a fair pile. He went out at the same time as a huge guy who'd been just sitting there for some time, not playing any more for want of the wherewithal. Twenty minutes later the big guy who had been so unlucky came back and started gambling like crazy. I thought the winner must have lent him the dough, but still it seemed queer he should have lent him so much. When daylight came they found the winner dead, stabbed less than fifty yards from our place. I talked to Jojo about it, telling him what I thought.

'It's nothing to do with us,' he said. 'Next time, he'll watch out.'

'You're gaga, Jojo. There'll be no next time for him, on account of he's dead.'

'True enough: but what can we do about it?'

I was following José's advice, of course. Every day I sold my foreign notes, the diamonds and the gold to a Lebanese buyer, the owner of a jeweller's shop in Ciudad Bolivar. Over the front of his hut there was a notice 'Gold and diamonds bought here: highest prices given'. And underneath it 'Honesty is my greatest treasure'.

Carefully I packed the credit-notes payable on sight to my order in a balata'd envelope—an envelope dipped in raw latex. They could not be cashed by anyone else nor endorsed in any other name. Every gallowsbird in the village knew what I was doing, and if there was any type who made me feel too uneasy or who didn't speak French or Spanish, I showed him. So the only time I was in danger was during the game or when it ended. Sometimes that good guy Miguel came and fetched me when we stopped for the night.

For the last two days I'd had the feeling the atmosphere was getting tenser, more mistrustful. I'd learnt the smell in penal: when trouble was brewing in our barrack on the islands, you realized it without being able to tell how. When you're always on the alert, do you pick up waves put out by the guys getting ready for the rough stuff? I don't know. But I've never been wrong about things like that.

For example, yesterday four Brazilians spent the whole night propped up in the corners of the room, in the darkness. Very occasionally one of them would come out of the shadows into the hard light that shone on the blanket and lay a few ridiculous little bets. They never took the dice nor asked for them. Something else: *not one of them had a weapon that could be seen.* No machête, no knife, no gun. And that just didn't go with their killers' faces. It was on purpose, no doubt of it.

They came back this evening. They wore their shirts outside their pants, so they must have their guns up against their bellies. They settled into the shadows, of course, but still I could make them out. Their eyes never left the players' movements. I had to watch them without their noticing it; and that meant I must not stare straight at them. I managed by coughing and leaning back, covering my mouth with my hand. Unfortunately there were only two in front of me. The others were behind, and I could only get quick glances of them by turning round to blow my nose.

Jojo's coolness was something extraordinary. He remained perfectly unmoved. Still, from time to time he did bet on other men's throws, which meant the risk of winning or losing by mere unaided chance. I knew that this kind of gambling set him on edge, because it forced him to win the same money two or three times before keeping it for good. The disadvantage was when the game grew red-hot he became too eager to win and passed me over great wads of dough too fast.

As I knew these guys were watching me, I left my pile there in front of me for everyone to see. I didn't want to behave like a living safe-deposit today.

Two or three times I told Jojo, in quick crook's slang, that he was making me win too often. He looked as if he didn't understand. I had worked the lavatory trick on them yesterday and I had not come back; so it was no good doing it now—if these four types meant to move in tonight, they were not going to wait for me to return: they'd get me between the shack and the shit-house.

I felt the tension mount: the four images in each corner were more on edge than ever. Particularly one who kept smoking cigarette after cigarette, lighting one from the butt of the other.

So now I started making bancos right and left, in spite of Jojo's ugly looks. To crown it all I won instead of losing and, far from shrinking, my pile kept on piling up. It was all there in front of me, mostly in five-hundred-bolivar notes. I was so keyed up that as I took the dice I put my cigarette down on them and it burnt two holes in a folded five hundred. I played and lost this note together with three others in a two-thousand-bolo banco. The winner got up, said, 'See you tomorrow,' and went out.

In the heat of the game I took no notice of how the time passed, and then all at once to my amazement I saw the note there on the blanket again. I knew perfectly well who'd won it, a very thin bearded white man of about forty with a pale mark on the lobe of his left ear, standing out against the sunburn. But he was not here any more. In a couple of seconds I had put the scene together again: he'd gone out alone, I was certain of that. Yet not one of those four types had stirred. So that meant they had one or two accomplices outside. They must have a system of signalling from where they were that a guy was coming out loaded with cash and diamonds.

There were a good many men gambling standing up, so I could not make out who had come in since the thin guy left. As for the ones sitting down, they had been the same for hours and the place of the thin guy with the burnt note had been filled the moment he left.

But who had played the note? I felt like picking it up and asking. But that would be very risky.

I was in danger: no doubt about that. There before my eyes was the proof that the thin guy had got himself killed. My nerves were tense but they were under control; I had to think very fast. It was four in the morning: no daylight before six-fifteen, because in the tropics the sun comes up straight away, some time after six. So if something was going to happen, it would be between four and five. Outside it was as dark as hell: I knew, because I had just got up, saying I wanted a breath of fresh air in the doorway. I'd left my pile there where I sat, neatly stacked. I saw nothing unusual outside.

I came back and sat down calmly, but all my senses were on the alert. The back of my neck told me there were two pairs of eyes drilling into it.

Jojo rolled the dice, and I let other people cover his stakes. And now he began to have a fair-sized pile in front of him—something he hated.

The temperature was rising, rising; I felt that for sure, and in a very natural voice, not as if I were taking precautions, I said to Jojo in French, 'I'm dead certain there's trouble in the air, man: I can smell it. Get up at the same time as me and let's cover the lot with our guns.'

Jojo smiled as though I were saying something pleasant: he no more bothered about me than about someone else understanding French, and he said, 'My good friend, what's the sense of this damn-fool attitude? And just who's to be covered in particular?'

True enough. Cover who? And what reason could you give? Yet the balloon was just going to go up, that was certain. The guy with the everlasting cigarette had two full cups of rum and he tossed them straight off, one after the other.

It would be no good going out alone in the inky darkness, even holding a gun. The men outside would see me and I wouldn't see them. Go into the room next door? Worse still. Nine chances out of ten there was already a guy there: he could easily have got in by lifting one of the planks in the wall.

There was only one thing to do and that was to openly put all my winnings into my canvas bag, leave the bag there where I was sitting and go out and have a piss. They would not signal because I wouldn't have the dough on me. There was more than five thousand bolos in my pile. Better lose them than my life.

Anyhow, there was no choice. It was the only way to get out of this trap, which might snap to any minute.

I'd worked all this out very quickly, of course: it was now seven minutes to five. I gathered everything together, notes, diamonds, the aspirin tubes and all: everyone saw me. I deliberately stuffed this little fortune into the canvas bag. As naturally as could be, I pulled the strings tight, put the bag down about a foot from me, and so that everybody should understand I said in Spanish, 'Keep an eye on the bag, Jojo. I don't feel so good: I'm going to take a breath of air.'

Jojo had been watching all my movements; he held out his hand and said, 'Give it me. It'll be better here than anywhere else.'

Unwillingly, I held it out, because I knew he was putting himself in danger, immediate danger. But what could I do? Refuse? Impossible: it would sound very strange.

I walked out, my hand on my gun. I could see no one in the darkness, but I didn't have to see them to know they were there. Quickly, almost running, I made for Miguel's place. There was just a chance that by coming back with him and a big carbide lamp we might avoid the crunch. Unfortunately Miguel's was more than two hundred yards from our shack. I began to run.

'Miguel! Miguel!'

'What's the matter?'

'Get up quick! Bring your gun and your lamp. There's trouble.'

Bang! Bang! Two shots in the pitch-black night.

I ran. First I got the wrong shack—insults from inside and at the same time they asked me what the shooting was about. I ran on. Here was our shack—all lights out. I flicked my lighter. People came running with lamps. Nobody left in the room. Jojo was lying on the ground, blood pouring from the back of his neck. He was not dead, but in a coma. An electric torch they'd left behind showed just what had happened. First they'd shot out the carbide lamp, at the same time knocking Jojo out. Using the torch, they'd swept up the pile lying in front of Jojo—my bag and his winnings. His shirt had been torn off and the canvas belt he wore next to his skin ripped open with a knife or a machête.

All the gamblers had escaped, of course. The second shot had been fired to make them move faster. Anyhow, there had not been many of us left when I'd got up. Eight men sitting down, two standing, the four types in the corners and the kid who poured out the rum.

Everybody offered to help. Jojo was carried to Miguel's hut, where there was a bed made of branches. He lay there in a coma all the morning. The blood had clotted; it no longer ran out, and according to an English miner that was a good sign but also a bad one, because if the skull was fractured, the bleeding would go on inside. I decided not to move him. A miner from El Callao, an old friend of Jojo's, set off for another mine to fetch a so-called doctor.

I was all in. I explained everything to Mustafa and Miguel, and they comforted me by saying that since the whole business had been as you might say signalled hours ahead, and since I had given Jojo a clear warning, he ought to have followed my lead.

About three in the afternoon, Jojo opened his eyes. We made him drink a few drops of rum, and then, the words coming hard, he whispered, 'It's all up with me, mate: I know it. Don't let me be moved. It wasn't your fault, Papi; it was mine.' He paused for a while and then went on, 'Miguel, there's a can buried behind your pig-sty. Let the one-eyed guy take it to Lola, my wife.' His mind was clear for a few minutes after that, and then he relapsed into coma. He died at sunset.

Doña Carmencita, the fat woman from the first joint, came to see him. She brought a few diamonds and three or four notes she had found on the floor at our place during the morning. God knows hundreds of people had been there, yet not one of them had touched either the money or the diamonds.

Almost the whole of the little community came to the funeral. The four Brazilians were there, still wearing their shirts outside their trousers. One of them came up to me and held out his hand; I pretended not to see it and gave him a friendly shove in the belly. Yes: I had been right. The gun was just there, where I had thought it would be.

I wondered whether I ought to deal with them. Do it now? Later? Do what? Nothing: it was too late.

I wanted to be alone, but after a burial it was the custom to go and have a drink at every joint whose owner had turned up at the graveyard. They always came, all of them.

When I was at Doña Carmencita's she came and sat by me, with her glass of anis in her hand. When I put mine to my lips, she raised hers too, but only to hide the fact that she was talking to me. 'It was better him than you,' she said. 'Now you can go wherever you want in peace.'

'What do you mean, in peace?'

'Because everybody knows you always sold your winnings to the Lebanese.'

'Yes, but suppose the Lebanese is killed?'

'That's true. One more problem.'

I told Doña Carmencita the drinks were on me and walked off by myself, leaving my friends sitting there. Without really knowing why, I took the path that led to what they called the graveyard, a piece of cleared ground of about fifty square yards.

Eight graves there in the cemetery: Jojo's was the latest. And there in front of it stood Mustafa. I went over to him. 'What are you doing, Mustafa?'

'I've come to pray for an old friend—I was fond of him— and to bring him a cross. You forgot to make one.'

Hell, so I had! I'd never thought of it. I shook the good old Arab's hand and thanked him.

'You're not a Christian?' he asked. 'I didn't see you pray when they threw the earth on to him.'

'Well, I mean ... there's certainly a God, Mustafa,' I said, to please him. 'And what's more, I thank Him for having looked after me instead of sending me down the line with Jojo. And I do more than say prayers for this old man; I forgive him: he was a poor little kid from the Belleville slums, and he was only able to learn just one profession—shooting craps.'

'What are you talking about, brother? I don't understand.'

'It doesn't matter. But just remember this: I'm really sorry he's dead. I did try to save him. But no one should ever think he's brighter than the rest, because one day he'll find a man who moves faster than him. Jojo is fine here. He'll sleep for ever with what he loved, adventure and the wild landscape; and he'll sleep with God's forgiveness.'

'Yes, God will forgive him for sure, because he was a good man.'

'That's a fact.'

I walked slowly back to the village. It was true that I did not feel resentful towards Jojo, although he had very nearly been the death of me. His enthusiasm, his prodigious energy, and, in spite of his sixty years, his youth, and his underworld good breeding—'Behave properly, God almighty, behave properly!' And then I'd been warned. I'd willingly send up a little prayer to thank José for his advice. Without him I shouldn't be here.

Swinging gently in my hammock and smoking fat cigar after fat cigar, as much to soak myself in nicotine as to chase the mosquitoes away, I cast up my accounts.

Right. I had ten thousand dollars after only a few months of freedom. And both here and at El Callao I had met men and women of all races and backgrounds, every one of them full of human warmth. Because of them and this life in the wild, in this atmosphere so unlike that of the city, I'd come to know how wonderful freedom was, the freedom I'd fought for so hard.

Then again the war had come to an end, thanks to Charlie de Gaulle and the Yankees; in all this churning about of millions of people, a convict didn't amount to much. So much the better for me: with all these problems to settle, they would have other things to do apart from worrying about what I had been.

I was thirty-seven: thirteen years of penal settlement, fifty-three months of solitary confinement, counting the Santé, the Conciergerie and Beaulieu as well as the prison on the islands, the Réclusion. It was hard to put a label on me. I was neither a poor bastard only capable of working with a pick or a shovel or an axe, nor was I a type with a real trade that would let me earn a decent living anywhere in the world, as a mechanic or an electrician, say. On the other hand, I couldn't take on important responsibilities; I hadn't enough education for that. At the same time as your schooling, you ought always to learn a good manual trade: if school goes wrong, you can then always look after yourself in life. It was not that you felt better than a street-sweeper if you had a certain amount of education—I had never despised any man, apart from screws and pigs—but you couldn't sustain your role. You were between two stools—you felt that you had it in you to be happy, but that you couldn't get there. I had both too much education and not enough. Hell, that was hardly the brightest outlook in the world.

Then again, if you were an ordinary, normal man, how could you control your deep-down urges? I ought to look for peace and quiet, and live like the retired lags of El Callao; but what I felt right down inside me was a kind of explosion, a terrific thirst for life. Adventure drew me on with such force that I wondered whether I should ever be able to live a quiet life.

And it was true that I had to take my revenge, too: it was true I could not possibly forgive the people who had done me and my family so much harm. Calm down, Papi, calm down. You've got plenty of time. You must gradually learn to trust in the future. For although you've sworn to go straight in this country, here you are right out on the loose, forgetting your promise.

How hard it was to live like other people, obey like other people, walk in step with everybody else, rigidly conforming to the rules.

Take your choice, Papi: either you make up your mind to obey the law in this, God's own country, and you give up your revenge, or you decide you can't put your obsession behind you. And in that case, since you'll need much more money than you'll ever make by working, you must go on the loose again.

And after all I could very well go and look for this essential cash *outside Venezuela*. That's not such a bad idea, man. But it needs thinking over first. Let's get some sleep.

But before that I couldn't help going to the doorway and gazing for a long while at the stars and the moon and listening to the countless noises coming from the mysterious bush that surrounded the village with a wall as dark as the moon was brilliant.

And then I slept, rocking gently in my hammock, happy to the core in the knowledge that I was free, free, free, and *master of my fate.*

AT about ten the next morning I went to see the Lebanese. 'So I go to El Callao or Ciudad Bolivar, to the addresses you've given me, and they pay me your bills of exchange?'

'That's right: you can go off with an easy mind.'

'But what if they kill you too?'

'It doesn't matter, as far as you're concerned. You will be paid whatever happens. You're going to El Callao?'

'Yes.'

'What part of France are you from?'

'Round Avignon: not far from Marseilles.'

'Why, I've got a friend from Marseilles: but he lives a great way off. Alexandre Guigue is his name.'

'Well, what do you know! He's a close friend of mine.'

'Of mine, too. I'm glad you know him.'

'Where does he live, and how can I get there?'

'He's at Boa Vista. A very long and complicated journey.'

'What does he do there?'

'He's a barber. Easy to find him—you just ask for the French barber-dentist.'

'So he's a dentist too?'

I couldn't help laughing. Because I knew Alexandre Guigue very well: an extraordinary guy. He was sent down the same time as me, in 1933; we made the crossing together, and he had all the time in the world to tell me every last detail of his job.

One Saturday night in 1929 or 1930, Alexandre and a friend climbed quietly down from the ceiling of Lisbon's biggest jewel-shop. They had broken into a dentist's flat on the next floor up. To fix the geography of the building, to make sure the dentist went away every week-end with his family, and to take the prints of the lock of the front door and the surgery, they had had to go there several times and have stoppings put in their teeth.

'Very good work he did, too,' Alexandre told me, 'seeing the stoppings are still there. In two nights we had all the time we needed to shift the jewels and open two safes and a little steel cabinet, doing it neatly and without any noise. There was no identikit in those days, but the dentist must have been fantastic at describing people, because as we were on the platform leaving Lisbon the pigs jumped on us without any hesitation at all. The Portuguese court sent us down for ten and twelve years. So there we were, a little while later, at their penal in Angola, down under the Belgian and French Congo. No problem about escaping: our friends came to fetch us in a taxi. Like an idiot I went to Brazzaville: my mate, he chose Leopoldville. A few months later I was picked up by the French police. The French wouldn't give me back to the Portuguese: they sent me back to France and there I copped a twenty-year stretch instead of the ten they'd given me in Portugal.'

He made a break from Guiana. I'd heard that he had passed through Georgetown, and that he'd gone to Brazil through the bush, riding on an ox.

What if I went to see him? Yes: I'd go to Boa Vista. That was a brilliant idea!

I set off with two men. They said they knew how to get to Brazil, and they were to help me carry the food and bedding. For ten days and more we wandered about the bush without even managing to reach Santa Helena, the last mining village before the Brazilian frontier: and after a fortnight we found ourselves at Aminos, a gold-mine almost on the edge of British Guiana. With the help of some Indians we reached the Cuyuni river, and that led us to a little Venezuelan village called Castillejo. There I bought machêtes and files as a present for the Indians, and I left my so-called guides. I had to control myself so as not to smash their faces in, because in fact they no more knew those parts than I did.

In the end I found a man in the village who really did know the country and who agreed to guide me. Four or five days later I reached El Callao.

At last, exhausted, worn out, thin as a lath, I knocked on Maria's door at nightfall.

'He's here! He's here!' shrieked Esmeralda at the top of her voice.

'Who?' asked Maria from another room. 'And why do you

shout so?'

All stirred up by finding this sweetness again after the weeks I had just been through, I caught hold of Esmeralda and put my hand over her mouth to stop her answering.

'Why all this noise about a visitor?' asked Maria, coming in. A cry, a cry from the bottom of her heart, a cry of joy, of love, of hope fulfilled, and Maria threw herself into my arms.

When I had embraced Picolino and kissed Maria's other sisters—José was away—I lay there a long, long while beside Maria. She kept asking me the same questions: she couldn't believe I had come straight to her house without stopping at Big Charlot's or at any of the village cafés.

'You're going to stay a little while in El Callao, aren't you?'

'Yes. I'll fix things so I stay for some time.'

'You must take care of yourself and put on weight: I'll cook such dishes for you, sweetheart. When you go, even if it wounds my heart for ever—not that I blame you in any way, since you warned me—when you go, I want you to be strong, so that you can avoid the snares of Caracas as well as you can.'

El Callao, Uasipata, Upata, Tumeremo: little villages with names strange for a European, tiny points on the map of a country three times the size of France, lost at the back of beyond, where the word progress has no meaning and where men and women, young and old, live as people lived in Europe at the beginning of the century, overflowing with genuine passions, generosity, joy in life and kindness ... Almost all the men who were then more than forty had had to bear the most terrible of all dictatorships, the rule of Gomez. They were hunted down and beaten to death for nothing: any man in authority could flog them with a bull's pizzle. When they were between fifteen and twenty in the years 1925 to 1935, all of them were hunted like animals by the army's recruiting agents dragged off to the barracks. Those were the days when a pretty girl might be picked out and kidnapped by an important official and thrown into the street when he was tired of her; and if her family raised a finger to help her they were wiped out.

Now and then, to be sure, there were risings, suicidal revolts by men who were determined to have their revenge even if they died for it. But the army was always there at once, and those who escaped with their lives were so tortured they were crippled for the rest of their days.

And yet in spite of all that, the almost illiterate people of these little backward villages here still retained the same love for other men and the same trust in them. For me it was a continual lesson, and one that touched me to the bottom of my heart.

I thought of all this as I lay there beside Maria. I had suffered, that was true; I had been condemned unjustly, and that was true again; the French warders had been as savage as the tyrant's police and soldiers, and maybe even more devilish; but here I was, all in one piece, having just gone through a terrific adventure—a dangerous adventure, certainly, but how utterly fascinating! I'd walked, paddled my canoe, ridden through the bush; but as I lived it each day was a year, so full it was; that life of a man with no laws, free from all restraints, from all moral limits, all obedience to orders from outside.

So I wondered whether I was doing the right thing, going to Caracas and leaving this corner of paradise behind me. Again and again I asked myself that question.

The next day, bad news. The correspondent of the Lebanese, a little jeweller who specialized in gold orchids with Margarita pearls and in all kinds of other truly original little ornaments, told me he couldn't pay anything on my notes of credit because the Lebanese owed him a huge sum of money. OK, so I'd go and get my money at the other address in Ciudad Bolivar.

'Do you know this man?' I asked.

'Only too well. He's a crook. He's run off, taking everything, even some choice pieces I'd left with him on trust.'

If what this goddamn fool said was true, then I was even more broke than before I went off with Jojo. Fine, fine! Fate —what a mysterious business. These sort of things only happened to me. And done by a Lebanese, into the bargain!

Bowed down and dragging my feet, I came back to the house. To win those wretched ten thousand dollars I'd risked my life ten and twenty times over; and now not the smell of a sou was left to me. Well, well: that Lebanese did not have to load the dice to win at craps. Better still, he did not even bother to move—he sat there at home, waiting for the cash to be brought to him.

But my zest for life was so strong that I bawled myself out. You're free, free, free, man, and here you are whining about fate! You must be doing it for the laugh: you can't be serious. So maybe you did lose your banco; but what a marvellous caper it was! Lay your bets! The bank is broke! In a few weeks' time I'll be a rich man or a corpse! The furious suspense, as if I was sitting on the edge of a volcano keeping watch on the crater, but knowing that other craters might open up too—wasn't it worth losing ten thousand dollars for all that?

I was in control again now and I could see the position clearly enough. I'd have to hurry back to the mine, before the Lebanese buggered off. And since time is money, don't let's lose any. I'd go and find a mule, some stores and be on my way! I still had my gun and my knife. The only question was, would I find the way? I hired a horse—Maria thought it far better than a mule. The one thing that worried me was the idea of taking the wrong *pique*, because there were places where others came in from all directions.

'I know the paths: would you like me to go with you?' asked Maria. 'Oh how I should love that! I'd only come as far as the *posada*, where you leave the horses before taking to the canoe.'

'It's too dangerous for you, Maria. Above all, too dangerous coming back alone.'

'I'll wait for somebody who's returning to El Callao. That way I'll be safe. Please say yes, *mi amor*!'

I talked it over with José, and he agreed she should go. 'I'll lend her my revolver. Maria knows how to use it,' he said.

And that's how we came to be sitting there alone on the edge of the *pique*, Maria and I, after a five hours' ride—I had hired another horse for her. She was wearing breeches, a present from a friend, a *llanera*. The Venezuelan *llana* is a huge plain, and the women who live there are brave and untameable; they fire a rifle or a revolver like a man, wield the machête like a fencer and ride like an Amazon—yet in spite of that they are capable of dying for love.

Maria was exactly the opposite. She was gentle and sensual

and so close to nature you felt she was part of it. Not that that prevented her from knowing how to look after herself, with a weapon or without: she was courageous.

Never, never shall I forget those days of travelling before we reached the *posada*. Unforgettable days and nights when it was our hearts that sang after we were too tired to speak our happiness.

Never shall I be able to describe the delight of those dream-like halts when we played in the coolness of the crystal-clear water and then, still wet and mother-naked, made love on the grassy bank with butterflies and humming-birds and dragon-flies all round us.

We would go on, tottering with love and sometimes so filled with ecstasy that I felt myself to make sure I was still all in one piece.

The nearer we came to the *posada* the more closely I listened to Maria's pure natural voice singing love songs. And as the distance shortened, the more often I pulled in my horse and found excuses for another rest.

'Maria, I think we ought to let the horses cool a while.'

'At this pace, he's not going to be the one who's tired when we get there, Papi: we're the ones who'll be worn out,' she said, breaking into a laugh that showed her pearly teeth.

We managed to spend six days on the road before we came in sight of the *posada*. When I saw it, in a flash I was over-come with a longing to spend the night there and then go back to El Callao. The idea of having the purity of those six days of passion all over again suddenly seemed to me a thousand times more important than my ten thousand dollars. The desire was so strong it made me tremble. But even stronger, there was a voice that said, 'Don't be a lemon, Papi. Ten thousand dollars is a fortune, the first big wad of the amount you need to carry out your plan. You must not give it up.'

'There's the *posada*,' said Maria.

And against myself, against everything I thought and felt, I said the opposite of what I wanted to say. 'Yes, there's the *posada*. Our journey's over: tomorrow I leave you.'

Four good men at the paddles, and in spite of the current the canoe raced over the water. Every stroke took me farther from

Maria: and standing on the bank she watched me disappear.

Where was peace, where was love, where perhaps was the woman with whom I was fated to build a home and a family? I forced myself not to look back, for fear I should call out to the paddlers 'Let's turn around!' I had to go on to the mine and get my money and then head for other adventures as soon as possible so as to make enough for the great journey to Paris and back: if there was to be any return.

Just one promise: I'd not hurt the Lebanese. I'd just take what belonged to me, neither more nor less. He'd never know he owed this forgiveness to six days of travelling through paradise with the most wonderful girl in the world, Maria, the nymph of El Callao.

'The Lebanese? But I'm pretty sure he's gone,' said Miguel, having crushed me in his embrace.

I had found the shack closed, true enough, but the wonderful sign was still there: 'Honesty is my greatest treasure'.

'You think he's gone? Oh, the bleeding shit!'

'Calm down, Papi. We'll soon find out.'

My doubt did not last long, nor my hope. Mustafa confirmed that the Lebanese had gone: but where had he gone? It was only after two days of inquiry that a miner told me he had lighted out for Brazil with three bodyguards. 'All the miners say he's an honest man, for sure.' Then I told the story of El Callao and all I'd learnt about the disappearing Lebanese in Ciudad Bolivar. Four or five guys, including an Italian, said that if I was right, then they were broke. There was only one old character from Guiana who would not see it our way. According to him, the real thief was the Ciudad Bolivar Greek. We turned it this way and that for quite a time, but in my heart of hearts I felt I'd lost the whole packet for good and all. What was I going to do?

Go to see Alexandre Guigue at Boa Vista? It was a long way off, Brazil. You had to reckon about three hundred miles through the bush to reach Boa Vista. My last experience had been too risky—just a little farther, and it would have been my last journey. No: I'd fix things so I was in contact with the mine, and as soon as I learnt the Lebanese had come to the surface again I'd pay him a visit. Once that was settled, I'd be on my way for Caracas, picking up Picolino as I went by. That was the most sensible answer. Tomorrow I'd set off for El Callao.

A week later, there I was with José and Maria. I told them everything. Gently, kindly, Maria found the right words to restore my spirits. Her father urged me to stay with them. 'We'll raid the Caratal mine, if you like.' I smiled, and patted him on the shoulder.

No, really that did not appeal to me: I mustn't stay here. It was only my love for Maria and hers for me that could keep me in El Callao. I was more hooked than I had believed and more than I wanted. It was a strong, genuine love; but still it wasn't powerful enough to overcome my desire for revenge.

Everything was settled: I had fixed with a truck-driver and we were to leave at five the next morning.

While I was shaving, Maria slipped out and hid in her sisters' room. That mysterious sense that women possess had told her that this time it was the real parting. Picolino was sitting there at the table in the big room, washed and tidy, with Esmeralda standing next to him, her hand on his shoulder. I took a step towards the room where Maria was. Esmeralda stopped me. 'No, Enrique.' Then all at once she too darted to the door and disappeared.

José went with us as far as the truck. We did not say a word.

Caracas, and as quick as you can make it.

Farewell, Maria, little flower of El Callao: in love and tenderness you gave me much more than all the gold that ever came from the mines.

It was a tough journey, particularly for Picolino. Six hundred
miles and more; twenty hours of driving, not counting the
stops. We spent a few hours in Ciudad Bolivar, and then having crossed the splendid Orinoco on a ferry, we tore along, the
truck racing like crazy, driven by a man with nerves of steel;
which was just as well.

The next afternoon at four o'clock we reached Caracas. And
straight away there I was in the big city. The movement, the
crowds, the coming and going of thousands and thousands of
people, sucked me right in.

1929, Paris. 1946, Caracas. Seventeen years had gone by
without my having seen a genuine big city. A lovely city,
Caracas, beautiful with its one-storey colonial houses; and it
stretched right down the valley with the Avila mountains rising all round it. A city three thousand feet up, with an everlasting spring, neither too hot nor too cold.

'I trust you, Papillon,' said Dr Bougrat's voice in my ear,
just as though he were there, watching us drive into this huge,
swarming city.

Crowds of people everywhere, of all colours from the dark-
est to the lightest, without any complexes about race. All these
people, black, brick-red or purest white, were alive with a
happiness that went to my head in the first moments.

With Picolino leaning on my arm, we walked towards the
middle of the city. Big Charlot had given me the address of an
ex-lag who kept a boarding-house, the Pension Maracaibo.

Yes, seventeen years had gone by and a war had shattered
the lives of hundreds of thousands of men of my age in a great
many lands, including my own country, France. Between 1939
and 1945 Frenchmen had been prisoners, or they had been
killed or maimed. And you are here, Papillon, here in a big
city! You are thirty-seven, you are young and strong: look
around you at all these people, some of them poorly dressed—
they are laughing aloud. The singing was not just the sound of
the hit-songs played on records, it was in the hearts of all the
people. Of almost all, for of course you saw right away there

were some who were dragging not a ball and chain but something worse—the misfortune of being poor and of not knowing how to look after themselves in the jungle of a big town.

How beautiful it is, a great city! And it was only four o'clock now. What must it be like at night, with its millions of electric stars? Yet we were still only in a working-class district, and a pretty tough one, at that. I'd spend a little money for once. 'Hey there, taxi!'

Sitting there beside me, Picolino laughed and dribbled like a kid. I wiped his poor mouth; he thanked me with shining eyes, trembling, he was so moved. For him, being in a town, a great capital like Caracas, meant above all the hope of finding hospitals and doctors who could turn the wreck he had become into a normal man once more. The miracle of hope. He held my hand, while outside the streets went by and then still more streets with people and still more people, so many of them they entirely hid the pavement. And the cars, and the hooters, and the siren of an ambulance, the clang of a fire-engine, the bawling of the hawkers and the newsboys selling the evening papers, the shriek of a lorry's brakes, the ting-a-ling of the trams, the bicycle bells—all these shouts and the deafening noise around made us feel almost drunk. The din, made up of hundreds of different sounds, destroys some people's nerves, but it had the opposite effect on us; it woke us up and made us thoroughly understand that we were right back in the crazy rhythm of modern mechanical life and instead of being tensed up we felt wonderfully happy.

There was nothing surprising about the fact that it was the noise that struck us most. We had lived in silence so long. For it was silence that I'd known these last seventeen years, the silence of the prisons, the silence of the penal settlement, the more than silence of solitary confinement, the silence of the bush and of the sea, the silence of the little remote villages where happy people live.

I said to Picolino, 'We are coming into a foretaste of Paris —Caracas, a real city. Here they'll make you well, and as for me, I'll find my right path and work out my fate: you can be sure of that.'

His hand squeezed mine; a tear ran from his eye. His hand was so brotherly and affectionate that I held on to it so as not to lose that marvellous contact; and since his other arm was dead, it was I that wiped away my friend's tear.

At last we reached the place run by Emile S., the lag, and settled in. He was not there, but as soon as his wife, a Venezuelan, heard we were from El Callao she grasped what we were and gave us a room with two beds right away, and some coffee.

Having helped Picolino to have a shower I put him to bed. He was tired and over-excited. When I left he made violent signs: I knew he meant to say 'You'll come back, won't you? You won't leave me in the lurch, all by myself?'

'No, Pico! I'll just spend a few hours in the town: I'll be back soon.'

And here I was in Caracas. It was seven o'clock when I walked down the street towards the Plaza Simon Bolivar, the biggest in the city. An explosion of light everywhere, a magnificent pouring out of electricity, neon signs of every colour. What enchanted me most was the advertisements in coloured lights, flaming dragons that came and went like will-o'-the-wisps, flashing on and off like a ballet run by a magician.

It was a splendid square, with a huge bronze statue of Simon Bolivar on an enormous horse in the middle of it. He looked terrific, and the statue showed how noble he must have been. I walked right round him, the man who set Latin America free, and I could not help greeting him in my bad Spanish, speaking low so no one would hear. '*Hombre!* What a miracle it is for me to be here at your feet—at the feet of the Man of Freedom. A poor bastard like me, who has been fighting all the time for that freedom you personify.'

The *pension* was a quarter of a mile from the square, and I went back twice before I found Emile S. He said Charlot had written to tell him we were coming: we went out to have a drink so we could talk quietly.

'It's ten years now I've been here,' said Emile. 'I'm married, with a daughter, and my wife owns the *pension*. That's why I can't put you up for nothing; but you'll only pay half-price.' The wonderful solidarity of ex-cons when one of them is in a jam! He went on, 'Is he an old friend, that poor guy with you?'

'You've seen him?'

'No, but my wife's been telling me about him. She says he's an absolute wreck. Is he gaga?'

'Far from it, and that's what's so terrible. His mind is as clear as a bell, but his tongue and his mouth and his right side down to the waist are paralysed. That's the way he was when I first knew him in El Dorado. Nobody knows who he is or whether he's a con or a detainee.'

'I can't see why you want to drag this unknown type around with you. You don't even know if he's a right guy or not. And then on top of that, he's a burden to you.'

'I've realized that, these eight months I've been looking after him. In El Callao I found some women who took charge. Even so, it's not easy.'

'What are you going to do with him?'

'Get him into hospital if I can. Or find a room—rough, if need be, but with a shower and a lavatory—to look after him until I can find a place for him somewhere.'

'You got dough?'

'A little, but I've got to take care; because although I understand all they say, I speak Spanish badly and it's not going to be so simple to make things work out.'

'You're dead right: it's not easy here—more people wanting work than there are jobs. But anyhow, Papi, don't you worry: you can stay in my place the few days you'll need to find something.'

I got the message. Emile was generous, but he was unhappy about the whole thing. His wife must have drawn a pretty picture of Picolino with his tongue lolling out and his animal grunts. She must have thought of the impression he would make on the boarders.

Tomorrow I'd carry his meals up to our room. Poor Picolino, sleeping there next to me in your little iron bed. Although I pay for your board and lodging, they don't want you. People who are well don't like to see the sick, you understand. With your twisted face in front of them, they don't feel like laughing. That's life, all right. The group only accepts you if your personality brings it something, or else if you're so null and void you don't worry anybody at all. They'll put up with a living piece of furniture. But don't you worry, mate. Even if I'm not as gentle as the El Callao girls, you'll always have me by you; something better than a friend—a crook who's adopted you and who'll do everything he can to prevent you dying like a dog.

Emile gave me several addresses, but there was no job for me anywhere. And twice I went to the hospital to try to get Picolino in. Nothing doing. According to them there were no empty beds; and his papers, saying he'd been let out of El Dorado, were no help at all. Yesterday they asked me how he came to be under my care and why, and what was his nationality and so on. When I told the little shit of a clerk that the chief of El Dorado had put him in my charge and that I had undertaken to look after him, this is what the bastard produced: 'Well then, since he's been let out because you agreed to take care of him, all you have to do is to keep him where you live and have him treated there. If you can't do that, you ought to have left him at El Dorado.'

When he asked for my address I gave him a false one. I did not trust the silly bugger, an international example of the small-time official who wants to throw his weight about.

I moved Picolino: I moved him quick. I was desperate, both for him and for me. I felt I couldn't stay at Emile's any longer; his wife was moaning about having to change Picolino's sheets every day. Yet I did wash the dirty places every morning as well as I could in the washbasin; but they took a long time to dry and it was soon noticed. So I bought an iron and dried the places I had washed with it.

What was to be done? I couldn't be sure. One thing was certain—I had to find an answer quick. Now for the third time I'd tried to get him into a hospital with no result. It was eleven o'clock when we came out. Since that was the way things were, we'd have to set about it properly: I decided to devote the whole of that fine afternoon to my friend. I led him to the Calvario, a wonderful garden filled with tropical plants and flowers on a little hill plumb in the middle of Caracas.

Sitting there on a bench and admiring the splendid view, we ate *arepas* with meat in them and drank a bottle of beer. Then I lit two cigarettes, one for Pico, one for me. It was hard for Picolino to smoke: he drooled on his cigarette. He felt this was an important moment and that I meant to tell him something that might hurt him badly. His eyes were full of anxiety and they seemed to say 'Speak, speak right away. I can feel you've taken a big decision. Tell me; I beg you to tell me.' Yes: I could read all that in his eyes as plain as if it was written. It made me wretched, and I hesitated. At last I brought it out. 'Pico, it's three days now I've been trying to get you into a hospital. There's nothing to be done: they don't want you. You understand?'

'Yes,' said his eyes.

'On the other hand, we can't go to the French consulate without the risk of them asking the Venezuelans for an extradition order.' He shrugged his good shoulder. 'Listen: you've got to get well, and to get well you've got to be treated. That's the main thing. But you know I haven't got enough money to have you looked after. So this is what we'll do: we'll spend the evening together, and I'll take you to the cinema. Then tomorrow morning I'll take you to the Plaza Bolivar without any papers on you. There you lie at the foot of the statue and you don't stir. If they want you to stand or to sit up, you refuse. It's dead certain that after a minute they'll call a cop and he'll call an ambulance. I'll follow in a cab to see what hospital they take you to. Then I'll wait two days before coming to see you, and I'll come in visiting hours so as to mix with the crowd. The first time maybe I shan't talk to you, but as I go past your bed I'll leave you some cigarettes and a little money. OK? You agree?'

He put his good arm on my shoulder and looked straight into my face. His expression was an extraordinary mixture of sadness and gratitude. His throat contracted: he made a superhuman effort to force his twisted mouth to bring out a hoarse sound very like 'Yes, thank you.'

Next day, everything happened just as I had foretold. Less than a quarter of an hour after Picolino lay down at the foot of the Bolivar statue, three or four old men sitting under the shade of the trees told a cop. Twenty minutes later an ambulance came for him. I followed in a cab.

Two days later—no difficulty about mingling with the visitors and finding him—he was in the third ward I went through. A piece of luck: he was between two very sick patients and I could talk to him a while without any risk. He was flushed with joy at seeing me, and maybe he jerked about a little too much.

'They look after you all right?'

He nodded yes.

I looked at the chart at the foot of his bed. 'Paraplegia or malaria with secondary complications. To be checked every two hours.' I left him six packets of cigarettes, matches and twenty bolivars in change.

'Be seeing you, Pico!' Seeing his desperate and imploring eyes I added, 'Don't worry, mate; I'll come back and see you.' I mustn't forget that I'd grown absolutely necessary to him. I was his one link with the world.

I'd been here a fortnight, and the hundred-bolivar notes were disappearing fast. Fortunately I had decent clothes when I got to Caracas. I found a little room, cheap, but still too dear for me. No women anywhere on the horizon. Yet the girls of Caracas were lovely to look at, intelligent and full of life. The difficulty was getting to know them. This was 1946, and it wasn't the custom for women to sit in a café alone.

A big city has its secrets. To be able to take care of yourself, you have to know them; and to know them, you have to know the bright guys. And just who are these bright guys of the streets? A whole mysterious tribe with its own language, laws, customs and vices; its own ways of managing to make enough to live on for twenty-four hours every day. Earning a living, as honestly as possible: that was the problem, and it wasn't easy.

Like all the others, I had my own little ways, often good for a hearty laugh and far from wicked. For example, one day I met a Colombian I'd known in El Dorado.

'What are you doing?'

He told me just then he was earning his living by running a lottery for a magnificent Cadillac.

'Hell, so you've made your fortune already? You must have, to own a Cadillac.'

He choked with laughter: then he explained the job. 'The Cadillac belongs to the director of a big bank. He drives himself, gets there at nine prompt and parks like a good citizen a hundred or a hundred and fifty yards from the bank. There are two of us. One—not always the same, so we don't get spotted —follows him to the door of the bank where he sits on his arse all morning. If there's a hitch, a whistle you can't mistake for anything else: it's only happened once. So between the time he gets there and the time he goes, which is round about one, we put an elegant white streamer on the Cadillac, with red letters saying "On sale here: tickets that may win you this Cadillac. Winning numbers the same as the Caracas lottery. Draw next month." '

'Man, that's way out of the common run. So you sell tickets for a Cadillac that isn't yours? Christ, what a nerve! What about the pigs?'

'They're never the same; and seeing there's no vice in them, it never comes into their heads that maybe it's a swindle. And if they get a little too interested we give them a ticket or two and off they go, dreaming perhaps they'll win a Cadillac. If you want to make a little money with us, come along and I'll introduce you to my partner.'

'You don't think it stinks a trifle, clipping the poor?'

'Never on your sweet life. The tickets cost ten bolivars, so it's only well-off folk that can afford them. So there's no harm done.'

Once the partner had had a look at me, there was I, busy with this ploy. It's not very elegant, but you have to eat, sleep and be if not well dressed then at least clean. And I had to hold on to my reserve as long as possible—the few diamonds I'd brought from El Dorado and two five-hundred-bolivar notes that I hoarded like a miser in my charger, just as if I were still in penal. Because my charger was something I'd never left off carrying inside me, and for two reasons: my hotel was in a pretty rough part of the town and I might be robbed; and if I carried it in my pocket, I might lose it. In any case, it was fourteen years now I had had this charger in my colon, so a year more or less did not matter and that way I was easy in my mind.

The selling of the lottery tickets lasted more than a fort-night, and it would be going on still but for the fact that one day a very eager customer bought two tickets and examined every detail of this marvellous car he dreamt of winning. All at once he straightened up and cried, 'But doesn't this car belong to

97

Dr Fulano, the bank-director?'

Without batting an eyelid, the Colombian replied coolly, 'Just so. He put it into our hands to dispose of like this. He reckons a lottery will bring him in a better price than a straight sale.'

'Odd . . .' said the customer.

'But above all, don't mention it to him,' went on the Colombian, still very calm. 'He made us promise to say nothing, because he'd find it awkward if it was known.'

'I can't understand it: it's really most unusual for a man of his kind.'

As soon as he'd got far enough away, moving in the direction of the bank, we whipped off the streamer and folded it up. The Colombian vanished, carrying it, and I went to the door of the bank to tell our partner we were striking camp. Inside myself I was laughing like a hyena and I couldn't help hanging about not far from the door so as not to miss what I expected would be the sequel. It came off, all right. Three minutes later, there was the director together with the suspicious customer. He was waving his arms wildly and walking so fast I knew he was in a right fury.

They saw there was nobody left around the Cadillac, and surprised, no doubt, they came back slower, stopping at a café to have a drink at the bar. As the customer had not spotted me, I went in too to hear what they would say, for the laugh.

'By God, that was a nerve! Don't you think that was an infernal nerve, Dr Fulano?'

But the owner of the Cadillac, who, like all good Caraqueños, had a sense of humour, burst out laughing and said, 'When I think that if I had walked by they might have offered me a ticket for my own car! And that sometimes I'm so absent-minded that I might actually have bought it. You must admit it makes you laugh.'

Naturally enough, that was the end of our lottery. The Colombians vanished. For my part. I'd made close on fifteen hundred bolivars, enough to live on for over a month; which was important.

The days went by, and it was not at all easy to find anything worth while to do. This was the period when Pétain's supporters and the men who had collaborated with the Germans started reaching Venezuela from France, on the run from the justice of their own country. Seeing I didn't know enough about the possible distinction between collaborators and Pétainists, I lumped them all together under the label of ex-Nazis. So I did not associate with them.

A month went by and nothing much happened. At El Callao I had never thought it would be so hard to get myself going. I was reduced to selling coffee-pots from door to door; they were supposed to be specially designed for offices.

My patter was so glib and so bloody silly it nauseated me. 'You see, Señor Director, whenever your employees go out for a coffee [a usual custom in all Venezuelan offices] they waste an enormous amount of time, particularly when it's raining; and during this time you are losing money. With a coffee-pot in the office, you gain all round.' Maybe he might gain all round, but I didn't, because several of the bosses answered, 'Oh, in Venezuela, you know, we take life quietly, even in business. Indeed, that's why our people are allowed to go out for a *cafecito* in working hours.'

Then again, you look rather foolish walking about the streets with a coffee-pot in your hand: and I was doing just that when I bumped into Paulo the Boxer, an old Montmartre acquaintance.

'Why, what do you know? You must be Paulo the ...'

'And you're Papillon?'

He grabbed my arm and towed me into a café.

'Well, talk of coincidence—this is a coincidence, all right.'

'What are you up to, walking around the street with that coffee-pot?'

'I'm selling them: it's a bleeding disaster. What with getting it out and shoving it back again, the box tore just now.' I told him how things were with me and then I said, 'How about you?'

'Let's drink our coffee. I'll tell you somewhere else.'

We paid and stood up; I reached for my coffee-pot.

'Leave that where it is. You won't want it any more, I give you my oath.'

'You don't think so?'

'I know it, man.'

I left the vile pot on the table and we went out.

An hour later, in my room, after we had tossed memories of Montmartre to and fro, Paulo came to the point. He had a big job in a country not far from Venezuela. He knew he could rely on me. If I agreed, he'd take me on as one of his team.

'It's as easy as falling off a log—it's in the bag, man! I tell you very seriously, there are going to be so many dollars you'll need an iron to iron them out flat, so they don't take up too much room.'

'And where is it, this prodigious job?'

'You'll know when you get there. I can't say anything before.'

'How many will there be of us?'

'Four. One's already on the spot. I came here to fetch the other. You know him, by the way. He's a friend of yours: Gaston.'

'Right. But I've lost touch with him.'

'Not me,' said Paulo, laughing.

'You really can't tell me any more about the job?'

'Impossible, Papi. I've got my reasons.'

I thought quickly. Placed as I was, there wasn't much choice. Either I went on dragging about with a coffee-pot or some other goddamn nonsense in my hand or I went on the loose, with the possibility of getting hold of a packet and getting hold of it quick. I'd always known that Paulo was a sober, reflecting type, and if in his opinion there had to be four of us, then that meant this job was serious too. Technically, it would be a pretty piece of work. And that, I must admit, tempted me too. So what about it, Papi—banco?

'Banco!'

The next day we set off.

6: The Tunnel under the Bank

MORE than seventy-two hours of driving. We relieved one another at the wheel. Paulo took endless precautions: every time we filled up, the man who was driving put the others down three hundred yards from the pump and picked them up afterwards.

Gaston and I had been waiting half an hour in the driving rain, waiting for Paulo to come back. I was furious. 'You really think all this act is necessary, Paulo? Just look at us. We'll catch our bleeding deaths.'

'What a bleeding bore you are, Pápi, I had air put in the tyres, changed a back wheel and filled up with oil and water. You can't do that in five minutes.'

'I never said you could. But I tell you straight, I don't see the point of all these precautions.'

'Well I do, and I'm the boss. You may have had a thirteen-year-stretch in penal, but I copped ten of solitary in our loving homeland; so I don't think you can ever do enough in the way of precautions. Suppose there's a tip about a car, a Chevrolet with one man in it, say—well, it's not the same as a car with three men in it.'

He was right. Let's say no more about it. Ten hours later we reached the town we were aiming for. Paulo dropped us at the end of a road with villas on either side of it.

'Take the pavement on the right. The villa's called Mi Amor; it's along there. Walk in like you owned it, and inside you'll find Auguste.'

There was a garden with flowers, and a neat path leading to the door of a pretty little house. The door was shut: we knocked.

'Hi there, brothers, come right in,' said Auguste, opening the door. He was in shirt-sleeves; he was covered with sweat, and his hairy arms had earth on them. We told him Paulo had gone to park the car at the other end of the town. It made sense not to have a Venezuelan number-plate seen too often in the road.

'Did you have a good run?'

'Yes.'

No more than that. We sat down in the dining-room. I felt the decisive moment was coming and I was rather tense. Gaston had no more idea than I what the job was all about. 'It's a matter of trust,' Paulo had said in Caracas. 'Either you come along or you don't. Take it or leave it. Just one thing: it means more liquid cash than you've ever dreamt of.' OK: but now it was all going to have to be clear, open and exact.

Auguste gave us coffee. Apart from a few questions about our journey and how we were, not a word that shed any light at all. They were prudent, tight-mouthed, in this family.

I heard a car door slam in front of the house. It must be Paulo who'd hired a car with a local number-plate. Just so.

'Here we are,' cried Paulo, coming in and taking off his leather jacket. 'Everything's going just fine, boys.' Calmly he drank his coffee. I said nothing: I was waiting. He asked Auguste to put the cognac bottle on the table. Without any hurry, and still looking thoroughly pleased with life, he poured some for us; and then at last he came to the point. 'Well, boys, here you are on the spot: this is where we work. Listen, now: just in front of this little house, on the other side of the street you came by, there's the back of a bank. Its main entrance is on the big avenue that runs parallel with our little road. And the reason why you see Auguste's arms all covered with clay is because he knew you were idle, no-account bums, and he set to work so there would be less for you to do.'

'Do what?' asked Gaston, who was no fool but who was not very quick on the uptake.

'Not much,' said Paulo, smiling. 'Just dig a tunnel. It starts in the room next to this; it'll go under the garden, then under the street and come out just beneath the bank's strong-room. If my calculations are right. If they're not, then maybe we'll find ourselves nearer the street side. If that happens, we go deeper and try again for under the very middle of the strong-room.' A short silence; and then he said, 'What do you say about it?'

'Just a second, man. Give me time to think. It's not quite the kind of job I was expecting.'

'Is it a big bank?' asked Gaston: this was not one of his brighter days. If Paulo had set all this going, and on such a scale, it was certainly not just for three tins of liquorice.

102

'You walk by the bank tomorrow, and you'll have something to say,' said Paulo, roaring with laughter. 'Get this: there are eight cashiers. That gives you some idea of what they must handle by way of notes in the course of a day.'

'Christ!' said Gaston, slapping his thigh. 'So it's a real bank! Well, I am pleased. For once I'll be in on a big-time job, in keeping with my title of top-line crook.'

Still with his broad grin of happiness, Paulo turned to me. 'You got nothing to say, Papillon?'

'I don't need any titles. I'd rather stay just plain mister with enough dough to carry out a job I have in mind. I don't need millions. I'll tell you what I think, Paulo: it's a prodigious job, and if it comes off—*when* it comes off, I should say, because you must always believe in a job—we're set up for the rest of our lives with enough for the rent and the telephone. But ... There are a good many buts to get round. I can ask questions, boss?'

'As many as you like, Papi. I meant to talk over every part of the job with you anyhow. For although I'm the top man, since it was me who worked it out, each one of us is risking his freedom and maybe his life. So ask all the questions you want.'

'Right. The first is this: from the room next door, where the shaft is, how far is it to the pavement on this side of the road?'

'Exactly eighteen yards.'

'Second, how far from the edge of the pavement to the bank?'

'Ten yards.'

'Third, inside the bank, have you worked out exactly where the door to the strong-room is?'

'Yes. I've hired a safe in the customers' room. It's just next to the bank's own strong-room and separated from it by an armoured door with two wheel-locks. There's only one way in, and that's from the customers' room. You go from there into the main strong-room. One day, after I'd been down there a good many times, I was waiting for them to give me the second key of my safe and I saw the armoured door open. As it swung round, I caught a glimpse of the strong-room and the big safes lined up all round it.'

'Could you get an idea of how thick the wall was between

the two rooms?'

'It was hard to tell on account of the steel casing.'

'How many steps down to the strong-room door?'

'Twelve.'

'So the strong-room floor is about ten foot below street-level. What's your plan?'

'We must try and hit just under the wall between the two rooms. We can guide ourselves by the bolts under the floor of the strong-room—the ones that hold the safes. That way we get into both rooms at once with just one hole.'

'Yes, but since the safes stand right against the wall, you're likely to come out under one of them.'

'I hadn't thought of that. If that happens, all you have to do is to make the hole larger towards the middle of the room.'

'I think two holes would be better: one in each room, and each in the middle, if possible.'

'I think so too, now,' said Auguste.

'OK, Papi. We aren't there yet, you know: but it's just as well to think of these things well ahead. What next?'

'How deep's the tunnel going to be?'

'Three yards.'

'How wide?'

'Two foot six. You have to be able to turn round inside.'

'Have you reckoned the height?'

'A yard.'

'The height and the width are fine; but I don't agree with the depth. Six feet of earth overhead isn't solid enough. If a heavy truck goes by, or a steam-roller, it might collapse.'

'I dare say, Papi; but there's no reason why trucks or heavy stuff should come along this street.'

'Sure. But it doesn't cost us anything to make a shaft four yards deep. You do that, and you've got three yards of earth between the top of the tunnel and the street. Any objection? The only extra work is digging the shaft a yard deeper. It doesn't change anything about the tunnel itself. Then four yards down, you're almost certain of reaching the bank at the level of its foundations or even lower. How many storeys in the building?'

'Ground-floor and one over it.'

'The foundations can't be very deep, then.'

'You're right, Papi. We'll go down to four yards.'

'How are you going to cope with the strong-room? What about the alarm system?'

'As I see it, Papi, that's the main snag. Still, looking at it logically, systems are set up *outside* strong-rooms. So long as you don't touch a door, either of the bank or of the strong-room, it oughtn't to go off. And there can hardly be one right inside the rooms. Still, I think we'd better not touch the safes either side of the door to the customers' room nor the ones by the armoured door.'

'I agree with you. There is one risk, of course, and that is when you get to work on the safes the vibration might set things off. But taking precautions like you said, we've a pretty good chance.'

'Is that the lot, Papi?'

'You've thought of lining the tunnel?'

'Yes. There's a work-bench and everything we need in the garage.'

'Fine. What about the earth?'

'First we'll spread it out right over the whole garden, and then we'll make raised beds, and lastly a platform all along the walls a yard wide and as high as it'll go without looking queer.'

'Are there any inquisitive bastards round here?'

'On the right everything's fine. A tiny little old couple who apologize every time they see me, because their dog shits just outside our garden gate. On the left, not so hot. There are two kids of eight and ten who never quit their swing for an instant, and the silly little buggers fly so high they can easily look over the wall and see what's happening in our place.'

'But however high they swing they can't see more than part of the garden—they can't possibly see the stretch against their own wall.'

'True enough, Papi. OK. Now suppose we've made the tunnel and we're under the strong-room. There we'll have to make a big hollow, a kind of room, so as to hold the tools and be able to work properly, perhaps two or three of us together. And then once we've hit the centre of the rooms we'll make a space under each, two yards square.'

'Right. And what are you going to cut the steel of the safes with?'

'That's something we'll have to talk over.'

'You start.'

'Well, the job could be done with oxyacetylene: that's something I understand—it's my trade. Or there's the electric welder, and I understand that too. But there's a snag—you need 220 volts and this villa only has 120. So I decided to let another guy in on the job. But I don't want him to work on the tunnel: he'll come a couple of days before we move in.'

'What'll he come with?'

'Here comes my big surprise. Thermite is what he'll come with. He's a positive artist in the thermite line. What do you say to that, everybody?'

'It'll make five shares instead of four,' said Gaston.

'There'll be more than you can carry, Gaston! five or four, it's all one.'

'As for me, I'm in favour of the thermite guy; because if there are a dozen safes to open, it goes quicker with thermite than with anything else at all.'

'Well then, there's the all-over plan. Are you all in agreement?'

Everyone said yes. Paulo said one other thing: neither Gaston nor I should show our noses out of doors during the daytime on any pretext whatsoever. We could go out at night from time to time, but as little as possible and then very carefully dressed, with a tie and all. Never all four of us together.

We went into the room next door: it had once been an office. They had already dug a hole a yard across and three deep, and I was admiring the sides, as straight as a wall, when the thought of ventilation came to me. 'And what have you laid on for air down there?'

'We'll pump it down with a little compressor and plastic tubing. If the one working begins to suffocate, someone'll hold the tube to his face while he gets on with the job. I bought a compressor in Caracas—it's almost silent.'

'What about an air-conditioner?'

'I thought of that, and I've got one in the garage; but it blows the fuses every time you switch it on.'

'Listen, Paulo. Nobody can tell what may happen to the thermite guy. If he doesn't turn up, the oxyacetylene is slow and the electric welder is the only thing for the job. We have

106

to install 220 volts. To make it look natural, you say you want a deep-freeze and air-conditioning, etc., and a little circular saw in the garage as well, because you like arsing around with wood. There shouldn't be any difficulty.'

'You're right. There's everything to be said for putting in 220 volts. Well now, that's enough about the job for the moment. Auguste's the spaghetti king; as soon as it's ready, let's eat.'

Dinner was very cheerful. After we'd exchanged a few unpleasant memories, we all agreed that when talking about the past we'd never bring up stories about inside—only about happy things like women, the sun, the sea, games in bed, etc. We laughed like a pack of kids. Nobody had a second's remorse at the idea of attacking society in the shape of the greatest symbol of its selfish power, *a bank*.

There was no difficulty about installing the 220-volt current, because the transformer was close to the house. No problem at all. To finish the shaft, we gave up the short-handled pick, which was too awkward in such a confined space. Instead we cut out blocks of earth with the circular saw, prising out each block with a handy trowel and putting it into a bucket.

It was a titanic job, but little by little it advanced. In the house you could scarcely make out the zim-zim of the circular saw at the bottom of the shaft, now four yards deep. From the garden you heard absolutely nothing; there was nothing to be feared.

The shaft was finished. Today we started the tunnel, and it was Paulo, compass in hand, who dug the first yard through the very wet clayey earth that stuck to everything. We no longer worked half naked but in dungarees that come down under your feet. So when you came out and took the dungarees off, there you were as clean as a butterfly coming out of its cocoon. Apart from your hands, of course.

According to our calculations, we still had thirty cubic yards of earth to bring out.

'This is genuine convict's work,' said Paulo, when he was feeling rough.

But gradually we pushed on. 'Like moles or badgers,' said Auguste.

'We'll get there, mates! And we'll roll in cash for the rest of our lives. Isn't that right, Papillon?'

'Sure, sure! And I'll have the prosecutor's tongue and I'll get my false witness and I'll spring such a firework-display at 36, quai des Orfèvres! On with the job, boys—this is no time to talk bullshit or play belote. Here, lower me down the hole. I'm going to work another couple of hours.'

'Calm down, Papi. We're all of us on edge. Sure, it's not going fast, but we're getting on, and the jackpot's only fifteen yards ahead of us. Besides, we all have our problems. Look at this letter my friend Santos sent me from Buenos Aires.'

Paulo brought a letter out of his pocket and read it aloud. ' "Dear Paulo: Do you believe in miracles, mate? It's more than six months now and not only haven't you come to see your two chicks but you haven't even sent them a line either, not so much as a postcard. You just don't understand the world. They don't know whether you're dead or alive or what part of the globe you're in. It's no fun for me to go and collect in these conditions. Every Monday the battle gets worse—Hey there! Where's our man?—What's he doing? He's on a job, I swear it!—Oh, he's a bleeding wonder with his big-time jobs! He'd do better to stay here with us: we're sick of going to bed with the pillow—This is the last time we ever hand over our takings, you get that? Either he comes or we divorce!

' "So come on now, Paulo: make an effort and send a line. Don't you believe in miracles? One of these days you're going to lose your two chicks, and then no more dough. Your buddy, Santos." Well, I do believe in miracles, and the miracle's right there, ahead of us. And you and I, mates, with our intelligence and our guts, we're the ones who'll work this miracle. Still, let's hope my lovebirds will hold out long enough; we need their dough to finish off the job.'

'We'll all give them a present,' said Auguste, beaming at the idea.

'That's my pigeon,' said Paulo. 'I'm the artist who's carrying out one of the most elegant jobs ever conceived by a crook; and without knowing it, they provide the financial backing. After all, that's a very great honour for them.'

A big laugh, drinks all round, and I agreed to take a hand at belote-bridge to please the others and to relax a trifle.

No difficulty about carrying the earth out into the garden; it was eighteen yards long and ten wide, and we spread the stuff out over the whole width except for the garage path. But seeing the earth we dug was not the same as the topsoil, we had a truck-load of good garden loam brought in from time to time. Everything was going fine.

How we dug, and how we heaved up the buckets full of earth! We laid a wooden floor in the tunnel, because the water seeping in turned it to mud; and the buckets slid easily on these planks when you heaved on the rope.

This is how we worked. There was one man at the far end of the tunnel: with the circular saw and a little pick he filled a bucket with the earth and stones; another stood at the bottom of the shaft and pulled the bucket back along the tunnel; and at the top there was a third who hauled it up and emptied it into a rubber-wheeled barrow. We broke through the wall that divided the house from the garage, so the fourth man only had to take the barrow, wheel it out through the garage and appear quite naturally in the garden.

We worked for hours on end, spurred on by a furious urge to win—an enormous pouring out of energy. The far end of the tunnel was very hard to bear in spite of the air-conditioner and the blast of pure air coming down the pipe we carried rolled round our neck so as to take a suck every now and then. I was covered with little red heat-pimples; there were great blotches of them all over my body. It looked like nettle-rash, and it itched horribly. The only one who did not have it was Paulo, because he just looked after the barrow and spread the earth in the garden. When we came out of that hell-hole it took over an hour to recover even after a shower; then, breathing normally and covered with Vaseline and cocoa-butter, at last we felt more or less all right. 'Anyhow, we were the ones who started this labour of Hercules. Nobody makes us do it. So help yourself, bear it, shut your trap and Heaven will help you.' That's what I said to myself and what I said two or three times a day to Auguste whenever he began to beef about having got himself mixed up with this kind of a job.

For slimming, there's nothing to touch digging a tunnel under a bank. It's amazing how supple you get, bending, crawling and turning yourself inside out. In that tunnel, we sweated as much as if we had been in a sauna. If you do exercises in every conceivable position there's no danger of being over-weight; and you work up splendid muscles too. So there was everything to be said for it; and what's more, there at the end of the tunnel a magnificent prize was waiting—other people's money.

Everything was fine, except for the garden. With the level rising and rising, the flowers did not seem to grow but rather to sink; and that did not look altogether natural. If we went on, soon nothing would be seen but their petals. We hit on a remedy: we stuffed the flowers into pots and kept them flush with the earth as we dug it out. With the pots well covered nothing could be seen, and the plants looked as if they were coming right out of the surface.

This party was beginning to last rather too long. If only we could take turns at having a rest ... But there was no question of that. We all four had to be there to keep things running smoothly. With only three of us it would never end: and we'd have to store the earth in the house for the time being, which would be dangerous.

The trap-door over the shaft fitted to within a sixteenth of an inch. When we were resting, we could leave the room door open—not a thing could be seen. As for the hole in the garage wall, we covered it on the garage side with a huge wooden panel with handyman's tools hung on it, and on the house side with an immense Spanish colonial chest. So when Paulo had to have someone come to the house, he could do so without worrying at all. Gaston and I just hid in our first-floor bed-room.

For two days there had been non-stop torrential rain and the tunnel was flooded. There was close on a foot of water, so I suggested that Paulo should go and buy a hand-pump and the necessary piping. An hour later it was set up. Pumping as hard as we could (another form of exercise) we sucked up the water and poured it down the drain. A long, tough day's work for nothing.

December was coming nearer. If we could be ready by the end of November with our little room dug out and shored up, under the bank, that would be perfect. And if the thermite specialist appeared, there was no doubt Father Christmas would cram our stockings to the brim. If he did not turn up, then we'd decided to work with the electric welder. We knew where to find a set complete with all its fittings. General Electric turned out some terrific models. We'd buy it in another town much safer.

The tunnel crept on. Yesterday, 24 November, we reached the foundations of the bank. Only three yards to go and the room to make, that is to say about twelve cubic yards of earth to bring out. We celebrated with champagne, genuine *brut* from France.

'It tastes a bit green,' said Auguste.

'All the better. That's a good sign—it's the colour of dollars!'

Paulo summed up what there was left to do. Six days for bringing out the earth if there's not too much of it. Three days for the casing. Total, nine. 'It's 24 November today, so that brings us to 4 December. That's the big day, and we'll be sitting pretty. The bank shuts at seven in the evening on Friday, so we go into action at eight. We'll have the whole of Friday night, all day Saturday, Saturday night and the whole of Sunday. If all goes well, we ought to be able to quit the hideout at two in the morning on Monday. That makes fifty-two hours of work altogether. Everyone agreed?'

'No, Paulo, I don't agree at all.'

'Why not, Papi?'

'The bank opens at seven for the cleaners. At that moment the whole thing may turn sour for some reason or another: at seven in the morning, that is to say not long after we've left. This is what I suggest: we fix things so as to have finished the job by six on Sunday evening. By the time we've shared it out, it'll be round about eight. If we leave at eight, that will give us at least eleven hours' start if the thing blows up at seven, and thirteen hours if it hangs fire till nine.'

In the end everybody fell in with my suggestion. We drank our champagne, and as we drank it we put on records Paulo had brought—Maurice Chevalier, Piaf, the Paris of the little dance-halls ... Sitting there with his glass, each of us dreamt

111

of the great day. It was there, so close you could almost touch it with your finger.

Your bill, Papi, the bill you've got there engraved on your heart, you'll be able to have it paid in Paris pretty soon. If all goes well and if luck's with me, I'll come back from France to El Callao and fetch Maria. My father: that would be for later on. Poor, wonderful Dad! Before I go and embrace him I'll first have to have buried the man I was, the man on the loose ... It won't take long once I've had my revenge and I'm fixed up properly.

It was two days after our champagne celebration that the thing happened, but we didn't know it until the day after that. We'd been to look at a General Electric welding and cutting set in a neighbouring town. My mate and I, dressed very smoothly, set out on foot and joined up with Paulo and Auguste in the car about a mile away.

'We've deserved this trip, boys. Breathe it in, breathe it in deep: this is the wonderful air of freedom!'

'You're dead right, Paulo; we've certainly deserved it. Don't drive too fast; let's have time to admire the country-side.'

We split up and stayed in two different hotels, spending three days in this charming port stuffed with ships and swarming with cheerful, motley crowds. Every evening we all met. 'No night-clubs, no brothels, no girls off the street; this is a business trip, mates,' said Paulo. He was right.

Paulo and I went to look at the set, taking our time about it. It was terrific but it had to be paid for in cash and we hadn't the necessary. Paulo wired Buenos Aires and fortunately he gave the address of the hotel in the port where he was staying. He decided to take us back to the villa and then return by himself a day or two later to get the dough and the welder. We drove back, thoroughly set up by these three days of holiday.

Paulo dropped Gaston and me at the corner of our little road as usual. The villa was a hundred yards away. We were walking calmly along, pleased with the idea of seeing our masterpiece of a tunnel again, when all at once I grabbed Gaston's arm and stopped him dead. What was going on out-side the villa? There were cops, a dozen people milling around, and then I saw two firemen heaving earth out of the middle of the road. I didn't have to be told what had happened. The tunnel had been discovered!

Gaston began to tremble as though he had a fever, and then with his teeth chattering he stammered out, 'They've staved in our lovely tunnel! Oh, the bloody shits! Such a lovely tunnel!'

At this very moment a type with a pig's face you could tell a mile off was watching us. But the entire situation seemed to me so comic I burst out in such cheerful, genuine, open laughter that if the pig had had some slight doubt about us, it passed off straight away. Taking Gaston's arm I said out loud in Spanish, 'What a bleeding great tunnel those robbers have dug!'

And slowly we turned our backs on our masterpiece and walked away from the road—no hurry and no hitch. But now we'd got to get moving quick. I said to Gaston, 'How much have you got on you? I've nearly six hundred dollars and fifteen hundred bolivars. What about you?'

'Two thousand dollars in my charger,' said Gaston.

'Gaston, the best thing to do is for us to part right here in the street.'

'What are you going to do, Papi?'

'I'll go back to the port we came from and try to get a boat for no matter where—straight for Venezuela, if possible.'

We could not embrace one another there in the open street, but Gaston's eyes were as wet with emotion as mine as we shook hands. There's nothing that makes such a bond between men as the experience of danger and adventure.

'Good luck, Gaston.'

'Same to you, Papi.'

Paulo and Auguste went home by different roads, the one to Paraguay, the other to Buenos Aires. Paulo's girls no longer had to go to bed with their pillows.

I managed to get on a boat for Puerto Rico: from there I took a plane to Colombia and then another boat to Venezuela.

It was only some months later that I learned what had happened. A water-main had burst in the big avenue the other side of the bank and the traffic was diverted into the streets running parallel. A huge truck loaded with iron girders took our road, passed over our tunnel and plunged its back wheels into it. Shrieks, amazement, police: they grasped the whole thing in a moment.

7: Carotte: the Pawn-Shop

In Caracas it was Christmas. Splendid illuminations in all the big streets, cheerfulness everywhere, carols sung with the Venezuelans' marvellous sense of rhythm. For my part I was rather depressed by our failure; but I wasn't bitter. We'd gambled and we'd lost; but I was still alive and freer than ever. And then after all, as Gaston said, it was a lovely tunnel!

Gradually the atmosphere of these songs about the Child of Bethlehem seeped into me; and easy in my mind, my heart peaceful again, I sent Maria a telegram: 'Maria, may this Christmas fill the house where you gave me so much joy.'

I spent Christmas Day at the hospital with Picolino, sitting on a bench in the little hospital garden. I'd bought two *hallacas*, specialities they make only at Christmas, and they were the most expensive and the best I could find. I also had two little flat bottles of delicious Chianti in my pockets.

It was a Christmas of two men brought back to life, a Christmas ablaze with the light of friendship, a Christmas of total freedom—freedom even to splash money about as I had done. The snowless Christmas of Caracas, filled with the flowers of this little hospital garden: a Christmas of hope for Picolino, whose tongue no longer hung out now he was being treated, who no longer dribbled. Yes, a miraculous Christmas for him, since he distinctly—and happily—pronounced the word 'Yes' when I asked him if the *hallacas* were good.

But Lord above, how hard it was to make a new life! I went through some very tough weeks; yet I did not lose heart. I had two things in me: first, an unshakeable confidence in the future; and second, an unquestionable love for life. Even when it would have been more sensible for me to be worrying, a mere trifle in the street would make me laugh; and if I met a friend I might spend the evening with him, having fun like a twenty-year-old.

Dr Bougrat gave me a little job in his beauty-products laboratory. I didn't earn much, but enough for me always to be well dressed and almost elegant. I left him for a Hungarian woman who had a little yoghourt factory in her villa, and it was there that I met a pilot whose name I won't mention because at this moment he's in command of an Air France jet. I'll call him Carotte.

He was working for the Hungarian woman too, and we made enough to be able to have some fun. Every evening we'd stroll around the Caracas bars; and we often had a drink or two at the Hotel Majestic, in the Silencio district. It has vanished now, but at that time it was the only modern place in the city.

It was then, during one of those periods when you think nothing fresh can possibly turn up, that a miracle took place. One day Carotte vanished: a little while later he came back again, from the United States, with a plane—a little observation plane with two seats, one behind the other. A wonderful gadget. I asked no questions about where it came from: the only question I did ask was what was he going to do with it?

He laughed and said, 'I don't know yet. But we might be partners.'

'To do what?'

'No matter what, so long as we have fun and make a little dough.'

'OK. We'll look around.'

The sweet Hungarian woman, who couldn't have had many illusions about how long our jobs would last, wished us good luck; and then there began an utterly demented and extraordinary month.

Hey, that huge great butterfly—the things we did with her!

Carotte was an ace. During the war he used to fly French agents out of England, land them by night in fields guarded by the Resistance, and fly others back to London. He often came down with no more guidance than torches held by the men who were waiting for him. He was completely reckless, and he dearly loved a laugh. Once, without a word of warning, he banked so hard, right over, that I almost lost my pants, and all this just to frighten a fat woman who was quietly doing her business in the garden, her bottom bare to the winds.

I so loved that machine and our darting about in the air that when we had no money to buy juice, I brought up the brilliant

116

idea of turning myself into a plane-borne pedlar.

This was the only time in my life that I ever conned anyone. He was called Coriat and he owned a men's and women's clothes shop, the Almacen Rio. He was in business with his brother. Coriat was a medium-sized Jew, dark, with an intelligent head; he spoke very good French. His shop was well run and he was making money hand over fist. On the women's side he had all the newest, most fashionable dresses imported from Paris. So I had the choice of a whole range of very saleable merchandise. I persuaded him to let me have a quantity of blouses, trousers and dresses, on sale or return; they were worth a good deal of money and the idea was we would sell them in the remoter parts of the country.

We set off, going wherever we liked and coming back whenever it suited us. But although we sold our stuff pretty well, we didn't make enough to cover our expenses, and Coriat's share vanished in petrol. There was nothing left for him.

Our best customers were the whores, and of course we never failed to go round the brothels. It was a great temptation for them when I spread our things out on the dining-room table— garish blouses, the latest in the way of trousers, silk scarves, flowered skirts—and started my patter. 'And listen to what I say, ladies. This is not a useless luxury as far as you are concerned. If I may say so, it is more like a business investment, because the more attractive you are, the more the customers come crowding in. As for those ladies who just think of saving, I can tell them for sure that it's a deeply unwise economy not to buy from me. Why? Because all the really well-dressed girls are going to be dangerous competitors.'

There were some brothel-keepers who did not much care for our doing business this way; it made them feel bad to see money going into pockets other than their own. A good many of them sold 'professional equipment' to their girls—on tick, sometimes—and the bastards wanted to monopolize the profit.

We often went to Puerto La Cruz, because there was a good airfield at Barcelona, a town a short way off. The best-run, classiest brothel there had sixty women in it, but the boss was an ugly great sod of a man, vulgar, pretentious and obstinate. He was a Panamanian. His wife was a Venezuelan, and she

117

was charming; but unfortunately he was the one who gave the orders, and there was no question of even opening our cases for a quick look, far less of spreading things out on a table.

One day he went too far. He fired a girl then and there for having bought a scarf I was wearing round my neck. The argument turned nasty and the cop on duty told us to get out and never come back.

'OK, you fat shit of a phony ponce,' said Carotte. 'We shan't come back by land but we shall by air. You can't stop us doing that.'

I didn't understand the threat until next morning, when we were taking off at dawn from Barcelona and he said to me on the intercom, 'We'll go and say hello to the Panamanian. Don't be frightened and hold on tight.'

'What are you going to do?'

He made no reply, but when we came within sight of the brothel he climbed a little and then he dived straight for it at full throttle, shot under the high-tension cable just outside and roared over the corrugated-iron roof, almost touching it. Several of the sheets of iron were loose, and they flew off, displaying the rooms, with their beds and the people in them. We banked, climbed and flew back a little higher to contemplate the sight. I've never seen anything more utterly comic than those naked women and their naked customers, hopping mad in their lidless boxes, shaking furious fists at the plane, which had cut them short either in their games or in an exhausted sleep. Carotte and I laughed until we were almost sick.

We never went back, because now there would not only be a furious boss, but a furious pack of women too. Later I did find one girl who had the good taste to laugh at the whole thing with us. Apparently it had wreaked havoc, and in his rage the fat sod of a Panamanian had insisted on fixing the corrugated sheets on all the women's rooms himself, with enormous bolts.

Carotte and I were both devoted to nature and we often flew off just to look for beautiful places. That was how we came to find one of the real wonders of the world—Los Roques, about a hundred and fifty miles out at sea, a scattering of more than three hundred and sixty little islands, close together in an oval and forming a huge lake in the ocean. A calm lake, because the islands made a barrier, and its pale-green water was so clear you could see the bottom sixty or seventy feet down. Unfortunately in those days there was no landing-strip, and we flew the whole length and breadth of the cluster ten times before pitching on another island some twenty miles to the west, called Las Aves.

Carotte really was a wonderful pilot. I've seen him land on a steeply sloping beach with one wing touching the sand and the other sweeping the sea. Isla de Aves means the island of birds. There were thousands and thousands of them, and they had grey feathers except when they were young: then they were white all over. They were called bobos, because they were rather slow-witted and perfectly trusting. It was an extraordinary feeling, being there, just the two of us, stark naked on an island as flat as a pancake and being surrounded by birds that landed on you or walked about without the least fear, never having seen a man. We spent hours browning in the sun, lying on the narrow beach that ran right round the island. We played with the birds, taking them in the hollow of our hands; some were deeply interested in our heads, and gently pecked our hair. We swam, sun-bathed again, and when we were hungry we could always find crayfish warming themselves on the surface. We'd catch a few with our hands and grill them on the spot. The only difficulty was finding enough dry stuff for the fire, because almost nothing grew on the island.

Sitting there on that untouched beach, eating those succulent crayfish and drinking a full-bodied white wine—we always had a few bottles on board—with the sea, the sky and the birds all round us and nothing else at all, gave us such a feeling of paradise that we didn't have to speak to be wholly in touch with one another.

And when we took off again, before nightfall, our hearts were filled with sun and happiness and zest for life; we did not give a damn for anything, not even for finding the money for the petrol for the trip—a trip whose only reason was to let us live in a beautiful and unexpected world.

At Las Aves we discovered a huge sea-cave: at low tide its mouth was above the surface and light and air came in. I had a passion for this splendid grotto; you could swim into it, and inside the water was clear and shallow—not more than three feet deep. When you stood up in the middle and looked around, the roof and the walls seemed to be covered with cicadas. They weren't cicadas, of course, but thousands of little crayfish clinging to the rock. We sometimes stayed there a long while, never disturbing them. The only time we interfered was when a big octopus, a great lover of baby crayfish, put out an arm to gather a few. We jumped on him right away and turned him inside-out. There he could lie and rot, if he had the time, because he was an unusual treat for the crabs.

We often went to Las Aves and spent the night there. We each had a big electric torch and we gathered crayfish, each weighing about two and a half pounds, until we had filled two sacks with them. We dumped all the finery we were meant to be selling at Carlotta, the airfield in the middle of Caracas, and that meant we could bring back close on half a ton of crayfish. It was insane to load the plane like that, but it was all part of the fun. We could just about get off the ground, and as for gaining height, the stars were in no danger! We would labour up the twelve miles of valley from the coast to Caracas, just skimming the housetops; and there we would sell our crayfish at the ridiculous price of two bolivars fifty apiece. At least it paid for the petrol and kept us going. But when you go after crayfish with your hands you often get hurt, and sometimes we'd come back without any. It didn't matter; we never gave a damn—we were living to the full.

One day as we were on our way to Puerto La Cruz and not very far from it, Carotte said to me over the intercom, 'Papi, we're short of juice. I'm going to put her down on the San Tomé oil-company's field.' We flew over the strip to show we wanted to come down on their private landing-place, and the sods instantly ran a tanker full of petrol or water, God knows which, right out into the middle of the strip. Carotte had nerves of steel, and although I told him again and again I couldn't see where we could possibly touch down, he just said, 'Hold on, Papi,' and side-slipped towards a fairly wide road. He landed without bumping too much, but the speed carried him along towards a turning, and round this turning came a trailer filled with bullocks, tearing along as fast as it could go.

The shriek of the brakes must have drowned our shrieks of horror, because if the driver hadn't lost control and run his trailer into the ditch we should certainly have been done for. We jumped out of the plane and Carotte hushed the swearing driver—he was an Italian. 'Help us push the plane and you can beef later.' The Italian was still trembling all over and as white as a sheet. We helped him catch his beasts—they had escaped when the trailer came to pieces.

This prodigious landing made such a stir that the government bought Carotte's plane and made him a civilian instructor at the Carlotta camp.

My life as an airman was over. Sad. I'd had a few hours of lessons and I was coming on well. Never mind. The only one who came out of this business a loser was Coriat. The extraordinary thing was he never sued me. Some years later I paid him back every penny; and here I should like to thank him for the generosity of his attitude.

But at that particular moment, not only had I lost the plane and not only had my job with the Hungarian woman been taken by someone else but I also had to avoid the central parts of Caracas, because Coriat's shop was there and I had no wish to bump into him. So once more the position was far from brilliant. But I didn't care: those few weeks with Carotte had been too marvellous for me to regret anything at all.

Carotte and I often saw one another after that: we used to meet in a quiet little joint run by an old Frenchman who had retired from the Compagnie Transatlantique. One night when we were playing dominoes in a corner with a Spanish republican and an ex-lag, who now made a peaceful living by selling scent on tick, two men wearing sunglasses came in—we didn't know them—and asked if it was true that a Frenchman often came here, a pilot.

Carotte stood up and said, 'That's me.'

I examined these unknown types from head to foot and straight away, in spite of his dark glasses, I recognized one of them. I felt a sudden wave of emotion. I went up to him. Before I could speak he knew me. 'Papi!'

It was Big Léon, one of my best friends in penal. A tall guy with a thin face; a real man, open-hearted. This was not the moment to seem too friendly and he just introduced me to his side-kick Pedro the Chilean and said no more. We had a drink in a corner and Léon said he was looking for a light plane with a pilot and he had been told about this Frenchman.

'The pilot's here,' said Carotte, 'and I'm him. But the plane is not. It belongs to other people now.'

'That's sad,' said Léon laconically.

Carotte returned to his game of dominoes: someone else took my place. Pedro the Chilean went and stood at the bar, so we could talk quietly.

'Well, Papi?'

'Well, Léon?'

'The last time we met was more than ten years ago.'

'Yes. You were coming out of solitary just as I was going in. How are you doing, Léon?'

'Not bad, not bad at all. And you, Papi?'

Since it was Léon, I felt I could talk. 'I'll tell you straight, Léon: I'm more or less in the shit. It's not so easy to climb up the hill. It's all very well coming out of stir stuffed with the best intentions: life's so tough when you have no trade that all you think of is going on the loose again. Léon, you're older than me and you aren't the ordinary kind of lag. I can tell *you* what's on my mind. Speaking dead serious and dead straight, as far as I'm concerned I owe this country everything. I came back to life here and I've promised myself to respect this great community—to do the least possible number of things that could be criticized. But it's not easy. Yet I'm perfectly certain that even with my love for pulling things off I could set myself up here, starting from nothing and going straight, if only I hadn't a long bill to present to some people in Paris, *and I can't wait, in case those buggers should die before I get there.*

'When I see the young people of this country, utterly care-free and full of the joy of life, then in spite of myself I look back at all those years that were stolen from me, the best years of my life. And I see the black holes of the Réclusion, and the three years of waiting before the trial and after it, and that stinking penal where I was treated far worse than a mad dog. And then for hours, sometimes for whole days on end, I walk about the streets of Caracas turning it all over in my mind. I don't thank fate for having brought me here: no, that's not what goes on in my mind at all. I feel I'm back in those places where I was buried alive; I see them, I keep seeing them, and I go back to my *one, two, three, four, five, turn,* just as I did when I was buried there and walked to and fro like a bear in a cage. It's beyond my control; it's a real obsession. I can't bear the idea that those who unjustly put me through that hell should die in peace, without having paid.

'So when I'm walking along the streets like that, I don't look around like an ordinary man. Every jeweller's shop, every place that is sure to hold the money I need—I can't help casing it and working out just how I could get my hands on everything it contains. It's not because I don't feel like it that I haven't yet pulled anything off; there are jobs here so dead easy they almost cry out to be done.

'Up until now I've managed to keep a hold on myself; I've done nothing serious against this country that trusts me. That would be vile, as odious as raping the daughters of a house that had taken you in. But I'm afraid, yes I'm afraid of myself: I'm afraid one day I may not be able to resist the temptation of pulling off a big job. Because I'll never, never be able to scrape together the huge sum I need for my revenge, not by working honestly. Between you and me, Léon, I'm at the end of my tether.'

Big Léon listened to me in silence, gazing at me attentively. We had a last drink, hardly exchanging another word. He got up and gave me a time to come and have lunch with him and Pedro the Chilean the next day.

We met in a quiet restaurant with an arbour. The sun was shining.

'I've been thinking about what you said to me, Papi. So listen, and I'll tell you why we're in Caracas.'

They were only passing through, on their way to another South American country. There they were going to pay serious attention to a pawnshop, where, according to their own inquiries and information supplied by one of the chief employees, there was enough jewellery for each of them to come out with a very elegant fortune, once the jewels were turned into dollars. That was why they were looking for Carotte. They had meant to make him a proposition for his plane and himself; but now there was no point in talking about it.

'You can come in with us, if you like, Papi,' ended Léon.

'I've no passport and nothing much in the way of savings either.'

'We'll look after the passport. Isn't that right, Pedro?'

'It's just as if you had it already,' said Pedro. 'In a phony name: that way you'll officially neither have gone out of Venezuela nor come back.'

'What'll it cost, roughly?'

'Round about a thousand dollars. You got that much dough?'

'Yes.'

'Well then, seeing how you're placed, you shouldn't hesitate.'

A fortnight later there I was some miles from a South American capital, having hired a car the day after the job, busy burying a biscuit tin with my share of the jewels in it.

The carefully programmed operation had been simple. We went in through a tie shop next door to the pawnbroker's. Léon and Pedro had been there to buy ties several times so as to get a good look at the lock and fix the exact spot where they would make the hole in the wall. There were no safes, only cupboards armoured all round. We went in at ten p.m. on Saturday and we came out at eleven on Sunday night.

A smooth, well-run job. So there I was, a dozen miles from the town, burying my tin at the foot of a huge tree. I knew I should find the place again without any difficulty, because apart from the mark I had cut with my knife, the tree was easy to spot: the forest began just after a bridge, and the first tree of this forest, right by the road, was mine. Driving back, I threw the pick away some five miles along the road.

That evening we all met in a classy restaurant. We walked in separately and behaved as if we met by chance at the bar and then decided to have dinner together. Each one of us had hidden his share, Léon with a friend and Pedro in the forest, like me.

'It's much better for each to have his own private hole,' said Léon. 'That way, no one of us knows what the others have done with theirs. It's a precaution they often take in South America, because if the pigs pull you in, what they put you through is no kind of fun at all. Then if a poor guy starts to talk, why, he can only do the Judas on himself. So that's sewn up: tell me, Papi, are you satisfied with the share-out?'

'I think our rough estimate of each piece was dead right. Everything's fine: I've not a word to say against it.'

So all was satisfactory and everyone was pleased.

'Hands up!'

'Why, what the hell?' cried Léon. 'Are you crazy?'

No time for further observations: in a flash we were clubbed, handcuffed and wheeled off to the police headquarters. We hadn't even finished the oysters.

In that country, the pigs do not coddle you at all: the party went on all night. Eight hours at the very least. First questions: 'Do you like ties?'

'You go and bugger yourself.'

And so it went. By five in the morning we were nothing but lumps of bruised flesh. The pigs were furious at not having been able to get anything out of us: they frothed with rage. 'OK. Since you're all in a sweat and your temperature's too high, we'll cool you.' We could scarcely stand, but they tossed us into a black maria and a quarter of an hour later there we were in front of a huge building. The pigs went in and then we saw workmen coming out: the pigs must have asked them to leave. Then it was our turn to go in, each propped up by two pigs and almost dragged along.

An enormous corridor; steel doors right and left, each with a kind of clock over it: a clock with only one hand. Thermometers. Straight away I grasped that we were in the corridor of the deep-freeze of a big slaughter-house. We stopped at a place where there were several tables standing in the corner. 'Well, now,' said the chief pig. 'I'll give you one last chance to think it over. These are deep-freezers for meat. You understand what that means? So for the last time, where have you put the jewels and the other things?'

'We know nothing about any jewels nor about any ties,' said Léon.

'OK, lawyer. You can go first.'

The cops unbolted a door and opened it wide. A kind of icy fog came out and wafted down the corridor. Having taken off Léon's shoes and socks they shoved him in.

'Shut it quick,' said the chief, 'or we'll be frozen too.'

'Now, Chilean. Are you going to talk, yes or no?'

'I've nothing to talk about.'

They opened another door and pushed the Chilean in.

'You're the youngest, Italian [my passport had an Italian identity]. Take a good look at these thermometers. They show minus forty. That means that if you don't talk and we stuff you in there in a sweat, after the party you've been through, it's ten to one you'll catch pneumonia and die in hospital in less than forty-eight hours. I'm giving you one last chance, you see: did you rob the pawnbroker's by going through the tie shop, yes or no?'

'I've nothing to do with those men. I only knew one of them, long ago, and I just met them by chance in the restaurant. Ask the waiters and barmen. I don't know whether they had anything to do with this job, but I'm dead certain I didn't.'

'Well, Macaroni, you can perish too. I'm sorry to think of you dying at your age; but it's your own fault. You asked for it.'

The door opened. They shot me into the darkness, and hitting my head on an iron-hard side of beef hanging from a hook I fell flat on the floor: it was covered with ice an dhoar-frost. Immediately I felt the appalling cold seize upon my flesh, pierce right through and reach my bones. With a terrible effort I got to my knees, then, clinging to a side of beef, I stood upright. Every movement hurt, after the beating they had given us, but in spite of that I thumped my arms and rubbed my neck, cheeks, nose and eyes. I tried warming my hands under my armpits. All I had on was my trousers and a torn shirt. They had taken my shoes and socks too, and the soles of my feet hurt terribly as they stuck to the ice; and I felt my toes beginning to freeze.

I said to myself, 'This can't go on for more than ten minutes —a quarter of an hour at the most. Otherwise I'll be like one of these sides of beef: a lump of deep-frozen meat. No, no, it's not possible. They can't do that to us! Surely they can't freeze us alive? Stick it, Papi. A few minutes more and the door will open. That icy corridor will seem as warm as toast.' My arms were not working any more; I could no longer close

126

my hands nor move my fingers; my feet were sticking to the ice and I no longer had the strength to pull them away. I felt I was going to faint and in the space of a few seconds I saw my father's face, then the prosecutor's floating over it, but that was not so clear, because it merged with the faces of the cops. Three faces in one. 'How strange,' I thought. 'They are all alike, and they are laughing because they've won.' Then I passed out.

What was happening? Where was I? As I opened my eyes there was a man's face leaning over me, a handsome face. I could not speak, because my mouth was still frozen stiff with cold, but inside my head I asked myself what I was doing here, stretched out on a table.

Big, powerful, efficient hands rubbed me all over with warm grease and gradually I felt heat and suppleness coming back. The chief cop was watching, two or three yards away. He looked hot and bothered. Several times they opened my mouth to pour a drop of spirits into it. Once they poured too much; I choked and shot it out.

'There we are,' said the masseur. 'He's saved.'

They went on rubbing me for at least half an hour. I felt that I could talk if I wanted to, but I preferred keeping my mouth shut. I realized that over there on the right there was another body lying on a table the same height as mine. He was naked too, and they were rubbing and massaging him. Who was it? Léon or the Chilean? There had been three of us: but with me on this table and the guy on the other, that only made two. Where was the third? The other tables were empty.

Helped by the masseur I managed to sit up, and I saw who the other one was. Pedro the Chilean. They dressed us and put us into those padded overalls specially made for men who work inside deep-freezes.

The chief pig returned to the attack. 'Can you speak, Chilean?'

'Yes.'

'Where are the jewels?'

'I don't know anything.'

'And what about you, Spaghetti?'

'I wasn't with those men.'

'OK.'

127

I slipped off the table. I could only just stand, but once I was up I felt a healthy burning on the soles of my feet, and that pleased me although it hurt; and I felt the blood flowing inside me, racing round my whole body with such strength that it thumped in the farthest veins and arteries.

I thought that for one day I had gone as far in horror as possible: but I had got it wrong, quite wrong.

They put Pedro and me side by side, and the chief, who had now recovered his self-assurance, called out, 'Take off their overalls.'

They took them off, and there I was, naked to the waist: straight away I started shivering with cold again.

'And now take a good look at this, *hombres*.'

From under a table they dragged a kind of rigid parcel and stood it up on end in front of us. It was a frozen corpse, as stiff as a board. Its eyes were wide open and fixed, like two marbles: it was hideous to see, terrifying. Big Léon! They had frozen him alive!

'Take a good look, *hombres*,' said the chief again. 'Your accomplice wouldn't talk: so all right, we went all the way with him. Now it's your turn, if you're as stubborn as he was. I've been given orders to be merciless, because this job of yours is much too serious. The pawnshop is run by the state, and there's an ugly rumour in the town—people think it's a put-up job worked by some of the officials. So either you talk, or in half an hour you'll be like your mate here.'

My wits had not yet come back, and the sight so churned me up that for three long seconds I felt like talking. The only thing that prevented me was that I didn't know where the other hiding-places were. They'd never believe me and I'd be in worse danger than ever.

To my utter amazement I heard a very collected voice, Pedro's voice, say, 'Come on now; you can't frighten us with that stuff. Why, of course it was an accident—you never meant to freeze him; it was an error of judgement, that's all; but you don't want another error with us. One you can get away with; but three, three foreigners turned into blocks of ice, that mounts up. And I can't see you giving watertight explanations to two different embassies. One, OK. Three, it's too much.'

128

I could not help admiring Pedro's steely nerve. Very calmly the pig looked at the Chilean, not speaking. Then after a little pause, 'You're a crook, and that's for sure; but I have to admit that you've also got guts.' Turning to the others he said, 'Find them each a shirt and take them back to the prison: the judge will look after them. With brutes like this there's no point in going on with the party—it's a waste of time.' He turned his back and walked off.

A month later they let me out. The tie merchant admitted I had never been to his shop, which was true: the barmen stated that I had had two whiskies by myself, that I had already booked a table for one before the other two appeared, and that we had seemed very surprised to meet one another in this town. Still, they ordered me to leave the country in five days, because they were afraid that as Léon's so-called countryman (Léon also had an Italian passport) I would go and tell the consulate what had happened.

During the inquiries, we had been brought face to face with a guy I did not know but Pedro did—the pawnshop employee who had put him on to the job. The very evening we shared out, this silly bastard presented a girl from an all-night bar with a splendid antique ring. The pigs were tipped off, and they had no difficulty in making him talk: that was why Big Léon and Pedro were identified so quickly. Pedro the Chilean stayed there, stuck fast in this business.

I took the plane with five hundred dollars in my pocket. I never went near my hiding-place: it was too risky. I took stock, to see how things stood after the hideous nightmare I had just been through: the papers reckoned the pawnshop job at two hundred thousand dollars; even if they had exaggerated and doubled it, that still left a hundred thousand: so in my hole I had about thirty thousand. Since the value had been reckoned according to the amount lent on the jewels, that is to say half their real value, and if I sold them without going through a receiver, then by my calculations I should be the owner of more than sixty thousand dollars! So I had what I needed for my revenge, so long as I did not break into it for living. This money was sacred; it was for a sacred purpose,

129

and I must never use it for anything else *upon any pretext whatsoever*.

In spite of the horrible way it ended for my friend Léon, this job had been a triumph for me. Unless indeed I was forced to help the Chilean; but in a few months he was sure to send a trusted friend to collect his nest-egg for paying his lawyer and maybe for organizing a break. Anyhow, that was our agreement—each with his own hiding-place so that no one of us should be connected with the fate of the others. I hadn't been in favour of that method, but it was the customary way of working in the South American underworld—once the job was done, then each for himself and God for all.

And God for all … If it was really Him that had saved me, then He had been more than noble; He had been magnanimous. And yet God could not possibly have been the artisan of my revenge! He did not want me to take it, and that I knew. I remembered that day in El Dorado, the day before I was to be let out for good. I had wanted to thank the God of the Catholics, and in my emotion I had said to Him, 'What can I do to prove that I am sincerely grateful for your kindness?' And it seemed to me that I heard the words, just as though a voice were speaking to me, 'Give up your revenge.'

And I'd said no; anything else, but not that. So it could not have been God who took care of me in this business. Impossible. I'd had luck, that was all, the luck of the devil. The good Lord above had nothing to do with shit of that kind.

But the result—oh the result was there all right, buried at the foot of an ancient tree. It was a huge weight off my mind, knowing I possessed what I needed to carry out the plan I had been feeding my heart with these last thirteen years.

How I hoped the war had spared the sods who sent me down! Now all I had to do, while I waited for my D-day, was to look for a job and live quietly until I could go and unbury my treasure.

The plane was flying at a great height in a brilliant sky, way above a carpet of snow-white clouds. It was purity up here, and I thought of my people, my father, my mother, my family and of my childhood bathed in light. Beneath that white cumulus there were dirty clouds, a greyish, unclean rain—a fine image of the earthly world: that desire for power, that desire to prove to others that you are better than them, that dry, heartless desire you see in the kind of people who do not give a damn if they destroy a human being so long as by doing so something is gained or something is justified.

CARACAS again. It was with real pleasure that I walked the streets of this great living city once more.

I had been free twenty months now, and yet still I had not become a member of this community. It was all very well to say 'All you have to do is get a job': but, besides not being able to find any suitable work, I had difficulty in speaking Spanish, and many doors were closed to me because of this. So I bought a grammar, shut myself in my room and determined to spend however many hours it needed to speak Spanish. I grew angrier and angrier; I could not manage to hit the pronunciation, and after a few days I flung the book to the other end of the room and went back to the streets and the cafés, looking for someone I knew who could find me something to do.

More and more Frenchmen were coming over from Europe, sickened by its wars and political upheavals. Some were on the run from an arbitrary justice that varied according to the political climate of the moment; others were looking for peace and quiet—a beach where they could breathe without someone coming up every other moment to feel their pulse and see what rhythm it was beating at.

These people were not like Frenchmen; and yet they were French. These honest citizens had nothing in common with Papa Charrière or any of the people I had known in my childhood. When I was with them, I found they had ideas so different and so twisted in comparison with those of my young days that I was quite at sea. Often I'd say to them, 'I believe that maybe you shouldn't forget the past, but that you should stop talking about it. Is it possible that even now after the war is over there are supporters of Nazism among you? I'll tell you something: when you talk about the Jews, it's like seeing one race spew out hatred against another race.

'You're living in Venezuela, in the midst of its people, and yet you aren't capable of grasping their wonderful philosophy. Here there's no discrimination, either racial or religious. If anyone should be infected with the virus of revenge against the privileged classes the poorest class should be because of their wretched conditions of life. Well now, *that virus doesn't even exist in this country*.

'You aren't even capable of settling down to living for the sake of living. Is life made up of nothing more than never-ending battles between men who don't share the same ideology?

'Please, just you shut up. Don't come here as Europeans filled with notions of the superiority of their race, like explorers. True enough, you have had more intellectual training than the majority of the people here, but what of it? What good is it to you, since you're a more stupid bunch of sods than they are? As far as you're concerned education doesn't mean intelligence, generosity, goodness and understanding, but only learning things from books. If your hearts stay dry, selfish, rancorous and fossilized, what you've learnt doesn't mean a thing.

'God made the sun, the sea, the vast prairies and the bush, but did He make them just for you?

'Do you think you're a race pre-ordained to organize the world? When I look at you and listen to you, it occurs to me that a world run by poor sods like you will mean nothing but wars and revolutions. Because although you say you long for peace and quiet, you only long for it if it agrees with your point of view.'

Every one of them had his list of people to be shot, proscribed or shoved into gaol; and although it upset me, I couldn't help laughing when I heard these people, sitting in a café or the lounge of some third-rate hotel, criticizing everything and coming to the conclusion that they were the only ones who could really run the world.

And I was afraid, yes I was afraid, because I had a very real feeling of the danger that these newcomers brought with them—the virus of the old world's fossilized ideological passions.

1947. I'd come to know an ex-con by the name of Pierre-René Deloffre: he had only one object of worship, and that was General Angarita Medina, the former president of Venezuela, who had been overthrown by the last military *coup d'état*, in 1945. Deloffre was a high-powered character. Very active, but

133

open-hearted and enthusiastic. He brought all his passion to bear to persuade me that the people who had profited by this *coup d'état* weren't worth Medina's bootlaces. To tell the truth, he did not convince me; but since I was in a tricky position I was not going to cross him.

He found me a job through a financier, a truly remarkable guy called Armando. He came from a powerful Venezuelan family; he was noble-minded, generous, intelligent, well-educated, witty and unusually brave. There was only one drawback—he was burdened with a stupid brother, Clemente. Some of this brother's recent capers have made it clear to me that he hasn't changed in these last twenty-five years. Deloffre introduced me to the financier with no beating about the bush: 'My friend Papillon, who escaped from the French penal settlement. Papillon, this is the man I was telling you about.'

Armando adopted me right away, and with the directness of a real nobleman he asked me whether I was in need of money.

'No, Monsieur Armando; I'm in need of a job.'

I wanted to see how the land lay first; it was better to take one's time. What's more, I was not really short of cash for the moment.

'Come and see me at nine tomorrow.'

The next day he took me to a garage, the Franco-Venezuelan it was called, and there he introduced me to his associates, three young men full of life, ready to break into a furious gallop at the drop of a hat. Two of them were married. One to Simone, a magnificent Parisienne of twenty-five; the other to Dédée, a twenty-year-old blue-eyed girl from Brittany, as delicate as a violet and the mother of a little boy called Cricri.

They were good-looking, open types, frank and unreserved. They welcomed me with open arms, as though they'd known me for ever. Straight away they fixed me up a bed in a corner of the big garage, more or less curtained off and close to the shower. They were my first real family for seventeen years. This team of young people liked, cherished and respected me; and it made me all the happier because although I was a few years older I had just as much zest for life, just as much joy in living without rules and without limits.

134

I asked no questions—I didn't really have to—but I soon saw that not one of them was a genuine mechanic. They had a faint, a very faint notion of what a motor was: but even less than a notion as far as the motors of American cars were concerned, and they were the main or indeed the only customers. One of them was a turner, and that explained the presence of a lathe in the garage—they said it was for correcting pistons. Pretty soon I found that what the machine was really used for was changing gas-bottles so they would take a detonator and a Bickford fuse.

For the swarm of newly-arrived Frenchmen, the Franco-Venezuelan garage repaired their cars, more or less; but for the Venezuelan financier it fixed bombs for a *coup d'état*, a *golpe*. I didn't altogether care for this.

'Hell,' I said. 'Who's it in favour of and who's it against? Tell me about it.' It was evening; we were sitting there under the lamp and I was questioning the three Frenchmen—their wives and the kid had gone to bed.

'That's none of our business. We just fix the pots Armando asks us for. And that's fine by us, mate.'

'Fine for you, maybe. But I have to know.'

'Why? You earn a fat living and you have fun, don't you?'

'Sure. As far as fun goes, we have fun. But I'm not like you. They've given me asylum in this country: they trust me and they let me walk about as free as air.'

Hearing me talk like this in my position struck them as very odd. Because they knew what I had in the back of my head; they knew all about my obsession—I'd told them. But one thing I hadn't told them was about the pawnshop job. So they said to me, 'If this business comes off, you can make the money you need to carry out what you have in mind. And of course we don't intend to spend the rest of our lives in this garage. Certainly we have fun, but it brings in nothing like the solid cash we'd dreamed of when we came to South America.'

'And what about your wives and the kid?'

'The women know all about it. A month before the balloon goes up, they leave for Bogota.'

'They know all about it, then. Just as I thought: so they aren't too surprised at some of the things that go on.'

That same evening I saw Deloffre and Armando and I had a long talk with them. Armando said to me, 'In this country of ours, it's Bétancourt and Gallegos who run everything, under the cover of the phony A.D. [*Acción Democrática*]. The power was put into their hands by simple-minded soldiers who no longer really knew why they overthrew Medina—he was a soldier too, and he was more liberal and far more human than the civilians. I see the former Medina officials being persecuted, and there's nothing I can say; and I try to understand how it comes about that men who carried out a revolution with the slogans of "social justice and respect for all without the least exception" can become worse than their predecessors once they're in power. That's why I want to help bring Medina back.'

'Fine, Armando. I quite see that what you want above all is to stop the party now in power going on with their persecution. And as for you, Deloffre, you've got just one God, and that's Medina, your protector and your friend. But you listen to me, now: the people who let me, Papillon, out of El Dorado were this very party now in power. Straight after the revolution, the minute the new chief arrived he stopped the savage reign of terror in the settlement, stopped it dead. He's still there, I believe—Don Julio Ramos, a lawyer and a distinguished writer, the guy who let me out. And you want me to join in a coup against those people? No: let me go. You know you can rely on my keeping my mouth shut.'

Armando knew the tough spot I was in, and like a real gentleman he said to me, 'Enrique, you don't make the bombs; you don't work at the lathe. All you do is look after the cars and pass the tools when the panel-beater asks for them. So stay a little longer. I ask it as a favour; and if we make a move I promise you'll know a month ahead for sure.'

So I stayed there with those three young guys: they are still alive and they would be easily recognizable, so I will use the initials P.I., B.L. and J.G. instead of their names. We made up a splendid team and we were always together, living it up at such a pitch that the French of Caracas called us the three musketeers—as everybody knows, there were four of them. Those few months were the finest, the happiest and the live-

136

liest I ever spent in Caracas.

Life was one long laugh. On Saturdays we kept some elegant car belonging to a customer for our own use, saying it wasn't ready yet, and we drove down to one of the gorgeous beaches lined with flowers and coconut-palms to swim and have fun all day long. Sometimes, of course, we would meet the owner, far from pleased at seeing the car he thought was in the garage filled with all these people. Then gently, very gently, we would explain that we were doing this for his sake—that we could not bear the idea of giving him back a car not in perfect condition, and so it had to be tried out. It always worked, and no doubt the ravishing smiles of the girls helped a great deal.

On the other hand, we did have some bloody awkward situations. The Swiss ambassador's petrol-tank leaked: he brought the car in for us to solder the joint. I carefully emptied the tank with a rubber pipe, sucking out the very last drop. But apparently that wasn't enough, because as soon as the flame of the blowpipe touched it, the cow of a tank blew up, setting fire to the car and roasting it to a frazzle. While the other guy and I groped about, covered with black oil and smoke and just beginning to grasp that we had escaped from death, I heard B.L.'s calm voice saying, 'Don't you think we ought to tell our partners about this little mishap?'

He phoned the brothers, and the half-wit Clemente answered. 'Clemente, can you give me the number of the garage's insurance?'

'...'

'What for? Oh yes, I was forgetting. Because the Swiss ambassador's car caught fire. It's just a heap of cinders now.'

I don't have to tell you that five minutes later Clemente appeared at a brisk run, waving his arms about and hopping mad because in fact the garage was not covered in any way at all. It took three stiff whiskies and all the charm of Simone's amply-displayed legs to quieten him down. Armando only turned up the following day; he was perfectly calm, and this was his charming way of taking it—'Things happen only to people who work. Anyhow, don't let's talk about it any more: I've fixed everything with the ambassador.'

The ambassador got another car, but somehow we lost his custom.

From time to time, while we were living this zestful life, I thought about my little treasure lying there hidden at the foot of a tree in a republic well known for its frozen meat. And I put money aside for the fare there and back when the time came to go and fetch it. The knowledge that I had enough, or close on enough, to satisfy my revenge had completely transformed me. I no longer worried about making money, and I lived without care or worry of any kind; it was because of this that I could plunge so whole-heartedly into our musketeering life—plunge into it so deep that one Sunday afternoon at three o'clock there we were, all of us, bathing in a fountain in one of the Caracas squares with nothing but our drawers on. This time at least, Clemente rose to the occasion and had his brother's partners released from the police-station where they had been shut up for indecent exposure. By now a good many months had gone by, and at last it seemed to me safe to go and fetch my treasure.

So fare you well, buddies, and thanks for all your kindness: and there I was on my way to the airport. I got there at six in the morning; on arrival, I hired a car, and at nine I reached the spot.

I crossed the bridge. Christ above, what had happened? Had I gone mad, or was it a mirage? I stared around, but my tree was not there. And not only my tree but hundreds of others. The road had been made much wider, and the bridge and the stretch leading up to it had been entirely changed. Working it out from the bridge, I managed to more or less pinpoint the place where my tree and my wealth must have been. I was flabbergasted. Not a trace!

A kind of madness came over me, a stupid fury. I ground my heels into the asphalt, just as though it could feel anything. I was filled with an enormous overflowing rage and I looked around for something to destroy: all I could see was the white lines painted on the road—I kicked them, as if knocking off little bits of paint could destroy the road.

I went back to the bridge. The approach road the other side had not been altered, and judging from that I reckoned they must have shifted the earth to a depth of more than twelve feet. And since my loot had not been buried deeper than a yard, it can't have lasted long, poor thing.

I leant on the parapet and for a while I watched the water flow by. Gradually I calmed down, but still the thoughts whirled about inside my head. Was I always going to come unstuck like this? Should I give up trying to pull things off? What was I going to do now? My knees sagged. But then I got a hold on myself and I said, 'How many times did you fail before you brought off your break? Seven or eight times, right? Well, it's the same thing in life. You lose one banco, you go and win another. That's life, when you really love it.'

I didn't stay long in this country that felt itself called upon to change its roads so fast. It made me sick to think that a civilized nation didn't even respect ancient trees. And why, I ask you, why widen a road that was quite broad enough for all the traffic it had to carry?

In the plane taking me back to Caracas, I laughed to think that men can suppose they are the masters of their fate, that they imagine they can build the future and foresee what they'll be doing the next year or the year after. All so much balls, Papi! The brightest calculator, the cleverest imaginable organizer of his life is no more than a toy before fate. Only the present is certain: all the rest is something we know nothing about—something that goes by the name of luck, misfortune, destiny or indeed the mysterious and incomprehensible hand of God.

Only one thing really matters in life and that is never to admit you're beaten and to start up again after every flop. That was what I was going to do.

When I'd left, I'd said good-bye for keeps. Because once I'd dug up the loot I meant to go to other countries, not Venezuela, alter the jewels so they could not be recognized, sell them and move on to Spain. From there it would be easy to go and pay a call on Prosecuting Counsel and Co. So you can imagine the terrific uproar when the musketeers saw me turn up at the garage door. Dinner and a party-cake to celebrate my return, and Dédée put four flowers on the table. We drank to the re-formed team and life started off again at full throttle. But still, I was no longer as carefree as I had been.

I felt sure Armando and Deloffre had ideas about me that they were keeping back. It seemed to me that these must have something to do with the *coup d'état*, although both knew my position as far as that was concerned. They often asked me to come and have a drink or to eat at Deloffre's place. Wonderful food, and no witnesses. Deloffre did the cooking, and it was his faithful chauffeur, Victor, who waited at table. We talked about a great many things, but in the end the conversation always came round to the same subject—General Medina. The most liberal of all Venezuelan presidents; not a single political prisoner during his régime; no one persecuted because of his ideas; a policy of coexistence with all other states, all other régimes, even to the point of setting up diplomatic relations with the Soviet Union; he was good, he was noble, and the people so loved him for his simplicity that one day, during a celebration at El Paraiso, they carried him and his wife in triumph, like toreros.

By perpetually telling me about this wonderful Medina, who walked around Caracas with just one aide-de-camp and who went to the cinema just like an ordinary citizen, Armando and Deloffre almost persuaded me that any man with his heart in the right place would do anything to bring Medina back to power. They painted a very dark picture of the present government's injustice and its revengeful attitude towards a whole section of the population; and to make me like his marvellous president even more, Deloffre told me he lived it up with the very best of them. What was more, he was a personal friend, although he knew Deloffre had escaped from penal. I also noted the fact that Deloffre had lost everything in this last revolution. Some mysterious 'avengers' had wrecked his luxurious restaurant-cabaret where Medina and all the top people of Caracas often used to come to have dinner or sit around.

At last, almost won over—mistakenly, as I learnt afterwards —I began to think of taking part in the *coup d'état*. My hesitation vanished entirely (I have to say this because I want to be sincere) when I was promised the money and all the facilities I needed to set *my* plan of revenge in motion.

So this is how it was that one night Deloffre and I were sitting there at his place, me dressed as a captain and Deloffre as a colonel, ready to go into action.

It began badly. To recognize one another, the civilian conspirators were supposed to wear a green armband, and the password was *Aragua*. We were supposed to be at action stations at two in the morning. But then about eleven that night four guys turned up in the one horse-drawn cab left in Caracas: they were completely sozzled and they were singing at the top of their voices, to the accompaniment of a guitar. They stopped just in front of the house, and to my horror I heard them singing songs full of allusions to tonight's *coup d'état*—allusions as obvious as an elephant. One of them bawled out to Deloffre, 'Pierre! Tonight the nightmare comes to an end at last! Courage and dignity, *amigo*! Our Papa Medina must return!'

For goddamned utter foolishness you could not have asked better. The time between some lemon telling the pigs and the moment they came to call on us would be very short. I was hopping mad, and I had every reason to be: we had three bombs there in the car, two in the boot and one on the back seat, covered with a rug.

'Well, they're an elegant lot, your mates! If they're all like this, we needn't bother: we might just as well go straight to prison.'

Deloffre howled with laughter, as calm as if he were going to a ball; he was delighted with himself in his colonel's uniform and he kept admiring his reflection in the glass. 'Don't you worry, Papillon. Anyhow, we aren't going to hurt anyone. As you know, these three gas-bottles have got nothing but powder in them. Just to make a noise, that's all.'

'And what's going to be the point of this little noise of yours?'

'It's merely to give the signal to the conspirators scattered about the town. That's all. There's nothing bloody or savage about it, you see—we don't want to hurt anybody. We just insist upon them going away, that's all.'

OK. Anyhow, whether I liked it or not I was in this right up to the neck: so much the worse for me. It was not my job to quiver with alarm or be sorry: all I had to do was to wait for the given time.

I refused Deloffre's port—it was the only thing he drank: two bottles a day at least. He tossed back a few glasses.

The three musketeers arrived in a command-car transformed into a crane. It was going to be used to carry off two safes, one belonging to the airline company and the other to the Model Prison (the *Carcel Modelo*); one of the governors—or maybe the man in command of the garrison—was in the plot. I was to have fifty per cent of what was inside and I had insisted on being there when the prison safe was grabbed: they had agreed. It would be a sweet revenge on all the prisons in the world. It was a job very near to my heart.

A dispatch-rider brought the final orders: arrest no enemies; let them escape. Carlotta, the civilian airport right in the middle of the city, had already been cleared so that the chief members of the present government and their officials could get away in light planes without a hitch.

It was then that I learned where the first bomb was to be let off. Well, well, well: this Deloffre certainly went about things in style. It was to go off right in front of the presidential palace at Miraflores. The others were to explode one in the east and the other in the west of Caracas so as to give the impression that things were breaking out everywhere. I smiled to myself at the idea of the alarm and despondency we were going to cause in the palace.

This big wooden gate was not the official entrance to the palace. It was at the back of the building; the military trucks used it, and this way big shots and sometimes the president himself could come and go without being noticed.

Our watches were all set to the same time. We were to be at the gate at three minutes to two. Someone inside was going to open it a crack for just two seconds, long enough for the driver to make the noise of a toad with a little child's toy that imitated it very well. That was how they would know we were there. What was the point? I had no idea: nobody told me. Were President Gallego's guards in the plot and would they take him prisoner? Or would they be put out of action straight away by other conspirators already inside? I knew nothing about that.

One thing was certain: at two o'clock precisely I had to light the fuse leading to the detonator on the gas-bottle I had between my knees and then toss it out of the door, giving it a good shove so it should roll towards the palace gate. The fuse lasted exactly one minute thirty seconds. So I was to light it with my cigar, and the moment it started to fizz, shift my right leg and open the door, counting thirty seconds as I did so. At the thirtieth, start it rolling. We had worked out that as it rolled along, the wind would make it burn faster and that there would be only forty seconds before the explosion.

Although the bottle had no bits of iron in it, its own splinters would be extremely dangerous, so we should have to shoot straight off in the car to take shelter. That would be Victor the chauffeur's job.

I'd persuaded Deloffre that if there was a soldier or a cop near by, he, in his colonel's uniform, would order him to run to the corner of the street. He promised me he'd do just that.

We reached this famous gate at three minutes to two without any difficulty. We drew up along the opposite pavement. No sentry: no cop. Fine. Two minutes to two ... One minute to two ... Two o'clock.

The gate did not open.

I was all tensed up. I said to Deloffre, 'Pierre, it's two o'clock.'

'I know. I've got a watch too.'

'This stinks.'

'I don't understand what's going on. Let's wait another five minutes.'

'OK.'

Two minutes past two ... The gate shot open: soldiers came running out and took up their positions, weapons at the ready. It was as clear as gin: we had been betrayed.

'Get going, Pierre. We've been betrayed!'

It took more than that to knock Pierre off his perch: he seemed not to have grasped the situation at all. 'Don't talk bullshit. They're on our side.'

I brought out a forty-five and rammed it against the back of Victor's neck. 'Get going, or I kill you!'

I was certain of feeling the car leap forward as Victor stamped on the accelerator with all his force, but all I heard was this unbelievable remark: '*Hombre*, it's not you who gives orders here: it's the boss. What does the boss say?'

Hell: I'd seen some guys with guts, but never one like this half-caste Indian. Never!

There was nothing I could do because there were soldiers three yards away. They'd seen the colonel's stars on Deloffre's epaulette up against the window, so they came no closer.

'Pierre, if you don't tell Victor to get going, it's not him I'll put the chill on but you.'

'Little old Papi, I keep telling you they're on our side. Let's wait a little longer,' said Pierre, turning his head towards me. As he did so I saw his nostrils were shining with white powder stuck to them. I got it: the guy was stuffed full with cocaine. Fear came over me, yes, an appalling fear; and I was putting my gun to his neck when he said with the utmost calm, 'It's six minutes past two, Papi. We'll wait two more. We've certainly been betrayed.'

Those hundred and twenty seconds went on for ever. I had my eye on the soldiers; the nearest were watching me, but for the moment they were making no move. At last Deloffre said, 'Vamos, Victor: let's go. Gently, naturally, not too fast.'

And by a positive miracle we came out of that man-trap alive. Phew! Some years later there was a film called The Longest Day. Well, you could have made one called The Longest Eight Minutes out of that party of ours.

Deloffre told the driver to make for the bridge that runs from El Paraiso to the Avenida San Martin. He wanted to let off his bomb under it. On the way we met two trucks filled with conspirators who didn't know what to do now, having heard no explosion at two o'clock. We told them what was going on and that we had been betrayed: saying all this made Deloffre change his mind and he ordered the chauffeur to drive back to his place, fast. A mistake the size of a house, because since we had been betrayed, the pigs might very well be there already. Still, we went: and as I was helping Victor put my bomb into the boot I noticed that it had three letters painted on it: P.R.D. I couldn't help roaring with laughter when Pierre-René Deloffre told me the reason for them: we were taking off our uniforms at the time. 'Papi, never forget that whenever the business is dangerous you must always do things in style. Those initials were my visiting card for the enemies of my friend.'

Victor went and left the car in a parking-place, forgetting, of course, to leave the keys as well. The three bombs were not found until three months later.

No question of hanging around at Deloffre's. He went his way. I went mine. No contact with Armando. I went straight to the garage, where I helped carry away the lathe and the five or six bottles of gas that were lying about. Six o'clock: the telephone rang and a mysterious voice said, '*Francès*, get out all of you. Each in a different direction. Only B.L. must stay in the garage. You get it?'

'Who's that?'

He hung up.

Dressed as a woman and driven in a jeep by a former officer of the French Resistance I'd helped a good deal since his arrival, I made my way out of Caracas with no trouble at all and reached Rio-Chico, about a hundred and twenty-five miles away on the coast. I was going to stay there for a couple of months with this ex-captain and his wife and a couple of friends from Bordeaux.

B.L. was arrested. No torture: only a stiff, thorough-going but correct interrogation. When I heard that, it seemed to me the Gallegos and Bétancourt régime was not as wicked as they said; at least not in this case. Deloffre took refuge that same night in the Nicaraguan embassy.

As for me, I was still full of confidence in life, and a week later the ex-captain and I were driving the Rio-Chico Public Works Department's truck. Through a friend we'd got ourselves taken on by the municipality. We made twenty-one bolivars a day between us, and on that we lived, all five of us.

This road-making life lasted two months, long enough for the storm raised by our plot to die down in Caracas and for the police to turn their minds to the reports about a new one that was cooking. Very wisely they concentrated on the present and left the past to itself. I asked nothing better, because I had thoroughly made up my mind not to let myself be dragged into another job of that kind. For the moment, by far the best thing to do was to live here quietly with my friends, drawing no attention to myself.

In the late afternoon I often went fishing, to add to our daily rations. That evening I had hauled out a huge *robalo*, a kind of big sea-bream, and I was sitting on the beach, scaling it in no particular hurry and admiring the wonderful sunset. A red sky means hope, Papi! And in spite of all the flops I had had since I was let out, I began to laugh. Yes, hope must make me live and win: and it was going to do just that. But exactly when was success going to come along? Let's have a look at things, Papi: let's tot up the results of two years of freedom.

I was not broke, but I didn't have much: three thousand bolivars at the outside, the sum total of two years on the loose.

What had happened during this time?

One: the heap of gold of El Callao. No point in brooding over that: it was not a flop but something you voluntarily gave up so the ex-lags there could go on living in peace. You regret it? No. OK, then forget the ton of gold.

Two: craps at the diamond-mines. You nearly got yourself killed twenty times over for the sake of ten thousand dollars you never cashed in on. Jojo died in your place: you came out alive. Without a brass farthing, true enough; but what a terrific adventure! You'll never forget all those nights, keyed-up to the breaking-point, the gamblers' faces under the carbide lamp, the unmoved Jojo. Nothing to regret there either.

Three: the tunnel under the bank. Not the same thing at all: there really was no luck about that job. Still, for three months you lived at full blast twenty-four hours out of the twenty-four, just on what each hour brought in the way of emotion. Even if you got no more out of it than that, you don't have to be sorry for yourself. Do you realize that for three months on end, even in your dreams, you felt you were a dollar-millionaire with never a doubt about getting your hands on the dough? Doesn't that mean anything? Of course, just a trifle more luck might have given you a fortune; but on the other hand you might have been much more unlucky. Suppose the tunnel had caved in while you were at the far end? You'd have died like a rat or they would have caught you like a fox in its earth.

Four: what about the pawnshop and its fridges? No complaints—except for the Public Road Works of that bleeding country.

Five: the plot. Frankly, you were never really wholehearted about that business. These political jobs and those bombs that

146

might kill anybody—it's not your line. What it really comes to is that you were taken in first by the patter of two very nice guys and then by the promise of being able to carry out your plan. But your heart wasn't in it, because you never felt it was quite regular to attack the government that had let you out.

Still, on the credit side you had four months of fun with the musketeers, their wives and the kid; and you aren't likely to forget those days full of the joy of life.

Conclusion: I'd been unjustly imprisoned for thirteen years and almost all my youth had been stolen from me; and although I sleep, eat, drink and have fun, I never forget that one day I must have my revenge.

So, to put it in a nutshell, you've been free these last two years, and in these two years you've had countless experiences and terrific adventures. Better still, you've never even had to look for them: they came all by themselves. You've had wonderful love; you've known men of every kind who've given you their friendship—men you've risked your life with; and with all this, do you still keep moaning? You're broke, or nearly broke? What does that matter? Poverty's not a difficult disease to cure.

So glory be to God, Papi! Glory to adventure, glory to the risks that make you so vividly alive every day and every minute! You gulp it down like some marvellous drink that goes right to the bottom of your heart. And you're fit, which is the really important thing.

Let's wipe it all out and begin again, gentlemen. The chips are down! Make your last bets—this is it! Banco lost, banco again: banco again and again and again. Banco right along the line. But let your whole being thrill and quiver, singing a song of hope that one day you'll hear 'Nine on the nose! Rake it in, Monsieur Papillon! You've won!'

The sun was almost touching the horizon. Red in the evening, that meant hope. And sure enough I was crammed with hope and trust in the future. The breeze had freshened, and with a calmer mind I stood up, happy to be free and alive; my feet sank in the wet sand as I went back towards the house, where they were waiting for what I had caught for the evening meal. But all these colours, these countless touches of light and shade playing on the crests of the little waves stretching out for ever and ever stirred me so deeply, what with my remembering past dangers overcome, I couldn't help thinking of the creator of it all, of God. 'Good night, big guy, good night! In spite of all these flops, I still thank You for having given me such a beautiful day full of sun and freedom and, to finish it off, this marvellous sunset!'

ONE day, when I was making a quick trip to Caracas, a friend introduced me to a former Paris mannequin who was looking for someone to help her in a new hotel she had just opened at Maracaibo. I very willingly accepted the job of being her general-purposes man. She was called Laurence; I think she had come to Caracas to show a collection; and decided to settle in Venezuela. Six hundred miles lay between Caracas and Maracaibo, and that suited me fine; you never knew whether the police might re-open their inquiries into our *coup d'état.*

A friend gave me a lift, and after fourteen hours' driving I had my first sight of the lake of Maracaibo: they call it a lake, although in fact it is a huge lagoon nearly a hundred miles long and sixty wide at the broadest point, and it is joined to the sea by a channel about eight miles across. Maracaibo lies to the north, on the west bank of the channel, which is now linked to the east bank by a bridge; but in those days, if you came from Caracas, you had to cross on a ferry.

This lake was really extraordinary, dotted with thousands of derricks. It looked like a huge forest stretching away out of sight, a forest whose trees, all exactly lined up, allowed you to see as far as the horizon. But these trees were oil-wells, and each oil-well had an enormous pendulum that went to and fro all day and all night, never stopping, perpetually pumping up the black gold from the bowels of the earth.

A ferry-boat ran non-stop between the end of the Caracas road and Maracaibo, carrying cars, passengers and goods. During the crossing I hurried from one side to the other, absolutely fascinated by the sight of these iron pylons rising from the lake; and as I stared at them I thought that twelve hundred miles from here, down at the far end of the country in Venezuelan Guiana, the Good Lord had stuffed the ground with diamonds, gold, iron, nickel, manganese, bauxite, uranium and all the rest, while here He had filled it with oil, the motor of the world—with such enormous quantities of oil that these thousands of pumps could suck away day and night without ever sucking it dry. Venezuela, you've got no call to blame the Lord!

The Hotel Normandy was a splendid great villa surrounded by a carefully-kept garden full of flowers. The lovely Laurence welcomed me with open arms. 'This is my kingdom, Henri,' she said, laughing.

She had opened the hotel just two months before. Only sixteen rooms, but all luxurious, in the best taste, and each with a bathroom fit for the Ritz. She had designed all the décor herself, from the bedrooms to the staff lavatories, taking in the drawing-room, terrace and dining-room on her way.

I set to work: and it was no laughing matter being Laurence's right-hand man—she was under forty and she got up at six to see to her guests' breakfast or even make it herself. She was tireless, and all day long she hurried about, seeing to this and that, supervising everything, and yet still finding time to look after a rose-bush or weed a garden path. She had grasped life with both hands; she had overcome almost impossible difficulties to set this business going; and she had so much faith in its success that I was seized with a will to work almost as consuming as her own. I did everything I could to help her cope with the hundreds of difficulties that kept cropping up. Money difficulties, above all. She was in debt up to the neck, because to turn this villa into something like a luxury hotel she had borrowed every penny.

Yesterday, by a private deal I carried out without consulting her, I got something marvellous out of an oil company.

'Good evening, Laurence.'

'Good evening. It's late, Henri: eight o'clock already. I'm not blaming you, now; but I haven't seen you this whole afternoon.'

'I've been for a stroll.'

'Is this a joke?'

'Yes, I'm laughing at life. It's always good for a laugh, don't you think?'

'Not always. And at this time I should have liked your support: I'm in a bad jam.'

'Very bad?'

'Yes. I've got to pay for all these fittings and alterations, and although the place is running well, it's not easy. I owe a great deal.'

'Here comes the big surprise, Laurence: hold on. You don't owe anything any more.'

'Are you making fun of me?'

'No. Listen: you've brought me in as a kind of partner, and in fact I've noticed a good many people think I'm the boss.'

'What of it?'

'Well, one of the people who thought that way is a Canadian belonging to the Lumus Company, and a few days back he talked to me about a deal he thought we might make. I went to see him this afternoon: I've just come back.'

'Tell me quickly!' cried Laurence, her eyes wide with interest.

'The result is the Lumus Company takes your hotel, the whole of it, with full board, *for a year*!'

'It's not possible!'

'It is, I promise you.' In her emotion, Laurence kissed me on both cheeks and collapsed into a chair. 'Of course there was no question of *me* signing this terrific contract, so tomorrow they'll call you to their office.'

This contract meant that Laurence made a right little fortune out of the Hotel Normandy. The first quarter's advance alone let her pay off all her debts.

After the signing of the contract, Laurence and I drank champagne with the Lumus bosses. I was happy, very happy, as I lay there in my big bed that night. With the help of the champagne I saw life a fine rosy pink. Papi, you're no more of a fool than Laurence: so isn't it possible to get rich *by working*? And starting from almost nothing? Well, Christ above, this was a real discovery I'd made here at the Hotel Normandy. Yes, a real discovery, because in France, for the few years I'd been able to take a quick glance at life, it had always seemed to me that a working-man stayed a working-man all his life. And this completely wrong idea was even more wrong here in Venezuela, where the man who really wants to do something has every opportunity and every facility open to him.

This realization was very important for the carrying out of

my plan. It was not from love of money that I had gone for crooked jobs: I was not a thief out of a deep liking for theft. It was just that I'd never been able to believe it was possible to really get to the top in life starting from scratch—nor, as far as I was concerned, to get hold of a lump of money big enough for me to go and present my bill in Paris. But it *was* possible, and only one thing was necessary to start—a little bit of capital, a few thousand bolivars; and it would be easy to save that once I'd found a good job.

So there you are, Papi: no more crooked stuff, great or small. Let's go for plain, honest methods. Laurence succeeded that way: well then, so shall I! And if you can only bring this off, how happy your father will be!

The only snag was that if I went this way about it, I should need a good deal of time before being able to take my revenge: I could not scrape the necessary cash together in a day. 'Revenge is a dish you want to eat cold,' Miguel had said at the diamond diggings. I was certainly going to find out about that.

Maracaibo was on the boil. There was excitement in the air, and so many businesses, buildings of every kind and oil-refineries, were springing up that everthing, from beer to cement, was sold on the black market. Everything was snapped up right away—there was never enough to meet the demand. Labour was making money, jobs were well paid and every kind of business was doing well.

When there is an oil boom, a district's economy goes through two completely different phases. First comes the period before the wells begin to yield, the period of pre-exploitation. The companies turn up and settle in: they need offices, camps, roads, high-tension lines; they have to drill the wells, put up the derricks and pumps, etc. This is the golden age, golden for all the skilled workers and golden for every level of the community.

The people, the genuine horny-handed people, have banknotes in their pockets; they begin to discover the meaning of money and of security. Families start to get themselves organized, homes grow bigger or better and the children go to school in good clothes, often taken by companies' buses.

Then comes the second phase, the one that corresponds to my first view of the Maracaibo lake, with all I could see of it turned into a forest of derricks. This is the period of exploitation. Thousands of pumps, working away there by themselves, tirelessly sucking out millions of tons of black gold every day.

But this unbelievable great mass of dough does not pass through the people's hands: it goes straight into the coffers of the state banks or the companies. Things begin to grow sticky, staff is cut down to the strict minimum, there's no more money just floating around, all the active business is over. The coming generations will only know about it when they hear their grandfathers say, 'Once upon a time, when Maracaibo was a millionaire, there was a . . .'

But I was lucky. I came in for Maracaibo's second boom. It had nothing to do with the pumps on the lake, but several oil companies had just got new concessions running from the Perija mountains down to the lake and the sea, and they were wild with excitement. The moment might have been made for me.

I was going to dig in here. And I swore the hole I made would be a sizeable cavern. To succeed I'd work at anything I could lay my hands on to gather in every possible crumb of this gigantic cake. That's a sacred oath, Papi! My turn now to get to the top, taking the straight path. The straights are right after all; they manage to grow rich without ever going to gaol.

Good French cook, 39, seeks position with oil company. Minimum salary $800.

I'd learned the rudiments of cookery with Laurence and her chef, and I decided to try my luck. The advertisement came out in the local paper and a week later there I was as cook to the Richmond Exploration Co. I was sorry to leave Laurence, but she could not possibly pay me wages like that, not by a long chalk.

Now, having been through that school, I know a good deal about cooking; but when I first started my job I quaked in fear that the other guys in the kitchen would soon see the French cook knew precious little about saucepans. But to my surprise I soon grasped the fact that they too were all of a tremble in case the French cook should find out that they were only dish-washers, every last one of them! I breathed again; and all the deeper because I had a great advantage over them— *I owned a cookery-book, in French*. L'Escoffier, a present from a retired whore.

The personnel manager was a Canadian, M. Blanchet. Two days later he put me in charge of the cooking for the camp executives, a dozen of them—the big chiefs!

The first morning I showed him a menu like something out of the Ritz. But I pointed out that before I could prepare the food the kitchen would have to be better stocked. It was decided that I should have a separate budget, and that I should run it myself. I don't have to tell you I greased my own palm pretty handsomely when I did my buying; but still, the executives stuffed themselves heartily, no doubt about that. This way, everybody was happy.

Every evening I stuck up tomorrow's menu in the hall: written in French, of course. These grand-sounding names out of the cookery-book made a terrific impression. What's more, in the town I'd discovered a shop that specialized in French things, so what with Potel et Rodel's tins and my recipes I managed so well that the executive guys often brought their women-folk. Twenty would turn up instead of twelve. From one point of view it was a bloody nuisance, but from another, they took less notice of what I spent; because by the rules I was supposed to feed only the people on the list.

I saw they were so pleased that I asked for a rise—1,200 dollars a month, an increase of four hundred. They said no, but they gave me a thousand; and although I kept telling them it was wretched pay for a big-time chef like me, I let myself be persuaded.

Some months went by like this, but in time these set hours of work began to irk me like a shirt-collar that's too tight. I'd had about enough of this job and I asked the chief of the geologists to take me with him when he went out on a prospecting expedition into the most interesting regions, even if they were dangerous.

The point of these expeditions was to make a geological survey of the Sierra Perija, the mountain chain to the west of the lake of Maracaibo that divides Venezuela from Colombia. It is the country of a very fierce, warlike tribe of Indians, the Motilones: so much so that the Sierra Perija is often called the Sierra de los Motilones. Even now nobody knows just where this tribe came from: their language and their customs are quite unlike those of the neighbouring tribes, and they are so dangerous that even now, 'civilization' is only just beginning to make its way among them. They live in communal huts that house from fifty to a hundred people, men, women and children all mixed up together. Their only domestic animal is the dog. They are so wild that you hear of many cases where Motilones, captured by 'civilized' people, sometimes having been wounded, absolutely refuse to eat or drink; and although they may be well treated, they end up by killing themselves, biting the veins in their wrists with their front teeth, which are specially filed for tearing meat. Since the days I am talking about, the Franciscans have bravely settled on the banks of the Rio Santa Rosa, only a few miles from the nearest communal house. The Father Superior uses the most modern methods, dropping food, clothing, blankets and photographs of Franciscans over the huts from a plane. Even better, he parachutes straw figures dressed in Franciscan robes, the pockets filled with different kinds of food and even tins of milk. No fool, the good Father: the day he turns up on foot, they'll believe he's dropped from heaven.

But when I asked to take part in these expeditions it was back in 1948, a long time before those attempts at 'civilized' penetration.

As far as I was concerned, these expeditions had three positive advantages. In the first place, they meant a completely different life from the one I was leading in the kitchen of the Richmond Company's camp: and I had seen just about all I ever wanted to see of that. It would be an adventure starting again, but adventure on the level this time. There was real danger, of course, as there is in any adventure: quite often an expedition would come back short of one or two of its members, because the Motilones were highly skilled at archery: where a Motilone sets his eye, there he sets his arrow, as they say in those parts. But if you were killed, at least you were not eaten, because they were not cannibals. There was always that to be thankful for.

Second advantage: these three-week tours in the deep, unexplored, dangerous bush were very well paid. I'd make more than twice what I earned at my kitchen stove.

Third: I liked being with the geologists. They knew a great deal. Although I was well aware it was too late for me to learn enough to make me a different man, I had the feeling that I would not be wasting my time, going about with these scientists.

So, as a member of their expedition, I set off full of confidence and enthusiasm. No need for any cookery-books; I just had to know how to open tins and make bread and pancakes.

My new friend, the geologist in charge of the expedition, was called Crichet. He had been lent to the Richmond by the California Exploration Co. He knew absolutely everything about the oil side of geology, but he wasn't quite sure whether Alexander the Great came before Napoleon or after. In any case, he didn't give a damn in hell, one way or the other; he didn't need to know history to be very fit, to have a splendid wife, to give her babies and to provide his company with the geological information they needed. Still, I dare say he did know more than he let on—in time I learned to watch out for his sort of half-English humour, quite unlike what we were used to in my native Ardèche. We got along very well.

An expedition of this kind lasted between twenty and twenty-five days, with a week's leave when you got back. It was made up of a geologist in charge, two other geologists, and from twelve to eighteen porters and helpers—strength and discipline was all that was asked of them. They had their own tents and their own cook. I only looked after the three geologists. The men were not fools in any way, and among them there was a militant member of the left-wing *Acción Democrática* who saw the union laws were obeyed. His name was Carlos. There was a good over-all understanding, and I was the one who kept count of the overtime, which they always put down with absolute precision.

This first expedition fascinated me. Getting hold of geological intelligence about oil-fields is a very interesting business: the idea is to follow the rivers up into the mountains as far as possible, keeping to the passage they have cut through the rock. You go as far as you can in trucks, and then you take to jeeps. When there is no path any more, you paddle up the river in canoes; and when the river is too shallow you get out and shove, still going up as far as you can towards the source. The equipment is carried by the porters, about a hundred pounds a man; but the three geologists and the cooks don't carry anything.

Why go so far into the mountains? Because you see all the successive geological formations, just like in a school-book, along the course the river has dug out. You cut samples from the banks, sort them, label them, and pack them away in little bags. The geologists note the direction of the different layers sloping towards the plain. And so with these hundreds of geological samples taken from different places they draw up a map of the strata that should be found in the plain at a depth of say between three thousand and six thousand feet. And by working it out very carefully from all this information, one day they hit oil perhaps fifty miles away in some place where nobody has ever been, because they know in advance that the oil will be there at a given depth. Talk about the wonders of science—I was filled with admiration.

All this would have been fine if it hadn't been for the Motilones. Often members of the expeditions were killed or wounded by their arrows. This did not make recruiting any easier, and it cost the companies a great deal of money.

I went on several expeditions, and I had some marvellous experiences. One of the geologists was a Dutchman named Lapp. One day he was gathering alligators' eggs—they are very good, once they are dried in the sun. You can easily find them by following the track the alligator leaves as it crawls on its belly from the river to the dry place where it lays its eggs: it broods them for hours and hours. Taking advantage of the alligator's absence, Lapp dug up the eggs and calmly carried them back to the camp. He had scarcely reached our clearing before the alligator appeared, tearing along like a racing-car and coming straight for him. It had followed the robber's trail and was going to punish him. About ten feet long, it gasped hoarsely as it came, as if it had laryngitis. Lapp started to run, darting round and round a big tree; and I howled with laughter at the sight of this big guy in shorts bounding about

157

and bawling for help. Crichet and his men came running: two explosive bullets stopped the alligator dead. As for Lapp, he fell on his arse, as pale as death. Everybody was shocked by my behaviour. I told them there was nothing I could have done in any case, because I never carried a rifle—it got in the way.

That evening, while we ate my tinned dinner in the tent, Crichet said to me, in his sort of French, 'You not so young; at least thirty-four, eh?'

'Rather more. Why?'

'You living, you behaving like man of twenty.'

'Well, you know, I'm not much more. I'm twenty-six.'

'Not true.'

'Yes it is, and I'll tell you why. For thirteen years I was stuffed into a cupboard. So as I did not live those thirteen years then, I have to live them now. And since thirteen from thirty-nine makes twenty-six, I'm twenty-six years old.'

'Don't follow.'

'It doesn't matter.'

Yet it was true enough: my heart was that of a boy of twenty. I had to live it—those thirteen years that had been stolen from me; I needed them and I had to get them back. I had to burn them up, not giving a damn for anything at all, the way you do when you are twenty and your heart is filled with a crazy love for life.

One day, just before dawn, a scream jerked us all awake. As he was hanging up the hurricane-lamp he had lit before making the coffee, the men's cook had been struck by two arrows—one in his side, the other in his buttock. He had to be taken straight back to Maracaibo. Four men carried him as far as the canoe on a kind of litter; the canoe took him down to the jeep, the jeep to the truck and the truck to Maracaibo.

The day went by in a heavy, brooding atmosphere. We could sense the Indians all around us in the bush, though we never heard or saw them. The farther we went, the more we had the feeling we were right in their hunting-grounds. There was a fair amount of game, and as all the men had a rifle, every now and then they shot a bird or a kind of hare. Everyone was serious, nobody sang; and when they had fired a shot they stupidly talked very low, as though they were afraid someone might hear them.

Gradually a general fear came over the men. They wanted to cut the expedition short and go back to Maracaibo. Our leader, Crichet, kept on up the river. The union man, Carlos, was a brave guy, but he too felt uneasy. He took me aside.

'Enrique, what do you say to turning back?'

'What for, Carlos?'

'The Indians.'

'True enough, there are Indians: but they might just as easily attack us on the way back as if we go on.'

'I'm not so sure about that, Enrique. Maybe we're close to their village. Look at that stone there: they've been crushing grain.'

'There's something in what you say, Carlos. Let's see Crichet.'

The American had been through the Normandy landings; it took a lot to shake him, and he was completely in love with his job. When all the men were gathered together, he said we were in one of the richest districts for geological information. He lost his temper, and in his anger he said the one thing he never should have said—'If you're afraid, all right, go back. I'm staying.'

They all went off, except for Carlos, Lapp and me. But I stayed only on the condition that when we left we'd bury the equipment, because I did not want to carry anything heavy. Ever since I had broken both my feet in one of my unsuccessful breaks from Baranquilla, walking with a load made me tire very quickly. Carlos would see to the samples.

Crichet, Lapp, Carlos and I went on for five days without anyone else at all. Nothing happened, but I've never had a more thrilling and stirring time than those five days when we knew we were being watched twenty-four hours out of the twenty-four by God knows how many pairs of unseen eyes. We gave up when Crichet, who had gone down to the edge of the river to relieve himself, saw the reeds move and then two hands gently parting them. That wrecked his urge; but with his usual calmness he turned his back on the reeds as though nothing had occurred and came back to the camp.

He said to Lapp, 'I believe the moment has come for us to return to Maracaibo. We've got enough samples of rocks, and

I'm not sure it's scientifically necessary to leave the Indians four interesting samples of the white race.'

We reached La Burra, a hamlet of some fifteen houses, without trouble. We were having a drink, waiting for the truck to come and fetch us, when a drunken half-caste Indian of those parts took me aside and said, 'You're French, aren't you? Well, it's not worth being French if you're as ignorant as all that.'

'Ah? How come?'

'I'll tell you. You make your way into the Motilones' country, and what do you do? You blaze away right and left at everything that flies or runs or swims. All the men carry guns. It's not a scientific exploration: it's an enormous great hunting-party.'

'What are you getting at?'

'If you carry on that way, you'll destroy what the Indians look upon as their food reserve. They haven't got much. They just kill what they need for a day or two. Not more. Then again, their arrows kill with no noise—they don't make the other animals run away. Whereas you kill everything and you frighten away all the game with your shooting.'

It was not so foolish, what this guy said. I was interested. 'What'll you drink? It's on me.'

'A double rum, Frenchman. Thanks.' And he went on, 'It's because of this that the Motilones shoot their arrows at you. They say that because of you it's going to be hard for them to eat.'

'So we are robbing their larder?'

'You're dead right, Frenchman. Then again, when you go up a stream, have you never noticed that where it's narrow or where there's so little water you have to get out of the canoe and shove—have you never noticed that when you do so you destroy a kind of dam made of branches and bamboos?'

'Yes I have. Often.'

'Well, the things you destroy like that, never thinking twice, are fish-traps built by the Motilones; so there again you do them harm. Because there's a great deal of work in these traps. They are a kind of maze, and the fish that are running up the stream pass through zig-zag after zig-zag until they reach a big trap at the end, and then they can't escape. There's a wall of bamboos in front, and they can't find the entrance again,

160

because it's made of little creepers that the fish pushed aside to get in. The current pushes them back against the gate once the fish has passed. I've seen traps more than fifty yards long from one end to the other. Beautiful work.'

'You're right, absolutely right. You have to be vandals like us to smash work of that kind.'

As we travelled back I thought about what the rum-soaked half-breed had told me, and I made up my mind to try something. As soon as we reached Maracaibo, even before I went home for my week's leave, I left a letter for M. Blanchet, the personnel manager, asking him to see me next day.

He called me in, and there with him I saw the top geologist. I told them there would be no more killed or wounded in the expeditions if they would leave the management to me. Crichet would still be the official boss, of course, but I would be the one who saw to the discipline. They decided to have a try; Crichet had put in a report saying that if they could get higher up than the last expedition, that is to say into an even more dangerous region, they would find a real treasure-house of information. As to the pay for my new job, which would be in addition to being cook (I was still to be the geologists' chef), that would be settled when I came back. Of course I said nothing about the reasons why I could guarantee the expedition's safety, and since the Yankees are practical people they asked me no questions either—it was the result that mattered.

Crichet was the only one who knew about the arrangement. It suited him, so he fell in with the scheme and relied on me. He was sure I had found some certain way of avoiding trouble: and then the fact that I had been one of the three who stayed when all the others left had made a good impression.

I went to see the governor of the province and explained my business. He was friendly and understanding, and thanks to his letter of recommendation, I got the National Guard to give orders that the last post before the Motilones' territory should take all the weapons carried by the men on my list before letting the expedition through. They would think up some likely, comforting excuse. Because if the men knew back in Maracaibo that they were going into Motilone country unarmed, they wouldn't even start. I'd have to catch them short and con them on the spot.

It all passed off perfectly. At La Burra, the last post, their weapons were taken away from all the men except two, and I told those two never to fire except in immediate danger—never for hunting or for fun. I had a revolver, and that was all.

From that day on, there was no trouble whatsoever in any of our expeditions. The Americans got the message, and being for efficiency above all, they never asked me the reason why.

I got on well with the men and they obeyed me. My job fascinated me. Now, instead of smashing the fish-traps with our canoes, we worked round them, destroying nothing. Another thing: since I knew the Motilones' chief problem was hunger, every time we struck camp I left old tins filled with salt or sugar; and according to what we could spare, we'd also leave a machête or a knife or a little axe. When we came back through these camping-places we never found a thing. Everything had vanished, even the old cans themselves. So my tactics worked, and since nobody in Maracaibo knew what it was all about, there was a rumour that I was a *brujo*, a wizard, or that I had a secret understanding with the Motilones.

It was during one of these expeditions that I had an extraordinary lesson in how to fish—in how to catch a fish without bait, hook or line, just quietly picking it up on the surface. My teacher was a *danta*, a tapir, an animal bigger than a large pig. Sometimes they'll be more than six feet long. It was one afternoon, when I was near the stream, that I saw one for the first time. It came out of the water, and I watched, keeping perfectly still so as not to frighten it. Its skin was rather like that of a rhinoceros; its front legs were shorter than its back ones; and over its mouth it had a short but distinct trunk. It went over to a creeper and ate a good deal of it: so it was a herbivore. Then I saw it go down to the stream again, walk in and go towards a stretch of slack water. There it stopped, and began to sort of belch, like a cow: so it was a ruminant. Then it brought up a green liquid through its trunk. Very cleverly it mixed this stuff with the water, stirring with its big head. I was still wondering about the reason for all this when a few minutes later, to my astonishment I saw fish come to the surface, belly uppermost, moving slowly as though they had been drugged or put to sleep. And then there was my *danta* taking the fish one by one, not hurrying at all; and calmly he ate them up. I was absolutely amazed.

After that, I had a try. I carefully marked down the creeper I had seen the *danta* eating, gathered an armful and crushed it between two stones, collecting the juice in a calabash. Then I poured it into a part of the river where there was no current. Victory! A few minutes later I saw the fish come to the top, knocked out. Just as they had done for the *danta*. There's only one precaution you have to take: if they are edible fish, you must gut them right away, otherwise they go bad in two hours. After this experiment, the geologists' table often had splendid fish dishes. There was one order I gave the men—never, in any circumstances, kill such a charming fisherman. Particularly as tapirs are perfectly harmless.

Sometimes, in these expeditions, I took a family of alligator-hunters along as guides, the Fuenmayors, a father and his two sons. This suited everybody, because the Fuenmayors knew the region very well; but if they were alone they would be an easy prey for the Motilones. Going along with the expedition, they guided us by day in exchange for their keep, and at night they hunted alligators.

They were people from Maracaibo, Maracuchos, very sociable souls. They spoke in a musical way; and they had a very high notion of friendship. There was a great deal of Indian blood in their veins and they had all the Indian qualities; very knowing and intelligent.

I had some wonderful, indestructible friendships with the Maracuchos, and I have them still. Both with the men and the women, because the women are beautiful and they know how to love and how to make themselves loved.

Hunting alligators, creatures seven to ten feet long, is a very dangerous business. One night I went along with Fuenmayor and his eldest son. The father sat at the back of this very narrow, very light canoe, steering, me in the middle and his son in front. It was pitch dark; all you could hear were the noises of the bush, and very faintly the lapping of the water against the canoe. We didn't smoke; we didn't make the slightest sound. The paddle that moved the canoe and at the same time steered it was never allowed to scrape against the side.

Every now and then we sent the beam of a huge electric torch sweeping the surface, and pairs of red dots appeared. Two red points: one alligator. In front of these eyes there would be the nostrils, because the eyes and the nose are the only two parts of an alligator that show when it is resting on the surface. The victim was chosen according to the shortest distance between the hunters and the red dots. Once it was selected we felt our way towards it with the light out. Old Fuenmayor was wonderfully skilful at fixing the alligator's exact position, just by one flash of the torch lasting no more than a second. We paddled quickly towards it, aimed the beam, and almost always the brute just lay there, dazzled. The beam stayed on the alligator until we were two or three yards away. In the front of the canoe young Fuenmayor kept his torch aimed with his left hand and with all the strength of his right arm he threw a harpoon weighted with twenty pounds of lead —the only thing that could pierce a hide as tough as that and go through to the flesh.

Now we had to get moving, because the second the alligator was harpooned it dived: we took our three paddles and rapidly made for the shore. You really have to jump to it, because if you give the alligator time it comes to the surface again, rushes for you and with one sweep of its tail capsizes the canoe, turning the hunters into a quarry for the other alligators, who've been warned by the turmoil. You have scarcely reached the bank before you jump out, rush for a tree and take a turn round it with the rope. He comes along, you feel him coming along to see what's holding him. He can't tell what's happening to him, apart from the pain in his back. So he comes to find out. Gently, without pulling, you take in the slack and pass it round the tree. He's going to come out—he's almost at the edge. Just as he emerges, young Fuenmayor, holding a thin, razor-sharp American axe, gives his head a tremendous crack. Sometimes it needs three to finish the alligator off. At each blow it gives a sweep with its tail that would send the axeman to heaven if it touched him. It may happen that the axe does not kill the alligator, and in that case you have to give slack right away so the brute can go off into deep water. Because it is so strong it would wrench out even a deeply planted harpoon: you wait a minute and then start heaving again.

That was a wonderful night: we killed several alligators, leaving them on the bank. At daybreak, the Fuenmayors returned and took the skin of the belly and the underside of the tail. The skin of the back is too hard to be of any use. Then they buried each huge creature—if they were thrown back they would poison the river. Alligators don't eat other alligators, not even dead ones.

I made several of these expeditions, making a good living and managing to save a fair amount: and then there occurred the most extraordinary event in my life.

WHEN I was in the solitary confinement cells at Saint-Joseph I used to take off for the stars and invent wonderful castles in Spain so as to people the loneliness and the terrible silence: often I would imagine myself free, a man who had conquered 'the road down the drain' and who had begun a new life in some big city. Yes, it was a genuine resurrection: I pushed back the tombstone that crushed me down in the darkness and I came back into the daylight, into real life; and among the pictures my mind thought up, there would appear a girl as good as she was beautiful. Neither tall nor short; blonde; hazel eyes with jet-black pupils sparkling with life and intelligence. She had a wonderfully drawn mouth, and her laugh showed brilliantly white and pearly teeth. A lovely, perfectly proportioned figure: and this woman, just as I saw her then, was one day to be mine for life.

I invented a heart for this goddess—the finest, the noblest, the most sincere of hearts, the richest in all the qualities that make a woman both one you love and one who is your friend. Without doubt, some day I should meet her, and then, joined to her for ever, I should be loved, wealthy, respected and happy for life.

Yes: there in the stifling damp heat that deprived the unhappy prisoners of the Réclusion of the least waft of living air, when, half smothered, I breathed in that unbearable steam that hurt my lungs—gasping in the hope of finding some hint of freshness—and when in spite of my weakness, my unquenchable thirst and the anxiety that wrung my heart, I took off for the stars where the air was cool and the trees had fresh green leaves, and where the cares of everyday life did not exist because I had grown rich, there, in every vision, appeared the one I called my *belle princesse*. She was always the same, down to the very last detail. Nothing ever varied, and I knew her so well that every time she stepped into these different scenes it seemed to me quite natural—wasn't it she who was to be my wife and my good angel?

Coming back from one of these geological trips, I decided to quit my room in the Richmond Company's camp and live right in Maracaibo. So one day a company truck set me down in a shady little square somewhere in the city centre, with a small suitcase in my hand. I knew there were several hotels or *pensions* thereabouts and I took the Calle Venezuela, a street in a very good position, running between the two main squares of Maracaibo, the Bolivar and the Baralt. It was one of those narrow colonial streets lined with low houses—one storey or at the most two. The heat was shattering, and I walked in their shade.

Hotel Vera Cruz. A pretty colonial house dating from the conquest: painted a pale blue. I liked its clean, welcoming look and I walked into a cool passage that gave on to a patio. And there, in this airy, shaded courtyard I saw a woman; and this woman was *her*.

It was her: I could not be wrong—I had seen her thousands of times in my dreams when I was a wretched prisoner. There she was; there was my *belle princesse* before me, sitting in a rocking-chair. I was certain that if I went closer I should see her hazel-coloured eyes and even the minute beauty-spot on her lovely oval face. And these surroundings— I had seen them too, thousands of times. So it was impossible that I should be wrong: the princess of my dreams was there before me; she was waiting for me.

'*Buenas dias, Señora.* Have you a room to let?' I put my bag down. I was certain she was going to say yes. I did not just look at her: I ate her up with my eyes. She stood up, rather surprised at being stared at so hard by someone she did not know, and came towards me.

'Yes, Monsieur, I have a room for you,' said my princess, in French.

'How did you know I was French?'

'From your way of speaking Spanish. Come with me, please.'

I picked up my bag and, following her, I walked into a clean, cool, well-furnished room giving straight on to the patio.

I cooled myself down with a shower, washed, shaved and smoked a cigarette; and it was only after that, as I sat on the edge of the bed in this hotel room, that I really came to believe

I was not dreaming. 'She's here, man, here, just a few yards away! But don't go and lose your head. Don't let this stab in the heart make you do or say anything bloody foolish.' My heart was beating violently and I tried to calm myself. 'Above all, Papillon, don't tell anyone this crazy story, not even her. Who could possibly believe you? Unless you want to get yourself laughed at, how can you possibly tell anyone that you knew this woman, touched her, kissed her, had her, years ago, when you were rotting in the cells of an abominable prison? Keep your trap shut tight. The princess is here: that's what matters. Don't worry: now you've found her, she won't escape you. But you must go about it gently, step by step. Just from looking at her, you can see she must be the boss of this little hotel.'

It was in the patio, a garden in miniature, that one splendid tropical night I said my first words of love. She was so completely the angel I had dreamt of so often that it was as though she had been waiting for me for years. Rita, my princess was called: she came from Tangier, and she had no ties at all to hamper me. Her brilliant eyes gazed at me, shining like the stars in the sky over our heads. I was frank: I told her I had been married in France, that I did not know just how things were at present, and that there were serious reasons why I could not find out. And that was true: I could not write to the *mairie* of my village for a statement of my position—there was no telling how the law might react to a request like that: maybe by a demand for extradition. But I said nothing about my past as a crook and a convict. I devoted all my strength and all the resources of my mind into persuading her. I felt this was the greatest chance in my life, and I could not let it go by.

'You are beautiful, Rita, wonderfully beautiful. Let yourself be loved, deeply loved for ever, by a man who has nobody in his life either, but who needs to love and be loved. I haven't much money, it's true, and with your little hotel you are almost rich; but believe me, I want our two hearts to be just one, for ever, until death. Say yes, Rita. Rita as beautiful as the loveliest flowers of this country, as lovely as the orchids. I can't tell you when or how, but although it may seem impossible to you, I've known you and loved you for years and years.

168

You must be mine, just as I swear I'll be yours, wholly and for ever.' But Rita was not an easy girl; and that did not surprise me. It was only after three days that she agreed to be mine. She was very shy, and she asked me to hide when I came to her room. Then one fine morning, without making any sort of announcement, we quite naturally made our love obvious and official; and quite naturally I stepped into the role of the hotel's boss.

Our happiness was whole and entire, and a new life opened before me, a family life. Now that I, the pariah, the fugitive from the French penal settlement, had succeeded in overcoming that 'road down the drain', *I had a home*, and a girl as lovely in her body as she was in her soul. There was only one little cloud in our happiness—the fact that having a wife in France, I could not marry her.

Loving, being loved, having a home of my own—God, how great You are to have given me all this!

Wanderers on the roads, wanderers on the seas, men on the loose who need adventure as ordinary people need water and bread, men who fly through life as migrating birds fly through the sky, wanderers of the cities who search the streets of the slums night and day, ransack the parks and hang around the wealthy districts, their angry hearts watching for a job to pull off, wandering anarchists, liberated prisoners, servicemen on leave, soldiers back from the front, fugitives hunted by an organization that wants to catch them and put them in a cell to wipe them out—all, all without exception suffer from not having had a home at one moment or another; and when Providence gives them one, they step into it as I stepped into mine, with a new heart, full of love to give and burning to receive it.

So I too, like ordinary people, like my father, like my mother, like my sisters, like all my family, I too had *my home* at last, with a girl who loved me inside it.

For this meeting with Rita to make me change my whole way of living, and for me to feel that this was the turning-point of my life, she had to be someone quite exceptional.

In the first place, like me she had reached Venezuela when she was making a break. Not a break from a penal settlement, of course, nor from prison, but still a break.

She had arrived from Tangier some six months before with her husband; he had left her about three months back to go and try some kind of adventure two hundred miles from Maracaibo—she didn't want to go with him. He left her with the hotel. She had a brother in Maracaibo, a commercial traveller who moved around a great deal.

She told me about her life, and I listened intently: my princess was born in a poor part of Tangier; her widowed mother bravely raised six children, three boys and three girls. Rita was the youngest. When she was a little girl, the street was her field of action. She did not spend her days in the two rooms where the seven members of the family had their being. Her real home was the town with its parks and its *souks*, among the dense crowds of people who filled them, eating, singing, drinking, talking in every conceivable language. She went barefoot. To the kids of her age and to the people of her quarter she was Riquita. She and her friends, a lively flock of sparrows, spent more time on the beach than at school; but she knew how to look after herself and keep her place in the long queue at the pump when she went to fetch a bucket of water for her mother. It was only when she was ten that she consented to put on a pair of shoes.

Everything interested her lively, inquisitive mind. She spent hours sitting in the circle round an Arab teller of tales. So much so that one story-teller, tired of seeing this child who never gave him anything always there in the front row, butted her with his head. Ever after, she sat in the second row.

She did not know much, but that did not stop her dreaming vividly about the great mysterious world where all those huge ships with strange names came from. To travel, to go far away —that was her great desire, her great ambition, and one that never left her. But little Riquita's idea of the world was rather special. North America was top America and South America bottom America: top America, that meant New York, which covered it completely. All the people there were rich and they were all film actors. In bottom America lived the Indians, who gave you flowers and who played the flute: there was no need to work there, because the blacks did everything that had to be done.

But apart from the *souks*, the camel-drivers, the mysterious veiled women and the swarming life of the port, what she liked most was the circus. She went twice—once by slipping under the edge of the tent, and once thanks to an old clown who was touched at the sight of the pretty barefoot kid; he let her in and gave her a good seat. She longed to go off with the circus; it drew her like a magnet. One day she would be the one who danced on the tightrope, making pirouettes and receiving all the applause. The circus was to leave for bottom America, and she yearned with all her heart to go with it—to go, go far off and come back rich, bringing money for her family.

Yet it was not the circus she went off with, but her family. Oh, not very far, but still it was a voyage. They went and settled at Casablanca. The port was bigger and the liners longer. Now she was sixteen. She was always dressed in pretty little dresses she made herself, because she worked in a shop, Aux Tissus de France, and the boss often gave her short lengths of cloth. Her dream of travelling could not fail to grow stronger, because the shop, in the rue de l'Horloge, was very close to the offices of the Latécoère airline. The pilots often dropped in. And what pilots! Mermoz, Saint-Exupéry, Mimile the writer, Delaunay, Didier. They were handsome, and what's more they were the greatest and the bravest travellers in the world. She knew them all and they all made passes at her; now and then she would accept a kiss, but that was all, because she was a good girl. But what voyages through the sky she made with them, listening to the stories of their adventures as she ate an ice in the next-door cake-shop! They liked her; they thought of her as their little protégée; they gave her small but highly valued presents; and they wrote her poems, some of which were published in the local paper.

When she was nineteen she married a man who exported fruit to Europe. They worked hard, they had a little daughter, and they were happy. They had two cars, they lived very comfortably, and Rita could easily help her mother and her relations.

Then in quick succession two ships loaded with oranges reached port with damaged cargoes. Two whole cargoes completely lost, that meant ruin. Her husband was deeply in debt, and if he set about working to pay his creditors, it would take him years and years. So he decided to slip off to South

America. It was not hard for him to persuade Rita to go with him, to make this wonderful voyage to a land of milk and honey where you could just shovel up the diamonds, gold and oil. They entrusted their little girl to Rita's mother, and Rita, full of adventurous dreams, waited impatiently to go aboard the big ship her husband had told her about.

The 'big ship' was a fishing-boat thirty-six feet long and sixteen wide. The captain, a somewhat piratical Estonian, had agreed to ship them to Venezuela without papers, along with a dozen other irregulars. Price: five hundred pounds. And it was in the crew's quarters of this old fishing-boat that Rita made the voyage, packed in with ten Spanish republicans escaping from Franco, one Portuguese escaping from Salazar, and two women, one a twenty-five-year-old German, the captain's mistress, and the other a fat Spanish woman, the wife of Antonio the cook.

A hundred and twelve days to reach Venezuela! With a long stop at the Cape Verde islands, because the boat leaked and during one spell of rough weather it very nearly sank.

While it was being repaired in a dry-dock, the passengers slept ashore. Rita's husband no longer trusted the boat. He said it was madness to launch out into the Atlantic in a rotten tub like that. Rita put courage into him: the captain was a Viking, she said, and the Vikings were the best seamen in the world; they could have total confidence in him.

Then an incredible piece of news. The Spaniards told Rita that the captain was a double-crosser, that he had made a deal with another group of passengers and that he was going to take advantage of their being ashore to set off for Dakar by night, leaving them there. Instant turmoil! They warned the authorities and went to the ship in a body. The captain was surrounded and threatened: the Spaniards had knives. Calm returned when the captain promised they should go to Venezuela. In view of what had happened, he agreed to remain under the constant supervision of one of the passengers. The next day they left Cape Verde and faced the Atlantic.

Twenty-five days later they came in sight of the Testigos islands, the most outlying point of Venezuela. They forgot everything, the storms, the sharks' fins, the backs of the playful dolphins rushing at the boat, the weevils in the flour and the business at Cape Verde. Rita was so happy she forgot the captain had meant to betray them and she hugged him, kissing him on both cheeks. And once again they heard the song the Spaniards had made up during the crossing; because wherever there are Spaniards there is always a guitar and a singer:

> A Venezuela nos vamos
> Aunque no hay carretera.
> A Venezuela nos vamos
> En un barquito de vela.

(We're going to Venezuela, although there is no road. We're going to Venezuela, in a little boat with a sail.)

On 16 April 1948, after a voyage of 4,900 miles, they reached La Guaira, the port of Caracas, fifteen miles from the city.

To call the health authorities aboard, the captain used a flag made out of a petticoat belonging to Zenda, the German girl; and when they saw the Venezuelan tender, all their sun-cooked faces beamed with joy. This was Venezuela: they had won!

Rita had held out splendidly, although she lost twenty pounds in weight. Never a complaint nor a sign of fear. Yet from time to time there had been plenty to worry about in that cockleshell right out in the full Atlantic! She had only faltered once, and even then no one had known about it. When she left Tangier, among the books she took along to amuse herself she had packed the one tale she should have left behind—Jules Verne's *Twenty Thousand Leagues under the Sea*. One day, in really rough weather, she had not been able to bear it any more and she tossed it overboard: night after night she had been dreaming that a giant octopus was dragging their boat, like the *Nautilus*, down to the bottom.

A few hours after their arrival, the Venezuelan authorities agreed to allow them into the country, although not one of them had any papers. 'We'll give you identity-cards later on.' They sent two who were ill to hospital, and they clothed, housed and fed the others for several weeks. Then each found himself a job.

That was Rita's story.

*

Wasn't it strange that I should have met the woman who had filled my horrible solitude in the Réclusion for two years, and then that this woman should have come here just as I did, making a break—although indeed a very different kind of break? Without papers too, and, just like me, generously treated by this nation?

Nothing came to disturb our happiness for more than three months. Then one fine day, unknown hands opened the safe of the Richmond Company, for which I was still organizing and running the geological expeditions. How the local pigs found out about my past I never did discover. But what is certain is that I was pulled in as suspect number one and shut up in the Maracaibo prison.

Naturally enough, Rita was questioned about me and that was how she suddenly learned everything I had hidden from her—and learned it from the pigs. Interpol had given them all the information. But still she did not leave me in the lurch and while I was in prison she helped me as much as she possibly could. She paid for a lawyer, he defended me, and in less than a fortnight got me out—charge dismissed. My complete innocence was established; but the damage had been done.

When she came to fetch me from the prison, Rita was deeply moved; but she was very sad, too. She did not look at me the same way as before. I sensed that she was really frightened—that she was hesitating about taking up with me again. I had the feeling that everything was lost. And I wasn't wrong, because straight away she said, 'Why did you lie to me?'

No, I must not, must not lose her. I'd never have another chance like this. Once again I had to fight, and fight with all my strength. 'Rita, you've just got to believe me. When I met you, I liked you so much, I loved you so much straight away, that I was afraid you wouldn't want to see me any more if I told you the truth about my past. You remember what I said about myself? Of course I made it up, but that was because I wanted to say only what I thought you would like to hear.'

'You lied to me . . . you lied to me . . .' she kept repeating, over and over again. 'And I who thought you were a decent man.'

She was crazy with fear, as though she were living in a nightmare. Yes, she's afraid, man, *she's afraid of you.*

'And who's to say I can't be a decent guy? I believe that like everybody else I deserve a chance of becoming good, honest and happy. Don't forget, Rita, that for thirteen years I had to fight against the most horrible prison system in the world. I love you with all my heart, Rita; and I love you not with my past but with my present. You must believe me: the reason why I didn't tell you the story of my life was just that I was afraid of losing you. I said to myself that although I'd lived crooked before, my future with you would be the complete opposite. I saw the whole of the road we were to travel together, hand in hand, and I saw it all clean and straightforward, all in lovely colours. I swear it's true, Rita, I swear by the head of my father, whom I've made to suffer so much.' Then I cracked, and I began to weep.

'Is it true, Henri? Is that really how you saw things? Is that really how you saw our future?'

I got a hold on myself; my voice was hoarse and broken as I replied, 'It has to be like that, because now in our hearts that's the way it is. Besides, you feel it in yourself. You and me—we have no past. All that matters is the present and the future.'

Rita took me in her arms. 'Henri, don't cry any more. Listen to the breeze—it's our future that is beginning. But swear to me that you'll never do another dishonest thing. Promise me you'll never hide anything from me any more and that there'll be nothing dirty in our lives to be kept hidden.'

We held one another tight, and I made my oath. I felt that my life's greatest chance was at stake. I saw that I should never have hidden from this brave, honest woman, that I was a man with a life-sentence, a fugitive from the penal settlement.

So I told her everything, absolutely everything. It was all on the move inside me, even the thing that had been gnawing at me for eighteen years and more—the fixed idea that had turned into an obsession: my revenge. I decided to lay it at her feet—to give it up as a proof of my sincerity. I could not make a greater sacrifice, a sacrifice of which she could not in any case grasp the importance; I heard myself doing it as if, by a miracle—as though someone else were speaking. 'To prove how much I love you, Rita, I offer you the greatest sacrifice I can make. From this very moment on, I give up my revenge. The prosecutor, the pigs, the false witness, all those people who made me suffer so—let them just die in their beds. Yes, you are right. To fully deserve a woman like you, I must—not forgive, because that's impossible—but put out of my mind this desire to punish mercilessly the men who tossed me into the penal cells. Here before you there is a completely new man: the old one is dead.'

Rita must have thought over this conversation all day, because that evening, after work, she said to me, 'And what about your father? Since you're now worthy of him, write to him as soon as you can.'

'Since 1933 neither he nor I have heard from one another. Since October 1933, to be exact. I used to see the convicts being given their letters, those wretched letters opened by the screws, those letters in which you could say nothing. I used to see the despair on the faces of the poor guys who had no mail at all, and I could make out the disappointment of the ones who read a longed-for letter and didn't find what they had hoped for in it. I've seen them tear letters to pieces and stamp on them; and I've seen tears fall on the ink and blur the writing. And I could imagine just what those damned letters from the penal settlement might mean when they got there—the Guiana stamp that would make the postman and the neighbours and the people in the village café say "The gaol-bird has written. There's a letter, so he's still alive." I could guess the shame of taking it from the postman and the pain when the postman said "Is your son getting along all right?" So I wrote my sister Yvonne just one letter, the only letter I wrote from penal, saying "Never expect to hear from me, and never write. Like Alfred de Vigny's wolf, I shall know how to die without howling."'

'All that belongs to the past, Henri. You'll write to your father?'

'Yes. Tomorrow.'

'No. Now—at once.'

A long letter set off for France, just telling my father what could be told without wounding him. I described no part of my sufferings; only my resurrection and my life at present. The letter came back: 'Gone away without leaving an address.'

Dear Lord above: who could tell where my father had gone

176

to hide his shame because of me? People were so evil they might have made life impossible for him.

Rita's reaction came at once. 'I'll go to France and look for your father.' I stared at her. She went on, 'Give up your exploring job; it's too dangerous in any case. While I'm away, you'll see to the running of the hotel.'

I had not got my Rita wrong. Not only was she ready to plunge unhesitatingly into the dangers of this long journey all by herself, but she had so much trust in me—in me, the ex-convict—that she would leave everything in my hands. She knew she could rely on me.

Rita had only rented the hotel, with an option to purchase. So in order to prevent it slipping out of our hands, the first thing to do was to buy it. Now I really learnt what it meant, struggling to make one's place in life by honest means.

I got the Richmond Company to let me go, and with the six thousand bolivars I received and Rita's savings we gave the owner fifty per cent of the price. And then began a positive battle day by day, and night by night, to make money and meet our instalments. Both she and I worked like crazy eighteen hours and sometimes nineteen hours a day. We were united by a wonderful will to win at all costs and in the shortest possible time. Neither she nor I ever mentioned our weariness. I did the buying and I helped with the cooking and I received the guests. We were everywhere at once, always smiling. We died on our feet and then we began again the next morning.

To make a little more money, I had a two-wheeled cart that I filled with jackets and trousers to sell in the Plaza Baralt market. These clothes were manufacturer's rejects, which meant I could buy them very cheaply at the works. Under the blazing sun I reeled off my patter, bawling like a jack-ass and putting so much energy into it that one day, tweaking a jacket to show how strong it was, I split it from top to bottom. It was all very well explaining that I was the strongest man in Maracaibo, but I sold precious few that morning. I was in the market from eight until noon. At half past twelve I hurried to the hotel to help at waiting in the restaurant.

The Plaza Baralt was the commercial heart of Maracaibo, one of the liveliest places in the town. At the far end, the church; at the other, one of the most picturesque markets in the world, a market where you would find anything you could possibly think of in the way of meat, game, sea-food and shell-fish, not forgetting big green iguanas—a lovely dish—with their claws twined so they could not escape; and there were alligator's, tortoise's and turtle's eggs, armadillos and *moro-coys*, a kind of land-tortoise, all sorts of fruit and fresh palm-hearts. The market of this ebullient town swarmed with people in the scorching sun—skins of every colour, eyes of every shape, from the Chinese slit to the Negro's round.

Rita and I loved Maracaibo, although it was one of the hottest places in Venezuela. This colonial town had a lovable, warm-hearted population that lived happily. They had a musical way of speaking; they were fine, generous people with a little Spanish blood and all the best qualities of the Indians. The men were fiery creatures; they had a very strong sense of friendship, and to those they liked they could be real brothers. The Maracucho—the inhabitant of Maracaibo—did not much care for anything that came from Caracas. He complained that they provided the whole of Venezuela with gold by means of their oil, and that the people of the capital always overlooked him: the Maracucho felt like a wealthy man who was being treated as a poor relation by the very people he had enriched. The women were pretty and rather small: faithful, good daughters and good mothers. The whole town seethed with life and the noise of living, and everywhere there was brilliant colour—the clothes, the houses, the fruit, everything. And everywhere movement, business, activity. The Plaza Baralt was full of street-traders and small-time smugglers who scarcely bothered to hide the liqueurs, spirits or cigarettes they were selling. It was all more or less among friends: the police-man was only a few yards away, but he would turn his back just long enough for the bottles of whisky, the French cognac or the American cigarettes to pass from one basket to another.

Running a hotel was no trifle. When Rita first came, she took a decision completely opposed to the customs of the country. The Venezuelan customers were used to eating a sub-stantial breakfast—maize cakes (*arepas*), ham and eggs, bacon, cream cheese. And as the guests were there on full board, the day's menu was written up on a slate. The first day she wiped the whole lot out and in her pointed hand she wrote 'Breakfast: black coffee or café au lait, bread and butter.' 'Well, what do you think of that?' the guests must have said: by the end of the week half of them had changed their quarters.

I turned up. Rita had made some alterations, but with my arrival it was a downright revolution.

First decree: double the prices.

Second decree: French cooking.

Third decree: air-conditioning throughout.

People were astonished to find air-conditioning in all the rooms and in the restaurant of a colonial house turned into a hotel. The clientele changed. First came commercial travellers; then a Basque settled in: he sold 'Swiss' watches entirely manufactured in Peru, and he ran his business from his room, selling only to retailers, who hawked them from door to door and all through the oil-fields. Although the hotel was safe, he was so suspicious that he had three big locks put on his door at his own expense. But in spite of the locks he noticed that from time to time a watch disappeared. He thought his room was haunted until the day he found that in fact there was a female thief, our bitch Bouclette. She was a poodle, and she was so cunning she would creep in without a sound, and right under his nose would knock off a strap for pure fun, whether it had a watch attached or not. So here he was, shrieking and bawling, saying it was me who had trained Bouclette to steal his things. I laughed till I could laugh no more, and after two or three rums I managed to convince him that I had nothing to do with his lousy watches and that I would really be ashamed of selling such phony stuff. Comforted and easy in his mind, he shut himself up in his room again.

Among our guests there were people of every possible kind. Maracaibo was full to overflowing, and it was almost impossible to find a room. A flock of Neapolitans went from house to house, swindling the citizens by selling them lengths of cloth folded in such a way that there seemed to be enough for four suits while in fact it would only run to two. They were dressed as sailors and they carried a big bag on their shoulder; they combed the town and the country round, above all the oil-fields. I don't know how these sharp-witted creatures discovered our hotel. As all the rooms were full, there was only one solution—for them to sleep in the patio. They agreed. Every evening they came back about seven and had a shower. They had dinner at the hotel, so we learned to make spaghetti à la napolitaine. They spent their money freely and they were good customers.

At night, we brought out iron bedsteads and the two little maids helped Rita make them up in the patio. As I made the Neapolitans pay in advance, every night there was the same argument—paying the price of a room for sleeping in the open was too much. And every night I told them that on the contrary it was perfectly logical and completely fair. To bring out the beds, put on the sheets, the blankets and the pillows and then take them all in again in the morning was a huge amount of work—beyond price. 'And don't you go on beefing too much, or I'll put up your rent. Because here am I, literally slaying myself shifting things in and out—all I make you pay is the cost-price of moving.'

They would pay up and we would all have a laugh. But although they were making a lot of money, the next evening the whole thing would start all over again. They beefed even more one night when it rained and they had to run in with all their clothes and their mattresses and sleep in the restaurant.

A woman who kept a brothel came to see me. She had a very big house two or three miles from Maracaibo, at the place called La Cabeza de Toro: the brothel was the Tibiri-Tabara. Eléonore was her name, and she was an enormous mass of flesh: intelligent; very fine eyes. More than a hundred and twenty women worked at her place—only at night.

'There are some French girls who want to get out,' she told me. 'They don't like spending twenty-four hours out of the twenty-four in the brothel. Working from nine in the evening until four the next morning, that's fine. But they want to be able to eat well and sleep in peace in comfortable rooms away from the noise.'

I made a deal with Eléonore: the French and Italian girls could come to our hotel. We could raise the price by ten bolivars a day without worrying: they would be only too happy to be able to stay at the Vera Cruz, with French people. We were supposed to take six; but after a month, I don't quite know how, we had twice as many.

Rita laid down iron-hard rules. They were all young and all lovely. It was absolutely forbidden to receive any male at the hotel, even in the courtyard or the dining-room. But in any case, there was no trouble at all: in the hotel these girls were like real ladies. In everyday life they were proper, respectable women who knew how to behave. In the evening, taxis came for them. They were transformed—gorgeously dressed and made-up. Discreet, without any noise, they went off to the 'factory', as they called it. Now and then a ponce would come from Paris or Caracas, drawing as little attention to himself as possible. His girl could see him at the hotel, of course. Once he had made his haul, collected his money and made his girl happy he would go off again as quietly as he had come.

There were often little things that were good for a laugh. A visiting ponce took me aside one day and asked to have his room changed. His woman had already found another girl who was willing to switch. Reason: his neighbour was a full-blooded, well-equipped Italian, and every night, when his girl came back, he made love to her at least once and sometimes twice. My ponce was not yet forty and the Italian must have been fifty-five.

'Man, I just can't keep up the pace with Rital, if you follow me. There's no getting anywhere near that kind of a performance. And my chick and me being next door, we hear the lot—groans, shrieks, the whole works. And as I can scarcely manage to stir my baby once a week, I ask you to imagine what I look like. She doesn't believe in the headache stuff any more; and of course she makes comparisons. So if it doesn't put you out, do this for me.'

I kept my laughter inside me, and moved by such an unanswerable argument, I switched his room.

Another time, at two o'clock in the morning, Eléonore called me up. The cop on duty had found a Frenchman who could not speak a word of Spanish perched in a tree opposite the brothel. The cop asked him how he came to be in that curious position—was he there to steal or what?—and all he answered was, 'Enrique of the Vera Cruz.' I jumped into my car and darted out to the Tibiri-Tabara.

I recognized the fellow right away. He was from Lyons and he had already been to the hotel. He was sitting there, and the madam too: standing in front of them, two grim-faced cops. I translated what he told me—he put it very briefly. 'No, the gentleman wasn't in the tree with the idea of doing anything wrong. It's just that he is in love with one of the women, but he won't say which. He climbed up to admire her in secret, because she won't have anything to do with him. It's nothing serious, as you see. Anyhow, I know him, and he's a good citizen.'

We drank a bottle of champagne: he paid, and I told him to leave the change on the table—someone would surely pick it up. Then I drove him back in my car. 'But what the hell were you doing, perched up in that tree? Have you gone crazy, or are you jealous of your girl?'

'It's not that. The trouble is the takings have dropped off without any reason for it. She's one of the prettiest there and she earns more than the others. So I thought I'd come and watch how often she went to work without her knowing. That way, it seemed to me, I'd soon find out if she was holding out on me and keeping back my money.'

Although I was sore at having been pulled out of bed in the middle of the night on account of a ponce, I roared with laughter at his explanation. This 'tree-perched pimp', as I called him from that time on, left for Caracas the next day. It was no longer worth his while keeping a check. The whole business had made a lot of noise in the brothel; like everybody else his woman knew all about it, but she was the only one who knew why her fancy-man had chosen just that tree—it was dead opposite her room.

We worked hard, but the hotel was a cheerful place, and we had fun all the time. There were some evenings, after the girls had gone off to their factory, when we made the dead speak. We all sat at a round table with our hands flat on the top, and each one called up the spirit he wanted to question. It was a good-looking woman of about thirty, a painter, who started these seances—she was a Hungarian, I think. She called up her husband every evening, and of course with my foot under the table I helped his spirit to reply: otherwise we'd be there yet.

She said her husband was tormenting her. Why? She could

not tell. At last one night the spirit came through by means of the table, and after that he never left it quiet. He accused her of having round heels. We all exclaimed that that was very serious, and that this jealous spirit might take a horrible revenge; all the more so as she was perfectly willing to admit that in fact her heels were quite round. What was to be done about it? We discussed it very gravely and we told her there was only one thing to do: at full moon she was to provide herself with a brand-new machête, stand stark naked in the middle of the patio with her hair down and no make-up on, having washed all over with yellow soap, but with no trace of scent and no jewels, clean from head to foot. Nothing but the machête in her hand. When the moon was right over the patio, casting no shadow except directly beneath her, she was to slash the air exactly twenty-one times.

It worked perfectly, and the night after the exorcism (we had laughed fit to burst, hidden behind the shutters) Rita said the joke had lasted long enough; so the table replied that from now on her late husband would leave her in peace and her heels could be as round as she liked, always provided she never slashed the air with a sword at full moon any more, because it hurt him too much.

We had a poodle called Minou, quite a big poodle, that had been given to us by a French guest who was passing through Maracaibo. He was always perfectly clipped and brushed, and the stiff, thick hair on the top of his head was cut in the shape of a tall, impressive fez. He had puffed-out thighs, shaved legs, a Chaplin moustache and a little pointed beard. The Venezuelans were astonished at the spectacle, and often one of them would overcome his shyness and ask what kind of an animal this strange beast might be.

Minou very nearly brought about a serious clash with the Church. The Vera Cruz stood in the Calle Venezuela; our street led to a church and processions often went along it. Now Minou loved sitting at the hotel door to watch the people walking about. He never barked, whatever happened in the street. But although he did not bark, he did cause a sensation; and one day the priest and the choir-boys belonging to a procession found themselves all alone, while fifty yards behind the faithful of Maracaibo stood massed in front of the hotel, gazing at this extraordinary object. They had forgotten to follow the procession. Questions ran through the group, and they jostled to see Minou close to; some were of the opinion that the unknown creature might very well be the soul of a repentant sinner, since it had sat there so quietly, watching a priest and his choir-boys all dressed in red go by singing heartily. At last the priest realized that things were very silent behind, and turning round he saw there was no one left. He came striding back, crimson with fury and bawling out his parishioners for their lack of respect for the ceremony. Alarmed, they fell back into line and marched off. But I noticed that some who had been most struck by the sight walked backwards so as not to lose a minute of Minou. After that we kept an eye on the Maracaibo paper, *Panorama*, for the date and the time when a procession should come along our street, so that we could tie him up in the patio.

It seems this was the season for incidents with the clergy. Two French girls left Eléonore's brothel and the hotel; they had made up their minds to be independent and to set up a little 'house' in the centre of the town where they would just work by themselves, the two of them. It was quite a good scheme, because like this the customers would not have to get their cars and drive six miles there and back to see them. To get themselves known, they had cards printed, saying 'Julie and Nana: conscientious work' and the address. They handed them out in the town; but instead of giving them directly to the men, they often slipped them under the windscreen-wipers of parked cars.

They had the bad luck to put two, one under each wiper, on the car belonging to the bishop of Maracaibo. This set off a hell of an explosion. To show the profane nature of their action, the paper *La Religion* published a picture of the card. But the bishop and the clergy were indulgent: the little brothel was not closed, and the ladies were only begged to be more discreet. Anyhow, there was no point in going on handing out the cards: after the free publicity in *La Religion* a very considerable number of customers hurried to the given address. Indeed, the crowd was so great that to provide a reasonable excuse for this troop of men at their door, the girls asked a hot-dog seller to wheel his barrow quite close, so it would look as if the queue was standing there to buy a *perro caliente*.

That was the picturesque side of life at the hotel. But we were not living our life on a planet far out in space: we were living it in Venezuela, and we were mixed up with the country's economic and political ups and downs. And in 1948 politics were not so peaceful. Gallegos and Bétancourt had been governing the country since 1945, in the first attempt at a democratic régime in the history of Venezuela. On 13 November 1948, scarcely three months after I had set to work with Rita to buy the hotel, there came the first shot directed against the régime. A major called Thomas Mendoza had the nerve to try a rising all by himself. He failed.

On the twenty-fourth of the same month the soldiers seized power in a *coup d'état* run with clockwork precision: there were almost no victims. Gallegos, the president of the republic and a distinguished writer, was forced to resign. Bétancourt, a real political lion, took refuge in the Colombian embassy.

In Maracaibo we lived through hours of very tense anxiety. There was one moment when all at once we heard a passionate voice on the radio crying 'Workers, come out into the streets! They want to steal your freedom from you, close down your unions and impose a military dictatorship by force! Everybody occupy the squares, the...' Click, and it was cut off dead, the mike snatched from the brave militant's hands. Then a calm, grave voice: 'Citizens! The army has withdrawn the power from the men to whom they entrusted it after having dismissed General Medina, because they made an unworthy use of their authority. Do not be afraid: we guarantee the life and property of one and all, without exception. Long live the army! Long live the revolution!'

That was all I saw of a revolution which caused no blood to flow at all; and when we woke up next day, there was the composition of the military junta in the papers: three colonels —Delgado-Chalbaud as president, Perez Jimenez and Llovera Paez.

To begin with, we were afraid this new régime would mean the suppression of the rights given by the former one. But nothing of the kind. Life went on just the same, and we scarcely noticed the change of government, apart from the fact

185

that the key-posts were taken over by soldiers.

Then two years later came the assassination of Delgado-Chalbaud. A very ugly business with two conflicting explanations. First theory: they meant to murder all three and he was the first to be killed. Second theory: one of the other colonels or both had him put out of the way. The truth was never known. The murderer was arrested, and he was shot and killed while he was being transferred to prison—a lucky shot that prevented any embarrassing statement. From that day on Perez Jimenez was the strong man of the régime; and he officially became dictator in 1952.

So our life went on; and although we never went out for any fun or entertainment or even a drive, this life and our eagerness to work filled us with a wonderful joy. For what we were building up by our labours was to be our home, the home in which we should live happily, having earned it ourselves, united as only two people can be when they love one another as we did.

And into this home would come Clotilde, Rita's daughter, who would be mine, and my father, who would be theirs. And to this house there would come my friends, to draw breath a while when they were in need. And in this home filled with happiness we would be so thoroughly contented that never again should I think of taking my revenge upon those who had caused so much suffering to me and my people.

At last the day came—we had won. December 1950: a beautiful document was drawn up at the lawyer's, and we were the owners of the hotel for good and all.

11 : My Father

Today Rita set off on her journey, her heart filled with hope. She was going to find out the place where my father had retired—where he had hidden himself.

'Rely on me, Henri. I'll bring you back your father.'

I was alone in the running of the hotel. I gave up selling trousers and shirts, although I could make quite a packet out of it in a few hours. But Rita had gone to look for my father, so I was going to look after everything not only as though she were there, but even better, twice as well.

To look for my father: *to look for my father*! My father, the schoolmaster of a village in the Ardèche; my father, who twenty years ago, *twenty years ago*, could not embrace his son, a convict with a life-sentence, when he came to see him in prison for the last time, because of the bars in the visiting-room. My father, to whom my wife Rita would be able to say, 'I have come as your daughter to tell you that by his own efforts your son has regained his freedom, that he has made himself a life as a good and honest man, and that he and I have built up a home that is waiting for you.'

I got up at five o'clock and went shopping with Minou and a twelve-year-old boy called Carlitos I had taken in when he came out of prison. He carried the baskets. In an hour and a half I'd done the buying for the whole day—meat, fish and vegetables. We came back both loaded like mules. Two women in the kitchen: the one twenty-four, the other eighteen. I dumped everything we had brought on the table and they sorted it out.

For me, the best moment in this simple life was at half past six in the morning, the time when I ate my breakfast in the dining-room with the cook's daughter on my knee. She was four; she was coal-black, and she would not eat unless she had her breakfast with me. All these things—her little naked body, still cool from the shower her mother gave her when she got up, her little girl's piping voice, her lovely shining eyes that looked at me so trustingly, the jealous barking of my dog, cross at being neglected, Rita's parrot pecking at its bread and milk by my coffee-cup—yes, all this really made breakfast the top moment of my day.

Rita? No letter. Why? It was more than a month now that she'd been gone. The voyage took sixteen days, true enough; but after all she'd been in France a fortnight now—had she still found nothing, or did she not want to tell me? All I asked for was a cable, a very short cable just to say 'Your father is well and he loves you still'.

I watched for the postman. I never left the hotel unless I had to in order to keep it running smoothly and I hurried over the shopping and the other business so as to be on the spot all the time. In Venezuela the people who bring telegrams have no uniform, but they are all young; so the moment any boy walked into the patio I hurried towards him, my eyes fixed on his hands to see if he was carrying a green paper. Not a thing. Most of the time they weren't even telegraph-boys, except on two or three occasions when some young fellow did appear with a green slip in his hand: I'd rush out, snatch the telegram and then see with a sinking heart that it was addressed to someone staying at the hotel.

This waiting and this lack of news made me all on edge and anxious. I worked till I dropped; I always had to be busy because I felt that otherwise I should not be able to hold out. I helped in the kitchen, I worked out extraordinary menus, I checked the rooms twice a day, I talked to the guests about no matter what and listened to them whatever they had to say. The only thing that mattered was filling up these hours and days so as to be able to endure the want of news and the waiting. There was only one thing I couldn't do—take a hand in the poker-game that started up about two o'clock every night.

There was only one really serious calamity. Carlitos got things wrong. Instead of buying paraffin for cleaning the kitchen, he bought petrol. The cooks swilled the concrete floor with a good deal of it and then, never suspecting a thing, they lit the stove. The whole kitchen blazed up with a vivid burst of flame, and the two sisters were burnt from foot to belly. I just had time to wrap a tablecloth round Rosa's little black girl and save her—not a second to spare. She was almost unhurt, but the other two were badly burned. I had them looked after in their room in the hotel and engaged a Panamanian cook.

Life in the hotel carried on as usual, but I began to be seriously worried about Rita's silence and her not being there.

Fifty-seven days she had been gone. But now in ten or twenty minutes she'd be back. There I was waiting for her at the airport. Why just that simple telegram—'Arrive Tuesday 15.30 flight 705. Love Rita'? Why nothing more? Has she not found anyone? I couldn't tell what to think any more, and I didn't want to make any more guesses.

Here she was, my Rita. Now at last I'd know. She was the fifth coming down the gangway. She saw me right away and we both waved at the same moment. She came towards me, just as usual. From forty yards I searched her face: she was not laughing, just smiling. No, she was not coming with a triumphant air: no, she hadn't waved as a sign of joy and victory but just naturally, to show she'd seen me. At ten yards I saw she'd come back beaten.

'Did you find my father?'

The question hit her point-blank, after no more than just a kiss, a single kiss after two months of separation. I couldn't wait any longer.

Yes, she had found him. He was lying in the graveyard of a little village in the Ardèche.

She showed me a photograph. A well-made cement tomb with J. Charrière on it. He had died four months before she got there. And all Rita brought me back was this picture of his grave.

My heart, which had seen my wife go off so full of hope, almost stopped at this appalling news. I felt a deep, wrenching pain inside me, the collapse of all those illusions I had had as a man who still sees himself as a little boy for his father. God, not only have You struck the whole of my youth but You have also refused to let me embrace my father and to hear his voice, which would have said, I am certain of it, 'Come to my arms, my little Riri. Fate has been unmerciful to you; the law and its penitentiary system have treated you abominably; but I love you still, I have never renounced you, and I am proud that you have had the strength to win in spite of everything and to become what you are.' Over and over again Rita told me the small amount of information she had been able to get almost by begging, the little she had been able to find out about my father's life after I was sentenced. I said nothing; I could not speak; something inside me was tied into a furious knot. And then all at once, as though a sluice had burst open, the idea of revenge came over me again. 'Pigs, I'll set off that trunk of dynamite at 36, quai des Orfèvres, not just to kill a few but as many as possible—a hundred, two hundred, three hundred, a thousand! And you, Goldstein, you perjurer, believe you me, you'll get what's coming to you, every last bit of it. As for you, prosecuting counsel, so eager to send me down, it won't take long for me to find a way of getting hold of your tongue and tearing it out with as much agony as you can suffer!

'Rita, we must part. Try to understand: they've utterly wrecked my life. They prevented me from embracing my father and having his forgiveness. I must have my revenge: they can't get away with this. This is our last night: tomorrow I go. I know where to find the money for the journey and to carry out my plan. The only thing I ask you is to let me take five thousand bolivars out of our savings for my first expenses.'

An interminable silence settled; I no longer saw Rita; her face disappeared behind the unfolding vision of the plan I had worked out so often.

What did I need to put it into action? Less than two hundred thousand bolivars, in fact. I'd asked too much before. I'd have plenty to spare with these sixty thousand dollars. There were two jobs I'd left alone so as to respect this country. First, El Callao with its heap of gold guarded by ex-lags. Then right in the middle of Caracas, the cashier of a big firm. He was a push-over: he carried large sums of money without an escort. The entrance to the building was perfect; so was the fourth-floor corridor: both were badly lit. I could work alone, unarmed, with chloroform. The only bloody inconvenience was that when the sums were very large three men carried them. Holding them up all by myself was not a hundred per cent safe. The easiest was El Callao, of course. There I could take just what I needed, half a hundredweight of gold, not more, and bury it. A simple job: I could go to bed with Maria, and when she was asleep I'd chloroform her so she would not wake up when I got up to do the job. I could come back to her bed without having been seen by anyone. Getting close to the guard would be easy, naked, painted black and on a pitch-dark night.

As for the getaway, that would have to be through British Guiana. I'd get to Georgetown with just a little gold melted down into nuggets—easy enough with a blow-lamp. I'd be certain of finding a buyer for the lot. The fence and I would carry out the deal on the basis of notes cut in two: he'd keep one half and only give it me when I delivered the goods on the British side of the Caroni, where I would have the stuff hidden. That way, there would be confidence all round.

It would be all right for me to show up in Georgetown, because when I left some years back I'd done so secretly. Coming back secretly too, if I was ever asked what I was doing—always a possibility—I could say I had spent those years way out in the bush looking for balata or gold, and that was why no one had seen me for so long.

I knew Little Julot was still there. He was a regular guy and he would put me up. Just one risk: Indara and her sister. I'd only go out at night; or better still not go out at all, but get Julot to do the deal for me. And I thought Big André was in Georgetown too, on a Canadian passport. Switching the photo, changing the stamp—nothing to it. If he wasn't there, then I'd buy papers from anyone who was broke or from a seaman at the Mariners' Club.

Transfer the dough to Buenos Aires through a bank; carry a certain amount in notes; take a plane from Trinidad to Rio de Janeiro. At Rio, change passports and get into the Argentine.

Once there, no problem. I had friends in Rio, ex-lags; and it must be easy to find former Nazis with their trunks full of papers. Leave for Portugal from Buenos Aires with four sets of passports and identity papers—different nationalities but all in the same name so as not to get muddled up.

From Lisbon, take the road into Spain and reach Barcelona; still travelling by road, into France on a Paraguayan passport. I spoke Spanish well enough by now for an inquisitive French gendarme to take me for a South American.

Half the money would have been transferred to the Crédit Lyonnais, the other half kept in reserve at Buenos Aires.

Every single person I contacted in Georgetown, Brazil and the Argentine would have to believe I was going to Italy, where my wife was waiting for me to start a business in some seaside resort.

In Paris I'd stay at the Georges V. Never go out at night: have dinner at the hotel and send for tea in my suite at ten. The same thing every day of the week. That's the hallmark of a serious type leading an exactly regulated life. In a hotel this kind of thing gets known right away.

I'd have a moustache, of course, and hair cut *en brosse*, like an officer. Only say what was strictly necessary and use a Spanish sort of French to say it. Have Spanish newspapers put in my pigeon-hole at the reception every day.

Thousands and thousands of times I'd turned over the questions of which man or which men to begin with, so that the three jobs would never be connected with Papillon.

The first to get their deserts would be the pigs, with the trunk stuffed with explosives at 36, quai des Orfèvres. There would be no reason to think of me if I did it cleverly. To begin with I'd have a look at the premises and check the exact time it took to go up the stairs to the report-room and then get back to the entrance. I didn't need anyone to work out the fuse for the detonator: I'd made all the necessary experiments at the Franco-Venezuelan garage.

I'd turn up in a van with *Maison So-and-so: Office Equipment* painted on it. With me dressed as a delivery-man and with my little crate on my shoulder, it should work easily. But when I first went over the place I'd have either to find some inspector's card on a door or manage to get hold of the name of an important character with his office on that floor. Like that I could say the name to the pigs on duty at the door; or indeed I could show them the invoice, as if I didn't remember who the trunk was for. And then all aboard for the fireworks. It would need diabolical bad luck for anyone to connect the explosion— a sort of anarchist's job, after all—with Papillon.

In that way Pradel would not be warned. To cope with him, and to prepare the trunk, the fuse, the explosives and the bits of old iron, I'd have taken a villa, using my Paraguayan passport if I hadn't managed to get hold of a French identity-card. I was afraid it might be too dangerous to get into contact with the underworld again. Better not risk it: I'd make out with the passport.

The villa would be near Paris, somewhere along the Seine, because I'd have to be able to get there by water and by road. I'd buy a light, fast little boat with a cabin, and it would have moorings right by the villa and on the banks of the Seine in the middle of Paris, too. For the road, I'd have a small, high-powered car. It was only when I got there and when I knew where Pradel lived and worked and where he spent his weekends and whether he took the métro, the bus, a taxi or his own car that I'd take the necessary steps to kidnap him and shut him up in the villa.

The main thing was to make dead sure of the times and the places where he was alone. Once he was in my cellar, I had him on toast. This prosecutor who, way back in 1931, at the trial, had seemed to say to me, with his vulture-look, 'You won't escape from me, young cock; I'm going to make use of everything that can look bad for you, all this ugly muck in your file, to make you seem disgusting, so that the jury will turn you out of society for good and all'—this prosecutor, who had brought all his abilities and all his education to bear to paint the vilest and most hopeless picture of a boy of twenty-four, and with such success that the twelve incompetent bastards of jurymen sent me to penal servitude for life—this prosecutor, I'd have to torture him for at least a week before he died. And at that he wouldn't have paid too dear.

The last to pay the bill would be Goldstein, the perjurer. I'd take him last, since he was the most dangerous for me. Because once I'd killed him, they'd look back over his life, and the pigs were not always half-wits—they'd soon see the part he had played in my trial. And as they'd know right away that I was on the run, it wouldn't take them long to figure out there might be a Papillon fluttering about in the Paris air. At that point everything, hotels, streets, stations, ports and airfields, would become extremely dangerous for me. I'd have to make my getaway quickly.

It would not be hard to pinpoint him and follow him, because of his father's fur shop. There were several ways of killing him, but whichever way I chose, I wanted him to recognize me before he died. If possible, I'd do what I had so often dreamed of doing—strangle him slowly with my bare hands, saying, 'Sometimes the dead come to life again. You didn't expect that, brother? You didn't expect my hands to kill you? Still, you win, because you're going to die in a few minutes, whereas you sent me down to rot slowly all my life until I died of it.'

I couldn't tell whether I'd manage to get out of France, because once Goldstein was dead things would be very dangerous. It was almost certain they would identify me. I didn't give a damn. Even if I had to die for it, they must pay for my father's death. I'd have forgiven them for my suffering. But the fact that my father should have died without my being able to tell him his boy was alive and had gone straight; the fact that maybe he had died of shame, hiding from all his old friends, and that he should have lain down in his grave without knowing what I was now—that, no, no, no! That I could never forgive!

During the very long silence while I went through every step of the action again to see there was no hitch anywhere, Rita had been sitting at my feet, with her head leaning against my knee. Not a word, not a sound; almost seemed to be holding her breath.

'Rita, sweetheart, I leave tomorrow.'

'You shan't go.' She stood up, put her hands on my shoulders and looked me straight in the eye. She went on, '*You must not go:* you can't go. There's something new for me too. I took advantage of my journey to send for my daughter. She'll be here in a few days. You know perfectly well the reason why I didn't have her with me was I needed a settled place for her. Now I've got one, and she'll have a father too—you. Are you going to run away from your responsibilities? Are you going to spoil everything we've built up with the love and trust between us? Do you think killing the men who were responsible for your sufferings and perhaps for your father's death is really the only thing to do when you compare it with what we have? Is that the only answer you can find?

'Henri, our fates are linked for ever. For my sake and for the sake of this girl who is coming to you and who I am sure will love you, I ask you to give up your idea of revenge for ever. Why, you'd made up your mind to do so. And now here's your father's death throwing you back down the road to ruin.

Just you listen to me: if your father, that upright, kind village schoolmaster who spent his life teaching thousands of children to be good, straight, industrious and charitable, and to respect the law—if your father could speak, do you think he would accept your idea of revenge and approve of it? No. He'd tell you that neither the cops nor the false witness nor the prosecutor nor the jurymen nor the warders were worth your sacrificing a wife who loves you and whom you love, and my daughter who hopes to find a father in you, and your good, comfortable home, and your honest life.

'I'll tell you how I see your revenge: it's this—that our family should be a symbol of happiness for everybody; that with your intelligence and my help, we should succeed in life by honest means; and that when the people of this country talk about you not one would say anything but this—the Frenchman is straight and honest, a good man whose word is his bond. That's what your revenge ought to be; and that revenge would be the best kind—the revenge of proving to them all that they were terribly mistaken about you; the revenge of proving that you managed to come through the horrors of prison unspoilt and become a fine character. That is the only revenge worthy of the love and the trust I have placed in you.'

She had won. All night we talked, and I learned to drain the cup to the dregs. But I could not resist the temptation of knowing every last detail of Rita's journey. She lay on a big sofa, exhausted by the failure of this long voyage and by her struggle with me. Sitting there on the edge of it I leant over her, questioning her again and again and again, and little by little I dragged out everything she had meant to hide.

At the very beginning, after she left Maracaibo for the port of Caracas where she was to take the boat, she had a foreboding that she was going to fail: everything seemed to combine to prevent her from leaving for France. Just as she was going aboard the *Colombie* she noticed that she lacked one of the necessary visas. A race against time to get it in Caracas, tearing along that dangerous little road I knew so well. Back to the port with the paper in her bag and her heart beating for fear the boat should leave before she got there. Then a terrible storm broke out, bringing landslides down over the road. It became so dangerous that the driver lost his head and turned back, leaving Rita there alone in the storm by the side of the road, among the landslides. She walked nearly two miles in the downpour and then by a miracle she found a taxi that was returning to Caracas: but at the sight of the landslides it turned back for the port. And from the port she could hear ships' sirens. In her panic she was sure it was the *Colombie* leaving.

Then when she reached her cabin at last, weeping with joy, there was some accident aboard and the ship could not leave for several hours. All this gave her a very uneasy feeling, as if it was the finger of fate.

Then the ocean: Le Havre, Paris, and without a stop, Marseilles. Marseilles, where she stayed with a woman she knew, and there the woman introduced her to a municipal councillor; straight away he wrote her a cordial letter to a friend of his called Henri Champel, who lived at Vals-les-Bains in the Ardèche.

Then the train and the bus again, and it was not until she reached these wonderfully kind Champels that Rita could draw breath and begin to organize her search, but she was not at the end of her difficulties.

Henri Champel took her to Aubenas, in the Ardèche, where Maître Testud, the family lawyer, lived. Ah, that Testud! A heartless bourgeois. In the first place he told her my father was dead—just straight out, like that. Then on his own initiative, without consulting anyone, he forbade her to go and see my father's sister and her husband, my uncle and aunt Dumarche, retired teachers who lived in Aubenas. Many years later they welcomed us with open arms, indignant at the thought that because of this wretched Testud they had not been able to have Rita to stay and to get in touch with me again. The same thing with my sisters: he refused to give their address. Still, she did manage to get this stony heart to tell her where my father had died—Saint-Peray.

The journey to Saint-Peray. There Henri Champel and Rita found my father's grave; and they learnt something else. After having been a widower for twenty years he had married again—a retired schoolmistress; this was when I was still in the penal settlement. They found her. The family called her Tante Ju, or sometimes Tata Ju.

A fine woman, said Rita, and with such a noble character that she had kept the memory of my mother alive in this new home. In the dining-room Rita had seen big photographs of my mother, whom I worshipped, and of my father. She had been able to touch and fondle objects that had belonged to her. Tante Ju, who now suddenly came into my life—although at the same time I felt I already knew her—had done all she could to let Rita feel the atmosphere she and my father had wanted to keep alive—the memory of my mother and the continual presence of that vanished little boy who was still Riri to my father.

November the 16th was my birthday, and every 16 November my father used to weep. Every Christmas there was a chair left empty. When the gendarmes came to tell them their son had escaped again, they almost kissed them for having brought such wonderful news. Because although Tante Ju did not know me, she had already adopted me in her heart as though I were her own son, and both she and my father shed tears of joy at hearing what was for them news of hope.

So she had received Rita more than kindly. Only one shadow: Tante Ju had not given her the address of my two sisters. Why not? I thought quickly. No doubt about it: she wasn't sure how they would take the news of my reappearance. Since she did not say to Rita, 'Hurry over and see them at such-and-such a place; they'll be wild with delight to know their brother's still alive and doing well, and to meet his wife' she must have had her reasons. Maybe Tante Ju knew that neither my sister Yvonne nor my sister Hélène, nor my brothers-in-law, would care to be visited by the wife of their brother, the escaped gaol-bird sentenced to life for murder. No doubt she did not want to take the responsibility of disturbing their peace.

They were married and they had children, and probably these children did not even know of my existence. Take care, she must have said to herself. It seemed to me that although throughout my thirteen years of penal I had lived with them and through them, they, on the other hand, must have spent those thirteen years doing their best to forget me or at least

197

trying to blot me out from their daily life. So all my wife brought back was a little earth from my father's grave and a photograph of the tomb where just four months before her coming my father had been laid to rest for ever.

Still, through Rita's eyes (for Champel had driven her everywhere) I did see the bridge of Ucel once more, the bridge of my childhood. I listened as she told me every detail about the big primary school where we had lived in the flat over the classrooms. Once again I could see the war memorial opposite our garden, and the garden itself, where a splendid flowering mimosa seemed to have kept itself in full bloom so that Rita, whose eyes drank in the garden, the memorial and the house, should be able to say to me 'Nothing, or almost nothing, has changed; and you've so often described the scenes of your childhood that I did not feel I was seeing something new but rather coming back to a place I already knew.'

Often in the evenings I would ask Rita to tell me some part of her journey all over again. At the hotel life went back to what it had been before. But deep inside me something inexplicable had happened. I had not felt this death as a forty-year-old man in the prime of life feels when he hears of the death of a father he has not seen for twenty years, but like a boy of ten—one who lives with his father, disobeys him, plays truant, and then on coming home, hears of his death.

Rita's daughter Clotilde arrived. She was over fifteen, but she was so frail and slight you would have said she was twelve. Long, thick, black, curling hair down to her shoulders. Her small jet-black eyes sparkled with intelligence and curiosity. Her little face was not that of a girl but of a child that might still be playing at hopscotch or with a doll. There was immediate sympathy between us. Right away she felt that this man who lived with her mother was going to be her best friend and that he would always love and protect her.

Since she had appeared, something new had come over me —the protective instinct, the wish that she should be happy and that she should look upon me if not as her father then at least as her surest support.

Now that Rita was back again, I did the shopping later, at seven. I took Clotilde with me, and we walked hand in hand.

with her leading Minou and Carlitos carrying the baskets. Everything was new for her, and she wanted to see it all at once. When she found something unexpected she piped up loud and clear to know what it was. What struck her most was the Indian women with their long shimmering robes, painted cheeks and shoes decorated with huge, many-coloured woollen pompons.

Having a child beside me, a child that trustingly grasped my hand whenever there was an imaginary danger, a little creature that leaned on my arm to make me understand that in the midst of this hurrying and shouting crowd, she felt completely protected, moved me deeply and filled me with a hitherto unknown feeling—the feeling of a father's love. 'Yes, little Clotilde, go forward into life with a trusting, easy mind; you can be sure that until the end I shall do everything I can to keep your path clear of thorns.'

And we would go happily back to the hotel, always with something amusing to tell Rita about what had happened to us or what we had seen.

I KNOW perfectly well that what the reader expects is my own personal adventures and not a history of Venezuela. Forgive me if I feel I should mention certain important political events that happened during the time I am writing about, because they had a direct influence on my life and on the decisions I took.

For many people Venezuela is just a country in South America (most aren't quite sure just where) that produces oil, a country exploited by the Americans as though it were a kind of American colony. This is far from true.

To be sure, the oil companies did have very great weight; but little by little the Venezuelan intellectuals have set the country almost entirely free from the influence of American policy.

At present Venezuela is completely independent politically, as it has proved by the attitude it has adopted at the United Nations and elsewhere. One thing all the political parties have in common is a great zeal for Venezuela's freedom of action with respect to all foreign countries. Thus, ever since Caldera came to power we have had diplomatic relations with every country in the world, whatever their political régimes.

It is true that economically Venezuela depends on its oil, but it has succeeded in selling it at a very high price and making the oil companies hand over as much as eighty-five per cent of their profits.

Venezuela has other things besides oil, such as iron and other raw materials; and Venezuela has men, a whole mass of men whose aim is to free their country entirely from all forms of economic pressure, wherever they come from. Men who have begun to prove and who will prove more and more that in Venezuela a democracy as good as any other can be set up, respected and preserved.

The young people in the universities long for nothing but social justice and the radical transformation of their country. They are full of faith, and confident of succeeding without doing away with the foundations of real freedom—confident of bringing happiness to the whole nation without falling into a dictatorship either of the extreme right or of the extreme left. I believe in the young people of this country: they will help to make it a nation that can be held up as an example, both for its truly democratic régime and for its economy, because it must not be forgotten that its huge resources of raw materials will soon be completely industrialized. When that happens, Venezuela will have won a great battle: and Venezuela *will* win it.

Venezuela is also an ideal country for the kind of tourism that must develop in the coming years. Everything is in its favour—its beaches of coral sand, shaded by coconut-palms; its sunshine, which beats all other countries; its fishing of every kind in a sea that is always warm; a cheaper cost of living than other countries; islands by the hundred; a welcoming, hospitable people without the least trace of a colour problem. At one hour's flying distance from Caracas you find the Indians, the lake villages of Maracaibo or the Andes with their everlasting snow.

In short, Venezuela is so rich in resources that the country scarcely needs a politician at the helm but rather a good accountant with a dynamic team who would use the currency provided by the oil for building factories to exploit this wealth and to increase the labour market for all who need work and who want it.

1951: once again, as I reach this date, I have the same feeling that I had then—the feeling of having nothing more to tell. You tell about storms and shooting the rapids of a swollen river; but when the water is calm and peaceful you feel like closing your eyes and resting on the placid current. But the rain comes pouring down again, the streams rise, the quiet water grows rough, the flood carries you away, and even if you longed to live in peace from everything, outside events have such an effect on your life that they force you to follow the current, avoiding the reefs and shooting the rapids in the hope of finding a quiet harbour at last.

After the mysterious killing of Chabaud at the end of 1950, Perez Jimenez seized power, although he hid behind Flamerich, the figure-head president of the junta. The dictatorship began. First sign: the suppression of the freedom of speech. The press and the radio were throttled. The opposition went underground and the terrible police, the *Seguridad Nacional*, went into action. The Communists and the *Adecos* (the members of the *Acción Democrática*, Bétancourt's party) were hunted down.

Several times we hid them at the Vera Cruz. Never did we close our doors to anyone at all; never did we ask for any man's identity. I was only too glad to pay my tribute to these followers of Bétancourt, whose régime had set me free and given me asylum. By doing this we ran the danger of losing everything, but Rita saw that we could not behave otherwise.

Then again, the hotel had become something of a refuge for Frenchmen in a jam—for Frenchmen who had reached Venezuela with little in their pockets and who did not know where to go. They could eat and sleep at our place without paying while they were looking for a job. This reached such a point that in Maracaibo they called me the Frenchmen's consul.

But in the course of these years there happened something very important for me, almost as important as my meeting with Rita—I renewed my ties with my family. As soon as Rita left, Tante Ju wrote to my two sisters. And all of them, both my sisters and Tante Ju, wrote to me. Twenty years had gone by, and the great silence was coming to an end. I trembled as I opened the first letter. What would there be in it? I dared not read. Would they reject me for ever, or would they . . .

Victory! These letters were a cry of joy—joy at knowing I was alive, earning an honest living, and married to a woman Tante Ju described with all the kindness she had felt. Not only had I found my sisters once again, but I had also found their families, who now became *my* family.

My elder sister had four fine children, three girls and a boy. Her husband wrote himself to say that his affection had remained unaltered and that he was more than happy to know I was free and doing well. And photos and still more photos, and pages and still more pages—the story of their lives and of the war and of what they had had to go through to bring up their children. I read every word, weighing and analysing to understand it thoroughly and savour all its charm.

And my childhood came to the surface after the great black

hole of the prisons and the penal settlement: 'My dear Riri,' wrote my sister. Riri ... I could hear my mother calling me and see her lovely smile. It seemed that judging from a photo I had sent them I was the image of my father. My sister was convinced that if I was like him physically I must be like him in personality. Her husband and she were not afraid of my turning up again. The gendarmes must have heard about Rita's journey in the Ardèche, because they came to ask them about me, and my brother-in-law replied, 'Yes indeed, we have news of him. He's very happy and he's doing fine, thank you very much.'

My other sister was in Paris, married to a Corsican lawyer. They had two sons and a daughter, and he had a good job. The same cry: 'You are free, you are loved, you have a home, a good position and you are living like everybody else. Well done, little brother! My children, my husband and I bless God for having helped you to come out a winner from that terrible prison into which they threw you.'

My elder sister suggested having our daughter so that she could go on with her studies in France. But what warmed our hearts most was the fact that not one of them seemed to be ashamed of having a brother who was an ex-convict who had escaped from the penal settlement.

To round off this influx of wonderful news, I managed to get hold of the address of my friend Dr Guibert-Germain, the former doctor of the settlement, who treated me as one of his family when I was on Royale, inviting me to his house, and protecting me from the screws. It was thanks to Dr Guibert-Germain that the solitary confinement at Saint-Joseph was done away with; and it was thanks to him that I was able to get myself transferred to Devil's Island and escape. I wrote to him, and one day I had the immense happiness of receiving this letter:

Lyons, 21 February 1952

My dear Papillon,

We are very glad to have news of you at last. For a long while now I have felt sure you were trying to get in touch with me. When I was in Jibuti my mother told me she had received a letter from Venezuela, although she could not say exactly who had sent it. Then, very recently, she sent me the letter you wrote through Mme Roesberg. So after a fair amount of trials we have managed to find you again. Since September 1945, when I left Royale, a good many things have happened.

... And then in October 1951 I was posted to Indo-China; I am to stay there for two years, and I leave very soon, that is to say on 6 March. This time I am going by myself. Perhaps when I am there, and according to where they send me, I may be able to arrange for my wife to come out and join me.

So you see that since the last time we met I have travelled a fair number of miles! I retain some pleasant memories of those days; but alas I have not been able to get in touch with any of the men I used to like asking to the house. For quite a long while I did hear from my cook (Ruche), who settled at Saint-Laurent; but since leaving Jibuti I have had no word. Still, we were very pleased to know that you were happy, in good health and comfortably established at last. Life is a strange thing; but I remember you never gave up hope, and indeed you were quite right.

We were delighted with the photograph of you and your wife—it shows that you have been really successful. Who knows, perhaps one day we may come and see you! Events move faster than we do. We see from the photograph that you have excellent taste: Madame seems charming, and the hotel has a very agreeable look. My dear Papillon, you must forgive me for still using this nickname; but it brings back so many memories for us!

... So there you have some idea of our doings, old fellow. We often talk about you, you may be sure, and we still remember that stirring day when Mandolini poked his nose into a place he should have left alone.*

My dear Papillon, I enclose a photograph of both of us; it was taken at Marseilles, on the Canebière, about two months ago.

And so I leave you, with all kinds of good wishes and hoping to hear from you now and then.

* This was Bruet, the warder who found the raft in the grave in *Papillon*.

My wife and I send our kind regards to your wife and our best wishes to you.

A. Guibert-Germain

And following that, a few lines from Madame Guibert-Germain: 'With my best compliments on your success and kindest wishes to you both for the New Year. Greetings to my protégé.'

Madame Guibert-Germain never did join her husband in Indo-China. He was killed in 1952, so I never saw him again, that self-effacing medico who, together with Major Péan of the Salvation Army and a handful of others, was one of the very few men at the penal settlement who had the courage to stand up for humane ideas in favour of the convicts; and in his case, to succeed in getting some results while he was serving there. There are no words fine enough to express the respect due to people like him and his wife. In opposition to one and all and at the risk of his career, he maintained that a convict was still a man, and that even if he had committed a serious crime he was not lost for ever.

There were also the letters from Tante Ju. These were not the letters of a stepmother who has never known you, but real motherly letters, saying things that only a mother's heart could think of. Letters in which she told me about my father's life up until the time he died, the life of that law-abiding schoolmaster, full of respect for the legal authorities, who nevertheless cried out, 'My boy was innocent, I know it; and these swine have had him found guilty! Where can he be, now that he has escaped? Is he dead or alive?' Every time the members of the Resistance in the Ardèche brought off an operation against the Germans, he would say, 'If Henri were here, he would be with them.' Then the months of silence during which he no longer pronounced his son's name. It was as though he had transferred his affection for me to his grandchildren, whom he spoiled more than most grandfathers.

I devoured all this like a starving man. Rita and I read all these precious letters that renewed the links with my family over and over again and kept them like positive relics. Truly I was blessed by the gods—all my people without exception had enough love for me and enough courage not to give a damn for what people might say and to tell me of their joy that I was alive, free and happy. And indeed courage was necessary, because society has a hard heart and it does not easily forgive a family for having had a delinquent belonging to it.

1953: we sold the hotel. In time the shattering heat had got us down; and in any case Rita and I loved adventure, and we did not mean to spend the rest of our days in Maracaibo. All the more so as I'd heard of a tremendous boom in Venezuelan Guiana, where a mountain of almost pure iron had been discovered. It was at the other end of the country, so we were up and away for Caracas, meaning to stop there a while and look into the situation.

One fine morning we set off in my huge green De Soto brake, crammed with baggage, leaving behind us five years of quiet happiness and many friends.

And once again I saw Caracas. But was this really Caracas? Hadn't we hit on the wrong town?

At the end of Flamerich's term Perez Jimenez had himself named president of the republic; but even before that he had set about turning the colonial town of Caracas into a typical ultra-modern capital. All this during a period of unheard-of cruelty, both on the side of the government and the underground opposition. Caldera (who has been president since 1970) escaped from a shocking attempt on his life: a powerful bomb was thrown into the room where he was sleeping with his wife and a child. By an absolute miracle not one of them was killed; and with wonderful coolness—no shrieks, no panic —he and his wife just went down on their knees to thank God for having saved their lives.

But in spite of all the difficulties he had to deal with during his dictatorship, Perez Jimenez entirely transformed Caracas, and a good many other things too.

The old road from Caracas to the Maiquetia airfield and the port of La Guaira was still there. But Perez Jimenez had built a magnificent and technically outstanding motorway that meant you could get from the town to the sea in less than a quarter of an hour, whereas it had taken two hours by the old road. In the Silencio district Perez Jimenez ran up enormous buildings the size of those in New York. And he built an astonishing six-lane motorway right through the city from one end to the other—not to mention the building of working- and middle-class complexes that were models of urbanism, and many other changes. All this meant millions and millions of dollars swirling about; and it meant that a great deal of energy burst out in this country that had been dozing for hundreds of years. Foreign capital came flowing in, together with specialists of every kind. Life changed completely; immigration was wide open, and fresh blood came in giving a positive beat to the country's new rhythm.

I took the opportunity of our stop in Caracas to get in touch with friends and to find out what had happened to Picolino. These last years I had regularly sent people to visit him and take him a little money. I saw a friend who had given him a small sum from me in 1952, a sum he had asked for so as to go and settle in La Guaira, near the port. I'd often suggested that he should come and live with us at Maracaibo, but every time he replied through his friends that Caracas was the only place with doctors. It seemed that he had almost recovered his speech and that his right arm more or less worked. But now nobody knew what had become of him. He had been seen creeping about the port of La Guaira and then he had completely disappeared. Perhaps he had taken a ship back to France. I never knew; and I have always kicked myself for not having gone to Caracas earlier to persuade him to come to me in Maracaibo.

Everything was clear: if we couldn't find what we wanted in Venezuelan Guiana where there was this terrific boom and where General Ravard had just set about the overflowing virgin forest and its enormous rivers with dynamite to show they could be tamed, we would come back and settle in Caracas.

With the De Soto full of luggage, Rita and I drove to the capital of the state, Ciudad Bolivar, on the banks of the Orinoco. After eight years and more I found myself once more in that charming provincial town with its kindly, welcoming people.

We spent the night at a hotel, and we had scarcely sat down on the terrace for our morning coffee when a man stopped ped in front of us. A man of about fifty, tall, thin and sun-dried; he had a little straw hat on his head and he screwed up his small eyes until they almost disappeared.

'Either I'm crazy or you're a Frenchman called Papillon,' he said.

'You're not very discreet, mate. Suppose this lady here didn't know?'

'Excuse me. I was so surprised I didn't even notice I was talking like a fool.'

'Say no more about it: sit down here, with us.'

He was an old friend, Marcel B. We talked. He was quite amazed to see me in such good form; he felt I had succeeded in doing well for myself. I told him it had mostly been luck, a great deal of luck; he didn't have to tell me, poor soul, that he had not made a go of it—his clothes did the telling. I asked him to lunch.

After a few glasses of Chilean wine he said, 'Yes, Madame, although you see me like this, I was a fine upstanding type when I was young—afraid of nothing. Why, after my first break from penal I reached Canada, and there I joined the Canadian Mounted Police, no less! I might have stayed there all my life, but one day I had a fight, and the other guy fell right on to my knife. It's God's truth, Madame Papillon. This Canadian fell right on to my knife. You don't believe me, do you? Well, I knew the Canadian police wouldn't believe me either, so I made my getaway that very minute, and going by way of the United States, I reached Paris. I must have been sold by some sod or other, because they picked me up and sent me back to penal. That's where I knew your husband: we were good friends.'

'And what are you doing now, Marcel?'

'I grow tomatoes at Los Morichales.'

'Do they do well?'

'Not very. Sometimes the clouds don't let the sun come through properly. You know it's there, but you can't see it. But it sends down invisible rays that slay your tomatoes for you in a few hours.'

'Christ! How come?'

'One of the mysteries of nature, mate. I don't know anything about the cause, but the result, I know that all right.'

'Are there many ex-lags here?'

'About twenty.'

'Happy?'

'More or less.'

'Is there anything you need?'

'Papi, I swear if you hadn't said that I wouldn't have asked for a thing. But I can tell you're not doing so badly—so excuse me, Madame, but I'm going to ask for something very important.'

The thought flashed through my mind, 'God, don't let it cost too much,' and then I said, 'What do you need? Speak up, Marcel.'

'A pair of trousers, a pair of shoes, a shirt and a tie.'

'Come on: let's get into the car.'

'That's yours? Well, my cock, you have had luck.'

'Yes, plenty of luck.'

'When are you leaving?'

'Tonight.'

'Pity. Otherwise you could have driven the bridal pair in your bus.'

'What bridal pair?'

'Of course! I never told you the clothes were to go to the marriage of an ex-lag.'

'Do I know him?'

'Don't know. He's called Maturette.'

'What did you say? Maturette?'

'Right. What's so extraordinary about that? Is he an enemy of yours?'

'Not at all, a great friend.'

I couldn't get over it! Maturette! The little fairy who not only made it possible for us to escape from the Saint-Laurent-du-Maroni hospital but who also travelled fifteen hundred miles with us in a boat on the open sea.

No question of leaving now. The next day there we were at the wedding, when Maturette and a sweet little coloured girl were married. We could not do less than pay the bill and buy clothes for the three children they had produced before going to the altar. This was one of the few times when I was sorry I had not been christened, because that stopped me being his best man.

Maturette lived in a poor district where the De Soto made a

sensation, but still he did own a clean little brick house with a kitchen, a shower and a dining-room. He did not tell me about his second break and I did not tell him about mine. Just one reference to the past: 'With a little more luck, we'd have been free ten years earlier.'

'Yes, but our fates would have been different. I'm happy, Maturette; and you look pretty happy too.'

We parted, our throats tight with emotion, saying 'Au revoir,' and 'See you soon.'

As Rita and I drove on towards Ciudad Piar, a town springing up by a deposit of iron they were getting ready to exploit, I spoke about Maturette and the extraordinary ups and downs in life. He and I had been on the brink of death at sea a score of times; we had been captured and taken back to prison; and, like me, he had copped two years of solitary. And now, as she and I were driving in search of some new adventure, not only did I find him, but I found him on the eve of his marriage. And to both of us at the same moment there came this thought: 'The past doesn't mean a thing; all that matters is what you have made of yourself.'

At Ciudad Piar we found nothing suitable and we went back to Caracas to look for some business that was doing well.

Very soon we found one that answered both to our abilities and our purse. It was a restaurant called the Aragon, right next to the Carbobo park, a very beautiful spot, and it was changing hands: it suited us perfectly. The beginning was tough, because the former owners came from the Canaries and we had to change everything from top to bottom. We adopted half-French, half-Venezuelan menus and our customers increased in number every day. Among them were plenty of professional men, doctors, dentists, chemists and barristers. Some manufacturers, too. And in this pleasant atmosphere the months went by without incident.

It was on a Monday, at nine in the morning, that the wonderful news reached us: on 6 June 1956 to be exact. The Ministry of the Interior informed me that my request for naturalization had been granted.

Now came the great day: it was my reward for having spent ten years in Venezuela without the authorities finding anything to criticize in the life I had led as a future citizen. It was 5 July 1956, the national holiday. I was to go and swear loyalty to the flag of my new country, the country that accepted me knowing my past. There were three hundred of us there in front of the flag. Rita and Clotilde sat in the audience. Hard to say what I felt, there were so many ideas milling about in my head and so many emotions in my heart. I remembered what the Venezuelan nation had given me—both material and spiritual help, with never a word about my past. I remembered the legend of the Iano-Mamos, Indians who live on the Brazilian frontier, the legend that says they are the sons of Peribo, the moon. The great warrior Peribo was in danger of being killed by his enemies' arrows, and he leapt so high to escape from death that he rose far into the air, although he had been hit several times. He kept on rising, and from his wounds there fell drops of blood that turned into Iano-Mamos when they touched the ground. Yes, I thought about that legend, and I wondered whether Simon Bolivar, the liberator of Venezuela, had not also scattered his blood to give rise to a race of generous, open-hearted men, bequeathing to them the best of himself.

They played the national anthem. Everybody stood up. I stared hard at the starry flag as it rose and tears flowed down my cheeks.

I, who had thought I should never sing another national anthem in my life, I roared out the words of the anthem of my new country with the others, at the top of my voice—'*Abajo cadenas . . .*'—Down with the chains.

Yes, it was today and for ever that I really felt them drop off, the chains I had been loaded with. For ever.

'Swear loyalty to this flag, which is now your own.'

Solemnly all three hundred of us swore it; but I am very sure that the one who did so with most sincerity was myself, Papillon, the man his mother-country had condemned to a fate worse than death for a crime he did not commit. Yes, although France was the land that bore me, Venezuela was my haven.

Now events moved very rapidly. As a Venezuelan I could have a passport, and I got one right away. I trembled with emotion when they handed it to me. I trembled again when I fetched it from the Spanish embassy with an elegant three months' visa. I trembled when they stamped it as I went aboard the *Napoli*, the splendid liner that was taking Rita and me to Europe, to Barcelona. I trembled when the Guardia Civil gave it back to me in Spain, with the entrance visa. This passport, which had made me the citizen of a country once more, was so precious that Rita had sewn a zip-fastener on each of my inside coat pockets so that I could not lose it whatever happened.

Everything was beautiful during this voyage, even the sea when it was rough, even the rain when it came driving across the deck, even the ill-tempered guy in charge of the hold who unwillingly let me go below to make sure the big Lincoln we had just bought was properly stowed. Everything was beautiful because our hearts were on holiday. Whether we were in the dining-room, at the bar, in the saloon, and whether there were people around us or not, our eyes kept meeting so we could speak without anyone hearing. Because we were going to Spain, right up by the French border, and we were going for a reason I had not dared to hope for these many years. And my eyes said to Rita, 'Thank you, Minouche. It's thanks to you that I'm going to see *my people* again. And it's you who are taking me to them.'

And her eyes said, 'I promised you that if you trusted me, one day you would be able to go and embrace your family wherever you liked and whenever you liked, without having anything to fear.'

For the purpose of this hurriedly prepared voyage was to see my family once more, on Spanish territory out of reach of the French police. It was twenty-six years since I had seen them. We were going to spend a whole month together, and they were coming as my guests.

Day after day went by, and I often went into the bows,

spending a long time there, as though this part of the ship were closer to our destination. We had passed Gibraltar; we had lost sight of land again; we were getting very near.

I settled myself comfortably in a deckchair and my eyes tried to pierce the horizon where any minute now the land of Europe would appear. The land of Spain, joined to that of France.

1930-1956: twenty-six years. I was twenty-four then; I was fifty now. A whole lifetime. My heart beat violently when at last I made out the coast. The liner ran on fast, carving a huge V in the sea, a V whose far ends spread and spread until gradually they vanished and melted into the ocean.

When I left France aboard *La Martinière*, that accursed ship which was taking us to Guiana—yes, when she steamed away from the coast I did not see it: I did not see the land, *my land*, drawing gradually away from me and for ever (as I thought then), because we were in iron cages at the bottom of the hold.

And now today here was my new passport in the pocket of my yachtsman's blazer, well protected by Rita's zip—the passport of my new country, my other identity. 'Venezuelan? You, a Frenchman, born of French parents—of schoolteachers, and from the Ardèche into the bargain?'

I was perhaps five—when my grandfather Thierry bought me a beautiful mechanical horse. How splendid he was, my lovely stallion! Almost red; and such a mane! It was black, real horsehair, and it always hung down on the right-hand side. I pedalled so hard that, on the flat, our maid had to run to keep up with me; then she would push me up the little slope I called the hill; and so, after another stretch of flat, I reached the nursery school.

Mme Bonnot, the headmistress and a friend of Mama's, welcomed me in front of the school; she stroked the long curly hair that came down to my shoulders like a girl's and said to Louis, the caretaker, 'Open the door as wide as it will go so that Riri can ride in on his splendid horse.'

I pedalled with all my strength and flew into the playground. First I made a great sweep right round it and then I gently dismounted, holding the bridle so it would not roll away. I kissed Thérèse, the maid, who handed Mme Bonnot my sandwiches. And all the other boys and girls, my friends, came to admire and stroke this wonder, the one and only mechanical horse in these two little villages, Pont-d'Ucel and Pont-d'Aubenas.

Every day before I set out, Mama told me to lend it to each one in turn: this I found rather hard, but still I did it. When the bell rang, Louis the caretaker put the horse away under the lean-to, and once we were in line we marched into school, singing 'Nous n'irons plus au bois'.

I know my way of telling my story will make some people smile; but you have to understand that when I am talking about my childhood it is not a man of sixty-five who is writing but a kid—it is Riri of Pont-d'Ucel who writes, so deeply is that childhood imprinted on his mind, and he writes with the words he used then.

My childhood ... A garden with gooseberries that my sisters and I ate before they were ripe, and pears that we were forbidden to pick before Papa said we could; but by crawling like a Red Indian so that no one could see me from a window in the flat I had my fill from the pear tree, and a belly-ache afterwards.

I was eight, but still I would often go to sleep on my father's lap or in my mother's arms. Sometimes, when she tucked me into my little bed, I would half wake up, put my arms around her neck and hold her tight, and we would stay like that for what seemed to me a long, long time, our breath mingling; and at last I would go to sleep without knowing when she left me.

How beautiful Mama was! Tall, slim, always elegant. You ought to have seen how she played the piano, even when I knelt on a chair behind her music-stool and closed her eyes with my little hands. Wasn't it wonderful to have a Mama who could play the piano without seeing either the music or the keys? Besides, Mama was never meant to be a schoolmistress. My grandfather was very rich and Mama and her sister Léontine had been to the most expensive schools in Avignon. It was not Mama's fault that my grandfather Thierry had liked living high; her father was very kind, but because he had loved living so well, giving splendid parties in Avignon and meeting too many pretty farmers' wives, Mama had no dowry, and she was forced to earn her own living.

My grandfather was terrific. He had a little goatee and a snow-white moustache. Hand in hand we went round the farms in the morning, and as he was secretary of the *mairie* ('He has to earn his tobacco-money,' said Tante Léontine), he always had papers to take to the peasants or to fetch from their homes. I noticed how right my aunt was when she said he always lingered at a certain farm where the woman of the house was good-looking. I was delighted, because it was the only farm where they let me ride the little donkey and where I could meet Mireille, a girl of my age who was much better at playing papa and mama than the girl next door at Pont-d'Ucel.

Eight, and already I was beginning to play the fool. Secretly I went to swim in the Ardèche. I had learnt by myself in the canal; it was deep, but it was only five yards across. We had no bathing things, of course, so we bathed naked, seven or eight of us, all boys together. Oh, those sunny days in the water of my Ardèche! The trout we caught with our hands! I never went home until I was quite dry.

1914. The war, and Papa was called up. We went with him as far as the train. He was going with the *Chasseurs Alpins*, and he would soon be back. He said to us, 'Be good children and always obey your mother. And you girls must help with the housework, because she is going to look after both classes, mine and hers, all by herself. This war won't last long; everybody says so.' And standing there on the platform the four of us watched the train go, with my father leaning half out of the window to wave and to gaze at us a little longer. Those four years of war had no influence on our happiness at home. We drew a little closer to each other. I slept in the big bed with Mama; I took the place of my father, who was fighting at the front.

Four years in the history of the world is nothing. Four years for a kid of eight was an eternity.

I was growing fast; we played at soldiers and at battles. I would come home covered with bruises and my clothes torn, but whether I had won or lost I always came home happy, never crying. Mama bandaged the grazes and put raw meat on a black eye. She would scold me a little, but gently, never shouting. Her reproaches were more like a whisper. 'Be kind, little Riri, your mama is tired. This class of sixty children is utterly exhausting. I am completely worn out, you see; it's more than I can manage. Darling, you must help me by being good and obedient.' It always ended with kisses and a promise to behave well.

Somebody was stealing our wood, stacked under the lean-to in the playground; and at night Mama was frightened. I cuddled close, putting my child's arm round her to make her feel that I was a protection. 'Don't be afraid, Mama; I'm the man of the house and I'm big enough to defend you.' I took down Papa's gun and slipped two buck-shot cartridges into it—he used them for wild boar. One night Mama woke up, shook me, and whispered in my ear, 'I heard the thieves. They made a noise, pulling out a log.' She was sweating.

'Don't be afraid, Mama.'

I got up very quietly, with the gun in my hands. With infinite care I opened the window; it squeaked a little and I held my breath. Then, pulling the shutter towards me with one hand, I unhooked it with the barrel; holding the butt against my shoulder, ready to fire on the thieves, I pushed the shutter. It opened without a sound. The moon lit up the courtyard as though it were day and I saw perfectly well that there was nobody at all in the playground. The heap of wood was still neatly arranged. 'There's no one, Mama; come and see.' And, clinging to one another, we both stayed at the window for some time, comforted by seeing there were no thieves and Mama happy at finding that her little boy was brave.

In spite of all this happiness, sometimes I would behave badly, although I did not want to hurt my adored mother; but I always believed, I always hoped, she would not know. A cat tied by the tail to a front-door bell; the water-bailiff's bicycle that we threw over the bridge into the Ardèche—he had gone down to the river to catch poachers fishing with a net. And other things ... Hunting birds with slings; and twice, when I was between ten and eleven, little Riquet Debannes and I went off into the country with Papa's gun to shoot a rabbit he had seen skipping about in a field. Getting the gun in and out of the house without my mother noticing, and twice at that, was a tremendous feat.

1917. Papa was wounded. He had many little shell-splinters in his head, but his life was not in danger. The news came by the Red Cross: a terrible shock. But no outcry; almost no tears. Twenty-four hours passed, Mama taught her class as usual—nobody knew a thing. I watched my mother, and I admired her. Normally I was in the front row in class; that day I sat at the back to keep an eye on all the pupils, determined to step in if any of them fooled about during lessons. By half past three Mama was at the end of her tether; I knew it, because we should have had natural science, but she went out, writing an arithmetic problem on the blackboard and saying, 'I must go out for a few minutes: do this sum in your arithmetic books.'

I went out after her; she was leaning against the mimosa just to the right of the gate. She was crying: my poor dear mama had given in.

I hugged her tight: and of course I did not cry. I tried to comfort her, and when she said to me, sobbing, 'Your poor papa is wounded,' just as if I did not know, my kid's heart found this reply, 'So much the better, Mama. This way the war is over for him and we can be sure he'll come back alive.' And all at once Mama realized that I was right.

'Why, that's perfectly true! You're quite right, darling; Papà will come back to us alive!'

A kiss on my forehead, a kiss on my cheek, and we went back to the classroom hand in hand.

The Spanish coast was quite visible, and I could make out the specks of white that must be houses. The coast was becoming more distinct, just like those holidays in 1917 that we spent at Saint-Chamas, where Papa had been sent to guard the powder-works. His wounds were not very serious, but the minute splinters could not be removed yet. He was classed as an auxiliary: no more front line for him.

We were all together again, full of happiness.

Mama was radiant: we had got right out of this horrible war; but for other people it was still going on, and she said to us, 'Darlings, you must not be selfish and spend all your days running about and picking jujubes; you must set aside three

217

hours a day for thinking of others.'

So we went with her to the hospital, where every morning she looked after the patients and cheered them up. Each of us had to do something useful—push a badly-wounded man in his wheel-chair, lead a blind patient about, make lint, write letters or listen to what the men confined to bed had to say about their families.

It was when we were going home in the train that Mama felt so ill at Vogué. We went to my father's sister at Lanas, about twenty miles from Aubenas—to Tante Antoinette, who was a schoolmistress too. We were kept away from Mama, because the doctor's diagnosis was some unknown infectious disease, presumably caught when she was looking after the Indochinese at Saint-Chamas. My sisters went to the Aubenas high school as boarders and I to the boys' high school.

It seemed that Mama was getting better. But in spite of everything I was sad, and that Sunday I refused to go out for a walk with the others. I was alone, and I threw a knife at a plane tree; almost every time it stuck there in the bark.

That was how I was spending my time, in the road almost opposite the school, low-spirited and depressed. The road came up from the Aubenas station, some five hundred yards away. I heard a train whistle as it came in, and then again as it pulled out. I was not expecting anyone, so there was no point in looking down the road to see the people who had got out.

Tirelessly I threw my knife, on and on. My steel watch showed that it was five o'clock. The sun was low now, and it was getting in my eyes; so I changed sides. And it was then that I saw death coming silently towards me.

Death's messengers, their heads bowed, their faces hidden behind black crêpe veils almost down to the ground: I knew them well in spite of their funeral trappings—Tante Ontine, Tante Antoinette, my father's mother, and then behind them the men, as though they were using the women as a screen. My father, bent almost double, and my two grandfathers, all of them in black.

I did not go towards them; I did not stir; how could I have done so? My blood was all gone, my heart had stopped, my eyes so longed to weep they could not bring out a single tear. The group stopped more than ten yards from me. They were

218

afraid—or rather they were ashamed: I knew it, I was certain of it, they would sooner be dead than face me and tell me what I already knew, because without having to utter a sound their black clothes told me 'Your mother has died.'

Who was with her? Nobody, since I, her greatest love, was not there. Dead and buried without my having seen her, dead without giving me a kiss. Papa was the first to come forward; he managed to stand almost straight. His poor face was a picture of the most desperate suffering and his tears fell without ceasing; still I did not move. He did not open his arms to me: he knew very well I could not stir. At last he reached me and embraced me without a word. Then at last I burst into tears as I heard the words, 'She died saying your name.' I fainted.

The war was over: Papa came home. A man called to see him; and they ate cheese and drank a few glasses of red wine. They numbered the dead of our region, and then the visitor said a dreadful thing: 'As for us, we came out of this war all right, eh, Monsieur Charrière? And your brother-in-law too. We may have won nothing, but at least we lost nothing either.'

I went out before he left. Night had fallen. I waited for him to go by and then I threw a stone with my sling, hitting him full on the back of the head. He went bellowing into a neighbour's house to have his wound dressed —it was bleeding. He did not understand who could have flung the stone at him, nor why. He had no idea that he had been struck for having forgotten the most important victim, the one whose loss could least be mended, in his list of the war-dead. My mother.

No, we had not come out of this accursed war all right: far from it.

And every year when term began again, I went back as a boarder to the high school at Crest, in the Drôme, where I was preparing for the entrance exam to the Aix-en-Provence *Arts et Métiers*.*

At school I grew very tough and violent. At rugby I played scrum-half and I tackled hard: I asked no favours and I certainly gave none either.

* Roughly equivalent to a college of industrial design and engineering.

Six years now I had been a boarder at Crest, six years of being an excellent pupil, particularly in mathematics; but also six years with no marks for good behaviour. I was in all the roughest stuff that went on. Once or twice a month, always on Thursdays, I had a fight: but Thursday was the day the boys' parents came to see them.

The mothers came to take their sons out to lunch, and then if it was a fine afternoon, they would stroll about with their boys under the chestnut trees in our playground. Every week I swore I would not watch the sight from the library window; but it was no good, I just had to settle down in a place from where I could see everything. And from my window I discovered that there were two sorts of attitudes, both of which made me furiously angry.

There were some boys whose mothers were plain or badly dressed or who looked like peasants. Those fellows had the air of being ashamed of them, the swine, the dirty little sods! It was perfectly obvious. Instead of going right round the courtyard or walking from one end to the other, they would sit there on a bench in the corner and never move. They didn't want anyone to see their mother and they were hiding her; the sods had already got some idea of what educated, distinguished people were like, and they wanted to forget their origins before they were *Arts et Métiers* engineers.

It was not hard to pick a quarrel with that type. If I saw one send his embarrassing mother away early and come into the library, I would go for him at once. 'Say, Pierrot, why did you make your mother go so soon?'

'She was in a hurry.'

'That's not true. You're a liar: your mother takes the train for Gap at seven. I'll tell you why you sent her off: it's because you're ashamed of her. And don't you dare tell me that's not true, you sod!'

In these fights I nearly always came out on top. I fought so often that I became very good with my fists. Even when I got more than I gave, I didn't give a damn—I almost liked it. But I never went for a weaker boy.

The other kind that sent me into a rage, the kind I fought most savagely, were the ones I called the swaggerers. These were the fellows with pretty, well-dressed, distinguished mothers. When you are sixteen or seventeen you are proud of showing off a mother like that, and they would strut about the yard, holding her arm and mincing and simpering until it drove me mad.

Each time one of them had swaggered too much for my liking, or if his mother had a way of walking that reminded me of my own, or if she wore gloves and took them off and held them gracefully in one hand, then I could not bear it: I went out of my mind with fury.

The minute the culprit came in I went for him. 'You don't have to parade about like that, you big ape; not with a mother dressed in last year's fashions. Mine was better looking, brighter and more distinguished than yours. Her jewels were real, not phony like your mother's. Such trash! Even a guy who knows nothing about it can see that right away.'

Naturally, most of the types I spoke to like this didn't even wait for me to finish before hitting me in the face. Sometimes this first swipe would go right to my head. I fought rough: butting, cow-kicks, using my elbows in the in-fighting; and joy welled up inside me, as though I were smashing all the mothers who dared to be as pretty and fine-looking as my mama.

I really could not control it; ever since my mother's death when I was nearly eleven, I'd had this red-hot iron inside me. You can't understand death when you are eleven: you can't accept it. The very old might die, maybe. But your mother, an angel full of youth and beauty and health, how can she conceivably die?

It was because of a fight of this kind that my life changed completely.

This guy was a pretentious type, proud of being nineteen, proud of his success in maths. Tall, very tall; no good at games because he swotted all the time, but very strong. One day, when we were going for a walk, he lifted a massive tree-trunk all by himself so that we could get at the hole where a fieldmouse was hiding.

And this fellow had really let himself go that particular Thursday. A tall, slim mother, in a white dress with blue spots. If she had been trying to imitate one of Mama's dresses she couldn't have done better. Big black eyes; a pretty little

221

hat with a white tulle veil.

And this engineer-to-be swaggered about the courtyard the whole of that afternoon, up and down, to and fro, round and round. Often they kissed; they were almost like lovers.

As soon as he was alone I started on him. 'Well, you're the wonder of the world, all right. You're as good at putting on a circus act as you are at maths. I didn't know you were such a ...'

'What's wrong with you, Henri?'

'What's wrong with me is that I just have to tell you that you show your mother like they show a bear in a circus, to amaze your buddies. Well, get this: I'm not amazed. Because your mother is just nothing at all compared with mine: she merely takes after the showy tarts I've seen during the season at Vals-les-Bains.'

'Take that back, or I'll spoil your face for you; and you know I hit hard. You know I'm stronger than you.'

'Trying to get out of it, eh? Listen: I know you're stronger than me. So to balance things, we'll have a duel. Each with compasses. Go and fetch yours and I'll fetch mine. If you're not a shit and if you can stand up for yourself, I'll be waiting for you behind the lavatories in five minutes.'

'I'll be there.'

A few minutes later he went down, my compass-point buried deep just under his heart.

I was seventeen when my father and I came out of the office of the examining magistrate in charge of my case. He had told my father that if he wanted to stop the proceedings he should make me join the navy. At the gendarmerie of Aubenas I signed on for three years.

My father did not really reproach me for the serious thing I had done. 'If I understand rightly, Henri,' he said—he called me Henri when he meant to be severe, 'and I believe what you say, you suggested fighting with a weapon because your opponent was stronger than you?'

'Yes, Papa.'

'Well, you did wrong. That is the way ruffians fight. And you are not a ruffian, my boy.'

'No.'

'Look at the mess you have got yourself into. Think of how you must have hurt your mother.'

'I don't think I hurt her.'

'Why not, Henri?'

'It was her I was fighting for.'

'What do you mean?'

'I mean I can't bear seeing other boys flaunt their mothers at me.'

'I will tell you something, Henri; it was not for your mama that this fight and all the others before it came about. It was not out of real love for her. The reason is that you are selfish; because fate had taken your mother from you, you would like it to be the same for all the other boys. I suffer too when another teacher comes to see me, arm in arm with his wife. I can't prevent myself from thinking of their happiness, of that happiness I too ought to have had. Only I am not jealous of them: on the contrary, I hope that nothing as horrible as what happened to me will happen to them.

'If you were really a reflection of your mother's heart, you would be happy at the happiness of others. Now, do you see, in order to get out of this you have to join the navy: three years at least, and they are not going to be easy ones. And I am going to be punished too, since for three years my son is going to be far away from me.' And then he said something that has always remained engraved on my heart: 'You know, my dear boy, you can become an orphan at any age. Remember that all your life.'

The *Napoli*'s siren made me jump. It wiped out that remote past, those pictures of my eighteenth year, when my father and I walked out of the gendarmerie where I had just enlisted. But immediately afterwards there rose up the unhappiest memory of them all, the moment when I saw him for the very last time.

It was in one of those grim visiting-rooms at the Santé prison—each in a barred box separated by a corridor a yard wide. I was racked by shame and disgust for what my life had been and for what had brought my father here into this wild-beast cage.

He had not come to reproach me for being suspect number

one in a dirty underworld job. He had the same ravaged face I had seen the day he told me of my mother's death, and he had come into this prison of his own accord to see his boy for half an hour, not to blame his bad behaviour nor to make him understand what this business meant for his family's honour and peace of mind, nor yet to say 'You are a bad son', but to beg my forgiveness for not having succeeded in bringing me up properly. What he said was the last thing I should ever have expected, the one thing that could touch my heart more deeply than all the reproaches in the world: 'I believe, Riri, that it is through my fault that you are here. Forgive me for having spoilt you too much.'

Nothing could have been more hostile than the iron discipline of the navy in 1923. The ratings were classed in six categories, according to their level of education. I was in the top, the sixth. And this seventeen-year-old boy, just out of the class preparing for the *Arts et Métiers*, could not understand or adapt himself to blind, instant obedience to orders given by quartermasters belonging to the lowest intellectual level.

I was in trouble right away. I could not obey orders that had no rhyme or reason. I refused to go on any specialized course, the normal thing for a man with my education, and I was at once classed among the *estrasses*, the undisciplined, the no-good 'unspecialized' types.

We were the ones who had all the nastiest, dullest, stupidest jobs. The potato-peeling fatigues, the heads, brass to polish all day long, the coaling, washing the decks: all for us.

'What the hell are you doing there, hiding behind the funnel?'

'We have finished washing the deck, quartermaster.'

'Is that right? Well, just you start again, and this time wash it from aft forward. And if it's not cleaner this go, you'll hear from me.'

A sailor is a fine sight, with his pompon, his jersey with its wide blue collar, his slightly tilted cap as flat as a pancake and his uniform made to fit properly. But we good-for-nothings were not allowed to have our things re-cut. The worse we were dressed and the drearier we looked, the better the quartermasters were pleased. In an atmosphere like this the awkward types never stopped thinking up quite serious offences. Every time we were alongside a quay, for example, we stole ashore and spent the night in the town. Where did we go? To the brothels, of course. With a friend or two I would fix things in no time at all. Right away we each had our tart: we not only made love for free, but she would also give us a note or two for a drink or a meal.

The punishments became more frequent. Fifteen days' detention; then thirty. To get our own back on a cook who refused us a bit of meat and a crust after the potatoes fatigue, we stole a whole leg of mutton, done to a turn, fishing it out with a hook we slid down a ventilator over the stove when he had his back turned: we ate it in the coal-bunker. Result: forty-five days in the naval prison; and there I was without a stitch in the Toulon prison-yard in midwinter opposite the wash-house with its huge basin of icy water into which we had to plunge.

It was a seaman's cap not worth ten francs that brought me up before the disciplinary board. Charge: destruction of naval property.

In the navy, everybody changed the shape of his cap. Not to destroy it—it was a question of being well turned out. You first wetted it, and then three of you would pull as hard as possible, so that when you put a piece of whalebone round inside it was as flat as a pancake. 'It's smashing, a right flat cap,' said the girls. Particularly a cap with a pretty carrot-coloured pompon on it, carefully trimmed with scissors. All the girls in the town knew it brought good luck to touch a pompon, and that you had to pay for touching it with a kiss.

The master-at-arms was a thick-headed brute—I became his pet aversion. He never left me in peace; he kept after me night and day. So much so that three times I went absent without leave. But never more than five days and twenty-three hours, because at six days you were put down as a deserter. And a deserter I very nearly was at Nice. I'd spent the night with a terrific girl and woke up late. One more hour and I should have been on the list. I scrambled into my clothes and left at a run, looking for a cop to get myself arrested. I caught sight of one, hurried over to him and asked him to arrest me. He was a fat, kindly old soul. 'Come now, boy, don't fly into a panic. Just you go back quietly to your ship and tell them all about it. We've all been young once.'

I told him one hour more and I was a deserter; but it was no good, he wouldn't listen. So I picked up a stone, turned to a shop window and said to the cop, 'If you don't arrest me, I'll smash this window in one second flat.'

'The boy's crazy. Come along, young fellow; the station for you.'

But it was for having stretched a cap to make it prettier that they sent me to the disciplinary sections at Calvi, in Corsica. No one can doubt that this was the first step towards the penal settlement.

They called the disciplinary section *la camise*, and you had a special uniform. As soon as you got there you went in front of a reception committee, and they decided whether you were to be rated a genuine *camisard*. You had to prove you were a man by fighting two or three seniors one after another. With my training at the Crest high school, it passed off pretty well. During the second fight, when my lip was split and my nose a bleeding mess, the seniors stopped the test. I was rated genuine *camisard*.

La camise. I worked in a Corsican senator's vineyards. From sunrise to sunset: no break, no little presents; the difficult types had to be brought to heel. We weren't even sailors any more: we belonged to the 173 Infantry Regiment at Bastia. I can still see that citadel at Calvi, our three-mile walk, pick or shovel on our shoulder, to Calenzana, where we worked, and our quick-march back to the prison. It was unendurable, we rebelled, and as I was one of the ringleaders, I was sent, along with a dozen others, to a still tougher disciplinary camp at Corte.

A citadel right up on top of the mountain: six hundred steps to go up and down twice a day to work at making a sports ground for the enlisted men near the station.

It was when I was in that hell, with that herd of brutes, that a civilian from Corte secretly passed me a note: 'Darling, if you want to get out of that horrible place, cut off your thumb. The law is that the loss of a thumb, with or without preservation of the metacarpal, automatically brings about transfer to the auxiliaries; but if this injury is caused by an accident in the course of duty, it brings about permanent incapacity for

226

armed service and therefore discharge. Law of 1831, circular of 23 July 1883. I am waiting for you. Clara. Address, Le Moulin Rouge, Quartier Réservé, Toulon.'

I did not delay. Our work consisted of digging about two cubic yards of earth out of the mountain every day and wheeling it off in barrows for fifty yards to a place where trucks took away everything that was not needed for levelling the ground. We worked in teams of two. I must not cut off my thumb with an edged tool, or I should be accused of self-mutilation, and that would cost me another five years of *camise*.

My Corsican mate, Franqui, and I started on the mountain at the bottom, and we dug a fair-sized cave into it. One more blow with the pick and everything above would fall in on me. The supervising NCOs were tough: Sergeant Albertini was always there, just two or three yards behind us. This made the job tricky, but there was this advantage—if all went well, he would be an impartial witness.

Franqui put a big stone with a fairly sharp edge under an overhanging piece; I laid my thumb on it and stuffed my handkerchief into my mouth so as not to let out the least sound. There would be five or six seconds for us to bring the whole mass of earth down on me. Franqui was going to smash my thumb with another stone weighing about twenty pounds: it could not fail. They would be forced to amputate it even if the blow did not take it off entirely.

The sergeant was three yards away from us, scraping earth off his boots. Franqui grasped the stone, lifted it up as high as it would go and brought it down. My thumb was a shattered mess. The sound of the blow mingled with the noise of the pickaxes all round and the sergeant saw nothing. Two swings with the pick and the earth came down all over me. I let myself be buried. Bellowing, shouts for help: they dug for me and at last I appeared, covered with earth and my thumb destroyed. And I was suffering like a soul in hell. Still, I did manage to say to the sergeant, 'They'll say I did it on purpose: you see.'

'No, Charrière. I saw the accident: I'm a witness. I'm tough but I'm fair. I'll tell them what I saw, never you fear.'

Two months later, discharged with a pension and with my thumb buried at Calvi, I was transferred to the No. 5 Depot at

227

Toulon, and there they let me go.

I went to say thank you to Clara at the Moulin Rouge. She was of the opinion that nobody would even notice the missing thumb on my left hand, and that I could make love as well with four fingers as with five. That's what really mattered.

'You've changed in some way, Riri. I can't quite tell how. I hope your three months with those undesirables have not left too many traces.'

There I was with my father in my childhood home: I had hurried back after my discharge. Was there some deep change in me? 'I can't tell you, Papa: I don't know. I think I'm more violent and less willing to obey the rules of life you taught me when I was a little boy. You must be right: something has changed in me. I feel it, being here in this house where we were so happy with Mama and my sisters. It doesn't hurt as much as it used to. I must have grown harder.'

'What are you going to do?'

'What do you advise?'

'Find a position as soon as possible. You're twenty now, my boy.'

Two exams. One at Privas for the post office; the other at Avignon for a civilian job in the military administration. Grandfather Thierry went with me.

Both the written and the oral parts went very well. I was playing the game: I had no objection to following my father's advice—I'd be a civil servant. It would be a proper, honourable life. But I can't help wondering how long the young Charrière would have stayed a civil servant with everything that was boiling up inside him.

When the morning post brought the results of the exam, my delighted papa decided to have a little party in my honour. A huge cake, a bottle of real champagne and a colleague's daughter invited to the feast. 'She would make a fine wife for my boy.' For the first time for ten years, the house bubbled with joy.

I walked round the garden with the girl Papa dreamed of as a daughter-in-law, a girl who might make his little boy happy. She was pretty, well brought up and very intelligent.

Two months later, the bombshell! 'Since you have not been

able to provide our central office with a good-conduct certificate from the navy, we regret to inform you that you cannot enter our service.'

After the letter came, shattering all his illusions, Papa was sad, saying very little. He was suffering.

Why go on like this? Quick, a suitcase and a few clothes: let's take advantage of the teachers' meeting at Aubenas and get out.

My grandmother caught me on the stairs. 'Where are you going, Henri?'

'I'm going somewhere where they won't ask me for a good-conduct certificate from the navy. I'm going to see one of the men I knew in the disciplinary sections at Calvi, and he will teach me how to live outside this society I was still stupid enough to believe in—a society that knows very well I can expect nothing from it. I'm going to Paris, to Montmartre, Grandmother.'

'What are you going to do?'

'I don't know yet, but certainly no good. Good-bye, Grandmother. Give Papa a big kiss from me.'

The land was coming very close, and now we could even see the windows of the houses. I was coming back to it after a very, very long journey to see my people: to see them after twenty-six years.

What were they like? For them, I was dead; for their children, I had never existed—my name had never been pronounced. Or perhaps just a few times, when they were alone with Papa. It was only during these last five years that they must gradually have given their kids some idea of Uncle Henri, who lived in Venezuela.

We had corresponded for five years; letters are all very well, but won't they be afraid of what people might say? Won't they feel rather nervous about meeting an escaped ex-convict of a brother at a rendezvous in Spain?

I did not want them to come out of duty; I wanted them to come with their hearts full of genuine feeling for me.

Ah, but if they only knew ... If they only knew—the coast was coming nearer slowly now, but how it had raced away from me twenty-six years ago—if they only knew how I had been with them all the time during those thirteen years of prison!

-If only my sisters could see all the visions of our childhood I had made for myself in the cells and the wild-beast cages of the Réclusion!

If only they knew how I kept myself going with them and with all those who made up our family, drawing from them the strength to beat the unbeatable, to find peace in the midst of despair, to forget being a prisoner, to reject suicide—if they only knew how the months, days, hours, minutes and seconds of those years of total solitude and utter silence had been filled to overflowing with the smallest events of our wonderful childhood!

The coast drew nearer and nearer; we saw Barcelona; we were about to enter its harbour. I had a wild desire to cup my hands and shout, with all my strength, 'Hey there! I'm coming! Come as fast as you can!' just as I used to call out to them when we were children in the fields of Fabras and I had found a great patch of violets.

'What are you doing here, darling? I've been looking for you this last hour. I even went down to the car.'

Without getting up I put my arm round Rita's waist; she bent down and gave me a little kiss on the cheek. It was only then that I realized that although I was going to meet my people full of self-questioning and full of questions to ask as well, there in my arms was my own private family, the family that I had founded and that had brought me to this point. I said, 'Darling, I was living over the past again as I watched the land come closer, the land that holds my people, the living and the dead.'

Barcelona: our gleaming car on the quay with all the baggage neatly in the boot. We did not stay the night in the great city; we were impatient to drive on through the sunlit countryside towards the French frontier. But after two hours my feelings overcame me so that I had to pull in to the side of the road—I could not go on.

I got out of the car: my eyes were dazzled with looking at this landscape, these ploughed fields, huge plane trees, trembling reeds, the thatched or tiled roofs of the farms and cottages, the poplars singing in the wind, the meadows with every possible shade of green, the cows with the bells tinkling as they grazed, the vines—ah, the vines with their leaves that could not hide all the grapes. This piece of Catalonia was exactly the same as all my French garden-like landscapes: all this was mine and always had been ever since I was born; it was among these same colours, these same growing things, these same crops that I had wandered hand in hand with my grandfather; it was through fields like these that I had carried my father's game-bag the days when he went shooting and when we urged on our bitch Clara to start a rabbit or flush a covey of partridges. Even the fences round the farms were the same as they were at home! And the little irrigation canals with their planks set across here and there to guide the water into one field or another: I did not have to go up to them to know there were frogs that I could bring out, as many as I wanted, with a hook baited with a piece of red cloth, as I had done so often as a child.

And I quite forgot that this vast plain was Spanish, so exactly was it like the valley of the Ardèche or the Rhône.

So there on the road between Barcelona and Figueras I began to sob. For a long time my tears flowed, until gently, very gently, Rita's hand stroked my neck and she said to me, 'Let us thank God for having brought us this far, so near to your France and only two or three days from meeting your own people.'

We stopped at the hotel nearest the French frontier. The next day Rita took the train to fetch Tànte Ju from Saint-Peray. I should have gone myself, but for the French police I was still a man who had escaped from Guiana. While Rita was away I found a very fine house at Rosas, right on the edge of the beach.

A few more minutes of waiting, Papi, and then you will see Tante Ju step out of the train, the woman who loved your father, and who wrote you such beautiful letters, bringing back to life your memories of those who loved you and whom you loved so much.

It was Rita who got out first. As carefully as a daughter, she helped her tall companion to climb down to the platform. And then two big arms enfolded me, two big arms pressed me to her bosom, two big arms conveying the warmth of life and a thousand things that cannot be expressed in words. And it was with one arm round Rita and the other round my second mother that we walked out of the station, quite forgetting that suitcases do not come with their owners unless they are carried.

It was eleven in the morning when Rita and Tante Ju arrived, and it was three the next morning when Tante Ju went to her bedroom, worn out by the journey, by her age, by emotion and by sixteen hours of uninterrupted exchange of memories; and it was there, when I went to say good-night, that she fell asleep in the hollow of my arm, her face as peaceful as a child's.

I fell into my bed and went straight to sleep, exhausted, without a breath of energy to keep me awake. The outburst of too great happiness is as shattering as the worst disaster.

My two women were up before me, and it was they who pulled me out of my deep sleep to tell me it was eleven in the morning, that the sun was shining, the sky blue, the sand warm, that breakfast was waiting for me and that I should eat it quickly so as to go to the frontier to fetch my sister and her tribe, who were to be there in two hours' time. 'Rather earlier,' said Tante Ju, 'because your brother-in-law will have been forced to drive fast, to prevent the family bullying him, they are so eager to see you.'

I parked the Lincoln right next to the Spanish frontier post.

Here they were! They were on foot, running—they had abandoned my brother-in-law back there in the queue by the French customs in his Citroën.

First came my sister Hélène, her arms out. She ran across the stretch of no-man's-land from the one post to the other, from France to Spain. I went towards her, my guts tied up with emotion. At four yards we stopped to look one another right in the face. Our tear-dimmed eyes said 'It is really her, my childhood Nène,' and 'It is really him, my little brother Riri from long ago.' And we flung ourselves into each other's arms. Strange. For me this fifty-year-old sister was as she had always been. I did not see her aging face; I saw nothing except that the brilliant animation of her eyes was still the same and that for me her features had not altered.

Our embrace lasted so long we forgot all about the others. Rita had already kissed the children. I heard, 'How pretty you are, Aunt!' and I turned, left my Nène and thrust Rita into her arms, saying, 'Love her dearly, because it is she who has brought me to you all.'

My three nieces were splendid and my brother-in-law was in great form. The only one missing was his eldest boy, Jacques, who had been called up for the war in Algeria.

We left for Rosas, the Lincoln in front, with my sister at my side. I shall never forget that first meal, with us all sitting at a round table. There were times when my legs trembled so that I had to take hold of them under the cloth.

1930–1956. So many, many things had happened, both for them and for me. Such a length of road, such a struggle to reach this point, and so many obstacles to overcome! I did not talk about the penal settlement during the meal. I just asked my brother-in-law whether my being found guilty had caused them a great deal of trouble and unpleasantness. He reassured me kindly, but I could feel how much they must have suffered, having a convict as brother and brother-in-law. 'We never doubted you, and you can be quite certain that even if you had been guilty we should only have been sorry for you; we would never have renounced you.'

No, I said nothing about penal, and I said nothing about my trial. For them and, I sincerely believe, for me too, my life began the day when, thanks to Rita, I buried my old self, the man out on the loose, to bring Henri Charrière back to life, the son of the Ardèche schoolteachers.

That August on the sands of Rosas beach went by too fast. I rediscovered the cries of my childhood, the laughter with no cause, the outbursts of joy of my young days on the beach of Palavas, where we used to go with my parents.

One month: thirty days. How long it is in a cell alone with oneself, and how terribly short it is with one's own people. I was literally drunk with happiness. Not only had I my sister and my brother-in-law again, but I had also discovered new people to love—my nieces, unknown only the other day, and now almost daughters to me.

Rita was radiant with joy at seeing me so happy. Bringing

us together at last, out of reach of the French police, was the finest present she could have given either them or me. I lay on the beach; it was very late—midnight, perhaps. Rita was stretched out on the sand too, with her head against my thigh; I stroked her hair. 'They all fly away tomorrow. How quickly it has passed; but how wonderful it was! One must not ask too much, darling, I know; but still, I'm sad at having to part from them. God knows when we'll see one another again. A journey like this costs so much.'

'Trust in the future: I'm sure we'll see them again one day.'

We went with them as far as the frontier. They were taking Tante Ju in their car. A hundred yards from the French border we parted. There were no tears, because I told them of my faith in the future—in a couple of years we should spend not one month of holiday together but two.

'Is it true, what you say, Uncle?'

'Of course, darlings, of course.'

A week later my other sister landed at Barcelona airport, by herself. She had not been able to bring her family. Among the forty-odd passengers coming out of the plane I recognized her at once, and after she had passed through the customs she came straight towards me without the least hesitation.

Three days and three nights—she could spend only a little while with us, so since we did not want to lose a minute, it was three days and three nights of memories almost without a pause. She and Rita liked one another at once, so we could tell one another everything—she her whole life-story and me all that could be told.

Two days later Rita's mother arrived from Tangiers. With her two fine, gentle hands on my cheeks she kissed me tirelessly, saying, 'My son, I am so happy that you love Rita and that she loves you.' Her face shone with a serene beauty in its halo of white hair.

We stayed in Spain too long, our happiness hiding the days that passed. We could not go back by boat—sixteen days was more than we could spare—so we flew (the Lincoln coming later by ship), because our business was waiting.

Still, we did make a little tour of Spain, and there in the hanging gardens of Granada, that wonder of the Arab civilization, I read these words of a poet, cut into the stone at the foot of the Marador tower: *Dale limosna, mujer, que no hay en la vida nada como la pena de ser ciego en Granada.* Give him alms, woman, because there is no greater sadness in life than being blind in Granada.

Yes, there is something worse than being blind in Granada, and that is being twenty-four, full of health and trust in life, undisciplined maybe and even not very honest, but not really corrupted through and through or at least not a killer, and to hear yourself condemned to a life-sentence for another man's crime: a sentence that means vanishing for ever without appeal, without hope, condemned to rot bodily and mentally, without having one chance in a hundred thousand of ever raising your head and of being a man again some day.

How many men whom a pitiless justice and an inhuman penitentiary system have crushed and destroyed inch by inch would have preferred to be blind in Granada! *I am one of those men.*

14: The Revolution

THE plane we had boarded at Madrid came down gently at Maiquetia, the Caracas airport, and there was our daughter waiting for us, together with some friends. Twenty minutes later we were back home. The dogs welcomed us enthusiastically, and our Indian maid, who was one of the family, never stopped asking, 'And how are Henri's people, Señora? And Henri, what did you think of Rita's mama? I was afraid you would never come back, with all those people over there to love you. Thanks be to God, here you are, all in one piece.'

The struggle for life went on. We sold the restaurant: I had begun to have enough of steak and chips, *canard à l'orange* and *coq au vin*. We bought an all-night joint, the Caty-Bar.

In Caracas an all-night bar is a place where the customers are all men, because it has its own girls to keep them company, talk to them and even more listen to them, drink with them, and if they are not very thirsty, help them on a little. It's quite a different kind of life from that of the day, much more intense and not in the least peaceful; but it is one where every night you discover something new and interesting.

Senators, deputies, bankers, lawyers, officers and high officials hurried in at night to let off the steam that had piled up during the day, when they had to keep a hold on themselves and put out an image of perfectly virtuous behaviour in their various jobs. And at the Caty-Bar each one showed himself as he really was. It was a bursting out, a throwing off of the social hypocrisy they were forced to observe, a refuge from business or family worries.

For these few hours every single one of them grew young again. With alcohol lending them a hand, they threw off their social chains and started right in on a life that left them free to shout and argue and play the Don Juan with the prettiest girls in the bar. In our place things never went farther than that, because Rita ran the bar very strictly and no woman was allowed out during working hours. But all the men enjoyed the presence of these girls who were kind enough to listen when they talked (they loved that) and to fill their hours of freedom with their beauty and their youth.

How often I have seen them at daybreak, all alone (because the girls left by another door), but nevertheless happy and easier in their minds. One was an important businessman and he was always at his desk by nine; he was a regular customer, and I used to walk to his car with him. He would put his hand on my shoulder, and waving the other arm towards the mountains of Caracas, sharp against the early-morning sky, he would say, 'The night is over, Enrique; the sun is going to rise behind the Avila. No hope of going anywhere else—everything is shut; and with the daylight we come face to face with our responsibilities. Work, the office, the slavery of every day is waiting for me; but how could we go on without these nights?'

Very soon I had another place, the Madrigal, and then a third, the Normandy. Together with Gonzalo Durand, a Socialist and an opponent of the régime who was ready night and day to defend the interests of night-club, bar and restaurant owners, we formed an association for the protection of places of this kind. Some time later I was made president, and we defended our members as well as we could against the abuses of certain officials.

I turned the Madrigal into a Russian joint, calling it the Ninoska; and by way of adding to the local colour I dressed a Spaniard from the Canaries as a Cossack and perched him on a horse, a peaceful horse, because of its great age. The two of them were to act as porters. But the customers started giving the Cossack drinks—he was bored stiff at half a dollar an hour—and, what was worse, they did not forget the horse either. Naturally, the horse didn't knock back glasses of whisky, but it dearly loved sugar dipped in spirits, particularly kummel. Result: when the old horse was drunk and the Cossack tight as a drum, they would tear off down our street, the Avenida Miranda, an important artery crammed with traffic, galloping right and left, the Spaniard shrieking 'Charge! Charge!' You can just imagine the scene: brakes jammed on so hard they almost tore up the asphalt, cars banging into one another, drivers bawling, windows opening and angry voices shouting about the din at that time of night.

To top it all, although I had only a single musician, he was not one of the ordinary kind. He was a German called Kurt Lowendal; he had a boxer's hands and he played the cha-cha on his organ with such zeal that the walls trembled even up to the ninth floor. I could hardly believe it, but the concierge and the owner took me up with them one evening to see: and it was no exaggeration.

My other joint, the Normandy, was really beautifully placed —right opposite the police headquarters. On one side of the street, terror and grilling, and on the other the gaiety of life. For once I was on the right side. Not that that prevented me from making things tricky for myself: I did the most dangerous thing I could—I acted as a secret letter-box for the prisoners, both political and criminal.

1958. For some months now things had been on the move in Venezuela: Perez Jimenez's dictatorship was limping badly. Even the privileged classes were dropping away from him, and the only supporters he had left were the army and the *Seguridad Nacional*, the terrible political police, who were making more and more arrests.

Meanwhile in New York the three most important political leaders, all in exile, had worked out their plan for seizing power. These were Raphael Caldera, Jovito Vilalba and Romulo Bétancourt. On 1 January an airforce general, Castro Leon, tried to get his men to rise, and a small group of pilots dropped a few bombs on Caracas, particularly on Perez Jimenez's presidential palace. The operation failed, and Castro Leon fled to Colombia.

But at two o'clock in the morning of 23 January a plane flew over Caracas. It was Perez Jimenez going off with his family, his closest associates and part of his fortune—a cargo of such value in people and wealth that the Venezuelans christened the plane 'the holy cow'. Perez Jimenez knew he had lost the game —the army had abandoned him, after ten years of dictatorship. His plane flew straight to San Domingo, where another dictator, General Trujillo, could only welcome his colleague.

For close on three weeks there were no police in the streets. Of course, there was pillaging and scenes of violence, but only against Perez Jimenez's supporters. It was a nation bursting out after having been muzzled for ten years. The *Seguridad Nacional*'s headquarters, opposite the Normandy, was attacked and most of its members killed.

During the three days that followed the departure of Perez Jimenez I very nearly lost the result of twelve years' work. Several people telephoned to tell me that all the bars, night-clubs, luxury restaurants and places frequented by the top supporters of Perez Jimenez were being broken into and sacked. We had our flat on the floor above the Caty-Bar. It was a little villa at the bottom of a blind alley, with the bar at street-level, then our living-quarters and then a flat roof over that.

I was determined to defend my house, my business and my people. I got hold of twenty bottles of petrol, made them into Molotov cocktails and lined them up neatly on the roof. Rita would not leave me: she was at my side with a lighter in her hand.

Here they came! A crowd of men, pillagers: more than a hundred of them. Since the Caty-Bar was in a blind alley, if anyone came along it, it meant they were coming to us.

They came closer and among the shouts I heard 'This is one of the Perezjimenists' places! Sack it!' They broke into a run, waving iron bars and shovels. I lit the lighter.

Suddenly the crowd halted. Four men with their arms stretched out were strung across the alley: they stopped the over-excited mob. I heard, 'We are workers, we belong to the people, and we are revolutionaries too. We've known these people for years. Enrique, the boss, is a Frenchman, and he's a friend of the people—he's proved it to us hundreds of times. Get out, there's nothing for you to do here.'

And they began to argue, but more quietly; and I heard these splendid men explain why they were defending us. It lasted a good twenty minutes, with Rita and me still on the roof, holding the lighter. The four must have persuaded them to leave us in peace, because the mob withdrew without any threats.

Lord, that was a close one! A close one for a good many of them, too, I may say. None of them ever came back.

These four men of the people, our defenders, worked for the Caracas Water Company. And it so happened that the side door of the Caty-Bar, down at the bottom of the alley, was right next to the entrance to the company's depot, the gate the tankers used when they went to supply places that were short of water. We often gave the men who worked there something to eat, and if they came for a bottle of Coke we said there was nothing to pay. Because of the dictatorship they almost never talked politics, but sometimes, when they had had a drink, a few would let out an incautious word—it was overheard and reported. Then they were either imprisoned or sacked.

Often either Rita or I had been able to get one of our customers to have the culprit let out or given back his job. In any case, among the senators, deputies and officers belonging to the régime, a good many were very kind and obliging. There were few who would not do a favour.

On that day the Water Company's men paid their debt to us, and they paid it with very great courage, because the mob was in no laughing mood. And the most extraordinary thing was that the same miracle happened for our two other places. Not a pane of glass smashed at the Ninoska. Nothing, absolutely nothing destroyed and nothing stolen at the Normandy, right opposite the terrible *Seguridad Nacional*, the hottest spot of the whole revolution, with machine guns firing in all directions and revolutionaries burning and pillaging the shops right, left and centre all along the Avenida Mejico.

Under Perez Jimenez, nobody had argued; nobody had done anything but obey. The press was muzzled.

Under his successor Admiral Larrazabal, everybody danced, sang, disobeyed to their heart's content, spoke or wrote anything that came into their heads, drunk with joy at being able to talk balls in total freedom with the accelerator right down.

The sailor was a poet into the bargain, an artist at heart, sensitive to the wretched position and the poverty of the thousands of people who came flooding into Caracas, wave after wave of them, as soon as the dictator had fallen. He thought up the Emergency Plan, which handed out millions to these unfortunate souls from the national funds.

He promised that there should be elections. He was dead straight, and he prepared them very fairly; but although the Admiral got in at Caracas, it was Bétancourt who won the election. Bétancourt had to face up to a tricky situation—not a

240

single day without some plot being hatched, not a single day without having to win a battle against the forces of reaction.

I had just bought the biggest café in Caracas, the Grand Café in the Sabana Grande: over four hundred seats. This was the café where Julot Huignard, the hammer-man of Lévy's jewellery shop, had said we should meet when we were in the corridor of the Santé way back in 1931. 'Keep your spirits up, Papi! We'll meet at the Grand Café in Caracas.' Here was I at the rendezvous. Twenty-eight years later, to be sure, but still here—and I owned it. But Huignard had not kept the appointment.

The political state of the country did not make Bétancourt's job an easy one. A vile, cowardly attempt on his life suddenly upset the still youthful democracy. Under the remote control of Trujillo, the dictator of San Domingo, a car stuffed with explosives went off right by the president as he was driving to an official ceremony. The head of the military household was killed, the chauffeur very badly wounded, General Lopez Henriquez and his wife horribly burnt, and the president himself had his forearms dreadfully injured by the flames. Twenty-four hours later, with his hands bandaged, he addressed the Venezuelan nation. It seemed so unbelievable that some people claimed that the man who spoke was his double.

In such an atmosphere Venezuela too, though blessed by the gods, began to be attacked by the virus of political passion. There were cops everywhere, and among the officials, there were some who made evil use of their political connections.

Officials belonging to different ministries came and badgered me many times. Inspectors of every kind appeared: inspectors of drinks, of municipal taxes, of this and of that. Most of them had received no training and they only had the job because they belonged to some political party or other.

What's more, since the government knew about my past, and since I was inevitably in contact with various bent types who passed through even though I lived honestly and had nothing to do with them in the way of business, and since on top of that I had been granted asylum here, while proceedings against me were still in force in France, the pigs took advantage of my position to carry out a kind of blackmail, playing on my past. For example, they dug up the murder of a Frenchman two years back, in which the killer had never been found. Did I know anything about it? I knew nothing? Wasn't it in my interest, considering my position, to know a little?

Oh, this was beginning to be a splendid party, this was. I had had about enough of these bastards. It might not be very serious for the moment, but if it went on and I blew up, God knows what would happen. No, no blowing up here, not in this country that had given me my chance of being a free man once more and of making a home for myself.

There was no point in going round and round the mulberry bush: I sold the Grand Café and the other joints, and Rita and I went off to Spain. Maybe I'd be able to start some kind of business there.

But I could not manage to get going. The European countries are too well organized. In Madrid, when I had obtained the first thirteen permits to open a business, they kindly told me I needed a fourteenth. It seemed to me that was just one too many. And Rita, seeing that I was literally incapable of living far from Venezuela and that I missed even the sods who badgered me, agreed that although we had sold everything, we should go back there.

15: *Camarones*

CARACAS once more. This was 1961, and sixteen years had passed since El Dorado. Night-life had changed a great deal in Caracas, and buying a joint as healthy, good-looking and important as the one I'd sold, the Grand Café, was impossible to find and even more impossible to build up. And then again there was a ridiculous law that the people who had bars and sold alcoholic drinks corrupted public morals: this meant all kinds of abuses and exploitation on the part of certain officials, and I didn't want to get back into that racket at all.

Something else was needed. I discovered not a mine of diamonds but a mine of very big prawns, the kind called *camarones*, and of even bigger ones called *langostinos*. And all this was back at Maracaibo once again.

We settled down in an elegant flat: I bought a stretch of shore and founded a company called the Capitan Chico, after the district that included my beach. Sole share-holder, Henri Charrière; managing director, Henri Charrière, director of operations, Henri Charrière; chief assistant, Rita.

And here we were, launched into an extraordinary adventure. I bought eighteen fishing-boats. They were big craft, each with a fifty-horsepower outboard and a net five hundred yards long. A crew of five to each boat. As one fully-equipped boat cost twelve thousand five hundred bolivars, eighteen of them meant a lot of money.

We transformed the little villages round the lake, doing away with poverty and the dislike for work (since the work I gave was well paid), and bringing a new life in place of the old listlessness.

These poor people owned nothing, so without any guarantee from them we gave one full set of fishing gear for each crew of five. They fished as they chose and the only undertaking they had to give was to sell me the *langostinos* and *camarones* at the market price less half a bolivar a kilo, because all the equipment and its upkeep was paid for by me.

The business ran at a tremendous pace, and it fascinated me. We had three refrigerated trucks that never stopped hurrying about the beaches to pick up my boats' catch.

I built a pier on the lake about a hundred feet long, and a big covered platform. Here Rita managed a team of between a hundred and twenty and a hundred and forty women who took off the heads of the *camarones* and *langostinos*. Then, washed and washed again in ice-cold water, they were sorted for size, according to how many would go to one American pound. There might be ten to fifteen, or twenty to twenty-five, or twenty-five to thirty. The bigger they were, the more they fetched. Every week the Americans sent me a green sheet which gave the market price for *camarones* each Tuesday. Every day at least one DC-8 took off for Miami, carrying 24,000 lb of *camarones*.

I should have made a lot of money, if I had not been such a fool as to take a Yankee partner one day. He had a moon face, and looked worthy, stupid and straight. He spoke neither Spanish nor French, and as I spoke no English, we could not quarrel.

This Yankee brought in no capital, but he had rented the freezers of a well-known brand of ice that was sold all over Maracaibo and in the neighbourhood. This meant that the *camarones* and the *langostinos* were perfectly frozen.

I had to look after the fishing, the supervision of my boats, the loading of each day's catch into my three refrigerated trucks and the payment of the fishermen: and I had to provide these considerable sums out of my own pocket. Some days I would go down to the beach with thirty thousand bolivars and come home without a cent.

All this was well organized; but nothing runs itself without a hitch, and I had a continual war with pirate buyers. As I've said, it had been agreed with the fishermen who used my equipment that I should buy their catch at the market price less half a bolivar a kilo, which was fair. But the pirate buyers risked nothing. They had no boats: they just had a refrigerated truck and that was all. They turned up on the beaches and bought *camarones* from no matter who. When a boat brought in eight hundred kilos of *camarones*, half a bolivar a kilo more made a difference of four hundred bolivars for my fishermen between what I gave them and what the pirate offered. You would have to be a saint to resist a temptation like that. So whenever they could, my fishermen took the pirate's money. That meant I had to protect my interests almost day and night; but I liked the battle—it gave me intense satisfaction.

When we sent our *camarones* and *langostinos* to the States, the payment was made in the form of a letter of credit, once the bank had seen the shipping papers and a certificate that the quality of the goods and their perfect deep-freezing had been checked. The bank paid eighty-five per cent of the total and the remaining fifteen per cent was received when Miami told Maracaibo that the consignment had arrived and had been found satisfactory.

It often happened that on Saturdays, when there were two plane-loads of *camarones*, my partner would go in one to accompany the consignment. On those days the freight cost five hundred dollars more and the Miami cargo-handlers did not work on Saturdays. So someone had to be on the spot to get the consignment out, loaded on to a refrigerated trailer and taken to the buyer's works, either in Miami itself or at Tampa or Jacksonville. And as the banks were closed on Saturdays there was no way of working the letters of credit: there was no way of insuring, either. But on Monday morning, in the States, the shipment sold for ten or fifteen per cent more. It was a sound venture.

Things were running smoothly, and I was delighted with my partner's elegant strokes of business when he flew off at the week-end. Until the day he did not come back.

By stinking bad luck, this happened at the season when there were few *camarones* in the lake: I had hired a big boat at the sea-port of Punto-Fijo to fetch a whole cargo of splendid crayfish from Los Roques. I'd come back loaded to the gunwales with extra-prime-quality goods; and I'd had their heads taken off right there. So I had a very valuable shipment, made up entirely of best crayfish tails, weighing from a pound and a half to a pound and three-quarters each.

And that Saturday two DC-8s loaded with crayfish tails paid for by me, the freight and all the rest paid for by me too, took off with this choir-boy and vanished into the clouds.

Monday, no news: none on Tuesday, either. I went to the bank: nothing from Miami. I didn't want to believe it, but I knew already: I had been done. As it was my partner who dealt with the letters of credit and as there was no insurance on Saturday, he had sold the whole consignment the moment he got there, and walked quietly away with the dough.

I flew into a terrible rage and went off to look for Moonface in America, with a souvenir for him in my pocket. There was no difficulty in picking up his trail, but at each address I found a woman who said he was her lawful wedded husband but she didn't know where he was. And this three times, in three different towns! I never did find my worthy partner.

There I was, flat broke. We had lost a hundred and fifty thousand dollars. We still had the boats, of course; but they were in poor condition: so were the outboards. And as this was a business in which you had to have a lot of ready cash to carry on day by day, we could not stand the loss, nor get on our feet again. We were pretty well ruined, and we sold everything. Rita never complained nor blamed me for having been so trusting. Our capital, the savings of fourteen years of hard work, more than two years of useless sacrifice and continual effort—everything was lost; or very nearly everything.

With our eyes filled with tears, we left the great family of fishermen and workers we had brought into being. They were appalled too; they told us how it grieved them to see us go and how grateful they were to us for having brought them a prosperity they had never known before these two years.

16: The Gorilla

THERE was a knock at the door (the bell was not working) and I went to open it. It was my buddy, Colonel Bolagno. He and his family had always called me Papillon: they were the only people in Venezuela to do so. All the others called me Enrique or Don Enrique, according to how I was doing at the moment. The Venezuelans have a feeling for that; they know straight away if you are prosperous or on the rocks.

'Hi there, Papillon. It's three years since we've met.'

'True enough, Francisco: three years.'

'Why haven't you been to see me in my new house?'

'You never asked me.'

'You don't ask a friend. He comes when he feels like it, because if his friend has a house it's his house too. To invite him would be an insult.'

I made no answer; I knew he was in the right.

Bolagno embraced Rita. He sat there with his elbows on the table, looking disturbed and uneasy: he had taken off his colonel's cap. Rita gave him a cup of coffee, and I asked, 'How did you find my address?'

'That's my business. Why didn't you send it to me?'

'A great deal of work and a great deal of worry.'

'You have worries?'

'All I want.'

'Then I've come at the wrong moment.'

'Why?'

'I came to ask you to lend me five thousand bolivars. I'm in a jam.'

'Impossible, Francisco.'

'We are ruined,' said Rita.

'Ah, so you're ruined? You're ruined, Papillon? It's true you're ruined? Is that why you did not come to see me, so as not to let me know about your worries?'

'Yes.'

'Well, just you let me tell you you're a sod. Because when you have a friend, he's there so you *can* tell him your worries and so you can rely on him to do something to get you out of a

247

hole. You're a sod not to have thought of me, your friend, to back you up and give you a hand. I heard about your difficulties from other people, and that's why I'm here to help you.'

Rita and I were so moved we scarcely knew where we were: we could not say a word, we were so touched. We had never asked anyone for anything and that was a fact; but there were a good many people I had helped a lot and who even owed me their jobs, and although they knew we were ruined not one had come to give us a hand in any way at all. Most were French; some straight, others bent.

'What do you want me to do for you, Papillon?'

'Setting up a business we could live off would cost too much. Even if you have the money, you couldn't spare it.'

'Go and get dressed, Rita. We'll all three of us go and eat at the best French restaurant in town.'

By the end of the meal, it was agreed that I should look for a business and tell him how much it would cost to buy. And Bolagno said, 'If I have the money, there's no problem; and if I haven't enough, then I'll borrow from my brothers and my brother-in-law. But I give you my word I'll get hold of what you need.'

All the rest of that day, Rita and I talked about his wonderful tact. 'When he was just a corporal at El Dorado,' I said, 'he gave me his only civilian suit, so that I could leave decently dressed; and now today here he is giving us a hand to make a fresh start.'

We paid our overdue rent and moved to a pleasant, well-situated café-restaurant in the top avenue of Las Delicias, still in the Sabana Grande district. It was called the Bar-Restaurant Gab, and that was where we were at the time of Long Charlie's arrival.

Charles de Gaulle, then president of the republic, came on an official visit, invited by Raul Leoni, the president of Venezuela.

Caracas and the whole of Venezuela celebrated the occasion. The people, the real people, the ones with horny hands, straw hats and rope-soled shoes, all these open-hearted people without exception were waiting, filled with emotion, to cheer

Charles de Gaulle.

The Gab had a charming covered terrace, and I was sitting there quietly drinking pastis with a Frenchman. He explained the mysteries of the processing of fish-meal; and in a low voice he also told me about an invention he was just perfecting—one that would bring him in millions, once it was accepted. The discovery was cinema in relief; he whispered and looked sideways to seem more confidential and also to tell me how much money I could invest in his researches.

It is always amusing to listen to the line of a guy that wants to do you, and his patter was so smooth and it so charmed me that I did not notice a neighbour pricking up his ears and leaning over to listen to us. Not until I unfolded a little note from Rita, who was at the cash-desk and who had sent it discreetly by one of the waiters: 'I don't know what you are talking about, but there's no doubt your neighbour is very interested in catching what you say. Looks like a foreign pig.'

To get rid of the inventor, I strongly advised him to carry on with his researches, and I told him I was so sure he would succeed that I should certainly have come in with him if only I had any savings, which was unfortunately not the case. He went away: I got up, turned round and faced the table behind me.

Sitting there I saw a well-built guy, too well-built and too well-dressed, with a tie and all, and a steel-blue suit; and there on the table in front of him, a pastis and a packet of Gauloises. No need to ask his trade; nor his nationality either.

'Excuse me, are those French cigarettes you are smoking?' I asked in Spanish.

'Yes: I'm a Frenchman.'

'Really? I don't know you. Tell me, you wouldn't be one of Long Charlie's gorillas, by any chance?'

The well-built guy stood up and introduced himself. 'I'm Commissaire Belion, in charge of the General's security.'

'Pleased to meet you.'

'And what about you? Are you French?'

'Come off it, Commissaire. You know very well who I am; it's not just by chance you're here on my café terrace.'

'But . . .'

'Don't go on. You put the Gauloises right out on your table

so that I should talk to you. Right or wrong?'

'Right.'

'Another pastis?'

'OK. I came to see you because since I'm responsible for the President's security, I'm getting the embassy to draw up a list of people who might have to leave Caracas before the General arrives. The list will be shown to the minister of the interior and he'll take the necessary steps.'

'I'm on the list?'

'Not yet.'

'What do you know about me?'

'That you have a family and that you are going straight.'

'What else?'

'That your sister is Madame X and she lives at such and such an address in Paris and that the other one is Madame Y, who lives in Grenoble.'

'After that?'

'That proceedings against you lapse next year, in June 1966.'

'Who told you?'

'I knew it before I left Paris, but it's been notified to the consulate here.'

'Why didn't the consul let me know?'

'Officially he doesn't know your address.'

'Well, thanks for the good news. Can I go to the consulate and be told officially?'

'Whenever you like.'

'But tell me, Commissaire, how come you're sitting on the terrace of my restaurant this morning? It's not just to give me the news about proceedings having lapsed, nor to let me know my sisters haven't changed their address, eh?'

'Correct. It was to see you. To see Papillon.'

'You only know one Papillon, the guy in the Paris police file, a heap of lies, exaggerations and twisted reports. A file that never even described the man I was before, still less the man I have become.'

'Quite sincerely I believe you: and I congratulate you.'

'So now you've seen me, are you putting me on the list of people to be expelled during de Gaulle's stay?'

'No.'

'Well now, do you want me to tell you why you're here, Commissaire?'

'That would be interesting.'

'It's because you said to yourself, a guy on the loose is always a guy on the lookout for dough: now although Papillon may have become a good citizen, he's still on the loose, he's still an adventurer. He might refuse a considerable sum for doing something against de Gaulle himself; but as for picking up a fat packet for just helping to prepare an attack—why, that's something else again, and very possible.'

'Go on.'

'Well, you've got it dead wrong, dear Commissaire. In the first place because I wouldn't get mixed up with any political crime, not even for a fortune; still less one against de Gaulle. Secondly, who could possibly gain by such a thing in Venezuela?'

'The OAS.'

'Right. That's not only very possible but even very probable. They've pulled things off so many times in France that in a country like Venezuela, it's a piece of cake.'

'A piece of cake? Why?'

'The way they're organized, the OAS men don't have to get into Venezuela by the ordinary ways, the ports or airfields. The land frontiers are enormous—Brazil, Colombia, British Guiana—not to mention a coastline of over a thousand miles. They can come in just when they want, on the day and at the time that suits them, without anyone being able to do anything about it. That's your first mistake, Commissaire. But there's another, too.'

'What's that?' asked Belion, smiling.

'If these OAS guys are as sharp as people say, they've taken great care not to contact the French living here. Because since they know the cops are going straight to the Frenchmen, their very first precaution must be to go nowhere near any single one of them. And don't forget, no evil-intentioned guy is ever going to stay in a hotel. There are hundreds of people here who'll let a room to no matter who without declaring him. So you see there's no point in looking for people who might make an attempt on de Gaulle's life among the Frenchmen here, crooks or not.'

When Belion left he told me to come and see him when I returned to Paris; and he behaved straight with me. Unlike some other Frenchmen I was not expelled from Caracas during de Gaulle's stay—a stay that passed off with no trouble at all.

And like a fool I went along and cheered de Gaulle.

And like a fool the mere presence of this great leader who had saved my country's honour made me forget it was that same country which had sent me to penal for life.

And like a fool I would have given one of my fingers to shake his hand or be there at the embassy's reception in his honour: a reception to which I was not invited, of course. But the underworld was able to take an indirect revenge, because some old retired French whores slipped in: they had turned over a new leaf, as you might say, by making a good marriage, and there they were with their arms full of flowers for de Gaulle's delighted wife.

I went to see the French consul, and he read me out the notification that proceedings against me lapsed next year. One year more and I'd go to France.

Our situation improved rapidly, and I went back into all-night bars, buying the Scotch Club in Chacaito, in the very middle of Caracas. This was an odd business because I went into it in the first place to come to the rescue of a poor French hairdresser who some ugly bastards were trying to strip. Later this Robin Hood caper paid off very well.

So for several years there I was living by night again. The Caracas night-life was growing more and more vulgar, losing that touch of bohemianism that was its charm. The men who lived it up were no longer the same, and these new customers lacked culture and good manners.

I stayed in the bar as little as possible and I lived in the street almost all the time, wandering about the neighbouring districts. I came to know the kids of Caracas, the urchins who drifted about all night looking for a few cents, and the wonderful inventiveness of these children whose parents lived in rabbit-hutches. Not always model parents, either; for there were a good many who, in their poverty, had no hesitation in exploiting their children.

And these kids bravely launched themselves into the night to bring home the amount required of them. They were any age between five and twelve; some were shoe-shine boys, others waited at the door of all-night joints, offering to guard the customer's car as he went in, and others rushed to open the car door ahead of the doorman. A thousand dodges, a thousand clever gimmicks to add bolivar to bolivar until they had ten or thereabouts so that at five or six in the morning they could go home.

Often, when a customer I knew was just going to get into his big car, I would urge him to be generous, using this formula, 'Be handsome, now! Think of the money you've spent in this joint—a hundredth part of what you've splashed about would be a godsend to this poor kid.' Nine times out of ten it worked, and the playboy would give the kid a ten- or twenty-bolivar note.

My best friend was called Pablito. He was rather small and thin, but he was tough and he fought older, bigger boys like a lion. For there were conflicting interests in this struggle for life, and if a customer had not specially pointed out one boy to guard his car, then when the man came out again, the quickest off the mark got the coin. That meant a pitched battle.

My little friend was bright, and he had learned to read from the papers he sold from time to time. There was none like him at outstripping all competition when a car drew up; and he was the quickest at running little errands—fetching things the bar was short of, like sandwiches or cigarettes.

Every night my little Pablito carried on the struggle so that he could help his grandmother: she was a very, very old grandmother, it seemed, with white hair, faded blue eyes and rheumatism—rheumatism so bad she could not work at all. His mother was in gaol for having crowned a neighbour with a bottle when he tried to steal her radio. And he, at nine, was the one and only breadwinner in the family. He would not let his grandmother, his little brother or his little sister come out into the streets of Caracas, either by day or by night. He was the man of the house, and he had to look after all his people and protect them.

So I helped Pablito when he had had a bad night or in cases of emergency, money for his grandmother's medicines, or for a taxi to take her to see a doctor at the free hospital.

'And she has these bouts of asthma too, my grandmother. So you realize what that costs, Enrique?'

And every night Pablito gave me a report on his grandmother's health. One day there was an important request: he needed forty bolivars to buy a secondhand mattress. His grandmother could not lie in a hammock any more, because of her asthma: the doctor said it compressed her chest.

He often used to sit in my car, and one day the policeman on guard was talking to him, leaning on the door and playing with his revolver: without the least bad intention he put a bullet into Pablito's shoulder. They rushed him to hospital and operated. I went to see him the next day. I asked where his hut was and how to get to it; he said it was impossible to find it without a guide, and the doctor would not let him get up in that condition.

That night I looked for Pablito's friends, hoping one of them would take me to his grandmother. The terrific solidarity of street-arabs: they all said they did not know where he lived. I didn't believe a word of it, because every day a whole gang of them waited for one another to go home together.

I was interested and puzzled, and I asked the nurse to call me when Pablito had a visitor she knew was one of the family or a neighbour. Two days later she phoned me and I went to the hospital.

'Well, Pablito, and how are you coming along? You look worried.'

'No, Enrique; it's only that my back hurts.'

'Yet he was laughing only a few minutes ago,' said his visitor.

'Are you one of his family, Madame?'

'No. I'm a neighbour.'

'How are his grandmother and the little ones?'

'What grandmother?'

'Why, Pablito's grandmother.'

'But Pablito hasn't got a grandmother.'

'Well, well, well.'

I took the woman aside. Yes, he had a little sister; and yes, he had a little brother: but no grandmother. His mother was not in prison: she was a wreck of a woman, very dim-witted.

That wonderful Caracas street-kid did not want his friend Enrique to know his mother was half-crazy, and he had invented this splendid asthmatic grandmother so that his buddy the Frenchman, giving because of her, might relieve his poor mother's unhappiness and distress.

I went back to my little friend's bed: he was ashamed to look me in the face. Gently I pulled his chin up: his eyes were closed, but when at last he opened them I said, '*Pablito, eres un tronco de hombre.*' (You're a real man.)

I slipped him a hundred-bolivar note for his family and walked out, thoroughly proud and pleased with myself for having such a friend.

1967: proceedings against me had lapsed. I left for France by myself; to keep the business running properly you had to have authority and courage and the power of making yourself respected: and only Rita could do that. She said to me, 'Go and embrace your people in their own homes; go and pray at your father's grave.'

I went back to France by way of Nice. Why Nice? Together with my visa, the French consulate in Caracas had given me a document notifying the lapse of proceedings; but as he handed them to me, the consul said, 'Wait until I have instructions from France about the conditions under which you can return.' They did not have to spell it out. If I went back to the consul and he had received the reply from Paris, he would tell me I was *forbidden the department of the Seine for life*. But I had the firm intention of taking a trip to Paris.

This way I avoided getting the notification; and seeing I had neither received it nor signed it, I would be committing no offence, unless the consul learned that I was off and told the police at the Paris airport to hand me the notification. Hence my two stops—I should arrive at Nice as though I were coming from Spain.

1930–1967: thirty-seven years had gone by.

Thirteen years of the 'road down the drain'; twenty-four years of freedom, twenty-two of them with a home, which meant that I could go straight, reintegrated into society.

In 1956, a month with my people in Spain, then a gap of eleven years, though during these eleven years our many letters had kept me in living contact with my family.

1967. I saw them all. I went into their homes, I sat at their table, I had their children on my knee and even their grandchildren. Grenoble, Lyons, Cannes, Saint-Priest and then Saint-Peray, where I found Tante Ju in my father's house, still faithful at her post.

I listened to Tante Ju as she told me why Papa had died before his time. He watered his garden himself and he carried the cans for hours and hours over a distance of more than two hundred yards. 'Just imagine that, my dear, at his age! He could have bought a rubber hose, but Lord above, he was as stubborn as a mule. And one day, as he was carrying these watering-cans, his heart failed.'

I could just see my father lugging those heavy cans all the way to his beds of lettuces, tomatoes and haricot beans. And I could see him obstinately persisting in not getting the hose his wife, Tante Ju, kept begging him to buy. And I could see him, that country schoolmaster, stopping to draw breath and to mop his forehead, advise a neighbour or give a botany lesson to one of his grandsons.

Before going to see his grave in the cemetery, I asked Tante Ju to go with me on his favourite walks. And we went at the same pace he used to go, following the same stony paths lined with rushes, poppies and daisies until a milestone, or some bees, or the flight of a bird would remind Tante Ju of some little happening long ago that had touched them. Then, quite delighted, she would tell me how my father had told her about his grandson Michel being stung by a wasp. 'There, Henri, do you see? He was standing just there.'

I listened, with my throat constricted, thirsty for more, still more of the smallest details about my father's life. 'You know, Ju,' my father had said to her, 'when my boy was very small, five or six at the most, he was stung by a wasp when we were out for a walk: not once, like Michel, but twice. Well, he never cried at all; and on top of that, we had the greatest difficulty stopping him going off to look for the wasps' nest to destroy it. Oh, Riri was so brave!'

I did not travel on into the Ardèche: I went no farther than Saint-Peray. For my return to my village I wanted Rita to be with me.

I got out of the train at the Gare de Lyon; and put my bags in the left-luggage office so as not to have to fill in a registration form at the hotel. And then once more there was the asphalt of Paris under my feet, after thirty-seven years.

But this asphalt was not *my* asphalt until I was in my own district, Montmartre. I went there by night, of course. The only sun the Papillon of the thirties knew was that of the electric lights.

And here it was, Montmartre: the Place Pigalle and the Pierrot café and the moonlight and the Passage Elysée des Beaux-Arts and the types whooping it up and the laughter and the tarts and the ponces that anyone in the know could tell straight off just by the way they walked, and the joints crammed tight with people at the bar. But all this was just my first impression.

Thirty-seven years had gone by: nobody took any notice of me. Who was going to look at an old man of sixty? The tarts might even ask me upstairs and the young men might be so disrespectful as to elbow me out of my place at the bar.

Just one more stranger, a possible client, a provincial manufacturer—that's what this well-dressed, tie-wearing gent must be; a middle-class guy, another who had lost his way at this late hour and in this dubious bar. You could see right away he wasn't used to being in these parts; you could feel he was uneasy.

Sure I was uneasy, and that was understandable. These were not the same people nor the same mugs; at the first whiff you could tell that everything was mixed up now, everything confused. Pigs, lesbians, phony ponces, pouffes, wide-boys, squares, blacks and Arabs; there were only a few types from Marseilles or Corsica, speaking with a southern accent, to remind me of the old times. It was a completely different world from the one I had known.

There wasn't even what there had always been in my time— tables with groups of poets, painters or actors, with their long hair that reeked of Bohemia, and an avant-garde intelligence. Now every silly little jerk had long hair.

And I wandered from bar to bar like a sleepwalker, and I climbed stairs to see if there were still the billiard-tables of my youth on the first floor, and I civilly refused a guide's offer to show me Montparnasse. But I did ask him, 'Do you think that since 1930 Montmartre has lost the soul it had in those days?'

I felt like slapping him down for an answer that insulted my own personal Montmartre: 'Oh, but, Monsieur, Montmartre is immortal. I've lived here forty years, seeing I came when I was ten, and believe me, Place Pigalle, Place Blanche, Place Clichy and all the streets running off them are just the same and always will be the same for ever.'

I fled from the dreary little sod and walked along under the trees on the raised part in the middle of the avenue. From here, yes—so long as you didn't see the people clearly, so long as you only saw their shapes—from here, yes, Montmartre was still the same. I went slowly on towards the very spot where I was alleged to have shot Roland Legrand on the night of 25–26 March 1930.

The bench, probably the same bench repainted every year (a public bench might perfectly well last thirty-seven years with its wood that thick), the bench was there, and the lamp-post was there, and the bar over the way was there, and the half-closed shutters on the house opposite, they were still there. But say something, won't you, wood and stone and tree and glass! You saw, you must have been there then, seeing you're here now; you were the first, the only, the true witnesses of the tragedy; you know very well the man who fired that night was not me. Why didn't you say so?

People went by, unconcerned; people went by, never noticing this sixty-year-old man leaning against a tree, the same tree that had been there when the shot was fired.

Twenty-four I was in 1930, when I used to run down the Rue Lepic, that street which I can still walk up pretty briskly. The ghost has come back in spite of you all; he's pushed back the gravestone under which you buried him alive. Stop, stop, you half-blind creatures passing by! Stop and have a look at an innocent man who was condemned for a murder in this very place, on this very ground, before these same trees and these same stones—stop and ask these dumb witnesses, ask them to speak out today. And if you lean close, if you beg them, implore them to speak, you will hear them just as I hear them, whispering faintly, 'No, this man was not here at half past three on the night of 25 to 26 March thirty-seven years ago.'

'Where was he, then?' the doubters will say. Simple: I was in the Iris-Bar, maybe a hundred yards from here. In the Iris-Bar, when an honest taxi-driver burst in, crying, 'There was a shot outside just now.'

'It wasn't true,' said the pigs. 'It wasn't true,' said the boss and the waiter of the Iris, prompted by the pigs.

Once again I see the inquiry; once again I see the trial: I could not avoid being brought face to face with the past. You want to live through it again, man? You really want to? Nearly forty years since and you still want to go through that nightmare again? You're not afraid this going back will make you long for a revenge you gave up long ago? Are you sure of your strength, sure that dipping yourself in this filth won't mean you cannot wait for dawn and the shops to open to buy a cabin-trunk and stuff it with explosives for you know where? No: I'm perfectly certain of it: not one of them has anything to fear from me—let them perish, if the worms haven't eaten them already.

Well, my old Papi, there's no difficulty about going through the Grand Guignol piece you were the hero of, and the victim. Sit down there, on this same green bench, the one that saw the killing just opposite the Rue Germain-Pilon, right here on the Boulevard de Clichy, by the Clichy Bar-Tabac, where the tragedy began after the inquiry.

It's the night of 25–26 March: half past three in the morning. A man comes into the Clichy and asks for Madame Nini.

'That's me,' says a tart.

'Your man's just been shot in the guts. Come on; he's in a taxi.'

Nini runs after the unknown guy, together with a girl-friend. They get into the taxi, where Roland Legrand is sitting on the back seat. Nina asks the unknown guy who told her to come too. He says, 'I can't,' and disappears.

'Quick, the Lariboisière hospital!'

It was only during the drive that the taxi-man, a Russian, learned that his passenger was wounded: he had not noticed anything before. The moment his fare was unloaded at the hospital he hurried off to tell the police what he knew: he had been hailed by two men arm-in-arm outside 17, boulevard de Clichy: *only one of them got in*—Roland Legrand. The other told him to drive to the Clichy Bar and followed on foot. This man went into the bar and came out with two women; then he vanished. The two women told him to drive to the Lariboisière hospital: 'It was during the trip that I learned the man was wounded.'

The police carefully wrote all this down; they also wrote down Nini's declaration that her boy-friend had played cards all that night in that same bar where she plied her trade, had played cards with an *unknown man*; he'd played dice and had a drink at the bar with some men, still *all of them unknown*; and that Roland had left after the others, *alone*. Nothing in Nini's statement to show that anyone had come to fetch him. He went out by himself, after the others, the unknowns, had left.

A commissaire and a cop, Commissaire Gérardin and Inspecteur Grimaldi, questioned the dying Roland Legrand in the presence of his mother. The nurses had told them his condition was hopeless. I quote their report, it's been published in a book written to pull me to pieces, with a preface and therefore a guarantee by a *Commissaire divisionnaire*, Paul Romain. Here it is. The two pigs are questioning Legrand:

'"Here beside you you have the police commissaire and your mother, the holiest relationship in the world. Tell the truth. Who shot you?"

'He replied, "It was Papillon Roger."

'We asked him to swear that he had really told the truth. "Yes, Monsieur, I have told you the truth."

'We withdrew, leaving the mother beside her son.'

So what happened on the night of 25 March 1930 was clear and straightforward: the man who fired was Papillon *Roger*.

This Roland Legrand was a pork-butcher and a ponce who put his girl-friend Nini out to work for him: he lived with her at 4, rue Elysée des Beaux-Arts. He was not really a member of the underworld, but like all those who hung around Montmartre and all the genuine crooks he knew several Papillons. And because he was afraid they might arrest another Papillon instead of the one who had killed him, he was exact about the Christian name. For although he was fond of living as a ponce, like all squares he also wanted the police to punish his enemy. A Papillon, sure: but Papillon *Roger*.

Everything came flooding back to me in this accursed place. I must have run through this file in my head a thousand times and more; I'd learned it by heart in my cell, like a Bible, because my lawyers had given it to me and I'd had time to engrave it on my mind before the trial.

So there was Legrand's statement before he died; and the declaration of Nini, his girl. Neither of them named me as the killer.

Now four men come upon the stage. On the night of this job they went to the Lariboisière hospital to ask:

(1) if the wounded man was in fact Roland Legrand
(2) what condition he was in

The pigs were told at once and they began a search. Since these men did not belong to the underworld and were not concealing themselves, they had come on foot and they left on foot. They were picked up as they were walking down the Avenue Rochechouart and kept in custody at the station in the XVIII arrondissement.

Their names were:

Georges Goldstein, 24; Roger Dorin, 24; Roger Jourmar, 21; Emile Cape, 18.

All the statements they made to the commissaire of the XVIII arrondissement station on the very day of the killing were fresh from the oven. Goldstein stated that in a gathering of people he had been told that a man called Legrand had been wounded—shot *three times* with a revolver. Thinking it might be his friend Roland Legrand, who was often in that district, he walked to the hospital to find out. On the way he met Dorin and then the two others and asked them to go with him. The others knew nothing about the business and they did not know the victim.

The commissaire asked Goldstein, 'Do you know Papillon?'
'Yes, a little. I've met him now and then. He knew Legrand; *that's all I can tell you.*'

So what of it? What does this Papillon mean? There were five or six of them in Montmartre! Don't get worked up, Papi. As I go through all this again, I'm still twenty-four and I'm re-reading my file in my cell at the Conciergerie.

Dorin's statement: Goldstein asked him to go with him to the Lariboisière to inquire after a friend *whose name he did not mention.* Dorin went into the hospital with him and Goldstein asked if the Legrand who had been brought in was seriously wounded.

'Do you know Legrand? Do you remember Papillon Roger?' asked the commissaire.

'I don't know Legrand, either by name or by sight. I do know a man called Papillon, having seen him in the street. He

262

is very well known and they say he is a terror. I know nothing more.'

The third man to be questioned, Jourmar, said that when Goldstein came out of the hospital, having gone in alone with Dorin, he said, 'It's certainly my mate.'

So before he went in, he was not sure about it, right?

The commissaire: 'Do you know Papillon Roger and a man called Legrand?'

'I know a man called Papillon who hangs around Pigalle. The last time I saw him was about three months ago.'

The same with the fourth thief. He didn't know Legrand. A Papillon, yes, but only by sight.

In her first statement the mother also confirmed that her son had said Papillon *Roger*.

It was only after these first statements that the really dirty business began. Up until then everything had been plain, clear-cut and exact. All the chief witnesses gave their evidence in complete freedom before a local commissaire without being prompted, threatened or guided.

In short, Roland was in the Clichy bar before the tragedy; and all the people present were unknown. They may have been playing cards or dice, which meant they were acquaintances of Roland's, but still they were unknown. What was odd and indeed disturbing, was that they remained unknown until the very end.

Second point: Roland Legrand was *the last to leave the bar, and he left it by himself*: his own girl said so. Nobody came to fetch him. A very little while after he went out he was wounded by an unknown man whom he positively identified on his deathbed as Papillon Roger. The man who came to tell Nini was also an unknown; and he too was to remain unknown. Yet he was the one who helped Legrand into the taxi immediately after the shooting—an unknown man who did not get in but who walked along with the cab as far as the bar where he was going to warn Nini. And this essential witness was to remain unknown for good, although everything he had just done proved that he belonged to the underworld, to Montmartre, and that he was therefore known to the pigs. Strange.

Third point: Goldstein, who was to be the prosecution's chief witness, *did not know* who had been wounded and went to the Lariboisière hospital to find out whether it was his friend Legrand.

The only clues as to this Papillon were that he was called Roger and that he was said to be a terror.

Were you a terror at twenty-three, Papillon? Were you dangerous? No, not yet; but maybe you were on the way to becoming both. And it's certain too that I was a tough guy, an 'undesirable' then; but it's also certain that at only twenty-three, I could not have become set for ever as one particular type of man. It's also certain that at that age, having been only two years in Montmartre, I could not have been either the head of a gang or the terror of Pigalle. Certainly I disturbed public order; and certainly I was suspected of having taken part in big jobs, but nothing had ever been proved against me. Sure they had pulled me in several times and grilled me pretty hard at 36, quai des Orfèvres, but without ever having been able to get anything out of me, neither a confession nor a name. Sure, after the tragedy of my childhood and after my time in the navy and after the government had refused me a steady career, I had made up my mind to live outside that society of clowns and to let them know it. Sure, every time I was picked up and grilled at the quai des Orfèvres for an important job they thought I was mixed up in, I insulted my torturers and humiliated them in every possible way, even telling them that one day I should be in their place, the shits, and that they would be in my power. So of course the pigs, humiliated through and through, might have said to themselves, 'This Papillon, we'll have to clip his wings the first chance we have.'

But still, I was only twenty-three! My life was not only mere resentment and rancour against society and the squares who obeyed its damn-fool rules: it was also *life itself*, continually on the move, sending off showers of sparks. It's true there was some serious nonsense; yes, but it was not wicked nonsense. Besides, when I was pulled in there was only one condemnation on my file: four months' suspended sentence for receiving stolen goods. Did I deserve to be wiped off the face of the earth just for having humiliated the pigs and just because I might turn dangerous one day?

And it all began at the point when the criminal police took

the business over. The word went round Montmartre that they were looking for all the Papillons—Little Papillon, Pussini Papillon, Papillon Trompe-la-Mort, Papillon Roger, etc.

As for me, I was just plain Papillon; or sometimes to avoid confusion, Charrière Papillon. But it was no part of my way of life to hobnob with the pigs, and I moved off fast: yes, that was true, I went on the run.

And why did you do that, Papi, since it wasn't you?

You ask that now? Have you forgotten that by the time you were twenty-three you had already been tortured several times at the quai des Orfèvres? You were never really fond of being knocked about, nor of all those exquisite tortures invented by the head pig of those days, the trough where they shove your head under the water until you are perishing for want of air and you don't know whether you're dead or alive, the pigs who give your balls five or six twists and leave them so swollen you walk like an Argentine gaucho for weeks on end, the paper-press in which they crush your nails till the blood spurts and they come off, the beating-up with a rubber truncheon that wounds your lungs so blood pours out of your mouth, and the twelve- or fifteen-stone porkers who jump up and down on your belly as if it was a spring-board. Is it your age, Papi, or have you lost your memory? There was not just one reason for going on the run right away, but a hundred. It was a break that didn't carry me too far, since I wasn't guilty. There was no need to go off abroad; just a little hide-out near Paris would be enough. Soon they'd pick up the Papillon Roger in question, or if not pick him up then at least identify him; and then fine, you jump into a taxi and you're back in Paris. No more danger for your balls or your nails or all the rest.

Only this Papillon Roger never was identified. There was no culprit.

Then all at once a wanted man was produced like magic. This Papillon Roger? Simple: you just wipe out the Roger and you pick up plain Papillon, the nickname of Henri Charrière. The trick's done: all that's left is to pile up the evidence. It's no longer a matter of an honest, impartial inquiry into the truth, but of the total fabrication of *a culprit*.

Policemen, don't you see, need *to bring off the solution of a murder-case* so as to deserve promotion in their very noble, very honest career. Now this Papillon has everything going for him as a culprit. He's young, and there is something of the ponce about him ... We'll say his girl's a whore. He's a thief, and he's been in trouble with the police several times; but he's either got off on a dismissed charge or he's been acquitted.

And then into the bargain the guy is an awkward sod; he's awkward when we arrest him, he sneers at us, humiliates us, calls his little dog Chiappe [chief of the Paris police in those days] and sometimes he says to our colleagues, 'You'd be well advised to grill a little more gently, if you want to reach retirement age.' These threats of punishing us one day for our 'modern' and 'thoroughgoing' methods of interrogation worry us. So go right in, man. We're covered on all sides.

So that was the sinister beginning of it all, Papi. Twenty-three you were, when these two lousy pigs flushed you out at Saint-Cloud on 10 April, while you were eating snails.

Oh, they went right in, all right! What drive, what zeal, what steadiness, what passion, what diabolical cunning to succeed in getting you into the dock one day, for the court to fetch you that blow—a blow that knocked you out for thirteen years!

It wasn't so easy to turn you into the guilty man, Papi. But the inspector in charge of the job, Mayzaud, a Montmartre specialist, was so eager to send me down that it was open war between him and my lawyers even in the court, as you can see in the papers of that time, with insults, complaints and foul blows; and ready to hand this accursed Mayzaud had the draper's son, the plump little Goldstein, one of those phony little bastards who lick the underworld's feet in the hope of being accepted. Very amenable, this Goldstein! Mayzaud (he said so himself at the trial) met him maybe a hundred times *by chance* during the inquiry. This precious witness *on the very day of the killing* stated that in a crowd of people he had heard that someone called Roland had got three bullets in the guts; he had then gone to the hospital to ask about the exact identity of the victim and the danger of his wound—a statement cross-checked by three friends who had nothing whatsoever to do with it; more than three weeks later, on 18 April, after many contacts with Mayzaud, this same Goldstein made the following declaration: 'That on the night of 25–26 March, before the killing, he had met Papillon [me] together with two un-known men' [still more?]. Papillon had asked him where Le-grand was. Goldstein: 'At the Clichy.' Papillon left him and straight away he went to warn Legrand. While he was talking to Legrand one of Papillon's two companions came in and asked Legrand to come outside. Goldstein himself went out a little later and saw Papillon and Legrand talking quietly; but he did not linger. Later, coming back to the place Pigalle, he *once more* met Papillon who told him he had just shot Le-grand and asked him to go to the Lariboisière and see what state he was in, and if he was still alive, to advise him to keep his mouth shut.

For of course, Papi, you who were described to the court as a terror, a member of the underworld all the more dangerous because of your intelligence and cunning; so would you in fact be such an idiot that having shot a guy right there on the boulevard, you would hang around the place Pigalle, right on the spot, until Goldstein comes that way again? Do you stand there like a milestone on some little Ardèche lane, so that the pigs only have to come trotting along to ask you how you are doing?

But this Goldstein was not such a fool as all that: the day after his statement he buggered off to England.

Meanwhile I stood up for myself stoutly. 'Goldstein? Don't know him. I may have seen him; may even have exchanged a few words with him like you do with people always around the same district, without knowing who you're talking to.' I really could not manage to fit a snout to that name; so much so that it was only when we were brought face to face that I succeeded in identifying him. And I was so taken aback that a little square I didn't know should make such a detailed charge against me, that I wondered what crime he could have com-mitted—nothing much for sure, he being such a dreary little sod—for the pigs to have such a hold on him. I am still won-dering; sexual offences? Cocaine?

Without him, without his successive statements that *every time* brought new material to the case the pigs were building up, without him nothing held together. Nothing.

And now there appeared something that at first sight looked miraculous but later turned out to be exceedingly dangerous—

indeed fatal. A diabolical police plot, a horrible trap that I and my lawyers fell into head first. I thought it meant safety, but it was disaster. Because there was nothing solid in the file: Goldstein's successive bits of evidence were all very improbable. The file had so little body to it that my alleged killing lacked even a motive. Since I had no cause to dislike the victim and since I was not raving mad, I was as out of place in this job as a hair in the soup; and any jury at all, even one made up of the dullest idiots on earth, could hardly fail to realize it.

So the police invented a motive: and the one who provided it was a pig who had been working Montmartre for the last ten years, Inspector Mazillier.

One of my lawyers, Maître Beffey, liked wandering about Montmartre in his off time; and he met this pig, who told him he knew what had really happened on the night of 25–26 March and that he was prepared to tell—and this implied that what he had to say would be in my favour. Beffey and I said, either he's motivated by professional honesty or else—which is more likely—there's some rivalry between Mayzaud and him.

And *we* called him as a witness. *We* did.

But what Mazillier had to say was not at all what we had expected. He stated that he knew me well, that I had done him many favours, and he added, 'Thanks to the information provided by Charrière I have been able to carry out several arrests. As for the circumstances in connection with the murder, *I know nothing about them.* Yet I have heard it said [Lord, how many 'I have heard it said's' we had during my trial!] that Charrière was the object of ill-will on the part of persons unknown to me who disapproved of his relations with the police.'

And there we were with the cause of the murder! I'd killed Roland Legrand during a quarrel because he was spreading it around Montmartre that I grassed, that I was an informer.

And when was this statement of Inspector Mazillier's made? 14 April. And when did Goldstein make his, the one that went back on his statement on the day of the killing? 18 April, *four days after Mazillier's.*

But the other judges—apart from the investigating magistrate Robbé, who was in the pigs' pocket from the start—the other judges were not ready to swallow the ugly brew prepared by these bastards. When the court of first instance was presented with this padded, elastic evidence, this mass of rumours, lies and prompted statements, they sensed there was something fishy about the whole thing. Because although you often put them all into the same bag, Papi, as if judges, pigs, jurymen, the law and the prison administration were all part of the same conspiracy you must admit that there have been some exceedingly honest judges.

As a result, the court *refused* to send me before the assizes with that phony file and sent all the evidence back to the investigating magistrate, insisting upon *further inquiry*.

The pigs were utterly infuriated; they found witnesses everywhere—in prison, just about to be let out or just having been let out. But the further inquiry produced nothing, absolutely nothing, not the slightest clue nor the least beginning of new and serious evidence.

In the end, without anything fresh—still a badly-made bouillabaisse with no rascasse—the file was at last allowed to be sent up to the assizes.

And now came the clap of thunder. Something happened that is almost never seen in the legal world: the public prosecutor, the man whose job it is to protect society and to get promotion by putting as many defendants as possible behind bars—the public prosecutor who had been given the brief to act against me, took it with the tips of his fingers, as though he were holding it with tongs, and put it back on the desk, saying, 'I shan't act in this case. It smells fishy and prefabricated: give it to someone else.'

How splendid he looked, Maître Raymond Hubert, when he came to tell me this extraordinary news at the Conciergerie! 'Can you imagine it, Charrière! Your file is so unconvincing, a prosecutor has refused to have anything to do with it and has asked for the brief to be given to someone else!'

... It was cool that night on the bench in the boulevard de Clichy. I walked up and down under the shadow of the trees; I did not want to walk into the light for fear of interrupting the magic lantern as it poured out these pictures from thirty-seven years ago. I turned up the collar of my overcoat. I pushed back my hat a little to air my head—the intensity of all this total recollection had made it hot and sweaty. I sat down again, pulled my coat over my legs, and then, with my back to the avenue I slid my legs over the bench and sat the other way round, my arms leaning on the back as they had leant on the rail of the dock during my first trial in July 1931.

Because there was not just one trial at the assizes for me. *There were two.* The first in July, the other in October.

It all went too well, Papi! The court was not blood-red, like a slaughterhouse; it was more like an enormous boudoir. In the flooding light of that marvellous July day, the hangings, the carpets and the judges' robes were almost pale pink. And in this court, a smiling, kindly, rather sceptical presiding judge, so little convinced by what he had read in the file that he opened proceedings like this: 'Charrière, Henri, as the indictment does not entirely correspond with what we should have liked to see in it, will you explain your case to the court and the jury yourself?'

The president of an assize court asking the defendant to lay open his case! You remember that sun-filled July assize and those wonderful judges? It was too good to last, Papi. Those judges conducted the proceedings with such impartiality, the president calmly and honestly looking for the truth, asking the pigs embarrassing questions, worrying Goldstein, pointing out his contradictions and allowing my lawyers and me to ask him awkward questions—it was too splendid; I tell you again, Papi, it was sunlit justice, a holiday-sitting with the judges in your favour.

There you could fight and stand up for yourself, Papi. Fight against whom? Oh, there was no lack of enemies—they were there in droves.

The first important witness, already primed by the pigs: the mother. I don't think it was out of bad faith that she had adopted the pigs' insinuations. She really did so unconsciously.

Now the mother no longer said that she and the commissaire had heard 'Papillon Roger', or that Legrand had added (when?) that a friend of his called Goldstein knew Papillon well. Now she stated that what she had heard was, 'It's Papillon: Goldstein knows him.' She had forgotten the *Roger* and she had added the 'Goldstein knows him', words that Commissaire Gérardin and Inspecteur Grimaldi did not hear. Odd that a commissaire should not write down something as important as that, don't you think?

Maître Gautrat, the lawyer appearing for the family, wanted me to ask the victim's mother to forgive me. I said to her, 'Madame, I do not have to ask your forgiveness because I did not kill your son. I express my sorrow for your grief; that is all I can do.'

But Commissaire Gérardin and Inspecteur Grimaldi changed nothing of their first statement: Legrand had said 'It was Papillon Roger', that's all.

And now the key witness came forward: Goldstein. This witness, a recording machine prepared at 36, quai des Orfèvres, had made five or six statements: three of them were used. Each one accused me; it did not matter if they were contradictory—each time they brought a fresh piece of wood to the framework the police were building up. Sitting there on the bench, I could see him as if he were just in front of me. He spoke in a low voice: he scarcely raised his hand when he said 'I swear it'. When he had finished his statement, Maître Beffey went for him. 'Goldstein, how many times have you met Inspector Mayzaud "by chance"? He himself states that he has met you and talked to you about this case "by chance" several times. It's curious, Goldstein. In your first statement you said you knew nothing about the affair; then you knew Papillon; after that you said you had met him on the night of the crime, before it was committed; then he tells you to go to Lariboisière and see how Legrand is getting on. How do you explain these differing statements?'

Goldstein's only reply was to repeat, 'I was afraid, because in Montmartre Papillon is terribly dangerous.'

I made a gesture of protest and the president said to me, 'Defendant, have you any questions to ask the witness?'

'Yes, Monsieur le Président.' I looked straight at Goldstein. 'Goldstein, turn this way and look me in the face. What is it that makes you lie and accuse me falsely? What crime of yours does Mayzaud know about? What crime are you paying for with these lying statements?'

The shit trembled as he looked me in the face, but he did manage to bring out the words 'I'm telling the truth' quite distinctly.

I could have killed the swine! I turned towards the court. 'Gentlemen of the court, gentlemen of the jury, the public prosecutor says I am an intelligent, sharp-witted, knowing character; but the witness's evidence shows me to be a perfect idiot and I'll prove it to you. Confiding something as important as this, telling a man you've just killed his friend means, if you are intelligent, that you must know him very well; whereas admitting such a thing to a man you don't know at all is the act of a total imbecile. Yet I don't know Goldstein.' And turning towards Goldstein I went on, 'Goldstein, please name one single person in Paris or in the whole of France who can say he has seen us talking together even once.'

'I don't know anyone who could testify to that.'

'Right. Please name a bar, restaurant or eating-place in Montmartre, Paris, or anywhere in France where we have eaten or drunk together even once.'

'I've never eaten or drunk with you.'

'Very well. You say the first time you met me that extraordinary night I had two men with me. Who were they?'

'I don't know them.'

'Nor do I, either. Now say quickly, without hesitating, where I told you to meet me to give me the answer—the answer you were to bring back from the hospital—and say whether you mentioned that place to the men who went with you. And if you did not mention it to them, why not?'

No answer.

'Reply, Goldstein. Why don't you reply?'

'I didn't know where to find you.'

Maître Raymond Hubert: 'So my client sends you on an errand as important as this—he sends you to find out Roland Legrand's condition, and you did not know where to give him the answer? It is as absurd as it is unbelievable!'

Yes, Papi, it was unbelievable all right; but it was even more unbelievable that the whole indictment had been allowed to be built up on the successive accusations of this dreary straight who, although carefully prepared by the pigs, did not even have wits enough to give a quick answer.

The president: 'Charrière, the police claim that you killed Legrand because he called you an informer. What have you to

272

say to that?'

'I've had dealings with the police six times and each time I came away with the charge dismissed or an acquittal, except for my four months' suspended sentence. I've never been arrested with another man; I've never had another man arrested. It is impossible to accept that when I am in the hands of the police I don't talk, and that when I'm at liberty I inform on my friends.'

'An inspector says you are an informer. Call Inspector Mazillier.'

'I state that Charrière was an informer, one who enabled me to arrest several dangerous individuals; and that this was known in Montmartre. As to the Legrand affair, I know nothing about it.'

'What have you to say to that, Charrière?'

'It was on Maître Beffey's advice that I asked for this inspector to be called at the inquiry: Maître Beffey had told me Mazillier knew the truth about the murder of Legrand. And now I see that both my counsel and I fell into a horrible trap. Inspector Mazillier, when he advised Maître Beffey to call him, said he knew all about the killing; my counsel believed him, and so did I. We imagined he was either an honest cop or that there was some rivalry between him and Mayzaud that led him to give evidence about this crime. But now, as you see yourself, he says he knows nothing about it.

'On the other hand, it's clear that the inspector's statements at last provided the missing motive for my alleged crime. This statement, coming from a policeman, was a godsend: it preserved the framework of the accusation and gave some body to an indictment that just didn't hold together. Because there's no doubt that without the help given by Mazillier, the indictment would have fallen to pieces, in spite of all Inspector Mayzaud's efforts. The dodge is so obvious that it's astonishing the prosecution should ever have used it.'

I fought on and I said, 'Gentlemen of the court, gentlemen of the jury, if I'd been a police informer, one of two things would have happened: either I should not have killed Raymond Legrand for calling me a grass—because a type as low as that takes such an insult without batting an eyelid—either I should not have killed him at all, or, if I had shot him, being furious, you can be dead certain the police would have played the game: they would never have gone out for my blood with all this zeal and all this clumsiness, because I was so useful to them. More than that, they would have closed their eyes or have fixed some gimmick that would have made it look as though I was acting in legitimate self-defence. Plenty of precedents of that kind could be quoted; but fortunately for me they don't apply. Monsieur le Président, may I ask the witness a question?'

'Yes.'

Knowing what I was up to, Maître Raymond Hubert asked the court to free Inspector Mazillier from his professional secrecy, otherwise he would not be able to reply.

The president: 'By its discretionary powers, the court releases Inspector Mazillier from his professional secrecy, and requires him, in the interests of truth and justice, to answer the question the defendant is about to put to him.'

'Mazillier, name one single man in France, the colonies or abroad you have arrested because of my information.'

'I cannot reply.'

'You're a liar, Inspector! You can't reply because there's never been one!'

'Charrière, moderate your language,' said the president.

'Monsieur le Président, I'm defending two things here, my life and my honour.'

But the incident went no farther. Mazillier withdrew.

And the other witnesses, how they came rolling up! All dressed in the same cloth, cut and sewn in the same fashion, all the handiwork of the pigs at 36, quai des Orfèvres, Paris.

And your last explanation, Papi, don't you remember that? The last and the most logical of them all. I can still hear it. 'Gentlemen, be straight with me and listen to what I have to say: Legrand got only one bullet; he was shot once only; he remained on his feet, he walked off alive, he was allowed to quietly take a taxi. That means the man who shot him did not want to kill him; otherwise he'd have fired four, five, six shots the way we do in the underworld. Anyone who knows Montmartre knows that. Right or wrong? So suppose it was me, and suppose I confess and say "Gentlemen, this man, for such-and-such a reason, right or wrong, had a row with me or accused

274

me of something; he put his hand in his pocket, and as he was an underworld type like me I was afraid so I fired just one shot to defend myself." If I said that, at the same time I'd be giving you the proof I didn't mean to kill him because he went off on his own feet and alive. Then I would end up by saying to you, "Since an inspector says I'm very useful to the police, I ask you to accept my confession and that what I have told you is true, and to treat the business as unintentional homicide." '

The court listened in silence: thoughtful, it seemed to me. I went on, 'Ten times, a hundred times, both Maître Raymond Hubert and Maître Beffey have asked me the question, "Was it you who fired? If it was you, say so. You'll get five years at the outside, maybe even less: you can't be sent down for more. When they arrested you you were twenty-three, so you'll still be very young when you come out." But, gentlemen of the court and gentlemen of the jury, I can't take that path, not even to save myself from the guillotine or penal servitude, *because I'm innocent and I've been framed by the police.*'

All this in that sunny courtroom where they let me explain things properly. No, Papi, it was too good; it was going too well; you felt that the court was worried and that victory was possible. Poor pretentious kid, couldn't you see it was too good to last?

For this was the point where Mayzaud quickly thought up a gimmick: one that beyond doubt showed his diabolical nature. Feeling he had lost the game and that his fifteen months of effort might be reduced to nothing, he did what was forbidden. During a pause in the hearing he came to see me in the room where I was alone among the *Gardes républicains* and which he had no right to enter. And he came up to me and he had the nerve to say, 'Why don't you say it was Corsican Roger?'

Completely taken aback, I said, 'But I don't know any Corsican Roger.'

He talked for a moment, walked quickly out, went to the prosecuting counsel and said to him, 'Papillon's just confessed to me that it was Corsican Roger.'

And now what this accursed Mayzaud wanted to happen did happen. The trial was stopped, in spite of my protests. Yet I still fought on and I said, 'For the last eighteen months Inspector Mayzaud has been saying there's only one Papillon in this case and that it's me; Inspector Mayzaud says there's no doubt that I am Legrand's killer; Inspector Mayzaud says he not only asserts it but that he's brought honest, unanswerable witnesses who prove my guilt without the shadow of a doubt. Since the police have found all the necessary witnesses and proofs against me, why is their whole framework collapsing? So isn't this whole mass of evidence a pack of lies? And is just one new name tossed into the arena enough for it to seem uncertain any more that Papillon is guilty? Since you say you've got all the proofs of my guilt, is it merely on the existence of some imaginary Corsican Roger that the trial is to be stopped and started all over again? Just because of some imaginary Corsican Roger, thought up by Mayzaud if you believe me, or thought up by me, if you trust him once again? It's impossible: I demand that the proceedings should go on: I demand to be judged. I beg it of you, gentlemen of the jury and Monsieur le Président!'

You'd won, Papi, you'd very nearly won; and it was the honesty of the prosecuting counsel that made you lose. Because this man, Cassagnau, stood up and said, 'Gentlemen of the jury, gentlemen of the court, I cannot proceed ... I no longer know ... The incident must be expunged ... I ask the court to put the trial back and order a further inquiry.'

Just that, Papi, just those three phrases of Maître Cassagnau condemned you on a phony indictment. Because if this upright lawyer had had something clear, straight and unanswerable in his hands, he would not have said 'Stop the trial, I can no longer proceed.'

He would have said, 'Just one more of Charrière's inventions: the defendant wants to lead us astray with his Corsican Roger. We do not believe a word of it, gentlemen; here I have everything that is required to prove Charrière guilty, and I shall not fail to do so.'

But he did not say that: and why not? Because in his conscience he did not fully believe in his brief, and because he must have begun asking himself questions about the honesty of the pigs who had put it together.

You were a kid of twenty-three: and that was how, at the very moment they were shamefully losing, the pigs pipped you at the post, knowing very well their Corsican Roger was pure boloney. They hoped that before the next assizes they could think up some other ploy. Their twisted minds reckoned that another court, another president, another prosecuting counsel and the atmosphere of the next assizes would not be so favourable to me, and that the boudoir would turn into a slaughterhouse.

The trial was stopped and they ordered a supplementary inquiry, *the second in this case.*

One of the newspapers said, 'Such a lack of conviction is most unusual.'

Of course the supplementary inquiry provided *no new facts whatsoever.* Corsican Roger? Of course he was never found. During this further inquiry the *Gardes républicains* were straight: when they were asked about the incident in July they gave evidence against Mayzaud. In any case, how could a man who proclaimed his innocence and who proved it logically and who felt the court favourably inclined towards him, how could this man throw the whole thing up and suddenly say 'I was there but I wasn't the one who fired: it was Corsican Roger'?

And what about the other trial, Papi? The next assizes, the last, the decisive hearing: there where the dry guillotine began to work, there where at twenty-four your youth and your faith in life received the great hammer-blow of a life-sentence; there where Mayzaud, sure of himself once more, apologized to the prosecuting counsel and admitted having made a mistake in July; there where you shouted at him 'I'll rip off your mask, Mayzaud!' ... do you really want to live through all that again?

Do you really want to see that courtroom again, and that grey, unhappy day? How many times do I have to tell you that thirty-seven years have gone by since then? Do you want to feel that savage blow on the jaw again, that swipe which forced you to struggle for thirty-seven years to be able to sit on this bench in the Boulevard de Clichy, in your Montmartre? Yes, indeed; I want to go down those first steps of the ladder that took me to the very bottom of the pit of human baseness, I want to go down them one by one again, so as to have a better notion of the road I have travelled.

You remember? You remember how different it was when

you came into the second courtroom, a good-looking boy in a perfectly cut double-breasted suit? Yet it was the same court.

In the first place the sky was so low and rainy they had to light the chandeliers. This time everything was draped in red, blood-red. Carpets, hangings, judges' robes—as if they had all been dipped in the basket that holds the heads of guillotined men. This time the judges were not about to go off for their holidays; they had just returned from them: it was not the same as July.

The old stagers of the law courts, the barristers and so on, know better than anyone how the weather, the time of the year, the character of the presiding judge, his mood that day, the mood of the prosecuting counsel and the jury, the defendant's and his lawyers' fitness—their form—can sometimes influence the scales of justice.

This time the president did not pay me the compliment of asking me to explain my case myself; he was quite satisfied with the monotonous voice of the clerk of the court reading out the indictment.

The twelve bastards who made up the jury had brains as damp and dreary as the weather; you could see that in their moist, dull, half-witted eyes. They eagerly supped up the boloney of the indictment.

There was absolutely nothing human about the prosecuting counsel, the purveyor-in-chief for the guillotine.

I felt all this the moment I came in and glanced quickly round the court. 'Look out, Papillon, it's not in a court like this that you're going to be able to stand up for yourself properly.' And I had sized it up exactly; during the two days the trial lasted they hardly let me speak at all.

And now came the same statements, the same evidence, as in July. No point in going over it in detail; it was the same party beginning all over again with the one difference that if I felt outraged and if I sometimes burst out, they shut me up at once.

Only one really new fact, the appearance of the taxi-driver Lellu Fernand, the witness for my alibi, who had not had time to give his evidence before the postponement in July—the only witness the pigs had never been able to find: a myth, according to them.

Yet he was an essential witness for me, because he had stated that when he went into the Iris Bar saying 'there's just been a shot', *I was there.*

Lellu confirmed his statement: they accused him of being a put-up witness.

Here on this green bench, fury seized hold of me again; I felt neither the cold nor the drizzle that had begun to fall.

Once again I saw the boss of the Iris Bar come into the witness-box and state I could not have been in his place when Lellu came in to say there had been a shot outside, because he had forbidden me to enter his bar a fortnight earlier. That meant I was such a bloody fool that in a job as serious as this, with my freedom and perhaps my life at stake, the alibi I gave was just the very place where I was not allowed to go! And his waiter confirmed his evidence. Naturally they forgot to add that permission to stay open until five in the morning was a favour granted by the police and that if they told the truth they would be going directly against the pigs, which would mean their closing-time would be brought back to two o'clock. The boss was defending his till and the waiter his tips.

Maître Raymond Hubert did all he could and so did Maître Beffey—a Maître Beffey so disgusted that he reached the point of open war with Mayzaud, who, in confidential police reports, tried to damage his standing as a barrister by giving details of sexual matters that had nothing to do with the case.

Now it was the end. I was the last to speak. What could I say? 'I'm innocent. I've been framed by the police. That's all.'

The jury and the court withdrew. An hour later they returned and I stood up while they went back to their places. Then in his turn the president rose: he was about to read the sentence. 'Prisoner at the bar, stand up.'

And so firmly did I believe I was in the court, here under these trees in the Boulevard de Clichy, that I jumped to my feet, forgetting that my legs were pinned against the back of the bench, which made me fall back on my arse.

So it was sitting, not standing as I ought to have been, that there under the boulevard trees in 1967, I heard the toneless voice of the president who, in October 1931, pronounced this sentence. 'You are condemned to penal servitude for life.

Guards, take the prisoner away.'

I was just about to hold out my hands; but there was no one to put on the handcuffs; there were no *Gardes républicains* beside me. There was no one except a poor old woman lying curled up at the far end of the bench, with newspapers on her head to protect her from the cold and the rain.

I untwisted my legs. Standing at last, I let them get over their stiffness and then, lifting the papers, I put a hundred-franc note into the hands of this old woman, sentenced to extreme poverty for life. For me, 'life' had only lasted thirteen years.

And still keeping under the trees in the middle of the Boulevard de Clichy I walked along to Place Blanche, pursued by the last image of that trial—myself standing to receive the unbelievable blow that wiped me out of Montmartre, my Montmartre, for nearly forty years.

I had scarcely reached that wonderful square before the magic-lantern went out, and all I saw were a few bums sitting there at the exit from the métro, squatting with their heads on their knees, asleep.

Quickly I looked round for a cab. There was nothing here to attract me, neither the shadow of the trees that hid the glare of artificial light nor the brilliance of the square, with its Moulin Rouge blazing away at full blast. The one reminded me too much of my past and the other shouted 'You don't belong here any more.' Everything, yes, everything had changed: get out quick if you don't want to see that the memories of your twenties are dead and buried.

'Hey! Taxi! Gare de Lyon, please.'

And in the suburban train that took me back to my nephew's, I went over all the newspaper articles that Maître Raymond Hubert gave me to read after my conviction. Not one of them could avoid speaking of the doubt that had hung over the whole case; *Le Journal* gave it the headline 'A Dubious Case'.

I looked up these papers when I came back to France. Here are a few samples. *Le Matin* of 27.10.31: 'Thirty witnesses were called. Perhaps one would have been enough—the unknown who put the wounded man into the taxi, told his "wife" and then vanished; but this unknown remains the unknown whom thirty successive testimonies will probably not succeed in identifying.'

La France of 28.10.31: 'The defendant replied calmly and firmly ... The defendant: "It grieves me to hear that," he said. "This Goldstein has not the least reason to wish me ill, but he is in the hands of Inspector Mayzaud, like so many others of his kind who have uneasy consciences, and that's the truth of it." '

L'Humanité of 28 October. This article deserves to be quoted at length.

Charrière-Papillon condemned to penal servitude for life

In spite of the persisting doubt as to the identity of the real Papillon, of the Papillon who is said to have killed Roland Legrand on the Butte one night in March, the jury of the Seine convicted Charrière.

At the beginning of yesterday's hearing, the witness Goldstein, upon whose statements the whole charge rests, gave evidence. This witness, who remained in continual contact with the police and whom Inspector Mayzaud said he had seen more than a hundred times since the tragedy, made his statements on three separate occasions, each deposition being more serious than the last. It is clear that this witness is a loyal helper of the criminal police.

While he was uttering his accusations, Charrière listened closely. When Goldstein had finished, Charrière cried, 'I don't understand, I don't understand this Goldstein: I have never done him any harm and yet he comes here and pours out lies whose only aim is to get me sent to penal servitude.'

Inspector Mayzaud was recalled. This time he claimed that Goldstein's evidence was spontaneous. But sceptical smiles were seen in court.

For the prosecution Siramy made a rambling closing speech in which he observed that there were several Papillons in Montmartre and even elsewhere. Nevertheless he asked for a conviction, though without being exact as to the sentence, which he left to the jury.

Maître Gautrat, representing the family, comically held up penal servitude as a school of 'moral betterment' and then asked that Charrière should be sent there for his own good, so as to be made an 'honest man'.

The counsel for the defence, Maîtres Beffey and Raymond Hubert, pleaded innocence. It did not follow that since Corsican Roger, otherwise Papillon, could not be found, Charrière, otherwise Papillon, was therefore guilty.

But after a long retirement the jury came back, bringing in the verdict of guilty, and the court sentenced Henri Charrière to penal servitude for life, awarding the family one franc damages.

For years and years I have asked myself this question: why did the police go all out for a little crook of twenty-three who they *themselves* said was one of their best helpers? I have only found a single answer, the only logical one: they were covering up for someone else; and this someone else was a *genuine informer*.

The next day, in the sun, I went back to Montmartre. I found my old haunts again, the Rue Tholozé and the Rue Durantin; and the market in the Rue Lepic; but the faces, the faces, where were they?

I went into 26, rue Tholozé to see the concierge, pretending to be looking for someone. My concierge had been a big fat woman with a hairy wart on her cheek. She had vanished, and a woman from Brittany had taken her place.

The Montmartre of my youth had not been stolen; no, everything was there, absolutely everything; but it had all changed. The dairy had turned into a laundromat, the local bar into a chemist's and the fruit shop into a self-service store.

The Bandevez bar, at the corner of the Rue Tholozé and the Rue Durantin, used to be the meeting-place for women from the post office in the Place des Abbesses; they came and drank their little glass of *blanc-cassis*, and to make them fly off the handle we solemnly reproved them for getting blind drunk while their poor husbands were working. Well, the joint was still there; but the bar had been moved to the other side and the two tables were no longer in their right place. What's more, the owner of the bar was a *pied-noir* from Algeria and the customers were Arabs or Spaniards or Portuguese. Where can the old boss have vanished to—the type from the Auvergne?

I went up the steps that lead from the Rue Tholozé to the Moulin de la Galette. At least the handrail had not changed: it still ended as dangerously as ever. It was here that I had picked up a poor little old man who had fallen on his nose, not seeing well enough to make out that the rail stopped so soon. I stroked the rail: I saw the scene again and I heard the old man thank me: 'Young man, you are truly kind and very well brought-up. I congratulate you upon it, and I thank you.' These simple words so disturbed me that I did not know how to set about picking up the gun I had dropped as I leaned over him; I did not want him to see that the good young man was maybe not as kind as all that.

Yes, my Montmartre was still there all right. It had not been stolen from me—they had just stolen the people, the pleasant smiling faces that used to say, 'Hi, Papillon, how are you doing?' Those, yes, those had been stolen from me, and I felt a terrible pang in my heart.

That evening I went into a rough bar. I chose the oldest of all the old guys there and I said to him, 'Excuse me, but do you know So-and-so?'

'Yes.'

'Where is he?'

'Inside.'

'And So-and-so?'

'Dead.'

'And So-and-so?'

'Don't know him. But you ask a lot of questions. Who are you?'

He raised his voice a little on purpose, to attract the others' attention. It never misses. An unknown type who just walks into a man's bar like that without introducing himself or having a friend—you have to find out what he's after.

'My name's Henri. I'm from Avignon and I've been in Colombia. That's why you don't know me. Be seeing you.'

I did not linger but hurried off to catch my train so as to sleep outside the *département* of the Seine. I took these precautions because at no price did I want them to notify me that

I was forbidden to be there.

But I was in Paris, I was there. You're there, man! I went and danced at the little places round the Bastille. At Boucastel's and at the Bal-à-Jo I shoved my hat back and took off my tie. I even had the nerve to ask a skirt to dance just as I used to do when I was twenty, and in the same way. And as we waltzed to the sound of an accordion almost as good as Mimile Vacher's when I was young, the chick asked me what I did for a living and I told her I kept a house in the provinces: so I was looked upon with great respect.

I went and had lunch at La Coupole, and as if I had returned from another world I was simple-minded enough to ask a waiter whether they still played bowls on the flat roof. He had been there twenty-five years but my question absolutely stunned him.

And at La Rotonde I looked for the painter Foujita's corner, but in vain: my eyes gazed hopelessly at the furniture, the lay-out of the tables and the bar, looking for something that belonged to the past: disgusted at seeing that everything had been turned upside-down and that they had destroyed everything I had known and loved, I walked straight out, forgetting to pay. The waiter grabbed my arm at the entrance to the Vavin métro just by, and as manners have been forgotten in France he bawled the amount of the bill into my face and told me to pay up quick if I didn't want him to call a cop. Of course I paid, but I gave him such a paltry tip that as he left he threw it at me. 'You can keep that for your mother-in-law. She must need it more than me!'

But Paris is Paris. As brisk as a young man I walked right up the Champs-Elysées and then right down again, the Champs-Elysées lit with thousands of lights, with that light of Paris that warms you through and through and casts its wonderful spell, giving you a song in your heart. Ah, life is sweet in Paris!

There was not the least over-excitement in me, not the least longing for violence as I stood there at the Porte Saint-Denis or in front of the old *L'Auto* office in the Faubourg Montmartre, where Rigoulot, then champion of the world, used to lift a huge roll of newsprint. My heart was quiet as I passed in front of the club where I used to play baccarat with Stavisky;

and I went to watch the Lido show alone and perfectly calm. And quietly I mixed in the turmoil of the Halles for a few hours—they, at least, were more or less the same as before. It was only when I was in Montmartre that bitter words rose in my heart.

I stayed eight days in Paris. Eight times I went back to the scene of that famous murder.

Eight times I stroked the tree and then sat on the bench.

Eight times, with closed eyes, I put together all I knew of the inquiry and my two trials.

Eight times I saw the ugly faces of all those swine who manufactured my conviction.

Eight times I whispered, 'This is where it all began, the theft of those thirteen years of your youth.'

Eight times I repeated, 'You have given up your revenge; that's fine; but never will you be able to forgive.'

Eight times I asked God that as a reward for giving up my revenge the same kind of thing should never happen to anyone else.

Eight times I asked the bench whether the false witness and the shifty pig had cooked up their next statement in this very place.

Eight times I went away, less and less bowed down, so that the last time I walked off as straight and supple as a young man, whispering to myself, 'You won after all, man, since you're here, free, fit, beloved and master of your future. Don't you go trying to find out what has happened to those other types—they belong to your past. You're here, and that's close on a miracle. God doesn't work them every day. You can be dead sure that of all the people concerned in this business, you're the happiest.'